S0-AHD-571

DIRECT MARKETING MANAGEMENT

DIRECT MARKETING MANAGEMENT

Mary Lou Roberts
University of Massachusetts/Boston
Paul D. Berger
Boston University

Prentice Hall
Englewood Cliffs, NJ 07632

2-9-95

LIBRARY OF CONGRESS
Library of Congress Cataloging-in-Publication Data

Roberts, Mary Lou.
Direct marketing management/Mary Lou Roberts, Paul D. Berger.

Includes index.
ISBN O-13-214784-X
1. Direct marketing. I. Berger, Paul D., 1943- . II Title.
HF5415.126.R62 1989
658.8'6--dc19 88-25240
CIP

Editorial/production supervision
and interior design: *Millicent Lambert and Douglas Ens*
Manufacturing buyer: *Margaret Rizzi*

Printed in the United States of America
10 9 8 7 6 5 4 3 2 1

ISBN 0-13-214784-X

Prentice-Hall International (UK) Limited, *London*
Prentice-Hall of Australia Pty. Limited, *Sydney*
Prentice-Hall Canada Inc., *Toronto*
Prentice-Hall Hispanoamericana, S.A., *Mexico*
Prentice-Hall of India Private Limited, *New Delhi*
Prentice-Hall of Japan, Inc., *Tokyo*
Simon & Schuster Asia Pte. Ltd., *Singapore*
Editora Prentice-Hall do Brasil, Ltda., *Rio de Janeiro*

To Our Families

Don, Greg, and Lynn,
Susan and Seth

Contents

5 CREATIVE STRATEGY AND EXECUTION, 122

Part Three Special Techniques of Direct Marketing

6 TARGETED MARKETING USING DATABASES, 147

11 TELEPHONE MARKETING, 295

12 DIRECT RESPONSE IN PRINT MEDIA, 329

Foreword

No marketer's crash kit is complete today if it is missing knowledge and experience in direct marketing. No matter what business you may be in, direct marketing can and should play a role, as a distribution channel, a focused communications channel, or an efficient way to search for new customers. The information explosion and the reduced cost of computer transactions have allowed direct marketing to expand rapidly and it has become the fastest growing activity today in major league marketing.

My marketing apprenticeship and career were spent with General Foods, one of the great package goods companies that prides itself on its marketing prowess. And with good reason! They built multibillion dollar businesses with mass merchandising, supported heavily by mass advertising. However, in the late 1970s their world began to change as mass markets fragmented, media costs rose rapidly, and the distribution system consolidated its power. Today, General Foods and other package goods marketers still rely heavily on advertising and promotion, but recognize the need to find fresh ways to reach their customers. They are learning quickly about direct marketing as an important new discipline in their marketing skills bag.

Despite its huge size, direct marketing is still a young industry and very much in its high-growth stage. In recent years, socioeconomic trends have favored direct marketing and will continue to do so for at least the next decade. Two-wage-earner households have little time for shopping, while at the same time, shopping is less fun with traffic problems, parking difficulties, and inadequate retail help. Buying via catalog, mail, or telephone is becoming second nature to those of us who have had good experience with the quality products and service we have received. The inevitable expansion of the home computer market will add to the growth momentum as a number of retailers can be directly accessed. The Trintex experiment of Sears and IBM may be a big step in this direction.

One of the benefits of such a young industry is that most of its pioneers are still active and influencing its development. They are a wonderful lot of creative, enthusiastic visionaries who make everyone want to believe in their new ideas: Lester Wunderman, the acknowledged dean of direct marketing with his "Book of the Month Club," Stan Rapp, Gerry Pickholtz, and many more. These are people with an idea who learned what worked and then made it work better.

Major innovation still abounds in direct marketing. Data suppliers such as Claritas broke new ground with PRIZM—clusters of similar-minded people in discontinuous zip codes, thus allowing highly targeted mailing. Jock Bickert, Chief Executive Officer of National Demographics and Lifestyles, learned how to compile lists of individuals with lifestyle information as a superior indicator of buying behavior. Such information is of great value to catalog and other mailers. And a whole new world is opening up, searching for creative ways to communicate with potential customers to encourage them to buy, repeat, or use more, from long-distance phoning to luxury cars or credit cards. Direct mail has been a significant key in the growth of competitive long-distance phone carriers, such as MCI or Sprint. At the other end of the spectrum, the Lincoln Division of Ford uses a sophisticated mail campaign with over one hundred variations to entice drivers of competitive cars to consider and test-drive a Lincoln next time they are in the market for a new car. Because the margin on a expensive car is substantial, focusing that much attention on a few prospects is sound strategy as a good investment that pays. American Express has its own distinctive competence, but one of its reasons for success is that it makes the best combined used of direct mail and traditional advertising. I certainly don't leave home without it!

Anyone who is looking at the front end of a marketing career and who feels challenged by opportunities to do new things has to be excited by direct marketing. As for those already hooked by the wonderful stimulation of marketing, here's the way to building direct marketing into your rich experience. Whether you are creative with ideas, words, or numbers, a rewarding adventure awaits you in direct marketing.

Good luck.

F. Kent Mitchel
President, Marketing Science Institute
Cambridge, Massachusetts

Preface

According to Peter Drucker, "Every practice rests on theory, even if the practitioners themselves are unaware of it."[1] In no area of marketing is this s true as it is in direct marketing. The field of direct marketing lacks conceptual frameworks which allow knowledge gained through experience to be organized for effective transmittal to the inexperienced. This has slowed the acceptance of direct marketing as a field worthy of study in management programs at all levels.

One of the chief objectives of this text is to provide a systematic approach to the study of direct marketing. We do not dwell on abstract theories, although where theory is needed we use it. We do, however, provide many conceptual models based on the best current thinking and practice in direct marketing. These will assist the student in organizing the multiplicity of managerial decisions and activities required to plan and implement direct marketing programs.

The other major objective of this book is to provide thorough coverage of the field. A chapter, or a major portion thereof, is devoted to each of the major managerial decision variables and media alternatives of direct marketing. Throughout the book examples and applications are drawn from a wide range of consumer, business, and not-for-profit marketing activities for both products and services.

There are, however, common marketing topics that are noticeably absent from this book. These subject areas—which include product planning, pricing, and some aspects of marketing research—cover activities which differ little, if at all, from general marketing to direct marketing. They are treated thoroughly in general and specialized marketing texts and their applications to direct marketing are quite straightforward.

[1]Peter F. Drucker, *Innovation and Entrepreneurship: Practice and Principles* (New York: Harper & Row, 1985), p. 26.

Because we have attempted to organize and integrate much information which has been published in fragmentary fashion, if at all, the writing of this book has been more dependent than most on the cooperation of many direct marketing practitioners. Scores of people whom we knew slightly or not at all have picked up their telephone only to find a curious author on the other end of the line. Almost without exception they have responded by sharing their hard-won knowledge with us in a most generous fashion. Many of them have also shared examples of their work or directed us to others who could, and we are grateful for that also.

We wish to single out for an expression of thanks three organizations in particular. The staff of the Direct Marketing Educational Foundation, especially Dr. Richard Montessi and Laurie Spar, has been consistently supportive. So has the staff of Hoke Communications, led by publisher Henry R. "Pete" Hoke, Jr. and Raymond Roel, editor of *Direct Marketing* magazine. Also, the staff of Persoft, Inc., with Richard Campbell as bellweather, has continually provided the most valuable kind of assistance and information access.

So many individuals have provided information and assistance that it is not possible to name them all. Mary Lou Roberts wishes to offer special thanks to Alan E. Lewis of Grand Circle Travel for introducing her to the field of direct marketing, to George Zahka of Marcoa/DR Group for continuing encouragement, and to my good neighbors at Hub Mail Advertising—especially Wallace Bernheimer, Al Silverstein, and Alan Sack—for many different kinds of assistance.

For providing thoughtful critiques of individual chapters we also express our gratitude to Daniel W. Pelley of The Historic Providence Mint, Dr. Connie Bauer of Marquette University, Lynn Jaffe of Boston University, Robert K. Russell of Maxwell Communication Corp., Charles A. Khuen and Dr. Harriette L. Chandler of the Adelie Corporation, Dr. Bernard Silverman of The Signature Group, and Marilyn Ewer of MKE Enterprises. Textbook reviewers are usually anonymous, but in the small world of academic direct marketing this was not feasible. Consequently we can pubicly thank Bruce Buskirk of Northwestern University, Bob Dwyer of the University of Cincinnati, and Jerry Kirkpatrick of Northwestern University for a host of valuable insights and suggestions. Special thanks is also due our production editor, Fred Dahl, who took charge of a complex project in midstream and saw it through with competence and good humor. And last but certainly not least, our sincere gratitude to Pat Bennett who assisted in many phases of the manuscript preparation and revision. Our editor, Whitney Blake, has been a constant source of strength and enthusiasm.

To all who have assisted us in this activity: We hope you recognize the value of your contributions to our understanding of direct marketing. To those who are just joining us in the study of this field: We hope you discover the kind of intellectual excitement we have found while exploring this little-known aspect of marketing.

Mary Lou Roberts
Paul D. Berger

Part One
Introduction to Direct Marketing

1 What Is Direct Marketing?

Recently a leading direct marketing firm prepared to interview graduating students at a large midwestern university. Working with the university's placement service, the firm listed several entry-level openings for telephone marketing sales representatives. It made available various pieces of corporate literature describing its rapid growth as a distributor of scientific and laboratory supplies and equipment, sold primarily through a large force of telephone marketing representatives located in branch offices throughout the country.

The detailed position description indicated that the newly hired reps would be responsible for developing business from dormant accounts, opening new accounts, and maintaining steady and profitable sales growth. Specific responsibilities included staying current on and implementing sales and promotional programs, acquainting customers with sales support services, and handling branch overflow calls—all in a professional manner. Qualifications for the positions were a four-year degree, preferably in business or marketing, and a commitment to an entry-level position in sales. The firm indicated some preference for persons who had held sales-related jobs while in college.

On the appointed day the recruiter arrived to find a number of students eagerly waiting to be interviewed. All of them were well prepared to discuss the challenges of selling supplies and equipment directly to business customers in the field. Unfortunately, none of them understood the nature of telephone marketing nor the broader field of direct marketing.

These students are not unusual. Both members of the general public and people in the business community tend to have incorrect or incomplete ideas of what direct marketing is. They receive a great deal of unsolicited mail; they are annoyed by telephone calls from a computer (who is sometimes, even more annoyingly, named Earnest); they see multitudes of consumer-goods catalogs, only a few of which contain merchandise that interests them.

Though these are indeed aspects of direct marketing, they are only surface manifestations of a highly developed set of marketing strategies and tactics. These strategies and tactics have been tested and refined over the years by both consumer and business-to-business direct marketers as well as by not-for-profit organizations. More recently, they have become important parts of the marketing plans of many corporations that are not "direct marketers" in the pure sense.

WHY IS DIRECT MARKETING SUCH A WELL-KEPT SECRET?

There is no single, completely satisfactory answer to this question, but several circumstances have contributed to the lack of awareness of direct marketing. First, many of the most prominent direct marketers have been entrepreneurs who have necessarily focused their energies on building businesses, not on spreading the word about direct marketing in the broader business community. Second, few business or communications schools have offered courses in direct marketing so students do not learn about the field or realize the career opportunities it offers. Finally, many marketing professionals have regarded direct marketing as a faintly disreputable activity, full of hucksterism and outright deception. They have been slow to recognize that direct marketing is now a discipline worthy of respect and thoughtful study.

Recently, however, direct marketing has begun to take its place within the domain of marketing. Individuals, businesses, and most of all the Direct Marketing Association and the Direct Marketing Educational Foundation have contributed to the growing awareness of direct marketing. More important, an increasingly competitive business environment has created a voracious demand for precisely targeted marketing strategies that require the use of direct marketing elements.

A DEFINITION OF DIRECT MARKETING

The most widely accepted definition is the one provided by the Direct Marketing Association:

> Direct marketing is an interactive system of marketing which uses one or more advertising media to effect a measurable response and/or transaction at any location.

There are four key elements of this definition that bear closer inspection. First, direct marketing is described as being an *interactive system*. That is, the marketer and the prospective customer engage in two-way communication. In many marketing situations the marketer attempts to communicate information to the target audience but has no opportunity to obtain precise feedback about the success of that communication. That can be described as one-way communication—the marketer speaking to the prospect. Consequently, the marketer must rely on measures of communications effectiveness, such as awareness or recall, rather than on measures of marketing effectiveness, such as sales.

A direct marketing activity always gives the individual target of the communication an opportunity to *respond*. There are many ways of allowing the prospect to respond, and they will be summarized later in this chapter. For now, it is also important to note that nonresponse also provides information to the direct marketer, information that can be used in planning the next marketing program.

The communication can take place at *any location*. That is, it is not necessary for the potential customer to come into a retail store or be visited by a salesperson. The contact can be made at any time and any place where there is access to communications media.

Of paramount importance is the fact that all direct marketing activities are *measurable*. A response, or lack thereof, can be associated with the individual prospect. The specific communication that prompted the individual to respond can be identified. As a result, the direct marketer knows to which communication the prospective customer responded and the exact nature of that response—a sale or a request for more information, for example.

This information is added to existing information about the individual in the direct marketer's database so that it will be available for the planning of the next marketing program. This is another way in which direct marketing provides an interactive system. The direct marketer analyzes customer data, uses it in planning new campaigns, and updates it after every customer contact. *This database of information is the key to effective direct marketing.* Table 1.1 summarizes the major differences between direct marketing and general marketing.

DIRECT MARKETING'S SPECIAL COMPETENCIES

As a result of these differences, there are some things that direct marketing does much better than general marketing. If you think about these special competencies for a moment, you will recognize that virtually all of them stem from the fact that the communications of direct marketers are directed at specific individuals, not at mass markets by way of mass media.

Precision Targeting. Through the use of carefully selected mailing lists and the information contained in customer databases, the direct marketer can direct communications to an individual consumer or a specific business customer who has been identified as a viable prospect. This reduces the waste inherent in many other types of communications that cannot be so precisely targeted.

TABLE 1.1 Key Differences Between Direct Marketing and General Marketing

General Marketing	*Direct Marketing*
Reaches a mass audience through mass media	Communicates directly with the customer or prospect
Communications are impersonal	Can personalize communications By name/title Variable messages
Promotional programs are highly visible	Promotional programs (especially tests) relatively "invisible"
Amount of promotion controlled by size of budget	Size of budget can be determined by success of promotion
Desired action either Unclear Delayed	Specific action always requested Inquiry Purchase
Incomplete/sample data for decision-making purposes Sales call reports Marketing research	Comprehensive database drives marketing programs
Analysis conducted at segment level	Analysis conducted at individual/firm level
Use surrogate variables to meaure effectiveness Advertising awareness Intention to buy	*Measurable*, and therefore highly *Controllable*

Personalization. The individual consumer can and should be addressed by name, while the business customer can be addressed by name and title. The ability to personalize extends beyond the mere use of names, however. Information from the data base can be used to select an appropriate appeal (for example, "April is the month to plant lily bulbs in New England" for the Connecticut resident who has previously purchased bulbs and perennials from a mailing by the nursery) or to encourage a customer who has purchased previously to buy a complementary product ("The glassware on p. 9 would go well with the china you recently bought").

Call for Immediate Action. Direct marketing copy calls for specific and immediate action, typically the purchase of a product or a request for more information about it. This call for immediate action works against the prospect's normal tendency to defer action, often permanently.

"Invisible" Strategies. The strategies and tactics of the direct marketer are less visible to competitors than are strategies that must be implemented in the mass media. Competitors can certainly keep abreast of one another's activities by, for example, making sure to be on their mailing lists. However, by the time the competitor receives the communication, so have customers, and it may be too late to retaliate effectively. Lack of visibility is especially important when testing direct marketing campaigns. A traditional test market invariably tips off the competition; the test of a direct marketing program may go unnoticed by competitors.

Measurability. The list would be incomplete without again stressing the importance of the measurability of direct marketing. By knowing precisely what worked and what did not, the marketer can allocate marketing dollars much more effectively.

THE DECISION VARIABLES OF DIRECT MARKETING

Just as in general marketing we talk about the 4 P's—product, price, promotion and place—we can identify a set of decision variables for direct marketing programs:[1]

Offer (which includes the product)
Creative
Media (which includes lists when applicable)
Timing/sequencing
Customer service

These decision variables form the basic framework around which this book is structured. Since they will be discussed in detail in later chapters, we will take only a brief look at them here.

Offer. The offer is the complete proposition made by the marketer to a prospective customer.[2] It includes the product (or service) itself, the price at which it is offered, any adjustments to the price, and other elements of the positioning strategy for the product.

The Healthy Home Cooking mailing package shown in Figure 1.1 offers the opportunity to subscribe to a new series of Time-Life Books. Subscribers will receive a free Lucite cutting board, an incentive that is closely related to the basic book offer.

[1] The first four decision variables were suggested by Edward L. Nash, *Direct Marketing: Strategy/Planning/Execution* (New York: McGraw Hill, 1982), pp. 16-30; and John Stevenson, "What Is Direct Marketing?" unpublished paper, Young & Rubicam, Inc., no date.

[2] Suggested by Bob Stone, *Successful Direct Marketing Methods* (Chicago: Crain Books, 1984), p. 43.

Creative. The creative component of the direct marketing program includes the copy platform, the graphic design elements, any involvement techniques, and production considerations such as personalization. The benefit-oriented copy in the Healthy Home Cooking mailing addresses current concerns that food be healthful, good-tasting, and easy to prepare. The graphics are crisp and contemporary in feeling, with illustrations well calculated to induce hunger in the reader. The recipe cards are an excellent involvement device, offering their own type of free trial. Although the letter is not personalized, the recipient's name (not "occupant") was used on the mailing label, as you would expect for a high-quality mailing package targeted to people with contemporary attitudes and lifestyles.

FIGURE 1.1 ***Healthy Home Cooking Mailing Package***

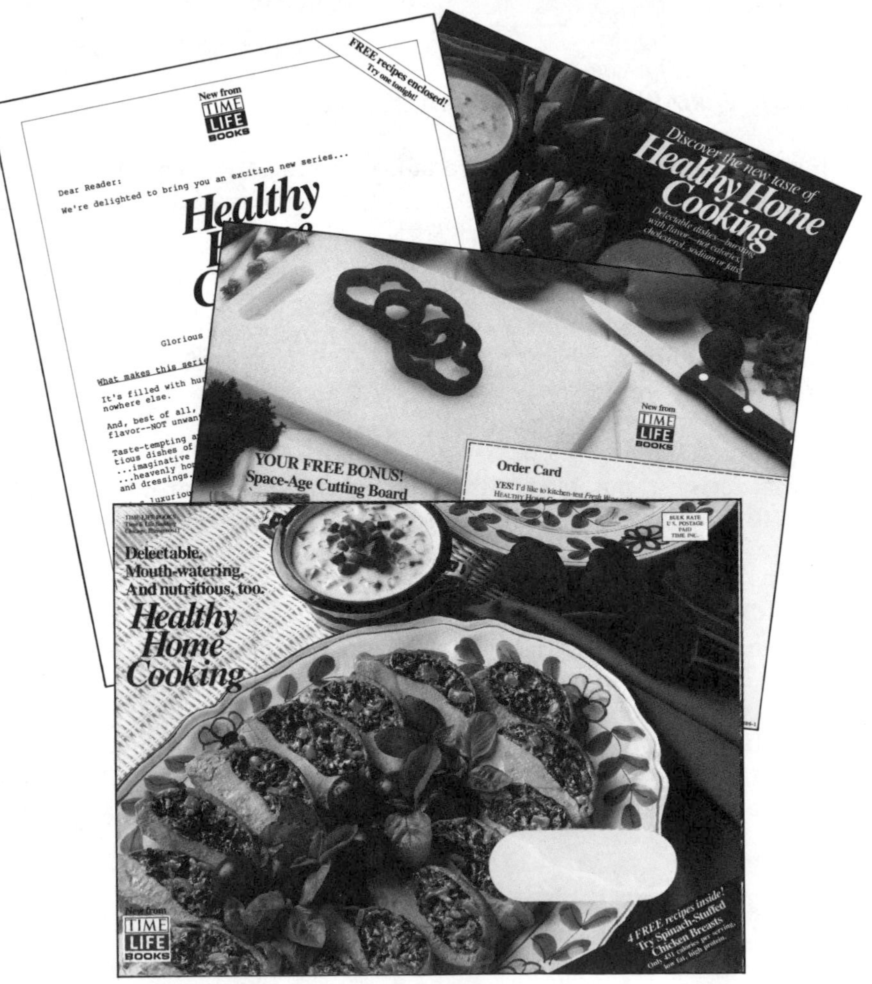

Source: Time-Life Books, Inc.

Media. The media available to direct marketing include all those used by general marketing as well as direct mail and telephone. Both direct mail and telephone usually require lists of actual or prospective customers. It is reasonable to assume that Time-Life used at least a portion of its own house list of purchasers of other book series and also rented outside lists. One measure of the success of this series of books is the notice in an issue of *Direct Marketing* magazine that the Healthy Home Cooking list of 24,283 active subscribers (apparently as of May 1986) had itself become available for rental through a list broker.[3]

Timing/Sequencing. Concerns about the timing and sequencing of direct marketing communications are in many ways similar to those for general advertising. These concerns include one-shot messages versus campaigns, pulsing versus a steady flow of communications, seasonal effects, and questions of how much repetition is enough.

Part of the conventional wisdom of the direct marketing industry is an estimate of the relative importance of these four decision variables in creating a response (see Figure 1.2). Reaching the right person accounts for 50 percent of a program's impact. The offer and the timing are next at 20 percent each. The creative elements account for only 10 percent. This estimate comes as a surprise to many people, especially those who are committed to the creative side of advertising communications.

Stop and think about it, though. If the message does not reach the proper target—the target for which it was designed—it has little chance of being effective. Likewise, if the product or the way it is valued is not right for the target customer, or if the message arrives at an inappropriate time, the probability of generating a response will be decreased. The creative elements, important though they are, cannot be effective unless the other variables are implemented correctly.

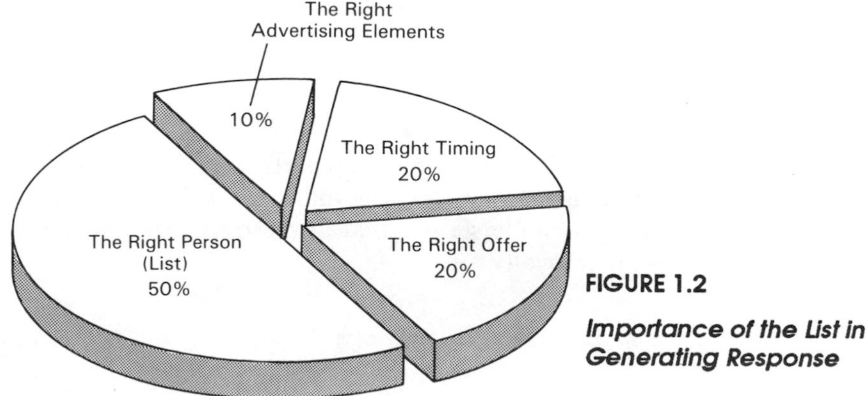

FIGURE 1.2

Importance of the List in Generating Response

[3] "DM Marketplace," *Direct Marketing*, August 1986, p. 88.

Customer Service. The fifth major variable—customer service—has not been explicitly recognized in previous discussions of key direct marketing decision elements. This is true even though Lester Wunderman, one of the senior statesmen of direct marketing, is reputed to have observed long ago that "direct marketing turns a product into a service."

The importance of service cannot be overstated. The *types of customer services* offered—toll-free telephone numbers, free limited-time trial, acceptance of several credit cards, for example—are important techniques for overcoming customer resistance to buying via direct-response media. Even more important is the *level of customer service* provided—the speed and accuracy of order fulfillment, handling of customer inquiries and complaints, and guaranteed returns policy, for example. Next to the quality and performance of the product itself, the services available in connection with its purchase and use are the prime determinant of customer satisfaction. The level of customer satisfaction is, in turn, a prime consideration in the decision whether to re-purchase.

Excellent customer service includes problem prevention as well as problem resolution. Neiman-Marcus, the Dallas-based specialty retailer, goes to great lengths to try to prevent customer problems with merchandise ordered by mail or by phone:

> Neiman-Marcus sends a first-class mailing to customers confirming the details of any complex order (e.g., engraved items). Customers are asked to immediately call the 800 number if any errors are found. This minimizes the shipment of incorrect orders (e.g., wrong message engraved) and thereby decreases the expense of responding to consumer complaints. During periods of peak telephone orders (e.g., Christmas), Neiman-Marcus sends a mailgram to ensure that customers are aware of their order's status.
>
> Neiman-Marcus representatives who process telephone orders receive special briefings on product aspects which might lead to "unmet" customer expectations. For instance, if the actual color of a dress differs slightly from what is shown in the catalog, the telephone representative advises the customer of this difference. Also, representatives provide advice and help customers select clothes that will "go together." In this manner, product returns are reduced and consumer satisfaction is increased.[4]

As this example implies, and as many experts have found, expenditures on customer service may actually make operations more profitable instead of being a drain on profits. Certainly service that leads to satisfaction is an investment in long-term customer loyalty.

[4] *Consumer Complaint Handling In America: An Update Study, Part II* (U.S. Office of Consumer Affairs, 1986), p. 14.

GENERIC OBJECTIVES FOR DIRECT MARKETING PROGRAMS

Each direct marketing program or campaign should, of course, have specific and measurable objectives. It is useful, however, to think about four broad types of objectives that direct marketing programs can achieve. These broad classes of objectives are:

Sale of a product or service
Lead generation
Lead qualification
Maintenance of customer relationships

Most of the direct marketing communications we are accustomed to receiving as consumers are designed to accomplish the sale of a product or service. The Healthy Home Cooking mailing actually aims to sell not just one, but an entire series of books (a continuity program).

Business marketers sell many products using direct marketing techniques, but they are often also concerned with producing well-qualified leads (prospective customers) for their field salespeople. As we will discuss in Chapter 14, this is becoming increasingly important as the cost of a field sales call rises. Leads are generated whenever a prospect requests additional information as a result of a direct marketing communication. When prospects answer questions or engage in any other behavior that indicates that they have a genuine intention to buy, they become "qualified prospects." Expensive or complex consumer products,—insurance policies, for example—are also sold by this two-stage process.

In addition, business marketers frequently engage in activities that are clearly recognizable as communications with customers who may not now be in the market for their products. Newsletters and seminars that update customers on product and service developments, share customer use experiences, and explain new applications are examples of this type of communication. The newsletter from the Industrial Division of the Polaroid Corporation shown in Figure 1.3 is designed to provide information about new products. Its contents include an introductory letter emphasizing Polaroid's concern for customer service and a feature written by a customer that describes a successful product application.

These types of communications are less common in consumer markets, but they do exist. Orvis, the Vermont sporting goods and outdoor clothing cataloger, sends a newsletter to recent buyers. One edition, 40 pages long, included articles on the production of Harris Tweed, fly fishing in Georgia, and one feature article, plus several promotional items about the famous Orvis fly fishing school. The last 15 pages were devoted to sale items.

FIGURE 1.3 ***Newsletter from the Industrial Division of Polaroid Corporation***

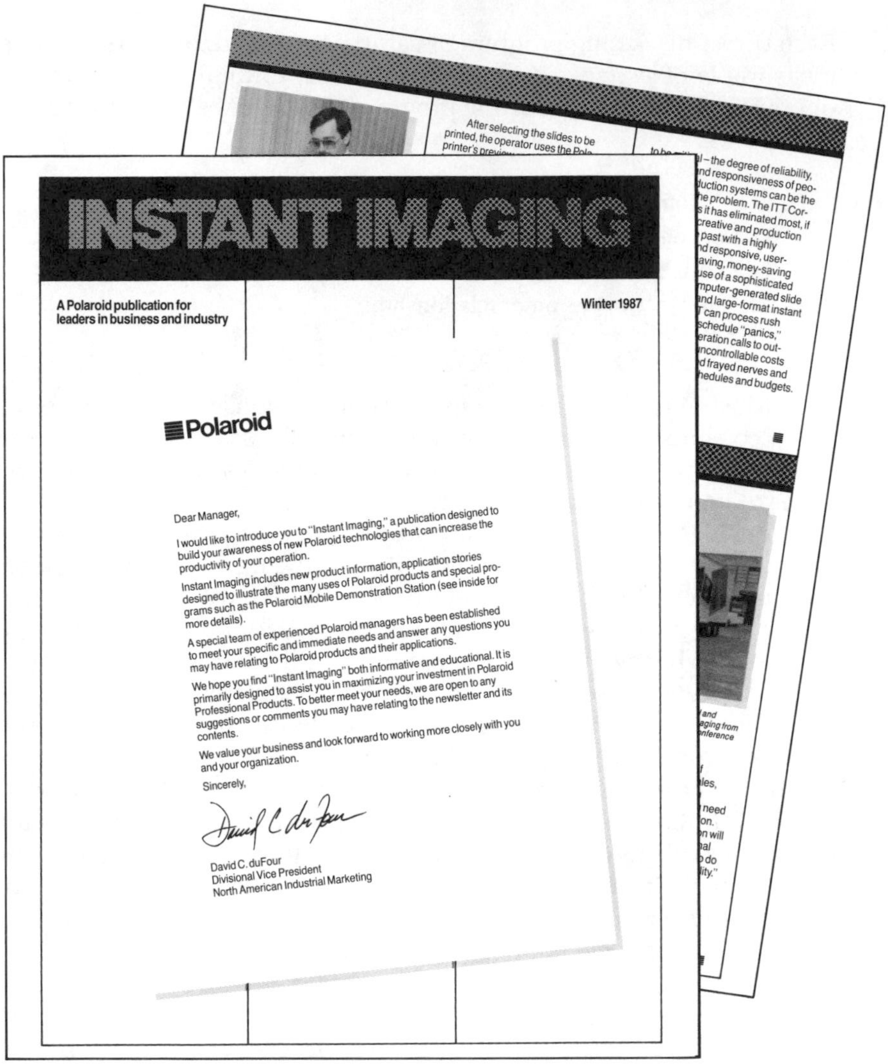

INSTANT IMAGING

A Polaroid publication for leaders in business and industry

Winter 1987

Polaroid

Dear Manager,

I would like to introduce you to "Instant Imaging," a publication designed to build your awareness of new Polaroid technologies that can increase the productivity of your operation.

Instant Imaging includes new product information, application stories designed to illustrate the many uses of Polaroid products and special programs such as the Polaroid Mobile Demonstration Station (see inside for more details).

A special team of experienced Polaroid managers has been established to meet your specific and immediate needs and answer any questions you may have relating to Polaroid products and their applications.

We hope you find "Instant Imaging" both informative and educational. It is primarily designed to assist you in maximizing your investment in Polaroid Professional Products. To better meet your needs, we are open to any suggestions or comments you may have relating to the newsletter and its contents.

We value your business and look forward to working more closely with you and your organization.

Sincerely,

David C. duFour
Divisional Vice President
North American Industrial Marketing

Source: Courtesy Polaroid Corporation.

Not as easily recognizable as customer relations devices are many of the catalogs and other mailers produced by most retailers today. Many of these communications are not designed primarily to sell products (although you can buy the products by telephone or mail), but rather are designed to encourage customers to come into the store to shop.

THE SIZE AND SCOPE OF THE DIRECT MARKETING INDUSTRY

To appreciate the growing role of direct marketing in our economy we must describe its relative magnitude and rate of growth. This is not as easy as it sounds because there is considerable disagreement about many of the statistics used to describe the industry.

There is agreement on the fact that U.S. Census Bureau data considerably understate the size of the industry. This is because the Census of Business classifies each business unit according to its primary activity. For example, even though a department store makes a noticeable proportion of its sales through mail and telephone orders, it is classified as a retail store and its entire sales volume is credited to that category.

In the absence of definitive government statistics, various groups attempt to collect data. Unfortunately, because they lack the government's resources and ability to compel firms to provide information, even the widely accepted statistics that we quote here may not be completely accurate. It is highly unlikely, however, that refinement of these statistics would change the overall picture of this large and dynamic industry.

Sales Generated by Direct Marketing

The Direct Marketing Flow Chart shown in Figure 1.4 presents an overview of the structure of the direct marketing industry and the size of its component parts. It presents two kinds of numbers—(1) sales generated by each major type of selling activity and (2) media expenditures.

The absolute numbers—billions of dollars!—are difficult for most of us to comprehend. Figure 1.5 presents the sales data in relative terms. It is quite clear that field selling and retailing predominate as mechanisms for generating sales. Mail-order and telephone sales account for only 1.4 percent of the total, with vending machines generating an even smaller sales volume.

Another way to think about the importance of direct marketing is in terms of its *rate of growth*. Table 1.2 compares the rates of growth of retail store sales to the basic categories of nonstore store retail sales, using the higher industry estimates of sales.

Included in the nonstore category is direct selling, which is personal selling to consumers in their homes or other nonretail locations. The catalog/direct advertising category is the fastest-growing, outpacing even the growth of sales in retail stores.

That pattern is expected to continue for the next few years. According to figures compiled by Arnold Fishman for *Direct Marketing* magazine, retail sales growth was about 5 percent in 1986 while mail-order sales increased by 10 percent.[5]

[5] Arnold Fishman, "The 1986 Mail Order Guide," *Direct Marketing*, July 1987, p. 47.

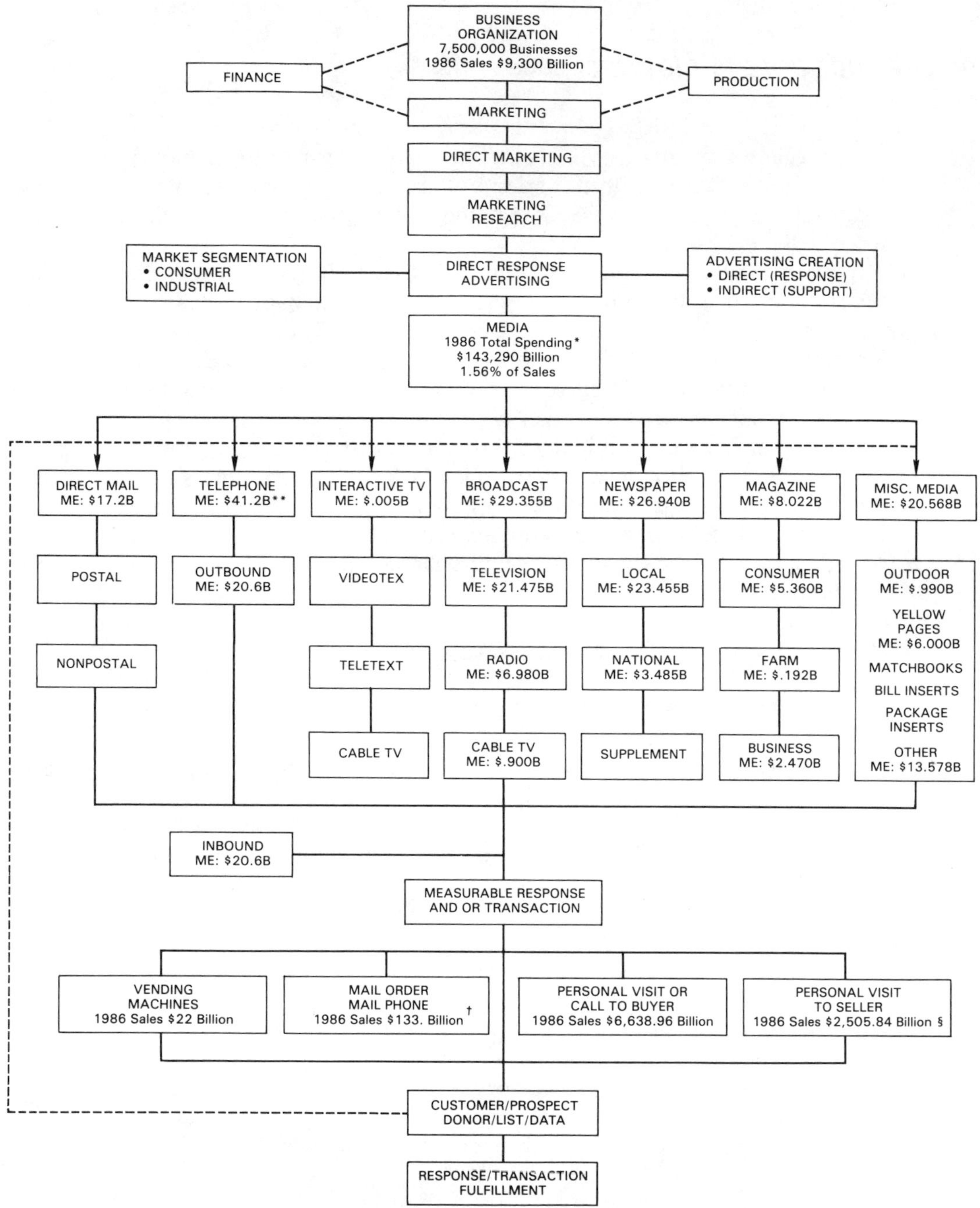

FIGURE 1.4 ***Direct Marketing Flow Chart***

* Arnold Fishman, U.S. Census, Robert Coen, McCann Erickson (media figures); (dollars in billions; ME-media expenditures). ** Rudy Oetting, Telephone Marketing Resources, NYC and AT&T: approx. 1/2 = inbound calls, 1/2 = outbound. † The mail order sales figure includes approx. $33B of charitable contributions not included in the $9.33B total. § Personal visit to seller includes all retail consumer product and service sales; total excludes $870B investment spending minus $75B in net exports.

Source: Martin Baier, Henry R. Hoke, Jr., and Robert Stone, in *Direct Marketing Magazine* (April 1987), p. 29. From *Direct Marketing Magazine*, 224 Seventh Street, Garden City, New York 11530-5771.

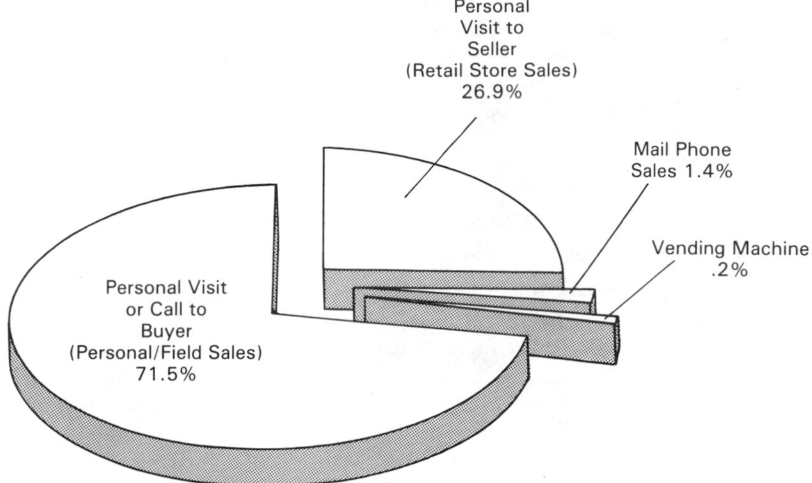

FIGURE 1.5 ***Direct Marketing Sales Data***

When we look at statistics for business-to-business marketing separately, the strength of direct marketing is even more apparent (see Table 1.3). Direct marketing accounts for almost one-third of all business-to-business marketing and advertising expenditures, and although reliable statistics are difficult to obtain, that percentage appears to be growing.

Finally, we should also point out that the not-for-profit sector is a major participant in the direct marketing industry, both for fund-raising and for audience development. Nonprofit organizations make extensive use of direct marketing techniques, and many of them are very sophisticated in their applications. According to one expert, "Non-profit marketers learned a long time ago the lesson that commercial direct marketers are just learning; that the real advantage is in the long-term pay-out. The profit is in the small, selective appeal to the right audience, not the huge mass mailing to everybody under the sun."[6]

TABLE 1.2 Five-Year Compound Annual Growth Rates (1980–1984)

Retail stores	6.4%
Non-store Retailing	
Vending machine	4.7%
Direct selling	3.2%
Catalog/direct advertising	9.5%

Source: U.S. Department of Commerce, Census of Business.

[6] Len Strazewski, "Non-Profits Learn Long-Term Lesson," *Advertising Age Special Report,* July 27, 1987, p. S-1.

TABLE 1.3 Business-to-Business Marketing Communications Expenditures (1984–1985)

Direct marketing	$ 30,850,000	32.9%
Trade shows	21,000,000	22.4%
Incentives	15,065,871	16.0%
Advertising	8,589,371	9.2%
Sales promotion	7,616,900	8.1%
Sales force management	5,920,000	6.3%
Public relations	2,405,300	2.6%
Research	2,190,200	2.3%
TOTAL EXPENDITURES	$ 93,637,642	

Source: Adapted from "Here is What Business–to–Business Marketers Spend Their Money On. We Think." *Business Marketing*, no date, p. 2.

Nonprofit organizations are making effective use of multimedia campaigns involving not only direct mail but also telephone, direct-response space and broadcast, and videotaped promotions. Direct mail is the most popular medium for the nonprofits, which mailed out 10.9 billion pieces in 1985—20.9 percent of all third-class mail.[7] A considerable portion of the estimated $87.22 billion in charitable contributions made in 1986 can be attributed to direct-response fund-raising efforts.[8]

THE MEDIA OF DIRECT MARKETING

The statistics in the Figure 1.4 describe total media expenditures by all marketers, not just by direct marketers. Keeping in mind that we cannot separate the expenditures of direct marketers from those of general marketers with a high degree of precision, we will concentrate on how direct marketers use the media.

Many people are surprised to learn that telephone is probably the largest advertising medium. Telephone marketing experts estimate that approximately half of the $41.2 billion spent on this medium is for outgoing calls, with the other half representing incoming calls for purchases and customer service. Television is next, followed closely by newspapers. The miscellaneous category, which includes outdoor media and the Yellow Pages, is also quite large. Direct mail and magazines are smaller in terms of media expenditures.

Figure 1.6 shows a detailed breakdown of media expenditures, excluding telephone. The only direct-response medium broken out is direct mail. Account-

[7] Strazewski, "Non-Profits Learn Long-Term Lesson," pp. S-1, S-2.

[8] Estimate by the American Association of Fund-Raising Counsels, quoted in "Charitable Giving Moves to New Heights," *Fund Raising*, July 1987, p. 12.

ing for almost 17 percent of media expenditures and with a 10.6 percent growth rate in 1986, direct mail is a rapidly growing medium.

Virtually all of the media shown in Figure 1.6 can be used to transmit direct marketing offers. It is important to remember that, while many of the media are used by both general marketers and direct marketers, the direct marketer uses and evaluates the effectiveness of the media differently.

Let's take a brief look at each of the primary media and their role in direct-response marketing. Developing and implementing direct marketing programs in each of these media will be the subject of several later chapters in the book.

Telephone

The telephone is an indispensable medium for direct marketers of both consumer and business products. We are probably all familiar with many of the consumer applications of this medium. The consumer makes outgoing calls to obtain

FIGURE 1.6 ***U.S. 1986 Media Advertising Breakdown***

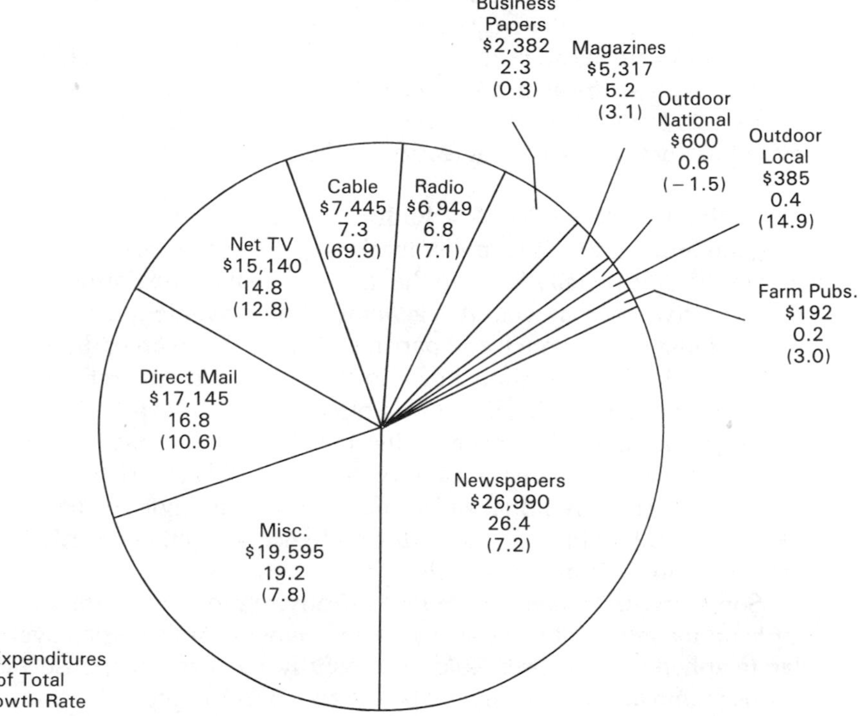

Dollar amount in millions and percent of total; numbers in parentheses notes percent change from 1985.

Source: Direct Marketing (July 1987), p. 20, McCann-Erickson.

information, order merchandise, and request follow-up service. The consumer receives incoming sales and service calls, plus solicitations of many kinds from nonprofit organizations.

The telephone is especially critical to many business marketers today as they strive to make their sales effort cost effective. Telephone sales and service representatives are used in conjunction with a field sales force or are, increasingly, taking over the entire responsibility for the sale of some business products. Telephone marketing will be discussed in Chapters 11 and 14.

Broadcast and Electronic Media

Direct-Response Television. Long the province of the late-night pitchman selling vegetable slicing machines, inexpensive sets of kitchen knives guaranteed to last a lifetime, and smokeless ash trays, direct-response television has gained respectability in the last few years. It is now a vehicle for marketing a wide variety of goods and services. Large national advertisers such as Time-Life have found prime-time direct-response television sufficiently effective to devote a portion of their promotional budget to it. Cable television is also becoming increasingly popular with direct-response marketers.

The ultimate in direct-response television, of course, are television shopping programs such as those on the Home Shopping Network. These programs were riding a wave of enthusiasm in the mid-1980s, but it is too early to tell whether they will become a permanent feature of the direct-response landscape.

Direct-Response Radio. Radio has not traditionally been considered a strong medium for direct-response marketing. The reasoning has gone something like this: "People usually listen to the radio while they are doing something else—working, driving, whatever. It is generally not convenient for them to stop what they are doing, find a pencil and paper, and write down an address or a telephone number. Besides, by the time they find the pencil and paper, the ad is over."

Radio has shown itself to be an effective direct-response medium from its early days, however, and even in the television era it has advantages to offer marketers. One attraction is its ability to reach highly segmented audiences. The current emphasis on regionalization of marketing strategies by national marketers makes the local nature of the radio audience attractive. Furthermore, direct-response radio is cheaper than television.

Some products have an obvious affinity to radio, or more accurately, to the people on the move who are heavy radio listeners. Both paging systems and cellular telephones have been sold successfully by direct-response radio. Direct-response radio and television will be discussed in Chapter 13.

Videotex. Videotex is, along with cable television, one of the emerging electronic media that are just beginning to achieve widespread acceptance by consumers. Public access videotex applications include CRT (cathode ray tube) displays of daily schedules in hotels and flight information in airports (some of which are now accepting advertising). Videotex can also be transmitted to television sets or personal computers. A tremendous amount of information—and merchandise—can be made readily available to consumers and businesses through this medium. The emerging electronic media have such great potential impact for the future of direct marketing that they will be treated in detail in Chapter 16.

Space Advertising in Print Media

Newspapers and Magazines. Display advertising in both newspapers and magazines is used by a wide variety of product and service marketers. All three advertisements in Figure 1.7 appeared in the same issue of *The Wall Street Journal*. Let's consider the objectives and target market strategies of the three very different companies that used the *Journal* as one of their media vehicles. The "tummy trimmer" ad appears to be aimed at busy executives, both male and female. The executive aircraft, which features a much higher price tag, is clearly aimed at a select few companies and their top managers. The printer ad is relevant for a large number of personal computer users and is designed to appeal particularly to users of a popular spreadsheet program.

A direct-response space advertisement always includes at least one reply mechanism. The aircraft and exercise equipment ads feature toll-free telephone numbers and the "tummy trimmer" ad also provides a mailing address in very small print. The printer ad has a coupon as well as a toll-free number. Notice that callers of this toll-free number are provided with the name of the nearest dealer; a sales representative does not try to close the sale over the telephone. A call to the aircraft manufacturer is also unlikely to result in a strong sales pitch, but for different reasons. Think for a moment about the training and knowledge necessary to handle calls about the printer by simply providing the name of the nearest dealer versus the expertise necessary to deal with requests for information from potential purchasers of executive aircraft.

Specialty Advertisements in Print Media

Newspaper Inserts. Daily, and especially Sunday, newspapers are vehicles for the dissemination of preprinted inserts, most often using four-color printing, often on glossy paper stock. These inserts are an important advertising vehicle for many branded products and mass merchandisers.

Bind-ins and Blow-ins. These advertisements, usually in the form of postal reply cards, are found in most magazines today (frequently hampering the reader's efforts to keep the magazine open to the desired page). These cards may support the adjacent advertisement; that is, the ad presents basic information about a sophisticated new copying machine, for instance, and the card invites the reader to send away for additional information or to request a sales call. Frequently, though, the cards are stand-alone advertisements for a familiar product such as a subscription to a well-known magazine, perhaps the magazine in which the card is found. The cards can be stapled into the magazine (bind-ins)—more expensive, but less likely to be lost. They can also literally be blown in by specialized machinery—cheaper, but more easily lost.

Bingo Cards. Most trade journals, and many general-interest magazines, contain reader service cards, affectionately known in the trade as *bingo cards*. The reader can use these cards to send away for additional information from advertisers in that issue of the magazine. Bingo cards do provide a real service to some

FIGURE 1.7 ***Print Display Advertisements in* The Wall Street Journal, *May 12, 1987.***

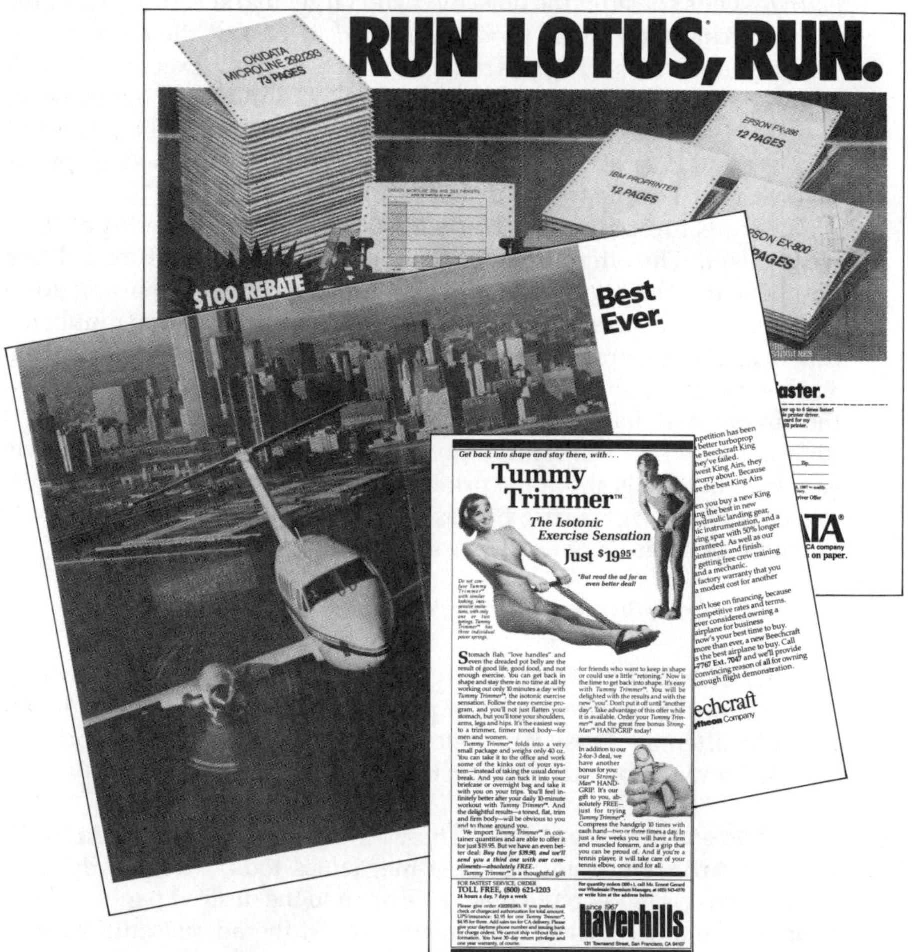

Source: "Run Lotus, Run" ad, from Okidata, Mt. Laurel, NJ; "Best Ever" ad, from Beechcraft, Whichita, KS; "Tummy Trimmer" ad, from Haverhills, San Francisco, CA

readers and some advertisers, but they tend to attract many respondents who are merely information seekers, not potential purchasers.

Specialty Advertisements in Various Media

There is a wide variety of miscellaneous direct-response devices. Figure 1.8 pictures several examples of specialty advertisements as they are used by various divisions of American Express.

Bang-Tail Envelopes and Bill/Package Stuffers. Direct marketers are quick to take advantage of any opportunity to transmit a direct-response offer to a prospective customer without incurring postage cost. The package in which your last mail-order purchase arrived probably also contained a brochure, a mini-catalog, or the current issue of the entire catalog. A bill from a retailer or a credit

FIGURE 1.8 ***Specialty Promotions: Personal Card Take–One Display and Parts of the American Express TRS 1987 Sweepstakes Mailing***

Source: Reprinted with permission of American Express Travel Related Services Company, Inc..

card statement often contains a number of brochures as well as an offer presented on the over-sized (bang-tail) flap of the envelope.

Coupons and Samples. Both coupons and samples can be transmitted by a wide variety of media—newspapers, magazines, mail, and home delivery are frequently used options. Although you might initially wonder why coupons and samples qualify as direct marketing media, both are increasingly being used in ways that allow marketers to track them and to build and expand marketing databases with the information they provide.

Direct Mail

Solo Mailings. A wide variety of marketing communications can be included under the heading of solo mailings. Solo mailings are generally understood to be any mailing piece that emphasizes a single product or service, as the Healthy Home Cooking mailer does.

The development of campaigns featuring one or more solo mailings will be discussed in Chapter 9.

Catalogs. Catalogs contain a line of merchandise—general or specialty, narrow or deep. We are all familiar with consumer catalogs. What many people do not realize is how extensively catalogs are being used as a sales tool in business-to-business marketing. The many issues involved in the development and management of consumer catalogs will be discussed in Chapter 10, and business-to-business catalogs will be covered in Chapter 14.

THE LARGEST DIRECT MARKETING FIRMS

To help us better understand the nature of the industry, let's take a look at the types of firms that make up the direct marketing industry.

The Bureau of the Census counted 12,200 firms whose primary business was selling products and services by mail in 1985.[9] This category, as explained earlier, does not include many companies that do a large volume of business via direct marketing. Table 1.4 shows the ten largest direct marketing firms as measured by direct-response sales volume. The list contains well-known and respected firms plus others that, although large, are less visible because they are primarily direct marketers. The list looked different in 1984, when Montgomery Ward's catalog operation and Gulf Oil's mail order division were still in existence, together accounting for over $1 billion in mail-order sales.[10]

[9] *Third Class Mail: Serving A Changing Society* (Direct Marketing Association, 1987), p. 4.

[10] Arnold Fishman, "The 1985 Mail Order Guide," *Direct Marketing*, July 1986, p. 26.

The Role of Service Agencies in the Direct Marketing Industry

Sellers of products and services, both large and small, are not the only players in the direct marketing industry. Several types of service firms also make important contributions to the industry.

There are three basic groups of service firms: general advertising agencies (whose primary business is serving media advertisers), full-service direct response agencies (whose primary business is serving direct marketers), and specialized direct-response service firms (which perform one or more specialized functions such as printing or list brokerage). Of course, it's not really this simple because there is overlap, especially between the general and direct-response agencies.

In recent years the general advertising agencies have become increasingly concerned about providing their clients with integrated communications programs, often on a global basis. This has led to feverish acquisition of com-

TABLE 1.4 Largest U.S. Direct Marketers in 1986

Company	*Products*	*Mail-Order Sales ($ millions)*
Sears, Roebuck & Co.	General merchandise, insurance, auto clubs	2,061.8
J. C. Penney	General merchandise, insurance	1,931.9
Time, Inc.	Books, magazines, cable TV	1,867.7
United Services Automobile Association	Insurance	1,589.4
GEICO	Insurance	1,395.6
Reader's Digest	Books, collectibles, general merchandise, magazines	1,250.0
Primerica (formerly American Can)	Audio-video,food, gardening, general	1,133.1
Capital Holding	Insurance	1,024.4
American Automobile Association	Auto clubs, insurance	1,000.0
Otto-Versand (Spiegel)	General merchandise	890.0

Source: Arnold Fishman, "The 1986 Mail Order Guide." *Direct Marketing*, July 1987, p. 40.

TABLE 1.5 Direct Response Ad Agencies U.S. Gross Billings

Top 10 Agencies Reporting Fees and Commissions Only	*In Millions* 1986	1985
Wunderman, Ricotta & Kline	224.5	175.7
Ogilvy & Mather Direct	207.4	172.0
MARCOA DR Group Inc.	110.0	101.0
Chapman Stone & Adler Inc.	97.0	99.5
Grey Direct International	94.0	81.8
Kobs & Brady Advertising Inc.	81.0	70.3
Rapp & Collins Direct Response Group	80.1	83.5
FCB Direct	78.4	60.6
Barry Blau & Partners	63.1	42.5
Top 10 Agencies Reporting Fees, Commissions, Internal Production Revenues		
The Direct Marketing Group Inc.	138.7	101.6
Krupp/Taylor	64.8	50.4
The Direct Marketing Agency Inc.	60.4	63.4
Epsilon	47.8	35.8
Customer Development Corp.	40.5	35.4
Direct Mail Corporation of America	40.0	39.8
Computer Marketing Services Inc.	37.5	26.4
Grizzard Advertising Inc.	13.7	8.1
Manus Services Corp.	12.4	12.5
Marketing Communications Inc.	11.7	13.0

Source: Reprinted from *Marketing News*, April 24, 1987, published by the American Marketing Association.

panies, among them direct-response agencies. Table 1.5 has two different rankings of agencies, first on the more traditional basis of media commissions and fees and the second on production costs (costs such as data processing or print production). The second group of agencies may be unfamiliar to you, but the first one includes several names you have probably heard in discussions of general advertising.

What is remarkable is the small number of service firms that specialize in some aspect of direct marketing. Stevenson counts "17 major software suppliers, 14 list/database compilers, 13 research and analysis companies, [and] 73 service

[11] John Stevenson, "The Next Direct Marketing," *Direct Marketing*, October 1986, p. 162.

bureaus."[11] This suggests that the service sector of the direct-response industry is very concentrated.

Figure 1.9 gives two views of suppliers of specialized services in the direct response industry. Stevenson, in compiling information from an industry directory, found 428 listings for agencies and service firms involved in direct marketing. As indicated in Figure 1.9a, some firms are listed under multiple headings. After the general category "agencies," the greatest number of listings of firms providing specialized direct marketing services is for "Consultants and [personnel] Recruiters"—242; and the smallest is for Envelope Suppliers—25.

Figure 1.9b shows the functions the 73 service bureaus were performing for their clients. All did list merge/purge (to be discussed in Chapter 4), but beyond that, the bureaus performed a wide variety of services related to direct marketing.

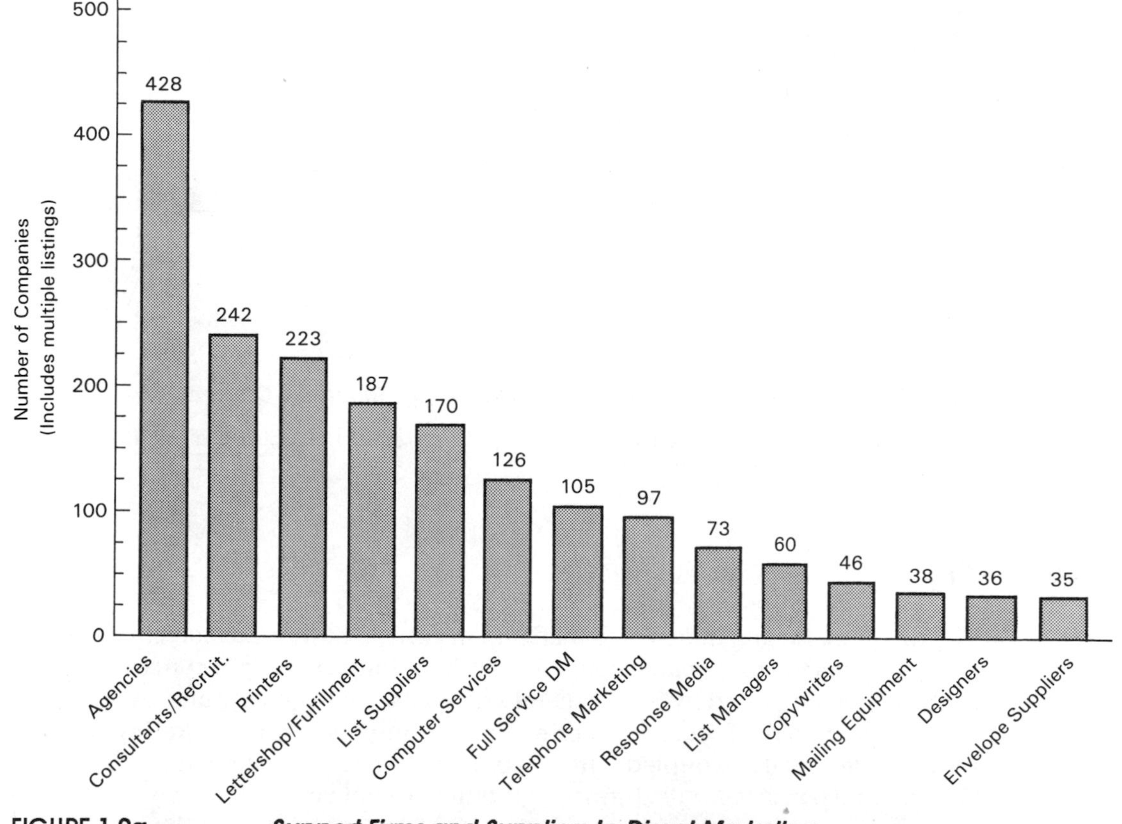

FIGURE 1.9a ***Support Firms and Suppliers to Direct Marketing***

Source: John Stevenson, "The Next Direct Marketing," *Direct Marketing*, October 1986, pp. 158-167. Used with permission of John Stevenson.

Function	% of Total Companies (N = 73)
Merge Purge D.P.	100
Lettershop	42
Product Fulfillment	30
Analysis	26
Telemarketing	15
Consulting	14
Software Sales	11
Creative	11
List Rental	7
Model Development	6
Research	6
System Development	1

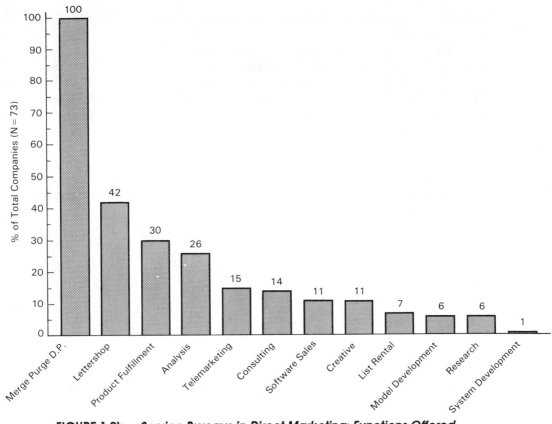

FIGURE 1.9b ***Service Bureaus in Direct Marketing: Functions Offered***

Source: John Stevenson, "The Next Direct Marketing," *Direct Marketing*, October 1986, pp. 158-167. Used with permission of John Stevenson.

SUMMARY

The direct marketing industry is made up of firms that rely exclusively on direct marketing and firms that are engaged in both traditional and direct marketing activities. It is supported by both general and specialized agencies and by specialty service providers. Direct marketing is the only type of marketing that is measurable, and that, coupled with its ability to hone in on precise market targets, is largely responsible for its dramatic growth in recent years. This growth has occurred in firms classified as "general marketers" as well as in firms that use direct-response methods to conduct all of their business. The direct marketing industry is a dynamic part of the total marketing industry and will continue its rapid evolution and growth for many years to come.

DISCUSSION QUESTIONS

1. In your own words, give a definition of direct marketing. How is direct marketing, as you have defined it, different from general marketing?
2. What does direct marketing do especially well compared to general marketing?
3. What are the decision variables of direct marketing?
4. Why is direct marketing growing so rapidly? Do you think it will continue to do so? Why?
5. Name some businesses that use aspects of direct marketing described in this chapter. Before reading this chapter, would you have thought of them as direct marketers? Why or why not?

SUGGESTED ADDITIONAL READINGS

1. Herbert Katzenstein and William S. Sachs, *Direct Marketing* (Columbus, Ohio: Charles E. Merrill Publishing Company, 1986).
2. Jim Kobs, *Profitable Direct Marketing* (Chicago: Crain Books, 1979).
3. Edward L. Nash, *Direct Marketing: Strategy/Planning/Execution* (New York: McGraw-Hill, 1982), pp. 16-30
4. Edward L. Nash, *The Direct Marketing Handbook* (New York: McGraw-Hill, 1984).
5. Bob Stone, *Successful Direct Marketing Methods*, 4th ed. (Chicago: National Textbook Company, 1988).

APPENDIX 1

DIRECT MARKETING AROUND THE WORLD

The United States is generally thought to be in the forefront of most aspects of direct-response marketing, but many of the same trends experienced in this country are driving the development and growth of direct marketing in industrialized nations around the world. These countries have the technological infrastructure necessary to support direct-response activities—sophisticated postal systems, computerized databases, credit card systems, toll-free telephone numbers, and growing electronic communications systems. At the same time they are experiencing demographic change, especially the entry of women into the labor force, and resulting lifestyle changes similar to those in the United States. Although data are difficult to obtain, it is probably safe to assume that business marketers in these industrialized countries are experiencing rapid increases in the cost of field sales calls, just as U.S. companies are. The world's largest direct marketers are still consumer-goods companies, however, as shown in Table 1.

The trend toward globalization of marketing efforts is affecting everyone. Most major corporations are multinational in scope, and U.S. firms are stimulating use of direct marketing techniques by their foreign subsidiaries. As advertising agencies and other marketing service firms have increasingly found themselves serving companies with operations in many parts of the world, they have accelerated their growth and acquisition strategies in order to provide

TABLE 1 World's Ten Largest Mail-Order Companies

Rank	*Company Name*	*Country*	*Year of Data*	*Mail-Order Sales ($MMs)*	*Type of Merchandise*
1	Sears, Roebuck & Company	United States	1985	2,809	General
2	Great Universal Stores	United Kingdom	1985	2,787	General
	Otto Versand	West Germany	1982	2,726	General
4	Schickedanz	West Germany	1982	2,079	General
5	Time, Inc.	United States	1985	1,863	Publishing
6	J.C. Penney	United States	1985	1,769	General
7	United Automobile Association Sevices	United States	1985	1,421	Insurance
8	Mobil	United States	1985	1,295	General
9	Colonial Penn	United States	1985	1,081	Insurance
10	GEICO	United States	1985	1,073	Insurance

Source: Arnold Fishman, "1988 International Mail Order Guide," *Direct Marketing*, August 1986, p. 42.

worldwide coverage for their clients. This, too, is providing access to direct marketing expertise in many parts of the world.

There are, however, major differences in the nature and stage of development of direct marketing activities in various countries around the world. These differences can be stated in terms of the size of the direct-response industry, customer acceptance of direct marketing activities, the availability of mailing lists and sophisticated databases, the kinds of services provided by postal and telephone systems, and governmental regulation.

It is important for marketers to understand both differences and similarities in direct marketing activities in countries where the industry is becoming established. What follows is a country-by-country summary of the status of the direct marketing industry for countries for which reasonably current data are available.

CANADA[1]

Though Canada is the world's second-largest country in terms of land area, its population was less than 26 million in 1987, about the same as that of the state of California. Although Canada is considered an English-speaking country, French is the primary language of 25 percent of its people. About 80 percent of Canadians live within 100 miles of the U.S. border, where they are able to receive U.S. radio and television. The eastern provinces contain the majority of the population and industry. The western provinces are sparsely populated, and businesses there are far behind their eastern counterparts in the use of direct marketing. Each of the ten provinces has consumer protection laws that can affect direct marketing activities.

Although Canadian culture is similar to that of the United States in many ways, Canada's small population and multiple ethnic groups make direct marketing very different. For example, the market is not large enough to support specialty catalogs. The few catalogs in existence have had to exert a broad appeal in order to be successful. As a general category, however, catalog sales lead all other types of consumer direct marketing in terms of sales dollars.

In Quebec, all advertising, including direct mail, must be in French as well as in English, which increases its cost. For sizable ethnic groups (Italians, Chinese, Ukrainians, Vietnamese, and others), mailing lists by language are not generally available. List availability is not considered adequate; only 584 lists were available in 1987, compared to about 50,000 in the United States. Because of the small population, lists are not large enough to allow for testing followed by roll-out of the revised campaign. Consequently, Canadian direct marketers have to place a great deal of emphasis on marketing research.

Canadian telephone and postal services are technologically sophisticated but expensive. Both WATS lines and toll-free numbers cost roughly twice as much as they do in the United States. There is a shortage of experienced telephone market-

[1] Gloria Savini, "Ode to Canada!" *Direct Marketing*, May 1987, pp. 28-31; Arnold Fishman, "1985 International Mail Order Guide," *Direct Marketing*, August 1986, p. 42.

ing managers and representatives. Canada's six-digit alphanumeric postal code is as powerful as the United State's Zip + 4. Both first- and third-class postal rates are higher than in the United States, and there is no nonprofit rate available. A three-tier third-class system is planned, and this will reduce rates for many mailers.

The single biggest hindrance to the growth of direct marketing in Canada appears to be a shortage of qualified persons at all levels.

BRAZIL[2]

With a population of 139 million (almost 40 percent of whom live in rural areas) and 31.1 million households, Brazil is a sleeping giant for direct marketing. A number of obstacles have slowed its growth, but in recent years direct-response activity has increased. One enabling factor has been a decrease in the country's inflation rate, although a recurrence of hyperinflation is a continuing concern. Reliable statistics are not available, but growth is occurring in both consumer and business markets, where lead-generation campaigns are just beginning.

More than 100 lists are available, but their quality is not uniformly good, resulting in multiple mailings to the same address and low response rates. Difficulties are compounded by the fact that inflation makes it difficult for catalog marketers to hold prices stable through a selling season. Direct-response print advertising is used to build in-house lists. Telephone marketing is new and growing. Some direct-response television is also used. Consumer attitudes toward direct marketing are now known.

Another obstacle has been the reluctance of many Brazilian advertising agencies to recommend direct marketing to their clients. Governmental regulation poses no problem, however; there are no laws restricting the use of direct marketing.

EUROPE[3]

According to one senior direct-response agency executive, direct marketing in Europe "is just starting to take off. It reminds me of the U.S. in the late 1970s." That view is supported by the sales figures in Table 1, which indicate that the largest European direct marketers deal in general merchandise, while in the United States general merchandise is rapidly being replaced by specialty retailing. Although penetration of direct marketing is lower in Europe than in the United States (see Table 2) and varies a great deal from country to country (Table 3), another direct marketer concludes that "in the state of the art, they're not behind the U.S.

[2] "Direct Marketing World Survey," *Direct Marketing*, April 1987, p. 34; "Direct Marketing Makes International Waves," *Advertising Age*, January 12, 1987, pp. S-14-S-16.

[3] Lori Kesler, "U.S. Agencies Stake Claims Around the Globe," *Advertising Age*, January 12, 1987, p. S-2; Fishman, "1985 International Mail Order Guide," pp. 42-43.

TABLE 2 U.S./European Mail-Order Spending

Country	*Avg. Annual Mail-Order Dollars Per Capita*
Unites States	$642
West Germany	124
Switzerland	82
United Kingdom	67
France	53
Finland	50
Denmark	40
Netherlands	33
Norway	22
Belgium	20
Italy	9
Spain	4

Source: Lori Kesler, "U.S. Agencies Stake Claims Around the World," *Advertising Age*, January 12, 1987, p. 1.

Note: Based on 1984 and 1985 data. *European Marketing Data & Statistics 1986–1987, 1984 International Fact Book* on DM, DMA.

at all. In creativity and graphics they may be a little ahead. They're not afraid to take a chance, to work with a little more panache." A substantial proportion of European ad budgets is devoted to direct mail (see Table 4), with an unknown portion of broadcast and print expenditures going to direct-response advertising. Because of the high cost of postage, European direct marketers have been forced to become more sophisticated than their U.S. counterparts in the use of direct-response newspaper advertising, and several countries are clearly further along in the exploitation of interactive electronic marketing (videotex).

United Kingdom[4]

Direct marketing is growing rapidly in Britain, fueled by market fragmentation and the desire of packaged-goods marketers to use their promotional dollars more effectively.

[4] Michael York Palmer, "ACORN Segmentation Analysis of Direct Mail Makes Interesting Conclusions," *Direct Marketing*, November 1986, pp. 156-157; Michael York Palmer, "Mail Order Outstripping Retail Sales," *Direct Marketing*, December 1986, pp. 112-113; "First Direct Marketing Centre in the U.K.," *Direct Marketing*, October 1986, p. 214; "Grocery Shopping from the Easy Chair," *Direct Marketing*, May 1987, pp. 78-82; Direct Marketing World Survey," pp. 32-40; "Direct Marketing Makes International Waves," pp. S-12-S-14.

TABLE 3 Addressed Direct Mail Items per Household

Country	1981	1982	1983	1984	1985
Belgium	87	96	114	125	132
Denmark	62	64	67	71	74*
Finland	86	87	95	111	119
France	72	77	79	86	93*
Ireland	10	12	12	13	18
Netherlands	102	103	103	135	171
Portugal	NA	24	16	16	17
Sweden	110	113	119	128	116
Switzerland	126	134	144	147	152
United Kingdom	49	52	52	60	62
West Germany	119	118	119	126	123*

*estimate

Note: Services Postaux Europeens.

Source: Lori Kesler, "U.S. Agencies Stake Claims Around the World," *Advertising Age,* January 12, 1987, A1-5B p. 16.

In 1985, direct mail was the third-largest advertising medium, behind print and television, and was experiencing the fastest growth. True, some of the growth in expenditures over the last few years has come from increases in postal rates, but real growth has been considerable. Much of the recent growth in direct mail is ap-

TABLE 4 Proportion of European Advertising Budgets Devoted to Each Medium

Medium	1984	1985	1986*
Tv and radio	25%	22%	21%
Newspaper and magazine	44	46	46
Direct Mail: unaddressed	25	24	15
Direct Mail: addressed	26	25	26
All other media	39	39	37

*estimated

Note: Services Postaux Europeens.

Sources: Lori Kesler, "U.S. Agencies Stake Claims Around the World," *Advertising Age,* January 12, 1987, p. 19.

parently attributable to increasingly sophisticated marketing databases and to the deregulation of financial services markets in 1986.

Telephone marketing is growing rapidly but expenditures are still small compared to those for direct mail. Inbound telemarketing—mainly inquiries and orders generated by direct-response advertising—is experiencing a favorable environment. British consumers, however, view outbound telemarketing with hostility.

Each of the 20.6 million households in the United Kingdom (whose total population in 1986 was 56.4 million) received 0.8 piece of mail per week in 1985, with more affluent households getting considerably more than the average. New specialty catalogs are appealing to female consumers who had not previously been direct-mail buyers. In 1985, mail-order sales grew at a more rapid rate (10.5 percent) than retail store sales (8.7 percent).

The British Post Office actively markets direct-mail services and has kept increases in postal rates below the rate of inflation. Seventy percent of direct mail takes advantage of cheaper second-class postal rates. There is also a successful videotex operation in the United Kingdom. It transmits information over the telephone, and an adapter allows that information to be displayed on a television screen. With about 70,000 terminals and an audience of about 400,000, Prestel offers between 600 and 700 different services to its subscribers.

The importance of the industry in Britain is evidenced by the creation of a Diploma in Direct Marketing at the Kingston Polytechnic Business School. The first educational program of its kind in Europe, it serves both college students and practitioners and assists in curriculum development for other educational institutions. Established with the cooperation of the British Direct Marketing Association, the program also sponsors research and maintains library facilities.

France[5]

Direct marketing apparently started slowly in France because of consumer attitudes/shopping patterns and governmental restrictions, but recent growth has made up for the slow start. In 1986, direct marketing accounted for 25 percent of 1986 advertising expenditures equivalent to $7.5 billion. Consumer mail-order sales accounted for only 2.5 percent of retail sales, but grew by 25 percent in 1986, a year marked by a number of terrorist attacks on retail stores.

France's population in 1987 was 54 million (19 million households). The scope of consumer mail order has traditionally been limited, with 24 percent of consumer mail order sales represented by books and other published materials. That percentage is expected to decline as sales of other merchandise categories grow. Catalogs are becoming more upscale and are beginning to target upscale males as well as females. Consumer attitudes toward direct mail are considered

[5] "Direct Marketing Report—France, Spain, Italy and Israel," DMA Release No. 800.4, January 1984; "Direct Marketing Makes International Waves," pp. S-10-S-12; "Direct Marketing World Survey," pp. 38, 40.

favorable: 80 percent of French people report that they open and read direct-mail advertisements.

Recent regulatory changes that have affected direct marketing include:

- Green numbers, the French equivalent of the 800 number, were first made available in 1984.
- Direct-response television advertising using toll-free numbers was first permitted in February 1986.
- Third-class postal rates are now available to direct marketers. (Previously the only option had been first-class mail.)
- Direct marketers have had access to the telephone list only since 1985. They do not have access to other governmental data, including census data, auto registrations, and utility subscribers.

The list situation in France is far from satisfactory. There are only about 350 consumer lists available, and related databases do not appear to be extensive. There are only 10 business lists in existence, but these are described as very effective. The other major impediments to the growth of direct marketing in France are the shortage of trained personnel and business's lack of understanding of direct marketing.

The significance of all other direct marketing accomplishments in France, however, pales in comparison to the development, beginning in 1981, of the national videotex system, Teletel. This system is based on the Minitel terminal (and is often referred to as Minitel) and is sponsored by the government-owned telecommunications system. Terminals are loaned to high-volume consumer telephone users in areas where the Electronic Telephone Directory Service has replaced the paper telephone book, as well as to consumers designated by commercial service providers such as banks and newspapers. It can also be rented for $12 per month.

As of mid-1986, there were 1.8 million installed Minitel terminals and nearly 2.5 million hours were being logged on the system each month. (For comparison, British Telecom's videotex service, established in 1980, has 70,000-90,000 users, and West Germany's, begun in 1983, has about 52,000.) In September 1986, there were over 3,000 services and systems available to users, with a new service being established every 2 days. Seventy-two percent of the time logged on the system is related to consumer-oriented services, with the national electronic telephone directory being far and away the most used service. While electronic shopping appears to be growing in popularity, especially among time-pressured consumers, it still represents only a small percentage of total sales. One large cataloger reports that of its 100,000 daily orders, 45 percent are made by mail, 52 percent by telephone, and 3 percent by Minitels, even though that system is available 24 hours a day.

Business use of the system is significant and increasing: 700,000 of the Minitels are used in businesses, with the distribution sector being the heaviest user. Retailers use the system for verifying consumer credit cards and checks, for inventory control and replenishment, for analysis of operations, and for sales to consumers. Publicly available electronic kiosks are also popular. Wholesalers use the system extensively for communications of all kinds with their dealer network.

According to two French communications experts, "The most important victory of Minitel has been in winning over the noncomputer literates to the use of advanced technologies in their day-to-day life.[6] The French government also hopes that this creation of a technologically literate society, along with the hardware and software developments spawned by the system, will enable France to move into the twenty-first century as a leader in world technology.

West Germany[7]

Direct marketing is well established in West Germany, which has numerous large mail-order houses, generally favorable public attitudes, and increasing sophistication in areas such as list segmentation. The most current statistics indicate that expenditures on direct-response advertising are increasing at an annual rate of 7-10 percent as compared to slightly over 4 percent for advertising in general. Over 80 percent of all West German firms use direct-response elements in their communications programs. As shown in Table 1, two of the world's ten largest mail-order firms are based here.

With a 1985 population of 61 million, West Germany represents a large, affluent market. Catalogs are very popular with both urban and rural consumers, and magazines and direct-response television are also used extensively. The postal system is considered very efficient.

There are many consumer protection laws that affect the operations of mail-order firms, and West German privacy laws are among the strictest in Europe. Firms that transmit data to other companies must register with the government. Any firm that maintains a database must have an employee charged with protecting privacy rights and that employee must submit reports to the government. The amount and type of data about customers that can be made available to other firms are severely limited.

Belgium[8]

Belgium, with a population of 9.8 million people (3.6 million households), had only a few traditional users of direct-response marketing, primarily publishers and financial services companies, before 1986. Since that time there has been a

[6] George Hanon and Edith Pointeau, "Minitel Videotex in France: What We Have Learned," Direct Marketing, January 1987, p. 68.

[7] Barbara Lewis, "Direct Marketing Report—West Germany, Austria, Switzerland," DMA Release No. 800.3, January 1987; Fishman, "1985 International Mail Order Guide," pp. 42-46; "*Direct Marketing* Moving into European Fast Lane," *Advertising Age*, May 12, 1986, pp. 36, 38.

[8] "Direct Marketing World Survey," p. 32; "Direct Marketing Makes International Waves," pp. S-21-S-22.

noticeable increase in interest among businesses of various types. Direct response accounted for $48 million in sales in 1985 (less than 1 percent of retail sales) and 17 to 20 percent of total advertising expenditures.

The two primary media are direct mail and couponing in space advertising. There is no commercial TV in Belgium and hence no direct-response television advertising. Telephone marketing is in its infancy but growing rapidly. There are between 150 and 200 lists available to direct marketers.

As of early 1987, there was no legislation regulating direct mail or telephone marketing, but it seems likely that in the near future there will be privacy legislation governing the uses of databases.

Switzerland[9]

Mail order has been accepted in Switzerland since the late 1800s. One out of every three Swiss citizens shops by mail, and attitudes toward mail order are positive.

The early use of direct marketing is attributed to the multilingual population and resulting high advertising costs. The marketer in Switzerland must create campaigns in three languages-German, French, and Italian. The small population of this country (6.4 million people and 2.5 million households in 1987) adds to the difficulty of making advertising cost effective. One-third of all advertising expenditures are now devoted to direct marketing, with 85 percent of these allocated to direct mail.

The volume of direct mail per household, estimated by the Swiss Post Office to be 11.5 pieces per week, is quite high for a European country, and response rates are falling. The Swiss Direct Marketing Association maintains a list of persons who do not wish to receive unsolicited mail, but its use is voluntary. As of 1987, there was no governmental regulation of direct mail or telephone marketing and a preferential rate for mail weighing less than 50 grams was offered. The number of lists available is not known, but a number of list brokers are active in the country.

There is little commercial time available on Swiss television channels, and commercial radio is in its infancy, so broadcast direct marketing is not a major factor in the industry. Direct-response advertising is found in both newspapers and magazines.

Holland[10]

Although few current statistics are available, Holland is another European country in which direct marketing got an early start. In 1979, direct marketing advertising expenditures were greater than those of France, which has a population

[9] Lewis, "Direct Marketing Report—West Germany, Austria, Switzerland; "Direct Marketing World Survey," p. 40; "Direct Marketing Makes International Waves," pp. S-25-S-26.

[13] Murray Raphel, "Direct Mail in Italy? Bene! Bene!" *Direct Marketing*, February 1988, p. 100; "Direct Marketing World Survey," pp. 34-36; "Direct Marketing Makes International Waves," p. S-21.

base more than three times that of Holland (14.6 million people and 5.5 million households in 1987). By 1986, direct marketing expenditures were estimated to be 39 percent of all advertising expenditures. Another indicator of rapid growth is the 100 firms known to be users of direct marketing. There are as many as 250 consumer and 1,200 business lists available.

Austria[11]

In spite of strict privacy laws that forbid the transfer of personal information, including age, financial and credit status, political and religious affiliation, purchase profiles, and frequency of purchase, direct marketing is growing in Austria. Lists are widely available, but because of the privacy restrictions cannot be segmented as easily as in other countries.

Consumer attitudes toward mail order are quite favorable: 40 percent of the country's 7.5 million people bought by mail in 1984, and 80 percent of Austrian companies use direct-response techniques. Toll-free numbers are just becoming available and are not yet widely used for ordering. The mail is considered reliable although slow and expensive. The rest of the media infrastructure is well developed, but broadcast advertising to children is strictly regulated.

Experts predict continuing growth and development of the direct marketing industry. There is considerable interest in the possibility of electronic shopping by computer.

Italy[12]

The direct marketing industry in Italy is small and consequently experiencing a rapid growth rate (approaching 30 percent in recent years). Telephone marketing is growing the most rapidly, up 50 percent in 1986, followed by direct mail (30 percent), catalogs, and business-to-business (both 20 percent). Approximately 30 Italian firms account for the bulk of direct-response advertising.

Consumer mail-order sales were $850 million in 1985, about 1 percent of total retail sales. In both 1984 and 1985, mail-order sales grew more rapidly than did department store sales. Appliances and furniture were the original staples of Italian mail-order marketing. In recent years, however, the focus has shifted to clothing, which appeals to the fashion-conscious Italian consumer and provides higher margins. Sales of mutual funds by mail have also grown rapidly since the passage of enabling legislation. The 1986 population of Italy was 57 million persons in 14 million households, providing a market of moderate size for mail-order marketers.

[11] Lewis, "Direct Marketing Report—West Germany, Austria, Switzerland"; Emanuel Soshensky, "Direct Marketing in Austria Is Expected to Grow Despite Harsh Privacy Restrictions," *DM News*, December 1, 1985, pp. 6-7.

[12] "Direct Marketing Report—France, Spain, Italy and Israel"; Raphel, "Direct Mail in Italy?", pp. 100, 102; "Direct Marketing World Survey," p. 36; "Direct Marketing Makes International Waves," pp. S-18-S-19.

Business-to-business direct marketing is used by subsidiaries of American companies such as IBM and by a growing number of domestic companies. There are only 80 consumer lists available, but there are 1,800 business lists. List brokers do not operate in Italy; each firm rents its own list.

Consumer attitudes toward mail order are generally favorable, with 70 percent of respondents in a recent survey saying that they like to receive mail. Attitudes toward telephone marketing are unknown. Telemarketing has not been used much in consumer markets (toll-free numbers were not due to be available until the spring of 1987). There is a bulk postal rate available (fifth class), but Italian mail service has historically been both expensive and unreliable.

Italy lags behind the United States and a number of countries in Western Europe in the development of direct marketing, but experts see increasing interest among businesses of all kinds.

Sweden[13]

The direct-marketing industry in Sweden is a clear beneficiary of the government's extensive records on its populace. Every Swede is assigned a ten-digit identification number, which allows the collection of extensive demographic data on individuals. Privacy laws in Sweden are not strict, and this information is made available to companies for a fee. Consumer attitudes toward direct mail are generally favorable, and business marketers are major users of the medium.

The small population (8.4 million people living in 4 million households) and the ready availability of lists and data have stimulated recent annual growth rates in direct marketing expenditures (they are now approaching 20 percent). The growth of mail order is also facilitated by the affluence of the population and the predominance of two-wage-earner households. Mail-order sales accounted for 6.4 percent of Sweden's total retail sales in 1985. Telephone marketing is just coming into widespread use, but advertising on radio and television has not been permitted.

Norway[14]

Norway is currently experiencing the most rapid increase in the growth of direct mail of any European country: it has almost doubled in the past 6 years. Databased direct-mail marketing is still in its early stages, however, with only 50 companies using it.

Norway had a population of 4.1 million persons (1.7 million households) in 1987. There are 120 consumer lists and 5 large business databases, but government

[13]Lewis, "Direct Marketing Report—Norway, Sweden, Finland and The Netherlands"; "Direct Marketing Makes International Waves," pp. S-10-S-12; "Direct Marketing World Survey," pp. 38, 40.

[14] Lewis, "Direct Marketing Report—Norway, Sweden, Finland and The Netherlands"; "Direct Marketing World Survey," pp. 38, 40; Murray Raphel, "Norway: Europe's Fastest Growing User of Direct Mail," Direct Marketing, December 1987, pp. 118, 120.

registers are not made available to the Norwegian direct-marketing industry. Advertising in print media is available, but firms can engage in telephone marketing only to their own customer list. Radio and television advertising are not permitted. While consumers are generally favorable toward direct marketing, each household receives only 117 pieces of mail per year.

Finland[15]

Finland, with a population of 4.9 million people (1.89 million households), is just beginning to experience rapid growth in direct marketing. Expenditures increased 25 percent in 1987 and now account for 11 percent of all advertising spending. More than 60 companies are active in the field.

List bartering has been common among Finnish companies, but a privacy law that went into effect at the beginning of 1988 has caused the emphasis to shift to compilation of large-scale lists. Business marketers are heavy users of direct mail. Consumers are extremely favorable toward direct mail, and personalization is very important to its success. Print media and television are also available to direct marketers, but there is no commercial radio. All advertisers must obey general acceptability guidelines.

AUSTRALIA[16]

Direct marketing offers major advantages in a country with a large land area and a relatively small population (15.9 million people in 1986). In spite of some difficulties, total direct marketing expenditures have been growing at a rate of 10 percent per year for the past decade, with business-to-business direct marketing expected to grow 25 percent a year for the next few years.

Australian consumers have been skeptical about direct marketing; many of them perceive it as "junk mail." The Australian Direct Marketing Association, in cooperation with Australia Post and Telecom, has begun a program called Operation Integrity to educate consumers about the benefits of direct mail.

List availability is fair, with about 1,000 consumer and business lists in existence. Australia Post publishes a list catalog and offers other services to encourage the use of direct mail. The quality of lists, however, is often poor, resulting in many duplicate mailings that aggravate the problem of consumer distrust.

Direct marketing expenditures in 1986 were about $230 million, resulting in sales of about $1.65 billion. Direct mail, much of it lead-generation programs in both consumer and business markets, accounted for over 38 percent of total ex-

[15] Lewis, "Direct Marketing Report—Norway, Sweden, Finland and The Netherlands"; "Direct Marketing World Survey," pp. 38, 40; Murray Raphel, "The Big Finnish...Is Just the Beginning," Direct Marketing, April 1988, pp. 80, 81, 84.

[16] "Direct Marketing Makes International Waves," pp. S-17-18; "Direct Marketing World Survey," p. 32.

penditures and 53 percent of sales. Magazines and newspapers accounted for 24 and 9 percent of expenditures, respectively. Direct-response television is relatively new, and expenditures in that medium were about 7 percent of the total. Direct-response radio accounted for less than 0.5 percent. Toll-free telephone numbers have only recently become available, but telephone marketing is growing appreciably, especially in business markets.

There are no special laws restricting direct marketing, but federal and state consumer protection laws apply to all transactions.

JAPAN[17]

Japan, with a 1985 population of 120.7 million people (36.5 million households) is also experiencing significant growth in direct marketing despite significant problems. Growth in total expenditures of about 10 percent per year is expected to continue through 1990, but sales in 1986 were only 1 percent of the country's total retail sales. In the past most direct marketing was targeted to consumers, but business use is beginning to show rapid growth (about 20 percent per year).

List availability is a major problem. Only about 200 usable consumer and 100 business lists are known to direct marketers. Recording of Japanese names is difficult, and the existence of different character sets makes computerization and conversion from one set to another error-prone. Consequently, less than half of the lists are computerized. Japanese firms are less willing to rent their customer lists than are their counterparts in other countries.

One result is that print media, especially newspapers, are important for two-step programs in which names are captured and then mailed. Direct mail is expensive, with bulk postage rates only recently available. Still, it is cost effective when a good list exists. There is considerable resistance on the part of Japanese consumers to unsolicited telephone marketing calls, but toll-free numbers are now available (though expensive), and the volume of in-bound calling is growing, even though credit cards are not widely used in Japan.

Japanese consumers have traditionally been wary of direct mail, partly because of unsatisfactory experiences with direct selling, which is a major component of retailing in Japan, but acceptance is growing rapidly. This is true of both Japanese-based companies and foreign companies that market their goods through catalog centers in department stores.

There are no laws specifically restricting the use of direct marketing, but concerns about privacy are growing.

[17] "Direct Marketing Makes International Waves," pp. S-22–S-24; "Direct Marketing World Survey," p. 36; "The Japanese Go on Mail-Order Shopping Spree," *Business Week*, September 7, 1987, p. 44.

2

Strategies for Direct Marketers

The decision variables discussed in Chapter 1 are the heart of the short-term planning process for direct marketing. But it is also important for direct marketers to take a longer-term perspective on what constitutes success in their particular line of business. Without thoughtful long-term strategic planning they will find it difficult to cope with competition and marketplace change. Even extremely successful firms are hard put to manage the changes that occur at such a rapid rate in today's business environment.

TUPPERWARE: ADAPTING TO CHANGING MARKET CONDITIONS[1]

Tupperware has long been a pioneer and leader in the direct sales of plastic containers via the "home party plan." Tupperware had enjoyed an enviable record of growth in sales and profits until the early 1980s, when a slide began.[2] Between 1983

[1] The discussion of Tupperware is based on David W. Cravens, Gerald E. Hills, and Robert B. Woodruff, *Marketing Management*, (Homewood, Il.: Richard D. Irwin, 1987), pp. 286-288; "How Tupperware Hopes to Liven Up the Party," *Business Week*, February 25, 1985, pp. 108-109; "Tupperware: Sales Rebound Under Way," *Advertising Age*, March 3, 1986, p. 32; "Dart & Kraft: Why It'll be Dart and Kraft," *Business Week*, July 7, 1986, p. 33; Jerrold Ballinger, "Tupperware in Shift to Direct Response," *DM News*, May 1, 1987, p. 2.

[2] Until 1980, Tupperware was a division of Dart Industries, a diversified consumer products firm. In 1980 Dart merged with the Kraft Corporation in a move that was designed to bolster the sagging profit margins of Kraft's stagnant food products business. In 1986 Tupperware, West Bend appliances, Hobart food-service equipment, and Wilsonart laminates were sold off to a group of private investors, becoming Premark International. One reason for Tupperware's sale was said to be faltering profit margins.

and 1984 sales decreased 6 percent to $777 million and profits fell 27 percent to $139 million.

A number of factors could be blamed for this decline, most of them common to the entire direct-sales industry. The industry is counter-cyclical; when the economy is weak and unemployment is high, there is an abundance of sales representatives; and when the economy is strong and jobs are plentiful there is a shortage of sales reps. This has been true ever since the industry was founded, but new developments have further aggravated the situation.

The primary development has been the continuing, and apparently permanent, influx of women into the labor force. These women are for the most part, no longer available to be Tupperware dealers and managers. Their time-pressured lives also leave them little time to attend the home parties on which Tupperware had based its success. Other demographic changes, including more single-person and single-parent households and an aging population, have also affected the market for Tupperware.

In addition, Tupperware containers represent a mature industry. With about 80 percent of the market in 1985, Tupperware's products are familiar to consumers, negating the need for the demonstration that is the heart of the home party. Price competition also intensified as the market matured, with competitors selling their products in mass-merchandise outlets for as much as 40 percent below Tupperware prices.

Facing these difficult changes in their operating environment, Tupperware managers could have reacted in many different ways. They could have followed their competitors into supermarket and mass merchandise outlets. They could have drastically lowered their prices. They could have intensified their attempts to recruit sales representatives. They could have simply continued to operate in the same way, hoping things would improve.

Instead, a new top-management team chose two primary approaches to regaining profitability. First, they introduced a major new product line—the Ultra 21 line of freezer-to-oven-or-microwave cookware. This line has margins that are considerably higher than those of older products and was designed to excite consumer interest.

Second, they made a number of major changes in Tupperware's time-honored marketing approaches. The traditional home party was not abandoned, but dealers were encouraged to arrange shorter parties in other locations such as health clubs and work. Advertising expenditures were greatly expanded, from $2 million in 1984 to $15 million in 1986. Before 1985 the objective of Tupperware advertising was to attract sales representatives. In 1985 the advertising focus was on promoting the new Ultra 21 line. And in 1987 the company also began to test the use of direct-response television to provide leads for dealers.

Management's approach to its dealer network was also revised. Today there is a greater emphasis on the training of Tupperware dealers and managers; in addition to their sales commissions, managers are now paid for time spent training dealers. Recruitment of new dealers is still stressed, but emphasis is on productivity, rather than on numbers. Incentives such as group life and health insurance and smaller steps between bonuses are being offered to dealers.

Early results suggest that the strategy is paying off. Reported sales for 1986 were $822 million, a reversal of the downward trend that had been in effect for a number of years.

THE NATURE OF STRATEGIC MARKETING

A strategy such as Tupperware's, which appears to be successfully guiding a firm that had been faltering in a complex, dynamic environment, is arrived at only after careful consideration of numerous issues. Further, it is developed in the context of the overall strategic direction of the larger organization to which the business belongs.

Planning takes place at several levels in the strategically managed firm. At the corporate level, *strategic planning* establishes broad directions for the guidance of all parts of the organization. At the next level, *strategic market planning* is done for individual "businesses" within the firm. Finally, plans are developed for individual functions within the operating unit. Figure 2.1 portrays the nature of and relationships between the various levels of business planning.

This chapter focuses on the second level—strategic market planning. In this way we set the stage for the remainder of the book, which focuses on individual elements at the third level—operational planning for the direct marketing function. Strategic market planning is discussed first also because the direct marketing

CORPORATE STRATEGIC PLAN

Corporate Mission and Objectives
Centralized Resource Allocation
Performance Monitoring
Diversification Planning

STRATEGIC MARKETING PLAN

Business Definition
Systematic Evaluation of Alternatives
Tailored Objectives

OPERATIONAL MARKETING PLAN

Marketing Program Plans
Budgets

FIGURE 2.1

LEVELS OF STRATEGIC PLANNING

Source: Adapted from Day, *Strategic Market Planning* (St. Paul, MN: West Publishing Co., 1985), p. 7.

manager is likely to be either a major contributor to, or the manager responsible for, this plan.

Whether at the corporate level or at the individual business level, a strategic plan has the same set of components. The difference is in the scope of the operations covered by the plan. The basic elements of a business strategy are shown in Figure 2.2. As you study these elements, notice that the first six apply to all businesses, whether they have one unit or many. The last two elements apply only to multiunit businesses.

The product-market in which the business competes. This includes products offered, markets served, and the degree of vertical integration.

The level of investment. The level of investment will depend on whether the strategic objectives are growth, maintenance of an existing position, harvesting, or liquidating.

The sustainable competitive advantage. The core concept in strategic market management is a distinctive advantage that can be sustained over time in the face of competition.

The distinctive competencies and assets. Distinctive competencies are the things that a business does especially well. Distinctive assets are assets that are strategically important and are strong relative to the competition.

The strategic objectives. These objectives should reflect long-term goals and the types of effort required to develop distinctive competencies and assets.

The functional-area policies needed to compete in the selected product-markets. Policies for functional areas such as marketing, production, and finance form the basis for strategy implementation. They also ensure that the functions and various subfunctions will be coordinated with one another in support of the strategy.

The allocation of resources over business units. Both financial and nonfinancial resources must be allocated among the different business units.

The creation of value by having business units that support and complement one another, known as synergy. A multiple-unit organization can achieve an overall impact that is greater than the sum of the impacts of each of its individual units.

FIGURE 2.2 ***Elements of a Business Strategy***

Source: Adapted from David A. Aacker, *Strategic Market Management* (New York: John Wiley & Sons, 1984), pp. 4-6.

IDENTIFYING THE STRATEGIC BUSINESS UNIT[3]

The strategic marketing plan involves essentially the same set of activities, but at a lower organizational level, that of a strategic business unit (SBU). Before strategic market planning can begin, the SBU must be defined. How to divide a large organization into planning units is often not obvious. The units must be neither too small nor too large to be meaningful for planning purposes.

The ideal SBU is "any organizational unit that has (or should have) both a defined business strategy and a manager with sales and profit responsibility."[4] Sometimes the business units within an organization seem obvious: a firm that publishes a number of trade periodicals, for instance, might manage each one as a separate business. Usually, however, the identification of the SBUs is not so easy. IDG Communications, a subsidiary of International Data Group and the world's largest publisher of computer-related newspapers and magazines, is a good case in point. With over 100 publications in 34 countries, IDGC is organized into multiple units in both its domestic and international operations.

To qualify as a strategic business unit an entity within a larger organization must have a number of identifiable characteristics.

The SBU must serve an external as opposed to an internal market. When you look at the IDGC domestic organizational chart (Figure 2.3), the nature of some of the company's served markets is obvious just from the name of the division. When you study the chart more closely, the logic with which publications have been grouped together is generally clear. However, two of the divisions, The Marcomm Group and International Marketing Services, appear to be service providers, not publishing divisions.

The Marcomm (Marketing Communications) Group makes available a number of services to the publishing divisions: circulation promotion (direct-mail planning, creative and production services), list management, sales promotion, marketing research, and public relations. Its services are billed to the client publication within IDGC. It operates as an autonomous unit with bottom-line responsibility.

The other nonpublishing unit, International Marketing Services, sells advertising in IDGC publications around the world to U.S. firms that want to sell computer-related products in foreign countries where IDGC's publications appear. This unit receives what is essentially a media commission for each ad placed, but this is not sufficient to cover the unit's costs of operation. It lacks both the bottom-

[3] This discussion of SBUs is based on: George S. Day, *Strategic Market Planning* (St. Paul, MN: West Publishing Co., 1985), pp. 41-42; David A. Aaker, *Strategic Market Management* (New York: John Wiley & Sons, 1984), pp. 8, 9; promotional materials of International Data Group; interview with Jack Edmonston, president of The IDG Marcomm Group.

[4] David A. Aaker, *Strategic Market Management*, p. 8.

FIGURE 2.3 *The IDGC Domestic Organizational Chart as of 1987*

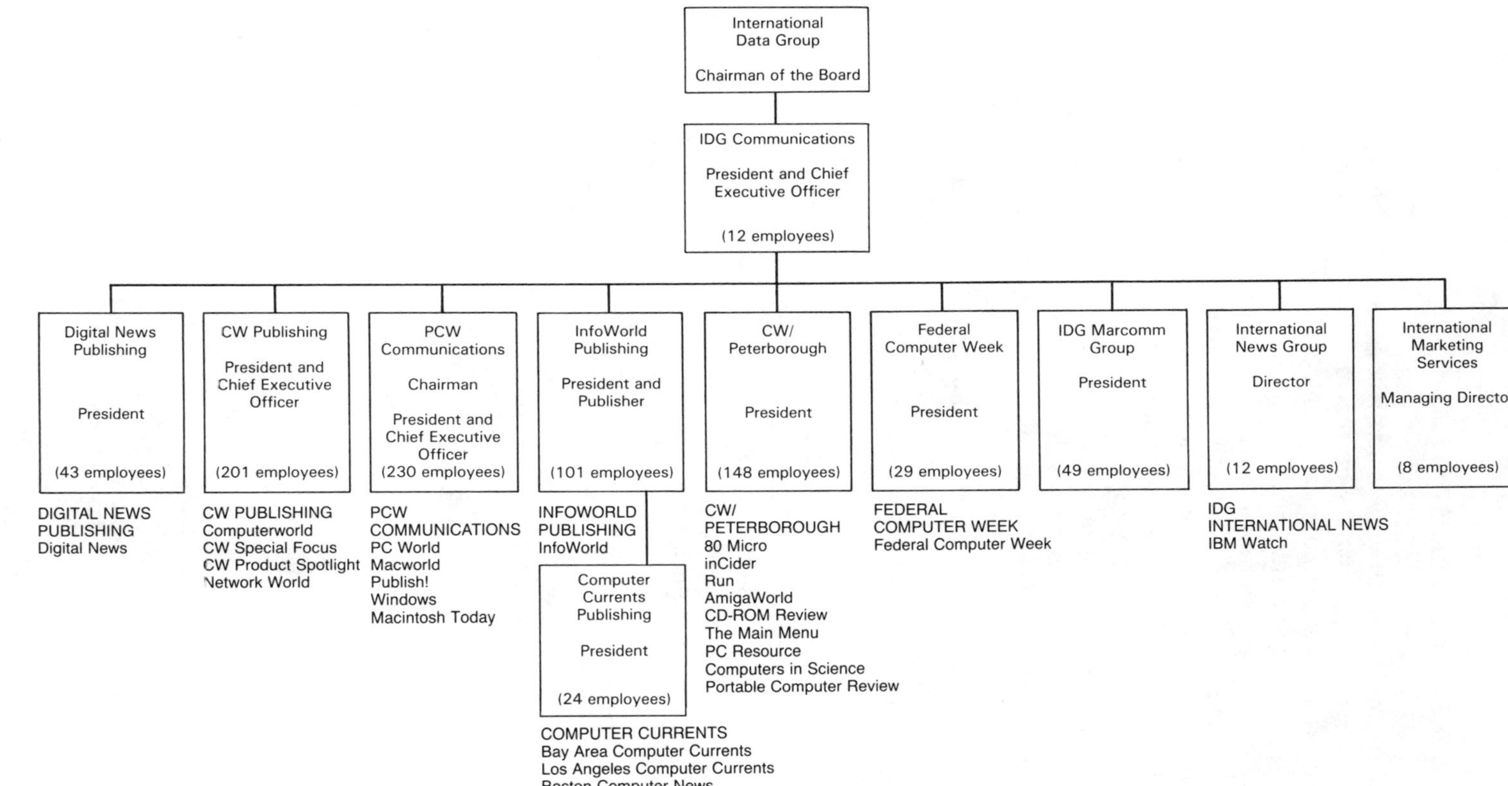

line responsibility of the Marcomm Group and its flexibility of operations, and does not qualify as a strategic business unit. Instead, it is a service provider within IDGC.

The SBU should have a distinct group of customers and competitors, both of which are different from those of other SBU's within the firm. Some of IDGC's divisions serve very broad markets, while others serve very specialized ones. CW Publishing is responsible for *Computerworld* and other products that serve information systems professionals in medium to large organizations, while PCW Communications and CW/Peterborough publish magazines for users of specific brands of personal computers.

Management of the SBU should have control over the factors that are critical to success in its industry. At IDGC each division has its own management structure, which exercises a great deal of autonomy. For example, each division establishes its own editorial policy and marketing plans and controls its own production facilities.

One good indication that an SBU is largely in control of its own destiny is managerial freedom to purchase a resource from outside the firm even though that resource is available internally. Other divisions of IDGC can obtain services from the Marcomm Group or from outside suppliers, usually on the basis of competitive bids. Likewise, the Marcomm Group can and does bid on jobs outside the company.

The SBU should be strategically autonomous. That is, its strategy should be independent of the strategies of other SBUs. Strategic autonomy is important to the operations of IDGC in the United States, but even more critical for its international operations. IDGC has achieved an unusual degree of success in international publishing (see Fig. 2.4 for international organizational chart) by persistently pursuing start-up opportunities around the world, by hiring talented local management and allowing it to operate freely, and by systematically eliminating unsuccessful operations. If you question whether IDGC could be equally successful in the international marketplace without a combination of managerial freedom and financial control, consider its operation in the People's Republic of China.

That operation is a joint venture between IDGC and the Chinese government—unusual in and of itself. Circulation management and advertising sales are even more unusual. *China Computerworld* must apply to the postal authorities for a permit for each issue of the biweekly magazine months in advance. The permit must specify the exact number of magazines that will be mailed and the exact number of pages that will appear in the issue.

Further complicating things, direct-mail promotion to solicit advertising in the publication is not allowed. Advertising is solicited by space ads in the publication itself. A hard-to-forecast amount of advertising space is sold; the number of pages available for advertising have been specified months in advance in the per-

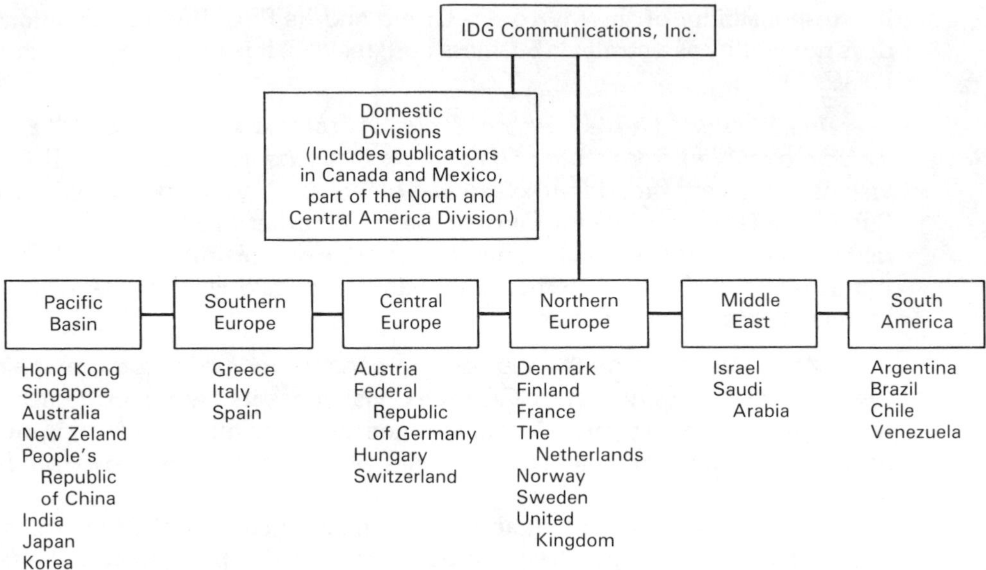

FIGURE 2.4 ***The IDGC International Organizational Chart as of 1988***

mit application. The unfortunate result is usually more advertising than the publication can accommodate.

There is one more interesting operational quirk—the Chinese post office handles the circulation for the magazine. *China Computerworld* knows how many subscribers it has, but it doesn't know who they are because the post office won't release their names!

Somehow *China Computerworld* does eventually get paid for the subscriptions. Exactly how that happens is unclear to managers in U.S. headquarters.

Could a headquarters management team effectively establish strategies and exercise close operational control over this unit?

In order for a manager to have clearly measurable sales and profit responsibility, it is helpful if the profitability of the SBU can be measured by real sales and costs as opposed to transfer costs between divisions of the firm. Ideally, it should have its own dedicated operations for marketing and sales, production, product development, and accounting. In practice, however, cost effectiveness often dictates that SBUs share some or all of these facilities and operations. While the resulting joint costs make it more difficult to evaluate the SBU as an investment center, and therefore to determine return on investment or return on assets managed, the prime concern is that the SBU make sense in terms of strategy development.

Theory vs. Practice

The distinction between corporate strategic planning and strategic marketing and the concept of the strategic business unit seems straightforward. However, it often turns out to be less clear-cut in practice.

You should also recognize that many of the concepts covered in this chapter are similar to concepts of strategic planning that you may have studied in another course, perhaps one in business policy. The overlap is real and unavoidable, but keep in mind that we are talking about a different level of analysis—the strategic business unit.

THE BASES OF SUSTAINABLE COMPETITIVE ADVANTAGE

The activity of strategic marketing planning is centered around the concept of achieving and sustaining a *competitive advantage*. According to Porter, "The fundamental basis of above-average performance in the long run is sustainable competitive advantage." [5] We can think of competitive advantage, in the words of one British businessman, as "only do[ing] for our customers what we can do better than others." [6] This includes both the concept of meeting customer wants and needs and the reality of competition. The essence of strategic marketing is the search for the set of factors that will yield a profitable competitive advantage in the long run.

Types of Competitive Advantage

There are three types of competitive advantage that a marketing operation can possess—lowest delivered cost, differentiated offering, and a protected niche. It can rely on only one of these types of advantage or on some combination of them. The types of advantage are: [7]

Lowest Delivered Cost. Having the lowest delivered cost is usually the result of size (economies of scale) and of tight control of costs. A low-cost position is ordinarily achieved only as a result of considerable effort over a period of time.

One area that offers direct marketers great potential for economies of scale and/or cost efficiencies is their data-processing systems. San Antonio-based USAA (formerly United Services Automobile Association) was one of the first insurance companies to recognize that it must automate the handling of responses

[5] Michael E. Porter, *Competitive Advantage* (New York: The Free Press, 1985) p. 11.

[6] George S. Day, *Strategic Market Planning, (St. Paul, Minn.: West Publishing Co., 1985), p. 25.*

[7] This discussion of types of competitive advantage is based on Day, *Strategic Market Planning*, pp. 26–28.

to its direct mail promotions and collections activities as well as its customer service activities.

During the 1970s USAA began to develop a customer database and installed computer terminals to give its service representatives easy access to the database. Over the years it has continued to refine the database and its uses. As a result, it has achieved a low-cost position that is widely recognized. The National Insurance Consumer Organization, located in Alexandria, Virginia, recommends USAA's Universal Life Policy to consumers "largely because automation lets the company do sales and service over the telephone, eliminating agents that boost premiums."[8] In addition, *Consumer Reports* ranks USAA at or near the top in terms of customer satisfaction with the handling of claims on automotive and homeowner policies.

Economies of scale and cost control are often enhanced by investment in increased productivity. It is estimated that American Express spends between $300 million and $400 million annually on its telecommunications and computer systems. These systems provide rapid transaction approval and direct customer services such as replacement of lost or stolen AmEx traveler's checks through automated teller machines (ATMs). Equally important, they allowed the company to achieve a 50 percent growth in the number of card holders during the late 1970s and early 1980s without a corresponding increase in losses from fraudulent credit card usage, an important cost element in the credit card business.[9]

Differentiated Offering. There are a number of ways in which a direct marketer can distinguish its offering from those of its competitors.

Offer a product that is truly unique or that is perceived by its customers as providing superior value for dollars spent. L. L. Bean developed a unique product in 1912 when he sewed leather uppers onto rubber bottoms to create the Maine Hunting Shoe. Today a number of other suppliers of outdoor clothing offer a similar boot or shoe. However, L. L. Bean still provides a superior value in the eyes of many customers by offering a superb blend of concerned personal service and a state-of-the-art order-fulfillment system that ships orders within six days of receipt with a high level of accuracy.[10]

Create a strong brand or firm image. Bean's consistency over the years in terms of product quality, unwavering dedication to customer satisfaction, and its 24-hour-a-day, 365-days-a-year retail store have created for it extremely high levels of consumer awareness and customer preference. Although the firm has experienced increasing competitive pressure in recent years, its high level of customer loyalty has enabled it to continue to thrive in a crowded marketplace.

[8] "Information Power," *Business Week*, October 14, 1985, p. 112.

[9] "American Express Plays Its Trump Card," *Business Week*, October 24, 1983, p. 132.

[10] "The Rustic Pitch Pays Off in Catalog Sales for L.L. Bean," U.S. *News & World Report*, March 25, 1985, pp. 61-62.

Offer a full line of merchandise that satisfies all customer needs in the product category. Many specialty marketers offer deep merchandise lines in narrow product categories. Few attempt to offer assortments that are both broad and deep.

Until the early 1980s there were five major companies with general-merchandise catalogs that offered both breadth and depth. By 1986, only one remained. Alden's left the field in 1982, followed by Montgomery Ward's in 1985. As early as 1976, Spiegel eliminated its focus on general merchandise and began to concentrate on upscale products for the working woman. About the same time, Penney's moved from a general-merchandise catalog to a number of specialty catalogs featuring apparel, home furnishings, and electronics. Only Sears was left.

Sears continues to offer its Big Book, considering it worthwhile both in terms of the sales and the retail store traffic it generates. Additionally, the presence of the Big Book allows Sears to build targeted lists that support its specialty catalogs.[11] Its total array of catalogs is now composed of over 50 books in five categories:

1. Major catalogs—two seasonal Big Books and Christmas books
2. Seasonal books—five different "seasons"
3. Targeted sale books—lawn and garden, back-to-school, etc.
4. Monthly sale supplements—general merchandise assortments
5. Specialty catalogs—apparel, business, recreation, etc.

The experience of Sears and the other general catalog merchants suggests that, in an era of intense competition and narrow profit margins for mass-marketed merchandise, firms cannot afford the luxury of marketing to customers who have no interest in that particular product category. Even Sears, with its massive resources, does not circulate its Big Book to its entire customer base.

The need to offer customers an extensive selection within a product category suggests that specialty merchandisers rather than general merchants will continue to dominate the catalog field. Even firms that rely on mailings featuring individual products, such as Garden Way (gardening equipment) and Franklin Mint (collectibles), specialize in one or more product categories in order to maintain the image they desire in the minds of their customers.

Both business's demand for cost efficiency and the customer's demand for time efficiency suggest that specialty direct marketers will continue to predominate.

Being the first to offer innovative products or services desired by customers The Sharper Image, described by one writer as the "Toys 'R' Us for baby-boomers,"[12] has succeeded by doing just that. The company began in 1977 by selling a useful but hard-to-find digital stopwatch for joggers via space advertising in

[11] C. E. Bjorncrantz, "Sears' Big Book: Dinosaur or Phoenix?" *Direct Marketing*, July 1986, p. 73.

[12] "Pied Piper for Yuppies," U.S. *News And World Report*, May 26, 1986, p. 36.

Runners World. By 1979 founder Richard Thalheimer was able to issue his first catalog. Since then, the catalogs have featured such items as a $950 suit of armor and a $7,900 jukebox. In the lower price range (for Sharper Image, at least) items have included a $249 telephone camouflaged as a duck decoy, a $179 pocketknife, a $499 television set the size of a paperback book, and a $119 pogo stick.

Thalheimer and his staff of buyers go to great lengths to keep the merchandise in the catalog fresh and innovative, rejecting anything that smacks of the ordinary. The result has been rapid growth for the catalog.[13]

Securing access to lists or other media that allow the firm to reach a larger proportion of its most valuable target customers. This is the equivalent of wide distribution coverage for the traditional marketer.

Many direct marketers are concerned that lists, especially the most productive ones, are being used excessively, perhaps to the point of diminishing returns. While many direct mailers do quite well relying on rental lists, the search for other sources of profitable names has intensified.

Lands' End has been an aggressive user of full-page space advertisements in upscale magazines to build its customer base. The ads are designed to stimulate a request for a catalog, not to generate an immediate sale. Most other catalog marketers generate responses from smaller ads, often only a few column inches in size. Lands' End has been willing to incur the higher costs of full-page ads to portray a quality image. The firm hopes that this unconventional tactic will attract responses from the kind of people who do not appear on rental lists. The ad shown in Figure 2.5, by contrasting in-store to mail-order shopping, is especially well designed to encourage non-mail-order buyers to request a catalog. It also creates an overall image of quality merchandise and customer service.

The ultimate customer access may eventually turn out to be electronic transaction systems. As we will discuss in more detail in Chapter 16, these systems have taken off rather slowly in the United States. However, the potential of interactive communications via TV, telephone, and personal computer for the marketing of consumer goods and services in the home or in a retail setting can hardly be overstated.

Occupying a Protected Niche. Kotler[14] has described the requirements for a niche as follows:

- The niche must be of sufficient size and purchasing power to be profitable.
- The niche must have growth potential.
- It should be of negligible interest to major competitors.

[13] "Entrepreneur's Slick Catalog for Affluent Is Pacing the Growing Direct-Mail Business," *The Wall Street Journal*, March 1, 1984, p. 31; John Grossmann, "Richard Thalheimer: Expanding the Sharper Image," *American Way*, July 8, 1986, pp. 44-49.

[14] Philip Kotler, *Marketing Management*, 5th ed. (Englewood Cliffs, N.J.: Prentice Hall, 1984), p. 411.

Why we call ourselves Lands' End, Direct Merchants.

These days, on top of everything else, you don't need the added frustrations you often face when you go shopping.

Threading your way through traffic into parking lots, in distant suburbs. Shouldering your way through crowded malls into stores well-stocked with goods, but staffed too sparingly to serve you well.

Lacking clerks who know the stock, you paw over counters, and shuttle hangers back and forth on racks.

Finally, when you've found what you want, there's that added wait while a cashier communes with her computer, recording everything about the item sold except that you've been standing in line waiting to pay for it.

There has to be a better way. And there is.

Shop with Lands' End, Direct Merchants.

We call ourselves direct merchants because we provide a straight line service, from us to you, with *no middle men* (or *middle-persons,* if you prefer.) Our way lets you shop at leisure in your home. From a colorful catalog. 24 hours a day, 365 days a year. By mail if you like. But, better still, by phone.

You pay no toll. No parking fees. You burn no gas. You lose no patience. And you have direct access to an astonishing array of quality products, about which we give you no-nonsense information, and which we offer at no-nonsense prices.

We didn't originate this method of shopping. But not a day goes by but what we at Lands' End ponder ways to re-invent the system, simplify it, refine it, or add to it when appropriate.

We roam the world in your behalf.

The search for quality is endless at Lands' End. And we go to the four corners of the earth in quest of it. In so doing, we practice a tough philosophy. Simply stated, it goes like this:

First, *quality.* Then, *price.* And always, always *service.*

Once an item seems right for our customers, as direct merchants we seek out the prime quality source; the one not only best suited to manufacture it, but the one that can make it most efficiently as well.

When we're sure we can offer you Lands' End quality at a Lands' End price, we pass the word on to you promptly in our catalogs. If we can't price a quality item so it's to your advantage to buy it from us, we don't offer it. But we continue to search for a new prime source of that item. And occasionally—as with our soft luggage lines—we undertake to make the items ourselves.

Millions use us. Millions more could.

We have served and satisfied millions of customers, but there remain millions more of you who have never experienced our direct service.

If you're among the latter group, why not try us now? Let us prove to you that you can trust us, too.

Ask us to send you a catalog by return mail. Better still, call us right now on our toll-free number (800-356-4444). We have over 100 friendly, well-informed operators waiting to answer your call personally, 24 hours a day. They're trained to serve you, and serve you they do. With answers to questions on sizes, styles, shipments and prices. On colors, on care, on delivery. Should an item be temporarily out of stock, they'll tell you and suggest an alternative. (Including, if need be, referring you to a respected competitor.)

What can you lose?

Understand, we're not all things to all shoppers. We don't initiate or pursue fads. We don't start or ride trends. We deal in clothing and accessories that know no time or season.

And every item we sell is GUARANTEED. PERIOD. If you are not completely satisfied with any item you buy from us, at any time during your use of it, return it and we will refund your full purchase price.

Call us right now, and let us begin to serve you. From our brand-new Catalog, featuring pages of solid values we can ship to you within 24 hours, or we'll know the reason why, and so will you.

Lands' End, Direct Merchants. The exciting new way to shop in today's world.

LANDS' END®
DIRECT MERCHANTS

of fine wool and cotton sweaters, Oxford button-down shirts, traditional dress clothing, snow wear, deck wear, original Lands' End soft luggage and a multitude of other quality goods from around the world.

Please send free catalog.
Lands' End Dept. J-09
Dodgeville, WI 53595

Name ____________
Address ____________
City ____________
State ________ Zip ________

Or call Toll-free:
800-356-4444

FIGURE 2.5 ***Lands' End Advertisement***
Source: Lands' End Dogeville, WI 53595

- The firm must possess the skills and resources to serve the niche effectively.
- The firm must build up enough customer goodwill to be able to defend itself against an attacking major competitor.

The Sharper Image is an example of niche marketing in the catalog area. Its merchandise mix is composed primarily of electronic and luxury household and personal-care products. It is targeted at the young and affluent single person or household. It is not alone in this category; catalog competitors include both other specialty catalogs, such as Markline, and catalogs that have a broader mix but many similar products, such as Adam York. However, *The Sharper Image* was the first to make a real impact in this specialty area and has maintained a dominant position.

Niches can quickly become crowded, however. Insurance marketers are often among the first to become aware of important demographic trends. One such trend is the increasing size and affluence of the elderly population in the United States. Consequently, a number of insurance companies have designed products such as low-cost, guaranteed-acceptance life insurance to be sold to older people through direct-response media such as mail or television. This niche appears to have many competitors, and it will be interesting to see if all can be profitable in the long run.

Organizational Resources and Skills

None of these competitive advantages occurs by accident, or more accurately, without consistent nurturing by management over time. Underlying these advantages are two basic assets of the organization: superior resources and superior skills.

Resources. *Resources* are the more tangible of these assets. For the direct marketer the following resources are the most important.

Access to its base of customers and prospects. This resource will be discussed in detail in later chapters. Here we will just note that it is composed of the following elements:

- An extensive and accurate mailing list
- A detailed database providing relevant and up-to-date information on customers and prospects
- Analytical techniques and models capable of extracting from the database the critical information on which to base managerial decisions.

Each of these elements is so important that a chapter, or a major portion of one, is devoted to it in this book. But a discussion of the success of Bloomingdale's mail-order catalog will provide some useful insights at this point.

Bloomingdale's By Mail began in 1980, its initial base consisting of the store's 19,000 credit card holders and telephone buyers. An aggressive space advertising campaign in print media increased that number to over one million in just a few years.

Each customer's name and address is maintained in a master file that also includes date of last purchase, the number of purchases made, and the total dollar value of the purchases. This information is recorded by any well-managed mail-order firm. However, because of its retail origins, from the very beginning Bloomingdale's By Mail captured detailed transaction information directly from its order-entry system. Instead of having only aggregate data about purchases (total value of purchase, for example), it has the same detailed data you would see on a retail store sales transaction slip.

This detailed information, plus extensive secondary data on sociodemographic characteristics, has allowed BBM to engage in sophisticated statistical modeling of the information in its database. One result has been the segmentation of its million-plus active customers into three mutually exclusive merchandise categories: (1) some ready-to-wear lines, menswear, and fashion accessories; (2) other ready-to-wear lines, cosmetics, gifts, and tabletop items; and (3) home furnishings, daywear, and children's wear. Using this merchandise segmentation scheme, BMM can design a specific catalog for each segment and time the mailing of that catalog appropriately for the merchandise being offered. The result is a profitable business in a relatively small but fashion-conscious and affluent market. [15]

Strength in multiple channels and/or media. Multiple ways of reaching customers may be desirable; for example, firms like Bloomingdale's have both catalog and retail operations. The complexity of products and/or markets may also dictate multiple avenues of customer contact; for example, the business marketer who uses a combination of direct mail, telephone marketing, and field selling.

Adequate capital or access to it. Direct marketing has long been regarded as a field in which entrepreneurs can succeed with a good idea and a minimal amount of capital. While there are indeed flourishing direct-response businesses that were begun on a shoestring, this is becoming harder to do every year. At a minimum, a distinctive product line, efficient order-fulfillment systems and equipment, and sophisticated information processing systems are necessary for success today. These systems can be quite expensive and require a scale of operation far more extensive than a "basement business" to achieve profitability.

A dependable source of merchandise (or the ability to perform services) that customers want at the proffered price. This requirement implies unique products (or services) that have high value relative to their cost to the customer.

Low-cost manufacturing and order-fulfillment systems. As it becomes harder and harder to obtain unique products, more direct marketers are integrating backward into manufacturing. This allows them to design and make their own exclusive merchandise. Order-fulfillment systems must meet the dual criteria of high

[15] Gary Ostranger, "Bloomie's Database Marketing," *Direct Marketing*, October 1986, pp. 94-105.

levels of customer service (few stockouts that cause back orders; accurate order filling) and inventory-carrying and order-processing costs that do not detract from profitability.

Skills. Tangible resources tend to be easier for competitors to duplicate than *intangible skills*. The following are among the skills that can be a source of competitive advantage for the direct marketer:

More accurate knowledge about customer needs, behaviors, and decision-making processes. How this knowledge can be accumulated in a database and analyzed to aid management decisions will be discussed in Chapters 4 and 6. Marketing research can also be of great value, and more direct marketers have been engaging in formal marketing research in recent years.

Better customer service. It can be argued that direct marketing converts all products to services because of the time and place utilities it creates. If this is true, customer service becomes a—perhaps the—key element of direct marketing strategies. State-of-the-art technology makes it easier to provide superior customer service, but trained and highly- motivated personnel are absolutely essential.

When L. L. Bean admonished customers in an early catalog, "We wish to call your attention to the fact that throwing away a pair of used Maine Hunting Shoes is about the same as throwing away a $5 bill," he laid the foundation for a level of customer service that generates great customer loyalty. Even today, Bean will take a customer's 14-year-old boots and, for $22.75, provide new rubber soles and other repairs that make them as good as a new pair costing $64.75. They repair approximately 10,000 pairs of Maine Hunting Shoes each year, refusing to repair them only, in the words of one employee, if "the manure is wet and dripping off of them."[16]

There are, then, numerous skills and resources that can form the basis of a competitive advantage for the direct marketer. Having determined that the organization has, or can develop, one or more bases of competitive advantage, the direct marketer must evaluate the advantage on two criteria: its value to the customer and the organization's ability to sustain it.

Value can be evaluated on four dimensions:

1. Does the advantage offer benefits that are genuinely desired by customers? Even better, will the benefits strongly influence the customers' decision-making processes?
2. Is the advantage important to a sizable customer segment?
3. Is it of sufficient value to cause customers to buy at the offered price?
4. Is the same advantage readily obtainable from competitors?

[16] *U.S. News and World Report*, March 25, 1985, p. 62.

The ability to sustain a competitive advantage depends on the competition as well as on the strategies and execution of the firm itself. If competitors who are strong and well financed choose to pursue similar strategies, it will be more difficult for the firm to achieve and maintain profitability. It is also important to recognize that many of these sources of competitive advantage are available to the general marketer who makes use of selected direct marketing techniques.[17]

Since a competitive advantage does not occur by accident, all firms that wish to cultivate strong and enduring advantages should systematically engage in strategic market planning.

THE STRATEGY PLANNING PROCESS

There are a number of stages in the strategy planning process. Some of them can take place concurrently but, as suggested by Figure 2.6, for the most part they are sequential.

To better explain this series of activities, we will use a hypothetical product line in a hypothetical firm as our example.[18] This hypothetical firm—call it OmniVideo— distributes all kinds of videocassettes, including feature films and music videos. It also produces informational tapes on a variety of self-help/self-improvement subjects for consumer and educational markets. Eighty percent of OmniVideo sales are made to retail video outlets whose primary business is video rentals. Twenty percent of sales are made to retailers who sell tapes to consumers for their own video libraries. The latter is referred to in the industry as the sell-through market.

OmniVideo reaches both the rental and the sell-through markets with a field sales force supported by promotional mailings. We will concern ourselves with strategic market planning for a new division of OmniVideo, Fitness and Leisure. The F&L Division has all the characteristics necessary to qualify as a strategic business unit (SBU) within OmniVideo—an external market, an identifiable group of

[17] For a discussion of some of the ways in which aspects of direct marketing can be integrated into general business strategies, see F. Robert Dwyer, "Direct Marketing in the Quest for Competitive Advantage," *Journal Of Direct Marketing,* Winter 1987, pp. 15-22.

[18] The information in this section is based on: "Boom Continues for VCR's," *Marketing & Media Decisions,* July 1985, p. 6; "American Video Sharpens Up Its Image," *The Economist,* October 12, 1985, pp. 88-89; Mark Trost, "VCR Sales Explosion Shakes Up Industry," *Advertising Age,* January 9, 1986, p.14; Michael G. Harvey and Janes T. Rothe, "Video Cassette Recorders: Their Impact on Viewers and Advertisers," *Journal Of Advertising Research,* December 1985/January 1986, pp. 19-27; "Mom-and-Pop Videotape Shops are Fading Out," *Business Week,* September 2, 1985, pp. 34-35; Jolie Solomon, "Working at Relaxation," *The Wall Street Journal,* April 21, 1986, pp. 1D-2D; Laura Landro, "Videocassette Makers Bid to Turn Movie Renters Into Movie Buyers," *Wall Street Journal,* December 2, 1986, p. 33; Jeffrey A. Tannenbaum, "New Compact Disks With Video Are Coming—But Will They Sell?" *The Wall Street Journal,* May 4, 1987, p. 35; Steve Sternberg, "VCRs: Impact and Implications," *Marketing & Media Decisions,* December 1987, pp. 100-107; interview with William K. Couture, branch manager, Artec Distributing, Inc., Canton, MA.

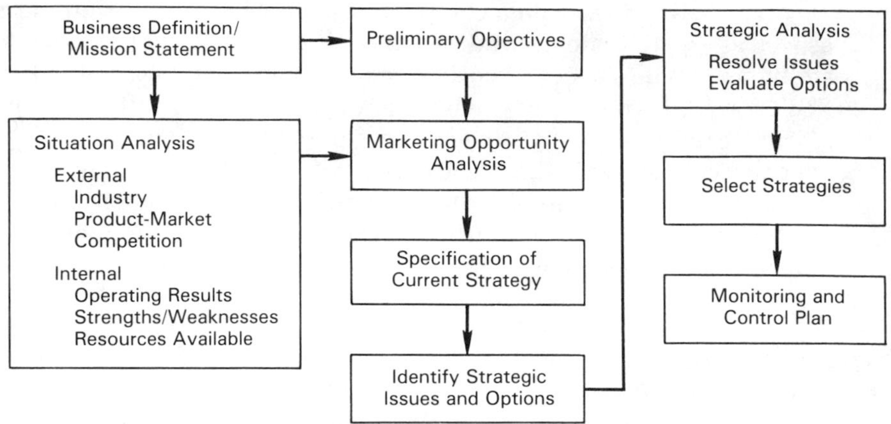

FIGURE 2.6 ***The Strategy Planning Process***

customers and competitors, and management that is reasonably autonomous in terms of both operations and strategy.

The F&L Division must develop its own strategic market plan within the context of the overall strategy set forth by OmniVideo. The basic elements of that strategy are summarized in Figure 2.7

Business Definition

Once management of the F&L Division has thoroughly acquainted itself with the corporate mission and strategy statement, its next step will be to develop a business definition for the division. This can be viewed as the mission statement. The business definition must state clearly and concisely the nature and scope of the division's current activities and anticipated growth directions. Elements frequently contained in a business definition are:

- The generic customer need that the unit has been established to fulfill
- The nature of the product offered and the market for which it is intended
- The unit's distinctive competence or asset

After carefully considering the nature of the division's business—what it is now and what management wishes it to be—F&L management arrived at the following business definition:

> The Fitness and Leisure Division attempts to meet the full range of consumer needs for videocassettes that provide information, instruction, and guidance for a wide variety of individual and team sports and fitness programs, and self- in-

Corporate Mission:

To serve the entertainment and self-help needs of households equipped with videocassette recorders by making videotapes available for both rental and sale to ultimate consumers and to sell selected videocassettes in educational markets.

Corporate Objectives:

1. By 1990, to achieve a 15 percent share of the videocassette distribution business and to produce 10 percent of the nonmusic videocassettes.
2. To achieve a 10 percent growth in sales to the video rental market each year and a 20 percent growth in sales of cassettes intended for resale to the ultimate consumer.
3. To be a major supplier to all retail video chains and franchises and to mass-merchandise chains which sell prerecorded videocassettes.

Financial Priorities:

In order to achieve the desired rate of growth in sales and market share it will be necessary to invest heavily in the most rapidly - growing segments of our business. For the three-year period 1988–1990, those are expected to be the Educational Division and the Fitness and Leisure Division.

Divisional Goals:

(n) The target objectives for the Fitness and Leisure Division for each of the years 1988, 1989, and 1990 are:

Sales: a 25 percent growth in dollar volume of tapes intended for resale and a 15 percent increase in dollar volume of tapes destined for rental.

Margins: divisional contribution, before allocation of corporate operational and administrative expenses, of 22 percent.

Market Share: by the end of 1990, to hold a 20 percent share of the self-help videocassette market.

Backward Integration:

Between 1988 and 1990 a substantial proportion of the cash flow from the business will be invested in state-of-the-art production facilities in order to provide complete production capabilities for the division. During this period, acquisition of a producer of blank videocassettes will also be investigated.

FIGURE 2.7 ***Major Elements of OmniVideo Strategy***

> struction for a multitude of activities in and around the home. Over the next 3 years the Division aims to become one of the three largest distributors of F&L videocassettes and to become well established as a producer of high-quality cassettes for this market.

Assuming that this business definition is sound and realistic, it will provide guidance for the remainder of the strategy formulation process.

Defining the Product-Market

For strategic market planning purposes, it is unrealistic to analyze products in isolation from the specific markets they serve or to analyze markets without consideration of the product. Consequently, in identifying product-markets at least three factors should be considered:

1. Product substitutability. For strategic purposes, the relevant set of products is the set within which customers consider substitution appropriate *for a particular use.*
2. The benefits sought from use in the particular situation.
3. The customers who need such benefits and who engage in such uses.

> The product-market being served by the F&L Division of Omnivideo includes physically active consumers who wish to improve their skills in sporting activities or to engage in a guided exercise or other fitness program in their own home. It also includes those who wish to learn or improve a craft or skill in their home. F&L will meet the needs of both customers who wish to purchase videos and those who wish to rent them.

External Situation Analysis

Having defined its product-market, the Fitness and Leisure Division must analyze its current situation, both internal and external to the firm, in general terms and especially in terms of its product-market. At a minimum, external situation analysis will include the product-market situation, competition, and the general business environment as it affects the product. Since the rental and purchase of F&L videocassettes is dependent on household ownership of a VCR, management began by studying the current level and nature of VCR ownership and usage.

In 1985 $3.2 billion worth of VCRs, about 12 million units, were sold. Sales remained at 12 to 13 million units in 1986. Over 25 percent of all U.S. homes had a VCR in 1985, and that number exceeded 50 percent in 1987. Consumers reported using their VCRs primarily to record programs for later viewing, either because they were unable to watch TV when the program was aired or because they wanted to watch two programs that were on at the same time. A substantial number of people also indicated that renting prerecorded tapes was an important reason for having a VCR. The importance of all uses of VCRs tended to decline after consumers had owned them for 12 months.

A substantial number of consumers reported shifting the time of their TV watching and also watching more TV as a result of having a VCR. They reported going out to the movies less frequently and entertaining at home more frequently since they had purchased the VCR.

Industry studies indicated that the average VCR-owning household is no longer primarily young, well-educated, affluent, and living in wealthy urban or suburban areas. There is now heavy ownership among singles, 18-to-24-year-olds, and households in the $27,000 to $32,000 income range. A recent study concluded that the VCR is no longer a plaything of the wealthy but has become a home entertainment mainstay.

After examining the available data on the VCR market, F&L executives concluded that there was still considerable opportunity for growth. First, they noted that VCR penetration was only expected to be about one-half of U.S. households by the end of 1987, far from the 98 percent of households penetrated by television. Penetration was projected to increase at 5 to 10 percent per year for the next few years, reaching almost 70 percent by 1990. Second, they recognized that the current uses of VCRs were primarily entertainment-oriented and revolved to a great extent around television programming and feature films. They saw great potential in encouraging the use of video for active pursuits as opposed to passive viewing.

Videocassettes can be sold either prerecorded or blank. The major use of blank cassettes is for recording off the air. Sales of cassettes were $760 million in 1985, with 85 percent going to consumers and 15 percent to producers of prerecorded videocassettes.

The consumer market for prerecorded videocassettes initially developed as a rental market, with about 90 percent of the business at retail being rental. In 1985 the retail video market was $4.6 billion, with $950 million (21 percent) being sales to consumers. In 1986 the market was $5.6 billion with $1.6 billion (29 percent) being sales.

The rental market was primarily served by retail video stores. In the late 1970s most of the stores were small single-unit independents. Multi-unit stores, many of them franchises with several hundred locations nationwide, now dominate this market.

By 1985, many of the retail video stores were experiencing substantial competition from mass merchants, including discount stores, convenience stores, and supermarkets. These mass merchants were not a serious threat to the video stores' rental business because they usually had a limited selection. However, their buying and promotional power made them a major factor in the sale of videocassettes. The mass merchandisers sold movies for $29.95, which video stores typically priced at $79.95 and special promotions sometimes drove the price as low as $19.95. The video specialty stores could not compete with this type of loss-leader pricing. In addition, consumers intended to use the movies over a long period of time, and therefore did not consider rental an option except for trial viewing.

F&L management also noted that videos were being added to the catalogs of book sellers such as Brentano's and B. Dalton. They had also heard that some major producers were considering videocassette catalogs aimed at the consumer market, and they wondered if this would become a major distribution alternative in the near future.

Competition in F&L's product-market had to be broadly defined. It could include all planned fitness and planned and unplanned leisure-time activities. Direct competition included movie-going and television viewing. Television had become a more complex competitor with the growing popularity of cable and pay TV, which provided consumers with a plethora of viewing choices.

Direct competitors of the F&L division included both producers and distributors of videos. Producers ranged from the specialty organization (Jane Fonda's exercise tapes or Jack Nicklaus's golf instruction tape) to the large producer of multiple types of videos. The distribution structure for self-help tapes was much less organized than the structure that served the rental market, where approximately 20 of about 1,000 distributors and buying groups controlled almost 85 percent of the market. Specific information on competitors in the self-help market was not available in any organized form, but after conversations with trade organizations and other observers of the industry, top management was reasonably confident that there were many small producers and distributors, none of whom held a dominant market position.

The most important aspect of the external macro environment to F&L was the effect of consumers' attitudes and values on their use of leisure time. The health and fitness boom showed no real signs of abating, although there were changes from time to time such as a recent shift away from jogging toward walking. Self-development and self-improvement were important in both sports and fitness related activities as well as in other types of leisure pursuits.

Consumers who engage in home improvement and home decorating projects do so primarily to save money, but they also see these activities as a way of expressing their creative abilities and individuality. Expressing creativity and individuality, as well as doing something nice for family and friends, is also important to people who engage in arts and crafts or who wish to improve a skill such as cooking or woodworking.

Internal Situation Analysis

OmniVideo itself is an entrepreneurial organization that is still in a rapid growth phase. It prides itself on being able to spot trends and react quickly to them and on a small, hard-working cadre of managers who function effectively without multiple supervisory layers of management.

The F&L Division itself is new and consequently has no past performance to evaluate. At present, management of the division consists of a general manager; managers of operations, marketing, and finance; and analysts and administrative assistants. Most of the personnel were transferred from other OmniVideo divisions to F&L, although the general manager and the marketing manager were recruited from similar positions in other firms. The average age of managers in the division is 32, and none of the managers considers his or her current position a final career objective. They are all committed to seeing their division and OmniVideo as a whole become dominant forces in their industry. Also, because the division is new, there is no past strategy statement on which to base their current activities.

F&L management summarized the results of the situation analysis as follows:

- The market for prerecorded videocassettes is large and will continue to grow for the next few years as a result of the continued penetration of VCRs.
- The market for F&L's product line is in its early stages, lagging far behind the entertainment market. There appears to be substantial consumer interest in this type of product.
- Competition at both the producer and distributor levels is fragmented, consisting of many small firms, none of which holds a dominant position in the broad market for self-help videos.
- At the retail level, specialty video stores still dominate the rental business, but mass merchants are performing more effectively in selling videocassettes. This is especially true of self-help videos.
- As a new division of a rapidly growing and solidly financed company, F&L has the skills and resources to compete effectively in its defined market.

Marketing Opportunity Analysis

In assessing the possibilities open to it, an SBU must consider both the *opportunities* that exist and the *threats* that may prevent it from taking advantage of the opportunities. F&L management has identified these opportunities in its product-market:

- To develop a diversified line of videotapes that meet a wide variety of needs for self-help and self-improvement.
- To produce tapes that are interesting, educationally sound, and have good "production values," i.e., have high-quality video and audio.
- To utilize or establish a distribution structure that achieves the widest possible distribution coverage.
- To establish an image for quality and reliability, first in the minds of retailers of prerecorded videocassettes, and as soon as feasible, in the minds of ultimate consumers.
- To investigate the feasibility of reaching the ultimate consumer directly at the earliest possible time both to avoid overdependence on retail distribution in a few large mass-merchandise chains and to solidify a position in the minds of the ultimate consumer.

F&L managers realized that these opportunities might be summarized as the chance to become a dominant force in an emerging industry before it becomes well organized and intensely competitive. They also recognized that there were substantial threats that might make it difficult to take advantage of this opportunity:

- A slowing or a halt in the penetration of VCRs into U.S. households. This would reduce the potential size of their market.
- Entrance of a larger, better-financed competitor that would quickly achieve market dominance.
- A major shift in consumer lifestyles that would reduce the demand for their product.
- A substantial recession in the national economy which would reduce the discretionary income households could allocate to the purchase of videocassettes.
- The emergence of new technology—for example, compact disk technology permitting video as well as audio reproduction— that would make their product line and production facilities obsolete.

F&L management realized that the factors identified as major threats were all external and uncontrollable. It would be necessary to continually monitor these areas. At the same time, all currently available information indicated that none of the threats were imminent, and they felt confident that they possessed the skills and resources necessary to take advantage of the market opportunity.

Identifying Strategic Issues and Options

Having conducted the situation analysis and organized the information they had obtained in the form of a market opportunity analysis, F&L management was ready to move from the relatively comfortable area of fact gathering and analysis to embark on the difficult area of developing strategies. They knew that strategy development would be especially difficult because they were pioneering in a relatively new segment of the industry and had little in the way of known successes and failures to guide them. Over-aggressiveness might lead to major mistakes, but over-cautiousness might lead to lost opportunities and a permanent "also-ran" position in the industry. Consequently, F&L management approached this stage of the planning process very thoughtfully.

The major strategic issues that concerned them centered around the nature of their initial product line, distribution policies, and production processes. Recognizing that price ranges at both the retail and the wholesale level were already established, they considered price a constraint rather than a strategic issue at present. Promotion, now almost entirely point-of-purchase and retail cooperative advertising, was not now a major strategic issue, but management realized this would probably change as more competitors entered the field.

Management's deliberations resulted in the following major strategic options:

- To focus on a specific segment of the market or to develop a broad product line.

- To sell through retail outlets or directly to the consumer. If retail outlets are targeted, should they use distributors or should they develop their own field sales force?
- To invest in their own production facilities initially or to sub-contract much of the production.

Each major option is then broken down into several more detailed options. For example, in looking at the option of whether to develop a focused product line or a diverse one, the management team identified over 20 possible market segments, defined as specific types of activities that appealed to different target markets. They carefully worked their way through each option, evaluating it on the basis of divisional objectives and management's assessment of its feasibility.

Selection of Strategies

After lengthy deliberation and a number of conferences with corporate management, the outline of the division's initial strategy began to emerge:

- Their product line would focus on specific market segments that were not currently being addressed in four general areas: sports, individual fitness, ethnic cooking techniques, and home improvement and repair.
- They would concentrate on obtaining distribution in major mass-merchandise chains. It had been determined that the regular OmniVideo sales force could handle the bulk of the sales activity, but that specialty distributors might be needed to reach specialty retailers such as sporting goods chains. The division had neither the expertise nor the personnel necessary to attempt to market directly to the consumer at present.
- They would subcontract initial filming of tapes for the present, but would do all editing and final production in-house in order to achieve the desired level of quality.
- Pricing would be competitive, but marketing efforts would concentrate on product quality and service to retail customers in an attempt to avoid price-cutting and destruction of profit margins.
- Emphasis would be placed on cooperative promotions with retail chains in an effort to establish the name of the OmniVideo Fitness & Leisure Division in the minds of consumers.

General guidelines for strategy execution and monitoring and control were also established:

- Development of the product line would avoid areas where "big names" were required to produce best-selling tapes (e.g., golf and tennis instruction and the already crowded aerobics field).

- F&L executives would be active participants in selling to major national chains as one method of actively monitoring developments in the market.
- Within the next year a specialist in direct marketing would be hired to begin experiments in reaching F & L's markets directly.
- F&L management would formally review progress toward reaching objectives and the continuing appropriateness of strategies on a quarterly basis.

SOME FINAL THOUGHTS ON STRATEGIC MARKET PLANNING

Our example was deliberately kept fairly simple to provide a general overview of the basic process of strategic market planning. It ignored some of the more complex theoretical and analytical issues that frequently arise, especially in SBUs with a diverse product line and products in many stages of the product life cycle. Even so, it strongly suggests that strategic market planning is a complex activity, requiring an extensive fact base and creative thinking and analysis.

It may have occurred to you to ask if all firms need the detailed strategic marketing process described in this chapter. Yip has examined this question by comparing firms with more advanced strategic planning processes to those with less advanced processes.[19] He finds that strategic planning has less value when either the corporation or the SBU have the following characteristics:

- The sources of competitive advantage are primarily tactical, not strategic. This is likely to occur when the firm is marketing low-involvement products that lead to routinized purchasing behavior.
- Technological change in the industry is minimal.
- The product line is relatively homogeneous.
- The industry is not particularly sensitive to economic cycles, environmental change, and competitive activity.
- There are few opportunities for synergy through integrated management of shared resources (fulfillment operations that are shared by a number of operating units, for example).

Evaluation of these characteristics may help a firm design a planning process based on its own specific needs. If design of a strategic market planning process is approached in this manner, firms and SBUs may avoid planning systems that become a net cost to the organization rather than a source of competitive advantage.

SUMMARY

In recent years the strategic planning process, whether carried out at the corporate or at the SBU level, has come to be understood as the search for sustainable com-

[19] George S. Yip, "The Role of Strategic Planning in Consumer-Marketing Businesses," Working Paper (Cambridge, MA.: Marketing Science Institute, 1984), pp. 36-39.

petitive advantage. The process can become complex and time-consuming, so some managers are understandably wary of it. However a firm chooses to carry out these activities, an in-depth knowledge of the environment in which the business operates, its market, and its competition, as well as strategic thinking about the challenges and opportunities it faces, are necessary to succeed in today's dynamic business world.

DISCUSSION QUESTIONS

1. Explain the differences between corporate strategic planning, strategic marketing planning, and operational marketing planning. Under which activity does the development of specific direct response programs fall?
2. What is a strategic business unit? How does the concept of the SBU affect the process of strategic marketing planning?
3. Think of a direct marketing business with which you are familiar. What do its bases of competitive advantage appear to be?
4. In your own words, describe the basic steps in the strategic marketing planning process.

SUGGESTED ADDITIONAL READINGS

1. Thomas Byrne, "Strategic Planning for Financial Services Providers," *Direct Marketing*, August 1986, pp. 72-75.
2. Jim Kobs, "Marketing Strategies for Maximum Growth," *Direct Marketing*, May 1987, pp. 32-39, 155.
3. Raymond E. Taylor and L. Lynn Judd, "Environmental Forecasting for Direct Marketing," *Journal Of Direct Marketing Research*, Winter 1987, pp. 115-125.

Part Two
Direct Marketing Decision Variables

3

Offer Planning and Positioning

In Chapter 1 we briefly discussed the five decision elements of direct marketing—offer, creative, media, timing/sequencing, and customer service. Now we are ready to explore one of those elements—the offer—in depth.

We defined the offer as the complete proposition made by the direct marketer to the prospect. The next step is to break the offer down into its component parts and examine each one. Before we do that, however, let's ask just how important it is to "get the offer right."

Figure 3.1 shows an offer from the Historic Providence Mint for a series of 12 porcelain plates depicting vanishing barns from throughout the United States. The mailing package consisted of a 4-page letter, a testimonial letter, a brochure, an order card featuring the free gift offer, and a business reply envelope. The brochure showed each plate, emphasized the attractiveness of the entire series, profiled the artist, and provided information about the producer of the plates. The outer envelope had an attractive sketch of a rural scene and featured the free gift offer.

The offer variation tested was a single payment of $39.50 for each plate versus a bimonthly payment of $19.75. Both versions were money-with-order (MWO) offers. Seventy-six thousand of each version of the package were mailed to names from Historic Providence Mint's house list and a number of rental lists that were being tested. For each list used, names were assigned to the two test cells on an every-other-name basis (often referred to as an *A/B split*). The results of the test are shown in Table 3.1.

You can easily see that while the response rate was higher for the bimonthly payment offer, both the conversion rate[1] and the retention rate were higher for the single monthly payment offer. The bimonthly payment offer had better front-end results, but the single monthly payment offer had sufficiently higher conversion and retention rates to make it the more profitable offer.

Bi monthly payment: 311 initial orders x .75 x .68 = 158 series customers.
Single monthly payment: 265 initial orders x .85 x .78 = 176 series customers.

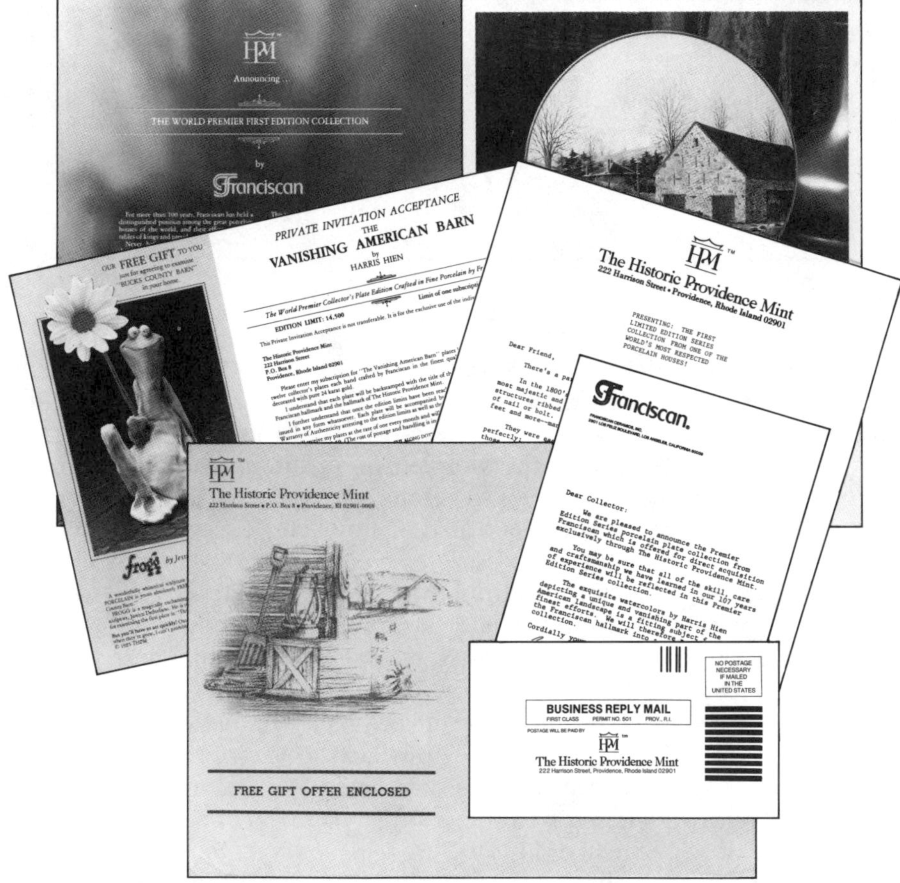

FIGURE 3.1 ***Mailing Package for Plate Series of Vanishing Barns of the United States***

Source: Historic Providence Mint, Providence, RI 02901.

[1] *Conversion rate* ordinarily refers to the percentage of inquirers who actually purchase. In this case, because it is a cash-with-order offer, the conversion rate refers to the number of initial customers who continued with the series by taking the second plate. Retention rate refers to the number of series customers (i.e., those who took the second plate) who actually completed the series.

TABLE 3.1 Results of Test of Two Offers

	Response Rate	*Conversion Rate*	*Retention Rate*
Bi-Monthly pymts.	.41%	75%	68%
Single monthly payment	.35%	85%	78%

In other words, the number of initial orders times the conversion rate times the retention rate equals the number of customers who complete the series. The difference in profitability between the two offers provides a concrete example both of the value of testing and also of the importance of looking at back-end results instead of just at front-end response. It also suggests a slightly different approach to testing from the approach that will be described in Chapter 8 in which a control package (the most successful previous mailing package) is the standard against which a change in the marketing program is measured.

It is vitally important to test variations in the offer that represent a good chance of improving results. Experts have frequently pointed out that changes in offers may result in increases in response rate from 20 percent to 100 percent or more. However, as the Historic Providence Mint example shows, it does not take a huge percentage difference in response rate to make a noticeable difference in profitability, especially when the offer is for a series of purchases.

ELEMENTS OF THE DIRECT MARKETING OFFER

It is useful to classify the elements of the direct marketing offer into those that are required (must be present in every offer) and those that are optional (may be included or not, depending on strategy and costs). This classification assumes that the objective is order generation on the basis of this offer alone. If the objective is, say, to have the prospect request information, all the elements listed as required may not be necessary. We will return to that issue later in the chapter.

The basic elements are listed under the categories of "Required Elements" and "Optional Elements" in Table 3.2. Keep in mind that there can be many variations within these basic elements.

The Required Elements

Product/Positioning. Once the product for the direct marketing campaign has been chosen, the issue becomes how best to present the product to the target audience. How to present—or position—a product is such an important topic that the last portion of the chapter will be devoted to it. Suffice it to say at this point that the positioning chosen will define the product's image in the mind of the prospect.

Table 3.2 Elements of the Offer

Required Elements	*Optional Elements*
Product/positioning	Incentives
Price	Multiple offers
Length of commitment	Customer's Obligations
Terms of payment	
Risk-reduction Mechanisms	

Source: Adapted from Herbert Katzenstein and William S. Sachs, *Direct Marketing* (Columbus, OH: Charles E. Merrill, 1986) p. 206; Caroline Zimmermann, "The Proposition," in Edward L. Nash, ed., *The Direct Marketing Handbook* (New York; McGraw-Hill, 1984), pp. 81, 82.

There are times when the manager should consider changing the product itself to create a more effective offer. In the case of a tangible product, one or more of its attributes can be changed. For example, a catalog of art items may be offering an expensively framed print that is not selling well and management may decide to test an offer of the print alone, without the frame. In the case of a service, changes are usually easy to make. A cable television franchise may find its customers resistant to the inclusion of a particular movie channel as part of the basic subscription package. If the franchise's agreement with the supplier does not prevent it, the cable company can offer the movie channel as an option. Both these changes would obviously affect the price of the product being offered.

Price. When establishing the base price for a product, direct marketers, like general marketers, follow one of three basic pricing policies:

1. A *penetration* price implies setting a low price to encourage a high volume of sales.
2. A *skimming* price implies setting a high price in order to obtain a high margin on each unit sold.
3. A third policy, often referred to as *sliding down the demand curve,* implies establishing a high price for the initial offer and then making planned reductions in price for succeeding offers.

These policies obviously provide only general guidelines for actual price setting. A detailed discussion of the pricing process is beyond the scope of this book, but the topic is well covered in marketing principles and marketing management texts. Other pricing issues of importance to direct marketers are covered in retailing texts. Direct marketers, like general marketers, must remember that the perceived value of the good to the prospective customer and its costs to the marketer establish the upper and lower boundaries within which the actual price must be set. They must also remember that price is another determinant of the image of the product and the firm that offers it.

Length of Commitment. Offers can involve either a single transaction or a series of transactions over a period of time. Perfume purchased from a self-mailer sent by a local department store, a book bought through an ad in a trade magazine, a piece of software purchased from a distributor's catalog—all of these are examples of a one-time commitment. Offers that involve multiple transactions over a period of time, such as the Historic Providence Mint plate series, are called *continuity offers*. There are a number of kinds of continuity offers:

Fixed-term offers. Newspaper and magazine subscription offers feature a fixed number of issues for a stated price, payable at the beginning of the service. For magazines, the term is fairly standard—a year—with shorter terms used in introductory offers and discounts offered for longer-term subscriptions. Magazines are the classic example of a fixed-term offer; so much so, in fact, that other types of fixed-term offers are sometimes referred to as "subscription offers."

Automatic shipment plans. The Time-Life mailing for the Healthy Home Cooking Series discussed in Chapter 1 and the Historic Providence Mint plate series are examples of this type of continuity offer. In an automatic shipment plan, purchase of the first item signals acceptance of the series and triggers automatic shipment of remaining items—every other month, for example. Shipment of the series will continue until it is completed or until the purchaser cancels. This type of offer is also referred to as a "till forbid" offer.

The Historic Providence Mint plate series is an effective variant of an automatic shipment plan. Shipment of additional plates in the series is "automatic" only for credit card users who can be charged at the time of shipment. Customers who pay cash are required to pay before the shipment is made.

Club plans. The true club plan, originated by the Book-of-the-Month Club, adds an element of choice to the automatic shipment plan. The advance bulletin allows the member to choose the recommended selection, an alternative, or no shipment at all for that time period. The Book-of-the-Month Club uses a type of club plan called the *negative option*, meaning the recommended selection will be shipped unless the customer refuses it within a stated period of time. It is also possible to structure a *positive option*, requiring the customer to reply affirmatively before any shipment is made, but experts agree that such a plan does not usually work because it makes it too easy for the customer to effectively say "no" by not replying. This is a violation of the basic direct marketing rule, which says, "Make it easy to say yes!" Club plans generally involve some type of commitment—a requirement that the customer purchase a minimum amount of the product within a certain period of time.

The Book-of-the-Month Club offer shown in Figure 3.2 is a variant in this type of offer. The offer provides a choice of attractive front-end incentives—four best-selling books for $1 each or one of three book series (*The Story of Civilization, The Oxford English Dictionary,* or *The Second World War*) for prices ranging from $37.95 to $49.95. It also waives the customer's obligation to purchase four books within the next two

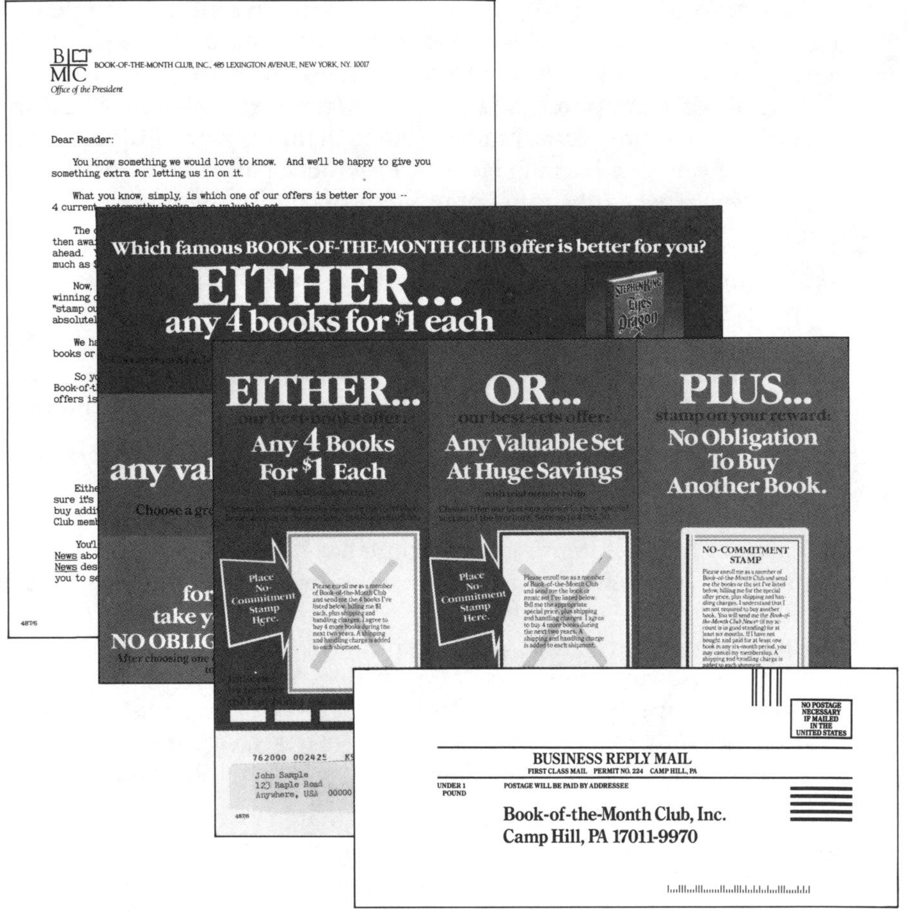

FIGURE 3.2 ***Book-of-the-Month Club Offering***

years by using as an involvement device a "no-commitment stamp" found on the order form.

Terms of Payment. Most direct marketing offers provide a variety of payment options, including cash, cash on delivery (COD), and credit cards. Some upscale catalogs allow purchasers to divide the price into two or three payments without incurring an interest charge. Other offers feature more traditional installment payments with interest.

All direct marketers agree that the size of the average order is larger when customers use credit cards. Estimates of how much larger range from 15 to 30 percent. On the other hand, COD is becoming a less favored payment option because of its cost and inconvenience if the customer is not at home when delivery is attempted. Additionally, the rate of refusals of COD shipments is high.

Risk-Reduction Mechanisms. There are many ways by which marketers can reduce the perceived risk of purchasing a particular product by direct response without first having had a chance to examine it. Guarantees, warranties, and free trial offers are among the most common. For example, Sears has operated from the very beginning with a "satisfaction guaranteed or your money back" policy.

Free trial, ordinarily an opportunity to use the product in the purchaser's home or business for a specified period of time with the right to return it free of charge during that period, is also common. The Fingerhut offer shown in Figure 3.3 was for "free trial" of the merchandise, contingent on credit approval.

For certain types of products, the seller may include some type of "value protection" in the offer. The concern that sells rare stamps may guarantee to repurchase them at the selling price for a stated time or even indefinitely. The "collectibles" firm may guarantee a stated value within a certain period of time or they will repurchase the item or series. Firms selling off-price or discount merchandise may offer to refund the difference or, occasionally, the entire purchase price if the purchaser can find the exact same merchandise at a lower price within a stated time period.

Perceived risk, which can be either economic or social in origin, can be reduced by presentations that help overcome some of the disadvantages of not being able to see and touch the actual merchandise. In upscale mailings or catalogs fabric samples are sometimes included so that customers can evaluate both color and quality. Frequently, long copy describing the product in great detail helps lessen the sense of unfamiliarity.

The Optional Elements

The optional elements of the offer can be described as ways of *enhancing the value of the offer* to the prospective customer. By providing a higher perceived value, these elements create a sense of urgency that helps to overcome the natural human tendency to defer a decision. Direct marketers long ago learned the lesson that a purchase postponed is most often a purchase not made.

Incentives. The variety of incentives that can be offered to make the proposition more attractive is limited only by the imagination and funds of the direct marketer. In a very general way, we might classify these incentives as free gifts, free information or samples, sales or discounts, and sweepstakes or contests.

Think carefully about what you intend to accomplish by including an incentive as part of the offer. Is it to reward the prospect for a request for information, for examining the product on a trial basis, or for actually purchasing the product? Do you want to use the incentive to increase the size of your average order—by offering merchandise at sale or discount prices, by offering an incentive for purchases above a certain amount, or by offering a series of gifts as the size of the purchase increases? Is it important to get a sample of the product itself into the hands of the prospect? Are you using the incentive to try to increase the response rate or to build excitement and involvement?

With regard to free gifts, the generally accepted rule among direct marketers is that the gift should be related to the product being sold. Beyond that, creativity and cost take over. What will work best? Only testing can answer that question with any degree of certainty. Some direct marketers recommend testing one gift;

FIGURE 3.3 ***Fingerhut Mail Package***

Source: ©Fingerhut Corporation, St. Cloud, MN 56395

if that works, add a second; and keep adding them until you reach a point of diminishing returns. Fingerhut, a general-merchandise mail-order marketer, has long used multiple gifts successfully. Figure 3.3 shows an offer in which five free gifts were used as incentives to either acquire new customers or to reactivate old ones. The gifts all came under the general heading of "housewares," as did most of the merchandise offered for sale. Notice the use of a sticker (to be transferred from the outer envelope to the order form) as an involvement device.

Free gifts may also be used to reward current customers for providing names and addresses of prospects. This is often referred to as a "get-a-friend" offer.

Sale or discount merchandise may be offered as a promotional activity, as part of normal merchandising practice, or for reasons related to other aspects of direct marketing strategy.

Sales, especially discounts offered for promotional reasons, are quite frequent. The trade paper offers a limited-time subscription (2 or 3 months, perhaps) at a steeply discounted price. The bank offers new customers free checking accounts for the first 2 months. A coupon offers an especially attractive introductory price for a new consumer packaged good.

Most direct marketers have overstocked, end-of-season, or just generally slow-moving merchandise that must be moved. This can be done by establishing outlet stores or selling the items in bulk to other firms. But often this merchandise is offered to the regular customer base as a sale or discounted item. You have probably noticed that many catalogs feature sale merchandise on special pages in the middle of the catalog.

Occasionally, you will see merchandise offered at such a low price that your reaction is, "Either this is a really poor-quality product or there is another reason for this offer." One example is full-page ads that appeared in one of the Sunday news magazines over a considerable period of time. Each ad has featured a sporting goods item, apparently of good quality, at a price so low as to be completely unrealistic. One hypothesis is that the firm had no idea what it was doing and must have been losing mega-money. That seems unlikely, since they ran the ads on a seemingly irregular basis over several months. A better hypothesis is that the firm was actually building a list of persons who purchase sporting goods by mail!

Free samples or information are usually part of a multistage sales process. Computer software dealers offer "demonstration disks" for new software products that give the prospect an opportunity to experience the main features of the program. The rare coin dealer offers a booklet explaining the criteria for judging the value of rare coins. The home furnishings dealer offers a videotape of various interior decorating approaches, featuring new merchandise and trends in home decor. This type of approach should increase the prospect's knowledge and interest, making it more likely that a sale can be closed by either personal sales effort or a follow-up direct-response offer.

Contests and sweepstakes are a specialty promotional field in and of themselves. They can be extremely effective in many types of direct marketing situations, but they are also fraught with risks, both legal and monetary.

Multiple Offers. Often a mailing or a space advertisement will feature more than one product. Perhaps the most common type today, especially in business markets, is the card deck. Promotions for 20 to 30 different products, most printed on business reply postcards, are combined in a single mailing. Each offer stands on its own, but the set of offers is targeted to a particular market—business executives, doctors, computer professionals, etc. The American Express card deck shown in Figure 1.8 on page 19 is an example of a consumer version.

Another reason for developing multiple offers is product complementarity. A business marketer may offer computer software for medical billing purposes and include in the offer an initial supply of the preprinted business forms needed to produce the bills. The objective of this type of offer might be to increase the average order size or simply to enhance customer satisfaction by providing all the requirements for successful product use.

A financial services firm may include information about Individual Retirement Accounts (designed for persons who wish to supplement their existing pension plans) and information about Keogh Plans (designed for the self-employed) in a broadly targeted mailing. This type of offer should have "something for everyone" who is interested in retirement income planning, no matter what the person's employment status.

Customer's Obligations

With some offers, the customer assumes an obligation by accepting the offer. The Book-of-the-Month Club offer in Figure 3.2 obligates customers to purchase four books over a 2-year period. Other types of obligations are registration of warranties and a requirement to have periodic servicing performed.

OBJECTIVES AND THE OFFER

Given the great variety of possible options, how should the direct marketer go about developing one or more offers to be tested?

The first step is to clearly establish the marketing objectives of the individual offer. These are just some of the possibilities:

- To attract new customers
- To obtain repeat business from the existing customer base
- To produce sales leads:
  - for an established product
  - for a new product
- To raise funds for a nonprofit organization

This list is far from exhaustive. Remember, the more specific the objective, the better guidance it will provide in structuring the offer.

The marketer must also determine how financial objectives will affect the criteria for determining whether the offer is successful. Is this offer alone expected to produce a profit? Or is a profit dependent on repeat sales (e.g., continued purchase of tapes or records)? Is the offer viewed as an investment in building the base of prospective customers? Is it part of a multistage sales process, such as sales-lead generation, that cannot be directly evaluated in terms of profitability? In other words, will the success of this specific offer be evaluated over a short or a long time horizon?

The direct marketer must clarify the marketing and financial objectives in order to make a decision that balances front-end (short-term) responsiveness against back-end (longer-term) effectiveness. An example will show why.

Say that a magazine is deciding whether to offer a 3-month introductory subscription for $8 or a 12-month subscription for the regular price of $48. The 12-month offer would allow respondents to cancel at any time and receive a full refund for the unused portion of their subscription.

Assume that the magazine has a gross margin, before subscriber acquisition cost, of 10 percent, or $4.80, based on the regular price. The acquisition cost per subscriber for this magazine averages $6.

It is immediately clear that the magazine would not make money on 12-month subscriptions. It would lose even more money on the 3-month trial subscription:

Regular subscription revenue	$ 48.00
Less: gross margin	4.80
Product cost (12 months)	43.20
Acquisition cost	6.00
Total direct costs (12 months)	$ 49.20
Loss on 12-month subscription	$ 1.20

Product costs for 3 months = $10.80 ($43.20/4)

Product cost (3 months)	$ 10.80
Less: Trial subscription revenue	8.00
	2.80
Plus: Acquisition cost	6.00
Loss on 3-month trial subscription	$ 8.80

This hypothetical example makes the economics of the 3-month trial subscription look very unfavorable. The example is oversimplified, however. For one thing, the response rate should be higher for the 3-month trial (less perceived risk!) than for the regular 12-month subscription, making the assumption of equal acquisition costs incorrect. The cost for a 3-month trial should actually be lower than

$6, so the front-end of the 3-month subscription would probably look quite favorable. On the other hand, subscribers who accepted the 3-month offer would have to be contacted much sooner to renew their subscriptions, meaning increased renewal cost (which, by the way, should be considerably lower than the initial acquisition cost, assuming that the subscribers are satisfied and renew at a high rate). That is one of the back-end considerations.

Another back-end consideration is the number of cancellations on the 12-month offer. Cancellations can be quite high, making the loss greater than it appeared to be on the front end and, even worse, providing a smaller customer base for renewal efforts.

In this example no incentives were offered. Think about what might have happened if an attractive free gift had been included:

- The inclusion of a free gift with the 3-month offer would probably increase the response rate even further. That would be good—even though it makes the offer more expensive—if subscribers really like the magazine and renew over a period of several years. In other words, it would be a good investment in repeat business.
- The inclusion of a free gift with the 12-month offer would probably increase the response rate to that offer also. That would also be good, wouldn't it? The 12-month offer brings in more revenue and doesn't incur renewal costs as soon, right? But remember, the 12-month offer has a cancellation privilege (and, of course, the customer gets to keep the free gift). What if a lot of people accept the offer just to get the gift, then cancel immediately? The answer is obvious—the magazine would lose a lot of money! This happens more often than you might expect.

This illustrates the difference between a hard offer and a soft offer. A *hard offer* is one in which the product essentially stands on its own feet; there are no incentives, and perhaps even a small cost attached to the reply. A *soft offer* is one that is as attractive as possible and that makes it as easy as possible for the prospect to take action. "Hard" and "soft" are not absolutes; they are relative. Figure 3.4 contains suggestions for hardening or softening offers. The important point is that with a hard offer, the number of responses will be smaller, but their quality will be higher; with a soft offer, there will be a large volume of initial responses, but many of these responses will be unproductive.

There is one more way in which the marketing objectives can affect the choice between these two hypothetical offers. If one objective is to quickly ascertain the likelihood of success or failure of the product itself—say, the offer is for a new magazine—the 3-month trial offer will allow management to assess the renewal rate more quickly than the 12-month offer will.

Designing an offer is not simple. There are a multitude of factors to consider. Direct marketers will, however, be much less likely to make major blunders in designing offers if they keep objectives, not the mechanics of the offer, paramount at all times.

To Harden an Offer, You Can:

- Make it harder to order (telephone number not toll-free, business reply envelope not included, customer must ask for more information).
- Make payment terms more stringent.
- If price is not mentioned (e.g., a lead-generation offer), mention it. If price is mentioned, emphasize it.
- Tell more about the product, especially any negative features.
- Charge for something that could be offered free (charge for the first catalog, don't place postage on the business reply envelope).
- In a lead-generation program, tell them a salesperson will call.

To Soften an Offer, You Can:

- Make the payment terms less stringent.
- Offer advance credit approval.
- Offer an incentive. If you have been offering one incentive and find it is working, try offering two.
- Make it as easy as possible to respond (fill in the recipient's name and address on the postage-paid response card so all the person has to do is drop it in the mail; keep your toll-free number in operation 24 hours a day, 7 days a week).
- Add a game, contest, or involvement device—a rub-off spot, stamps that are to be stuck on the appropriate squares, a riddle or puzzle to be solved.
- Run a sweepstakes. Even direct marketers who personally dislike them admit they work.

FIGURE 3.4 ***Offer Hardeners and Softeners***

Source: Adapted from Edward L. Nash, *Direct Marketing* (New York: McGraw-Hill, 1982) pp. 74-75; Bob Stone, *Successful Direct Marketing Methods*, 3rd ed. (Chicago: Crain Books, 1984), pp. 58-60; Caroline Zimmermann, "The Proposition," in Nash, *Direct Marketing Handbook*, pp. 87-88.

PLANNING OFFERS FOR MULTISTAGE MARKETING PROGRAMS

The classic multistage offer is a two-stage offer in which the respondent first requests more information and then is contacted by mail, telephone, or in person to close the sale. Actually, there can be more steps; for example, an inquiry, followed by a detailed mail package, followed by a qualifying telephone call, followed by a personal sales call.

Marketing and financial objectives play an equally crucial role in structuring multistage offers. Additionally, the direct marketer can plan a progression of incentives, or can build up to a major incentive, in a way that produces harder leads at each succeeding stage.

A FEW MORE WORDS ABOUT COSTS

In planning an offer, it is important to distinguish between its fixed and its variable costs. Whether we are discussing a mailing, a space ad, or a broadcast ad, *fixed costs* are those that do not change with the volume of responses, whereas *variable costs* do change with the volume of responses. In general, the same is true of telephone marketing costs, except that there we have the added factor of time expended per call.

Fixed costs generally include production costs (copy writing, graphic design, printing, filming, recording, etc.) and media costs (time, space, list rental, postage, etc.). Remember that even though these costs are defined as "fixed" *for a specific direct-response* program, management has a great deal of discretion in terms of the actual costs. An expensive four-color mailing package with several components printed on high-quality paper becomes a fixed cost *once management has decided on that specific package design*. Management should remember that:

1. Once the production and media decisions have been made, the costs are essentially fixed for that program, whether it is successful or not.
2. High costs, or even high quality in a *technical* sense, do not necessarily make a direct-response program successful.

Variable costs, as we have said, are those that vary according to the volume of responses. Costs of merchandise and incentives will ordinarily vary directly with the number of responses. Other costs will vary, but not necessarily directly. These are often the back-end costs of honoring guarantees, dealing with returns and/or cancellations, collection costs, and other aspects of customer service. Because these costs vary indirectly, they are difficult to predict. We cannot stress too strongly that these costs can escalate rapidly as a result of a poor-quality product or a poorly structured offer. If a test is involved, poor planning and/or execution can make the results of the test difficult to read.

In 1986 Murjani International, Ltd., tested a video catalog for its Coca-Cola clothing line. Produced in the style of a contemporary music video, it probably cost at least $40,000 plus $5 per unit for duplicating and mailing individual tapes. When a sample of people who watched the video were questioned, 9 percent indicated that it had encouraged them to purchase the product. The problem was that virtually all of them bought at a retail store instead of purchasing directly and providing Murjani with a higher gross margin.

Why? One company executive suggested that it might have helped to include a direct-response incentive, perhaps a rebate on the cost of the tape. That didn't seem to be the major problem, however, because Murjani actually received a 4 percent rate of response (which is pretty good) on their toll-free telephone number. Unfortunately, the telephone operators hadn't been properly trained to provide the needed customer service for this fairly high-ticket line of fashion merchandise. Because they couldn't answer questions about sizes, colors, and the like, few people bought.[2]

WHAT MOTIVATES PROSPECTS TO RESPOND?

There are many considerations in structuring an offer, many individual elements that can be included. In the final analysis, the direct marketer can ascertain which of the available offers works best by testing alternative offers and going with the winner.

Testing, as we will discuss in detail in Chapter 8, is a critical aspect of the discipline of direct marketing. The ability to know which offer (or which list or mailing date or whatever) works best is the feature that most distinguishes direct marketing from general marketing.

Testing provides tremendous opportunities to improve the productivity of direct marketing programs. However, it is not the entire answer. Direct marketers need to understand the attitudes, values, and motivations of customers and prospects just as general marketers do. Testing can only help select the best offer from the available set of offers. Understanding customer/prospect motivations and behavior will help the direct marketer structure better offers initially.

Marketing and consumer behavior texts frequently contain extensive discussions of motivation theory. Most students are familiar with Maslow's hierarchy of motivations, and many are also aware of other approaches to understanding human motivation. The problem for marketers is that these theories are borrowed directly from the behavioral sciences without the necessary adaptations that would make them applicable to specific marketing situations.

In 1978 Fennell set forth a marketing-specific typology of motivations[3] that has been further developed by Rossiter and Percy.[4] Figure 3.5 shows the eight basic purchase motivations. The motives are divided into three categories—negative, mildly negative, and positive.

For our purposes, it is sufficient to think of motives as forces that cause people to try to achieve a desired state of being. These forces, or drives, can cause a person to try to *avoid* a particular situation or outcome regarded as unpleasant or even dangerous (a negative motivation). If the situation or outcome is seen as pleasant

[2] Joanne Lipman, "Need a Commercial Break? Viewers Take Ads Home to Play on VCR's," *The Wall Street Journal*, June 5, 1987, p. 27.

[3] Geraldine Fennell, "Consumer's Perceptions of the Product-Use Situation," *Journal of Marketing*, 42 (1978): 38-47.

[4] John R. Rossiter and Larry Percy, *Advertising and Promotion Management* (New York: McGraw-Hill, 1987), pp. 169 - 174.

	Negative Origin
Problem removal	Prospect experiences problem; seeks product to remove it.
Problem avoidance	Prospect anticipates future problem; seeks product to prevent occurrence.
Incomplete satisfaction	Prospect not satisfied with current product; seeks a better one.
Mixed approach-avoidance	Prospect likes some things about product but not others; tries to find product to resolve this conflict.
	Mildly Negative Origin
Normal depletion	Prospect is out of stock or low; seeks to maintain normal inventory.
	Positive Origin
Sensory gratification	Prospect seeks physical gratification/enjoyment.
Intellectual stimulation	Prospect seeks psychological gratification; to explore or master situation.
Social approval	Prospect sees opportunity for social rewards/personal recognition through use of product.

FIGURE 3.5 ***Basic Purchase Motivations***

Source: Adapted from John R. Rossiter and Larry Percy, *Advertising and Promotion Management* (New York: McGraw-Hill, 1987), p. 170.

or attractive, the person will be motivated to *approach* it. There are also times when the individual is merely motivated to *maintain* the status quo.

Home security systems are one product category where an avoidance motive—to prevent the negative outcomes resulting from fire or theft—is likely to be operative. Attractive travel opportunities suggest approach, while purchase of disability insurance may be motivated by a desire to maintain an established standard of living.

Thinking carefully about what would motivate the target prospect to respond to the offer will help the direct marketer develop more effective offers. There is one more thing to keep in mind when conducting this analysis. Motives affect both the decision to purchase a product category (disability insurance) and the decision to purchase a specific brand within that category (a specific firm's disability insurance policy). Sometimes the motivation will be the same at both category and brand levels; sometimes it will not be. Be sure to separate the two levels conceptually in order to be as clear as possible about motivations for purchase. This type of analysis will lead directly to a consideration of the appropriate positioning for the product.

THE IMPORTANCE OF POSITIONING

The desired positioning for the product should be an important consideration throughout all stages of the development of an offer and its creative execution. According to Kotler, "Positioning is the act of designing a company's product and marketing mix to fit a given place in the consumer's mind."[5] Positioning is only relevant to a clearly defined market—the product-market discussed in Chapter 2. Positioning is also relevant only to target customers—it does not matter whether persons outside the defined target market like the product's presentation or find it attractive. Only the target customers matter when evaluating the effectiveness of a positioning strategy.

There are two basic approaches to developing a positioning strategy. One is to rely on managerial judgment about what constitutes the most effective positioning. The other is to conduct marketing research at one or more points in the process of developing the strategy.

Unquestionably, marketing research is needed to develop the best positioning strategy. Experience suggests that managers often, perhaps even usually, would not select the positioning strategy that research finds to be best. One reason seems to be that managers find it difficult to view their own products objectively or in the same manner as prospective customers view them. The discussion of purchase motivations in the preceding section is based on *consumer perceptions* of the needs products satisfy in actual use. Either the uses or the needs may differ from management's expectations; hence managerial and customer perceptions of the product may differ.

A discussion of the techniques used to conduct positioning research is beyond the scope of this book.[6] We will not complicate our discussion of positioning strategy by continually referring to the need for research and the types of research needed, but trust that students will recognize that most of the issues we discuss in the remainder of this chapter can be more completely understood with the aid of good marketing research.

POSITIONING ALTERNATIVES

Conventional wisdom says that products can be positioned in terms of their benefits or attributes (a copying machine with automatic feed and collating), their particular uses or users (personal copiers for individuals or small businesses), or against a specific product category or competitor (the copier with the lowest repair frequency). However, a recent study by Crawford uncovered other types of

[5] Philip Kotler, *Marketing Management*, 5th ed. (Englewood Cliffs, NJ: Prentice-Hall, 1984), p. 272.

[6] For a detailed discussion, consult Chapter 7, "Product Positioning," in Glen L. Urban, John R. Hauser, Nikhilesh Dholakia, *Essentials of New Product Management* (Englewood Cliffs, NJ: Prentice Hall, 1987).

positionings in widespread use among both consumer and business marketers.[7] Figure 3.6 contains a complete list of positioning alternatives that are available equally to general marketers and direct marketers.

Crawford called the new type of positioning he discovered *surrogates* or substitutes. The nature of this type of positioning is that "the marketer does not describe the features/benefits, but instead says something about the product that permits the reader/listener to reach individual conclusions." [8] He reasons that this type of positioning is particularly effective because it lets the reader infer attributes/benefits of the product—presumably those the individual would most like the product to possess. Following Fennell's reasoning about applying the purchase motivation categories to the development of positioning strategies, the surrogate positionings would allow for a broader positioning that does not rely on explicit claims about attributes/benefits. The result could be appeal to a broader target market. In Crawford's study, benefit positioning was used most frequently (32 percent) in the ads studied, followed by the general category of surrogates (23 percent), then attribute positioning (19 percent). Twenty-six percent of the ads had no identifiable positioning. Figure 3.7a and 3.7b show a number of direct response space ads that demonstrate some of the positioning alternatives.

Crawford cites a number of strategic implications that emerged from the complete study:

- Surrogate positioning should be considered, especially for products with little or no physical differentiation.
- Positioning should be consistent over all elements of the marketing program.
- The positioning approach should be sustained over a considerable period of time.
- There will probably be more types of positioning developed as managers become more experienced with this powerful marketing tool.

THE PROCESS OF DEVELOPING A POSITIONING STRATEGY[9]

The complex activity of developing an effective positioning strategy can best be handled by dividing it into distinct steps. Aaker and Myers have provided a useful approach which can be modified slightly for the direct marketing environment. It consists of seven steps:

1. Identify the competitors.
2. Determine how the competitors are perceived and evaluated.

[7] C. Merle Crawford, "A New Positioning Typology," *Journal of Product Innovation Management*, 4 (1985), pp. 243-253.

[8] Crawford, "A New Positioning Typology," p. 247.

[9] This section is based on David A. Aaker and John G. Myers, *Advertising Management*, 3rd ed. (Englewood Cliffs, NJ: Prentice Hall, 1987), pp. 132-146.

Product Attributes/Benefits

Product Features: A characteristic, usually tangible, of the product itself.

Product Benefits: A satisfaction received from use of the product.

Direct—directly attributable to use of the product

Indirect—indirectly attributable to use of the product

Surrogates

Nonpareil: Without equal; top quality.

Parentage: origin—maker, seller, performer, etc. A parentage positioning can be stated in terms of:

Brand—because it comes from that line of branded products

Company—because it comes from that particular company

Person—because it was created by a particular person

Manufacture: The manner in which the product is made. A manufacture positioning can be stated in terms of:

Process—how it is actually produced

Ingredients—the ingredients it contains

Design—superior functioning as a result of the way the product is designed

Target: Because the product was made specifically for people/firms like you. A target positioning can be stated in terms of:

End use—how or the situation in which it will be used

Demographic—created for a group of people who can be defined demographically

Psychographic—created for a group of people who can be defined in terms of life-style

Behavioral—created for a group of people who can be defined in terms of a specific behavior

Endorsement: Credible spokesperson(s) says it is good. Endorsement can be made by:

Expert—person with appropriate credentials/knowledge

Emulative/object of emulation—a role model or person the target would like to imitate

Rank: Market leader.

Experience: Long or frequent use gives credibility to its claims. The experience can be of several types:

Other market—in another market

Bandwagon—sheer numbers

Time—over an extended period of time

Competitor: Alike or similar to another successful product.

Predecessor: Similar to an earlier product that was popular.

FIGURE 3.6 ***Product-Positioning Alternatives***

Source: Adapted from C. Merle Crawford, "A New Positioning Typology," *Journal of Product Innovation Management*, 4 (1985): 243 - 253.

3. Determine the competitors' positionings.
4. Analyze the target market.
5. Select the desired segment.
6. Develop alternative positionings.
7. Implement the positioning strategy and monitor its effectiveness.

Identify the Competitors

If a strategic analysis has been performed, this step will already have been accomplished. It is identical to the definition of the product market and identification of the competition in the strategy development process.

Determine How the Competitors Are Perceived and Evaluated

Knowledge of how competitors are perceived and evaluated rests upon two pieces of information: (1) what attributes/benefits customers use to judge competitive products; and (2) how satisfactory customers perceive each product to be on each attribute/benefit. Since there are many attributes/benefits on which products can be judged, determining the few that are actually important to customers is not an easy task. Aaker and Myers discuss various research-based approaches in their chapter on "Attitude and Market Structure."

Determine the Competitors' Positionings

Knowing how each of the competitive products is evaluated on each of the determinant (important) attributes/benefits effectively defines its positioning. This is often expressed as a mapping of products on dimensions that represent the important attributes/benefits. Figure 3.8 shows a hypothetical perceptual map for soft drinks in which taste (sweet/tart) and heaviness (light/heavy) are the dimensions (attributes) and a number of brands are arrayed on these two dimensions. Although perceptual mapping is a technique commonly used in general marketing—as in this example—there do not appear to be any published applications in direct marketing.

Analyze the Target Market

This step requires determining what segments exist in a particular product market. The assumption, based on the findings of many studies, is that customers tend to use the same set of attributes/benefits to evaluate all the products in a category, but that these same customers have distinctly different preferences for different attributes/benefits. It is the difference in preferences that creates market segments. One way to approach the search for an unserved or underserved market segment is to look for a set of attributes/benefits that customers want, the firm can

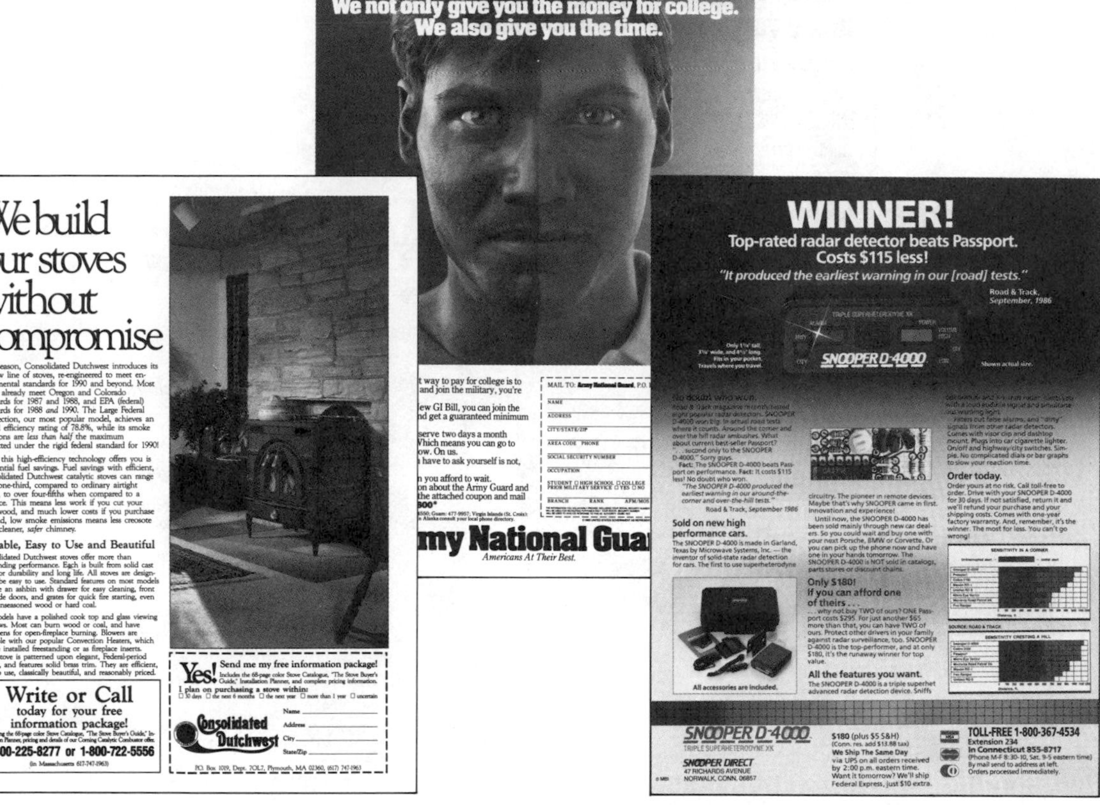

FIGURE 3.7a ***Print Advertisements***

Source: Consolidated Dutchwest, Plymouth, MA 02360; Army National Guard, Washington, DC; and Snooper Direct, MBI, Inc., Norwalk, CT 06857.

deliver, and its competitors cannot deliver. Once it is established that the firm's product can deliver those attributes/benefits, the question becomes: Will customers believe that it can deliver? If the attributes/benefits are not being successfully delivered by a competitive product, that is even better. Frequently a product will be able to establish a distinctive positioning simply by emphasizing desired attributes/benefits that no other product has seen fit to emphasize. Remember, this crucial step in developing a positioning strategy is based on understanding what customers want, not what management thinks they want!

Select the Desired Segment

Positioning represents a firm commitment to serving a specific market segment. How does the marketing manager identify an unserved or underserved market segment?

FIGURE 3.7b ***Print Advertisements (continued)***

Source: Seymour of Sycamore, Inc., Sycamore, IL 60178; Charles Schwab & Co., Inc., San Francisco, CA 94104; and Applied Business Technology Corp., New York, NY 10013

Think in terms of a product-market map, and look for "gaps" in product availability on one or more dimensions. Gaps indicate two possibilities. The first is that no product is serving that particular need or set of needs—which means an opportunity exists. The second is that no one (or at least not a sufficiently large group of customers) has that particular set of needs—which means there is no opportunity.

Even if an opportunity exists, questions remain. Management must ask: Are we capable of serving that particular segment of the market? Do we have the skills and resources? Is our image appropriate (or can we make it so)? Is the market segment attractive? Is it large enough to be profitable? Does it have a satisfactory rate of growth? Can we reach the purchase decision makers in a cost-effective fashion?

If all these questions are answered affirmatively, management has located a market segment in which they can effectively position the product—and they can develop one or more positioning alternatives that should appeal to that market segment.

Develop Alternative Positionings

The value of testing alternative positionings can be seen clearly in the National Geographic Society's experience with a new book, *Discovering Britain and Ireland*. Member survey data had indicated sufficient interest to warrant publication of the book, even in the face of intense—and often steeply discounted—competition from a multitude of pictoral books about Great Britain. The marketing task was to position the volume to achieve a profitable level of sales in a crowded market.

Two quite different positioning approaches were tested (see Figure 3.9). One was an appeal to the armchair traveler interested in the history and culture of the British Isles. The four-color brochure featured a romantic landscape complete with medieval castle and carried the message, "Tradition is all around you . . . and the

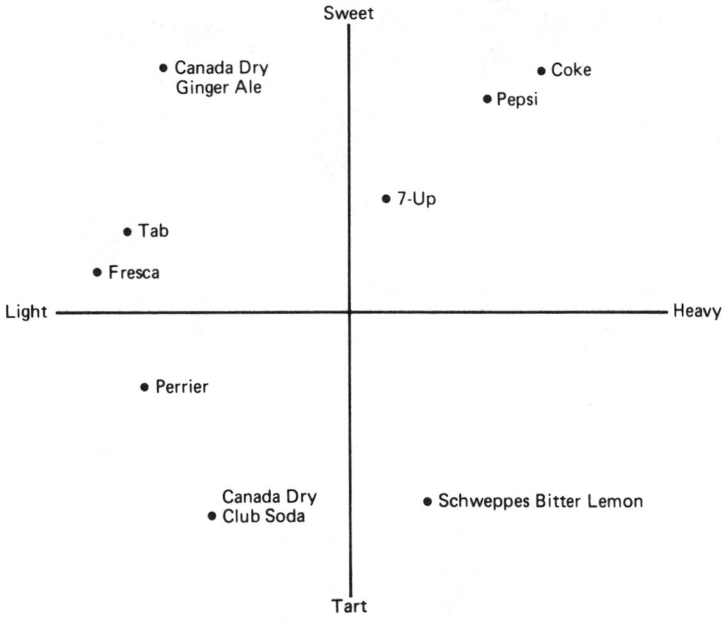

FIGURE 3.8 ***A Hypothetical MSD Map for Soft Drinks.***

Source: Glen L. Urban, John R. Hauser, and Nikhilesh Dholakia, *Essentials of New Product Management* (Englewood Cliffs, N.N.: Prentice Hall, 1987), p. 116.

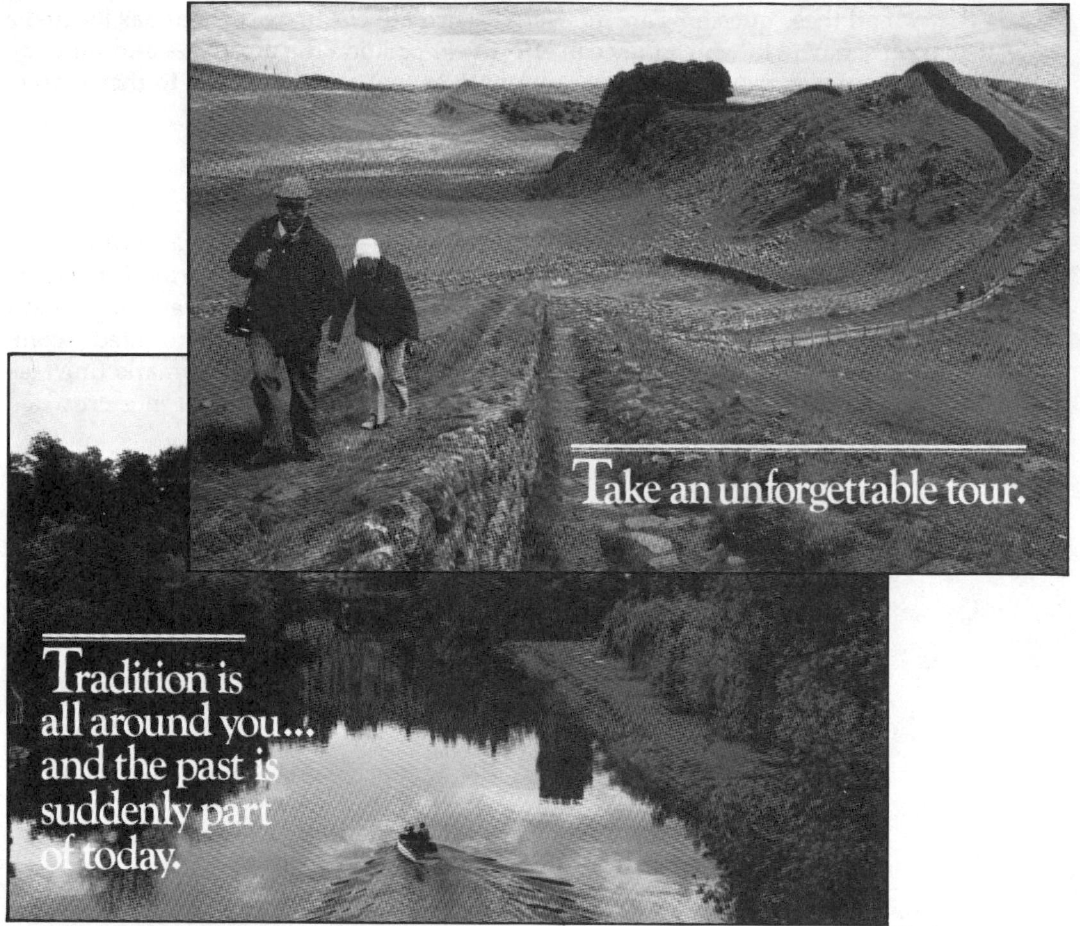
Take an unforgettable tour.
Tradition is all around you... and the past is suddenly part of today.

FIGURE 3.9 ***Two Mailing Packages: Discovering Britain and Ireland***

Source: National Geographic Society, Washington, DC 20036

past is suddenly part of today." This offer tested the volume at $22.95 for the regular edition and $32.95 for the deluxe edition.

The second positioning approach was a more active appeal to "Take an unforgettable tour." The brochure featured a mature couple hiking along Hadrian's Wall in northern England. The prices tested for this version of the offer were also $22.95 and $32.95.

In each of the two versions a "publisher's letter" (also called a "lift letter"; see Chapter 9) reinforced the positioning approach, but the other elements of the package—four-page letter, order form, outer envelope, and brochure contents—were identical. Which would you pick as the winner in the test?

The winner was the "Hadrian's Wall" package; it beat the "Castle" package by 8–24 percent, depending on the list. According to *Direct Marketing* magazine, use of the winning package resulted in an acceptable cost per order and a volume of sales that made it the most successful National Geographic title in four years.

Implement the Positioning Strategy and Monitor Its Effectiveness

The positioning selected will have a major impact on many elements of the overall marketing program.

- It will affect the manner in which the offer is structured and how the various elements of it are implemented.
- It will affect the creative execution, which must portray in both words and visuals the desired image.
- It will affect the choice of media vehicles, both to reach the chosen target market and to provide an appropriate context for the product as positioned.
- It will affect the types of customer services offered.

The degree to which the positioning of the product in the minds of the target market matches management's desired positioning should be evaluated at regular intervals to ensure that the positioning remains appropriate to the needs of the target market as it changes and evolves over time.

A FEW LAST THOUGHTS ON POSITIONING

If it is done well, positioning will create for a product an image, perhaps even a "personality." Positionings can be modified, but not easily, so much thought should be given to choosing an appropriate positioning strategy initially. When doing so, it will help to keep these points in mind:

- Don't try to be something you are not. Be realistic in assessing your firm's and your product's capabilities. You can be sure that your prospective customers will be!
- If the positioning is working, stick with it. Modified positionings—even worse, frequently modified positionings—cannot be as sharp and clear as a single positioning, maintained with absolute consistency.
- For maximum impact, see that the positioning permeates all your marketing communications.

Avoid these positioning traps: [10]

[10]Adapted from Michael L. Rothschild, *Marketing Communications* (Lexington, MA: D. C. Heath, 1987), pp. 158–160.

Trap 1: Positioning head-on against the industry leader. It is very difficult to compete with an established product on its own territory. Instead, establish your own territory.

Trap 2: "Me too" positionings. The positioning should not be a weak image of another product's position, offering some trivial differentiating feature or benefit. Again, carve out your own area of distinctiveness.

Trap 3: Factory-driven positionings. This trap arises when a firm produces a product to utilize manufacturing capacity or an available technology. It is hard to position a product successfully if no one really wanted it in the first place.

Trap 4:- Being "something for everybody." If you try to be something for everyone, you usually end up being nothing to anybody. An undifferentiated marketing strategy suggests an unsegmented market—a difficult thing to find today.

Trap 5: Line-extension positionings. A product that relies on a strong, pre-existing product for much of its image in the customer's mind will obviously suffer if the original product declines in popularity.

Trap 6: F.W.M.T.S.. This acronym stands for "forgot what made them successful." If it isn't broken, don't fix it!

SUMMARY

The offer and the product positioning it establishes are central to the execution of the direct marketing strategy. The direct marketer must choose carefully among the variety of offer and positioning alternatives available. Both the marketing and the financial objectives of the program will affect the way in which the offer is structured.

DISCUSSION QUESTIONS

1. What are the required offer elements? The optional elements? What role does each play in developing an offer?
2. What do the terms front-end and back-end mean? How are they relevant to offer planning?
3. Why would a direct marketer choose to use a hard offer instead of a soft offer? When might a soft offer be better?
4. Looking at the motivations described in Figure 3.5, can you think of a product which strongly appeals to each motive?
5. What is the meaning of positioning? How is it important in the process of offer development?

6. Bring in a direct mail piece or a direct-response ad from a magazine and be prepared to identify the offer elements it contains. How is the product positioned?

SUGGESTED ADDITIONAL READINGS

1. Robert B. Settle and Pamela L. Alreck, *Why They Buy: American Consumers Inside and Out* (New York: John Wiley & Sons, 1986).
2. Al Ries and Jack Trout, *Positioning: The Battle for Your Mind*, revised ed. (New York: McGraw-Hill, 1986).
3. Glen L. Urban, John R. Hauser, and Nikhilesh Dholakia, *Essentials of New Product Management* (Englewood Cliffs, NJ: Prentice Hall, 1987)..

4

List Selection and Segmentation

INTRODUCTION

It has been said that you will lose money sending a terrific piece to a lousy list, but make lots of money sending a lousy piece to a terrific list. Perhaps this is a myth perpetuated by list compilers and brokers. Certainly product manufacturers would argue that the product is the key, and copy writers would probably insist that the copy is the important thing. Still, nobody denies that the list is a crucial ingredient in determining the profitability of the overall direct marketing effort.

There are many definitions of a list, and quite a few of a mailing list. At this point, think of a mailing list as the names and addresses of prospects to whom your copy could feasibly be sent. Note the word feasibly as a qualifier.

Direct marketers should be aware of all feasible lists. However, it is even more important to select lists that are profitable, if not in terms of dollars, at least in terms of providing ample information that can be used to enhance future list selection decisions. But, even if we limit the meaning of profitability to dollars, it's not always easy to specify the criterion function to be used in choosing among feasible lists. Should we use "response rate" as the guiding value? Or should we use "dollars of profit per name"? Or "dollars of profit per dollar spent"? Or should we use simply "total dollars"? The answer can be any of the above, depending on just how we formulate the choice.

We begin this chapter by discussing the types of lists available and describing aspects of each type. Then we walk down various paths through the list rental process. We next consider the economics of mailing lists and the choice among feasible lists. Finally, we explore certain facets of segmenting lists, that is, breaking out a list into subsets with different characteristics, notably different profit/cost/response parameters.

TYPES OF LISTS

There is no standard way to categorize the different types of lists. The most common breakdown of list types is: response lists, compiled lists, and house lists.

In oversimplified terms, *response lists* are lists of people who have some identifiable product interest, like martial arts equipment, investment advice, or X-rated videotapes, and have a proven willingness (or at least not a total aversion) to buy by mail. The reason these lists are called response lists is that the list members have indeed responded to a mailing.

Compiled lists are lists of people whom we do not know are willing to buy by mail, but who have some identifiable characteristic or set of characteristics, like being a lawyer, a male member of a bridge club, or a self-reported viewer of an UFO. Compiled lists are often broken down into two subcategories: compiled business lists and compiled consumer lists. The reason these lists are called compiled is that somebody (or a computer) has actually compiled them. That is, the names are not found in one place through any sort of "natural selection," as, say, a list of members of a gun club would be.

A *house list* is usually defined as a list of customers who have bought from the company. Actually, a better way to express the notion of a house list is to say that it is a list derived from the company's own files. It may include the names of people who aren't really customers, and who have never been customers but who once made an inquiry.

THE LIST RENTAL PROCESS

Ninety-nine percent of all lists a company uses outside of its own house list are rented lists. Of course, some lists a company rents are house lists of *other* companies. On rare occasions a list is bought rather than rented. Less rarely—in fact, with increasing frequency over the past several years—two companies will *exchange* house lists, or to maintain an equity of sorts, one company will exchange a number of names from its house list for a different number of names from the other company's house list. The equity issue arises when, for example, one company's list is more up-to-date than the other company's. Actually, list exchanges can be lumped together with list rentals in most ways.

List Brokers

The list rental process begins with list brokers. These people provide a service analogous to that of a real estate broker. They work for both sides, the list renter and the list owner, and it is the latter who pays their fees, just as the seller of a home pays the real estate broker's commission. The list broker must be aware of most available lists; the general tendency is for list owners to make their lists available to any reputable broker who has a potential renter. This is similar to what is called "multiple listing" in real estate transactions. Some renters use one list broker; others use many list brokers. The list broker advises the renter which lists are good buys for the renter's needs, and ideally provides some help in the entire direct marketing process. Brokers have a wealth of experience to offer the renter, partially based on their service to other clients, yet they are careful not to breach any confidence concerning the choices, results, and strategies, of any other clients.

List Compilers

Where do all these lists come from originally? Many are house lists of companies, but the majority are compiled lists. There are essentially two ways of creating a compiled list. Using telephone directories, government census data, and other sources of information, list compilers put together a list of people having some specific set of properties (e.g., female heads of households). *Building up a list* this way is the older method. Today most lists are compiled in a reverse approach. Instead of using many distinct sources to build up a list having special characteristics, large list compilers have an enormous master file of names and using computer technology *cull out a list* with the desired special characteristics.

List Managers

A list owner may contact a list broker to convey that he has a list for sale. Or if the owner deals with several brokers, has several distinct lists available, or rents his lists somewhat frequently, he may prefer to hire a list manager who will interact with the list broker and keep track of all aspects of the process relevant to the owner. This list manager is ideally not just an administrator, but also an innovator who can suggest how the owner should market or segment his list. When the list owner is also a list compiler, the list manager/list compiler distinction is likely to be blurred.

List Rental Agreements

Certain written and unwritten rules are typically part of the list rental process. Generally, lists are rented for one-time use. The renter may not retain any names for later use, except for the names of responders. The mailing piece must be agreed to by the list owner before it is mailed out. Without this condition, an unscrupulous renter could offer a loss-leader deal just to get a large number of responders, and thereby get to keep a large number of names as his forever. (Actually, this could be a dubious economic decision for the renter, even if he could get away with it, because many people respond to loss leaders but don't "convert" when offered products on which the company *would* make a profit.) The list owner must also okay the date of the mailing. This condition allows the owner to make sure that sufficient time elapses between the renter's mailing and any mailing he may wish to conduct himself.

How can a list owner or manager be sure that the renter will not defy the agreement and use the list more than once? The one-time use rule is so universally accepted that it would be rare for a renter to violate it; the person or company that did breach the agreement would never again find a source from which to rent another list. Nevertheless, list owners and managers frequently seed lists—that is, insert a few dummy names, or names with an identifiable incorrect middle initial. Whenever these pieces are received, the owner is informed. The authors know one list manager whose dog gets a great deal of mail addressed to different variants of his name.

The price charged for a list rental depends on the list's quantity and quality. The quantity aspect is generally dealt with by pricing on a per-thousand basis. There are some exceptions to this rule for lists that are relatively small. Also, one must rent a minimum number of names so that fixed costs can be allocated over a sufficiently large base.

The quality aspect is more complex. It involves, among other factors, uniqueness (i.e., nobody else in the world has these names together on one list), specificity, and good old-fashioned supply and demand. Most lists rent for between $30 per thousand names and $125 per thousand names. Many lists, especially those available from large list compilers (e.g., Metromail), offer a large number of segmentation options for an additional price. A list renter often wants only certain zip codes, only women, only hotline names (people who made a purchase within the last 30 days or some other short-time period), or some combination of a large number of available segmentations.

Direct Mail List Rates and Data, a semiannual publication by Standard Rate and Data Service, Inc., lists available lists and their rates. The lists are cataloged in a variety of ways (e.g., by market, by owner). There are other lists of lists. All contain data cards noting certain relevant facts about each list to be managed, rented, or brokered. The main elements of a data card are: (1) the number of names on the list; (2) the type of list; (3) the price of the list; (4) the source of the list; (5) the minimum number of names that must be rented; and (6) the segmentation options (the selects available). Data cards also contain some general facts about the list (e.g., percent women). For a sample data card, see Figure 4.1.

List Processor

After a list (or a list segment) has been selected, arrangements must be made about the mechanics and format of the delivery (type of labels, magnetic tape, location to which to deliver, etc.). The next step is often to hire a *list processor.* The customary task of the list processor is to eliminate duplicates from a collection of more than one list (called *merge/purge*). Then a system of allocating these duplicate names to lists for the purpose of payment is devised. Usually, a renter must agree to pay

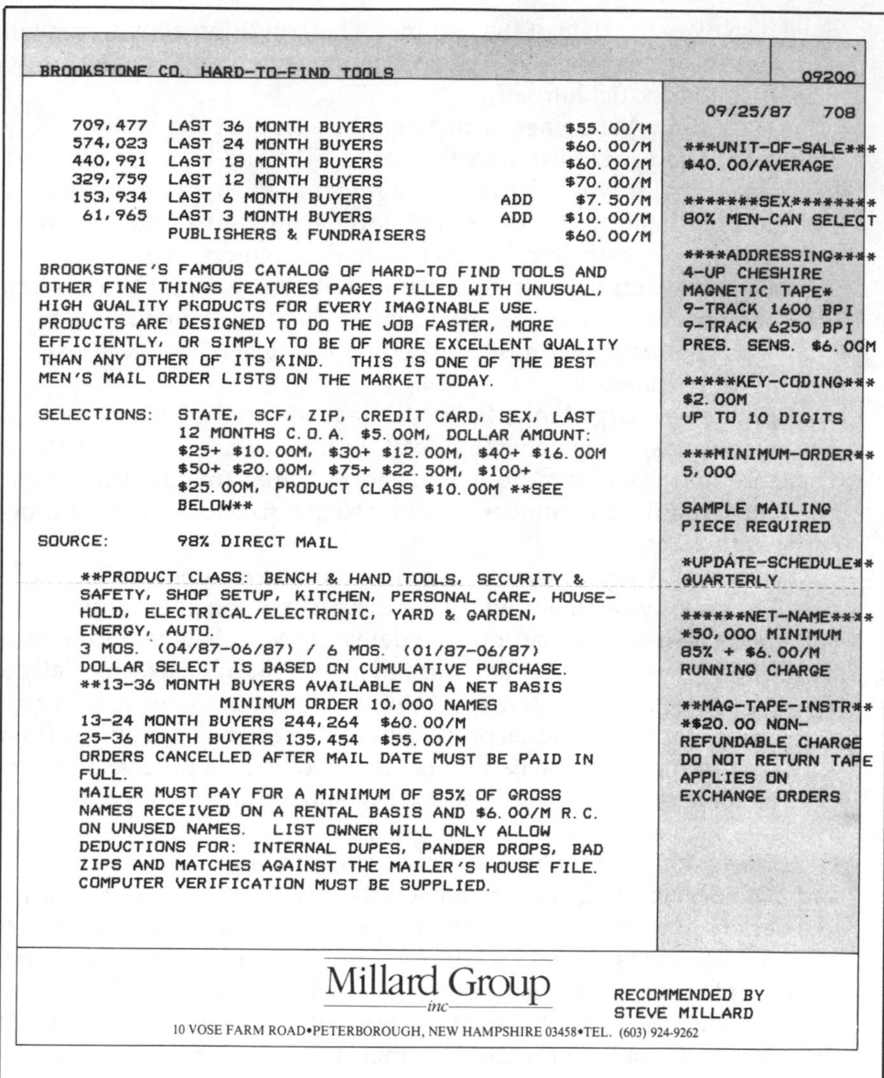

BROOKSTONE CO. HARD-TO-FIND TOOLS 09200

709,477	LAST 36 MONTH BUYERS		$55.00/M
574,023	LAST 24 MONTH BUYERS		$60.00/M
440,991	LAST 18 MONTH BUYERS		$60.00/M
329,759	LAST 12 MONTH BUYERS		$70.00/M
153,934	LAST 6 MONTH BUYERS	ADD	$7.50/M
61,965	LAST 3 MONTH BUYERS	ADD	$10.00/M
	PUBLISHERS & FUNDRAISERS		$60.00/M

BROOKSTONE'S FAMOUS CATALOG OF HARD-TO FIND TOOLS AND OTHER FINE THINGS FEATURES PAGES FILLED WITH UNUSUAL, HIGH QUALITY PRODUCTS FOR EVERY IMAGINABLE USE. PRODUCTS ARE DESIGNED TO DO THE JOB FASTER, MORE EFFICIENTLY, OR SIMPLY TO BE OF MORE EXCELLENT QUALITY THAN ANY OTHER OF ITS KIND. THIS IS ONE OF THE BEST MEN'S MAIL ORDER LISTS ON THE MARKET TODAY.

SELECTIONS: STATE, SCF, ZIP, CREDIT CARD, SEX, LAST 12 MONTHS C.O.A. $5.00M, DOLLAR AMOUNT: $25+ $10.00M, $30+ $12.00M, $40+ $16.00M $50+ $20.00M, $75+ $22.50M, $100+ $25.00M, PRODUCT CLASS $10.00M **SEE BELOW**

SOURCE: 98% DIRECT MAIL

**PRODUCT CLASS: BENCH & HAND TOOLS, SECURITY & SAFETY, SHOP SETUP, KITCHEN, PERSONAL CARE, HOUSEHOLD, ELECTRICAL/ELECTRONIC, YARD & GARDEN, ENERGY, AUTO.
3 MOS. (04/87-06/87) / 6 MOS. (01/87-06/87)
DOLLAR SELECT IS BASED ON CUMULATIVE PURCHASE.
**13-36 MONTH BUYERS AVAILABLE ON A NET BASIS
MINIMUM ORDER 10,000 NAMES
13-24 MONTH BUYERS 244,264 $60.00/M
25-36 MONTH BUYERS 135,454 $55.00/M
ORDERS CANCELLED AFTER MAIL DATE MUST BE PAID IN FULL.
MAILER MUST PAY FOR A MINIMUM OF 85% OF GROSS NAMES RECEIVED ON A RENTAL BASIS AND $6.00/M R.C. ON UNUSED NAMES. LIST OWNER WILL ONLY ALLOW DEDUCTIONS FOR: INTERNAL DUPES, PANDER DROPS, BAD ZIPS AND MATCHES AGAINST THE MAILER'S HOUSE FILE. COMPUTER VERIFICATION MUST BE SUPPLIED.

09/25/87 708

UNIT-OF-SALE
$40.00/AVERAGE

*******SEX*******
80% MEN-CAN SELECT

****ADDRESSING****
4-UP CHESHIRE
MAGNETIC TAPE*
9-TRACK 1600 BPI
9-TRACK 6250 BPI
PRES. SENS. $6.00M

*****KEY-CODING***
$2.00M
UP TO 10 DIGITS

***MINIMUM-ORDER**
5,000

SAMPLE MAILING PIECE REQUIRED

*UPDATE-SCHEDULE**
QUARTERLY

******NET-NAME****
*50,000 MINIMUM
85% + $6.00/M
RUNNING CHARGE

MAG-TAPE-INSTR
*$20.00 NON-REFUNDABLE CHARGE
DO NOT RETURN TAPE
APPLIES ON EXCHANGE ORDERS

Millard Group inc

RECOMMENDED BY STEVE MILLARD

10 VOSE FARM ROAD•PETERBOROUGH, NEW HAMPSHIRE 03458•TEL. (603) 924-9262

FIGURE 4.1 ***List Card from the Brookstone Hard-to-Find Tools Catalog***
Source: Brookstone Company, Petersborough, NH 03458.

for a minimum of 80 or 85 percent of the names provided, even if only a smaller percentage is usable because of duplication. This often occurs even after routine allocation of names to lists (e.g., if 1,000 names are on the same two lists and no other list, 500 are allocated to each of the two lists). On occasion, the arrangement provides that payment will be made only for names not present on any other list being used by the renter. Both this arrangement and the one in which there is a set minimum percent of names that must be paid for are called *net agreements*. A newer type of arrangement, called a *net net agreement*, provides that the renter will pay only for those names he *chooses* to mail to. The net net agreement allows the renter to do his own independent analyses instead of relying on a priori selections. He can statistically or otherwise study the list, and *then* decide whom to mail to.

Other services provided by list processors are: (1) list cleaning—getting rid of "nixies," or incorrectly addressed pieces that would be returned by the postal service; (2) list suppression—removing names with known undesirable characteristics (e.g., deadbeats, people who have requested that their names be removed from mailing lists); (3) data overlay—matching names against certain response or demographic traits; and (4) a variety of services in the high speed computer area.

There are two other types of agreements that should be mentioned here. The first has already been alluded to —exchanging lists. This can be viewed as similar to bartering, except that occasionally the issue of market share and competitive advantage becomes involved. Sometimes a company will exchange lists with another firm they would never allow to *rent* their list. In other words, reciprocity is a requirement. The second is cooperative mailings. In this case, a group of noncompeting companies each puts a piece in an envelope that is mailed out. A variation is a joint mailing, in which each company puts its own self-contained envelope into one larger envelope.

We end this section of the chapter with a look at three advertisements (see Figure 4.2). The first is an ad of a *list owner* (Norm Thompson) for his list, offering traditional selects as well as selects by product. The second is an ad for a *list compiler* (Research Projects of Woodbury, Connecticut), offering a large variety of compiled lists. The third is an ad for *list manager* services (Fred E. Allen, Inc., of Mt. Pleasant, Texas), featuring a list of satisfied customers—a frequent component of ads in all aspects of marketing.

ECONOMICS OF MAILING LISTS

Before we take up the economics of mailing lists, we want to note that our discussion will be somewhat different for each of the following situations:

1. We are offered a list for rent. We either rent this list or we don't. The list in question is not competing with any other choice, and the decision on this list is independent of all other considerations.
2. We are choosing among many lists. We can choose, at most, only a subset of the available choices.

The first situation is cleaner, so we will consider it first. Then we will extend the discussion to the second situation. We acknowledge that our description of situation 1 is a bit too idealized, in that it's unlikely that any significant decision

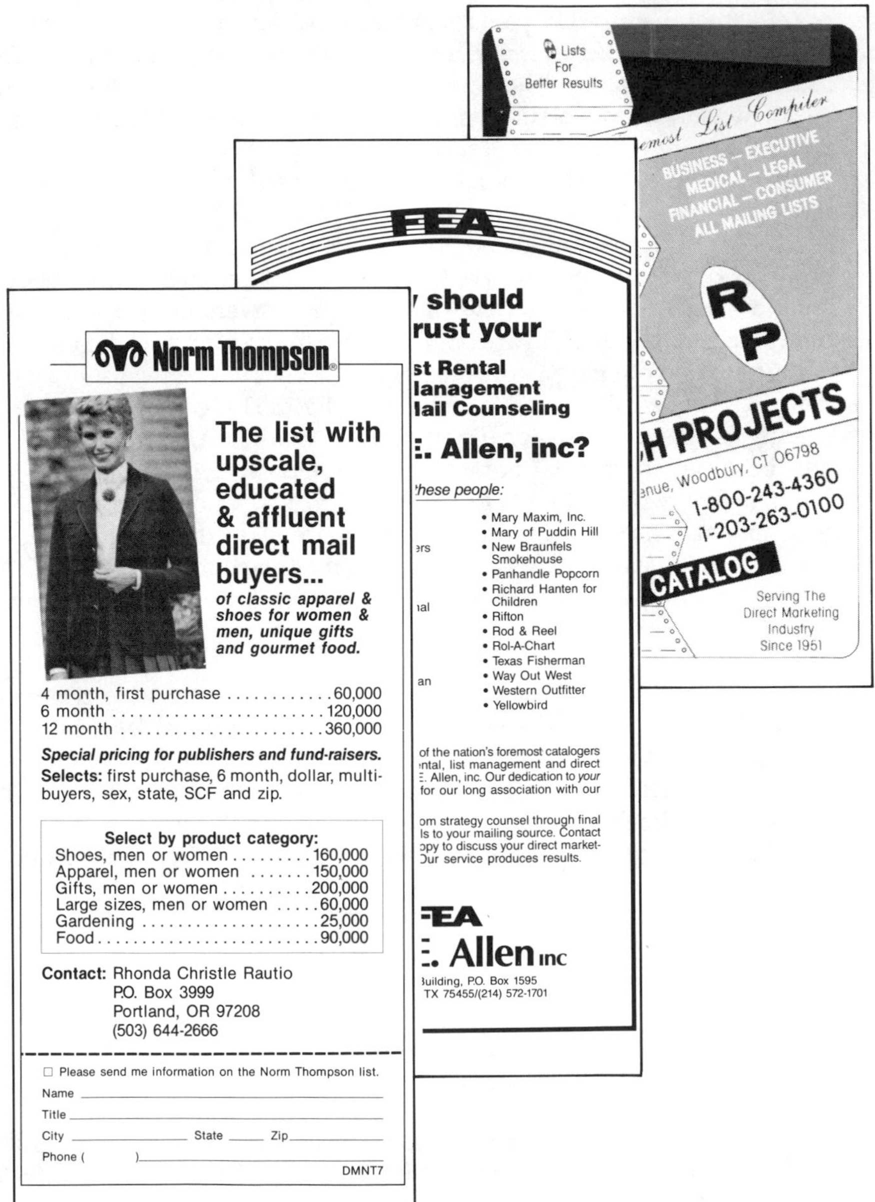

FIGURE 4.2

Sources: Norm Thompson ad—*Direct Marketing,* July, 1987, p. 83
Research Projects ad—*Direct Marketing,* January, 1987, p. 76
Fred E. Allen ad—*Direct Marketing,* December, 1986, p. 113

is truly independent of other company decisions. However, our intent is to look at the economics of a mailing list in isolation.

Assume that we have an ongoing mail-order business and offer a specific product for which an order is virtually always for one and only one unit of the product, and also that the lifetime value of a buyer is just the single sale. We have a good handle on our variable profit per order, which is revenue per order less variable costs per order (these costs include production costs and handling costs, both incoming and outgoing, and postage outgoing for orders). Further assume that we have never a bad debt or a return. Given these conditions, should we rent the offered list or not? Let's detail the decision process:

Let N = number of names on the list
Let S = selling price of the one item making up an order (sum for all items if discussing multi-item order)
Let H = handling cost per order
Let M = variable profit per order (equals $S - H$ – manufacturing cost)
Let R = rental cost per thousand names of the list
Let C = in-the-mail cost per piece (name) mailed
Let F = fixed cost associated with renting the list (can include any fixed costs involved in filling orders)
Let p = estimated response rate (a value from 0 to 1)

Then, if we do rent the list, our overall gain by having done so, G, is:

$$\begin{aligned} G &= p \times M \times N - N \times R / 1000 - C \times N - F \\ &= [\, p \times M - R / 1000 - C \,] \times N - F \end{aligned} \qquad (4.1)$$

If $G > 0$, rent the list.

Now consider what happens to G in equation 4.1 if we relax some of our earlier simplifications. If it is relevant to consider the lifetime value of a buyer, L, as opposed to just counting the profit of this one sale, M, simply replace M by L in equation 4.1. If it is thought that the list in question differs from the company's experience in terms of the value of M or L, the desired value will have to be estimated. If the M or L value is not the same for all customers, an expected value or average value is to be used.

If the customer is allowed to make returns, and r = the proportion of purchases returned, by how much will profit be reduced? If we suppose that we return the customer's entire outlay, including the part due to handling, we reduce G by $N \times r \times p \times (S + H)$. We would then have:

$$G = [\, p \times M - r \times p \times (S + H) - R / 1000 - C \,] \times N - F$$

If a proportion, b, of the nonreturned orders will not be paid for (i.e., will be bad debts), the term $p \times M$ needs to be replaced with $p \times M \times (1 - r) \times (1 - b)$, and G would be:

$$G = [p \times M \times (1-r) \times (1-b) - r \times p \times (S+H) - R/1000 - C] \times N - F$$

This expression may look complicated, but it's really just a case of plugging in values and performing arithmetic. The real problem is that we don't know the values of p, r, and b. These unknown values would have to be estimated by using the company's past experience, in order to evaluate G and see if it's greater than zero.

If we do decide to rent the list, we would probably not mail the entire list all at once. Instead, we would mail an initial 5,000 or 10,000 names, note the values of p, b, and r, and then decide whether to mail the rest of the list, to terminate mailing the list, or to mail another (larger) portion of the list. If we do mail another portion of the list, we would then decide among the same three choices. This process is called *pyramiding* or *rolling out*.

Since the list is to be tested, and thus not completely mailed if initial results are unsatisfactory, a simple decision based on whether G is greater than zero is not the mathematically optimal decision process *if we include uncertainty and averages in our analysis.* But for all practical purposes, G should be used for the decision. The G test is more conservative than the mathematically optimal decision process under uncertainty. Actually, the preceding analysis can be viewed in the context of the decision to rent the quantity that will be used in a test mailing. Certain terms of the equations would change to reflect the savings realized when test results are not as good as originally estimated, and the mailing is therefore terminated, as well as the gain in expected profit that would occur because only when initial results are encouraging enough do we go forward with a rollout. Nonetheless, the essence of the analysis would remain intact.

How would our analysis change if the issue is not the relatively simple one of deciding whether or not to rent a particular list, but rather one of choosing the optimal subset from a set of many eligible lists? First of all, why not just rent all lists with a G that is greater than zero? In considering this question use the simplifying, though unrealistic assumption that each of the eligible lists contains no names that appear on any other list. Under this assumption, renting all lists with a G greater than zero (i.e., all profitable lists) seems to be the obvious answer. True, cash flow considerations might not permit us to rent *all* profitable lists, at least simultaneously, but this drawback could be overcome by setting a benchmark of G> some modest positive value as a hedge against risk. Remember that we can envision the decision problem as one in which we must choose which lists to test, rather than which to completely mail.

In the real world, of course, our simplifying assumption that no list duplicates names on any other list would not hold. As more lists are rented for testing, the amount of duplication would increase. Duplication could be eliminated by merge-purge techniques, but the cost would have a negative effect on profitability. If we rented lists under an agreement to pay for 85 percent of the names regardless of the actual duplication rate, each additional list would likely yield a smaller and smaller rate of new names. Thus the rental cost per name would, in percentage terms, rise at a marginally increasing rate.

If, on the other hand, we only have to pay a rental fee for those names we actually mail, this increased rental cost per name would not occur. However, we would then have the burden of allocating payments to list owners for names that appear on more than one list. There are various ways to do this, some fairer than others; but all require additional software, and the result will probably be unhappiness on the part of some list owners (which could lead to bad feelings). The allocation method thought to be fairest allocates payment as follows: For a name on only one list, the total payment goes to that list owner; for a name on two lists, each list is credited with one-half a name; for a name on three lists, each list is credited with one-third of a name; and so forth. The problem with this system is that because lists are rented at different prices, one list owner is paid more than another list owner *for the same name.* Some people would like to see a system that pays higher amounts for names that are on only one list. That lists are not all priced alike supports this argument. They also argue that payments for names that appear on more than one list should be equal for all owners of those lists, on the grounds that each list offers the same profit potential to the renter for that name.

It should be noted here that the overlap in names from one list to another can be put to advantage by the list renter. If you note different response rates for names on only one list, names on two lists, and so on, you may be able to use that variable for future analysis.

LIST SEGMENTATION

Once you decide on a list, there is no rule that every name on it need be mailed. You may have the option of renting only a specified portion of a broker's list—for example, just the males—or you may choose a particular subset of your own house list for a specific mailing. In either case, the process is called *segmentation.*

Advantages

What are the advantages of segmenting your list? If you mailed, say, to half the names on your house list, *chosen randomly*, you would generate about half the sales that would be produced by mailing to the entire list. Obviously, there is no advantage in this kind of segmentation. But suppose you could find a way to choose half the list so that the mailing generates 90 percent of the sales that would have been generated by mailing to the entire list. That would be an enormous advantage. In fact, depending on the economics of the situation, mailing to 50 percent of the list and generating 60 percent of the sales that would have come from mailing to the entire list could be quite an advantage.

Let's analyze how this could be done. Suppose you discover that when you break up your list into five equally sized, mutually exclusive and collectively exhaustive age groups, each of the five promises to yield a different response rate for a particular offering. For simplicity, we will assume that profit per sale is the same for all responders and future considerations are negligible. Though you cannot know the response rates prior to the mailing, by mailing a pilot sample of names and applying sophisticated statistical analysis, you can obtain a reasonably precise estimate of the five values. Suppose those values turn out to be as follows:

Group A—4 percent
Group B—3 percent
Group C—2 percent
Group D—1 percent
Group E—.5 percent

Suppose further that the net profit per sale excluding mailing cost is $20, and the in-the-mail cost per piece is 28 cents. A little math will show why you would want to mail only to groups A, B, and C. For group A, expected profit per piece is $.04 \times \$20 = 80$ cents; for group B, $.03 \times \$20 = 60$ cents; for group C, $.02 \times \$20 = 40$ cents; for group D, $.01 \times \$20 = 20$ cents; and for group E, $.005 \times \$20 = 10$ cents. Clearly, you would not mail to groups D and E because the in-the-mail cost exceeds the expected profit for these groups. You might consider mailing to groups A, B, and half the names (randomly chosen) of group C. Thus your mailing would be 50 percent of the total list—but this would be the *best* half of the list, not the random half we discussed earlier. What percent of the sales that would be generated by mailing to the entire list will be generated by mailing to this best half of the list?

$$\{4 + 3 + .5(2)\} / \{4 + 3 + 2 + 1 + .5\}$$

$$= 8 / 10.5$$

$$= .762$$

$$= 76.2 \text{ percent}$$

Formerly, segmentation was done on the basis of "gut" feel, without the aid of a computer. Even today, it is still done this way at some smaller companies. But high-speed computers that can deal with large lists in a relatively short time, relatively cheaply, have revolutionized segmentation for large direct marketers.

Two whole new industries have developed, one to provide information for segmentation purposes, the other to perform the segmentation analyses. In the simplified example we used, only one variable was considered—age—and it had only five levels. In actual practice, segmentations are based on hundreds of variables, each having many different possible values. We will refer to a variable on which a segmentation is performed as a *major characteristic,* and to each of the levels of a major characteristic as a *category.* Typical major characteristics are ones that deal with previous purchase behavior (e.g., date of most recent purchase by mail of the company's products), demographics (e.g., age), geographical factors (e.g., zip code), and psychographics or lifestyle characteristics (e.g., degree of concern with nutritional eating habits).

Factors Affecting Segmentation Benefits

Two major factors will determine the benefit to be gained from performing a segmentation analysis, which is defined as a selection of different subsets of a list, with anticipated differences in likelihood to purchase or in amount of purchase. One factor is the amount of information available on each member of the list. The other is the sophistication, or ability to discriminate, of the statistical or other type of technique used to actually perform the analysis. Obviously, everything else being equal, the more information we have on list members, the greater will be our ability to distinguish those who will respond from those who will not, or those who will provide large revenue from those who will provide small or no revenue. Less obvious, perhaps, is the fact that some analytical techniques will yield better results than others, and that the computer hardware and software used will affect the analysis. There is at present no universal agreement about which techniques are better—or even what "better" means. It is likely that no single technique or methodology is better in all instances.

Before discussing these two factors, we will consider some basic facts about what segmentation won't do and the parameters that determine the amount of benefit one can expect from segmentation.

First of all, segmentation will not make a buyer out of a nonbuyer. However, it should eliminate from your mailing, a number of nonbuyers, and this is quite an advantage. Let's see why. The number of pieces to be mailed is usually fixed by some budget figure. Instead of mailing pieces to all the names on one list, segmentation allows you to choose the superior segment(s) of one or several lists. Thus you will generate a higher percentage of sales for the mailing. Even if the total number to be mailed is not fixed by budget constraints, you would save a lot by conducting a segmentation analysis and eliminating the names of unlikely prospects.

Second, segmentation will not change the underlying nature of the direct marketing economics of your company. If the mailing cost per piece is X percent of the revenue per purchase, this will not alter, unless the segmentation is geared toward identifying people who buy more when they buy, instead of toward identifying people who are more likely to buy.

One parameter that is very important in determining the potential benefit of segmentation is the mailing cost. As we have seen, segmentation saves mailing costs by identifying and eliminating unlikely prospects from the mailing list. Where the mailing cost is very small per unit, of course, the savings will be less from segmentation. This does not mean that segmentation has *no* benefit, only that your cost-benefit analysis would probably show that it is not worthwhile to pay for extra-delicate discrimination.

Another important parameter is the extent to which you have a targeted customer. If your customer base is not very distinct, a segmentation analysis will result in a less focused profile. It will then be more difficult to break out the stronger names. For example, if males and females are just as likely to respond to an offering, then gender will not provide any discriminatory power. But if you know that males over 65 years of age are the most likely group to respond to an offer, then the major characteristics of age and gender will be good discriminators.

Segmentation Characteristics

There are many major characteristics that are routinely used for segmentation purposes. There are others that are used less often, mainly because of unavailability, and still others that are specific to a particular company or list.

Within the group of major characteristics measuring previous purchase behavior, the primary bases of segmentation are *recency* of last purchase, *frequency* of purchase (also known as multihistory), and *monetary amount* spent on the purchase(s). Many people consider these three variables—known as RFM—to be the most important in determining the likely profitability of mailing to an individual.

Recency of last purchase is represented by either the number of consecutive mailings without a response or the actual number of months since the most recent purchase. This variable relates solely to names previously mailed.

Frequency of purchase may be represented simply by the number of previous purchases made (by mail) for the product(s) involved or from the company itself, or by the proportion of mailings to which the person responded. The former measure is used more often, but the latter is more helpful, as it discriminates between the person who has responded 3 times out of 5 mailings received, and the person who responded 4 times, but out of 18 mailings received.[1]

Monetary amount may be represented by the total amount of dollars the person spent on all purchases or by an average dollar amount per purchase. Again, the former measure is used more often, but the latter is more helpful because it discriminates between the person who has made ten purchases for a total of $100, and a person who has made four purchases for a total of $97.

Of the major characteristics in the demographic group, some of the most frequently used are sex, age, income, education, title code (e.g., Mr., Mrs., Ms., Dr., Rabbi), and family structure (e.g., number of people in household, number of children, number of wage earners). Of the major characteristics in the geographic group, some of the more frequently used are state lived in, zip code (more discriminating than state, but requiring a larger number of names on the list for statistical analysis to be of any value), sectional center, and overlay data pertaining to the neighborhood (or census tract or block) of residence, (e.g., percentage Hispanic or single-family households, educational level of the neighborhood).

The usefulness of major characteristics in the psychographic group depends on what information is available, and this varies considerably. Examples of psychographic characteristics pertaining to individuals are jogging, playing ten-

[1]A note of clarification: This comment is appropriate only for persons who are already multiple buyers.

nis, and degree of concern with nutritional eating. Examples pertaining to the neighborhood are mobility index (degree of stability of the residents of a neighborhood) and number of doctors per capita.

One other major characteristic that is often a good discriminator is the source code, that is, where the name came from (e.g., *TV Guide's* subscription list, direct inquiry, house file of previous purchasers). This characteristic is especially useful when the list to be segmented is a combination of other lists, either rented, compiled, or in-house.

The decision concerning which major characteristics will be used in the segmentation process is based first on what information is available from the house list, and second, on whether it is considered desirable to purchase various overlay geographic and psychographic information. Once the major characteristics have been settled on, the next step is to decide how to split them up into separate categories. This involves determining both the number of categories to be used and the class limits of those categories. A characteristic that naturally falls along a continuum, like age or recency of last purchase, can either be treated as a continuous variable or split up into discrete categories.

Segmentation Techniques

Once you know what major characteristics you will be using and how you will split them up, the next step in the segmentation analysis is to decide on a technique for actually performing the analysis. When only one characteristic (variable) is being used, the decision is easy to make. Find the response behavior for different values (levels) of the variable, rank-order the values, and determine a cutoff point by considering expected profit, what's allowed by budget constraints, etc. However, when there are two or more major characteristics, a choice must be made among a variety of different statistical methods or techniques (or a combination of them). As we noted earlier, there is no agreement about which method is the best in general, or even in any particular circumstance; in fact, there is no agreement about the definition of best. We will describe and discuss the most frequently used methods.

A Simple Technique. A simplistic method which has no formal name works as follows. You split each major characteristic into categories by gut feel, scan your data set (names on the list to be analyzed), assign points to each category of each characteristic in accordance with its differential response behavior, and then add up the points for each name on the list.

For example, assume the objective is to rank-order your list of names on the basis of available data so that you can decide who on the list should receive an expensive piece of mail. There are three major characteristics: time since last purchase (recency), number of purchases made in the last 5 years (frequency), and total amount of dollars spent over the last 5 years (monetary). You decide to consider the following categories of each characteristic:[2]

Recency	*Frequency*	*Monetary*
1. Within 6 months	1. 0	1. $ 0
2. 6–12 months	2. 1–3	2. 1–100
3. 12 + months/never	3. 4+	3. 101–500
		4. 500+

You are using data from last year's mailing at the same season as the mailing being considered, and response rate is the criterion of interest. The overall response rate last year was 5 percent. Now look at each category of each characteristic to determine the category's response rate. Note that the response rates for the individual categories will likely *not* average 5 percent, since the categories are not generally of equal proportions in the list. You obtain the following response rates by category:

Recency	*Response Rate*	*Differential (from 5%)*
1.	7.3%	+ 2.3
2.	5.2%	+ 0.2
3.	3.9%	− 1.1
Frequency		
1.	2.1%	− 2.9
2.	6.3%	+ 1.3
3.	7.7%	+ 2.7
Monetary		
1.	2.1%	− 2.9
2.	5.1%	+ 0.1
3.	5.9%	+ 0.9
4.	8.1%	+ 3.1

You are now able to classify each list member into one of the $3 \times 3 \times 4 = 36$ mutually exclusive, collectively exhaustive groups and add up the member's differential values. For example, John Smith with a recency of 8 months, a frequency of 2, and a monetary of $86, has a score of:

$$S = +.2 + 1.3 + .1 = 1.6$$

[2]For illustration purposes, we have used only a few categories. In the real world, each characteristic would have more categories.

Mary Jones, with a recency of 14 months, a frequency of 1, and a monetary of $131, is worse on the recency value, the same on the frequency value, and better on the monetary value. Her overall score would be:

$$S = -1.1 + 1.3 + 3.1 = 3.3$$

Therefore she is a better prospect than John Smith.

This method has one major advantage—simplicity. Its major disadvantage is that it does not account for *redundancy*, also called *overlap, double counting,* and, by statisticians, *multicolinearity*. For illustration purposes, a blatant exhibition of this notion was incorporated into the above example. The first category of frequency (0) and the first category of monetary ($0) are complete synonyms: every person with a frequency of 0, and only those people, are in the monetary category of $0; and the only people with $0 monetary are those with 0 frequency. Note that each category has the same response rate—2.1 percent. However, the $(2.1 - 5.0) = -2.9$ value is being *counted twice,* when it really *should be counted only once.* That is, if we consider all frequency/monetary combinations (ignoring recency for a moment), the 0/$0 combination would have a response rate of 2.1 percent and be 2.9 percent below the overall average of 5 percent, *not* $(2.9 + 2.9) = 5.8\%$ *below this overall average.*

Most double counting is not so complete as this one. This example contains partial overlap between the 0 frequency, $0 monetary, and 12+ recency categories. *All* of the 0 frequency/$0 monetary people have 12+ recency; but only some of the 12+ recency people are the 0 frequency people. The only way there will be no double counting at all is when the major characteristics are all mutually independent. Characteristics are independent if knowing the category a person is a member of in one characteristic gives no indication which category that person is a member of in the other characteristic. This is a condition one hardly ever meets in practice. To return to our example, if you know that someone is 12+ recency, you surely also know that person is more likely to be a 0 frequency person.

All of the other segmentation techniques that we will discuss avoid this serious problem.

Multiple Regression Analysis (MRA) Multiple regression analysis is a technique that develops a scoring formula that predicts some aspect of purchase behavior. With our criterion of response rate, MRA would provide an estimated probability of response for each list member. For our example of three major characteristics, an equation in the following form would be found:

$$Yp = a + b1 \times X12 + b2 \times X13 + b3 \times X22 + b4 \times X23 + b5 \times X32 + b6 \times X33 + b7 \times X34$$

where a and the b's are constants found to provide the best fit to the data, and Xij is a 1 if the person is a member of category j of major characteristic i, and 0 otherwise. Note that one category of each major characteristic (category 1 of each) is not represented by an X variable; this is a purposeful omission, and is part of the technique. For John Smith, who was in recency category 2, frequency category 2, and monetary category 2, we would assign for recency $X\,12 = 1$ and $X\,13 = 0$, for frequency $X\,22 = 1$ and $X\,23 = 0$, and for monetary $X\,32 = 1$, $X\,33 = 0$, and $X\,34 = 0$. For Mary Jones, who was in recency category 3, frequency category 2, and monetary category 3, we would assign $X\,12 = 0$, $X\,13 = 1$, $X\,22 = 1$, $X\,23 = 0$, $X\,32 = 0$, $X\,33 = 1$, and $X\,34 = 0$. The Yp is the predicted probability that the person will make a purchase. A value of $Y = 1$ is used as input to the MRA if the person made a purchase from the (previous) mailing used as input data, and $Y = 0$ is used if the person did not make a purchase. MRA uses calculus to truly perform an optimization and determine the constants that best fit the data. It should be noted that having two categories that have 100 percent overlap is unwise; in fact, it adversely affects the performance of the regression analysis (overlap less than 100 percent, however, does not have the same adverse effect). If there were only one characteristic, the regression scoring equation would have coefficients for each category equal to the differential response rate of that category from the omitted category. The Yp value for each category would equal its response rate. If frequency were the only characteristic in the earlier example, the resulting scoring equation would be:

$$Yp = .021 + .042 \times X\,22 + .056 \times X\,23$$

Note the correspondence between the predicted probabilities of purchase and the actual response rates. A person with 0 frequency would have $X\,22 = 0$ and $X\,23 = 0$; Yp is $.021 + 0 + 0 = .021$ (response rate was noted as 2.1 percent). A person with frequency 1-3 has $X\,22 = 1$ and $X\,23 = 0$; Yp is computed to be $.021 + .042 + 0 = .063$ (response rate was 6.3 percent). A person with frequency 4+ has $X\,22 = 0$ and $X\,23 = 1$; Yp is $.021 + 0 + .056 = .077$ (response rate was 7.7 percent).

For all practical purposes, you cannot perform a multiple regression analysis without a computer and a software package that includes MRA. Once you have everyone's Yp, the names can be rank-ordered and/or subjected to a variety of profitability analyses. Furthermore, the b coefficients provide information as to which categories auger better or worse for purchase likelihood (by their sign and magnitude).

Figure 4.3 is an illustration of one method of anticipating the degree of success of a segmentation analysis, as measured by number of responses, by using MRA on data from a past mailing. The horizontal axis indicates the (top) percent of the rank-ordered list mailed (e.g., "40" refers to mailing the top 40 percent as rank-ordered). The vertical axis represents the number of responses realized as a fraction of the total number of responses that would be realized if the entire list were mailed (e.g., "0.8" means 80 percent of the responses that would be realized from 100 percent of the list). The 40/0.8 point on the curve thus indicates that the top 40 percent of the rank-ordered list generated 80 percent of the responses of the entire list.

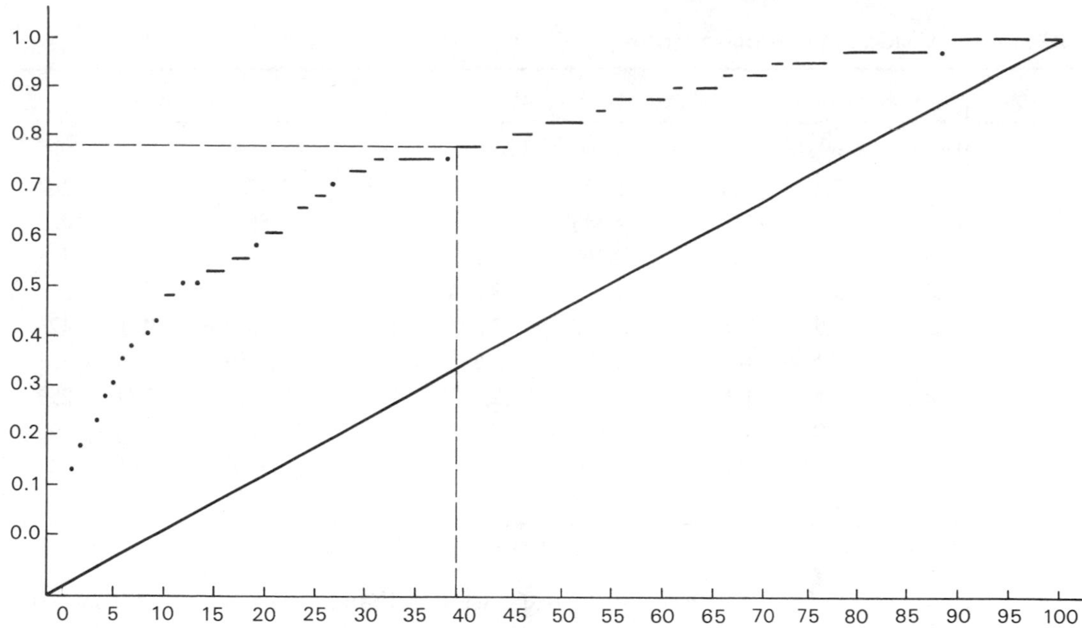

FIGURE 4.3 ***Response as a Fraction of Total List Response***
Source: Used with permission of Persoft, Inc.

Table 4.1 shows the results of an MRA-generated scoring model by decile, being applied in validation mode; i.e., the scoring equation is applied to a set of names not part of the set from which the scoring equation was generated. The results go well beyond response rate, and consider sales and profits. The term lift refers to the ratio of decile cumulative result to result if the total list is mailed. For example, the response lift of 304 (decile 1) is the ratio of 15.2 percent to 5.0 percent, multiplied by 100; the sales lift of 308 (decile 1) is the ratio of 6,252 to 2,031, again multiplied by 100.

Multiple regression analysis is considered by many to be the best and most versatile of all the statistical techniques available for direct marketing list segmentation.[3]

Multiple Discriminant Analysis (MDA). Another technique used for list segmentation is multiple discriminant analysis. MDA is useful only when the dependent variable is categorical—meaning, generally, when the dependent variable is response/no response—although it can also be used when the dependent variable is classified into more than two categories (e.g., no response, small monetary amount, large monetary amount), or into two categories that do not per se divide

[3] So stated by Richard Courtheoux of Kestenbaum and Company in "Advanced Techniques for Applying List Segmentation," *Mailing Lists: A Practical Guide* (New York: Direct Marketing Association, 1984).

TABLE 4.1 Validation of Scoring Model

	Response Cum			*Sales Cum*			*Profit Cum*		
Decile	*Percent*	*Resp %*	*Lift*	*Per 1000*	*Sales/K*	*Lift*	*Per 1000*	*Prof/K*	*Lift*
1	15.2	15.2	304	6,252	6,252	308	1,376	1,376	1262
2	11.6	13.4	268	4,543	5,398	266	863	1,119	1027
3	5.5	10.8	216	2,200	4,332	213	160	800	734
4	4.0	9.1	182	1,660	3,664	180	(2)	599	550
5	3.3	7.9	158	1,353	3,202	158	(94)	461	423
6	2.7	7.1	142	1,101	2,851	140	(170)	356	327
7	2.5	6.4	128	1,071	2,597	128	(179)	279	256
8	2.1	5.9	118	903	2,385	117	(229)	216	198
9	1.7	5.4	108	748	2,203	108	(276)	161	148
10	1.1	5.0	100	484	2,031	100	(355)	109	100

Source: Paula Ames, Kestenbaum & Co.,Chicago, in DM News/Catalog Business, July 1, 1987. ©1987

by response (e.g., no response or response less than $10, response at least $10). MDA, like MRA, yields a scoring equation (or more than one equation if there are more than two categories for the dependent variable) that relates to the probability of a person being in a particular category. The technique has many similarities to multiple regression analysis, especially when there are only two categories into which names are being classified.

Log Linear Modeling (LLM). The third technique that results in a scoring equation is log linear modeling. LLM is a relatively new and complex technique. Like MDA, it is suitable for categorical data, but far less software has been developed for LLM than for MDA.[4] A discussion of how LLM compares with some other of the available techniques appears later in this section.

Other techniques used for list segmentation do not provide a scoring equation (which allows a complete rank ordering of an entire list of names). Rather, they attempt either to cluster (bunch together) groups of names that will act similarly with respect to whatever dependent variable is used as the criterion or when no response-related data are available, to find groups with similar profiles.

Cluster Analysis. Cluster analysis considers the input data (generally geographic, demographic, or psychographic) and clusters names into like groups. Its main use in the area of segmentation is to identify groups with similar traits; cluster analysis might identify a certain neighborhood in Atlanta, another in Buffalo, and a third in Newark that should be clustered together for purposes of analyzing response behavior.

[4]The basic idea of LLM and its potential application in the general field of marketing is discussed in W. S. DeSarbo and D. K. Hildebrand, "A Marketer's Guide to Log Linear Models for Qualitative Data Analysis," *Journal of Marketing, 44,* (Summer 1980), 40–51.

PRIZM (Potential Rating Index by Zip Marketing), developed by Claritas Corporation, considers 35,600 zip codes and clusters each into 1 of 40 zip markets. Each zip market is labeled with a catchy name, and represents a like group of geographical areas. For example, one of the 40 labels is "Black Enterprise"; the concise definition of this cluster is "upscale, white-collar, black families in major urban fringes." Rose Harper has noted that a marketer can profit from using a service like PRIZM in conjunction with his internal file of customers to answer the question: Who is my customer?[5] She notes a dozen examples of the catchy PRIZM labels:

Blue Blood Estates
Money and Brains
Young Influentials
Young Suburbia
God's Country
Urban Gold Coast
Blue-Collar Nursery
Bunker's Neighbors
Olf Brick Factories
Malboro Country
Back-Country Folks
Hard Scrabble

Similar types of service are available to business-to-business marketers.[6]

Automatic Interaction Detection (AID). Another technique for list segmentation that belongs to the cluster family is automatic interaction detection. An exploratory data-analysis technique developed at the University of Michigan's Survey Research Center, AID considers the relationship between a dependent variable and a number of potential independent variables. It is very much like cross-tabulation analysis; it does not assume linearity (e.g., that the change in probability of purchase is a constant for each added year of age) or additivity (that the effects of different characteristics can be added, as opposed, for example, to requiring multiplication). Most other segmentation methods—MRA, MDA, and LLM—make at least some of these assumptions.

AID deals with categorical variables. Its main strength is its ability to discover interaction effects among the variables (i.e., the effect of one independent

[5]Rose Harper, *Mailing List Strategies* (New York: McGraw-Hill, 1986), pp. 82–83.

[6]Some of the companies that provide this kind of overlay service (either for the consumer or business-to-business market or both) are: Donnelly Marketing Information Services of Stamford, CT (Cluster-Plus); CCX of Arkansas (Focus-Master); CACI of New York City (ACORN); National Decision Systems, Inc., of Encinitas, CA (Vision); Yankelovich, Clancy Shulman of Westport, CT (Monitor); SRI International (VALS); R. L. Polk of Detroit, MI; Lifestyle Selector of Denver, CO.; Metromail of Lincoln, NE; Demographic Research Co. of Santa Monica, CA.

variable on the response variable not being the same for all levels of other independent variables). AID analysis is often referred to as a *tree analysis* because it subdivides the list of names into successive segments that are depicted as a pyramidal or tree-like structure. AID seems to require a relatively large data base in order to provide useful results, but many lists and most data bases in direct marketing applications are sufficiently large to use AID.

Chi Square Automatic Interaction Detection (CHAID). An extension of AID is a technique called chi square automatic interaction detection, which was developed by Dr. Gordon Kass. It overcomes one major limitation of AID, in that it allows the finding of segments that are of three or more levels of a variable, whereas AID is limited at each stage to finding segments that respond either high or low. In fact, CHAID automatically determines just how many levels there ought to be and what those levels are. Statistical Innovations of Belmont, Massachusetts, has developed computer software for performing a CHAID analysis, called SI-CHAID. A limitation of SI-CHAID is that an analysis is restricted to at most 30 independent variables and at most 15 levels of each independent variable. Figure 4.4 shows the results of a CHAID analysis applied by Jay Magidson, founder of Statistical Innovations, to the adoption of a new telecommunication service.

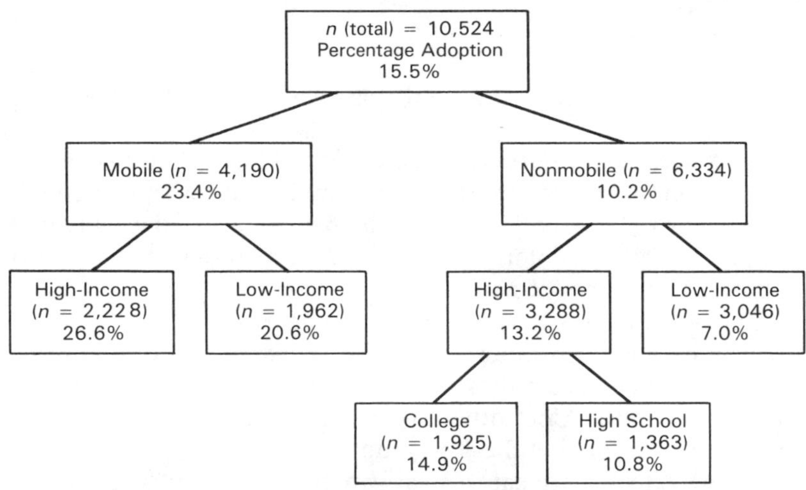

FIGURE 4.4 ***CHAID Analysis for New Telecommunication Device***

Source: Jay Magidson, "Some Common Pitfalls in Causal Analysis of Categorical Data," *Journal of Marketing Research, 19* (November 1982), 461–471.

Note: It was a coincidence that the branching off the mobile section was the same as the branching off the nonmobile section. "College" and "high school" mean completion of those levels of education.

Classification and Regression Trees (CART). CART is a combination of elements of AID and elements of multiple regression analysis. A treelike group of segments is formed, and MRA is used to split each division of the list of names into a further subdivision.

Comparison of Segmentation Techniques. There is not a great deal of literature comparing the various segmentation techniques. A study by Blattberg and Dolan compared (1) MLR with continuous independent variables; (2) MLR with dummy (categorical) variables; (3) first-order LLM (no interaction); (4) saturated LLM (all interactions); and (5) AID (indirectly).[7] The primary criterion used in this study was the predictive ability of the respective models. Secondary criteria were interpretability of results, simplicity of use, computer cost, and data-preparation cost.

The conclusions of the study were as follows:

1. The first-order LLM and the dummy variable MRA models dominated the other two models (linear regression and saturated LLM).
2. With respect to the two MRA models, the benefits of decreasing the number of parameters to be estimated are outweighed by the costs of misspecifying the model. (In particular, the assumption of a *linear* relationship between the independent variables, age and education, and the dependent variable, response rate, was clearly incorrect.)
3. With respect to the two LLM models, the introduction of the interaction terms (in going from the first-order model to the saturated model) reduced the performance of the model.
4. The first-order LLM model and the dummy variable MRA model performed about equally well.

As for the comparison of LLM with AID, it must be noted that using LLM required a reduction in the number of independent variables, which using AID did not. However, even after this reduction, LLM generally outperformed AID by a sizable margin. For example, over a variety of examples in which the top-ranked 20 percent were mailed, LLM resulted in about 10 percent more respondents than AID. Both techniques, though, did far better than random selection.

Blattberg and Dolan reached three general conclusions: (1) LLM models do have a valuable application in marketing; (2) if the main concern is predictive ability, ordinary least-squares regression with a dichotomous dependent variable may well be the most appropriate analytical tool; and (3) if the percentage of predicted probabilities falling outside the 0 to 1 range is small, dummy variable regression is likely to be most effective.

A key to remember. Do not lose sight of the fact that for any segmentation to be possible using *any* technique, variables must be identified for which different

[7]Robert C. Blattberg and Robert J. Dolan, "An Assessment of the Contribution of Log Linear Models to Marketing Research," *Journal of Marketing*, Spring 1981, pp. 89–97.

values (levels) have differential response characteristics (rate, dollars, repeat-response likelihood, etc.).

The MORE/2 System. This section on list segmentation would not be complete without a discussion of a relatively new product called MORE/2, produced by PERSOFT, Inc., of Woburn, Massachusetts. MORE/2 combines the three elements of an expert system for list segmentation—dynamic list updating and automatic file maintenance, sophisticated analytical capabilities for list segmentation, and useful managerial reports and tracking of results.

List updating and file maintenance are often underrated aspects of an expert system for list segmentation. There are more horror stories about disasters caused by lack of data integrity than about any other problem. This is especially true in the area of direct mail because of the acute dynamics of the important variables involved. Unfortunately, the analytical/statistical capabilities of the segmenting process are often the only aspects of the system given close scrutiny. Frequently neglected are back-end analysis (e.g., what happened in the last mailing?) and rigorous analysis for prospecting decisions. Recognizing this, PERSOFT designed MORE/2 to provide a series of reports that pinpoint what happened, tell how what happened compares to the past, and identify emerging trends.

We present here two examples of reports that MORE/2 provides its clients. These reports are illustrated for two potential segmenting variables: recency and state.

Recency is defined in our example as the number of months elapsed since the list member's previous order by mail from Company XYZ. There are 10 categories:

0–3 months
4–6 months
7–9 months
10–12 months
13–24 months
25–36 months
37–48 months
49–60 months
61+ months
Unknown

People who have never ordered by mail from Company XYZ would be in the 61+ category. For a variety of reasons (e.g., a recorded value that is obviously an error), there are people for whom the date of last order is unknown, and would be in the Unknown category.

State reflects location of mailing address, and has 54 categories: the 50 states plus the District of Columbia, Puerto Rico, the Virgin Islands, and Guam.

The first report, *Characteristic Performance Analysis*, lists the response rate for each category, rank-ordered from high to low. The report for, say, the 2/1/87 mailing, uses a random sample of about 50,000 names. Actually, the sample size is 49,078, or 1 percent of the number of people mailed. Figure 4.5 is this report's analysis for the characteristic recency. The 10 categories are listed by response rate, and the quantity mailed, number of orders, and response rate (in percent) are noted. Figure 4.6 is this report's analysis for the characteristic state. Categories for which there were no responses have blanks for the number of orders and response percent.

The second report, *Characteristic Trend Analysis*, compares, for a characteristic, results over past mailings, category by category. The comparison is over a maximum of six past mailings. These need not be the most recent mailings, but could, for example, be the past six Christmas mailings. (Company XYZ would choose which past mailings.) Figure 4.7 is this report's analysis for the characteristic recency. It shows five consecutive mailings, the fifth being the 2/1/87 mailing. The categories appear in routine consecutive order as entered onto the data base. The merit ratio (last column) is defined as 100 times the ratio of the response percent of the category to the overall response percent of that particular mailing; thus, if the five mailings have different overall response rates, the merit ratio values are still meaningful in considering the performance of a category over time. Note that the 49–60 month category in the third mailing listed has a *lower* response percent than in the second mailing listed (1.408 versus 1.526), but has a *higher* merit ratio (132.330 versus 127.591).

Figure 4.8 is a portion of the *Characteristic Trend Analysis* report for the characteristic state. Four consecutive states, Nevada, New York, Ohio, and Oklahoma are shown. Note that for Nevada and to a lessor degree for Oklahoma, the number of pieces mailed is relatively low and the number of orders sparse, and that a

---------CHARACTERISTIC--------			QUANTITY	ACTUAL MAILING PERFORMANCES ORDER	RESPONSE
NO.	VAL	DESCRIPTION	MAILED	RESPONSE	PCT
021	DT LST ML ORD				
	11	DT LST ML ORD 0-3 MOS	1,258	51	4.054
	10	DT LST ML ORD 4-6 MOS	795	31	3.899
	09	DT LST ML ORD 7-9 MOS	1,142	40	3.503
	08	DT LST ML ORD 10-12 MOS	1,239	30	2.421
	07	DT LST ML ORD 13-24 MOS	3,579	72	2.012
	06	DT LST ML ORD 37-48 MOS	2,368	29	1.225
	05	DT LST ML ORD 25-36 MOS	3,037	33	1.087
	04	DT LST ML ORD 61+ MOS	9,099	65	.714
	03	DT LST ML ORD 49-60 MOS	2,081	14	.673
	02	DT LST ML ORD UNKNOWN	24,480	97	.396

FIGURE 4.5 ***MORE Characteristic Performance Analysis/Recency***

--------CHARACTERISTIC--------			QUANTITY	ACTUAL MAILING PERFORMANCES	
NO.	VAL	DESCRIPTION	MAILED	ORDER RESPONSE	RESPONSE PCT
045	STATE				
	37	STATE = NEW MEXICO	224	6	2.679
	16	STATE = HAWAII	151	4	2.649
	58	STATE = WYOMING	118	3	2.542
	33	STATE = NORTH DAKOTA	90	2	2.222
	18	STATE = IDAHO	142	3	2.113
	23	STATE = LOUISIANA	451	9	1.996
	12	STATE = DELAWARE	151	3	1.987
	34	STATE = NEBRASKA	204	4	1.961
	45	STATE = RHODE ISLAND	256	5	1.953
	54	STATE = VERMONT	267	5	1.873
	56	STATE = WISCONSIN	681	12	1.762
	41	STATE = OKLAHOMA	345	6	1.739
	55	STATE = WASHINGTON	657	11	1.674
	29	STATE = MISSOURI	728	12	1.648
	26	STATE = MAINE	372	6	1.613
	27	STATE = MICHIGAN	1,387	22	1.586
	07	STATE = COLORADO	985	15	1.523
	38	STATE = NEVADA	136	2	1.471
	36	STATE = NEW JERSEY	2,173	31	1.427
	03	STATE = ALABAMA	494	7	1.417
	06	STATE = CALIFORNIA	4,850	67	1.381
	21	STATE = KANSAS	331	4	1.208
	47	STATE = SOUTH DAKOTA	87	1	1.149
	42	STATE = OREGON	450	5	1.111
	05	STATE = ARIZONA	477	5	1.048
	17	STATE = IOWA	391	4	1.023
	10	STATE = CONNECTICUT	1,790	18	1.006
	35	STATE = NEW HAMPSHIRE	1,222	12	.982
	24	STATE = MASSACHUSETTS	3.567	34	.953
	02	STATE = ALASKA	213	2	.939
	40	STATE = OHIO	1,539	14	.910
	09	STATE = DIST OF COLUMBIA	336	3	.893
	19	STATE = ILLINOIS	1,705	15	.880
	50	STATE = TEXAS	2,392	20	.836
	46	STATE = SOUTH CAROLINA	359	3	.836
	32	STATE = NORTH CAROLINA	899	7	.779
	13	STATE = FLORIDA	1,832	13	.710
	39	STATE = NEW YORK	4,042	27	.668
	51	STATE = UTAH	150	1	.667
	22	STATE = KENTUCKY	328	2	.610
	28	STATE = MINNESOTA	1,271	7	.538
	30	STATE = MISSISSIPPI	186	1	.538
	25	STATE = MARYLAND	1,373	7	.510
	43	STATE = PENNSYLVANIA	3,373	13	.385
	52	STATE = VIRGINIA	2,084	6	.288

FIGURE 4.6 ***MORE Characteristic Performance Analysis/State***

FIGURE 4.6 *(Continued)*

NO.	VAL	DESCRIPTION	QUANTITY MAILED	ORDER RESPONSE	RESPONSE PCT
045		STATE			
	20	STATE = INDIANA	826	2	.242
	48	STATE = TENNESSEE	498	1	.201
	14	STATE = GEORGIA	1,748		
	57	STATE = WEST VIRGINIA	257		
	04	STATE = ARKANSAS	207		
	31	STATE = MONTANA	173		
	44	STATE = PUERTO RICO	79		
	53	STATE = VIRGIN ISLANDS	24		
	15	STATE = GUAM	7		

ACTUAL MAILING PERFORMANCES

NO.	VAL	DESCRIPTION	MAIL ID	QUANTITY MAILED	ORDER RESPONSE	RESPONSE PCT	MERIT RATIO
021		DT LST ML ORD					
	02	DT LST ML ORD UNKNOWN	1	28,577	135	.472	44.029
			2	27,912	167	.598	50.000
			3	27,085	128	.473	44.454
			4	19,271	177	.918	57.590
			5	24,480	97	.396	42.082
	03	DT LST ML ORD 61+ MOS	1	4,232	36	.851	79.384
			2	7,106	74	1.041	87.040
			3	7,052	56	.794	74.624
			4	7,323	59	.806	50.564
			5	9,099	65	.714	75.876
	04	DT LST ML ORD 49-60 MOS	1	1,693	25	1.477	137.779
			2	1,769	27	1.526	127.591
			3	1,633	23	1.408	132.330
			4	1,709	27	1.580	99.121
			5	2,081	14	.673	71.519
	10	DT LST ML ORD 4-6 MOS	1	1,403	58	4.134	385.634
			2	825	41	4.970	415.551
			3	689	27	3.919	368.327
			4	1,229	56	4.557	285.884
			5	795	31	3.899	414.346
	11	DT LST ML ORD 0-3 MOS	1	2,009	55	2.738	255.410
			2	1,121	63	5.620	469.899
			3	1,719	83	4.828	453.759
			4	1,055	92	8.720	547.051
			5	1,258	51	4.054	430.818

FIGURE 4.7 ***MORE Characteristic Trend Analysis/Recency***

ACTUAL MAILING PERFORMANCES

------CHARACTERISTIC------ NO. VAL DESCRIPTION	MAIL ID	QUANTITY MAILED	ORDER RESPONSE	RESPONSE PCT	MERIT RATIO
045 STATE					
38 STATE = NEVADA	1	141	0		
	2	157	0		
	3	144	1	.694	65.225
	4	110	2	1.818	114.052
	5	136	2	1.471	156.323
39 STATE = NEW YORK	1	4,429	40	.903	84.235
	2	4,172	63	1.510	126.254
	3	4,009	51	1.272	119.548
	4	3,238	63	1.946	122.082
	5	4,042	27	.668	70.988
40 STATE = OHIO	1	1,969	28	1.422	132.649
	2	1,874	29	1.547	129.347
	3	1,743	23	1.320	124.060
	4	1,257	28	2.228	139.774
	5	1,539	14	.910	96.705
41 STATE = OKLAHOMA	1	430	7	1.628	151.865
	2	394	3	.761	63.628
	3	369	3	.813	76.409
	4	288	7	2.431	152.509
	5	345	6	1.739	184.803

FIGURE 4.8 ***MORE Characteristic Trend Analysis/State***

difference of one order either way would lead to a large percentage change in the order percent and merit rating. Therefore, for these states, this particular report is of limited value.

Many other managerially useful reports are routinely generated by the MORE/2 system.

MORE/2 is designed primarily to operate at service bureaus. However, MORE/2 can be fruitfully utilized by individual firms engaging in national direct marketing activities. Lists are examined on a name-by-name basis, and names are analyzed and ranked from most-likely-to-respond to least-likely-to-respond. With MORE/2, a service bureau can process one million names for one client in less than 45 minutes.

Clearly, user-friendly, statistically superior software development is at the leading edge of research in the area of list selection and segmentation analysis.

SUMMARY

The list is an important element of the direct marketing mix. There are many types of lists; except for a house list, lists are usually rented on a one-time basis. There are professionals who specialize in enhancing the list rental process: list brokers, list compilers, list managers, and list processors.

List segmentation, or mailing a selected subset of a list, can improve the economics of mailing lists. A variety of variables in the areas of previous purchase behavior, demographics, and psychographics may be available as segmentation characteristics. Once choosing these characteristics, there are many segmentation techniques that can be used to perform the segmentation analysis. These include some simple techniques, as well the more sophisticated techniques of multiple linear regression, multiple discriminant analysis, log-linear modeling, cluster analysis, automatic interaction detection, and classification and regression trees.

DISCUSSION QUESTIONS

1. Can you suggest some useful sources that can be used for compiling lists?
2. Describe some variables that would be especially useful for segmenting a list consisting of subscribers to *Time* magazine.
3. How important is it to have the result of a segmenting technique be a specific scoring equation?
4. What is the relationship between segmenting for purposes of determining whom to mail to, and segmenting for the purpose of list prospecting (i.e., determining the best lists to rent)?

SUGGESTED ADDITIONAL READING

1. Leo Breiman and others, *Classification and Regression Trees* (Belmont, CA: Wadsworth International Group, 1984).
2. Chaim Ehrman, "Estimating the Probability of Lists' Rollout Success from Test Results," *Journal of Direct Marketing Research, 1* (1986), 95–104.
3. John J. Kennedy, *Analyzing Qualitative Data* (New York: Praeger, 1983).
4. Jim Mammarella, "Psyching Out List Overlays," *Direct Marketing* (February 1986), pp. 46–51.
5. John Neter, William Wasserman, and Michael Kutner, *Applied Linear Regression Models* (Homewood, IL: Richard B. Irwin, Inc., 1983).
6. Leonard Quenon, "Using Household Level Data for File Segmentation," *Journal of Direct Marketing Research, 2* (1987), 43–56.

5

Creative Strategy and Execution

As you read the title of this chapter, some of you probably said, "I can't draw and I don't want to be a writer, so why do I have to study the creative part of direct marketing?" It's a good question, and there are at least two good answers to it:

1. All direct marketing managers are involved in the creative process in some way. At the very least, they participate in the development of the creative strategy and approve the final creative execution.
2. All direct marketing managers—all managers, for that matter—have opportunities to be creative, whatever their job titles. There can never be enough truly creative ideas for strategies, products, alternative offers, product positioning, customer services—in fact, for all aspects of direct marketing.

The point is that two kinds of creativity are important to successful direct marketing. The first is the kind businesspeople usually think of when they hear the word creativity. It involves layout, art, and copy that effectively communicate a message. The second has, in recent years, come to be known as *managerial creativity*. We might think of it as "finding new solutions to old problems."

The major part of this chapter is devoted to a discussion of the traditional approach to the creative process in the direct marketing environment. First, however, we will look briefly at the general subject of creativity, and then more specifically at managerial creativity.

WHAT IS CREATIVITY AND WHO HAS IT?

Many myths and false stereotypes interfere with the typical manager's understanding of the subject of creativity. The purpose of this section is to break away from the myths and stereotypes and acquaint you with a small portion of the best current thinking on the subject of creativity.

A Definition of Creativity

There are many definitions of creativity, but the one set forth by Amabile gives considerable food for thought:

> A response will be judged as creative to the extent that (a) it is both a novel and appropriate, useful, correct, or valuable response to the task at hand and (b) the task is heuristic rather than algorithmic. [1]

The (a) part of that definition is pretty straightforward, but interesting for the emphasis it places on the applicability of the creative solution to the situation for which it is intended. Genuine creativity is not "creativity for creativity's sake," but a unique solution to a real problem.

The (b) part contains two terms that sound like refugees from a statistics or a computer class—"heuristic" and "algorithmic." What do they mean in this context? *Heuristics* are rules of thumb, approximations that are used when precise solutions are either impossible for some reason or theoretically possible but prohibitively expensive to obtain. You might think of heuristics as commonsense rules or as decision rules developed on the basis of hard-to-quantify experience.

Algorithms, on the other hand, are precise and mechanistic formulas or series of steps that will lead to the solution of a problem. Solve the formula correctly, follow the series of steps precisely, and you will have the answer to the problem. Since this is a mechanistic (though sometimes difficult) process, it does not qualify as creativity.

The Creative Process

What, then, is the process an individual uses to come up with a unique and applicable solution to a problem? Many processes have been suggested in the literature of the social sciences. These processes are based on various psychological theories and/or on observation and analysis of the way uniquely talented individuals (e.g., Charles Darwin, Marie Curie, Albert Einstein) approached major

[1] Theresa Amabile, *The Social Psychology of Creativity*, quoted in Michael Ray and Rochelle Myers, *Creativity in Business* (Garden City, NY: Doubleday, 1986), p. 4.

discoveries. Marcus and Tauber synthesized a number of these theories and developed a five-step model of the creative process.[2]

1. Sensing. The first activity is sensing. This is the problem-recognition step. Assume that the product manager for a four-volume set of science reference books for secondary school students realizes that the mail campaign for the set is slowly "wearing out." That is, the response rate has declined steadily with each mailing over the last 3 years until the mailings are barely breaking even. Worse still, many of the initial purchasers are not completing the set, making the back end of this program unprofitable. Management has indicated that the series will be discontinued unless it can be returned to its former level of profitability within 6 months—a very clear problem definition.

2. Preparation. The second step in the process is preparation. In this stage the manager or creative specialist gathers all information that is pertinent to the problem. Our hypothetical product manager first analyzes the market and the competition. The market is of sufficient size and there are only two direct competitors, both of whom the product manager judges to have a weaker product at a higher price, but to have a very attractive direct-mail package.

The product manager commissions focus groups with users of the product and their parents and a series of in-depth interviews with secondary school science teachers and professors of education who are experts in science curricula. The primary research uncovers no major flaws in the product; in fact, respondents, both adults and children, voice considerable enthusiasm for the product.

3. Incubation. The product manager is ready for the third stage—incubation. In this stage the manager simply assimilates all the information, organizes it mentally, and attempts to understand its meaning and all its implications. The manager's conclusion at the end of this stage is quite clear: There is nothing wrong with the product; the marketing campaign has simply worn out.The product needs a new, attractive, hard-hitting mailing package.

4. Illumination. That was only the first part of the answer to the problem. Just what kind of mail package will produce the results the manager needs? The manager is now seeking illumination—the "Big Idea" that will turn the situation around for this book series. He is convinced that incremental changes to the current package will not do the trick—a breakthrough idea is required.

At this stage some experts recommend that the person searching for a creative solution get away from the problem for a while. The idea is not to keep struggling and try to force a solution to emerge, but to simply let the brain lie fallow, like a rich plot of soil. Then, when the person least expects it—perhaps while work-

[2] Burton H. Marcus and Edward M. Tauber, *Marketing Analysis And Decision Making* (Boston: Little, Brown and Company, 1979) pp. 198-200.

ing on a different task or while taking a shower or lying in that strange state between sleep and wakefulness—inspiration will strike.

There is much anecdotal support for this recommendation to get away from it for a while, but keep two things in mind:

1. None of the experts suggest that inspiration will strike unless intensive preparation has been done. The person seeking inspiration *must* immerse himself or herself in the factual information relating to the problem *before* sitting back and waiting for lightning to strike. This recommendation is in no way a prescription for laziness or for not doing one's homework!
2. There is a warning to managers inherent in this recommendation, and that is that it is counterproductive to force unrealistic deadlines on creative activities. Creative specialists *must* have time to absorb the available information, to let it gestate, and then to polish the creative concept that emerges.

This is not an argument for no deadlines, just for reasonable ones. Managers who consistently expect "instant creativity" will get just what they deserve—a poor creative product. At the same time, creative people who cannot meet deadlines will also achieve a rather predictable outcome—unemployment. The point is that good creative work demands cooperation and understanding between direct marketing managers and creative specialists.

After mulling over the situation for a while, our product manager comes up with a solution. It centers around a new package format: a rewritten letter, the addition of a lift letter (see Chapter 9 for a description), and a totally new graphics approach. The "Big Idea" is the offer of an attractive incentive for completion of the set—a high-quality wooden book holder especially designed for the four-book series. The book holder should encourage people to complete the set, the key to profitability for the offering.

5. Verification. The final step in the Marcus and Tauber process is verification—evaluating the creative idea or concept that has emerged. By this we do not mean testing in the direct marketing sense—that will come later—but simply asking yourself whether the idea is novel, appropriate, useful, correct, and valuable in the current situation.

All our product manager's ideas for improving the book offer seem reasonable. They will be tested in the direct marketing setting to see if they do indeed solve the problem. You may be saying to yourself that the product manager's ideas are not very original; they certainly don't seem earth-shaking. Yet in a real situation, comparable to the hypothetical one we have just described, similar changes resulted in a campaign that exceeded its sales objectives by ten times!

Who Possesses Creativity?

Many tests purport to measure creativity and each has its adherents and its detractors. There are, however, two built-in problems with creativity tests. First, most of them measure only one dimension of creativity, though Guilford identified 24 different creative abilities or functions, and implied that each one must be tested for separately.[3] The second problem stems from the first. Say you decide to take one of these creativity tests and find that you rate "below normal" or something of the sort. Despite the fact that there are many kinds of creativity and the test you took probably measured only one, what is likely to happen? You will say, "Well, I'm not very creative." You've just labeled yourself, and you've probably also created a self-fulfilling prophecy—since you don't believe that you have any creative powers, you won't attempt to do anything that you believe requires "creativity."

Instead, consider this quote from *Dun's Review:*

> Strictly speaking, scientists point out, it is inaccurate to speak of creativity as a trait that some people have and others don't. Everyone is to some degree creative. Even chimpanzees, faced with the problem of retrieving a banana from a high shelf, can assemble an ingenious (for a chimpanzee) collection of chairs, tables and sticks adequate to the task. When psychologists speak of creativity, they are actually talking in relative terms. The human mind is taught from birth to accomplish certain tasks in specific ways. Creativity is simply the degree to which one can think of different, more effective approaches.[4]

Predictably, but rather sadly, this article then goes on to present a 75-item creativity test that requires responses to each item on a 3-point agree/disagree scale! (Businesspeople have a seemingly irrepressible urge to quantify the unquantifiable.)

After reviewing a number of approaches used by businesses in an attempt to stimulate creativity, the article concludes:

> In creativity tests on individuals of all ages, creativity scores invariably drop about 90% between ages five and seven, and by age forty an individual is only about 2% as creative as he was at age five. This suggests to many psychologists that the almost total emphasis on logical thought in education may effectively suppress creativity. The hope of creativity research is that what is trained out can be trained back in.[5]

MANAGERIAL CREATIVITY

Retraining in creativity is precisely what is being attempted by numerous individual consultants and firms, including a few sizable ones like Synectics and

[3] J. P. Guilford, "Creativity: Retrospect and Prospect," *The Journal Of Creative Behavior*, Summer 1970, pp. 149-168.

[4] "Business Probes the Creative Spark," *Dun's Review*, January 1980, pp. 33-38.

[5] "Business Probes the Creative Spark," p. 38.

most notably in recent years by Professors Michael Ray and Rochelle Myers at Stanford University.[6]

Ray and Myers maintain that every individual possesses creative resources; they call this resource *Essence*. But they argue, that each individual's creativity is "inhibited by fear, negative personal judgment, and the chattering of your mind. Your creative Essence is often blocked by what is called the false personality, the ego or the external self."[7] In other words, creativity is inhibited by fear of social disapproval.

Ray and Myers do not promote group creativity techniques such as brainstorming, lateral thinking, or Synectics. These techniques have their place; they can produce useful new ideas under the proper leadership. However, they are oriented toward solving a particular problem; they do nothing to promote individual creativity on an ongoing basis. Ray and Myers focus on the individual, not the organization, and on creativity as an integral part of business life, not as a random occurrence.

To give you a taste of their approach, consider the process they have evolved for what they term *surrendering*. This is similar to the idea of "getting away from it for a while" suggested in the preceding section. However, Ray and Myers make it more concrete. Their concept of surrendering is two-dimensional; you surrender to your inner creative Essence; you also surrender striving to force a solution. Their process is as follows:

1. *Drop mental striving.* Ray and Myers describe "striving" as "apprehension, anxiety, tension, competition, anticipation."[8] Drop the picture of yourself as tense and pressured; replace it with one of yourself as happy and fulfilled.
2. *Apply yourself to a task.* In general, the most rewarding work is that which is done for the sheer joy of doing it. When your current assignment is "just not happening," Ray and Myers recommend that you "get to work on something (almost anything) productive, with the simple (even foolish) confidence that the work that's in front of you is part of your answer."[9] They suggest that concentration on the task at hand, whatever it happens to be, will release your creative powers.
3. *Maintain a spirit of inquiry*—about yourself and your own mental processes, not just about the world around you. As you begin to feel more confident in your own creative processes, you will become better able to surrender to them.
4. *Acknowledge that you don't know how it's going to turn out.* For goal-oriented businesspeople, who have been taught that it is desirable to strive for a predetermined outcome, this may be the hardest step of all. The advantage is that the creative outcome may be superior to the predetermined one. And, very importantly, you won't have "burned yourself out" getting there.

[6] Michael Ray and Rochelle Myers, *Creativity in Business* (Garden City, NY: Doubleday, 1986).
[7] Ray and Myers, Creativity in Business, p. 9.
[8] Ray and Myers, *Creativity in Business*, p. 29.
[9] Ray and Myers, *Creativity in Business*, p. 30.

This four-step process is only one of a number of avenues to releasing inner creativity that Ray and Myers discuss, but it will give you an idea of what getting in touch with your inner creativity can entail. Ray and Myers' book is, to our knowledge, the only complete published description of a creativity-enhancing program for managers. If their ideas sound trite or even silly to you, bear in mind that many managers have had the same reaction when they were required to attend training sessions on creativity. Some have become believers; of course, others have remained skeptical. Why don't you be your own judge? Read *Creativity in Business* and try several of the recommended techniques to see if any of them works for you. Most creativity experts suggest that everyone try a variety of techniques because no one technique appears to be right for every individual.

DEVELOPING CREATIVE STRATEGIES

The first portion of this chapter was an argument for creativity in *all* phases of direct marketing. Indeed, the importance of a sound underlying business strategy and a solid plan for each direct marketing program cannot be overstated. Yet, when all is said and done, a great deal of the responsibility for success or failure rests with the creative strategy and execution. Schultz, Martin, and Brown have emphasized the importance of the creative element of advertising in terms that apply equally to direct marketing campaigns:

> With all the previous planning steps taken, it would seem that the next step, determining or formulating the sales message to be delivered to customers and prospects for the product or service, should be quite simple. Unfortunately, just the opposite is true. This is the most difficult step by far unless you are blessed with a unique product or service. Yet this is where the practical success or failure of the campaign actually occurs. Quite simply, if the sales message is not clear, does not provide a benefit, or does not solve a problem for prospective purchasers, then the advertising campaign is bound to fail. . . . If the sales message is poor, weak, or ill-conceived, the campaign will fail or certainly not come close to reaching its potential.[10]

We will make a somewhat arbitrary but useful distinction between creative strategy and creative execution. The *creative strategy* is a formal description of the message you wish to convey and the audience to whom you wish to convey it. *Creative execution* is the combination of layout, copy, and graphics that accomplishes the creative strategy.

Direct marketing managers and creative specialists work together to come up with a successful creative product. It is the responsibility of the manager to ensure that the creatives have all relevant information about the product and the direct marketing plan. It is the responsibility of the creatives to assist in the

[10] Don E. Schultz, Dennis Martin, and William P. Brown, *Strategic Advertising Campaigns*, 2nd ed. (Chicago: Crain Books, 1984), p. 231.

development of the creative strategy and to put together a creative execution that carries out the marketing objectives and plan. Finally, it is the responsibility of the manager to approve the creative product. When managers and creatives work together closely, the results are more likely to be satisfactory, as in a recent direct-mail campaign by Apple Computer.

Apple is a company founded on innovation that stresses both creativity and accountability in its marketing programs. Referring to the importance of creativity in Apple's direct-response programs, which play an important role in the company's overall marketing strategy, Apple's manager of consumer advertising and an advertising agency executive say:

> In each of our three market segments (consumer, business and education), our direct response efforts must complement a corporate and segment strategy. We want our tactics to include strong offers targeted to the most responsive audience. Of equal importance to offers and audiences is the rather simple notion that if they don't read it, they can't respond. And that is the importance of break-through creative—creative that works its way through the information clutter in a compelling fashion. [11]

The Creative Strategy [12]

Every creative group, whether part of an agency or an internal service provider, has its own approach to developing a creative strategy, but all have five basic steps:

1. Develop the key selling concept.
2. Define the primary marketing problem.
3. Specify the desired action.
4. Fashion the message strategy.
5. Take account of corporate/divisional requirements.

Key Selling Concept. The key selling concept is the primary product benefit as seen from the customer's perspective. It is the positioning strategy translated into the language of the customer. The strongest appeal will be one that promises to solve a genuine problem experienced by the target audience or that offers a genuinely-desired benefit.

When the Apple IIGS (G stands for "graphics" and S stands for "sound") was introduced in 1986, Apple had an installed customer base of 3 million. They had experimented with mailings to this installed base—which they creatively refer to

[11] Murray R. Bowes and Linda Reed Tsien, "Selling Apples by Credit Card," *Direct Marketing*, June 1987, p. 61.

[12] The discussion in this section is based on Schultz, Martin, and Brown, *Strategic Advertising Campaigns*, pp. 239-245; Michael L. Rothschild, *Marketing Communications* (Lexington, MA: D.C. Heath, 1987), pp. 185-189; "Direct Mail Copy—The Marketing and Creative Process," DMA Release 310.1, January 1984.

as "IBM's" (!) for installed base mailings—very successfully. Apple recognized that the customers in this installed base were the best prospects for a product line extension that provided superior capabilities, including greatly increased computing power, almost 100 percent software compatibility, state-of-the-art graphics, and sound. The mailing piece they produced had as its objective convincing owners of Apple IIe's to upgrade to the Apple IIGS and owners of older Apple models to purchase the new model. (See Figure 5.1). This was a traffic-building mailing for Apple dealers, not an attempt to sell by mail order.

Primary Marketing Problem. Defining the primary marketing problem, the next step, reverses the perspective by looking at the situation from the marketer's point of view: What is the chief problem faced by the marketer in developing a successful marketing program?

In the case of the Apple IIGS direct-mail campaign, it appears that two key problems greatly concerned Apple marketing and advertising executives. The first was how to reach the best prospective customers with their message. The second was how to come up with a breakthrough creative execution.

Desired Action. The next step in the development of the creative strategy is to specify the action desired from the prospect. The execution of a program that is intended to close a sale will be different from the execution of a program that aims to produce a large quantity of sales leads, which, in turn, will be different from the execution of a program that aims to produce high-quality leads.

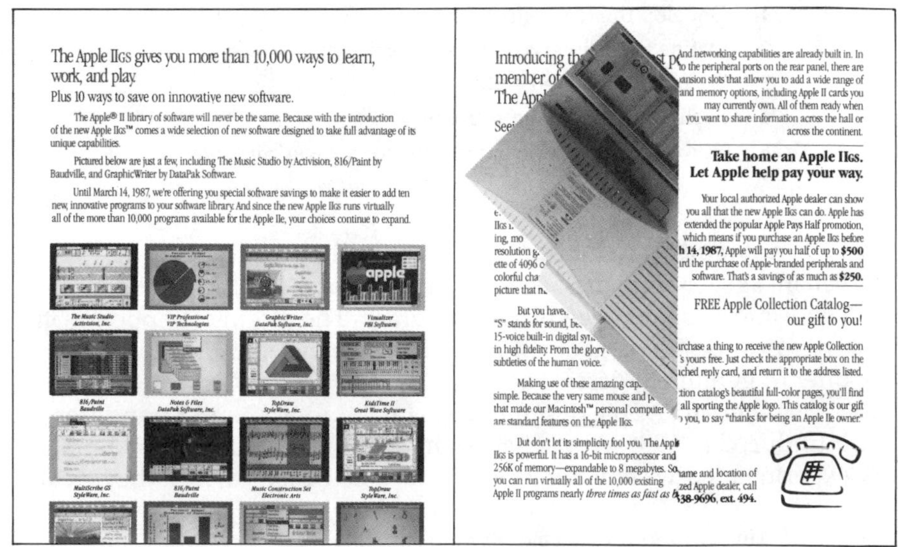

FIGURE 5.1 ***The Apple IIGS Mailer***
Source: Apple Computer, Inc., Cupertino, CA 95014

The program that is intended to close a sale must cover all phases of the selling process, from spelling out the product benefits to developing credibility to detailing the terms of sale. The program that has as its objective producing a large quantity of sales leads will stress the product benefits but probably not mention price. It may offer an attractive premium. And the program that aims to produce high-quality leads will offer more detailed information and might mention any drawbacks the product has. It also might make it more difficult to respond by not including a reply card or coupon, for example.

A program (such as the Apple IIGS mailing) that aimed to build retail store traffic would not be designed and executed to actively encourage orders by mail or telephone. Instead, it might well offer a discount coupon to be used only in the store or a gift available only at the store. Apple went a step further, creating an Apple Credit Card that could be used only to purchase Apple products. As an added incentive, purchasers of new computers could purchase $500 worth of peripherals and software for $250.

Fund-raising or patronage appeals for nonprofit organizations may require somewhat different types of action. A patronage appeal may actually be a sales effort when it attempts to sell tickets to an event or a series of events. Fund-raising appeals will have different characteristics depending on whether they are directed to first-time or repeat donors and whether they are seeking larger or smaller amounts of money.

Message Strategy. The next step is to develop the detailed message strategy. This involves several substeps:

- Describe the target market.
- Describe the selling task in relation to the competition.
- Describe the selling task in terms of the product's benefits.
- Give reasons why product delivers the benefits.
- Specify the desired tone or mood.

The *description of the target market* should cover several aspects:

- Demographics, geographics, and psychographics
- Media-use patterns
- Purchase and use patterns for the product and/or brand

This information should ordinarily come directly from the marketing plan, unless, for some reason, it needs to be updated.

In the case of the Apple IIGS mailing, the target market had been identified by previous direct-response programs. The key program took place in the fall of 1985, when the Apple Credit Card, offering preapproved credit of up to $2,500 for the purchase of an Apple computer system, was mailed to 15 million heads of household. The initial universe for the credit card mailing was 36 million names obtained from credit bureaus and subjected to geodemographic analysis. Through various multivariate statistical analyses, the initial universe was reduced to a final set of 15 million prime prospects. In general terms, these could be described as middle- to upper-income families with children between the ages of 7 and 17 who are concerned about the education of their children. The target market for the Apple IIGS mailing was refined, through similar types of analyses now made more powerful as a result of a continually expanding database, to 1 million (out of the 3 million installed base) upper-end households, as well as some educational and business customers.

The next step in developing the message strategy is to *describe the selling task in terms of the competition*. In other words, how do you want your product to be perceived in relation to its direct competitors? To a large extent, the answer to this question about the desired positioning vis-à-vis the competition also should be found in the marketing plan.

Next, the message strategy statement should spell out the *product benefits* in detail. The key selling concept—the primary benefit to be stressed—has already been identified. Now it is time to list the set of benefits that have been selected, on the basis of the positioning strategy, as sales appeals for the current program. Apple portrayed the IIGS as a computer that was more powerful than the company's earlier models, but just as easy to use and which had the added benefits of high-quality graphics and digitized sound.

As the benefits are being described, it is also important to develop a set of supporting *reasons why* the product delivers those benefits. These reasons why will be used to establish the credibility of the product and the offer. The greater the commitment the prospect is being asked to make—a purchase, a sales call, a donation—the more critical is credibility.

Reasons why may be linked to tangible attributes of the product: the materials from which it is made, its design, the manufacturing process used. Credibility is often derived from an association with the company or brand name. (Notice the similarity to some of the types of positioning discussed in Chapter 3.) The Apple mailing used a letter from the company's executive vice president to lend additional credibility to the offer.

Reasons why may also be developed in the form of testimonials from satisfied users. This is often a very effective way of developing credibility.

Finally, to complete the message strategy section, the *tone or mood of the program* should be specified. The primary determinant of this tone or mood is the brand personality (image) of the product. David Ogilvy says:

> Products, like people, have personalities, and they can make or break them in the market place. The personality of a product is an amalgam of many things—its name, its packaging, its price, the style of its advertising, and, above all, the nature of the product itself.
>
> Every advertisement should be thought of as a contribution to the brand image. It follows that your advertising should consistently project the *same* image, year

> after year. This is difficult to achieve, because there are always forces at work to change the advertising—like a new agency, or a new Marketing Director who wants to make his mark.[13]

Direct marketing has historically been less concerned than general marketing and advertising with issues like brand personality. However, as communications clutter has increased, these issues have become more important to direct marketers.

It is traditional to talk about the tone or mood of an advertisement or promotion as either rational or emotional. There are a number of problems with these two terms: they are difficult to define and measure; no ad is entirely one or the other; and the two terms do not seem to correlate very well with possible purchase motivations.

An improvement may be the informational/transformational schema introduced by Puto and Wells[14] and subsequently expanded upon by Puto.[15] Consider the definitions of the two terms by Puto and Wells:

> We define an informational advertisement ... as one which provides consumers with factual (i.e., presumably verifiable), relevant brand data in a clear and logical manner such that they have greater confidence in their ability to assess the merits of buying the brand after having seen the advertisement. An important aspect of this definition is that an advertisement can be designed with the intention of providing information, but it does not become an informational ad unless it is perceived as such by consumers ....
>
> For an advertisement to be judged informational ... it must reflect the following characteristics:
>
> 1. Present factual, relevant information about the brand.
> 2. Present information which is immediately and obviously important to the potential consumer.
> 3. Present data which the consumer accepts as being verifiable.
>
> A transformational advertisement is one which associates the experience of using (consuming) the advertised brand with a unique set of psychological characteristics which would not typically be associated with the brand experience to the same degree without exposure to the advertisement. Thus, advertisements in this category "transform" the experience of using the brand by endowing this use with a particular experience that is different from that of using any similar brand....
>
> For an advertisement to be judged transformational, it must contain the following characteristics:

[13] David Ogilvy, *Ogilvy On Advertising* (New York: Crown Publishers, 1983), p. 14.

[14] Christopher P. Puto and William D. Wells, "Informational and Transformational Advertising: The Differential Effects of Time," *Advances In Consumer Research*, Vol. XI, ed. Thomas Kinnear (Provo, UT: Association for Consumer Research, 1984), pp. 638-643.

[15] Christopher P. Puto, "Transformational Advertising: Just Another Name for Emotional Advertising or a New Approach?," *Proceedings Of The Division Of Consumer Psychology, 1985 Annual Conference*, ed. Wayne D. Hoyer (Washington, D.C.: American Psychological Association), pp. 4-6.

1. It must make the experience of using the product richer, warmer, more exciting, and/or more enjoyable, than that obtained solely from an objective description of the advertised brand.
2. It must connect the experience of the advertisement so tightly with the experience of using the brand that consumers cannot remember the brand without recalling the experience generated by the advertisement.[16]

Puto and Wells present a 23-item scale that can be used to classify an ad as high transformation/ low information, low transformation/ high information, high transformation/ high information, or low transformation/ low information. The scale has been tested and validated with television commercials. There seems to be no reason why it would not be just as effective when used in conjunction with print advertising, especially direct mail.

The message strategy is the core of the creative strategy. It cannot be considered in isolation, however. The three preceding steps in formulating the creative strategy—key selling concept, primary marketing problem, and action desired—are all necessary to create the depth of understanding required for a successful message strategy.

Corporate/Divisional Requirements. The final step in developing the creative strategy—*corporate/ divisional requirements*—is somewhat mechanical but essential nonetheless. In order to achieve some consistency in the "look" of all their promotional materials, and to ensure that the company and product are correctly and recognizably identified, most large firms have specific requirements for logos, brand names, and other identifying information. These requirements may involve such aspects as placement and size of the required information.

Some types of products must also meet legal requirements of one kind or another. A good example is the required warnings on cigarette packages, in which the actual copy used, placement of the warning label, and size of the warning label must all meet federal standards.

These requirements must be noted in advance so they can be effectively integrated into the creative execution. A last-minute discovery that something of this nature must be included can throw an otherwise effective creative execution into chaos.

CREATIVE EXECUTION

Once the creative strategy statement is in place, the translation of that strategy into the actual promotional piece can begin. Think of the creative execution as involving three reasonably distinct phases: copy, graphics, and layout.

[16]Puto and Wells, "Informational and Transformational Advertising," p. 638.

Direct-Response Copy

It is generally agreed that successful direct-response copy is different from general advertising copy. "It's long," is the difference most often mentioned. That is frequently true but very superficial.

John Caples, a retired vice-president of BBD&O who spent over 40 years in advertising and direct marketing, is regarded by many as the dean of direct-response copywriters. He has many strong opinions about what makes good copy in general and direct-response copy in particular:

On length of copy: "Ads with lots of facts are effective. And don't be afraid of long copy. If your ad is interesting, people will read all the copy you can give them. If the ad is dull, short copy won't save it." [17]

On being straightforward: "Direct writing outpulls cute writing. Don't save your best benefit until last. Start with it. You will have a better chance of keeping your reader with you." [18]

On imagery: "A skillful copywriter does not depend on the reader's imagination to visualize all the possible benefits of various product features .... He creates a word-picture that makes crystal-clear the specific advantages of every feature."[19]

On product features and benefits: "When you receive an assignment to write an ad for a product, your first step should be to study the product's features .... In writing your copy, your job is to translate these features into benefits."[20]

On speaking directly to the prospect: "Make believe you are writing a letter to your best friend. Put down the words 'Dear Joe.' Then tell Joe everything you want him to know about a wonderful new product you have just discovered .... Then turn your letter into an ad." [21]

Caples has much more to say about what works and what doesn't. He was a student of all aspects of advertising—comparing ads that pulled well with those that did not, ads that were used over and over with those that wore out quickly, headlines that worked with those that did not, and words that improved ads with those that didn't. After he learned what worked and what didn't, he tried to find out why—and that is probably the secret of his success.

There are differences in writing copy for the various direct-response media, and we will discuss them in the chapters that deal with each medium. Here we

[17] John Caples, *How To Make Your Advertising Make Money* (Englewood Cliffs, NJ: Prentice Hall), 1983), p. 16.

[18] Caples, *How to Make Your Advertising Make Money*, p. 16.

[19] Caples, *How to Make Your Advertising Make Money*, p. 84.

[20] Caples, *How to Make Your Advertising Make Money*, p. 85.

[21] Caples, *How to Make Your Advertising Make Money*, p. 180.

B.

THE ONLY SOLAR-POWERED WALKWAY LIGHT. This is the only walkway light that is solar-powered for illumination of gardens and paths without external wiring. The photovoltaic panels recharge the built-in NiCad batteries during the day —eliminating the need for frequent battery changes—and a photosensor activates the unit automatically at dusk for soft accent lighting. It remains lighted until the stored power is depleted (up to five hours per night during summer months, less during winter months with shorter days). The light may be mounted on a 20-inch stand with angling bracket (included) or set flush with the ground. Comes with one replacement bulb. Weather-resistant anodized aluminum housing. Height (without stand): 5 inches. Width: 6¼ inches. Depth: 5 inches. Weight: 2.45 pounds.
32619K . . . . .$59.95 **Postpaid and Unconditionally Guaranteed**

The Only Solar-Powered Walkway Light

FIGURE 5.2 ***The Solar-Powered Walkway Light***

will mention two contemporary copywriters' points of view that may help you understand, and therefore create, better direct-response copy.

Turley describes direct response copy as reason-why copy.[22] The direct-response copywriter is trying to motivate the prospect to take some action. The prospect needs reasons why he or she should take that action; reasons why his or her life will be less satisfying if the action is not taken. It may require long copy to present all those reasons in a compelling fashion. But remember, long copy is not the objective; it is sometimes the result of satisfying the communications objectives.

In a recent article, Hatch[23] compared the copy used by six different catalogs for the same solar-powered outdoor light and found only one emphasized benefits throughout. Describing the headline, Hatch said that,

> "in just five words, the writer hits the three major benefits on the nose: "Light Patios, Walkways Without Wiring" .... The key sentence in the body copy [is]: "To install it, just push the non-rusting aluminum leg into the soil." None of the other writers points out so clearly how easy these are to put in the ground... The headline has one or two or three—or more—bold promises in good-size, easy-to-read boldface type. Every adjective or adverb is carefully and brilliantly chosen to slip one more benefit into the prospect's mind."[24]

Notice that this is short copy doing an excellent sales job.

[22] Brian Christian Turley, "What's So Different About Direct-Response Copywriting?" *Direct Marketing*, March 1985, pp. 34-36.

[23] Denison Hatch, "Match the Copy to the Catalog," *Dm News/Catalog Business*, July 1, 1987, pp. 20, 48.

[24] Hatch, "Match the Copy to the Catalog," pp. 20, 48.

Direct-response copy does not have as its primary objective creating awareness or building an image. Rather its primary objective is to incite the prospect to take the desired action. That is really what makes direct-response copy different.

Graphics

The graphics of a direct-response promotion, whatever the medium being used (except, of course, radio), have a communications role to carry out, just as the copy does. There are several ways in which graphics can contribute to overall communications effectiveness:

- Communicating an important selling point quickly and effectively
- Attracting the attention of the target customer
- Directing attention to other elements of the promotion—e.g., the copy or a response device
- Communicating an idea that is difficult to verbalize
- Providing credibility for the selling points

There are two basic types of graphics; artwork and photography. Photography can be done either on location or in a studio.

Although artwork is used extensively in direct-response programs, photography is the norm in most applications because it offers greater detail and more credibility. This is especially critical when the objective is to close a sale on the basis of the direct-response promotion alone.

To add excitement and to portray products in settings appropriate to their use, the trend in recent years has been to on-location photography, especially for upscale catalogs. Shooting on location may well be cost effective, but remember it adds greatly to the time and cost of developing the promotion.

Gosden suggests four myths about graphics that are well worth keeping in mind:[25]

Myth 1: Costly graphics produce better results. Whether we are talking about four-color, bleed pages, page after page of graphics, or any other expensive technique, the question is simply: Is it cost effective?

Before you spend a bundle testing a very expensive graphics approach, think about the nature of the costs being incurred. The photography, design, and production set-up costs are fixed, no matter what the size of your production run. Elaborate graphics will therefore add less per unit to a large mailing and might be more easily justified than they would for a smaller mailing.

Other types of graphics decisions may result in variable costs—manual insertion into the envelope, for example, instead of machine insertion. This type of operation may be manageable and cost effective for a small program but not for a large one.

[25] Freeman F. Gosden, Jr., *Direct Marketing Success* (New York: John Wiley & Sons, 1985), pp. 151-153.

Myth 2: Graphics always improve communications effectiveness. A picture is not always worth a thousand words. Graphics are a wonderful communications device, but when they become overly elaborate, they can detract from the copy and harm overall effectiveness. Be especially careful of fancy type, particularly the kind with large serifs (the flourishes at the end of the main stroke on some characters) and reverse type (light copy on a dark background).

Myth 3: A picture is self-explanatory. Not if people don't look carefully or if they misinterpret it. Picture captions help to ensure that the correct inference is made.

Myth 4: Color is always desirable. Again, this is a matter of cost effectiveness. Let your decision on whether to develop an expensive program for testing be governed by common sense. Some products—food comes immediately to mind—need color for an effective (mouth-watering) presentation. Some objectives—lead generation, for example—may not require the impact of an expensive four-color presentation.

Gosden adds, "Year after year, the simpler packages seem to outpull the fancy, screaming, art-award generating, so called high-impact direct mail pieces."[26] Perhaps simplicity itself is appealing.

Layout

Layout refers to the manner in which the various components of the promotional piece are arranged on the page. There are several generally-accepted principles of layout design.

- *Balance* refers to a distribution of elements on the page that is visually pleasing. "Pleasing" does not necessarily mean symmetrical; in fact, total symmetry can be boring.
- *Clarity* suggests a design that is clean and straightforward, conveying the message without confusion or misunderstanding.
- *Simplicity* implies that anything that does not contribute to the message should be eliminated. Prospects should be able to grasp the message of the visual elements just as readily as they read the copy.
- *Proportion* is the manner in which the various elements relate to one another and to the background on which they appear.
- *Eye flow or movement* describes the placement of the various elements so they lead logically from one to another.
- *Contrast* is obtained by using different shapes, sizes, densities, and colors or tints to provide appeal and interest.
- *Unity* means that the entire promotional piece works together as an integrated whole to convey the desired message.

[26] Gosden, *Direct Marketing Success*, p. 154.

A mechanistic approach will not produce an outstanding product. Aaker and Myers quote an art director who distinguishes between simply "arranging elements on a page" and "visualizing an idea":[27]

> The former is a designer's (or layout man's) feat; his innate sense of composition, balance, color is brought fully into play. On the other hand, presenting the clearest visual interpretation requires a strong desire to communicate with the audience, a flair for the dramatic, the ability to think in pictorial terms (usually referred to as "visual sense") and, probably most significant, a firm understanding of the advertiser's goal.[28]

Managing the Creative Execution

During the creative execution and production stages, the direct marketing manager must coordinate and manage several diverse activities, each of which is being carried out by a separate person or group. Unless all these people are fully supplied with information, and unless all of them work together harmoniously, the final product will not be satisfactory.

Throckmorton likens the marketing manager to the conductor of an orchestra.[29] The basic "score" is arranged in this fashion:

1. The pure Creative Section with its copy and graphics does not play first. Marketing planning and the creative strategy come first. Creative specialists should be involved in the planning phases—providing information about past campaigns and what worked and what didn't; helping to formulate marketing research issues and receiving the results of the research; and actively participating in the development of the creative strategy.

2. The Production Section and the Media Section are equally creative and privileged to play as the marketing score requires and as the conductor indicates. Whatever medium or media are being used, production and media specialists should become involved at the very beginning of the creative execution. This will help them to develop a complete understanding of the program, and therefore to know what will be required of their group and when. Allow genuine interaction among the various creative groups. When they are sufficiently involved with and informed by the copy and graphics groups, for example, production people can identify which creative concepts are going to cause delays or unanticipated expense. Then the three groups can work together to revise the concept, or if a concept (like the Apple IIGS mailing) is judged worthy of special production techniques, production can plan ahead for the extra time and effort required.

[27] David A. Aaker and John G. Myers, *Advertising Management*, 3rd ed. (Englewood Cliffs, NJ: Prentice Hall, 1987), pp. 377-378 and William A. Cohen, *Building a Mail Order Business*, 2nd ed. (New York: John Wiley & Sons), pp. 345-347.

[28] Aaker and Myers, *Advertising Management*, 3rd. ed., pp. 377-378.

[29] Joan H. Throckmorton, "The 5 Basic Steps of Managing Successful Creative Interaction," DMA Release #300.2, January 1984.

The point is not to leave production and media in the dark until their specific activity is to begin. They can contribute much more if they are brought in during the creative planning stages of the project.

3. Many sections can and should work together in certain segments of the score. When and how depends on the score itself. In other words, the requirements of the marketing and creative strategies will dictate when and how various creative groups should work together. Throckmorton suggests that when this interaction is effective, "serendipitous" results may occur. The production group suggests a different mail format, an artist suggests a different approach to some element of the offer, a list specialist suggests a different appeal to a particular market segment—and these suggestions are tested and prove to be the most effective.

4. The program will give every section a fair and reasonable time to play, but since it runs on a time schedule, the program must begin and end within a predetermined time frame. Deadlines are more likely to be met without numerous last-minute crises if all creative and production groups work together rather than being isolated from detailed knowledge of what the other groups are doing.

The creative and production people should be kept informed about the campaign. Let them know how it is going and involve them fully in the post-campaign analysis. A good manager is willing to share the glory of a successful campaign with the various groups responsible for it and to ask for their critique and suggestions when a campaign fails to meet objectives. This is simply good participative management.

JUDGING THE CREATIVE EFFORT[30]

Judging the creative execution is the most difficult managerial task of all because there are no hard-and-fast rules, no "right" or "wrong." There are, however, executions that carry out the creative strategy and those that do not.

A good manager does not simply guide the development of the creative strategy, turn it over to the creatives, and wait for the final result. A good manager stays involved without interfering in the creative process.

One way to do this is to review the progress at several predetermined points. It makes sense to have a formal review of the creative concept, the rough execution, and the final execution. The checklist shown in Figure 5.3 suggests criteria that should be used in the review.

The Creative Concept Review

The creative concept is the main theme for the promotion. At this stage it is important for the manager to consider how well the theme ties in with the image

[30] Schultz, Martin, and Brown, *Strategic Advertising Campaigns*, pp. 283-287; L. William Black, "Evaluating the Creative Package from the Client Side," DMA Release #300.3, January 1984.

Does the Execution Carry Out the Creative Strategy? The creative strategy establishes the overall direction which the creative execution should follow. Management should, however, be alert for the—very rare—'breakthrough' creative concept that suggests that the strategy itself should be revised.

Will the Execution Appeal to the Target Audience? It is not important that you personally or management in general "likes" the creative execution; it is vital that it strikes a responsive chord in the minds of the prospects.

Would You Say This to a Prospect in Person? If you wouldn't—either because it might be offensive or simply because you just wouldn't speak directly to the prospect this way—rethink the execution.

Is it Written from the Prospect's Point of View or from the Marketer's Point of View? Don't let ego get in the way!

Is the Execution Clear, Concise, Complete, and Convincing? These can be considered the '4 C's' of advertising and promotion.

Does the Execution Get and Hold the Prospect's Attention? Clutter exists in all media today—in the mailbox as well as on television. One important task of the creative execution is to break through that clutter.

If Time or Space Is Limited, Make the Message Single-Minded. It is better to present one compelling message than many weak ones which are not persuasive.

Make Sure Management Knows Exactly What the Creatives Have in Mind. hether it is a complex mailing piece or a direct response television commercial, be sure that the exact nature of the finished product is clear.

If There Are Several Creative Pieces, Make Sure They All Work Together Effectively. This is not to say they should all be the same or similar, but that they should all contribute materially to conveying the desired image, the message, and/or to encouraging the prospect to take the desired action.

Does the Execution Overwhelm the Message? The substance of the message is more important than the manner in which it is conveyed. Great promotional pieces convey the substance in a way that strikingly draws attention to the message itself.

Is the Request for Action Clear and Specific? Don't leave the prospect guessing about the action requested . . .

FIGURE 5.3 ***Checklist for Judging Creative Execution***

Source: Adapted from Martin, Schultz, and Brown, pp. 283-287 and John M. Keil, *The Creative Mystique* (New York: John Wiley & Sons, 1985), pp. 85-123.

If a Reply Device Is Used, Is It Simple and Easy to Use? . . . and make it easy for the prospect to take that action!

Do Let the Cost of the Proposed Execution Influence You. Don't accept an execution that has little chance of being worth its cost—and don't reject a great idea just because it will be expensive.

FIGURE 5.3 ***(continued)***

of an established product and the rest of its current promotions. Good promotional strategies use each promotional element to deliver the same image, if not exactly the same message. Every element of the strategy reinforces every other element, so that a unified and consistent message is delivered to the target audience. Figure 5.4 shows an L. L. Bean space advertisement and two Bean catalog covers. The Bean catalog has long had a recognizable look; the space ad was carefully designed to convey this look.

The Rough Execution Review

At this stage the entire promotional piece exists in rough form. That is, the copy has been drafted, the graphics have been rendered in sketch form, and the layout has been planned. This is the time to ask critical questions about production as well as about the likely effectiveness of the finished piece.

Since the promotion is now available in tangible, if not finished, form, this is the time to be sure that it can be executed on time and on budget. The production people should be thoroughly involved in the review at this stage. If the promotion must be cleared by the legal department (which is usually a requirement), this should be done before the project moves on to the final execution.

The Final Execution Review

For any kind of print production, the promotional piece at the final execution stage is often described as a mechanical. A *mechanical* is a camera-ready piece of artwork with copy and graphics pasted up on sheets of artboard—in other words, the finished layout. For broadcast, the copy has been finalized, and for television, a storyboard has also been prepared with shots and cuts specified.

Major changes in the promotional piece at this stage, are likely to cause delay and additional cost. Still, it is the manager's responsibility to review the final execution very carefully to make sure that no errors have crept in and that all elements that were planned have been completed—correctly.

FIGURE 5.4 *The Recognizable Look of L. L. Bean*

Source: Courtesy L. L. Bean.

A WORD ABOUT CREATIVE AWARDS

No chapter on creative strategy would be complete without mention of the continuing controversy surrounding awards for creative excellence. This controversy exists in direct marketing just as it does in general advertising. Are award-winning campaigns necessarily successful in meeting their objectives?

A recent article in *Advertising Age* quoted a highly regarded direct marketing copywriter on the subject:

> Don't try to equate winning a contest with sales results. A contest prize in a creative field means that a number of judges—your peers, usually—liked your work. It does not necessarily mean that more bakers will buy your shortening or more plumbers will buy your hardware. Your hard-nosed customers won't automatically be impressed with the things that impressed your judges. . .With direct mail we don't really need a panel of judges. The marketplace is prosecutor, judge and jury, all in one.[31]

Perhaps the best comment on creative excellence comes from a respected general advertiser, Malcolm McDougall. When asked what his expectations were of young people entering the creative end of the business, he replied that they should be fundamentally salespeople, not show business people. They should love the business and use their talent, flair, and originality "to create a customer, not advertising." [32]

SUMMARY

Creativity should be a vital part of all managerial activity. In direct marketing, high-impact creative work is increasingly important to break through media clutter. Managers, creatives, and other direct marketing specialists must work together to produce direct-response promotions that embody creative strategies as well as creative executions. Managers have a special responsibility to understand and guide the creative process and to ensure that its final results are appropriate to the objectives of the direct-response program.

DISCUSSION QUESTIONS

1. What is the difference between managerial creativity and creativity as it is usually thought of by marketers?
2. Explain the process of developing a creative strategy.
3. What are the three basic aspects of creative execution?

[31] John Francis Tighe, "Winning Ads Don't Always Sell," *Advertising Age*, August 5, 1987, p. 32.
[32] Interview with Mr. McDougall, July, 1987.

4. Why is it important for all specialist groups that will be involved in a direct marketing program to participate in its creative development? What groups of specialists would you expect to be involved?
5. How should a direct marketing manager go about judging a creative execution?
6. Bring a direct-response promotion to class and be prepared to present your analysis of the creative strategy behind it and a critique of its creative execution.

SUGGESTED ADDITIONAL READINGS

1. Stephen Baker, *Systematic Approach to Advertising Creativity* (New York: McGraw-Hill, 1979).
2. John Caples, *Tested Advertising Methods* (Englewood Cliffs, NJ: Prentice Hall, 1974).
3. David Ogilvy, *Ogilvy on Advertising* (New York: Crown Publishers, 1983).
4. Michael Ray and Rochelle Myers, *Creativity in Business* (Garden City, NY: Doubleday, 1986).
5. Don E. Schultz and Stanley I. Tannenbaum, *Essentials of Advertising Strategy,* 2nd ed. (Lincolnwood, IL: NTC Business Books, 1988), Chapters 5 and 6.

Part Three
Special Techniques of Direct Marketing

6

Targeted Marketing Using Databases

The definition of direct marketing presented in Chapter 1 described it as "an interactive system of marketing." This interactivity is made possible by the existence of a marketing database. The database is the very essence of direct marketing.

A direct marketing database can make many marketing activities more cost effective. It may also allow some types of analyses or actual marketing programs that would be impossible otherwise. Specifically, a database allows the marketer to:

- Identify the most profitable customers
- Obtain more business from them
- Identify and qualify the best prospective customers
- Convert them to actual customers
- Identify past customers who are still prospects
- Reactivate them
- Identify the organization's most profitable products
- Develop appropriate promotional and pricing policies
- Identify new market opportunities
- Develop new strategies for tapping those markets
- Measure the effectiveness of advertising and promotion
- Reduce waste and increase productivity
- Evaluate the effectiveness of channels of distribution and individual channel members

- Decrease costs and increase sales volume.[1]

Notice two things about these sets of benefits of databased marketing:

1. All the major functions of marketing are included. In other words, a database can affect all aspects of marketing operations.
2. Direct marketing activities are not specified in any of the benefits. Marketing programs designed to capitalize on this new information will often involve direct marketing elements, however. This is simply because the marketing database allows for analysis and identification at the level of individual customers, prospects, or distributors. Targets can then be reached with individualized direct marketing efforts. This is the realization of "interactive system of marketing."

A FUTURISTIC TWIST TO MAIL-ORDER MARKETING[2]

Let me introduce you to John World, a Spiegel customer of the not-too-distant future. Dr. World lives in a small town in Midwestern America. He has a thriving practice, but today is Wednesday, his usual day off.

Spiegel is aware of this, so we've arranged for him to receive a small, attractive box from us in his morning mail. A little puzzled, since he hasn't ordered anything from Spiegel recently, he opens the box to see what's inside. He's even more surprised when he finds that Spiegel has sent him a videocassette tape with the intriguing title "Invitation to Adventure."

Enclosed with the videocassette is a short letter from me. In it I explain to Dr. World that he has been a terrific Spiegel customer. I list two or three of the major items he has purchased from us and tell him that since I understand he is a doctor with a thriving practice in a small community—and since cars and driving are one of his passions—he might find the enclosed tape worth viewing.

This is not just a guess, one we hope will be lucky. Spiegel knew that Dr. World loves sports cars, and that he can afford one. We understand that he cannot find the luxury autos he likes in his small hometown. And we predict that he will be curious enough to pop that cassette into the tape player we know he owns.

And we're right. He's dazzled and delighted by what unfolds before his eyes.

The videotape highlights the mystique of the British-built personal luxury car—the Jaguar. The tape takes Dr. World from his living room chair, and drops him in the driver's seat. He is behind the wheel of a sleek sedan, touring some of the most spectacular roads in America. The tape then takes him to England, to the plant where the Jaguar is assembled. He sees the care and craftsmanship that go into each model. He hears Jaguar engineers and assemblers talk about the

FIGURE 6.1

[1] These sets of database benefits were adapted from Charles A. Khuen and Harriette L. Chandler, *An Automated Approach to Increasing Sales and Marketing Productivity and Profitability* (Cambridge, MA: Adelie Corporation, 1985), p. 3.

[2] From a speech delivered by Henry A. Johnson, president and CEO of Spiegel, Inc., printed as "Computer Technology is Key to Segmentation and Service," in *Direct Marketing*, June 1985, pp. 66-69, 119.

love and dedication that go into each step of the creation and building of a Jaguar. And he relates these vignettes to his own longing for a sports car.

The tape ends with an offer that he can't resist. By calling a special Spiegel number, Dr. World can arrange to have the Jaguar of his choice, colors and equipment exactly the way he'd like it, delivered to his home for a 30-day trial period.

If he wants to return the car at the end of that month, he pays a $500 rental charge. If he decides to keep the car, he receives a free bonus gift—an all-expense-paid vacation for two to the countryside the Jaguar in the videotape toured so dramatically.

No surprise to us, he orders the 30-day trial. The Jaguar is delivered and Dr. World falls in love with it. John World, successful small town doctor, lives out his fantasy. And he remembers Spiegel as the one who made it possible....

The story of Dr. World and the Jaguar is a look into the future. It is an example of the ultimate power that computer technology can give the direct marketer. This power is already within our reach. *We have the ability to put together product and service offers that are more exciting and creative than anything we've ever imagined. We will meet not only the obvious needs of our customers, but also their hidden wants and desires by more effectively utilizing the power of the computer.*

FIGURE 6.1 ***(continued)***

WHAT IS A DATABASE?

In Chapter 4 we discussed mailing lists and their role in direct marketing programs. A database is just another name for a mailing list, isn't it? No, it is not. Ownership of a mailing list is the *first step* toward establishing a database, *but it is not a database.*

A database contains information about customers and prospects that has often been collected over a considerable period of time. Consider for a moment just a few of the databases that contain information about you:

- *Student records.* Every school you have ever attended has records containing information on your background and academic performance. The Educational Testing Service has a more limited set of data that includes your college entrance test scores.
- *Employment records.* Every organization for which you have ever worked also has a record containing data on your background, salary, and the amount withheld from your wages for taxes.
- *Automobile registration records.* If you own a car, both the state in which the car is registered and your insurance company have records containing background information on you, descriptive information about your car, and a history of your traffic citations and accidents. Notice that the state and the insurance company are keeping essentially the same information related to your automobile, but they are keeping it for different purposes and probably in slightly different formats.

None of these examples mentions the word *computer*. The concept of a database does not require the use of a computer. Practically speaking, however, it is impossible to effectively maintain a database of useful size without a computer. It is safe to assume that all marketing applications involve computerized databases.

Also note that none of the examples we have cited is a database designed primarily for marketing purposes. But just consider the number of firms which would like to have the mailing list of students currently enrolled at your school or of persons who have just purchased new automobiles (which some states do make commercially available).

AN EXAMPLE OF A MARKETING DATABASE

Let's take the example of an airline that has designed a database to keep track of members of its frequent flier program. This database contains a considerable amount of data on each member including mileage accumulated under the plan, hotel and rental car usage, and mileage-based awards claimed.

The airline can manipulate this data in a number of ways that will produce managerially useful information. It can analyze the travel patterns of individual members. Knowing that Mr. Smith travels frequently between Dallas and Chicago, for example, will allow the airline to target him for information about special mid-week fares between Dallas and Chicago or a tie-in promotion with a hotel in Chicago during the month of August. (The airline knows from the zip code of his home address that Mr. Smith lives in a suburb of Dallas, and therefore may be interested in the Chicago hotel promotion, but not in the corresponding one in Dallas.)

Because Mr. Smith is already accessible to the airline, they may wish to collect other data about him, perhaps on his satisfaction with flights and with specific airline services, his use of other carriers, and his decision-making process for both business and pleasure travel. Because Mr. Smith can be addressed by name, and because the airline can stress the value of his opinion as a member of the frequent flier plan, the probability that he will reply to a request for information is greater than if he were merely a randomly selected member of the general population.

The airline may segment its frequent fliers in a variety of ways in order to obtain especially pertinent information. If Mr. Smith has not flown on the airline for an unusually long period of time, the airline would be well advised to ask him why. If it is because of a change in his job requirements, there is nothing that can be done. If, however, he has changed his airline preference, knowing why he has done so may give the airline some insight into the success of competitive activities or the failure of their own.

In other words, the airline can manipulate the information it already has to help it better understand the behavioral patterns of its frequent customers. It can also collect and store additional information, which may be attitudinal as well as behavioral. This additional information can either be general (requested of all or most of the frequent fliers) or specific (requested of only those who have not flown on the airline for the past 3 months, for example).

Using all the information, from whatever source, that is contained in the database, the airline can develop marketing programs that will appeal to a substantial portion of its frequent fliers. It can then promote these programs directly to the fliers who have a high probability of responding instead of wasting its promotional dollars on those who have a low probability of response.

By now you should have a feel for the wide variety of valuable marketing programs that can be carried out with great efficiency if a marketing database is available. You may have been wondering, though, if the cost and effort of establishing and maintaining a complex database are worth the benefits.

WHEN IS A DATABASE COST EFFECTIVE?

The cost of manipulating and storing information is one of the few costs that have declined substantially in recent years. These cost decreases are quite significant, especially since computing power has been rising at the same time. Today, more firms have an opportunity to implement a wider variety of computer applications because processing time is shorter and costs are lower for any individual application.

Hardware, however, is not the only cost that management should recognize when considering whether to establish a marketing database (or any other computer application, for that matter). The *software* cost for the database management system (discussed in the next section) can also be substantial, particularly if the firms develops its own proprietary software.

If the system is to be used in locations remote from the central processing facility, there will be additional costs for *communications hardware* and *software* and *processing stations*.

There are also likely to be *human resources costs*, both for additional training for existing personnel and for the hiring of new personnel, some of whom will be highly trained and experienced, and therefore expensive.

Existing software and data files will probably have to be *converted* so they will work properly on the new database system. This can be expensive and time-consuming, and can result in considerable inconvenience and delay to existing users.[3]

Finally, there is an interesting phenomenon associated with successful system installations that is well recognized but whose magnitude is difficult to assess. Successful applications breed ideas for additional applications. There is a snowball effect, so that, before long, a system that was more than adequate for existing applications is hopelessly overloaded. Management should consider buying either initial excess capacity or an easily expandable system or both to keep total long-

[3] Fred R. McFadden and James D. Suver, "Costs and Benefits of a Data Base System," *Harvard Business Review*, January-February 1978, pp. 131-139.

run system costs in line. Even when accelerated growth in system use is planned for, management may well find that actual growth is greater than anticipated.[4]

Since total costs for a database system can be substantial, careful thought should be given to the types of situations in which a database will be especially valuable. Several such situations can be identified:[5]

- *Repeat-purchase situations characterized by:*
  - *Moderate to high dollar value.* The purchase must provide sufficient gross margin to cover all its promotion costs, including the database.
  - *Purchase cycle of moderate length.* Onetime or infrequent purchases do not present a need for databased marketing unless the infrequent purchase is so large and profitable that it is advisable to maintain the account history in depth. Also, very frequent purchases of convenience goods may offer little opportunity for specialized marketing promotions; neither are they likely to produce the margin needed to support those promotions.
- *A segmented (or segmentable) market.* Few markets today are so small or so homogeneous that segmentation cannot improve marketing effectiveness. However, the stronger the segmentation in a particular market, the more valuable the database that allows the marketer to reach that segment directly with specialized offers and appeals.
- *Customers who cannot be reached cost effectively by mass media.* Despite the proliferation of specialized media, many valuable markets are identifiable only on the basis of behavioral variables for which there is no direct media counterpart (e.g., Rolls-Royce owners, ultra-prestige credit card holders, frequent business travelers).
- *Ability to obtain names and addresses of customers and prospects in machine-readable form.* Records in a database can, of course, be maintained by using only a unique identification number. Practically speaking, however, if the marketer wishes to collect information about the consumer or the business account over time, the name is needed. A unique identifying number will still be used because names are not unique. If the customer or prospect is to be reached by direct mail, a correct mailing address is obviously essential.
- *Opportunities to increase the volume of business from existing customers.* One such opportunity could be obtaining a greater share of these customers' purchases in product categories from which they are currently purchasing. Another could be cross-selling, that is, persuading customers to purchase additional products from the firm's product line.

Most organizations would find that at least some of these situations apply to their marketing experience, and many organizations would find that all or most of them apply. This suggests two things. First, most marketers will find a database valuable in making their programs more cost effective. Second, where an organiza-

[4] J. Daniel Couger, "E pluribus computum," *Harvard Business Review*, September-October 1986, p. 88.

[5] The following list was adapted from Epsilon promotional materials.

tion finds many opportunities for targeted marketing using databases, it should be possible to establish priorities on the basis of incremental profit (incremental revenues minus incremental costs).

Now that we have presented general ideas about the nature and usefulness of marketing databases, we will look at both the marketing and technical requirements for the development, maintenance, and use of databases.

THE COMPONENTS OF A DATABASE SYSTEM

A marketing manager does not have to be a technical expert in order to make effective use of databased marketing. However, the manager must have a general comprehension of database technology in order to understand what it can do (and, at times, what it cannot readily do) and to be able to work effectively with management information systems (MIS) managers and technical personnel.

First, let's look at a formal definition of a database:

> A database is a shared collection of interrelated data designed to meet the varied information needs of an organization.[6]

This is a straightforward and useful definition, but we need to understand in some detail the elements that make up a database system.

Figure 6.2 illustrates the various components of a database system. Let's take a brief look at each of these elements.[7]

The *user group* consists of all requesters of data. Each user is allowed one or more types of access to the system—read only, add/delete, or modify. A user requests data through the database management system (DBMS).

A *DBMS* is a software system that handles all requests for data. In most database environments it serves multiple users at the same time. It also performs other functions, such as replacing damaged data with backup data and keeping track of system usage.

The *database* is the place where the data are physically stored.

The *data dictionary/directory (DD/D)* stores the definitions of the data items in the data base. It defines each item in terms of its name, its length, and the form in which it is stored.

Application programmers write the programming language (COBOL, BASIC, etc.) code that allows users to access and process the data. In the past, an application program was required to support all data requests. Today, high-level fourth-generation languages such as ORACLE allow users to access the data without an application program.

[6] Fred R. McFadden and Jeffrey A. Hoffer, *Data Base Management* (Menlo Park, CA: Benjamin/Cummings, 1985), p. 3.

[7] The following discussion is based on McFadden and Hoffer, *Data Base Management*, pp. 20-22.

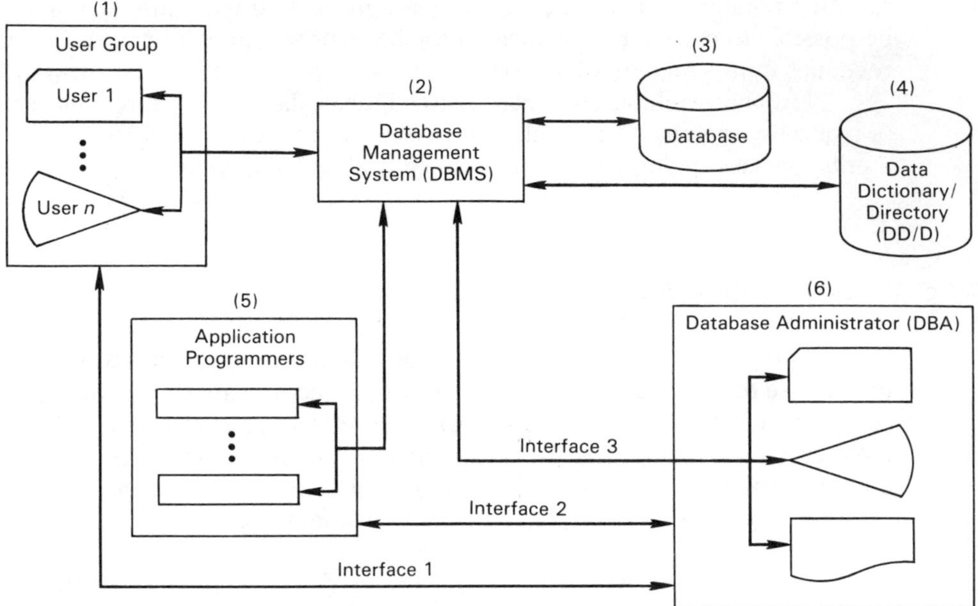

FIGURE 6.2 ***Various Components of a Database System***

Source: From *Data Base Selection, Design, and Administration* by Jon D. Clark, p. 6. Copyright© 1980 by Praeger Publishers, New York. Reprinted by permission of Praeger Publishers.

The *database administrator* (DBA) is the manager who is in charge of the database system. This individual is responsible, in consultation with users, for defining the data needs of the organization and for carrying out all of the activities that lead to satisfactory performance of the database.

CHARACTERISTICS OF A DATABASE

The activities required to manage a database are extremely technical and outside the purview of the typical marketing manager. However, an understanding of the characteristics that are necessary to the effective functioning of a database will help marketing managers to appreciate the advantages a database offers to a marketing operation. These characteristics are:[8]

- *Data independence.* The application program or user is protected from changes in the way the data are organized, stored, or accessed. The user should be able to

[8] The following discussion is based on Alfonso F. Cardenas, *Data Base Management Systems*, 2nd ed. (Newton, MA: Allyn and Bacon, 1985), pp. 12-16, 83-94.

continue to run the application program without even being aware that a change has been made in the physical or logical structure of the database.

- *Shareability and nonredundancy of data stored.* All qualified users are assured access to required data via the database. This eliminates the need for the maintenance of similar data files in various parts of the organization (redundant data). Very importantly, it also means that users throughout the organization are using equally current and valid data.
- *Relatability.* A record contains information about an individual (for example, your *student record,* as described earlier). Just as the data items on a single record are related to one another (in our example, they are related in the sense that they all pertain to you), so are records often related to one another. For instance, if either of your parents attended your school, there is a logical relationship ("child of alumnus") and it should be possible to represent this relationship in the database by indicating the connection between the parent's and the child's records.
- *Integrity.* The correctness of the data must be ensured. This involves maintaining control over access to the data and over editing of it, carrying out technical procedures that help to maintain the correctness and consistency of the data, and maintaining back-up data and systems.
- *Access flexibility.* This means being able to easily and efficiently access the data in a variety of ways suited to the needs of the user. It also implies the use of conventional programming or English-like query languages to enhance the ability of the nontechnically trained user to retrieve data or to simply browse through the system. Access flexibility also makes the tasks of database administration easier.
- *Security.* The database must be protected against unauthorized or malicious access and actions. There are various types of access (read only, add/delete, and modify) that may be granted to an individual user. Users may also be allowed to access the entire database or only a portion of it. There must be procedures in place to assign, control, and remove permissions to access the database.
- *Performance and efficiency.* The system must function smoothly at a level of cost that is acceptable to users. The larger the database becomes and the more individual users are concerned only with small subsets of the database (these two situations tend to go together), the more strain is placed on performance and efficiency. High levels of technical skill are needed to maintain a large database at peak efficiency in the face of the often conflicting demands of different user groups. The larger the database, the more difficult it is to make changes without disturbing the smooth functioning of the entire system.
- *Administration and control.* There must be centralized authority and responsibility for management of the system. Because of the large number of users and their different requirements and levels of technical proficiency, it is imperative that responsibility for the system be vested in one or a very few highly skilled database administrators. These administrators must be well-trained technical specialists who have the ability to work well with different types of people and groups from technical and nontechnical specialties.

ESTABLISHING A DATABASE

The process of establishing a database as seen from the point of view of a user such as a marketing manager is illustrated in Table 6-1. If the system is well designed and managed, the use of existing data to develop marketing programs generates new data that, in turn, can lead to additional marketing programs.

TABLE 6-1 Process of Creating a Database

1. Capture, organize, and maintain existing marketing data
2. Conduct research and analysis
3. Develop promotional program
4. Execute the program
5. Fulfill inquiries/orders/follow up leads
6. Capture new data and integrate it into existing database

Source: Adapted from promotional materials of Epsilon Data Management, Inc., 50 Cambridge St., Burlington, MA 01803.

Every contact with a customer should be *captured* and *recorded* in the database. This is a deceptively simple idea that can turn quite complicated in practice. The following situations are fairly typical:

- *A firm that is organized around the concept of direct marketing* (e.g., a catalog merchant) *usually performs this function well.* Each inquiry or order is recorded in the customer's file. Each contact also provides an opportunity to verify the accuracy of basic information such as mailing address.
- *General marketers often do not perform this function well.* In fact, many do not attempt to perform it at all.
- *Retailers record every charge transaction in considerable detail.* This information is used for accounting and financial purposes, including customer billing, inventory control, and departmental profitability analysis. Unfortunately, it is often relatively inaccessible to marketing management, either because the financial functions have priority within the system or because the data are not organized appropriately for marketing's needs.
- *Financial services firms often provide another example of sequestered data.* An individual may have several kinds of accounts with a particular bank—a checking account, a money market fund, and a personal line of credit. In most banks each of these financial products is the responsibility of separate departments, each of which has separate customer accounts systems. Consequently, it may well be impossible to draw a complete profile of the business a customer does with the bank. This makes it more difficult to cross-sell other financial products—for example, to encourage the customer with a substantial money market fund balance to consider another type of investment vehicle such as a mutual fund.
- *Business marketers have similar problems.* The order-processing and accounts receivable functions often have a wealth of information about customer pur-

chases that is not accessible to marketing management. Field salespeople are aware of the status of current negotiations, but they often do not have a satisfactory way of providing that information to management, even if they desire to do so. Some possible consequences include:[9]

- *A prospect is on the verge of committing to buy the firm's Model 324 widget.* The day before the sales rep is scheduled to call, hoping to close the sale, the prospect receives a direct-mail promotion offering the Model 324 at a special introductory price that is 15 percent less than the price the sales rep is able to offer. The prospect is irritated and decides not to buy the widget at all.
- *A telephone sales rep receives an incoming call requesting information about the Model 626 widget.* The telephone rep asks the standard questions and sends the standard information to the person who has inquired. Unfortunately, the telephone rep did not know that another division in the inquiring firm has been using the 626 widget for several years and could have given it a strong recommendation.

The lesson is that the marketing manager must identify internal sources of data and develop systems to capture the data for input into the database. If additional data are needed the marketing manager must commission *research* to obtain it and then work with the database administrator to ensure that the data will be available in the form needed when needed.

The contents of a database for a fund-raising application (presumably a not-for-profit organization) is shown in Table 6-2. Examine it carefully, noting both the large number of individual data items and the fact that many of these items will have multiple occurrences and therefore multiple entries. *Raw data alone will not contribute to more effective marketing programs. The data must be converted to useful information.* The following quote from Walter Wriston, former chairman of Citicorp, highlights the importance of this step.

> The incessant production of new data and its instantaneous communication create a paradox: information, the thing that eliminates uncertainty, now increases everybody's feeling of insecurity because of the failure to convert data into knowledge.[10]

Once an organization begins to systematically collect data, it quickly finds itself confronted with huge amounts of it. Conventional statistical techniques—ranging from the most elementary types of presentation (e.g., histograms) to simple descriptive statistics (e.g., means and medians) to more complex multivariate techniques (e.g., multiple regression)—may be extremely useful in analyzing these data and indicating which items are most relevant for decision-making purposes.

[9] The following examples were adapted from Charles A. Khuen and Harriette L. Chandler, *Improving the Productivity of Telemarketing: Making Each Call Count Through Integration* (Cambridge, MA: Adelie Corporation, 1986).

[10] Source: Walter B. Wriston, "The World According to Walter," *Harvard Business Review*, January/February 1986, pp. 65-66.

TABLE 6.2 Fund-Raising Marketing Database Elements

Name Block	*Address Block*	*General Donor Information*	*Donor Interactions*		*Market Research*
Individual Name Title and Suffix Personal Salutation Company or Foundation Name	Street Address (Name) City, State, Postal, and County Codes Date of Last Change Business Address City, State, Postal, and County Codes Mail and Address Status Codes	1. *Organizational Data* Approach Code Affiliations Chapter/Branch Code Donor/Member Code Origin Code, Date 2. *Donor Profile Data* Telephone Number (Home, Business) Special Interest Code Original Source and Date	1. *Gift History* Dates Amounts Source Codes Fund Allocation Use Code Acknowledgment Code 2. *Pledge History* Dates Amounts Number of Payments Interval Between Payments Source Codes Fund Allocation Use Code Acknowledgment Code 3. *Membership* Date Amount Begin Date Expiration Date Fund Allocation	4. *Tickets* Date Amount Series Section Row Seat Number(s) Number of Seats 5. *Direct Mail* Dates Package Codes Date Response Received 6. *Memorial History* Name and Date 7. *Volunteer History* Name and Date Assigned 8. *Activity History* Fulfillment Action Premiums Shipped 9. *Comment History* English Comments Date of Comment Type of Comment	1. *Donor Profile Survey* Date of Response Coded Answers to Questions 2. *Secondary Database Classification(s)* PRIZM© 3. *Demographic Profile* Occupation/Title Date of Birth Sex Family Structure Education 4. *Psychographic Profile* Program Preferences Giving Motivation Interests & Lifestyles

Source: Copyright 9/1/84 Epsilon Data Management Inc.

Suppose a science museum has a database with the elements described in Table 6-2. The museum wishes to profile the individuals who are its frequent donors so it can better target a direct-mail campaign to attract new donors. With the aid of regression analysis, it is discovered that being a member of the museum, attending at least four times a year, having children under 12 or over 21 years of age, and being educated beyond a bachelor's degree are the variables that best explain propensity to become a donor to the museum.

Armed with this information, the marketing director of the museum can develop a *targeted marketing program,* such as a direct-mail campaign that will appeal to this particular target group. Because it is carefully targeted, it should be cost effective.

Once the program is *implemented,* donations will be received by the museum. As the donations are *received and acknowledged,* a record is established for each new donor in the database. Thus new data are *captured,* completing one cycle of marketing activities and allowing for the beginning of another. There will be more data for the next analytical step, which should enhance the program's ability to produce useful and reliable results.

SOME SUCCESSFUL DATABASED MARKETING PROGRAMS

Databased marketing is such a new activity that the marketing manager has few sources of information on exactly how to plan and implement programs. Certainly the most valuable applications come about because of managerial problems that are difficult to resolve effectively without rapid access to large quantities of accurate information. It is becoming apparent to many observers, however, that the number of useful applications is limited only by the manager's resources and, perhaps even more, by the manager's creativity.

The descriptions of marketing situations and programs that follow are meant to stimulate your thinking about the possibilities of databased marketing.

A MULTINATIONAL, MULTILINGUAL SALES SUPPORT SYSTEM[11]

Companies often find it difficult to transmit information to their salespeople in a way that is both timely and efficient. When this happens, sales usually suffer.

This was precisely what happened to a Fortune 100 manufacturer of containers and the packaging equipment used to assemble and fill them. In addition

[11] This section was adapted from Patrick J. Yanahan, "How Salesmen's 'Computerized Catalogs' Cured a Communication Mess," *Industrial Marketing,* March 1983, p. 68. Reprinted with permission from *Business Marketing,* formerly *Industrial Marketing*. Copyright Crain Communications, Inc.

to selling new equipment, the company rebuilt traded-in machinery and sold it as used equipment. Company salespeople received a printed listing of the used equipment inventory every six months. By the time they got the inventory list it was outdated. To find out exactly what equipment was available and what condition it was in, salespeople had to contact warehouses all over the world by telephone and telex. This was so difficult and frustrating that most of them gave up, forgoing the substantial commissions to be achieved through equipment sales, and just sold the faster-moving container products.

An audit revealed millions of dollars worth of used equipment on the firm's books that was moving slowly, if at all, and generating little cash flow. An advertising program was suggested as a possible solution to this problem.

Instead, the company developed a computerized inventory reporting and ordering system. It linked a centralized database with more than 200 cities in the United States and all continents except Africa via telephone lines and satellite links. The system was installed in three phases:

1. The on-line database was first made accessible to field sales support personnel. The database was cross-indexed by many product attributes, including equipment type, size of package produced, speed, age of equipment, and physical location. A salesperson could make a single telephone call to a sales support person, request information on product availability by attribute(s), and receive a quick and accurate answer. As salespeople saw their professionalism—and along with it their commissions—increase, they quickly became sold on the system. Consequently, the second phase of the program went smoothly.
2. In the second phase salespeople were trained to use data terminals themselves. The applications software was very user friendly with extensive prompts to guide users through the system. Only 8 to 10 hours of training were required to learn to use the system. Direct use allowed salespeople to put a hold on equipment in inventory while a customer's credit check went through and headquarters approved the terms of sale. As they saw their effectiveness further improved, the salespeople became comfortable using the system directly.
3. The final phase saw multilingual reports and operations capability, management summaries produced on demand, and enhancements to the system that allowed changes in report format and content without major reprogramming activities.

This system was instituted at slightly less cost than had been budgeted for the advertising program originally proposed as the solution to the company's difficulties. The company had a communications problem, all right; but the problem was internal communications, not external communications. The solution was to make existing information available directly to the persons who needed it, when they needed it, and in the form in which they needed it. Salespeople quickly saw the value of the system, and those who were initially computer illiterate became its biggest proponents.

Farm Journal—Reaping a Rich Database Harvest[12]

According to the president of *Farm Journal*, "There's no real secret to target market publishing; we're trying to deliver to the individual reader the information that matters while eliminating the information that doesn't matter." That simple statement masks a sophisticated and complex publishing operation.

FJ is aware that each farm in the United States is unique in terms of size and method of operation. *FJ*'s database has been created to chronicle that uniqueness so the editors can target their editorial matter and offer their advertisers the opportunity to do the same.

As of October 1986, the *FJ* database contained 2.5 million names and addresses, with 1.4 million telephone numbers. It had 1.25 million names of farmers with complete and current demographic data; 900,000 of these subscribed to the journal. The demographic data for each farmer include whether the farmer is an owner or an operator, types of crops, acreage, types and sizes of livestock herds, and computer ownership. Demographic data are collected for each new subscriber and are updated every time the subscriber renews or sends in a reader service card. *FJ* also operates three telephone centers that are used to update information on subscribers and prospects.

Founded in 1877 to serve farmers in the Philadelphia area, by 1915 the *Farm Journal* had become a national publication with a circulation of 1 million. In 1953 it became the first farm magazine with regional editions, having recognized that the concerns of the cotton farmer in Georgia were quite different from those of the corn farmer in Iowa. Following the same line of reasoning, management created the first demographic edition of *FJ* in 1962. Much of the impetus for *Hog Extra* came from advertisers who had products or services targeted to the hog producer. These advertisers knew that only one out of every four farmers was raising hogs, and they did not want to buy the entire circulation of *FJ*. *Hog Extra* (circulation 120,000) was soon followed by *Beef Extra* (circulation 260,000) and *Dairy Extra* (circulation 100,000). Later *Top Producer* was added to serve 175,000 of the large, high-income farmers.

The magazine had still not realized its full potential for targeted publishing, however. In the middle 1970s *FJ*'s printing company, R. R. Donnelley & Sons, presented them with the opportunity to virtually build a customized magazine for each individual subscriber. The technique that allows this ultimate in customization is called *Selectronic® binding and imaging*.

The May 1984 issue of *FJ* was produced in 8,896 different versions of the magazine involving various combinations of advertising, editorial, and circulation

[12] The information and quotations in this section are from Dale E. Smith, "Database Harvest," *Direct Marketing*, October 1986, pp. 64-68. © Direct Marketing Magazine, 224 Seventh St., Garden City, NY 11530—800/645-6132.

wrappers for expiring subscriptions. The ink-jet printing used in this process eliminates the need for mailing labels by printing directly on the magazine and allows personalized messages on the circulation wrappers.

Subscriber reaction to the customized magazine format has been positive. Mailed queries to the paid subscribers of *FJ* have asked whether they wished to continue to receive whichever one(s) of the new publications for which they qualify. Response rates have run between 25 and 40 percent.

The amount of up-to-date information about its subscribers that *FJ* has can be used to advantage in a number of areas.

Advertising. Besides the national edition, there are six regional editions and eight "crop" editions that are distributed in geographical areas where certain crops are concentrated. If advertisers wish to use self-contained advertising units (an insert, for example), they may purchase any demographic breakdown allowed by *FJ*'s data base. An advertiser might wish to reach all wheat farmers but no one else. This information is included on the tape which controls the Selectronic® binding, and the advertiser reaches the target without waste circulation.

List Rental. *FJ* has created a profitable business in list rental by offering a variety of services to customers. Many of them involve some sort of a demographic overlay onto the customer's list.

For example, a manufacturer might need information in order to provide better dealer support. The manufacturer's dealer list is put into *FJ*'s database and a demographic analysis of the farm population in each dealer's trading territory is produced. After the customer has been provided with information about his own customer base, *FJ* can either develop a custom advertising program or provide assistance in a direct-mail effort or both.

Personalization. Selectronic® imaging allows ink-jet printing of personalized messages on demographic inserts. In addition, it is used to print a personal message requesting cooperation in the updating activity on circulation wraps when demographic information is being collected.

FJ's database and the uses that are being made of it are the result of years of investment and development. The payoff appears to have been realized in the current farm crisis. Despite the bad times in American agriculture, *Farm Journal* has remained prosperous.

Meeting the Special Challenges of Marketing Ethical Pharmaceuticals[13]

Our final example of a successful databased marketing program deals with the application of not only database technology but also one of the more recent

[13] This section is based on David Heaney and Dave Fish, "Integrating 'High Tech' into Your Marketing Operation," *Medical Marketing and Media*, October 1984, pp. 17-22.

hardware developments—the portable or lap-top personal computer—to meet a variety of marketing information needs and improve marketing programs. The problems (and opportunities) faced by this marketer of ethical pharmaceuticals are fundamentally the same as those encountered by many other marketers.

Ethical pharmaceuticals are sold by prescription only through channels of distribution that usually include wholesalers, drugstores, and health-care institutions. Physicians are key elements of the channels since they must prescribe the drugs.

Pharmaceuticals marketers have a number of problems that are common to large marketing operations:

- Centralized marketing management with geographically dispersed sales management and field sales representatives who work without direct supervision.
- Very large product lines, frequently containing thousands of individual products.
- Different market, competitive, and cost structures for different products or product lines, often resulting in wide variances in gross margins among products.
- Multiple channels of distribution with varying product and service requirements and often different levels of profitability.

In addition, the key role of the physician presents special problems:

- Physicians need information about new product introductions and new uses or information regarding existing products. They obtain some of this information from medical journals and at conferences, but the pharmaceutical sales rep (known as a *detail person*) is an important and highly credible source.
- Important as the detail person is as a source of information, physicians' busy schedules usually allow no more than 15 minutes for a sales call in which the detail person tries to present two or three products out of their total line.
- Since sales are made by drugstores or health-care institutions, it is difficult for the marketer to trace them to specific physicians. It is therefore especially difficult to measure the effectiveness of promotional activities, including detailing.

Several things were needed to increase the effectiveness of the overall marketing and sales operation of this ethical pharmaceutical manufacturer. All of them revolved around a centralized database that would store every contact—personal, mail, and so on—between the pharmaceutical firm and every physician, drugstore, health-care institution, and wholesaler with whom it did, or wished to do, business.

In developing the database, the pharmaceutical firm took special pains to deal with the problem of having a huge number of drugs to detail and very little time to detail them during each visit. Since a majority of physicians have specialized practices, each tends to prescribe a limited array of drugs. To identify this array for each physician in its database, the firm sent a questionnaire requesting this information to every physician it dealt with.

Over 75 percent of the physicians responded to the questionnaire. This unusually high response rate can be explained by the fact that physicians recognize the importance of receiving information on the drugs that figure prominently in their practice. Once the firm had this information in hand, it could detail the most heavily prescribed drugs to each physician and promote less heavily prescribed drugs by direct mail. Thus physicians receive only the information they need and do not have to contend with information about drugs they do not prescribe. This should help to create a very positive perception of the pharmaceutical firm.

In addition, the company's databased marketing system has one relatively unusual feature that undoubtedly will become much more common in the near future. Each detail person is equipped with a portable personal computer providing two-way communication between the detail person and the centralized database. The portable computer is plugged into a telephone each night, and at a pre-arranged time in the early-morning hours, it dials the main computer and sends and receives information. The detail person can send sales call data for inclusion in the database and messages to be delivered to electronic mailboxes. He or she can receive such information from the database as physician profiles (including prescription patterns), call reports and sales summaries, and messages from headquarters or local offices. The portable computer also allows the detail person to utilize software that provides information for territory management and call scheduling.

The depth and timeliness of the information provided to the detail people by this system is highly unusual outside the pharmaceutical industry. Unusual also is the currency of reports available to marketing and sales management. Reports that once were done on a weekly or monthly basis, and which became available long after the week or month had ended, are now available on a daily basis. Each manager can request necessary reports on his or her own computer terminal.

The information on which these reports are based seems to be more reliable also. It is much easier for the detail people to enter information on their portable pc's than it was to fill out the old paper forms. Moreover, the detail people know that since the information goes directly into the central database instead of to some office where it could be misplaced, it will always be available in time to affect management decisions.

Furthermore, the centralized database allows management to perform some analyses that were previously impossible. Company sales data at the zip code level can be compared with retail sales data supplied by outside sources such as Neilsen, providing a much more detailed picture of marketing effectiveness.

MANAGING INFORMATION

These three extended examples provide a fascinating glimpse of the potentiality of databased marketing to greatly improve existing marketing programs and to develop new ones. Lest it seem that applications like the ones described are a natural outcome of sophisticated technology, a word of caution is in order.

The road to effective use of marketing databases is littered with the skeletons of projects that either failed completely or failed to reach their full potential. Why should this be so?

There are as many specific reasons as specific projects, but there is clearly one overriding problem—a communications failure between marketers and information systems personnel. Representatives of the two functions neither speak the same language nor approach problems in the same manner.

Information systems people speak a language sprinkled with technical terminology and acronyms. Most managers lack the technical competence to decode this jargon. Worse still, many are so intimidated by it that they do not demand a clear, nontechnical presentation of the issues.

Technical specialists respond that managers must have a rudimentary knowledge of information systems and applications if they are to understand the issues involved. Many managers have not taken the time to become "computer literate."

Both sides are at fault, and both must take steps to remedy the situation. Many firms now require their managers to take computer training programs, not so they will become computer users, but so they will understand computer system and information management issues. Likewise, many information systems personnel are being given training in management. More important for the long term, most management students are now required to take at least one MIS course.

Improved training and communications may help bridge the gap between the long-term strategic orientation good managers bring to problem solving and the project orientation that is more common among technical personnel. Information is a strategic resource in today's world, and its development and management must be viewed from a strategic perspective.

There is no easy solution to the problems marketing managers and information systems specialists find in communicating with one another as they attempt to develop and implement effective databased marketing systems and programs. Alert students, recognizing both the problem and the potential, will prepare themselves to function well in a management environment where productive use of information is a requirement for success.

SUMMARY

The centralized marketing database is the focal point of the direct marketing operation and is an increasingly important element of the programs of general marketers. Marketing managers need to understand the tremendous potential databases have to help them develop more effective marketing programs and to target them more precisely. Although marketing managers will never be required to become technical experts, they will have to learn to be comfortable operating in a database environment.

DISCUSSION QUESTIONS

1. Explain, in your own words, the meaning of the term database.
2. How can a retail store use its customer database for marketing purposes?
3. Explain to the owner of a small business how to establish a database.
4. What does the statement, "Information is a strategic resource in today's world" mean? Do you agree or disagree with this statement?
5. For the next few days make a list of business activities you observe that could be providing information for marketing databases.

SUGGESTED ADDITIONAL READINGS

1. James, Martin, *An End-User's Guide to Data Base* (Englewood Cliffs, NJ: Prentice Hall, 1981).
2. Stan Rapp and Tom Collins, *MaxiMarketing* (New York: McGraw-Hill, 1987).
3. Roy Schwedelson, "New Wave Database," *Direct Marketing*, March 1988, pp. 40-41, 58.

7

The Process of Fulfillment

"The best copy, the best graphics, and the wisest choice of lists are all sheer waste of money, time, and talent if it is not followed through with really outstanding fulfillment." This quote by Robert Dorney[1] expresses many people's view of the importance of the process of fulfillment. Fulfillment has been defined in a variety of ways by different people, but all definitions have at their core the activities involved in fulfilling a customer's order after it has been received.

ELEMENTS OF FULFILLMENT

Some definitions of fulfillment encompass a larger circle of activities than others. The following list blends the most important elements contained in the various definitions:

1. Order-form issues
2. Receiving orders
   a. Mail orders
   b. Telephone orders
3. Processing of orders
4. Inventory policy
   a. Inventory costs
   b. Inventory management

[1]Robert D. Dorney, "Proper Fulfillment—Image with the Proper Stuff," *Direct Marketing*, July 1985, p. 28.

5. Warehousing issues
   a. Site selection/sizing/configuration
   b. Receiving
   c. Storing/stock location
   d. Picking
   e. Packing
   f. Shipping
6. Customer Service
7. Planning and control
   a. Data collection
   b. Standards
   c. Reports
   d. Plans

Any system that is designed to deliver goods has aspects of communication, inventory, warehousing, and transportation. Order-form issues and, in part, receiving orders are in the communication category: they involve a direct connection of some sort with the customer. The processing of orders initiates what is sometimes called *physical distribution* or *physical fulfillment*, a term that includes inventory, warehousing, and transportation issues. Customer service is another element of communication. Planning and control transcend this categorization and pertain to all aspects of fulfillment.

Some situations include a larger proportion of one aspect of fulfillment than of another. A magazine publishing operation may have no inventory or warehouse considerations (the magazines are sent from the printer directly to the customer), but may still have an extremely large concern with database management aspects of the order-processing element of fulfillment. To put fulfillment into perspective within the set of direct marketing activities, consider that what separates the "transactional" (selling) aspects of the direct marketing operation from most aspects of the fulfillment activities of a direct marketing operation is that the transactional aspects are essentially profit centers, while the fulfillment operations are primarily cost centers.

This perspective is useful, but still leaves unclarified whether database operations should be included as fulfillment activities. Katzenstein and Sachs take the position that they should not.[2] They use the example of an insurance company, and while acknowledging that extensive direct marketing takes place, they maintain that since the company does "not deliver tangible products, there is no physical distribution in the traditional sense, hence no fulfillment."[3]

[2]Herbert Katzenstein and William Sachs, *Direct Marketing* (Columbus, OH: Merrill Publishing Company, 1986).

[3]Katzenstein and Sachs, *Direct Marketing*, p. 397.

They go on to state: "Linking data base operations with physical distribution activities [i.e., calling both fulfillment] only heaps confusion on confusion."[4]

We will take the broader view in this chapter and consider fulfillment to include many database operations and some activities that take place prior to receiving an order (e.g., ensuring that order forms are clear to the customer and that perforations tear neatly), as well as the handling of inquiries and the planning and control function.

ORDER-FORM ISSUES

For every offering, products for sale must be numbered, different variations (color, size, etc.) must be distinguished, and other facts (payment method, shipping method, etc.) often need to be indicated. Therefore, consideration must be given to the design of the order form, not only so that the customer will clearly perceive all aspects of placing an order, but also so that errors will be reduced in the processing of orders by the seller. When customers think of "quality," they mean not only traditional product quality, but also the quality of service. One important aspect of service is timely order processing, and this may not be possible unless the order form and all instructions that pertain to it are clear and simple.

Whether or not order-form issues are officially considered part of the fulfillment process is not really important. Certainly, nobody would argue that the people concerned with fulfillment operations should be involved in the designing and writing of the order form. No reference is intended here to the core of the *creative* process, nor to such decisions as pricing, payment options, and delivery options. These issues are covered elsewhere in this text. Our sole concerns here are clarity and simplicity.

Clarity ensures that customers will know precisely what it is they are purchasing. *Simplicity* involves such devices as separated checkoff boxes (or their equivalent) for different sizes and colors and other variations, and a specific place with sufficient space for a clear capturing of the buyer's name and address. A great many order-processing errors result from incorrect capturing of buyers' names and addresses. This fact seems to be fostering increased use of preaddressed labels. An alternative that seems to decrease errors in capturing correct names and addresses is to provide an individual box for each and every letter and number to be written (along with an instruction to please type or print).

What we have said so far pertains to mail orders. For telephone orders, the problems involve voice clarity and correct verbal transmission.

[4]Katzenstein and Sachs, *Direct Marketing*, p. 397.

RECEIVING ORDERS

In the early days of direct marketing, nearly all orders were received by mail. Most current solicitations give customers a choice between mailing or phoning in an order. In recent years, the percentage of orders that come in by phone has been increasing, dramatically for large mail-order firms. At Sears, over 85 percent of the orders are received by phone. The ease of obtaining low-cost 800 (toll-free) numbers is the dominant reason for this trend.

Mail Orders

Orders are not the only mail that a direct marketing firm receives. Hence, the first step in dealing with incoming mail is to sort it into categories. One possible set of categories is by function. For example:

1. Payments
2. Orders
3. Other correspondence

Another possible set of categories is by size. For example:

1. Postcard size
2. Standard-size preaddressed material (usually for orders)
3. Other sizes

Whichever category contains payments should be subdivided into different forms of payment. For cash payments, special logging-in procedures should be used to ensure adherence to laws pertaining to cash transactions (e.g., if product delivery will not take place within the allowable 30 days, the customer has to be informed and given the option to cancel the order) and to maintain supervision and security. For credit card payments, validation procedures must be undertaken for transactions exceeding a certain amount (this amount varies by firm). Once the transaction is validated, a set of procedures for logging the charge and transferring funds from the credit card agency to the firm is put into effect. Every firm has to have a policy concerning the clearing of personal checks. The time needed for check clearing adds a relatively large amount to the turnaround time of an order, and needs careful monitoring.

There are machines, which can be bought or rented, that slit envelopes; some even use suction to remove the contents from the envelope. There are other machines that imprint checks and enhance quick check processing. One way or another, the mail orders need to be separated from the rest of the mail and be readied for order processing, and mail payments need to be separated by form of payment and sent on their respective paths of collection.

Telephone Orders

The ideal is to have order-taking telephone lines answered 24 hours per day. If this is not economic, a decision has to be made whether to have an answering machine in use during off-hours.

A good telephone-order program retains the best aspects of ordering by mail: a written record of the buyer's name, address, and choice of product; payment method (with correct credit card information, if applicable); and other supporting information. The person who takes the call records all this information directly onto a regular order form, or preferably, a mock order form on a computer terminal, (the latter avoids handwriting errors). Answering machines present a problem because they do not permit the resolution of ambiguity, which would, presumably, be revealed through the two-way communication process of live order taking.

When a customer calls The Sharper Image, the initial contact is a recording that asks the caller to dial a certain single digit if the purpose of the call is to place an order. This separates out the order-giving calls from the remaining calls (the latter follow different routes). Once this digit is dialed, a person comes on the line and solicits the information required on the order form. Each order taker has an on-site terminal in front of him or her into which the information is entered (typed). As each piece of information is given by the buyer, it is repeated by the order taker to ensure correct vocal transmission. When the product information is given by item number, the order taker states the item description (which appears on the terminal a moment after the item number is entered). At the end of the entire order, the order taker reiterates all the information entered into the computer and asks the caller to confirm that it is correct.

Whether a firm uses this system of entering the order into a computer while the caller is still on the telephone, or a system whereby the information is recorded onto an order form for later entry into the computer, the situation at this point is the same as that reached when the order is received by mail and then entered into the computer. (If there is no computer involved in the order-taking process, the order entry takes place in an analogous way.)

PROCESSING ORDERS

The first step in order processing has in many ways merged with the order-receiving process. In processing a mail order, the initial step is to enter it onto the computer. The same is true for a telephone order, although, as we have seen, the trend is to log it on the computer while taking down the customer's information. After the order is entered into the computer, the remaining steps of order processing depend on what the computer is programmed to do with the order data.

Ideally, the computer now performs a variety of parallel tasks. Customer files are checked to see if the customer made previous purchases or was for some other reason (e.g., made an inquiry) already in the database. During this task, the computer can also be performing a credit check (if past data are available), and updating the customer's record if his or her name is already in the database, or entering the name with accompanying purchase information in the database if the name is new. If the dollar size of the order is sufficiently large, the computer can conduct an outside credit check. If payment was via personal check, the name/order may be sent to a holding file, to be uploaded to the main order file when bank verification is received. (Note that customer file maintenance has a longer-range purpose than processing the immediate order. It can supply current records whenever management wants to analyze the house list, rent it out, or generate reports based on it.)

Either simultaneously with, or just after receiving the results of the credit check, inventory files record decrements for the items ordered and any stockouts noted (plus any action taken with respect to customer notification). In a more sophisticated system, not only the items ordered, but also the inventory of boxes and/or other required packaging will be decremented. Depending on the size of the item(s) and mode of transportation (delivery), even an allocated slot within the delivery system could be decremented.

Concurrently, the computer will generate for the warehouse hard copy of picking documents and shipping labels, as well as invoices to accompany the order. Notification of other offerings is usually included with the order. Many direct marketers believe that the accuracy and promptness of the hard-copy portion of order processing is the key to timely and proficient fulfillment.

INVENTORY POLICY

Even if the number of orders equals or (even better) exceeds expectations, and even if each order has a delightfully high contribution, there will be no immediate benefit—in fact, there may ultimately be a loss—if the item(s) ordered are not in stock. If the customer cancels the order because he or she thinks there has been an unreasonable delay in shipment, there is an actual loss attributable to administrative costs, plus an opportunity loss attributable to forgone profit. Even if the customer does not cancel the order and the item is ultimately shipped, costs may be increased because, for example, the stockout item had to be shipped in a separate package instead of as part of a multi-item order.

The general concepts of inventory policy are similar in all inventory environments. In some cases, the inventory to be managed relates mostly to raw materials; in other cases, to goods in process; in yet other cases, to finished goods. Our discussion envisions a finished-goods environment where, in essence, items are being resold to mail- or phone-order customers. It is an equivalent situation when a traditional retailing company sells by direct marketing: the company "buys" the finished goods from itself and "resells" them to the customer.

Inventory Costs

As is true of many marketing decisions, the inventory decision primarily involves balancing different costs. These are (1) stockout costs, (2) order costs, and (3) carrying costs.

Stockout costs are the costs associated with not having an item in stock at the moment it is needed. This item may be on order, meaning there will be a "lead time" between the placement of the replenishment order and its actual delivery, or not yet ordered, meaning there will be an even longer wait for replenishment. Stockout costs were mentioned earlier in terms of increased shipping costs and lost sales (when a customer cancels an order). The opportunity loss of a stockout is a difficult value to arrive at. Will a specific customer cancel his or her order? If the customer cancels this order, will that customer also refuse to place any more orders with the firm? What is the value of future orders lost this way? Because of all these uncertainties, the opportunity loss part of the stockout cost must be looked at in a probabilistic way and expressed as an "expected value" or average value. Even then, the value arrived at is not very robust. After all, there aren't many data around on what people buy in a lifetime (or, in this case, would have bought in a lifetime but didn't).

Order costs refer to costs that are proportional to the number of orders, without regard to order size. These would be such costs as paperwork, the fixed-cost portion of telephone calls, materials handling, and certain transportation costs. It is not easy to arrive at the specific value of the order cost. What is the cost of somebody's time filling out paperwork if that person is on salary? Nobody would say that it's zero, even though it may result in no incremental cash outlay. Certainly, a significant portion of the order cost can be determined only by an allocation of fixed costs, and most allocations of fixed cost are somewhat arbitrary. Nevertheless, a ballpark figure can be determined.

Carrying costs involve such costs as warehouse rental, capital cost (i.e., forgone interest), insurance premiums, any taxes levied on inventory, and costs due to deterioration, pilferage, and obsolescence. In other words, a carrying cost is any cost that varies proportionally with the average or maximum level of inventory. All of the carrying costs mentioned above are at least approximately proportional to the average inventory level, except for the warehouse rental cost, which often is proportional to the maximum level of inventory.

Inventory Management

Inventory policy is primarily concerned with determining, for each item, the answer to two basic questions:

1. How often should we order the item to be replenished?
2. What quantity should we order?

There are two basic systems for managing inventory; the Q system and the P system. Under the Q system, the amount to be ordered is fixed (i.e., the same for every order), but the time between orders varies. In other words, whenever the inventory level falls to a predetermined level, an order is placed. The amount that should be ordered each time so as to minimize total inventory-related costs is called the *economic order quantity* or EOQ. What level of inventory will trigger a reorder depends upon the lead time for the order to be delivered, as well as on the expected demand pattern during the lead time.

Under the P system of managing inventory, the time between orders is fixed; it is the amount ordered each time that varies. The inventory level at the trigger time is noted, and an order is placed for that quantity that will bring the level up to a predetermined amount. This amount depends on lead time and demand during lead time.

Each system has certain advantages and disadvantages. The Q system requires much closer monitoring of the inventory levels. Usually, high-priced items are good candidates for the Q system, since they tend to be closely monitored anyway. Indeed, the advantage of the Q system is that it generally requires less *safety stock*, or buffer inventory (the difference between what is on hand and what is expected to be demanded before replenishment). This buffer inventory is a positive value (as opposed to being zero) because of the stockout cost discussed earlier in this section. The optimal level of safety stock is determined by the relative cost of a stockout. Of course, a lower level of safety stock with the same probability of stockout means a lower overall carrying cost without other costs increasing.

Entire texts have been written on the subject of inventory policy. Precise treatment depends upon such questions as whether lead time for delivery of an order is variable or fixed, whether or not demand is reasonably constant over time, whether quantity discounts are available, and some other product-specific issues. Detailed treatment of this material is beyond the purpose of this text.

In an environment with a very large number of items inventory policy will often lump together groups of items, so as not to have to actually monitor each and every item with respect to EOQ and/or reorder times. Sometimes it is useful to institute an A, B, C system in which there are different classes of items and all that fall within a class are treated alike. The most popular classification is by the magnitude of an item's carrying cost. An item's carrying cost, in turn, is usually closely related to its wholesale or retail price—a fact that makes items easy to classify.

Ideally, a firm does ongoing demand forecasting so that inventory management can take place in a maximally informed environment.

WAREHOUSING ISSUES

The core of what is usually referred to as *physical fulfillment* involves all the activities connected to the warehouse operations. This set of activities begins with the *receiving* of incoming items at the warehouse.[5] After the received items are processed, their *storing* in the warehouse takes place and the location is noted for later reference. When an order comes in for one or more items, the next step is *picking* and gathering the items from their respective locations. The items then need *packing*. Finally, the package needs *shipping*. We will discuss each of these activities.

In a start-up situation, of course, all of these activities are preceded by consideration of where to locate the warehouse, its size (volume), and its dimensions. These start-up issues can be very complex. We will discuss them only briefly, from the perspective of the different costs and other considerations that must be traded off. This perspective should give you some insight into the activities of physical fulfillment.

Site Selection/Sizing/Configuration

When it comes to choosing a *site* for one or more warehouses, the main factors that need considering are of two types. One type concerns the macro location of the facility (e.g., which quadrant of which state); the other type concerns the particular site within that location. In most cases, a warehousing operation will involve more than one location. Many times, the total area being served is broken down into separate territories, each to contain one warehouse. Thus each warehouse is able to be independently located within a territory. We then have several so-called single-warehouse-location problems. The basic objective is to choose locations that minimize incoming and outgoing transportation costs. This, of course, requires knowing or forecasting points of origin of demand. The choice of the individual site involves a trade-off between the costs of land rental or purchase, real estate and other taxes, and such factors as adequacy of utilities, community attitude, and potential for expansion.

The *size* of the warehouse refers to its volume. Determining a minimum size is a complicated issue affected by many factors, such as the materials-handling system employed, the (anticipated) throughput of volume per time period, and the particular unit size of the items stored (beyond the total throughput volume). Certainly, the lower limit on minimum required size is the anticipated maximum volume of inventory.

The *configuration* of the warehouse first involves determining the ceiling height. Here there is a trade-off between construction and equipment costs and materials-handling costs. Once the height is determined, the next step is to decide on the best length and width, assuming the product of the two (the area) is fixed. That is, should the warehouse be a square, or if not, which particular rectangular shape should it be? This determination involves a trade-off between materials-handling costs and perimeter construction costs. It also involves consideration of dock requirements and design.

[5]The term *warehouse* is being used here to denote a generic storage location.

Now you can see why start-up issues are complex. We will assume for the rest of this section that the warehouse already exists with a definite size and configuration.

Receiving

Items arrive at the warehouse from a variety of sources. They have to be logged in, they have to be inspected for quantity and possibly quality, and they have to be stored. The basic objectives are to record arrivals accurately, to be able to easily and quickly call up an item's location, and to minimize subsequent handling of items either for purposes of relocation or retrieval for shipment.

The issues involved in receiving items at a warehouse are really no different from those involved in receiving food deliveries at a restaurant or office supplies at a work station. In all these other situations one must be concerned about the receiving workers' purposeful recording of incorrect amounts of goods received, as well as about security during the receiving process.

Storing/Stock Location

Once goods are received at the warehouse, they must be stored. The particular choice among storing units (e.g., various types of shelving and racks) and the related lift equipment will depend on the size and configuration of the warehouse. A firm or division whose prime focus is on direct marketing should rely on the advice of a person with warehousing experience when making these choices because they are more qualitative than others considered in this section.

The issue of stock *location* is more amenable to analytical resolution. Indeed, it is so appropriate for quantitative analysis that it has been the subject of a great deal of attention in the literature over the past 20 years, including the *Harvard Business Review* and the very quantitative journal *Management Science*.[6] There have been three approaches to determining stock location: intuitive, heuristic, and algorithmic.

The *intuitive approach* basically involves two criteria: (1) more popular items are located nearer the outbound point (i.e., the higher the item's turnover rate, the nearer the item's storage location is to the outbound point), (2) items are located according to size (i.e., the smaller the size, the nearer the item's storage location is to the outbound point. This strategy results in the largest number of items being near the outbound point). A third criterion, used on occasion, is a blend of the first two: the distance from the outbound point is rank-ordered by the ratio of volume to turnover. The larger the ratio, the nearer to the outbound point the item is stored. This criterion would rank two items equally if one item had half the turnover of the other, but also half the volume of the other. None of these criteria

[6]The first discussion of stock location in the marketing literature was Ronald M. Ballou, "Improving the Physical Layout of Merchandise in Warehouses," *Journal of Marketing*, *31* (1967), p. 67.

guarantees an optimal solution in terms of cost and time minimization, but they are superior to having no system at all for choice of location.

The *heuristic approach* implicitly recognizes the difficulty of finding a truly optimal solution. A heuristic is a rule that has been shown empirically to often result in a solution not too far from the optimal solution, but with much less computational time (and therefore less expense) than needed to find the optimal solution.[7]

The third type of approach to this problem of warehouse or facility layout is the *algorithmic approach*. An algorithmic solution usually refers to a rule (most often mathematical) for solving a problem that results in an *optimal* solution in accordance with some predetermined criterion. For the problem at hand, the usual methodology proposed is in the linear programming or graph theory family. Using this approach almost always requires high-speed computer facilities and very accurate knowledge or forecast of demand.

In the direct marketing environment, where the products being sold and/or the demand patterns are often undergoing modest if not continual change, either an intuitive or a heuristic approach to warehouse layout is warranted.

Picking

Picking the individual items and combining them to make up the full order is an operation second in labor intensity only to the packing operation. Some of the decisions to be made in the picking operation are similar to those required in other multi-item order environments. We are all familiar with the ordering process for a traditional fast-food operation. Imagine that there are four registers and four workers, each qualified to work the register and/or to actually "pick" the order (gather all ordered foods and drinks together). Should management assign two workers to be register persons only and two to be pickers only, or should there be four registers operating, each worker being both a register person and a picker, in sequence? If there are two register persons and two pickers, should a specific picker work only with a specific register person? This set of issues is usually analyzed and decided on the criterion of minimization of "expected time to (customer's) receipt of order."

In the warehouse environment the choice set is analogous. Should one person pick an entire order (individual order pick)? Or should different people be assigned to pick different sets of products or in different areas of the warehouse, all meeting at some central point? The answers to these questions depend on a variety of considerations, many of which are dealt with in the queuing theory and simulation literature.

[7]An early heuristic model was C. R. A. F. T. (Computerized Relative Allocation of Facilities Technique), discussed, among other places, in E. Buffa, G. Armour, and T. Vollman, "Allocating Facilities with CRAFT," *Harvard Business Review*, Vol. 42, April 1964. Other, more recent heuristics are noted in D. Bowersox, *Logistical Management*, 2nd ed. (New York: MacMillan, 1978); and D. Lambert and J. Stock, *Strategic Physical Distribution Management* (Homewood, IL: Irwin, 1982).

Packing

Packing is the most labor-intensive of the physical fulfillment activities. It includes the boxing and packaging of individual items, boxing the different items in an order together, wrapping the order, and addressing or labeling the order. Sometimes items that are received at the warehouse need to be individually packaged, (often referred to as *prepackaging*). This packing of individual items can be done at the time of the item's arrival at the warehouse, at the time of the item's inclusion in an order, or at slack times (whether planned or not). The decision will depend upon the predictability of the demand for other labor activities, as well as on such issues as how fragile an item is and the degree to which it is susceptible to spoilage.

The packing of an order often involves an assembly line. The particular division of labor (separation into different stations along the assembly line) may vary from one warehouse to another, but the following sequence is typical:

1. Check individual items to see if the order is correctly constituted and that each item is properly packaged.
2. Stuff the items together into a premade carton or other type of container and seal the carton.
3. Wrap the carton.
4. Label or otherwise address the package, and dispatch it to the shipping area for stamping/metering and the beginning of the delivery process.

Shipping

The final element in the physical distribution part of fulfillment is getting the package delivered to the customer. Most packages sent to consumers (as opposed to business-to-business transactions) by direct marketers weigh under 50 pounds and are often called *parcels*. Delivery of these parcels is usually arranged through United Parcel Service (UPS); a Direct Marketing Association survey in the early 1980s showed that 90 percent of the responding catalog mail order companies shipped with UPS, using UPS for 97 percent of their packages. Other delivery possibilities are the U.S. Postal Service (USPS) and Federal Express and similar private services. Some firms truck their packages from their warehouse to various post offices to qualify for local zone parcel post rates. Parcel post can be used for packages that do not qualify for UPS because of their size, weight, or location.

Some warehouse operations are large enough in volume to have UPS or USPS trucks either pick up at the warehouse or station a trailer there. In fact, some warehouses actually contain USPS facilities (i.e., a post office).

CUSTOMER SERVICE

If all the fulfillment elements we have covered thus far were always carried out perfectly, and if no customer ever misunderstood the conditions of an offer and never changed his or her mind, and if all products were of top quality and never got damaged en route, shipping would be the end of the transaction. In the real world, however, there are returns, lost and damaged shipments, missing and incorrect items in a shipment, and various other complaints, whether justified or not. These result in additional contact with the customer after the order is sent out. Handling these issues is a major part of what is called customer service.

The exact definition of, and duties covered by, customer service will vary both by company and by customer, but there is general agreement that customer service contains three basic components:

1. The timing of deliveries
2. The availability of the product
3. The quality of the delivery

The *timing of deliveries* has been alluded to previously. If deliveries are not timely, the customer may decide to cancel the order and the company will forfeit the corresponding profit. Orders that were purchased on impulse are more likely to be canceled if delivery is not timely. Also, certain costs are incurred if, under the law, customers must be notified when delivery will be delayed more than a given amount of time.

If a *product* is not *available* when ordered, this stockout will cause a delay in delivery. Also, extra costs may be incurred because of the need for separate delivery of and paperwork for the items not in stock. There is often tension between the people in the firm who want to realize cost reductions through reduced inventories and those who are responsible for traditional fulfillment.

The *quality of the delivery* refers to the arrival of the correct items in the correct colors, size, and so forth, as well as to the condition of the goods upon arrival. The costs and benefits of this component of customer service are qualitative, but surely any reasonable cost is warranted to ensure the maximum possible delivery quality.

Takeuchi and Quelch report that L. L. Bean has a successful customer-driven quality program.[8] A testimonial to the program is the fact that about 97 percent of a sample of 3,000 customers, when asked what they liked most about the company, listed "quality." Here are some of the things Bean reportedly does to enhance customer service:

[8]H. Takeuchi and J. Quelch, "Quality Is More Than Making a Good Product," *Harvard Business Review*, July 1983, pp. 139–145.

- They conduct regular customer satisfaction surveys.
- They track all customer complaints by computer.
- They guarantee a full refund if the customer is not 100 percent satisfied.
- They ask customers to fill out a short form telling why they are returning goods.

An increasingly prevalent view of the role of customer service in mail-order operations is that excellent customer service will not compensate for an inferior product, but that inferior customer service can nullify a terrific product. This view certainly suggests having a pro-active customer service program. Berry and Cooper list the following four steps to follow when developing a customer service program:[9]

1. Define the elements of customer service
2. Perceive the customer viewpoint
3. Design a competitive package
4. Establish performance controls

Step 1 involves determining what constitutes customer service: it includes, in one way or another, most of the fulfillment elements mentioned in this chapter. Step 2 calls for envisioning the benefits customers will realize from the elements of Step 1. Step 3 involves doing a cost-benefit analysis of the different elements of Step 1 and making the necessary trade-offs. In Step 4 a specific activity is names (e.g., shipping), a measure of performance, or MOP, is specified (e.g., delivery time from the warehouse to any household in continental United States), and a standard of performance, or SOP, is set up (e.g., 99 percent of orders will be delivered within 5 days, except during the Christmas season).

A critical aspect of a firm's customer service operations is its process for handling inquiries. Inquiries are made daily by potential customers who want information about products, warranties, costs, and other issues. Mail inquiries of this type must be separated from orders during the mail-sorting process. A similar sorting process is done for telephone inquiries.

The importance of inquiry handling for the direct marketing firm is twofold. First, for some inquirers, the decision whether to become a customer ("convert") will depend not only on the substance of the information received but also on the quality of the service received in response to the inquiry. Second, an efficient inquiry-handling system reduces the turnaround time for responding to an inquiry, which is very important when most sales are generated by leads that are followed up by sales telephone calls or visits, and improves the presorting of hot leads from dead ends.

Nobody has claimed that establishing and maintaining a customer service program is easy. It is feasible, however, if management realizes that customer service is no longer the sole purview of the manufacturing/operations group and

[9]D. Berry and S. Cooper, "Improve Company Operations with Quality Control System," *Direct Marketing*, 47 (1984), 50–60.

"quality" is not limited in meaning to product quality. Only when quality is equated with customer service, and thus made a co-responsibility of the marketing function, will true success be achieved in the company's mission.

PLANNING AND CONTROL

It should be clear to you by now that a direct marketing operation involves many different functions and requires many different skills. Each of these functions has its own need for planning and control. Basically, *planning* is the activity of looking ahead to where you want to go and setting goals, while *control* is the activity of knowing where you are and measuring your growth toward these goals. There is usually one overall planning and control process for all the different elements of the fulfillment function, because of the need to treat this set of elements as a system to be globally optimized. For example, planning and controlling inventory management can be properly performed only in conjunction with planning for warehouse space, as well as with planning and control of stock location and virtually all the other physical fulfillment functions.

The planning and control process requires careful data collection and report generation. At a minimum, data are needed, by item, concerning sales, inventory, returns, customer service, credit, billing, and quality control. Data in these areas are broken down into operating statistics (e.g., daily number of orders received, weekly number of customer complaints, average number of days from order receipt to order shipping) and operating costs. Then the data are evaluated for degree of compliance with labor and other standards.

Data Collection

The operating statistics and operating costs should be collected by utilization of a software system, either one purchased off the shelf or one tailored to the particular fulfillment system. General information like the number of orders received should probably be collected on a daily basis. For some item-specific data, daily collection is called for; while for others, weekly or perhaps less frequent collection is sufficient, depending on the type of inventory policy employed and the turnover rate of individual items. Cost data should probably be tabulated over a somewhat longer time than sales related data.

Standards

Collecting and inspecting data would have little benefit unless there is a way of knowing what are "low numbers" and "high numbers," "good performances" and "bad performances." That is the reason for setting standards against which collected data can be sensibly compared.

Two types of standards are possible. One is a set of standards specific to the mail-order operation of a specific firm, the other a set of standards conceived as necessary for the long-run success of any mail-order business. Initially (before any data is available) firm/product specific standards must be estimated from knowledge of similar situations or firms. Soon, however, there are enough data to allow determination of reasonable standards for such things as time required to perform a task, proportion of items ordered that require backlogging, proportion of orders for which not every item is in stock, time from order processing to shipping, and time from shipping to receiving.

When the objective is to collect data on how long it takes workers to perform a given task, the process is called *work measurement*. There are formulas that tell us what sample size is required (i.e., how many times we need to time the duration of a task), and there is a vast literature on such issues as obtaining a random sample and margins of error. (Some of these formulas are discussed in Chapter 8 in a slightly different context.) A similar procedure is used for establishing standards for other metric quantities that do not, strictly speaking, come under "work measurement" (e.g., delivery time for an order once shipped, average number of items per order).

When the object is to collect data on the proportion of time a group of workers is engaged in a certain activity or set of activities, the process is called *work sampling*. A prominent example of work sampling is setting standards for the proportion of time workers engage in direct labor, indirect labor, and break times. This is a relevant notion for many aspects of a warehouse operation, and the literature abounds with formulas for required sample size and other useful considerations. (Again, Chapter 8 contains some related discussion.) Steps involved in establishing standards for other categorical quantities (i.e., proportions) that are not, strictly speaking, labor-related (e.g., proportion of items ordered that are not in stock when the order is received) are quite similar to the procedures of formal work sampling.

Standards that pertain to the mail-order business or industry as a whole are of a different nature. These are basically a combination of the results of industry surveys and the opinions of experts. Typical standards are: "A customer should receive a response to written correspondence by the next calendar week," "No more than 4 percent of orders should be back-ordered," and "Customers should receive an order within 21 business days from phoning it in." These statements should be thought of as goals to be striven for; if they are not considered achievable, there should be identifiable reasons why not.

Reports

For purposes of control, we develop standards and collect data to compare with the standards (and possibly to use for continual revision of standards). The comparisons can take many forms. Control charts (x-bar charts, R-charts, p-charts, pn-charts, c-charts, and u-charts) are often used to study performances over time. They are especially geared for identification of trends. Many times, the objective is to monitor a process and to flag *only* when something is amiss or when an "outlier" or "unusual observation" occurs. This concept, usually referred to as exception reporting, saves lots of paperwork and yet keeps management informed whenever its attention is required.

Planning

The planning process must consider three notions: (1) a description of what has happened in the past (most of the preceding discussion focused on this); (2) a delineation of what is expected to happen in the future, assuming no action is taken to change anything; and (3) a determination of what the planners (management) *want* to happen. The first notion can be used to establish the relationship between input variables and output variables. The second notion concerns the extrapolation of this relationship for future values of input variables. The third notion involves a comparison of the projected values of the output variables with what management has concluded it would like the values to be, an examination of the cost required to bridge the gap, and a cost-benefit or risk-reward analysis to determine whether to continue toward the goal.

USING AN OUTSIDE CONTRACTOR FOR FULFILLMENT SERVICES

Most people would agree that business operations are becoming more and more specialized. This trend is apparent in direct marketing operations. A larger and larger number of direct marketing firms (or direct marketing divisions of firms) are hiring outside contractors to perform their fulfillment operations.

Thomas Litle, president of Direct Order Sales Corporation of Nashua, New Hampshire, has listed the following significant advantages of hiring an outside contractor:[10]

1. It enables the hiring firm to concentrate on what it presumably does best—marketing and merchandising.
2. Fulfillment costs can be treated by the hiring firm as variable costs. These costs are then more predictable, and net profits will not vary so much with volume (and the firm will be exposed to less downside risk).
3. The hiring firm will have access to the best fulfillment software, which it otherwise might not be able to justify economically even if it has the personnel to take advantage of it.
4. The hiring firm will likely receive equivalent fulfillment services for a cost per order lower than the in-house cost per order.

The main disadvantage of hiring an outside contractor to perform the fulfillment function is loss of control and potential leaks of proprietary information.

[10]Thomas Litle, *Integrating Product and Management Information Fulfillment Operations for Profit*, Direct Marketing Association Manual Release 1400.3, July 1984.

Though direct marketing firms that have hired outside contractors for fulfillment services are still in the minority, this is surely an option that will receive increasing attention in the future. Selecting the right outside fulfillment contractor could have an impact on profits equal to that of other, more mainstream direct marketing activities.

SUMMARY

Effective fulfillment involves many different skills and requires balancing many different considerations. Nash lists the following four extreme "philosophies" of fulfillment and customer service:[11]

1. "Stop the deadbeats." (Giving highest priority to credit checking and the like, regardless of the resulting delays, cancellations, etc.)
2. "The customer is always right." (Giving highest priority to doing whatever the customer wishes, extending credit to everyone without a credit check, providing refunds without checking receipts, etc.)
3. "Cost efficiency *uber alles*." (Giving highest priority to cost minimization, regardless of customer service, delivery quality, etc.)
4. "A rolling stone gathers no moss." (Giving highest priority to maximizing turnover, regardless of costs, customer service, etc.)

A superior fulfillment operation is one that finds the right blend of these extreme philosophies, which correspond to the four key considerations of payment, customer service, cost, and sales volume.

An overview of the flow of the fulfillment process from the receipt of the order from the customer to the shipping of the order to the customer, along with the customer service and planning and control support activities, can be seen in Figure 7.1. Orders by mail and telephone are received and processed; payment issues are attended to and the central database is then notified about the particulars of the order. Warehouse documents are generated and the order is picked, packed, and shipped to the customer, and the inventory file in the central database is updated. Items are received from suppliers and stored in the warehouse; the inventory file is appropriately updated. Customer service activities are available to interact with the system; the planning and control functions are gathering data, generating reports, and monitoring the overall fulfillment process.

[11]Edward L. Nash, *Direct Marketing* (New York: McGraw Hill, 1982), pp. 378–380.

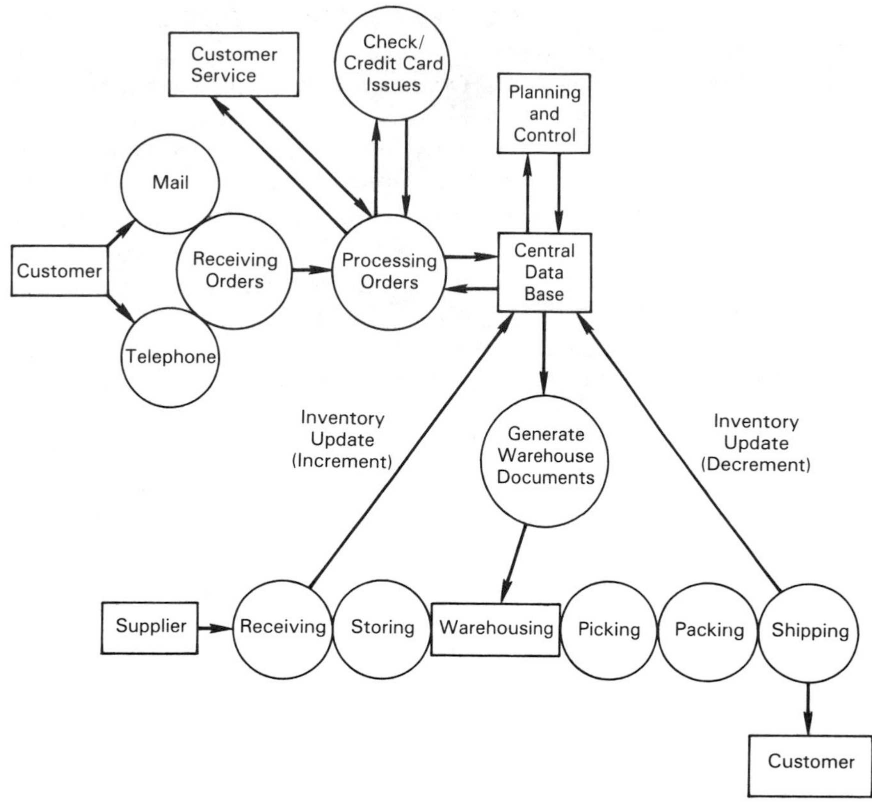

FIGURE 7.1 ***Flow of Fulfillment Process***

DISCUSSION QUESTIONS

1. Describe situations in which fulfillment operations are (a) relatively more important, and (b) relatively less important.
2. Why is there an increasing trend for the order taker, when taking orders on the telephone, to ask for the caller's telephone number?
3. Describe situations in direct marketing when demand patterns are (a) relatively more quick to change, and (b) relatively more stable.
4. What are the merits of the different options for organizing the picking operation in a warehouse with regard to security?
5. Suppose that individual items making up an order are stored in different warehouses. What are the various costs that must be considered in deciding whether to send out the items in separate packages versus arranging for the items to be sent together in one package?

SUGGESTED ADDITIONAL READING

1. L. Berry, V. Zeithaml, and A. Parasuraman, "Quality Counts in Service, Too," *Business Horizons*, May-June 1985, pp. 44–52.
2. G. Churchill and C. Suprenant, "An Investigation into the Determinants of Customer Satisfaction," *Journal of Marketing Research, 19* (November 1982), 491–504.
3. James Dilworth, *Production and Operations Management*, 3rd ed. (New York: Random House, 1986)
4. Christian Gronroos, "A Service Quality Model and Its Marketing Implications," *European Journal of Marketing, 18*, 4 , 36–44.
5. Robert McCoy, "Electronic Order Exchange Links Warehouse With Clients," *Direct Marketing*, September 1986, pp. 64–66.

8

Testing Direct-Mail Campaigns

REASONS FOR TESTING

Throughout this book you have read frequent references to the fact that direct marketing is the *measurable* element of the marketing discipline. This chapter covers another aspect of the measurability of direct marketing—the testing of direct-mail campaigns.

The basic philosophy of testing, as espoused by direct marketers, is a straightforward and very appealing one. Put simply, there is no reason to invest a large amount of resources in a direct-mail program unless there is a high probability of success. Because direct marketers have control over both outbound communication to their customers and prospects (how many pieces are mailed and to whom) and inbound communication from customers and prospects (responses), they are able to estimate that probability of success with a high degree of accuracy. Marketing effort can then be allocated to programs with the highest expected value, monetary or otherwise.

You may already have begun to realize that concepts from basic statistics courses will be important in studying direct-mail testing. Concepts that you have already learned, but perhaps have not applied to marketing situations, will be covered in this chapter. In addition, ideas about experimental design that are only briefly mentioned in most marketing research courses will be introduced and applied to direct marketing testing situations.

Much of the material in this chapter is based on lecture notes from QM 887—Experimental Design, a course developed and taught by Paul D. Berger at the Graduate School of Management, Boston University, and from the Direct Marketing Management Development Program.

THE NATURE OF DIRECT MARKETING TESTING

There is universal agreement among direct marketers about the importance of testing. Unfortunately, there is far less consensus about testing procedure and decision criteria. The approach we will take in this chapter combines elements of classical statistics, statistical decision theory, and financial analysis.

We can set forth three simple rules for developing effective tests:

1. All tests should be measured against the criterion of expected profit.
2. Decisions about the content of the test (which variables to test, when to conduct the test, for what period of time, etc.) should be based on sound marketing judgment.
3. Decisions about the design of the test (sample size, experimental design, choice and interpretation of analytical procedures, and selection of the "winning" variable or combination of variables) should be based on statistical theory.

Consider for a moment a possible situation: comparing the profitability of a high-margin, low-response-rate product with that of a low-margin, high-response-rate product. Without numbers we cannot be sure which one we would rather have, but we can be sure that we do not wish to make our decision based *on response rate alone.* With these rules as our guides, we can follow the procedure shown in Figure 8.1 for carrying out a test.

Before we examine the testing process in detail, however, we need to understand the concept of a "control" in direct marketing tests. The *control* is the package that thus far has performed best for the direct marketer. That package becomes the standard against which all other direct-mail campaigns are measured. The package is used without change until it is clearly beaten by another package. The winning package then becomes the control for future tests.

This seems to be, and indeed is, a very simple concept. However, designing, conducting, and analyzing results of tests to accurately determine the winner (the control package or the test package) is a complex subject, one to which we will devote the next section of the chapter.

THE TESTING PROCESS

Choose the Test Criterion

The first step is to choose the test criterion—the basis on which the results of the test will be compared. You will see many examples in which response rate is the chosen criterion. While response rate is undeniably important, it is not the direct marketer's real objective. Remember that we have established as one of our rules of testing that "all tests should be measured against the criterion of expected profit."

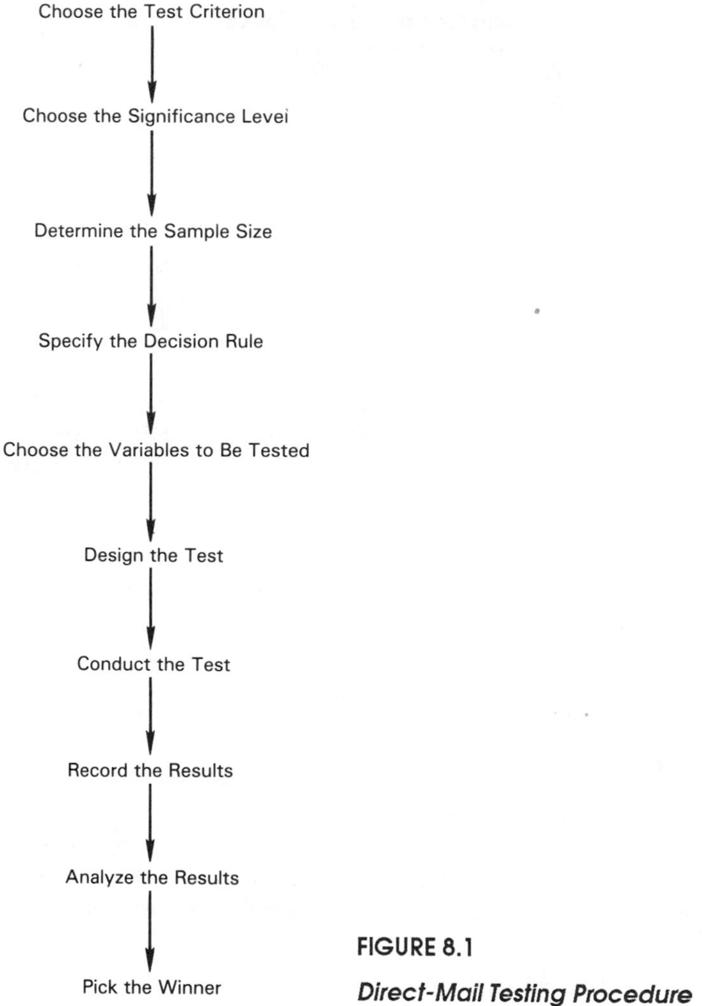

FIGURE 8.1

Direct-Mail Testing Procedure

In this chapter we will treat the criterion as if it were simply the profitability per customer of a single mailing. Actually, in a direct marketing environment we should compute the long-term value of a customer. That is often a fairly complex calculation,which is discussed in detail in Chapter 15.

We should remember, however, that the test criterion used in this chapter is an oversimplification of the concept of expected profitability over the life of the customer relationship.

Let us assume that we are testing a subscription-acquisition mailing for a newsletter. A simplified statement of the revenues and costs of this newsletter, on a per-subscriber basis, is shown in Table 8.1.

TABLE 8.1 Single-Subscriber Revenues and Costs—Newsletter Example

Subscription revenue (1-year subscription)	$10.00
Fulfillment cost (printing and mailing)	5.00
Gross margin	5.00
Average subscriber-acquisition cost	2.50
Operating costs	1.50
NET PROFIT BEFORE TAXES	1.00

To keep our example as simple as possible, we will use subscriber-acquisition cost as the test criterion. We can justify using acquisition cost instead of profitability in this instance because it appears to be the only cost likely to vary across customers, and therefore to affect profitability.

Response rate can be justified as equivalent to profitability when both *cost per person mailed* and *revenue per responder (customer)* are the same for all. An example of this would be two mailings (with, say, different themes or graphic approaches) of equal cost to produce and mail, competing to be the winner, to then be applied to a large number of names from which the two test mailings were a random sample. Of course, whether the winner is, indeed, profitable enough to warrant mailing to this large number of names is a separate decision that will be based on various profit considerations.

Remember, though, that we are using average acquisition cost to keep the numbers as simple as possible. What we really should do is compute the expected profitability of a customer over the time during which he or she can be expected to remain a subscriber. This "lifetime value of a customer," however, is a fairly complex topic, and will not be discussed in detail until Chapter 15.

Choose the Significance Level

This step in the process can easily be—and, in fact, usually is—passed over quickly by saying that we will use the traditional 5 percent significance level. However, the choice should be given more thought. If the cost of "going with the new" when, in fact, the "new" isn't really better is unusually costly, then a wiser choice could be to go with a smaller value of the significance level, say 2 or 1 percent. On the other hand, if the cost of "staying with the control" when, in fact, the "new" is substantially better has an unusually high opportunity loss, then a wiser choice could be to go with a larger value of the significance level, say 10 or even 20 percent. Sadly, there are also other considerations that are difficult to assess, but that bear on the best choice (for example, your a priori beliefs about whether the "new" is indeed better). Now you can understand why people so often simply go with the traditional value of 5 percent.

In our subscription-acquisition example, let's assume that we are very risk averse, and decide to choose a significance level of 1 percent. We know that the lower value for the significance level will decrease our chance of selecting the new package if it is really no better than the control.

Determine the Sample Size

The next step is to determine the size of the sample required for the mailing. This depends on three factors:

1. *The accuracy, often called precision, that we desire.* The only way we can achieve 100 percent accuracy is to sample the entire population with which we are concerned. This would then be a census. However, we obviously do not want to do this, for our objective is to determine whether the new package is better *before we invest substantial resources in its use.* Thus we must allow for some amount of sample error. *Sample error* here is the difference between the mean of the sample and the mean of the whole population from which we are sampling. The greater the sample error we are willing to tolerate, of course, the smaller the required sample size. Let's assume we are willing to accept a sample error of $.25. In other words, we are willing to be off in our estimate of the subscriber acquisition cost by +/- $.25.
2. *The confidence we insist upon having that we are meeting our desired accuracy.* We actually made that decision earlier when we chose a significance level of 1 percent. Our confidence level is 100 - 1 = 99 percent.
3. *The standard deviation of the acquisition cost.* This tells us how much variance there is from one value to another value, and hence the degree of likely sample error as a function of the sample size. Sometimes the standard deviation is known, often from past studies; more often it is unknown. In the latter case, we should conduct a small pilot study to estimate it.

Assume that in our case the standard deviation is known to be $1.00. The formula for determining our sample size is:

$$n = \frac{Z^2 sd^2}{e^2}$$

with our values of e = $.25, and sd = $1.00. The value of Z, found in a table of the standard normal distribution, is 2.6 for a confidence of 99 percent.[1] Consequently:

[1] When the standard deviation is assumed known, we use a standard normal distribution value. If the standard deviation is unknown, and estimated from a pilot sample, we should theoretically use a *t*-distribution value. However, when the pilot sample is at least 30 (and it always should be), the values from the two tables are essentially equal. From here on in this chapter we will use values from the standard normal distribution.

$$n = \frac{(2.6)^2(1.0)^2}{(.25)^2}$$

$$= \frac{(6.76)(1.0)}{.0625}$$

$$= 108.6$$

If we need 109 responses, then we must divide by the expected response rate to obtain the number to be mailed. We should choose the lowest response rate that seems realistic for this particular mailing to ensure an adequate number of responses. If a 2 percent response rate is the lowest reasonable expectation, we must mail:

$$= \frac{109}{.02}$$

$$= 5{,}450 \text{ packages}$$

Actually, to be risk averse, we really should mail a few more than the 5,450, just in case the response rate is unusually low for this particular sample. So, as a practical matter, 10 percent should be added to this number, giving us a value of about 6,000.

Specify the Decision Rule

Next we must state the decision rule. A decision rule is "simply a procedure that specifies the action to be taken for each possible sample outcome." [2] By specifying a decision rule *before* the test is conducted, we are trying to assure that the decision will be made objectively. To put it another way, we do not want to let the test results themselves influence our decision. The decision rule is usually set within the framework of what is called *hypothesis testing* and here specifies the values of the sample mean for which we will accept or reject the null hypothesis versus the alternative hypothesis.

What do we mean by "the null hypothesis"? We specify two hypotheses about the "state of the world"; actually, most of the time, and certainly in our example, the hypotheses are more modest in scope, being about values of a population parameter. Here the relevant population parameter is the expected subscriber-acquisition cost of the new package. The null hypothesis is the statement that has to be disproved. In other words, unless the evidence is overwhelming—or, in statistical terms, significant—against the null hypothesis, we will continue to believe in the null hypothesis. A useful way to think about this idea is to view the null hypothesis as getting the benefit of the doubt.

[2] Morris Hamburg, *Statistical Analysis For Decision Making*, 3rd ed. (New York: Harcourt Brace Jovanovich, 1984), p. 266.

In our situation, the control package has been delivering the best performance to date and has an average acquisition cost of $2.25. Thus when we hypothesize about the average of the new package's acquisition cost, we should set up a null hypothesis that states that this average is *no better (no lower) than for the control package*. This will guarantee that unless the evidence is clearly in favor of the new package, we will stay with the tried and true control package.

In statistical terms, we state:

$$H_0\text{: new package mean} >/= \$2.25$$

Note again that this essentially says that the new is not better (not lower) than the control. We don't want to reject this belief if the new is indeed no better than the control. However, there is always the chance that we could make this mistake. In statistical terms, it is called a Type I error. How could this error occur? Well, what if the new cost is higher (worse) than the control cost, but the "dice gods" for this one experimental mailing give us a result that shows a much smaller cost for the new package? Won't we get misled? Sadly, the answer is yes, although by our choice of a significance level of 1 percent, we have made the chance of such a thing happening very low. A corresponding example in the everyday world is that, while the average height of men is surely higher than the average height of women, in a sample we could have the women being taller just by the "luck of the draw."

The alternate hypothesis is essentially the complement of the null hypothesis; that is, the other possibility. Here the alternate hypothesis should have the meaning that the new package is *indeed* better than the control package by virtue of having a lower expected acquisition cost. In statistical terms, we state H_1, the alternate hypothesis, as:

$$H_1\text{: new package mean} < \$2.25$$

We want to reject the null hypothesis, and thus accept the alternate hypothesis, when there is evidence that the expected acquisition cost for the new package is less than that for the control package, which we know to be $2.25. Remember, our aim is to determine which package has the highest expected profit. We are using lowest acquisition cost as a stand-in for highest expected profit only because in the current situation they are equivalent.

We are now ready for the specific determination of the decision rule: i.e., for which values of the sample mean acquisition cost we should accept the null hypothesis, H_0, and for which values we should reject H_0 and accept the alternate hypothesis, H_1. Clearly, sample means that lead us to reject H_0 should be ones that are lower than $2.25, but not just any value under $2.25—only ones that are enough below $2.25 that it is likely they did not come out that way because of luck. After all, if the true mean of the new package is $2.26 or $2.27 (above $2.25 !), we could still get a sample mean of, say, $2.24. The decision rule requires finding a critical value, so that if $2.25 is the true expected acquisition cost for the new package, the chance is only 1 percent (the chosen significance level) that we would get a sample mean below it. The formula for this critical value, *C*, is:

$$C = \$2.25 - (2.33 \times sd)/(\text{sq. root } n)$$

Assuming that we get 109 responses (the number planned for), and recalling that *sd* = 1.0, we find:

$$C = \$2.25 - (2.33 \times 1)/(\text{sq. root } 109)$$

or

$$C = \$2.03$$

We will conclude that the new package has a lower acquisition cost than that of the control package ($2.25) only if the sample mean cost is below $2.03.

We should note that the appropriate value from the Z table used in the preceding formula is not the 2.6 we used in determining our sample size earlier in the chapter. This is because we will reject H_0 only if the sample mean is *below* the critical value (i.e., below $2.25); there is no corresponding rejection region above $2.25. All of our 1 percent Type I error is in the lower tail. Also, that is why we didn't get a critical value of $2.00 (.25 below $2.25, in line with the +/- $.25 chosen as a tolerable sample error). Our statistical analysis is portrayed graphically in Figure 8.2.

Choose the Variables to Be Tested

One of the cardinal rules of direct marketing testing is to "test the big things." According to Stone, "Trivia testing, e.g., testing the tilt of a postage stamp or testing the effect of various colors of paper stock, are passé. Breakthroughs are pos-

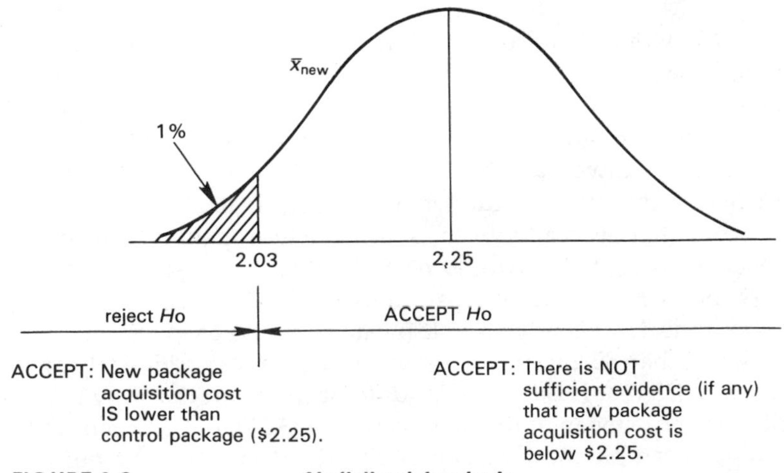

FIGURE 8.2 *Statistical Analysis*

sible only when you test the big things."[3] We can list a number of areas in which testing can provide results that can materially improve the likelihood of the success of a direct-mail program. They are:

The product or service itself
Product-positioning alternatives
List selection
Variations of the offer
Media options
Format of the promotional piece
Creative alternatives
Timing[4]

In testing the product or service itself, the direct marketer can test the appropriateness of a particular product for a given target market: Will this small portable kitchen appliance be a profitable addition to my catalog of housewares? Or the major question might concern alternative product attributes: Should we offer the product in avocado green as well as in off-white?

Product-positioning alternatives are derived from a study of the benefits and attributes of our product. The marketer of the small kitchen appliance may have two major positioning alternatives. Focusing on a benefit of using the product, the marketer could chose a positioning statement centered around "ease of use." Taking a tangible attribute approach, the positioning statement chosen could stress "low price."

In most tests the direct marketer will mail to at least a portion of the house list. Beyond that, the possibilities seem endless. Ordinarily, the direct marketer will test several lists in a single mailing.

There are a huge number of possible offer variations. The direct marketer can test, among others, different price levels, different premium offers (or no premium at all), and different warranty options. We discussed the many alternatives that are available in constructing the offer in Chapter 3.

As we noted in Chapter 1, all communications media are viable options for inclusion in a direct marketing program. Rarely, however, will all be used in a single campaign. Which, then, will work best in a particular situation? In the context of testing, the important thing to remember is that the cost of testing varies from medium to medium. It is relatively cheap to test variations in telephone scripts or of radio copy. Testing alternative lists is cost effective in both the direct-mail and telephone environments. It is more expensive, but still usually quite

[3] Bob Stone, Successful Direct Marketing, 3rd. ed. (Chicago: Crain Books, 1984), pp. 425-426.

[4] Stone, Successful Direct Marketing, pp. 425-426; Edward L. Nash, Direct Marketing: Strategy/Planning/Execution (New York: McGraw Hill, 1982), p. 211; Robert C. Blattberg, "Decision Rules and Sample Size Selection for Direct Mail Testing," DMA Release #610.1, October 1979.

feasible, to test variations in the direct-mail package—whether or not to include a brochure or a lift device, whether to use a plastic mailing sleeve or a printed, four-color mailing envelope. Testing different four-color magazine ads or different television ads can, however, become quite expensive. Testing in print and broadcast media will be discussed in Chapters 12 and 13, since the techniques are quite different from direct-mail testing.

There are two key issues for the direct marketer to keep in mind when testing media. The first is to consider not only the expense of testing but also the cost versus the benefit of continued promotion through a particular medium before deciding what to test. Second, the direct marketer should clearly distinguish between testing the medium itself (can this product be effectively sold by direct mail?) and testing a specific format in a specific medium (a mailing piece that executes a low-price positioning versus one that executes an upscale, ease-of-use positioning). The medium itself and the promotional formats that work in that medium are quite different questions, and the direct marketer should be clear about which is being tested. However, it is difficult to separate them even for purposes of discussion.

Nash suggests that while major creative alternatives such as a change in headline, illustration, or format are worth testing, "layout revisions or different copy treatments of the same theme usually show very little difference, presuming they were professionally executed in the first place." [5]

Timing can be a difficult issue when it comes to testing decisions. It is clear that timing can make a considerable difference in most direct-response situations. However, direct marketers must maintain a planned promotional schedule, which may not allow them to wait to run a test in a season that may be especially favorable. There is no simple solution to this problem. The element of timing should be built into the testing schedule in a manner that allows it to be studied but does not seriously interfere with the promotional schedule.

Nash summarizes the difficulties of deciding what to test by pointing out that selecting variables to test must be done methodically on the basis of the expected value of the information. He states that "the big differences—200 and 300 percent lift factors—almost always come from product positioning, offer changes, or the selection of different lists or publications."[6]

Design the Test/Analyze the Results

Designing the test when there are a number of variables to be tested can be a complex procedure. The second half of this chapter will deal with test design and analysis of test results.

[5] Nash, *Direct Marketing: Strategy/Planning/Execution*, p. 210.

[6] Nash, *Direct Marketing: Strategy/Planning/Execution*, p. 210.

Conduct the Test

Once the test design has been established, the test must be carried out. This means, in effect, conducting a direct-mail campaign just as described in Chapter 9. In fact, that is generally exactly what we are doing since most testing is done as an additional activity in an ongoing direct-mail campaign. Whether the test is full-scale or smaller-scale, all the planning, preparation, and execution that are necessary for a full-scale campaign are also necessary for a test. In order for even a small-scale test to be valid, *it must be implemented just as if it were a full-scale campaign.* To put it another way, the conditions of the test must exactly replicate the conditions of the full-scale campaign if the test is to be valid.

Record the Test Results

Of course, direct marketers always record the results of any contact with a customer in their database—correct? Yes, it is, but there is still a potentially fatal error lurking to catch the unwary direct marketer. The costs and revenues of the campaign itself (often referred to as the *front end*) are not the only issue. What goes on after the sale is made (the *back end*) can make a great deal of difference in the profit picture. An unusually high rate of returns or excessive service costs for products under warranty are two common examples of back-end costs that can quickly eat up profits. If the direct marketer fails to take these into account, the true results of the test can be grossly misstated.

For example, if we were testing two different pieces, for which one major difference is the prominent display of a toll-free number for no-hassle refunds, the mailing piece with the prominent display might induce a larger response rate (and thus a higher front-end profit), but *also* a larger number of returns for refund (and thus a far larger back-end cost). The mailing piece with the larger front-end profit could be the piece with the *smaller overall profit* if these back-end costs were (mistakenly) ignored.

Make the Decision/Pick the Winner

Returning to our subscription-acquisition example, let's assume that the results were as shown in Table 8.2.

TABLE 8.2 Average Subscriber-Acquisition Cost

	PACKAGE	
	Control	*Test*
Current (sample) mailing	$2.27	$2.10
Long-term	$2.25	NA

The average acquisition cost for the test package is lower than the long-term average acquisition cost for the control package. But, is it significantly lower?

Should we reject the null hypothesis that the acquisition cost of the new is (in reality) no lower?

To answer these questions we must perform a hypothesis test that asks whether the sample average acquisition cost falls into the acceptance region or the rejection (critical) region, these regions being established by our choice of significance level and sample size. Recall that we stated earlier in the chapter that the decision rule should be specified *before* the test is conducted. That's just what we did; look back at Figure 8.2, and the finding of the critical value that led up to the figure. All we need to do now is to note whether our sample average acquisition cost, $2.10, is above or below the critical value of $2.03. Obviously, $2.10 is above $2.03, and falls into the acceptance region.

We therefore accept the null hypothesis. This means that the evidence that the long-run average acquisition cost of the test package is lower than that of the control package is not sufficiently strong. We will continue to use the control package for the bulk of our mailings. However, we may wish to continue to test other packages (or even this test package again if no other viable possibilities present themselves) in an attempt to find one with a lower average acquisition cost.

Even if we had rejected the null hypothesis—that is, had found the cost of the test package to be significantly lower than the cost of the control package—we might not choose to make a radical change without further testing. We might do another test mailing, perhaps with a larger sample, to see if the results were repeated. If we had been testing a list, further testing might take the form of rolling out to a larger number of names on the list. If a variation on some other promotional element had been tested, the variation might be tested on additional lists before we made a final decision to accept it as the control.

THE NEED FOR EFFICIENT TEST DESIGNS

It should be clear from the preceding discussion of the testing process that the direct marketing manager welcomes information to support decisions on a wide variety of issues. The manager must identify the critical variables and test as many of them as possible. The limits of what can be tested are established by available funds and time.

The large number of variables that can be tested, coupled with the need to quickly develop and execute effective marketing programs in an increasingly competitive marketplace, puts a premium on efficiently designed tests. However, when the literature on the testing of direct-mail campaigns is carefully examined, two arguments stand out: (1) you should test *only one* variable at a time; or (2) you should test a *complete* mail package all at once (different offers, premiums, lift devices, etc.). When you test just one variable, you can ascertain the effect of that variable with a known degree of certainty. When you test an entire mail package, you know which package works best even though you do not know the effect of individual variables.

The argument about "just one variable at a time" is clearly in conflict with generally accepted statistical and experimental design techniques. The second argument is somewhat more difficult to refute, at least on a practical basis. It is the second approach—testing an entire mail package—that we have taken in the first section of this chapter. In describing a testing process focused on the expected profitability of competing packages, we have been looking at the performance of entire packages, not of their component parts.

Without doubt, the overriding need of the direct-mail marketer is to develop a package that works. There is simply not sufficient time to test even all of the variables that are likely to make a substantial difference in the profitability of the campaign. Creating a package that works is more important in the short run than finding out precisely what elements make it work (or, even better, *why* those elements make it work).

Unfortunately, this approach—which might well be called "finding the whats, not the whys"—adds little to our store of knowledge about how direct marketing really works. Put in practical terms, it does not help the direct marketer to *systematically* build a store of knowledge that will facilitate the rapid development of more effective direct-mail campaigns.

The remainder of this chapter will be devoted to a discussion of ways in which we can make tests more efficient—that is, obtain more information in return for the resources of time and money devoted to the test—without sacrificing ability to make statistically sound judgments about test results. The application of statistical techniques with which you are probably already familiar, coupled with some simple principles of experimental design, will enable us to develop a sense of what is possible. We will still, however, have only scratched the surface of the testing power that sophisticated multivariate analysis and complex experimental designs offer to the direct marketer.

A NON-NUMERICAL EXAMPLE

To better understand the issue of testing efficiency, we can look at an example that does not require numbers to make its point. Assume that our product is a small household appliance. We are faced with two issues: (1) the type of positioning to use (a convenience appeal vs. a status appeal); and (2) whether to use an expensive or an inexpensive premium as part of our offer.

Let's assume that we take the "one variable at a time" approach. First we will conduct a test, following all the steps described in the first section of this chapter, on the variable appeal. In order to be consistent with experimental design terminology, from now on we will refer to the variable as a *factor*.

Remember that this factor has two levels, convenience and status. The term *levels* refers to the values that the factor may take. These levels may be quantitative (e.g., an offer price of \$7.95 versus an offer price of \$5.95), or they may be qualitative, as in this case.

Since we are testing only one factor at a time, we hold the other factor constant. Assume that we decide to use the inexpensive premium and conduct the test on appeal by earmarking 20,000 pieces to receive the status appeal and 20,000 pieces to receive the convenience appeal, though all will receive the offer that includes the inexpensive premium. The particular profit values and/or response rates are not important to this example, so we simply note in Table 8.3 the number of mail pieces earmarked for the (so far) two cells.

TABLE 8.3

APPEAL	*PREMIUM*	
	Inexpensive (I)	*Expensive (E)*
Status (S)	20,000	0
Convenience (C)	20,000	0

Now consider testing the factor premium, which has two levels, inexpensive and expensive. Again, we hold the other factor constant, and fix appeal at the level status when testing premium.

We conduct this test of the two premiums by earmarking an additional 20,000 mail pieces to receive the expensive premium/status appeal combination. We already *have* 20,000 pieces earmarked for the inexpensive premium/status appeal combination. Thus we have earmarked 60,000 mail pieces as shown in Table 8.4.

TABLE 8.4

APPEAL	*PREMIUM*	
	Inexpensive (I)	*Expensive (E)*
Status (S)	20,000	20,000
Convenience (C)	20,000	0

To test the two appeals, we can use the results from the (S,I) and (C,I) cells of Table 8.4; the (S,E) cell cannot be usefully included to compare appeals. We have the statistical power of 40,000 mail pieces in terms of avoiding an erroneous conclusion about which level of appeal is superior.

To test the two premiums, we can use the results from the (S,I) and (S,E) cells of Table 8.4; the (C,I) cell cannot be usefully included to compare premiums. Again, we have the statistical power of 40,000 pieces in terms of avoiding an erroneous conclusion about which level of premium is superior.

Now consider the earmarking of mail pieces shown in Table 8.5. With the *same 60,000 mail pieces, but allocated as in the table,* we can test appeal using all four cells, thus getting the statistical power of *60,000* mail pieces in terms of avoiding an erroneous conclusion about which appeal is superior. Likewise, we can test premium using all four cells, here also getting the statistical power of 60,000 mail pieces. Thus the experimental design depicted in Table 8.5 uses the same 60,000

TABLE 8.5

APPEAL	*PREMIUM*	
	Inexpensive (I)	*Expensive (E)*
Status (S)	15,000	15,000
Convenience (C)	15,000	15,000

mail pieces as that shown in Table 8.4, but results in a far smaller probability of reaching an incorrect conclusion about which appeal level is superior and which premium level is superior.

This reduced chance of erroneous conclusions is reason enough to prefer the experimental design in Table 8.5 to that of Table 8.4. Yet there is another major advantage that the design in Table 8.5 has. What if, for example, the difference in response between the status appeal and the convenience appeal is not the same for the two types of premiums offered? The "one factor at a time" design gives us no way to assess this possibility. The design depicted in Table 8.5 *does* allow us to explore that possibility. If the impact of one factor is not the same for all the levels of another factor, we say that the factors have "interaction." We will see in the next section that the presence of interaction can be very important in determining the best overall combination of factor levels.

THE FACTORIAL DESIGN

The experimental design we will discuss in this section is called a *factorial design*. A factorial design "permits the experimenter to evaluate the combined effect of two or more experimental variables when used simultaneously"[7]. We will use a *complete factorial design* in our first examples—one in which all combinations of levels (values) of the factors under study are included. Later we will look briefly at a *fractional factorial design*—one in which only a portion of the combinations of levels of each factor are studied.

We will use the same two factors—appeal and premium. Appeal will have the same two levels—status and convenience. But in this example the premium factor will have three levels—no premium, an inexpensive premium, and an expensive premium. That gives us six experimental treatments—status/none, status/inexpensive, status/expensive, convenience/none, convenience/inexpensive, and convenience/expensive.

To avoid any timing bias, we must measure all experimental treatments simultaneously. Consequently, we will have a mailing divided into six equal parts. One-sixth of the names will receive a package using a status appeal and offering no premium, one-sixth will receive a status appeal with an inexpensive premium offer, and so on.

[7] B. J. Winer, *Statistical Principles in Experimental Design*, 2nd ed., (New York: McGraw-Hill, 1971), p. 309.

Note that a control package is not required for this type of experiment. The dependent (response) variable is profitability of the mailing, although discussion of the *precise* meaning of this term will occasionally arise.

You will soon see that, using this type of experimental design, we can measure the effect of the factor appeal as well as the effect of the factor premium. In addition, we can determine whether or not there is an interaction effect between the two factors. We will have done this with six experimental treatments, and we will have made all six experimental treatments from a single mailing, thus reducing the chance that unmeasured variables will affect the results of the test. This could well result in a substantial saving of both time and money as well as in improved information for decision making.

The technique we will use to analyze the effect of each factor and to determine whether or not interaction is present is called *analysis of variance*, often referred to as ANOVA.

ANALYSIS OF VARIANCE

Analysis of variance, like regression analysis, is one of the statistical techniques that falls into the category of "the general linear model." This model assumes an additive relationship between the variable we wish to predict (the dependent or response variable) and the variables (factors) that may be its determinants (the independent or predictor variable(s)).

Regression analysis measures the impact of each independent variable upon the dependent variable (the regression coefficients) and the overall predictive success of the set of independent variables (the R 2). ANOVA asks a different question: *What is the probability that a predictor variable could yield results different from simple random selection?* It also *allocates differences in dependent variable values for different experimental combinations to their sources* (here: appeal, premium, their interaction, other factors).

The logic behind ANOVA is precisely the same as that which underlies the concept of significance testing.[8] We are, then, merely extending the testing process covered in the first half of the chapter in a way that can encompass more variables (additional factors).

We are preparing to analyze the results of a test with two factors, appeal and premium; hence we use a two-way analysis of variance.

The three questions we intend to answer by performing this analysis of variance are:

[8] E. M.Uslaner, "Introduction," in Gudmund R. Iversen and Helmut Norpoth, *Analysis of Variance* (Beverly Hills, CA: Sage Publications, 1976), p. 5.

1. Are there systematic effects (i.e., differences in profitability) due to appeal alone (without any consideration of the possible effects of premium)?
2. Are there systematic effects due to premium alone (without any consideration of the possible effects of appeal)?
3. Are there systematic effects due neither to appeal alone nor to premium alone, but to the specific combination of a particular level of appeal with a particular level of premium?

Let's look at an example that illustrates the use of ANOVA and its interpretation. Assume that we have randomly assigned each name to one of the six experimental treatments, conducted a test mailing, and achieved the results shown in Table 8.6.

TABLE 8.6 Results of Test Mailing

Experimental Treatment	*No. Mailed*	*Response Rate*	*Profit per Order*	*Profit per Piece Mailed*
Convenience/ None	30,000	.009	$10.00	$0.09
Convenience/ Inexpensive	30,000	.018	10.00	0.18
Convenience/ Expensive	30,000	.020	9.00	0.18
Status/ None	30,000	.013	10.00	0.13
Status/ Inexpensive	30,000	.020	12.00	0.24
Status/ Expensive	30,000	.016	12.50	0.20

Though the terms "profit per order" and "profit per piece mailed" both take account of production and mailing costs, the criterion we wish to use—the one that really corresponds to "profitability of the mailing"—is "profit per piece mailed." This criterion eliminates any problems that could arise if the number mailed in each experimental treatment is different (whether by plan or perhaps because some got destroyed accidentally), and accounts for any profit-per-order differences that may arise for whatever reason (perhaps because of back-end costs). As we mentioned earlier, if production costs and mailing costs and profit per order are all the same for each experimental treatment, then response rate is equivalent to profit per mail piece.

Table 8.7 presents the test results in terms of our criterion.

TABLE 8.7

APPEAL	*PREMIUM*			
	None	*Inexpensive*	*Expensive*	*Row Means*
Convenience	.09	.18	.18	.15
Status	.13	.24	.20	.19
Column means	.11	.21	.19	
GRAND MEAN				.17

In order to illustrate the ANOVA process, we will perform the detailed calculations by hand; most often the calculations are performed via one of many software packages that exist for both mainframe and microcomputers.

We can measure the total variation in our data (i.e., how different all the data values are from one another) by adding the squared differences between each data value and the overall, or grand, mean of all the data values. This sum of squared differences is called the *total sum of squares* or *TSS*.

When performing an ANOVA, one usually first states a statistical model, which simply sets up an equation stating how the total variation in our data (*TSS*) is to be partitioned into its various sources. As we mentioned earlier, our sources in this analysis are appeal, represented by rows; premium, represented by columns; the interaction of these two factors; and error, the impact of all other factors not controlled in this test. The model would be written as follows:

$$TSS = SSBr + SSBc + SSIrc + SSE.$$

That is, the total sum of squares is equal to the sum of squares between rows (*SSBr*) plus the sum of squares between columns (*SSBc*) plus the interaction sum of squares (*SSIrc*) plus the error sum of squares (*SSE*).

First we will compute the *TSS*. Since it is the component parts of the *TSS* that we wish to find, we normally would not compute the *TSS* except as an arithmetic check. Recall that we add together the squared differences between each data value and the grand mean:

$$\begin{aligned} TSS &= (.09 - .17)^2 + (.18 - .17)^2 + (.18 - .17)^2 \\ &+ (.13 - .17)^2 + (.24 - .17)^2 + (.20 - .17)^2 \\ &= .0140 \end{aligned}$$

Don't be fooled into thinking that there isn't much total variability in the data just because this appears to be a "small" number. All numbers in an ANOVA are relative. If the values in our table were profit per 1000 mail pieces instead of profit per mail piece, the *TSS* would be 14,000.

Now we will compute the *SSBr*, the sum of squares between rows. We do this by subtracting the grand mean from each of the row means, squaring each, and summing; then we multiply this quantity by the number of data values in each row. The number of values per row in this case is 3, the number of columns.

$$SSBr = 3 \times [(.15 - .17)^2 + (.19 - .17)^2]$$
$$= .0024$$

Next we compute the *SSBc*, the sum of squares between columns. The reasoning is the same as for the *SSBr*. We subtract the grand mean from each of the column means, square each, add them up, and multiply by the number of data values in each column. There are 2 values in each column, the number of rows.

$$SSBc = 2 \times [(.11 - .17)^2 + (.21 - .17)^2 + (.19 - .17)^2]$$
$$= .0112$$

We now calculate the interaction sum of squares, *SSIrc*. This calculation is somewhat lengthy, but not difficult to do. For each cell value we subtract its corresponding row mean, also subtract its corresponding column mean, and add the grand mean. We square the resulting value, and these squared values are then added up. You may not "see" how this is indeed measuring interaction, because the description

(cell value – row mean – column mean + grand mean)

is really a shortcut for

[(cell value – grand mean) – (row mean – grand mean) – (column mean – grand mean)]

In this expression, we take the amount by which the cell value differs from the grand mean (the first subtraction term), eliminate any of this difference due to the row the value is in (adjusting for the row membership by the second subtraction term), and similarly eliminate any of the difference due to column membership. Putting aside the possibility of error for the moment, what could cause this expression's value to be nonzero? The only answer can be that particular combinations of rows and columns have special incremental effects that are not captured solely by considering the row by itself and the column by itself. This is precisely what is called *interaction*! Now—back to computing the *SSIbr*:

$$(.09 - .15 - .11 + .17)^2 + (.18 - .15 - .21 + .17) + (.18 - .15 - .19 + .17)^2$$
$$+ (.13 - .19 - .11 + .17)^2 + (.24 - .19 - .21 + .17) + (.20 - .19 - .19 + .17)^2$$
$$= .0004$$

Because there is no replication in this analysis (i.e., each cell has only one value), we are not able to compute a sum of squares due to error (*SSE*). Thus we must use the *SSIrc*, which really reflects interaction and error here, as if it is all error. A later example in this chapter does include replication, and thus a separate *SSIrc* and *SSE*.

Perhaps you have noticed that our three sums of squares add up to the *TSS*. The *SSBr* = .0024, the *SSBc* = .0112, and the *SSIbr* = .0004, for a total of .0140. This fact leads us to the final concept that must be examined before we can perform the ANOVA—*degrees of freedom*.

Each sum of squares must be normalized or averaged. Obviously, if there were 13 columns instead of the 3 columns we have in this example, we would have the *SSBc* be the sum of 13 terms instead of 3 terms. To make the *SSBc*, or any sum of squares term meaningful, we must take into account how many terms composed the sum. We do this, more or less, by dividing by the number of terms in the sum. We say "more or less" because the proper number to divide by is not exactly the number of terms, but rather the number of free terms in the sum. It is this idea of free terms that requires us to explore the concept of degrees of freedom.

Degrees of Freedom

There is no straightforward verbal definition of the concept of degrees of freedom, but a simple example should provide sufficient understanding. In the computations we have just made, both the row and the column means were compared with the grand mean. Looking back at Table 8.7 for a moment, we can see that the grand mean is $.17. The mean of the first row plus the mean of the second row, divided by 2, must equal the grand mean. If there are only two rows, and if we know the grand mean and the mean of row 1, the mean of row 2 has been determined; with the mean of the first row being $.15, the mean of the second row can only be $.19. No other value, added to $.15 and divided by 2, could equal $.17. In other words, when we know the grand mean and one row mean, the other row mean is not "free to vary." Consequently, we have one degree of freedom, (*one* row free to vary, *not two* rows free to vary).

The same reasoning applies to degrees of freedom for the columns in our test results. If we know the grand mean, and two of the three column means, the third column mean is not free to vary: two of the column means can vary, but once they are determined, the third one cannot vary. For the columns, then, we have two degrees of freedom.

Returning to the basic model presented earlier in this section, we have:

$$TSS = SSBr + SSBc + SSIr,c + SSE$$

The breakdown of degrees of freedom is equal to:

$$(rcn-1) = (r-1) + (c-1) + [(r-1)(c-1)] + rc(n-1)$$

where

r = the number of rows
c = the number of columns
n = the number of replications (*individual data values in each cell*)

In this example, we have r=2, c=3, and n=1. The degrees of freedom for error is thus 0. This corresponds with our earlier statement that with no replication (i.e., n=1) we cannot compute a separate error term.

There is a helpful check for determining whether the degrees of freedom have been calculated correctly. The total number of degrees of freedom is always one less than the total number of data points used in the ANOVA. There are six data points—the six cell values—in our example. The total number of degrees of freedom should therefore be five.

An analysis of variance is usually summarized in an ANOVA table. Let's construct an ANOVA table and continue the analysis of variance of the test results.

ANOVA Summary Table

TABLE 8.8 ANOVA Table for Household Appliance Test

Source	*Sum of Squares (SSQ)*	*Degrees of Freedom (df)*	*Mean Squares (MSQ)*
Rows	.0024	1	.0024
Columns	.0112	2	.0056
Error	.0004	2	.0002
TOTAL	.0140	5	

Table 8.8 is an ANOVA table with the information we have already computed filled in—all of the sums of squares and their respective degrees of freedom. We have three steps remaining:

1. *Compute the mean squares for each source of variability by dividing each SSQ by its respective degrees of freedom.* This is the normalizing or averaging step mentioned earlier. It can be likened to reducing all values to a per-unit basis so they can be meaningfully compared to one another.

2. *Calculate a value for F.* The mean square for error reflects only error, assuming the most conservative situation—that the error plus interaction is all error. If we find significant differences under this assumption, then we know that they would also have been significant if we did not assume all the error plus interaction was error. The mean square for rows reflects error plus row differences. The F value is a ratio of the mean sum of squares for rows divided by the mean sum of squares for error. Hence this ratio speaks to the issue of whether there are row differences. It is similar for columns. The F value for rows is (.0024/.0002) and the F value for columns is (.0056/.0002).

If there are no differences in, for example, rows, the F value for rows should be near 1.0. However, the average weight of two different, randomly chosen, but ostensibly the same, sets of people would almost surely not be identical (and thus the ratio would not equal exactly 1.0). We must decide how much above 1.0 is allowable before concluding that "it's beyond a reasonable doubt indicating real row differences." This is decided by traditional hypothesis-testing procedure, and thus depends on various points on the theoretical *F* distribution. The shape of the F distribution depends somewhat on the degree of freedom values of the sums of squares involved, but is for most degree of freedom values the shape shown in Figure 8.3.

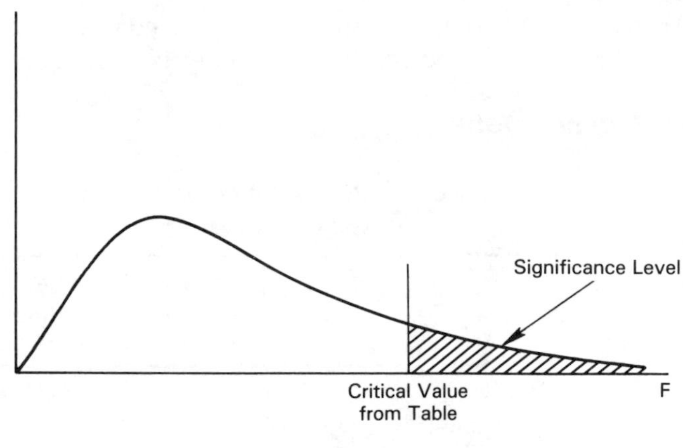

FIGURE 8.3 ***The F Distribution***

Most statistics texts have *F* table values for significance levels of .05 and .01, and occasionally other significance levels. The value from the *F* table (a small portion of which is reproduced in Figure 8.4) is our critical value. Values of our calculated *F* ratio smaller than the critical value lead us to accept the null hypothesis, and to conclude that there are no differences between the levels of the factor under consideration. Values of the *F* ratio that are larger than our critical value lead to rejection of our null hypothesis, and to the conclusion that there *are* differences between levels of the factor under consideration.

3. *Look up the F table value at the chosen level of significance and compare it to the calculated value of F.* In Table 8.9 we carry out these three steps and complete the ANOVA table.

Interpretation of the ANOVA Table

Now that we have completed the analysis of variance, what does it mean—statistically and managerially?

First, we have already pointed out that the error term (as we've called it) contains both error and interaction. However, when we note how small the mean

Denominator df_2	Numerator df_1									
	1	2	3	4	5	6	7	8	9	10
1	161.40	199.50	215.70	224.60	230.20	234.00	236.80	238.90	240.50	241.90
2	18.51	19.00	19.16	19.25	19.30	19.33	19.35	19.37	19.38	19.40
3	10.13	9.55	9.28	9.12	9.01	8.94	8.89	8.85	8.81	8.79
4	7.71	6.94	6.59	6.39	6.26	6.16	6.09	6.04	6.00	5.96
5	6.61	5.79	5.41	5.19	5.05	4.95	4.88	4.82	4.77	4.74
6	5.99	5.14	4.76	4.53	4.39	4.28	4.21	4.15	4.10	4.06
7	5.59	4.74	4.35	4.12	3.97	3.87	3.79	3.73	3.68	3.64
8	5.32	4.46	4.07	3.84	3.69	3.58	3.50	3.44	3.39	3.35
9	5.12	4.26	3.86	3.63	3.48	3.37	3.29	3.23	3.18	3.14
10	4.96	4.10	3.71	3.48	3.33	3.22	3.14	3.07	3.02	2.98
11	4.84	3.98	3.59	3.36	3.20	3.09	3.01	2.95	2.90	2.85
12	4.75	3.89	3.49	3.26	3.11	3.00	2.91	2.85	2.80	2.75
13	4.67	3.81	3.41	3.18	3.03	2.92	2.83	2.77	2.71	2.67
14	4.60	3.74	3.34	3.11	2.96	2.85	2.76	2.70	2.65	2.60
15	4.54	3.68	3.29	3.06	2.90	2.79	2.71	2.64	2.59	2.54
16	4.49	3.63	3.24	3.01	2.85	2.74	2.66	2.59	2.54	2.49
17	4.45	3.59	3.20	2.96	2.81	2.70	2.61	2.55	2.49	2.45
18	4.41	3.55	3.16	2.93	2.77	2.66	2.58	2.51	2.46	2.41
19	4.38	3.52	3.13	2.90	2.74	2.63	2.54	2.48	2.42	2.38

FIGURE 8-4 ***Portion of F–Table at .05 Significance Level***

square is, .0002, *relative to the other mean square terms,* we can be assured that there is no practically meaningful interaction between the factors, appeal and premium.

Second, it is clear that the F_{calc} for rows is much smaller than the appropriate critical value of *F*, while the F_{calc} for columns is much larger than its corresponding critical value. Consequently, we accept the null hypothesis for rows but reject the null hypothesis with regard to columns.

TABLE 8.9 ANOVA Table for Household Appliance Test

Source	*Sum of Squares (SSQ)*	*Degrees of Freedom (df)*	*Mean Squares (MSQ)*	F_{calc}	$F_{.95}$
Rows	.0024	1	.0024	12.00	18.51
Columns	.0112	2	.0056	28.00	19.00
Error	.0004	2	.0002		
TOTAL	.0140	5			

What does that imply? In ANOVA the null hypothesis is always that "All ______means are equal." For rows, then, it takes the form: "All row means are equal." Since we have accepted this hypothesis, we conclude that there are no differences between the different levels of the row factor. For columns, the null hypothesis is "All column means are equal," but we are rejecting it! We conclude that there is sufficient evidence in our results of differences among the column levels.

What are the managerial implications of the test results? Our conclusion that there is no meaningful interaction (if any at all) between the two factors, appeal and premium, in essence tells us that each factor's impact on profitability, if any, is independent of the other factor's impact. Or, to state the conclusion in other terms, each factor's impact can be viewed as constant across all levels of the other factor.

We found no statistically significant difference in profitability between the two types of appeal. The reader must understand that although it is true that the row means are not equal, the difference between them (.15 versus .19) isn't large enough to conclude that it didn't arise because of the "luck of the draw." In other words, it is not beyond a reasonable doubt that the difference is "real." Therefore, the choice between the two types of appeal should probably be based on considerations not relating to dollar/profit issues. This does not mean that we should not test these two appeals ever again! Probably we should at some point.

We did find a statistically significant difference in profitability among the three levels of premium. We can have confidence that all three levels are not equally profitable. Yet that doesn't totally solve our problem. Noting the three column means, our results are probably telling us: "Yes, the three aren't equally profitable; no premium (column 1) is inferior to the two others, but most likely the difference in profitability between the inexpensive premium and expensive premium is too close to call."

To perform tests on subsets of levels of a factor requires other statistical concepts beyond the scope of this chapter. The interested reader can find texts covering this subject in a library. The general topic to look up is "multiple comparison testing."

AN EXAMPLE WITH INTERACTION PRESENT

Let's assume that while the test mailing we have just described was being conducted and analyzed, the supplier of the appliance notified us that additional features had become available as a result of continued research and development. We can now have a timer added to the basic piece of equipment, and we can have the finish manufactured in either white enamel or stainless steel. There will be slight cost increases for both the stainless steel version and for the addition of a timer to either version. It is therefore important that the manager make a correct choice.

New features that force us to make additional decisions at this point are not particularly good news. We do not have time to do further test mailings to answer these product-design questions; the major selling season is near. Instead of testing, then, we will make our decision on the basis of a small, laboratory-type experiment that can be carried out in the time available.

For this example, assume that an experiment was designed and that 16 consumers were recruited to participate in this research. That is much too small a sample on which to make a decision, but again, a large volume of data would have made our computations exceedingly tedious.

The consumers were shown product prototypes and asked numerous questions about their attitudes and actual and intended behaviors. We are going to analyze only one question, however, the intention-to-buy question. This question was asked on a 7-point Lickert-type scale, with 1 being "Definitely Would Not Buy" and 7 being "Definitely Would Buy." The results are shown in Table 8.10, with the small numbers being individual responses and the larger numbers cell means. We randomly selected four consumers for each of the four cells.

TABLE 8.10 Results of Product-Feature Experiment

FINISH	*TIMER*		
	Without	*With*	*Row Means*
Enamel	2,3,2,3 2.5	3,3,2,4 3.0	2.75
Stainless	4,4,3,5 4.0	7,7,7,7 7.0	5.5
Column means	3.25	5.0	
GRAND MEAN			4.125

Following the same computational procedure that we used in the preceding example, we find:

$$SSQr = 30.250$$
$$SSQc = 12.250$$

Unlike the preceding example, however, we have replication in this experiment—4 data points per cell. We can therefore compute both an interaction sum of squares and an error sum of squares.

The *SSIcr* is computed by subtracting from each cell mean its corresponding row mean and its corresponding column mean and adding the grand mean. Each quantity is then squared. These quantities (there will be as many quantities as there are cells, in this case 4) are added together and the result is multiplied the number of replications.

$$4[(2.5 - 2.75 - 3.25 + 4.125)^2 + (3.0 - 2.75 - 5.0 + 4.125)^2$$
$$+ (4.0 - 5.5 - 3.25 + 4.125)^2 + (7.0 - 5.5 - 5.0 + 4.125)^2] =$$
$$4[(.625)^2 + (-.625)^2 + (-.625)^2 + (.625)^2] =$$

$$4(.390625 + .390625 + .390625 + .390625) = 4(1.5625) = 6.250$$

The interaction sum of squares is 6.250. Now we compute the error sum of squares. Each individual data point is subtracted from its cell mean. The resulting quantity is squared. All these quantities (there will be as many quantities as there are individual data points, in this case 16) are added together.

$$\begin{aligned}
&(2-2.5)^2 + (3-2.5)^2 \\
&+ (2-2.5)^2 + (3-2.5)^2 \\
&+ (3-3)^2 + (3-3)^2 \\
&+ (2-3)^2 + (4-3)^2 \\
&+ (4-4)^2 + (4-4)^2 \\
&+ (3-4)^2 + (5-4)^2 \\
&+ (7-7)^2 + (7-7)^2 \\
&+ (7-7)^2 + (7-7)^2 \\
&= (-.5)^2 + (.5)^2 \\
&+ (-.5)^2 + (.5)^2 \\
&+ (0)^2 + (0)^2 \\
&+ (-1)^2 + (1)^2 \\
&+ (0)^2 + (0)^2 \\
&+ (-1)^2 + (1)^2 \\
&+ (0)^2 + (0)^2 \\
&+ (0)^2 + (0)^2 \\
&= 5
\end{aligned}$$

The error sum of squares is 5. Now we are ready to construct the ANOVA table.

TABLE 8.11 ANOVA Table for Product-Feature Experiment

Source	*SSQ*	*df*	*MSQ*	F_{calc}	F_{95}
Rows	30.250	1	30.250	72.54	4.75
Columns	12.250	1	12.250	29.38	4.75
Interaction	6.250	1	6.250	14.99	4.75
Error	5	12	.417		
TOTAL	53.750	15			

It is clear from Table 8.11 that there are significant differences between rows and between columns, and that there is interaction between the factors. Let's pay special attention to the interaction—to what it is and to how we should interpret it managerially.

We said earlier in the chapter that the third question we had to answer in an analysis of variance was whether or not there were systematic effects due to neither appeal alone nor premium alone, but only to the combination of a particular level of one factor with a particular level of another factor. We are looking for a joint effect of two specific treatment levels that is different from the sum of the separate effects of each.

This is easier to understand if we portray it graphically, as in Figure 8.5.

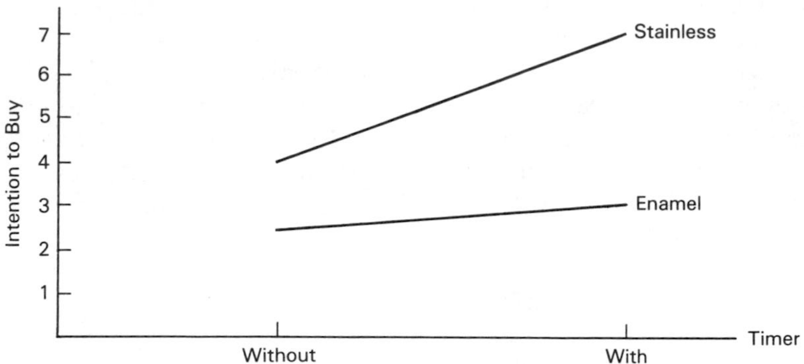

FIGURE 8.5. ***Graphic Representation of ANOVA Results for Product - Feature Experiment***

If there were no interaction, the lines in the figure would be parallel.

Looking back at the results of the product-features test, it is clear that the intention-to-buy score with the enamel finish increased only slightly when the timer was added. The intention-to-buy score with the stainless finish increased much more when the timer was added. This indicates the presence of interaction, and the analysis of variance shows that it is significant.

In fact, the ANOVA shows that the type of finish (without regard to timer) and the presence or absence of the timer (without regard to finish) are each also significant. Managerially, we can be confident that one particular level of each of these treatments creates a higher intention-to-buy score than the other, and the combination of the better levels of each factor creates yet a higher intention-to-buy score than the sum of the individual effects.

Consider the no timer/enamel cell. As we add the timer, we gain .5; as we go from enamel to stainless steel, we gain 1.5; when we make both moves, we gain not just (.5 + 1.5) = 2, but 4.5 (i.e., 7 - 2.5). The manager would obviously want to select that combination of features for the appliance—the stainless finish with the timer. This combination produces a significantly higher intention-to-buy score, so it would appear to be worth a slight cost increase to offer that version of the appliance. In this case, even without this positive interaction ("positive" because the gain is *more* than the sum of the two separate gains), the manager would still choose this combination.

A WORD ABOUT TESTING IN THE "REAL WORLD"

Except for the most statistically oriented among you, these examples of direct-mail tests and experiments probably seemed complex. Actually, they were kept very simple and very "clean." Much of the reasoning behind certain steps in the ANOVA procedure was not discussed, the amount of data was very small, and the numbers tended to come out even or pretty close to it. Nothing happened to distort the results of our experiments. Apparently all of our mailings were delivered, product was available to fulfill them, and the research technicians followed instructions in the laboratory experiment.

Would that it were always so in the real world! Obviously it is not, and all sorts of problems can make the results of real tests difficult to interpret. For insight into some of these problems, and for a statistically more sophisticated approach to analysis of variance, you might wish to read "Assessing a 'Real World' Mail Order Experiment" by John U. Farley and Philip D. Harvey.[9]

MORE SOPHISTICATED EXPERIMENTAL DESIGNS

This final section of the chapter provides a brief look at one advanced type of experimental design that is not widely understood but that holds great potential for the direct marketer.[10]

Think for a moment about our last two examples. Instead of relying on a small laboratory test, it would have been nice if we could have tested the two product features in the mailing in which we tested the appeal and the premium.

If we used a full factorial design and performed that test, what would it look like? We would have:

3 levels of premium x 2 levels of appeal x
2 types of finish x 2 levels of timer
= 24 treatment combinations!

It is not impossible to conduct a test that large, but it would be somewhat cumbersome, and certainly expensive.

The alternative is simply not to take measures on every cell in the full factorial design. For example, we might construct a design that looked like Table 8.12. In the table the x's represent the cells for which measurements would be taken; the other cells would not be measured. Reasonably enough, we call this design a *fractional factorial*. Such a test would be less expensive, easier to manage, and probably completed more quickly than would the corresponding full fac-

[9] *Current Issues and Research in Advertising*, ed. James H. Leigh and Claude R. Martin, Jr. (Ann Arbor: Division of Research, The University of Michigan, 1984), pp. 123-139.

[10] We can only give you a brief introduction to this design here. For more information you can consult an experimental design text.

TABLE 8.12

	Convenience				*Status*			
	Without/Timer		*With/Timer*		*Without/Timer*		*With/Timer*	
	ENAMEL	STAINLESS STEEL	ENAMEL	STAINLESS STEEL	ENAMEL	STAINLESS STEEL	ENAMEL	STAINLESS STEEL
No Premium	x			x		x	x	
Inexpensive Premium		x	x		x			x
Expensive Premium	x		x			x		x

torial. Would we lose anything by obtaining measurements for (in this case) only half the cells? Of course we would! The trick is not to lose anything important.

What managers often consider unimportant is what statisticians call higher-level interactions. These are interactions resulting from combinations of three or more factors.

For example, in the product-feature experiment we found a finish/timer interaction. If we combined the two experiments and did the full 24-cell factorial, we might find a three-way interaction—say, finish/timer/premium. Since we have four factors in the combined experiment, we might even find a four-way interaction—finish/timer/premium/appeal. Experience tells us, however, that in the real world the occurrence of higher-order interactions is infrequent. Also, would the direct marketer know what to do with that four-way interaction? Probably not; higher-level interactions are very difficult to interpret and for most people do not form a very comfortable basis for action.

If the higher-level interactions occur infrequently, and when they do are not particularly useful, why spend time and money to measure them? Most managers would not want to do so. They do, however, want information about the main effects of the treatments themselves—the effect of premium, the effect of timer, and so on—and of the two-way interactions (which occur reasonably frequently in the real world). The trick is to design fractional factorials that unambiguously measure the main effects and as many of the interactions (mostly two-way) as the manager wishes. In other words, the object is to measure all the potentially important effects and interactions, and accept as a penalty for not performing a *full* factorial the inability to measure the unnecessary ones. The design in Table 8.12 is not necessarily an efficient design in that sense, but analyzing it to see how good it is, and if we could do better, is beyond the scope of this chapter.

This version of a fractional factorial is called a *half-replicate* because it obtains measures for half the cells. It is also possible to do quarter-replicates, one-eighth-replicates, three-sixteenth-replicates and, in fact, replicates of virtually any fraction that leaves us an integral number of cells. Done correctly, these designs could provide the direct marketer with a great deal of testing power relative to the resources required.

SUMMARY

Testing is a powerful tool that allows the direct marketer to choose, with a known degree of statistical certainty, the most profitable mailing package or set of marketing variables. The testing process involves a number of steps: choosing a test criterion, determining the sample size, specifying the decision rule, selecting the variables to be tested, designing the test, conducting the test, recording the results, analyzing the results, and making a decision about which package or which set of variables to use. Good direct marketers test as many important program variables as possible, repeating tests on larger samples to ensure their validity. They can also employ experimental designs to increase the efficiency of their tests.

DISCUSSION QUESTIONS

1. Why do direct marketers test? What should they test?
2. Be able to define, in your own words, the following terms and explain their relevance in the testing process: test criterion, control, significance level, decision rule, hypothesis test.
3. Do direct marketers accept the results of any given test as the final answer? Explain.
4. What does the use of experimental design principles add to the testing process?
5. Choose a direct marketing situation and outline an appropriate testing procedure.

SUGGESTED ADDITIONAL READINGS

1. Virgil L. Anderson and Robert A. McLean, *Design of Experiments: A Realistic Approach* (New York: Marcel Dekker, 1974).
2. Mark L. Berenson and David M. Levine, *Basic Business Statistics: Concepts and Applications,* 3rd. ed. (Englewood Cliffs, NJ: Prentice Hall, 1986).
3. Harvey J. Brightman, *Statistics in Plain English* (Cincinnati: South-Western, 1986).
4. John U. Farley and Philip D. Harvey, "Assessing a "Real World" Mail Order Experiment," in *Current Issues And Research In Advertising,* ed. James H. Leigh and Claude R. Martin, Jr. (Ann Arbor: Division of Research, The University of Michigan, 1984), pp. 123-139.

Part Four
Direct Marketing Media

9

Developing Direct-Mail Campaigns

When most people hear the term *direct marketing*, they are thinking "direct mail"—mailing pieces that vary from a postcard announcing a sale to the glossy, multipart packages we used as illustrations in earlier chapters. The preceding chapters have emphasized that direct-response marketing is much more than direct mail, but direct mail is a key component of the industry—in some ways the standard to which all other types of direct-response efforts are compared.

In this chapter we discuss many types of mailing pieces, but we do not consider one type that could reasonably be included under the heading of "direct mail." Catalogs have become such an important aspect of direct marketing that we treat them separately, in the next chapter.

Direct mail is a venerable part of the marketing efforts of major companies all over the world. In an article in *Direct Marketing* magazine Hoge gives some fascinating insights into its role in the development of prominent corporations, and in some cases, entire industries:[1]

- Before the advent of mass production, automobiles were produced a few at a time in small shops in out-of-the-way locations. Most were sold by mail and delivered by railway express.
- The first trucks, buses, tractors, typewriters, and vacuum cleaners were sold by direct mail.
- Cyrus McCormick began to sell harvesters by mail in the 1840s. He maintained a database of purchasers and contacted them by mail. As he recruited dis-

[1] Cecil C. Hoge, Sr., "Mail Order's Lesser Role vs. Direct Marketing's Vastly Bigger One," *Direct Marketing*, May 1986, pp. 64-74, 149.

tributors, he provided dealer-support materials that encouraged them to do lead generation and follow-up.

- Thomas Edison sold many of his own inventions via mail order.
- Retailers were initially resistant to the idea of cash registers. John H. Patterson, founder of the National Cash Register Company, attemped to overcome this resistance by sending a mailing piece each day for 18 days. He analyzed responsiveness by type of business and developed separate mailings for each. As the field sales force grew, salespeople were provided with direct marketing tools.
- Although Eastman Kodak favored retail distribution of its cameras from the beginning, film processing was done by mail order. Customers sent the entire camera to Kodak; the film was removed and processed and a new roll of film inserted before the camera was returned to the customer.

Similar developments took place in England:

- Josiah Wedgwood sold china to dealers in "the colonies" by means of lavish catalogs. Wealthy plantation owners in the South, who had very limited access to retail stores, received their own catalogs.
- Chippendale furniture and Sheffield silver were also distributed by mail in various countries.

Hoge's vignettes go on. Even so, he forgot to mention that Sears once sold entire houses, more or less in kit form, to mail-order customers throughout the United States!

This is more than just an interesting glimpse of business history. These firms faced one or both problems common to fledgling industries: their market was small and geographically scattered and/or channels of distribution simply did not exist. Direct mail is a potential solution when either or both problems are present. It is not, however, a universal solution to all business woes or a sure-fire avenue to growth and profitability. Many of these firms moved away from mail order once distribution channels were set up or altered the nature of their direct-mail efforts as they established field sales forces.

THE ADVANTAGES OF DIRECT MAIL

Direct mail possesses all of the special competencies discussed in Chapter 1. In addition, it has some unique advantages compared to the other media of direct marketing. According to Stone, these advantages are:[2]

- *Selectivity.* Because of the ability to select mailing lists and to select especially desirable names from within those lists, direct mail can engage in precision targeting to a greater degree than any other medium of direct marketing.

[2] Bob Stone, *Successful Direct Marketing Methods*, 3rd ed. (Chicago: Crain Books, 1984), pp. 247-248.

- *Virtually unlimited choice of formats.* Direct-mail pieces or packages allow for a much wider range of choices in terms of format than do the other direct marketing media. However, there are potential constraints resulting from the inability of production equipment to handle some formats. (These are primarily constraints on creative execution, and are discussed in the appendix on print production.)
- *Personalization.* While some other media offer limited ability to personalize messages, direct mail offers the opportunity to personalize to any useful degree.
- *No direct competition.* In other media readers/listeners/viewers are ordinarily perusing the medium for reasons besides consumption of the advertising. When recipients open and read a piece of direct mail, there is no direct competition for their attention, at least for a limited period of time.
- *Most controllable.* The direct-mail manager is not dependent on the scheduling of other media for dissemination of promotional material. Barring error of some kind, the manager can control mail dates, the exact content of material sent, to whom it is sent, and so on. This means that the direct-mail medium lends itself to rigorous testing better than other media.
- *Unique capacity to involve the recipient.* A wide variety of involvement devices can be used to stimulate and retain the interest of the recipient while a decision to respond is being made. Remember that the recipe cards in the Healthy Home Cooking package described in Chapter 1 were an involvement device. So was the "No Commitment" stamp in the Book-of-the-Month Club offer in Chapter 3.

Direct mail can be used to advantage with present customers (e.g.,selling them additional items from your line), in prospecting for new customers (e.g., generating inquiries for additional information), with other relevant publics such as stockholders of a corporation (e.g., informative enclosures with dividend checks), and with members of your channel of distribution (e.g., product updates). In fact, Hodgson lists 49 specific ways direct mail can be used.[3]

When it is used to make a sale on the basis of the mailing alone, it is correctly termed *mail order.* (Actually, direct-response advertising in any medium that closes the sale on the basis of that ad alone is also mail order.) When direct mail is used for any purpose other than to close a sale, it is correctly termed *direct-mail advertising* or *direct-mail promotion* (or just *mail advertising* or *mail promotion*). In most instances in this chapter we will use the more generic term *direct mail.* Keep in mind that when one of the other terms is used, it has a more precise meaning.

"JUNK" MAIL?

Despite the positive benefits direct mail offers to the marketing manager, it has a poor image in many people's minds. It is frequently pointed out that "junk mail"

[3] Richard S. Hodgson, *Direct Mail and Mail Order Handbook,* 3rd ed. (Chicago: The Dartnell Corporation, 1980), pp. 72-78.

is any mail that does not interest the recipient. Presumably, then, one person's junk is another person's treasure!

Table 9.1 summarizes the responses of people questioned in a nationwide study. Some direct mailings were viewed negatively by most of the respondents, while other mailings did not have a negative connotation. In general, current mail-order buyers (defined as people who purchased at least once from a specific mail-order firm within the past 2 years) viewed most types of mailings less negatively than former buyers (purchased by mail from a specific firm but not within the last 2 years) and nonbuyers (never purchased from a mail-order firm). Free sample offers, merchandise offers from credit card firms, and catalogs got very low negative mentions. Former buyers and nonbuyers were even less negative toward free samples than buyers were.

TABLE 9.1 Percentage of Respondents Viewing Solicitations and Other Types of Mailings as Junk Mail

	Current Buyers Percent	*Former Buyers Percent*	*Nonbuyers Percent*
Solicitations to buy recreational land	82	90	84
Letters addressed to occupant or resident	82	85	84
Solicitations to invest money	80	81	82
Solicitations to buy insurance	79	84	84
Chance to win money, prizes, or sweepstakes	77	84	84
Letters with name inserted by computer	58	65	74
Solicitations from charities	44	45	49
Free samples offers	19	16	18
Merchandise offers from credit card companies	16	18	24
Catalogs from major department stores	6	5	9

Source: Edward Nash, *The Direct Marketing Handbook* (New York: McGraw-Hill Book Company, 1984), p. 437.

Additionally, this study found that nonbuyers were less likely than buyers or former buyers to agree with the following statements:

- Products offered by mail are of very high quality.
- There is an advantage to being able to spread your payments over time.
- I look forward to receiving a product after I have ordered it.
- Products offered happen to meet a particular need at a particular time.
- Products offered by mail are priced about the same or lower than the same or comparable products in retail stores.
- I have difficulty getting to retail stores to make purchases.

Another perspective on consumers' attitudes toward mail order is provided by the Simmons study of in-home shopping.[4] Panel data from a representative national sample of 431 homes captured both the in-home shopping done during the month of July 1984 and continuing payments for products and services previously purchased by mail or telephone. The study found that 48 percent of the homes purchased one or more products by mail or telephone during that month for a total of 941 transactions. Additionally, these homes recorded 1,160 payment transactions. Projecting these data, we arrive at the figure of $12 billion in sales generated by direct marketing (not just mail order) during that month. Taking seasonality into account (July is a slow month for retail sales), that would be $150 billion per year. That is somewhat higher than the conservative 1985 figures quoted in Chapter 1, but the methods of arriving at the estimates were quite different.

Table 9.2 shows what percentage of these in-home purchases were generated by each of the direct-response media. Direct mail accounted for just over 24 percent and catalogs for another 24 percent. Table 9.3 shows that apparel represented the largest percentage of the purchases. Since the seven categories of merchandise listed account for less than 50 percent of the total orders, it is clear that these households purchased a wide variety of merchandise categories through one of the direct-response media.

TABLE 9.2 Percent of Orders by Advertising Medium

Advertising Medium	*% of Total Orders*
Direct mail (other than catalogs)	24.2
Catalogs	24.1
Telephone	6.8
Circulars	6.7
Magazine ads	6.0
Newspaper ads	5.8
Yellow Pages ads	4.5
Take-ones	3.3
TV	3.1
Bill inserts	2.5

Source: Stan Rapp, "Simmons Study Takes a Peek at In-Home Purchasing Transactions," *Direct Marketing*, December 1984, pp. 36-40.

[4] Stan Rapp, "Simmons Study Takes Peek at In-Home Purchasing Transactions," *Direct Marketing*, December 1984, pp. 36-40.

TABLE 9.3 Most Popular Items Purchased

Catagory	*% of Total Orders*
Apparel	18
Magazine subscriptions	7
Home accessories	6
Home Maintenance	4
Kitchen Equipment	4
Home office supplies	4
Automotive accessories	3

Source: Stan Rapp, "Simmons Study Takes a Peek at In-Home Purchasing Transactions," *Direct Marketing,* December 1984, pp. 36-40.

The study found, not surprisingly, that households that averaged four or more pieces of mail a day were more likely to be headed by a person over 35 years old, have both husband and wife working, and be upscale in terms of both occupation and income (see Table 9.4). Sixty-six percent of the households reported themselves to be very or extremely satisfied with retail store shopping, while only 50 percent were equally satisfied with shopping by mail or by phone. Almost 60 percent of the households that were very satisfied with in-home shopping were also very satisfied with retail store shopping—and these households were above-average mail/telephone purchasers. About half of the participants reported some negative feelings about in-home shopping. Most wanted lower prices, no shipping charges, and faster delivery.

Taken together, these two studies suggest a good news/bad news situation for direct marketing in general and direct mail in particular. First, the good news. A large percentage of the population purchases (and, not incidentally, contributes

TABLE 9.4 Profile of Households Who Receive Four or More Pieces of Mail

	Total Households	*Household Head*			
		35-49	*50+*	*Income $35M+*	*Husband& Wife Work*
Received none	20.1%	12.8	22.8	12.3	11.9
Received four or more	31.3	34.3	35.8	44.1	37.5

Source: Stan Rapp, "Simmons Study Takes a Peek at In-Home Purchasing Transactions," *Direct Marketing,* December 1984, pp 36-40.

to nonprofit organizations) as a result of direct-mail solicitations. A large percentage of those who do are reasonably well satisfied with the experience.

The bad news is that a large percentage of the population does not purchase by direct mail. Parenthetically, that percentage is certainly not as large as the 52 percent you might infer from the Simmons study; a 1978 study by Ogilvy & Mather suggested that the percentage of non-mail-order buyers is about 19 percent.[5] The really bad news, however, is that these nonbuyers hold strongly negative attitudes toward mail order, so the likelihood of converting them into mail-order purchasers is slim.

One more perspective on the issue of junk mail: How many pieces of mail are actually sent through the postal system each year? Figure 9.1 shows total mail volume (140.1 billion pieces in 1985), first- class mail (72.4 billion), and third-class bulk mail (52.2 billion). Most direct mail, from both businesses and nonprofit organizations, is mailed third class. Significantly, third-class mail volume grew 132 percent in the decade from 1976 to 1985, while first class-volume grew only 39 percent.

That is, indeed, a great deal of mail. The job of the direct-mail manager is to find attractive products with both quality and value, to market them through pleasing direct-mail packages, to send them to the right individuals, and to give

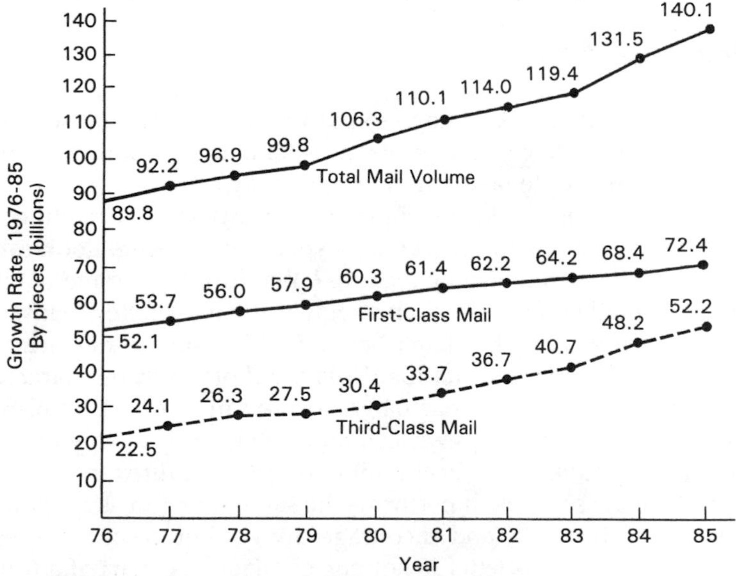

FIGURE 9.1 ***Growth of Third-Class Mail***
Source: Third Class Mail (monograph), p. 9, Direct Marketing Association.

[5] Quoted in John Stevenson, "The Next Direct Marketing," *Direct Marketing*, October 1986, p. 158.

the customer service that makes mail-order purchasing an entirely satisfactory experience. Admittedly, a big order, but that is what it will take to divorce the words "junk" and "mail" in the minds of the buying public!

THE "STANDARD" DIRECT-MAIL PACKAGE

We turn now to the formats available for direct mail. We will assume that there is such a thing as a "standard" direct-mail package, although, in reality, there is not (remember the advantage of virtually unlimited format choices). However, it is helpful to use a common package format as the basis for our discussion, and we call this the "standard." It includes:

- Outer envelope
- Letter
- Brochure
- Response device
- Reply device

We begin with the key sales component of the package—the letter.

The Letter

Direct-mail experts agree that the letter is the most important part of the direct-mail package. It presents the offer and communicates the sales message. It urges the reader to take action immediately.

The letter shown in Figure 9.2 was part of a mailing package sent as a response to inquiries generated by space advertising. Look carefully at the letter. What are its distinguishing features? Wouldn't you immediately recognize this as a direct-mail letter rather than a regular business letter? How?

For one thing, this letter has something similar to a headline—three lines in bold type before the salutation. This could probably be characterized as a Johnson Box, even though it isn't actually enclosed in a box. A Johnson Box (named after pioneer direct-mail copywriter Frank Johnson) is a copy block placed before the actual beginning of a direct-mail letter that captures the essential features of the offer in concise form. It performs the same function as a headline: it grabs the attention of the reader and encourages him or her to continue reading the letter.

Note that this letter is not personalized. As part of a fulfillment package, a personalized letter would be prohibitively expensive. "Dear Investor" captures the proper tone, however; this is being read by a person who is serious about making successful personal investments.

FIGURE 9.2 *Four-Page Fulfillment Letter*

Fidelity Investments

The Fidelity Building, 82 Devonshire Street, Boston, Massachusetts 02109
Fidelity funds are distributed nationally by Fidelity Distributors Corporation

Follow the "6 Steps To Fidelity Sector Investing" and find out for yourself if Fidelity Select Portfolios® could be a better way to pursue investment growth potential.

Dear Investor,

Here is the information you requested.

Please review it carefully. It will tell you why seeking investment growth with Fidelity Select Portfolios may be less risky, more convenient and more cost-effective than trading individual stocks.

Consider the unique investment opportunity Fidelity Select Portfolios offers.

Like many active investors, you know that regardless of where the market is headed, there will be times when some industry sectors outperform the stock market averages. While you may want to target your investment in a specific industry sector, you may not want to research and then choose from the many individual stocks available. And you may not wish to incur the risk or commissions normally associated with trading individual stocks.

Or perhaps you're currently investing in an equity mutual fund and value its traditional approach and professional management expertise. But you're looking for a more aggressive investment -- one that lets you target your investments to specific industry sectors.

Now there's an innovative opportunity: Investing in an industry sector portfolio.

Sector investing enables you to target your investment to specific industry sector portfolios -- comprised of a collection of stocks within that particular industry. This offers you the potential for greater returns -- at greater risk -- than mutual funds that invest in a broad range of industries. Sector investing through Fidelity Select Portfolios can provide you with . . .

(over, please)

-2-

Growth Potential. Fidelity Select Portfolios may offer you a way to try to outperform the stock market averages.

Industry Expertise. Each sector portfolio is managed by a Fidelity industry expert. That expert is responsible for choosing and managing a collection of potentially dynamic stocks within a particular industry. Forming the core of Fidelity's experienced research staff, these professionals know their specialized sector and the stock market.

Flexibility and Control. If you wish to take advantage of changing market conditions, you can reach a Fidelity representative to exchange your investments among any of Select's 35 industry sector portfolios by phone -- 24 hours a day. It costs just $10 per exchange.

Money Market Portfolio Option. For the times when you're undecided about which industry sector portfolio shows the greatest growth potential, Select offers you the convenience of a Money Market Portfolio. There you'll earn daily Money Market dividends while you decide on your next investment move.

Low Cost Transactions. Even with a 2% sales charge on purchases and 1% fee on redemptions, Select may provide you with a lower cost alternative to trading individual stocks.

Learn more about Fidelity Select Portfolios the Logical Way.

The enclosed Information Kit features the "6 Steps To Fidelity Sector Investing." These steps are each featured in a separate brochure designed to inform you about sector investing with Fidelity Select Portfolios and your potential for investment growth.

Fidelity developed these steps and the enclosed materials to make it more convenient for investors to learn about this innovative investment opportunity. Once armed with this information, you can decide whether investing with Fidelity Select Portfolios may be right for you.

Source: Courtesy of Fidelity Investments © 1987

FIGURE 9.2 ***Four-Page Fulfillment Letter***

-3-

These six logical steps are:

1. "Understand Sector Investing" -- Find out what sector investing is all about. Get answers to questions often asked by first-time sector investors. Understand the advantages and risks of investing in Fidelity Select Portfolios.

2. "Consider the Portfolio Choices" -- Look at the list of Select Portfolios to discover a wide range of industry sector portfolio choices. Then, examine profiles of each portfolio to help you decide which one or more may match your investment preferences.

3. "Check the Past Performance" -- See for yourself how many of the Fidelity Select Portfolios have performed in the past and compare this track record with the Standard & Poor's 500 index -- a widely recognized independent index of common stock prices.

4. "Know the Company" -- Understand Fidelity Investments -- its history, philosophy and direction. Find out why Fidelity has been entrusted with over $55 billion in assets.

5. "Count on Continuing Service" -- Once you've become a Fidelity Select Portfolios investor, you'll enjoy all of Fidelity's Investor Services -- plus a subscription to the Standard & Poor's Sector Trends newsletter. It's published for Select shareholders only, to help you take best advantage of sector investing.

6. "Read the Prospectus" -- It provides you with further details about Fidelity Select Portfolios to assist you in making an educated investment decision.

Remember: Fidelity Select Portfolios are aggressive in their search for capital appreciation, so share prices may be volatile.

Read your Information Kit
before opening your account.

You have information about the risks and potential rewards of Fidelity Select Portfolios at your fingertips. Read the "6 Steps to Fidelity Sector Investing" including the Prospectus. If you choose to invest, just complete the application attached to the Prospectus and mail it with your payment.

If you have any questions, please give us a call -- toll free -- at 1-800-544-6666 (in Massachusetts and Alaska, call collect 617-523-1919). A Fidelity representative will be able to answer your questions about Fidelity Select Portfolios.

You've taken the first steps toward potential investment growth by requesting the information in this kit. After thoroughly reading these materials, consider taking the next -- most important -- step by opening a Fidelity Select Portfolios account.

Sincerely,

Edward C. Johnson 3d
President

P.S. Remember, as a Fidelity investor, you'll have the support of all our investor services -- including access to a Fidelity representative 24 hours a day by phone. Plus, as a Select shareholder, you'll receive helpful information each month from Standard & Poor's Sector Trends newsletter -- published exclusively for Fidelity Select Portfolios shareholders to help you take the best advantage of sector investing.

Fidelity Distributors Corporation (General Distribution Agent)

SEL-ff1-10/86

Source: Courtesy of Fidelity Investments © 1987

Now look at the physical structure of the body of the letter. It follows the four rules set forth by mail-order copywriter Paul Bringe:[6]

1. It uses *short words*—almost all the words in the letter are of one to three syllables. There is no jargon; no complicated technical terms; just simple, straightforward English. Notice that this is true even though the letter is clearly targeted to an upscale population.
2. It uses *short sentences.* Bringe says that good sentences average about 12 words. Some will be shorter; some will be longer, but the average will be 12.
3. It uses *short paragraphs.* The paragraphs in this letter are no more than three sentences long. Bringe points out that a good paragraph can be just one sentence long.
4. It *looks easy to read.* That is partly the result of using short words, short sentences, and short paragraphs. It is also the result of using two ink colors—black with a rich-looking maroon (more upscale than the red ink used for many direct-mail letters) for the underlined sub-heads sprinkled liberally throughout the body of the letter. These break up the flow visually, creating more interest, and serve to highlight important parts of the message. The letter also uses indented blocks of copy to emphasize important points. Notice that when it wants to explain the six logical steps for deciding whether the product is right for the reader, it numbers them 1 through 6.

Notice some other things about this letter that are characteristic of a good direct-mail letter:

- Its tone is *personal.* The letter is not "folksy" or "cutsey," but is written as if one individual were speaking directly to another (just as a good salesperson would). This is not mass-media advertising; it is a letter to be read by one person at a time.
- It is *not* typeset. *Typewriter type* is used; large, easy-to-read type at that. Does a real letter look as if it has been printed on a printing press?
- It has a *postscript* that emphasizes important benefits as a final selling point. Direct-mail marketers know that even if most of the rest of the letter is not read, the postscript usually is. Use it for a final key message or a call to action on the part of the reader.
- It is signed by an individual in regular business-letter style.
- It is a four-page letter on regular business-size sheets (8 1/2 by 11 inches), folded. The length of a direct-mail letter will depend on the message you have to deliver and the audience to whom you are delivering it: Is the audience familiar with your firm and your product? How much informing, credibility building, and persuading need to be done? The issue is not length per se, even though many direct marketers seem to recommend long letters. Long letters can be successful;

[6]Quoted in Julian L. Simon, *How to Start and Operate a Mail-Order Business*, 4th ed. (New York: McGraw-Hill, 1987), pp. 260-266.

the 12-page fund-raising letter used in George McGovern's presidential campaign is a classic. But a short letter (a page or less) can also be successful if it delivers the right message to the right audience.

The Fidelity letter was mailed in response to inquiries based on space advertisements, presumably to people who were interested in (if not already purchasers of) stocks or mutual funds. Thus it wastes no time trying to convince them of the value of investing in equity instruments. Its objective is to close a sale or at least to provoke an inquiry to a telephone representative. It therefore has a fairly complex message to communicate, even though much of the complexity is reserved for the supporting folder (shown in Figure 9.3). The letter is no longer than absolutely necessary to communicate its message.

Notice that the Fidelity letter does not have:

- *Handwritten notes in the margin.* Handwritten notes would be inappropriate in an upscale letter about a very serious subject, though this technique is often used in consumer direct-mail letters.
- *Illustrations—drawings or photographs.* This is a letter, not a piece of sales-support literature. If visuals are needed, they belong elsewhere in the package.

So far, we have talked about the physical structure of a letter, aspects we can easily see and evaluate. These physical aspects merely implement the message the letter is designed to communicate. Now we will consider the communications approach taken in a direct-mail letter.

Many direct-mail copywriters like to follow the AIDA model. AIDA stands for:

Attention
Interest
Desire
Action

First you must get the prospect's *attention.* You do that by presenting the key selling point—offering the key benefit. In general advertising, this is often referred to as the unique selling proposition. The Fidelity letter actually offers the reader a "unique investment opportunity."

When you have the prospect's attention, you must then whet his or her *interest.* Don't just tell what the benefits of the product are, tell why—make the benefits credible. The Fidelity letter explains that its sector funds offer the benefits of investing in specific industries without the effort, cost, and risk of trading in individual stocks. It details specific benefits; it leads the reader through a series of support materials that provide in-depth information.

Next, instill in the reader a strong *desire* for the product—show why the prospect, the prospect's family, or the prospect's business will be better off with this product, why they absolutely must have it. Because the purchase of mutual

FIGURE 9.3 *Fidelity Investments Package*

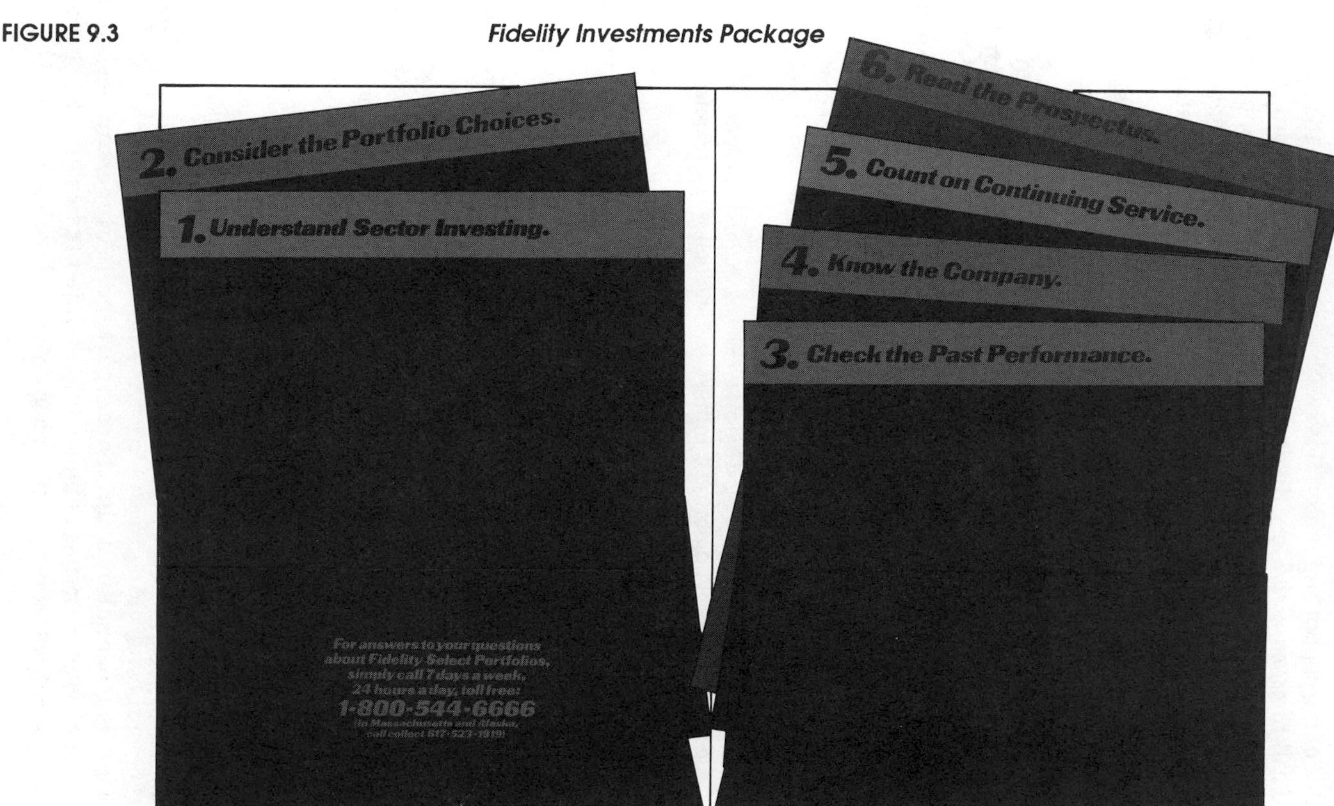

Source: Courtesy of Fidelity Investments ©1987.

funds is a complex consumer decision, the support material in the Fidelity package (Figure 9.3) carries a great deal of the burden of convincing the reader. The importance of the supporting material is emphasized just before the call to action.

The call to *action* is the key distinguishing feature of the direct-mail letter. Don't forget it or let it be weak. Don't just imply that the reader should do something—tell the individual exactly what you want him or her to do and encourage immediate action. Don't leave anything to the reader's imagination; be very specific about the action to be taken. In the Fidelity letter, the call to action is clear and it is accompanied by an invitation to call the toll-free number with any remaining questions. (If the reader still has "objections," the telephone representative will be able to "meet the objections" just as a field salesperson would.)

Stone suggests a seven-step approach to guiding a prospect through a series of stages that culminate in the desired action.[7] His formula is not meant to stifle creativity, but merely to guide it. Like any rule, it can sometimes be broken by an experienced copywriter who thoroughly understands the product and the audience and who comes up with a creative substitute. Stone's steps are:

1. *Promise a benefit in your headline or first paragraph—your most important benefit.* You are not writing a short story that builds to a climax. Unless you get the reader's attention and develop interest in the very beginning, the reader probably won't be around for your ending!
2. *Immediately enlarge on your most important benefit.* A good salesperson drives home the most important points in an enthusiastic and believable manner. Your direct-mail letter must do the same thing.
3. *Tell the reader specifically what he or she is going to get.* Be specific about product attributes so the customer develops a correct set of expectations about the product. Emphasize the benefits that are delivered by these attributes.
4. *Back up your statements with proof and endorsements.* After all, the reader knows this is advertising and is likely to view it with some cynicism. If you can provide testimonials from satisfied users, objective test results, or expert endorsements, the credibility of your message will be increased.
5. *Tell the reader what might be lost if action is not taken.* Give powerful and compelling reasons that will help to overcome the normal human tendency to defer action.
6. *Rephrase your prominent benefits in your closing offer.* A good sales presentation has a strong closing in which the salesperson summarizes the main selling points. The direct-mail letter should do the same.
7. *Incite action.* Now! Make the call to action strong and believable. If the reader puts the letter aside without acting, the battle is usually lost. Give good reasons why action should be taken, and make it easy to follow your instructions.

The Brochure

A letter is essential in a direct-mail package. A brochure—essentially a printed piece of four or six pages that is folded rather than stapled or bound—is optional but is frequently included. When should a brochure be used?

[7] Stone, *Successful Direct Marketing Methods*, pp. 272-273.

When there is a complex story to tell, when there are many attributes/benefits of the product that need to be explained, a brochure is needed. Even better, if the product can effectively be illustrated—preferably in use—a brochure may be the answer.

Again, there is no standard format for a brochure, but there are some useful guidelines. The brochure shown in Figure 9.4, which deals with a piece of software for computer-aided design/computer-aided manufacturing applications, illustrates a number of them. Because this is a six-page brochure, there was a little more latitude for creative graphics than if only four pages had been available.

The cover, page 1, is a simple benefit-oriented headline. The graphics are carried over onto page 5, which is actually the second page seen—or the first seen when the brochure is opened, if you want to think about it that way.

When the brochure is opened completely, pages 2, 3, and 4 are arrayed in a straight line. Thus all three surfaces are available to present a narrative that explains the product concept, its major benefits, and necessary technical details concerning hardware compatibility. The graphics help tell the story and lead the eye on through the narrative. Copy blocks are short; copy is broken up by the illustrations. This is done irregularly, not with a regular and boring sameness. Arrows highlight some of the main copy points, and also serve to move the eye along.

Page 6 simply repeats the name of the product, the positioning theme, and identifies the company.

Essentially, the story is told, the necessary selling points are made, on pages 2, 3, and 4. The other three surfaces are used for identity, positioning, and creative impact.

Notice some other things about this brochure:

- It is not written in a personal style. It is a piece of sales-support literature that can be used in ways other than as part of the fulfillment mailing from which it was taken.
- The brochure can stand alone if necessary. All the selling points are made in the copy of the brochure, even though they may well repeat the points included in the direct-mail letter. The different elements of the mail package may become separated, especially if more than one individual examines them. Each should be complete and self-contained.
- Graphics are used to show major features of the product. It is even better to show the product in use to emphasize benefits.
- Color was thought to be worth the added expense. This 8 1/2-by-11- inch brochure was produced on heavy, glossy paper stock, adding to the credibility of the presentation. The hard surface of this type of paper also allows for excellent color reproduction. As Stone says, "A two-color circular generally proves to be more effective than a one-color circular. Full-color is warranted in the promotion of such items as food, apparel, furniture, and other merchandise if the fidelity of color reproduction is good." [8]

[8] Stone, *Successful Direct Marketing Methods*, p. 287.

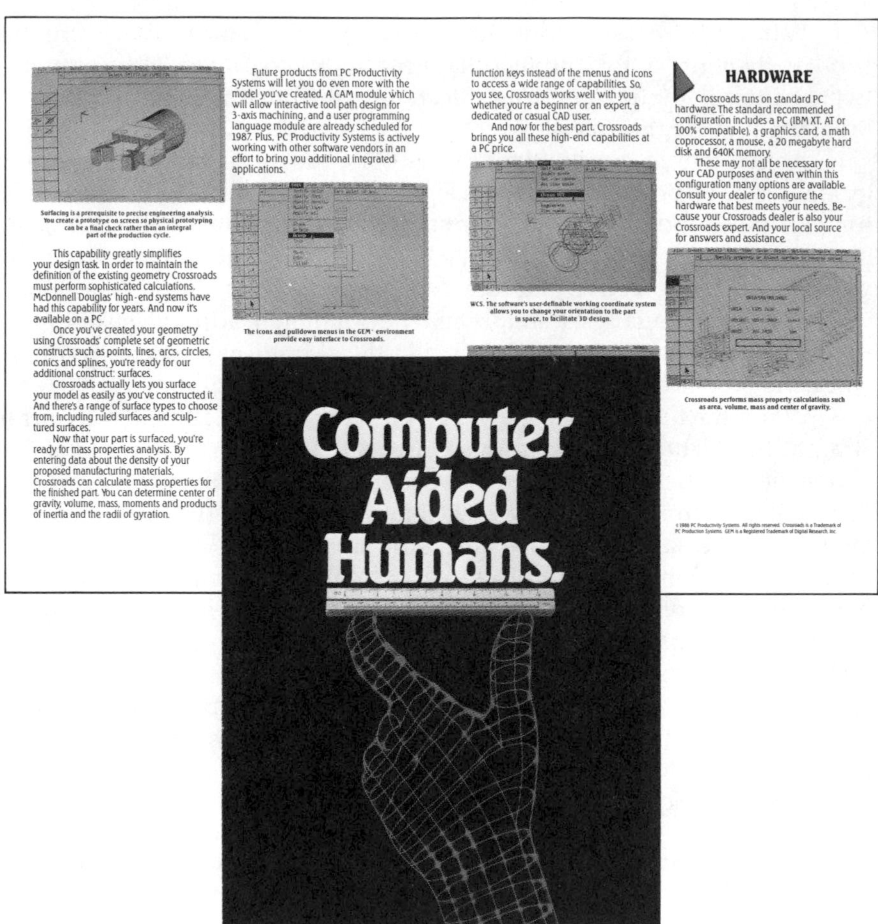

FIGURE 9.4 ***A Business-to-Business Brochure***

Source: Courtesy of Mc-Donnell Douglas Information Systems Group, St. Louis, MO 63166

A well-done brochure can deliver a sales message with a great deal of impact and credibility. Brochures, or some variant of them, are used in most business-to-business mailings. More costly and elaborate consumer mail packages also tend to have brochures. Brochures can be used in not-for-profit mailings, but care should be taken that they do not look too slick and expensive, for that may convey an image of spending too much money on frills and too little on delivery of services.

The Outer Envelope

Obviously, the outer envelope is the first part of the direct-mail package seen by the recipient. Equally obvious is the fact that the envelope must be opened—must be perceived as interesting enough to warrant opening—if the remainder of the direct-mail package is to have an opportunity to do its job. McLean believes that the envelope has 5 to 10 seconds to provoke sufficient interest to get the recipient to open it; otherwise it will be discarded unopened.[9]

Envelopes can be purchased from stock or made to order in an almost infinite number of sizes, colors, types, and materials. Before choosing an envelope (or any outer covering for a mailing piece), the direct marketer must be sure that it conforms to postal regulations. Printers and envelope suppliers appear to be logical sources of advice, but may not be experts on mailing procedures and regulations. When in doubt, consult the publications available from the USPS.[10] The envelope must also be large and strong enough to safely convey the material placed in it. Beyond these functional considerations, the outer envelope must do an effective marketing job. What makes an outer envelope effective?

The answer to that question depends on two aspects of your marketing program: the nature of your market and the nature of your offer. An upscale consumer market or a business market may respond better to a high-quality envelope that looks as much as possible like a regular business mailing. The prior relationship, or lack of one, with the recipient also makes a difference. According to McLean:[11]

- When selling to active customers, the envelope needs to suggest a new development worthy of their attention—a new product, a sale, etc.
- When soliciting inquiries from customers or prospects, one of two extremes usually works best—no copy or copy that reveals the complete nature of the offer.
- A "cold" sales message to prospects, especially ones unfamiliar with your product or your firm, is the most severe test of an envelope. Again, one of the two extremes is likely to work best—a plain envelope (whatever its size or shape) with just a standard business return address or an envelope with highly-involving copy and/or graphics. If you elect to use (or, more properly, to test) copy on your envelope, think of it as a headline.

Headlines can inform or promise a benefit. They can be phrased as a declarative statement or as a question intended to excite the curiosity of the reader; consequently, they are often referred to as *teasers*. Some examples:

- On the envelope of a consumer sweepstakes mailing: "Would you like to know how it feels to win $1,000,000?"
- On the wrapper of a small box delivered by UPS to a business address: "Our computer has 1.2M more megabytes of storage than our nearest competitor."

[9] Ed McLean, "Direct Mail Envelopes," in Edward L. Nash, ed., *The Direct Marketing Handbook* (New York: McGraw-Hill, 1984), pp. 479-493.

[10] The USPS has an informative booklet called the *Mailers Guide*, prepared by the Customer Services Department, and available at most post offices free of charge. If more detailed information is needed, all post offices have copies of the *Domestic Mail Manual* and the *International Mail Manual*.

[11] McLean, "Direct Mail Envelopes," pp. 483-490.

[When opened, the box revealed a set of plaster teeth that immediately started opening and closing (byting?).]

- On the envelope of a conservative fund-raising appeal: "Joan Baez wants you to throw this away!"
- Following up on an inquiry requires a statement on the envelope indicating "This is the information you requested." This is essential to differentiate it from unsolicited mailings.
- Envelopes containing subscription or membership renewal forms should identify the publication or organization. At the same time, they should look different from other mailings to the same individual. A "limited time" or "urgency" theme is often used for this envelope copy.
- Nonprofit organizations sending direct mail to an established patronage or donor base find that a straightforward businesslike envelope usually works best. When they are sending a "cold" mailing to a broader target audience, an envelope with teaser copy is more likely to be opened.

Envelope copy and graphics are important to the success of the mailing, and testing and refinement are essential to find what works best.

Another issue that is often raised with regard to the envelope is how the postage, whether third- or first-class, should be affixed. These are three choices: an indicia (a printed statement that the postage is to be paid by a numbered postal account), postage meter, or regular stamp. The best manner for affixing postage depends on the nature and objectives of the mailing itself. A postage stamp is the most personal, an indicia is the least. Metered postage looks businesslike.

Two points need to be made about postage. First, since the manner in which the postage is affixed may affect the response rate, it can and should be tested. Second, the question of how to affix the postage is not the same as whether to use first- or third-class postage. If the mailing is not expected (was not requested by the recipient) or if its timing can be established well in advance (renewal notices for publications), third-class mail is satisfactory. If the mailing was in any way requested by the recipient (an inquiry generated by advertising in any medium), or if timely delivery is essential for any other reason, first-class postage should be used.

All of these considerations suggest that the outer envelope has more than the utilitarian function of conveying and protecting the material inside. It is an integral part of the direct-mail package. As such, the design of the envelope should be in harmony with the characteristics of the offer, helping to convey the image and positioning that have guided development of the offer.

As you have read this section, you have probably recalled some envelopes you've found annoying or misleading, like the following:

- Envelopes that strongly resemble the overnight mail services of private companies and the USPS.

- Window envelopes allowing "Pay to the order of" to show. When opened, the nonnegotiable instrument is found to be tied to a purchase, entering a contest, or the like.
- Envelopes that state unequivocally that the recepient has won a prize. Inside you find that you must do something like visit a time-sharing condominium in the next state to "claim" your prize.
- Envelopes that convey a government-agency image—especially the one that looks like your overdue income tax refund!
- Envelopes whose appearance suggests a legal or other official notification.
- The last example is not an envelope, but it deserves to be included in this list. One of the authors received a postcard that looked very much like an order acknowledgment or a service completion announcement. It turned out to be an attempt to sell a 35mm camera for $12.88!

None of these mailings actually broke a law. And all must be effective in getting recipients to open them, or direct marketers wouldn't keep using them. But are they unethical? Some people argue very strongly that they are because they are designed to mislead, even if only until the envelope is opened or the postcard is read. They certainly show bad judgment and are good examples of the kinds of business practices that give all direct marketers a bad name.

The Response Device

A good salesperson always asks for the order, and does it in a way that is hard to refuse. The same is true of direct mail—make it clear what action is desired and make it easy for the recipient to take that action. There is more than one device for doing this:

- Simple order form or reply card
- Reply-O-Letter: a response card, often already filled out, inside a sleeve. All the recipient has to do is pull it out and drop it in the mail.
- Self-mailer: any mailing that does not have a separate envelope. It can contain a reply card (to be cut or torn out of the printed piece) or a reply envelope stapled or glued in.
- Bangtail envelope: an envelope with a second flap—actually, a perforated elongation of the envelope flap. The tail is a response device for an offer ancillary to the main purpose of the mailing (a bill stuffer, for example).
- A sticker or an actual Rolodex card to encourage telephone response.

The response device is so important that some direct-response copywriters design it before they write the main pieces of copy. Why? Once you have the response device in front of you, you know exactly what information the recipient must have and therefore are not likely to forget to include any important piece of information in the letter or brochure.

One creative approach that ties the response device to the main theme of the mailing package is a simple illustration of the product. Another is a colored paper stock that carries through the color theme of the mailing. Two- or four-color printing will make the response device more attractive. Or the printing can be superimposed over an illustration.

Other recommendations for making a response device both attractive and functional are:

- Design it so the eye moves easily through the form.
- Make sure it includes all the information the respondent needs to fill out the order/request accurately and promptly.
- Give the respondent plenty of room to write in the necessary information.
- Don't let the envelope flaps cover important parts of the form such as the instructions.
- Call the response device something besides an order form—a Free Trial Certificate, an Acceptance Slip, a Membership Card.
- Make it look important—some response devices look like bond certificates, others look like reply cards in a wedding invitation.
- Restate the offer, terms, and guarantee.
- Offer an opportunity to "trade up" (e.g., a two-year instead of a one-year subscription) or to order a "special."
- Use an involvement device.
- Display your toll-free number prominently for people who are in a hurry or don't like to fill out order forms.

The experts do not agree about the kind of response device that works best. Stone recommends order forms "with a busy, rather jumbled appearance and plenty of copy."[12] Others[13] think that elaborate response devices can be overdone and that a simple, straightforward one often works well.

In summary, the direct marketer needs a response device that is appropriate to the target market, the image and positioning of the offer, and the creative approach taken in the mailing package. Within these constraints, the direct-mail manager must test to find out which specific response device works best.

The Business Reply Envelope

The "business reply envelope" part of the direct mail package does not have to be an actual envelope. Every package must include some type of postage-paid

[12] Stone, *Successful Direct Marketing Methods*, p. 268.

[13] C. James Schaefer and William C. Allen, "Response Device Variations," in Nash, *The Direct Marketing Handbook*, pp. 473–474.

response device, but it can be a formal business reply envelope (BRE) or some other type of mailer.

Nash states flatly, "It does pay to have a reply envelope, even when the offer can be mailed back on a card."[14] Other experts have an "it depends" attitude. A reasonable hypothesis is that an envelope confers a certain importance and is worth the additional cost when that is the desired perception on the part of the respondent.

Other Inserts

A wide variety of inserts can be added to the standard direct-mail package to increase the response rate. (These add-ons are sometimes referred to as *peripherals*.) Turley[15] describes the following types of inserts:

Circulars, Folders, and Product Sheets. These three terms are used interchangeably by many professionals to designate a type of insert that is factual, perhaps even technical in nature. It is hard to precisely define this insert. It may be a single flat sheet; if folded, it usually unfolds to be no larger than the letter. It is designed to describe and give details about the product in a way that is more straightforward than the sales-oriented presentation of the letter or brochure. Consequently, it is less likely to be printed in four colors; ordinarily two-color printing (or even black and white for product sheets) is used. Since this type of insert is supportive of a sales objective, it contains more detail than is usually considered desirable in an inquiry-generation mailing.

The Fidelity letter described earlier was supported by a rather elaborate folder (Figure 9.3). Its design echos the six steps described in the letter, creating a very well coordinated mail package. Each of the six pamphlets in the folder has a different format to maintain reader interest.

No. 1 is four pages long, with two pages of questions and answers about the product and a fourth page listing "10 Reasons Why You Should Consider Investing in Fidelity Select Portfolios." No. 2 is eight pages long and describes the individual select portfolios in considerable detail. No. 3 is a single sheet showing comparative returns for some of the portfolios. No. 4 is essentially testimonials—favorable quotations about Fidelity from several of the nation's leading business publications. No. 5 is a single sheet describing a special newsletter that is sent free to everyone who invests in one or more of Fidelity's portfolios. No. 6 is the complete prospectus, 36 pages in length, with two additional pages for a foldout order form.

A number of details make this folder both easy to use and impressive:

[14] Edward L. Nash, *Direct Marketing: Strategy/Planning/Execution* (New York: McGraw-Hill, 1982), p. 305.

[15] Brian Turley, "Direct Mail Inserts," in Nash, *The Direct Marketing Handbook*, pp. 507-516.

- Each of the pamphlets is approximately 1 inch shorter than the one behind it, so when you place them back in the folder they all show. Also, it is hard to place them back in the wrong order.
- The firm's toll-free number is displayed on the folder itself and prominently on each of the pamphlets.
- A window in the back cover shows the mailing label under the words "Reserved for."
- The dominant color is a deep maroon—the same color used for the header and other emphasized copy in the letter.

It is worth noting that this package contained only the letter, the folder, and a business reply envelope. The outer envelope announced "Information You Requested About Select Portfolios." A simple, straightforward (but certainly not inexpensive!) presentation, done with the serious investor in mind.

Broadsides. A broadside, also hard to define, unfolds into a single large sheet, 17 by 22 inches or larger. Often it is inserted into a much smaller mailing package for impact and to provide a large surface on which to display product features, product in use, and numerous supporting blocks of copy. Broadsides often contain an order form, but this order form should not take the place of a separate response device.

Lift Letters. Often called *publishers' letters* because they were first used in that industry, these are undersized inserts that frequently begin "Don't open this unless you have decided not to accept this offer." Of course, the idea is that the reader will open and read it, providing one more opportunity to convince him or her of the value of the offer. The lift letter restates the offer, but from a different perspective. It should be signed by a different person from the individual who signed the main letter. Lift letters are reputed to sometimes generate substantial increases in response rate, perhaps as much as 25 percent.

Gift or Discount Slips. Also called *buck slips*, these inserts offer free gifts or price breaks or perhaps some last-minute information. Why make this a separate piece in the mailing? One reason is to test variations in the gift or discount. Another is that the slips can be implemented or discontinued quickly and cheaply, without changing the rest of the mailing package. Gift slips are usually smaller than most other items in the package, and should be designed to stand out. Don't forget that addition of a gift or discount will change the cost structure of your offer!

If you decide to use an additional insert, be sure it meets the following criteria:

- It is distinctive and stands out from the rest of the mailing. You do not even have to use the same type and grade of paper.

- It provides a different perspective on, not just a reiteration of, the selling points used in other pieces of the mailing.
- It has a built-in response device in case it gets separated from the rest of the mailing.
- Its copy and visuals are supportive of the main message, sharp, and easy to follow.
- It can be inserted into the package mechanically.
- It does not push the weight of the package over the limit for the amount of postage planned.

OTHER ASPECTS OF DIRECT-MAIL MARKETING

A number of other issues require decisions during the planning of the direct-mail program or when the package is being designed. Some of these issues will be affected by the format chosen, others will not.

Personalization

Remember that one of the things direct mail does especially well is deliver a personalized message. Let's consider two different types of personalization: the use of the recipient's name and individualized letters and/or packages.

If you possibly can, address the package to a person (not "Occupant" or "Patron") and use the recipient's name in the salutation of the letter. For a business-to-business mail package, also use the title of the intended recipient if it is available.

On the other hand, don't misuse the person's name! Don't use it (or the address) just to show you know it, rather than to enhance the sales message. "If it [the recipient's name] is forced into something, it's not going to lift response," according to one direct-response agency executive. "Only where you're trying to communicate that 'we know you, we're friendly, here's how we can help you' does it work. If you can create a whole scenario, it is extremely effective."[16]

Guardala gives some do's and don'ts for name use:[17]

Don't Mr. *Matthew* Smith will find thirty recipes each month in *Gourmet*.

Do Mr. Smith, the next four-star dining experience people will talk about in Boston could very well be at 42 Southlake Dr. The talk might well center around *your* truffled chicken, one of the 60-minute recipes you'll find in our free bonus issue of *Gourmet*.

Don't I'd like to send these slacks to 121 South River Dr. for a 15-day free trial, Mrs. Smith.

[16] Kevin T. Higgins, "Personalized Direct Mail Moves from Novelty to Standard," *Marketing News*, July 4, 1986, p. 7.

[17] Lucille M. Guardala, "Direct Mail Personalization," in Nash, *The Direct Marketing Handbook*, p. 502.

Do What's the advantage of our 15-day free trial offer, Mrs. Smith? Something no store in Dallas will let you do. When the slacks arrive at 121 South River Dr., wash them, wear them. If you think there's a better value in Dallas . . .

Don't The next twenty-six issues of *Time* are yours for 53 cents each, Ms. Jones.

Do Sitting in a chair at 95 Raff Avenue, you can take the pulse of world capitals in 60 minutes. That's how long it takes to keep up with the world in *Time* each week, Ms. Jones. All it costs, Damascus to Dayton, is 53 cents.

The other type of personalization (discussed in more detail in connection with databases in Chapter 6) is customization of the message. In direct-mail packages this is frequently accomplished by using a versioned or variable-paragraph letter. As the names suggest, individual letters are created from a selection of standard paragraphs. Theoretically, a huge number of paragraphs can be used, but realistically, the number is limited by the availability of information in the data base.

Beyond access to the technology (printers, software, and databases), what should you consider when deciding whether to use personalization in a mailing? Guardala lists eight important considerations:[18]

1. *Budget*. Personalization will cost more; how much more is a question to direct to the production experts. Once you know the answer, the question becomes: Will the increase in response rate be sufficient to justify the increase in cost?
2. *Product*. Personal, emotional motives and appeals are appropriate for some products but not for others. Financial services like insurance require decisions that are very personal in nature. Guardala suggests that copy about a wood-burning stove would not be enhanced by personalization.
3. *Target market*. The kinds of personalization that appeal to a downscale audience may be considered silly or even offensive by a more upscale group.
4. *Strategy*. If your approach is highly targeted, it is probably appropriate to use a personalized message.
5. *Lists/databases*. Does the necessary information exist in machine-readable form?
6. *Category history*. If the industry (e.g., insurance) or the technique (e.g., sweepstakes) has consistently used personalization, think carefully before disregarding the conventional wisdom.
7. *Universe*. Is the total market sufficiently large to make the entire program—test plus roll-out—viable?
8. *Timing*. It takes longer to produce a personalized mailing. Does the planned mail date leave sufficient time?

Personalization can be a very powerful technique. The local bank, in promoting home equity loans, points out that homes in your neighborhood have appreciated about x percent over the last 10 years. The letter goes on to say that you may therefore have as much as $*y* in equity, which you can obtain only if you sell your home or take out a second mortgage. That approach gets the reader's atten-

[18] Guardala, "Direct Mail Personalization," pp. 500-501.

tion! Bear in mind that it also requires a considerable amount of data gathering and list editing to make sure the appeal is accurate. Without accuracy, it would lose all impact.

The direct marketer should certainly evaluate the cost effectiveness of personalization. However, experience suggests that in most instances personalized messages will out-pull nonpersonalized ones.

Timing and Sequencing of Mailings

A truism of direct marketing is that you can't mail too frequently to your own customer base. While it is probably unwise to take that statement literally, many experts agree that most direct marketers could mail more frequently to their own customers and to their best lists. Precisely how frequently, though, is a question that has to be answered by each direct marketer through experimentation.

The first thing to understand is the response curve for orders (or inquiries) from mailings for a particular product or product line. In other words, how quickly do the responses come in? When can you expect to have received them all?

Simon quotes seven different studies of response times.[19] Unfortunately, they differ widely. Taking three of the consumer mailings that seem to have some surface similarity and doing some interpolating gives the following results:

End of 1st week	30-40 percent of responses received
End of 2nd week	58-73 percent of responses received
End of 3rd week	75-81 percent of responses received
End of 4th week	84-90 percent of responses received
End of 26th week	100 percent of responses received

Obviously, these ranges are far too broad to be of any real use; hence the warning that each direct-mail manager must track his or her own response curve. By the way, direct marketers measure from the date the first response is received (to compensate for postal irregularities), not from the date the mailing is dropped. This information is critical if you need to estimate total response rate before all responses have been received.

In fact, you will probably have to make a decision on remailing long before all responses have been received. Just how soon can you actually remail? Here again, unfortunately, the experts disagree. Simon quotes one as saying that if the response rate is twice break-even, mail again (the same offer to the same list) after 45 days. Another says 70 days! Two things seem clear: You can mail again more quickly than most people would expect; and the more successful the mailing, the more quickly you can remail the same offer to the same list.

Again, the only way to know how frequently you can remail—and this question is most critical for your house list—is to experiment. Carefully matched

[19] Simon, *How to Start and Operate a Mail-Order Business*, pp. 258-259.

sample groups and a considerable period of time will be necessary to arrive at a satisfactory answer.

The direct-mail manager must also be aware of seasonal effects on response rates. The product itself may be seasonal—a gift item or cold weather clothing, for example. Moreover, just as retail sales vary by month, so do mail-order sales. Figure 9.5 presents an index that can be used as a guide to non-product-related seasonal effects. You may be surprised to note that, in general, January is the best month for mail-order sales. The reason is not entirely clear, but direct marketers hypothesize that people relax after the Christmas season and spend some of their housebound winter moments engaging in mail-order shopping.

That the material in Figure 9.5 is only a very general guide is emphasized by seasonality studies of specific product categories. Harper presents the results of seasonality studies of ten different product categories.[20] These studies make two important points about seasonality: (1) there are distinct (and distinctly different) seasonal patterns for different product categories; and (2) these patterns change, usually gradually, over the years.

For example, for the category "business/finance," December has been the leading month, as measured by percent of total mailings, every year from 1980-1981 through 1984-1985. In 1984-1985 June was the second most popular month for this type of mailing, having risen from eighth place in 1980-1981.

For the category "parents and children," July has been the best month for each of these same five years, with August, December, and January also strong. Considerable change is also evident in the seasonality pattern for this category of mailings.

This category-based information is very useful to the direct-mail manager. Keep in mind two things, however. First, other considerations such as promotion schedules, frequency of mailings, and list availability can cause the marketer to schedule mail drops for times that are not optimal in terms of seasonality. Second, when evaluating results of mailings, seasonality effects should be taken into account.

Scheduling Execution of a Mail Order Package

The novice tends to seriously underestimate the time it takes to prepare a direct-mail package. The result is that either the planned mail date is missed (which may well lower the response rate) or the package is more expensive or shoddily put together because everything has been done on a rush basis. Plan ahead, and allow a little more time than you actually expect preparing the package will take.

The best advice for developing a schedule for the execution of a mail-order package is to start by estimating how long the most time-consuming element will

[20] Rose Harper, *Mailing List Strategies: A Guide to Direct Mail Success* (New York: McGraw-Hill, 1986), pp. 118-128.

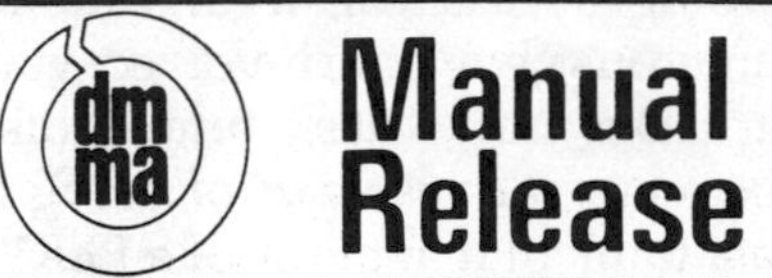

Release: 8302
Subject: Response by Months
Reprinted: February 1978

A Study Of Direct Mail Response By Months

NOTE: See also Release 2102

Recently Florence Wolf, Chicago, Illinois, conducted a survey among 40 direct response users throughout the country. After the results were tabulated, Florence was able to establish the following table of comparative response by months.

MONTH	PERCENT OF RESPONSE
January	100.0%
February	96.3%
March	70.0%
April	71.5%
May	72.0%
June	68.0%
July	73.3%
August	84.0%
September	79.0%
October	89.9%
November	80.0%
December	74.0%

(How to Read: February response was found to be 96.3% of the response obtained in January.)

Single Issue Price:
DMMA Members: $1.25
Non-DMMA Members: $2.00

FIGURE 9.5 ***Direct Mail Response***

require. List acquisition is frequently the most time-consuming element, often requiring from 6 to 8 weeks from initial contact to complete readiness. After you estimate the the time each element will require, plan backward from the most time-consuming elements.

A simple step-by-step schedule is insufficient for anything except a simple mailing by a small organization. If the mailing is more complex and/or if numerous people are involved, you need a very detailed day-by-day chart specifying tasks, start dates, completion dates, and persons responsible for each task. There are various ways of doing this—many firms use a daily calendar—but at least think of it in terms of a PERT chart. That is, some activities (e.g., identifying mailing lists and developing copy and graphics) can go on simultaneously. Other activities must be carried out consecutively. A trivial example is that the letter copy must be written before the printer can begin typesetting it.

AFTER THE SUCCESSFUL DIRECT MAIL PACKAGE . . .?

Because direct-response marketing allows the manager to know exactly what works and what does not, what is profitable and what is not, the search for something even better is unending. We close this chapter with two points of view, both very useful, on how to conduct that search.

In the chapter on testing (Chapter 8) we stated a number of times that certain elements of a direct-response program can greatly affect response rate, while others will have less effect. For a direct-mail package, the powerful elements are usually the product itself, the structure of the offer, product positioning, and list selection. How can you change any of these elements to make it more effective?

Stone suggests you ask yourself three types of questions as you try to develop possible improvements in your direct-mail package for testing:[21]

1. Can I add anything that will lift the response rate? An insert, a free gift, a contest, sweepstakes? (Just be sure you do not lift the response rate at the expense of depressing the profit!)
2. Can I extract anything from previous executions—some appeal, perhaps, that got buried in the earlier versions of the package, but which, if highlighted, might prove very effective?
3. Can I come up with an innovative approach to marketing this product? A blockbuster idea may be especially useful when a mail package has become old and tired.

One or more of these approaches should be employed with every mailing in a continuing effort to develop a new package that will beat the control.

Stevenson takes a different perspective.[22] Where Stone, correctly, encourages direct marketers to improve upon what they are already doing, Stevenson challenges them to look beyond their current approaches in an attempt to uncover new, untapped market segments. His reasoning is that if the "typical" (and there is really no such thing) response rate is 2 percent, what about the other 98 percent?

[21] Stone, *Successful Direct Marketing Methods*, pp. 284-285.

[22] John Stevenson, "98% Negative Database Holds Power of Expansion Benefits," *Direct Marketing*, March 1985, pp. 38-47.

You will recall from the chapter on mailing lists (Chapter 4) that direct marketers improve productivity by selecting only the best names and mailing to them. Whether we have 98 percent nonresponse from a mailing or whether we do not mail to the lowest 50 percent of a list, we have many names which represent an essentially untapped market. Consider just two possibilities.

Perhaps the nonresponders are potential customers, but for some reason are not yet ready to become actual customers. In terms of a frequently-used advertising model, they have not moved far enough up the "hierarchy of effects" (awareness, knowledge, liking, conviction, and purchase) to buy. If we approached them with a different mailing, one designed to coincide with their "readiness state" and move them along to the next stage in the hierarchy, could we gradually get them to the point of making a purchase? Experience suggests that we could, but success would require considerable knowledge about the individual prospect and a carefully designed campaign—not just a single mailing.

What if we decided to tap the 50 percent of our list of names who did not qualify for our initial mailing? Perhaps they have characteristics that would make them excellent prospects for another product in our line. Or maybe they would respond to another appeal or positioning. Our database contains a great deal of information about these people. Instead of just discarding them, we might conduct additional analyses to see if we could target them differently.

The point is to use everything you know and all the technology at your disposal to make your direct-mail programs more productive. A good direct marketing manager is never satisfied, even with success!

SUMMARY

Direct mail is the standard by which the entire direct-response industry is measured, for better or for worse. Direct-mail pieces can range from a simple postcard to a complex personalized mail package. Each part of the mailing must be appropriate for the target market and the direct marketer's objectives, and must be integrated with all other parts to deliver a cohesive message to the recipient. Continued testing and improved analytical methods hold the promise of increasing the productivity of the direct-mail effort.

DISCUSSION QUESTIONS

1. Explain the difference between direct mail, mail order, and direct marketing.
2. What do we mean by the "standard mail package"? What does it contain?
3. What are the most important characteristics of a good direct mail letter?
4. What are some of the additional inserts that may be included in a direct mail package? Why would a direct mail marketer use one of them?
5. How can a direct marketer increase the pulling power of a direct mail package?

6. Save all the direct mail you receive for a week or two. Sort the pieces into three piles—the ones you definitely would have opened, the ones you definitely would not have opened, and the ones you might have opened. Explain why each piece was assigned to that particular category. Now open the ones that attracted you and study their contents. What issues discussed in this chapter do you see illustrated in your own mail?

SUGGESTED ADDITIONAL READINGS

1. William A. Cohen, *Building a Mail Order Business*, 2nd ed. (New York: John Wiley & Sons, 1985).
2. Freeman F. Gosden, Jr., *Direct Marketing Success: What Works and Why* (New York: John Wiley & Sons, 1985).
3. Julian L. Simon, *How to Start and Operate a Mail-Order Business*, 4th ed. (New York: McGraw-Hill, 1981).

APPENDIX 9

PRINT PRODUCTION[1]

Commercial printers are fond of describing what they do as "putting ink on paper." While this is true, it is also an oversimplification of a very complex process. The purpose of this appendix is to provide a general overview of print production. These few pages can only introduce you to the process. Successful direct marketers must have a thorough grasp of the technical details of print production. Even the most experienced, however, work closely with their printer and pay close attention to this specialist's advice throughout a project.

Print production involves a number of steps. The actual printing is one of the last steps, not one of the first. However, earlier steps will be affected by the type of printing process used. The direct marketer must know what types of printing processes are available and decide which is most appropriate for a specific job before actual production begins.

TYPES OF PRINTING PROCESSES

There are five basic types of commercial printing processes—lithography or offset, gravure, letterpress, screen, and electronic ink jet. *Letterpress* is not often used for direct marketing applications. *Offset* is used for most direct mail catalogs and promotional packages because of its relative speed and economy. *Gravure* is used for high-volume applications ranging from upscale catalogs printed on high-gloss paper to mailers and inserts produced on newsprint. *Screen* is used to meet special graphics requirements. *Ink jet* is used for personalization of pieces already printed using another process or for low-volume or highly specialized jobs. Figure 1 summarizes the capabilities and most common uses of each of the basic processes.

The computer enthusiast will notice that the list of basic printing processes does not include desktop publishing—the combination of specialized microcomputer software and laser printers that can produce finished copy and artwork. Many marketers now prepare newsletters and black-and-white newspaper or magazine ads and direct mail pieces on desktop publishing systems. Improvements in both software and printers, including color capability, will rapidly broaden the range of applications. In most applications, however, desktop publishing will not replace conventional commercial printing; it will speed and perhaps simplify the makeup of the piece prior to printing.

[1]The information in this appendix is based on *Pocket Pal: A Graphic Arts Production Handbook*, 13th ed. (New York: International Paper Company, 1986); Katie Muldoon, *Catalog Marketing* (New York: R. R. Bowker, 1984), pp. 69–104; and Robert H. Jurick, "Lettershop Processing," in *The Direct Marketing Handbook*, Edward L. Nash, ed. (New York: McGraw-Hill, 1984), pp. 593–610.

FIGURE 1 ***Characteristics of Major Printing Processes Used by Direct Marketers***

Process	*Nature of Process*	*Appropriate Printing Surfaces*	*Preparation*	
			Copy	*Artwork*
Lithography (also called offset, offset lithography)	Printing image is captured on a plane (flat) surface which has been chemically treated so the image is receptive to ink and the nonprinting surface is nonreceptive to ink Printing image is offset from a plate to a rubber blanket before being transferred to paper	Sheet-fed or web-fed paper; heavy stock through newsprint	Photo-ready mechanicals which include both copy and artwork	
Gravure	Printing image (ink) captured in wells on the surface of a cylinder, then transferred directly to paper Paper run between ink-bearing cylinder and impression cylinder; as cylinders rotate the ink is transferred to the paper	Web-fed paper; packaging materials; heavy stock through newsprint	Art and copy prepared and submitted separately; exact preparation depends on publication requirements.	
Letterpress	Uses metal type set by hand or machine in a heavy metal frame; type is then locked into place; rollers ink the raised surfaces of type; ink is then transferred directly to paper	Sheet-fed or web-fed paper; packaging materials	Choose typeface; type copy, refer to copyfitting table for space requirements	Photoengravings or plates
Screen	Utilizes screen of silk, nylon, dacron, or stainless steel Stencil protects nonprinting image Thick ink spread over screen and forced through onto the surface to be imprinted	Virtually any surface; paper, wood, metal, cloth, etc.	Stencil prepared manually, photomechanically, or by some combination of the two	
Electronic/ Ink Jet	Processes are similar in that no printing plate or cylinder is used; instead, image stored in digital form in computer and reproduced for each copy printed Electronic processes use laser beam to transfer image to a drum from which it is developed by toner and transferred to paper (similar to copying machine) Ink jet uses many tiny nozzles through which ink is sprayed onto the paper	Primarily sheet-fed paper	Keyed into the computer; may be entered into any computer and transmitted to another via any data transmission method	

Typical Applications	Advantages	Disadvantages	How to Recognize
Sheet-fed: Books, catalogs, cards, posters, coupons, packaging *Web-fed:* Business forms, preprinted, sales support literature, books, magazines, catalogs	Eliminates need for expensive preparation of copy and artwork; rapid completion of jobs; good type reproduction	Images can be distorted; color can vary slightly	Seen under magnifying glass, edges of characters are smooth
Sunday newspaper supplements, preprints, catalogs	High speed with consistent color reproduction; can use a wide range of paper stock	Economical only for high-volume jobs	Seen under magnifying glass, edges of characters are serrate
Smaller sheet-fed equipment: Letterhead, envelopes, invitations, small brochures *Larger sheet-fed equipment:* Books, catalogs, packaging	Can be used for short, medium, or long runs (on different types of presses); economical for jobs which are mostly copy.	Reproduction of artwork is expensive	Seen under magnifying glass, there is a heavy ring of ink around each character
Banners, posters, billboards, counter displays and many others	Simple equipment; only practical process for many applications	Not economical for long runs	Thick layer of ink; may be able to see texture of screen
Addressing, coding, personalized letters, short publishing runs	Versatile; only practical process for some applications such as personalized pieces.	Images may be inconsistent	Dot pattern clearly visible in some applications

Computers can decrease the number of steps necessary to prepare a job for printing in other ways. Material can be produced by anything from simple word-processing software to sophisticated computer-aided design systems. It can be transmitted to the printer's equipment in ways which range from physically sending film or a floppy disk to using satellite telecommunications facilities. Just keep in mind that these are "high-tech" ways of performing basic tasks that are required before the printer finally "puts ink on paper."

Whatever processes are used for preparation and printing, the advice of a skilled, experienced printer is essential. Follow the advice in Chapter 5 and involve the printer and other production experts in the creative process itself. The results in terms of finished product, cost, and ability to stay on schedule will be far superior to just taking a completed creative execution to the printer and saying, "Here it is!"

THE PRODUCTION FLOW

Figure 2 represents the flow of work as it moves through the production process beginning with the creative concept and ending with the mail drop—the point at which the finished piece is put into the postal system. In this appendix we will assume a direct-mail piece, but the basic production process is the same for other types of printed material such as catalogs and newspaper inserts.

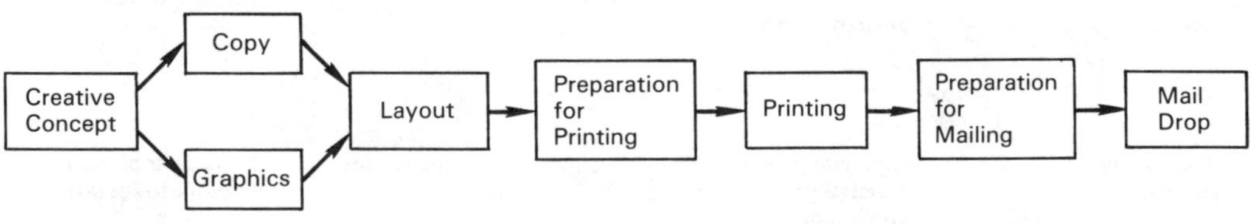

FIGURE 2

Creative and Layout

As discussed in Chapter 5, the creative concept provides direction to all the specialists involved in producing the final product. After the creative concept has been clearly articulated, the next step is to actually write the copy, take the photographs, and prepare the artwork. We have just discussed copy and artwork for direct-mail pieces in Chapter 9, and these subjects will be further discussed when we cover each of the other direct marketing media.

After the copy has been written and the photography and artwork has been completed, a layout is prepared to show the exact size and position of each element on every page. The layout doesn't have to contain finished copy and artwork, but the dimensions and positionings must be exact. If the layout is not correct, nothing that follows it will be either, so it should always be approved by the program manager before further work is done.

Preparation for Printing

The next step is to prepare both the copy and artwork for printing using the layout as a guide. Some of these activities differ greatly depending on the printing process and whether color is being used.

The preparation of copy is commonly referred to as *typesetting*, although that term is an historical anachronism. It refers to the activity of setting individual metal characters in metal grids, by hand in the early days of printing and later by machine and computer. The grids are then installed on the printing press. Rollers transfer ink onto the surface of the metal type and the image is transferred directly to the paper. This is the essence of the letterpress process which has been replaced by faster and more economical processes. Still, the term typesetting lingers on. Today copy is most often entered on a typewriter-like keyboard or other input devices that are part of specialized typesetting equipment, or it is photographed from camera-ready text.

Graphics preparation is complex and highly technical, but the basic concept can be explained simply. Whether the graphics consist of photographs or artwork, they are described as continuous-tone material (as opposed to line material—copy or simple line drawings). For the commonly used printing processes, these continuous tones must be converted to halftones. Halftones are a series of dots of varying intensity and size. There will be one halftone for each color used.

To see what a halftone is, look at a photograph in a catalog under a magnifying glass. You will see that the photograph is made up of tiny dots. These dots are relatively large and produce grainy, indistinct pictures. More expensive printed pieces use smaller dots on less porous paper and produce cleaner, sharper images, but the principle is the same. If the artwork is rendered in black and white, the dot pattern is differing densities of black dots on a white background. The device that controls the density of the dots is called a screen.

When color is used, a separate screen must be made for each color. To oversimplify, a screen is made for each of the basic colors—red, yellow, and blue.[2] These three colors plus black produce all the color gradations you see in printed pieces, and hence the term *four-color printing*. Any combination of two to four of these colors can be used to produce the desired effect. The process of creating a screen for each color is called *color separation*. When the piece is printed, each color will be applied separately, one on top of the other, to produce the final color image.

For some applications precise color is not essential. For other applications, such as photographs of fashion apparel, it is critical. To ensure that the final color will be acceptable, the direct marketer should always view and approve the photography before the separations are made and, later, the separations themselves. This sounds simple, but it isn't. There are a number of ways of viewing the separations, none of which exactly replicates the look of the subject. The way

[2]This is an oversimplification, because only one primary color can be removed from a continuous tone at a time. Removing red leaves blue and green (cyan); removing blue leaves red and green (yellow); removing green leaves red and blue (magenta). These three colors—cyan, yellow, and magenta—plus black are the four colors actually used in the printing process.

chosen for each job will depend on budget, time available, the separator's capabilities, and the importance of exact color. Ask as many questions as needed to make sure that your expectations of the final product are realistic and that they will be met. This is good advice at any stage in the production process, but is especially important for the color separations.

The next step is to bring the copy and graphics together into a final assembly or press layout. The final product of this stage is a paper or mylar (thin plastic) sheet with the negative of each element, copy or graphics, taped in place. The material behind each negative is cut away, and it is ready for the final pre-press step. A plate or cylinder is prepared from the assembly and transferred to a proof press.

A proof press run will be made to produce samples for the marketer's approval. Substantial changes at this point in the process are expensive, but it is the last chance to make them. Small adjustments can often be made while the job is actually on press, but they will be refinements, not changes.

FINISHING AND BINDING

After the items have come off the press, there are still two steps to complete in any but the simplest job--binding and finishing.

Depending on the nature of the finished piece, binding may include any or all of the following steps:

- *Scoring* puts a crease in the paper so it will be easier to fold.
- *Folding* may be as simple as creating a single-fold pamphlet. It may be as complex as creating sixteen separate pages from one large image on a *web-fed press* (a press that uses a continuous roll of paper instead of single sheets). When a sheet has been folded, it is called a *signature.*
- *Gathering* arranges the signatures in the proper order.
- *Stitching* fastens the signatures together.
- *Trimming* or cutting sizes the pages to the correct dimensions.

There are many activities possible in the finishing stage. They include *embossing* (producing a raised image), *die-cutting* (cutting special shapes), *varnishing,* and *laminating,* among others.

Most of the activities in the binding and finishing stages are automated in medium- to large-printing plants.

PREPARATION FOR MAILING

A printed piece—or more likely, several printed pieces waiting to become part of a mailing package—now exists. Another series of activities is needed before the package is complete and ready to be mailed. These are often referred to as *lettershop activities*. They may be performed in a separate establishment called a lettershop, or they may be handled by the printer's bindery. The major lettershop activities are:

- *Bursting* (separating multipart forms)
- *Folding*, if not done as part of the printing process or if additional folds are needed
- *Inserting* material into mailing envelopes
- *Stamping* or *metering*
- *Labeling* (affixing preprinted mailing labels)
- *Personalization* (printing names, addresses, source codes, salutations, and so forth, on already-printed mailing pieces)
- *Sorting* (by zip code and carrier route)
- *Tieing* (banding together zip-code-sorted mail into bundles that will travel intact to the Post Office nearest the final destination)
- *Bagging* (loading into bags acceptable to the carrier, usually the U.S. Postal System)
- *Loading* onto skids or pallets for transportation to the Post Office.

Again, most of these activities are completely automated in lettershops that handle even a moderate volume of direct mail. A mail package that is not designed to make use of the automated equipment (for example, a card that fits into the envelope so tightly that it cannot be inserted by machine) or a job that is too small for efficient use of the equipment will usually incur substantial additional costs in manual labor.

Large lettershop operations and printers have a postal annex on the premises. This will allow the job to be put into the mail stream a day or more earlier than it would if the mailing had to be trucked to the post office.

THERE IS A GREAT DEAL MORE...

While we have described the print production process from beginning to end, we have done so in a very general fashion. We have not discussed, for instance, two of the major decisions that become very technical very quickly--what kind of paper, and what typeface. We have not delved into the technical complexities which abound at each stage in the process. Also, we have not described in any detail the rather large number of separate suppliers that can be involved in a single job and how to ensure that they work together properly.

If it all seems a little overwhelming, there are two pieces of good news. The first is that good suppliers have an abundant supply of patience and are quite willing to explain and answer questions. Discuss your job with each supplier early and often. You will learn and your job will benefit.

Second, because a particular type of direct mail tends to be most appropriate for a particular type of printing process, most direct marketers do not need to become experts in all the different processes. That makes the situation much more manageable, especially for the beginner.

While good production cannot compensate for poor strategy or creative execution, ineffective management of the print production process can doom a promising campaign to failure. Successful direct marketers must select competent suppliers, work closely with them, and remain involved during each stage of the print production process.

10

Catalog Marketing

THE DEVELOPMENT OF CATALOG MARKETING

> In 1869, E. C. Allen of Augusta, Maine, had an idea. Americans had been buying products by mail from the time of George Washington, but no company was wholly dedicated to sales by mail, and most of those which dabbled in mail orders usually carried only a single line of products. So Allen hit on a plan to sell nationally a selection of specialty items ranging from recipes for washing powder to engravings and to do it only by mail. He founded the *People's Literary Companion*, whose object, despite its title, was commercial, not educational.
>
> In its second year, Allen's paper, priced at fifty cents a year, sold 500,000 copies. There was big money in the mails! [1]

The history of direct marketing does not record the fate of the *People's Literary Companion* beyond its successful second year of operations, but all of us know that some of its early competitors became mainstays of the American household.

The first of those American institutions began when Aaron Montgomery Ward established a general-merchandise catalog in 1872. A single sheet of paper with a headline reading "The Original Wholesale Grange Supply House," it was targeted at midwestern farmers who were upset by the high prices of goods they purchased compared to the low prices they received for their farm products.

The second came into being in 1886 when a Minnesota railroad agent named Richard Sears purchased an unclaimed shipment of $25 watches for $12 each and resold them to other agents along the line for $14 each. Encouraged by this suc-

[1] Gordon L. Weil, *Sears, Roebuck, USA* (Chicago: Stein and Day, 1977), p. 61.

cess, he began a catalog of watches and jewelry in 1888. By 1896, Sears had formed a partnership with Alvah C. Roebuck and they issued a 140-page general-merchandise catalog.

The success of the Sears and the Ward catalogs rested with the American farmer, who found high prices and limited selections at the local general store, often after traveling several hours for the privilege of buying there. The early catalog businesses were also bolstered by the development of the railroad network and the U.S. postal system.

Although no figures exist, it seems there was a steady growth in the catalog field during the first half of the twentieth century. Several successful catalogs were established during this period, including Spiegel (1904), L. L. Bean (1912), and Eddie Bauer (1920).

The next major growth era in catalog marketing occurred after World War II with the establishment of successful specialty catalogers including Spencer Gifts, Sunset House, Foster and Gallagher, Hanover House, and many food and nursery companies. Most of these catalogs supplied household items, clothing, and gifts to the middle-class mass market.

The increasing affluence and sophistication of the middle class market led to the next major step—and the recent explosive growth—in catalog marketing. The initiator of this movement was probably Roger Horchow, who established The Horchow Collection in 1974. This was the first in a wave of upscale catalogs that, according to one journalist, "look more like coffee-table books than anything as utilitarian as advertising, and...are far better read."[2]

As in all other aspects of direct marketing, valid statistics are difficult to obtain for catalog sales, but according to consultant Arnold Fishman catalog sales grew 10 percent in 1986 while retail sales grew 5.2 percent. The rate of catalog sales growth was as high as 17.5 percent in the early 1980s.[2a]

Another indicator of the size of the catalog marketing field is the listing of sales figures for the largest catalog houses shown in Table 10.1. Not only are the absolute sales figures impressive, but some of these houses are experiencing dramatic growth. Some of the larger catalog firms have not fared so well in recent years, however. Alden's (1981 sales of $320 million) went out of business in 1982. Montgomery Ward (1984 catalog sales approaching $1 billion) ended its catalog operation in December of 1985. Smaller but long-successful firms such as Sunset House (1949–1984) have also disappeared from the scene.

As the number of catalog firms has grown in recent years and competition has intensified, many catalog firms have come and gone—some so quickly that they left virtually no trace. The typical reasons for failure include undercapitalization, lack of knowledge of the marketplace, insufficient customer base, and poor order fulfillment.

The failure of catalog giants like Alden's and Montgomery Ward can be attributed to their lack of recognition of the changing nature of the U.S. consumer

2 "Catalogue Cornucopia," *Time*, November 8, 1982, p. 74.

[2a] Janice Steinberg, "Cacophony of Catalogs Fill All Niches," *Advertising Age*, October 26, 1987, p. S-2.

TABLE 10.1 The Largest Catalog Retailers

Companies are ranked by 1986 total catalog sales in millions of dollars.

Company	Sales
Sears	$3,711.4
J. C. Penney	2,332.0
Spiegel	882.2
Brylane[1]	475.0*
L. L. Bean	367.8
Fingerhut[2]	316.0*
Lands' End	265.0
Hanover House[3]	256.0
Avon(New Hampton Inc.)	216.2
General Mills[4]	200.0*
Foster & Gallagher[5]	185.0*
Inmac	143.0
Sharper Image	59.3
Williams-Sonoma	55.2
CML Group[6]	52.6
Gander Mountain	52.3

*Estimate.
[1]Subsidiary of Limited Inc.
[2]Division of Primerica.
[3]Division of Horn and Hardart.
[4]Through two catalogs: Eddie Bauer and Talbots.
[5]Breck's and Spring Hill Nurseries.
[6]Includes Carroll Reed.

Source: Blunt Ellis & Loewi Inc., Milwaukee, WI 53202; Table appeared in *The Wall Street Journal*, Nov. 24, 1987, p. 6.

marketplace in the 1960s and 1970s. The marketplace had become too competitive for huge general-merchandise catalogs to remain profitable. Also, catalogs with relatively downscale customer profiles like Alden's found it difficult either to remain profitable serving that customer base or to alter their merchandise and marketing efforts to serve a more upscale market. Image upgrading is not impossible, however, as witnessed by Speigel's successful turn around. Specialty catalogs targeted to niche markets, such as The Sharper Image (consumer electronics), Williams-Sonoma (kitchen equipment), and Brookstone (hard-to-find tools), now dominate the field.[3]

[3] The description of the development of catalogs was based on: C. E. Bjorncrantz, "Sears' Big Book: Dinosaur or Phoenix?" *Direct Marketing*, July 1986, pp. 71-75; "Ward Closes the Book," *Fortune*, September 2, 1985, p. 10; Stephen J. Sansweet, "Management Mistakes Plus Old Problems Led to Collapse of Alden's," *The Wall Street Journal*, January 6, 1983, pp. 1, 12; "New England Direct Marketing Day," speech delivered by Maxwell Sroge (catalog conultant and owner, Sroge Publishing, Colorado Spring, CO) March 1985.

THE APPEAL OF CATALOGS

Consumers seem to purchase from catalogs for the same reasons that they purchase through the mail in general—primarily unique merchandise and convenience. More specifically, Muldoon attributes the recent upsurge in catalog sales to the increase in women in the work force and the concurrent increase in two-income families, more precise targeting to specific consumer needs, the discovery of catalog shopping by many households during the energy crisis of the middle 1970s, and the continuing population shift away from central cities.[4] Figure 10.1

Age Bracket:
35–55 years.
Sex:
85% female. Exceptions include American Express and The Sharper Image.
Marital Status:
50% of the female purchasers are married; 50% are single, divorced, or widowe.d
Employment Status:
55-60% are employed outside the home.
Combined Family Income:
$40,000 annually.
Discretionary Income:
55% are from a two-income household.
Property Status:
65% are homeowners.
Charge Account Status:
Average 3.2 per customer (excluding gasoline credit cards). Most common are MasterCard, Visa, American Express, and department/specialty store credit cards.
Mail-Order Purchase Frequency:
5.1 times per year.
Attitude Toward Mail-Order Buying:
Positive.
Average Dollar Order:
$60–$100.
Educational Level:
Average 2.6 years of higher education. Married mail-order buyers have a lower level of education than do non-married.

FIGURE 10.1 ***Profile of the Upscale Catalog Shopper***

[4] Katie Muldoon, *Catalog Marketing* (New York: R. R. Bowker, 1984), pp. 2-5.

presents a profile of the upscale catalog shopper compiled from a number of research studies.

Tucker lists eight key factors in the generic appeal of mail order. Ranked by order of importance, they are:[5]

1. Convenience
2. Desirability (of merchandise)
3. Credibility of catalog name
4. Catalog presentation (graphics and quality reproduction)
5. Succinct, informative copy
6. Psychological use of color
7. Timing of mailing (seasonality)
8. Previous mail-order fulfillment experience.

A small-scale empirical study[6] asked respondents to rate the importance of 29 catalog attributes suggested by published material, catalog professionals, and consumers. One group of respondents, labeled "uninvolved catalog shoppers," did not place much importance on any of the attributes. The remainder, the "involved catalog shoppers," were able to discriminate among the attributes. From their data seven factors describing important catalog attributes were obtained (Figure 10.2).

Tucker refers to a focus group study in which

> mail-order customers reflected an amazing level of sophistication in terms of appreciation for quality catalog format and presentation. They were harshly critical of cheaper papers and expressed dislike of low-quality (color) separations and printing. They demonstrated a preference for catalogs with plus covers as opposed to self-covers[7] and recognized changes in format, fashion trends, and new directions. Subtle deviations from established catalog companies were noticed and commented on.[8]

This quote highlights another important aspect of catalogs—they are a visual medium. Informative and persuasive copy is important, but catalog appearance, layout, and graphics are the key success factors.

Consumers also recognize that catalog shopping has some drawbacks. When *Consumer Reports* asked nearly 100,000 of its subscribers what the major disadvantages of mail-order buying were, they replied:[9]

Can't see merchandise in advance	60%
Have to wait for merchandise	13%
Postage and handling costs	13%
Difficult to return merchandise	9%
Difficult to comparison-shop	5%

[5] Jo-Von Tucker, "Catalog Sales," in Edward L. Nash ed., *The Direct Marketing Handbook* (New York: McGraw-Hill, 1984), p. 664.

[6] Mary Lou Roberts, "Consumer Perceptions of Catalogs," unpublished manuscript.

[7] Covers of heavier paper stock as opposed to the same paper as used for the pages of the catalog.

[8] Tucker in Nash ed., *The Direct Marketing Handbook*, p. 664.

[9] "Mail-Order Buying," *Consumer Reports*, October 1982, pp. 514-521.

FIGURE 10.2 ***Catalog Attribute Factors for Involved Catalog Shoppers***

Attractive Catalog:
- Interesting background photography
- Attractive models
- Printed on quality paper
- Colorful, eyecatching pictures
- Well-displayed merchandise
- Pre-selected merchandise assortment

Ease of Use:
- Simple order form
- Easy to match photos with description
- Easy to read and understand
- Well-displayed merchandise
- Uncluttered format

Value for Dollars Spent:
- Reasonable prices
- Products are good value for the money

Convenience I:
- Ensures timely receipt of merchandise
- Accepts most credit cards
- It is easy to order merchandise

Variety/Description:
- Examples of different colors and fabrics available
- Lists materials and content of products
- Many sizes, colors, and styles available

Convenience II:
- Toll-free number for ordering
- Quick delivery options (such as Federal Express)
- Offers different methods of payment (COD, installment)

Reputation:
- Products have well-known brand names
- Company is well-known

Unique Merchandise:
- Products not easily found elsewhere
- Products are unusual

Low Risk:
- Money-back guarantee or warranty

The rapid growth of the catalog field in recent years has made the job of the catalog marketing manager even more challenging. In considering the whole process of marketing through catalogs, we can divide the manager's concerns into two major areas:

1. The front end, which includes all marketing decisions—targeting and positioning, merchandise selection and presentation, pricing, and so on.
2. The back end, which involves order processing and fulfillment.

Back-end operations, which are essentially the same for all direct marketing media, were discussed in Chapter 7. This chapter concentrates on the front end, or marketing, of a catalog.

We should also note that catalogs are an increasingly important medium for business marketers. While this chapter will deal primarily with consumer catalogs, the basic marketing principles also apply to business-to-business catalogs. The specifics of business catalog marketing will be discussed in Chapter 14.

THE CROWDED CATALOG MARKETPLACE

The day when a poorly targeted, poorly focused catalog could have even a minimal level of success is past. Stone urges catalog marketers to "think of the mailbox as a crowded marketplace where many vendors are milling around, setting up displays of their wares."[10] To stand out amid the mailbox clutter, a catalog must have a distinctive point of view and presentation.

The day when an undercapitalized catalog operation could achieve success is also gone. Estimates of the amount of capital needed to begin a catalog business typically range from $1 million to $2 million, but may be as high as $3 million to reach a mass market. This is a far cry from the romantic image of the entrepreneur with more creativity than cash.[11]

Catalog marketing has evolved from a romantic enterprise to a complex, disciplined process. Figure 10.3 presents the series of decisions that must be made by the catalog marketer.

DEVELOPING AND MARKETING CATALOGS

Developing the Catalog Concept

The distinctive point of view and presentation that are a major factor in the success of a catalog stem from the basic catalog concept. The catalog concept is a con-

[10] Bob Stone, *Successful Direct Marketing Methods,* 3rd ed. (Chicago: Crain Books, 1984), p. 305.

[11] Jerrold Ballinger, "Whatever Happened to the Kitchen Table Startup?" *DM News/Catalog Business,* February 1, 1987, pp. 12-14.

FIGURE 10.3 ***The Catalog Development and Marketing Process***

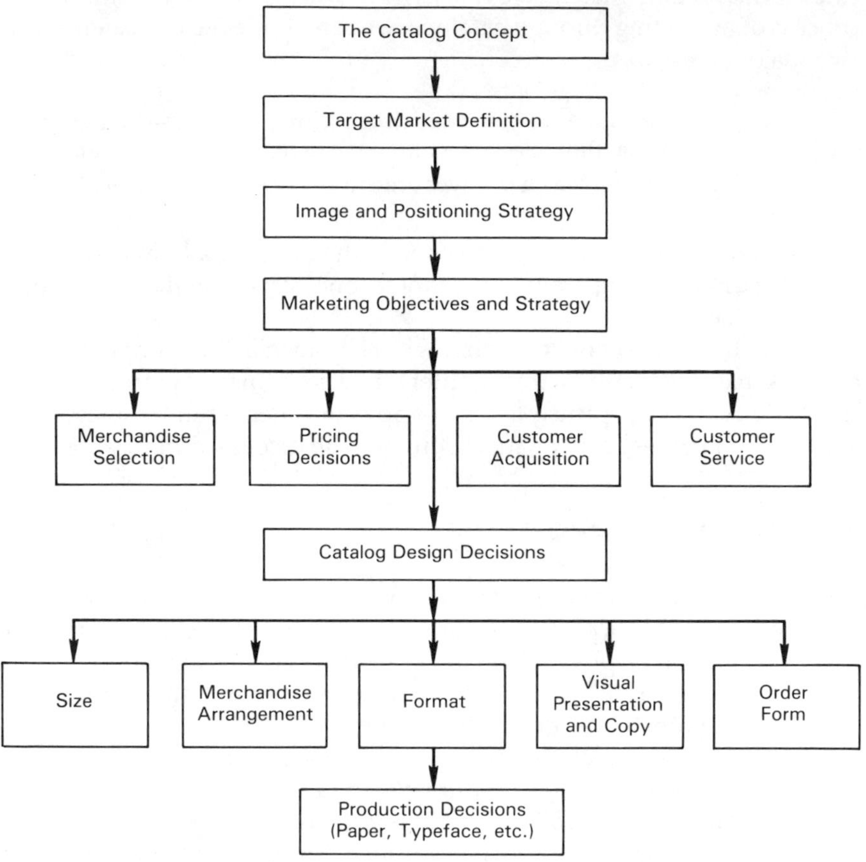

cise statement of the catalog's reason for existence. Many catalogers have presented to the public an explicit statement of their business philosophy that provides a description of the core concept of their business.

Perhaps the best known of these is an often-repeated quote that sums up the philosophy of L. L. Bean, founder of the catalog that bears his name. The Bean ad shown in Figure 10.4 presents the philosophy in a attractive format that encourages readers to send for a Bean catalog.

A catalog's concept defines the limits of the business and identifies the area in which the business intends to excel. Developing a concept that is neither too narrow (limiting the catalog's appeal) nor too broad (introducing irrelevant merchandise and confusing the catalog's image) is critical for long-term success. The concept may be translated into a catalog theme—Norm Thompson's "ESCAPE from the ordinary," for example.

The prospective customer knows what to expect from a catalog that states its purpose clearly. An explicit statement of purpose also serves to focus the efforts of all personnel involved in the production of the catalog.

Defining the Target Market

As in all marketing endeavors, a clear profile and an in-depth understanding of the target customer are essential. The existing catalog operation should continually add to and refine its knowledge about its customers as discussed in Chapters 4 and 6. The beginning catalog operation must define its target market on the basis of the concept statement. This requires sound managerial judgment and is increasingly the subject of marketing research by catalog marketers.

Earlier in the chapter a generic profile of the catalog customer was presented. This is a useful starting point for many catalogs, but it is much too broad for specific guidance. Moreover, it is not an accurate representation of the customer of some specialty catalogs. The Sharper Image, for example, has a customer base consisting predominantly of males between the ages of 25 and 50 with average incomes of $93,000. Their average order size was $145 in 1985.[12]

Image and Positioning Strategy

Stone insightfully refers to the catalog as a "paper store."[13] This is a useful comparison because there has been a great deal of research identifying the major dimensions of the retail store image.

What we mean by store image is "the way in which the store is defined in the shopper's mind, partly by its functional qualities and partly by an aura of psychological attributes."[14] Catalog image, then, would simply be the physical and psychological attributes of a catalog as perceived by its target customers.

Table 10.2 shows how many of the dimensions of retail store image can be duplicated in a catalog.

Except for the fact that a catalog does not have a physical store location (even though many catalog companies do have retail outlets), catalog image can be evaluated on dimensions similar to those used for evaluating retail store image.

What this tells the catalog marketer is that decisions concerning each of these dimensions will affect the image portrayed by the catalog. For example, in establishing pricing policies, the marketer will have to decide such issues as the overall level of prices, the number of price points, whether to engage in comparison pricing, and whether to feature price reductions. Decisions to engage in premium

[12] Arnold Fishman, "The 1985 Mail Order Guide," *Direct Marketing*, July 1986, pp. 26-44, 97.

[13] Stone, *Successful Direct Marketing Methods*, 3rd ed., p. 305.

[14] Pierre Martineau, "The Personality of the Retail Store," *Harvard Business Review*, 36 (January-February 1958): 47.

FIGURE 10.4 ***L.L. Bean***

NOTICE

I do not consider a sale complete until goods are worn out and customer still satisfied.

We will thank anyone to return goods that are not perfectly satisfactory.

Should the person reading this notice know of anyone who is not satisfied with our goods, I will consider it a favor to be notified.

Above all things we wish to avoid having a dissatisfied customer.

Reprinted from an L.L. Bean 1912 circular.

Customer Satisfaction: An L.L. Bean Tradition

Back in 1912, when Leon Leonwood Bean first mailed out his circulars, he included a notice that appears above. Satisfying customers has always been an L.L. Bean tradition.

For the past 76 years, L.L. Bean has been supplying quality apparel, footwear and equipment to men and women who enjoy the outdoors. Our customers know us for the practical and functional merchandise we sell and for our "treat others as we would like to be treated" customer service. And they appreciate us because we offer the services that mail order customers value most. We guarantee 100% satisfaction, we pay shipping and handling charges, and we offer TOLL-FREE order and customer service numbers.

We guarantee 100% satisfaction. From the beginning, L.L. guaranteed each product "to give perfect satisfaction in every way." Today our guarantee is as strong and as unconditional as ever. We'll accept returns at any time for any reason. Your purchase will be replaced, or we will refund your money or credit your credit card. We simply do not want you to have anything from L.L. Bean that is not completely satisfactory.

We pay all regular shipping and handling charges. L.L. didn't like to ask his customers to pay extra to do business with him. So, L.L. Bean pays the postage on all regular deliveries within the United States unless otherwise stated in our catalogs. This means substantial savings to mail order customers because unlike other catalogs, the price listed is the only amount you pay. There are no additional charges.

We offer TOLL-FREE Order and Customer Service numbers. When you browse through our catalogs, you'll notice another cost-saving feature: our toll-free phone numbers. Call to place an order, request a catalog, or to check on an existing order. There's never a charge to you and our phone lines are open 24 hours a day, 365 days a year.

Send for our FREE fully illustrated catalogs. They feature a full range of active and casual apparel and footwear. Outdoor sporting equipment, home and camp furnishings, practical and functional gift ideas. Order anytime, night or day, by phone or by mail. Our Customer Service and Telephone Representatives are always here to serve you. We maintain large inventories and ship promptly. And each order is sent postpaid and arrives unconditionally guaranteed.

☐ **Please send FREE Catalogs**

Name ____________________

Address ____________________

City __________ State ______ Zip __________

L. L. Bean, Inc., 1255 Casco St., Freeport, ME 04033

L.L.Bean®

Source: : L.L. Bean, Freeport, ME 04033

pricing with no reference to competitive prices and not to offer merchandise in the catalog at sale prices will contribute to an upscale image. Be careful about implying too much from a single image dimension, however. Comparison pricing of moderately priced merchandise that is presented in a very attractive manner could be successful in creating a "value" image as opposed to a "downscale" one.

TABLE 10.2 Characteristics of Retail Store and Catalog Image

Retail Store	*Catalog*
Merchandise assortment - - - - - - - - - - - - - >	
Customer services - - - - - - - - - - - - - - - - - >	
Pricing policies - >	
Customer communications - - - - - - - - - - - >	
Institutional reputation - - - - - - - - - - - - - - >	
Store clientele	Perception of catalog clientele
Store personnel	Customer service personnel
Physical attributes (atmosphere)	Appearance of catalog
Store location	

Source: Adapted from Barry Berman and Joel R. Evans, *Retail Management*, 3rd. ed. (New York: Macmillan, 1986), pp. 358–360; and Jay D. Lindquest, "Meaning of Image," *Journal of Retailing*, Winter, 1974–1975, pp. 29–37.

The Marketing Strategy

In developing a marketing strategy for a catalog, a basic set of marketing-mix variables—merchandise selection, pricing, customer acquisition, and customer service policies—applies.

The objectives of a specific catalog stem from the catalog's place in the overall marketing program of the firm. A catalog will often, though not always, have as its primary objective the *sale of merchandise*. But since many catalogers also have retail outlets, an equally important objective for these marketers may be to *promote the retail stores*.

Retailers face essentially the same situation. Many retailers use their catalogs primarily as vehicles to *attract customers to their retail outlets*. Sales made directly from the catalog are viewed as incremental and are not strongly pushed. Others, such as the Bloomingdale's By Mail operation described in Chapter 2, are operationally separate and have their own separate *sales objectives*.

Large marketers of brand-name products and services may use *sales incentive* catalogs. General Mills has for many years used its Betty Crocker catalog to encourage repeat purchases. More recently, firms like Citibank have entered the field of incentive marketing. Citibank's Citidollars program features a catalog of merchandise available at discounted prices to customers who have accumulated credits through use of their Citibank Visa and MasterCards.

Business marketers also use catalogs in a variety of ways: to make *direct sales* of low-ticket merchandise, supplies, and accessories; to *support the field sales force;* and to *support the dealer network.*

Some aspects of the catalog will change—for instance, more or less detailed and descriptive copy—vary according to the marketer's objectives, but the same general aspects of catalog marketing apply regardless of the specific objectives of the catalog.

Merchandise Selection

The importance of unique merchandise to the success of a catalog has already been mentioned. How does the catalog marketer locate and evaluate merchandise to include in the catalog?

This question is more easily answered by the established than by the new cataloger for at least two reasons:

1. The profitability of each item from previous catalogs is known; profitable items will ordinarily be retained for the next edition.
2. The demographic and purchase profile of the catalog's customers is well known.

Without this information, the new cataloger must rely on judgment in selecting merchandise for the catalog.

Like retailers, catalog marketers can visit merchandise marts and shows in major cities including New York, Chicago, Dallas, and Los Angeles. (Most of these are open to buyers only; consumers are not allowed.) The new cataloger will have to seek out merchandise resources; the successful one will be besieged with manufacturers and inventors who wish to sell through a well-known catalog. Once attractive merchandise is located, however, both will face the same problem—choosing the correct assortment to appear in each edition of the catalog.

Stanley Marcus of Neiman-Marcus has been quoted by Tucker as saying that "mail order works because it is a preedited selection of merchandise."[15] By this he means that the skilled marketer makes the initial selection of an appropriate set of merchandise, thereby making the customer's final choice easier. Tucker goes on to say that "in a typical high-ticket catalog of thirty-two pages plus cover, an ideal maximum number of products would be 120 to 140."[16] Catalogers tend to err on the side of including too many items rather than too few. Crowding in too many items makes it difficult to display each to its best advantage. Figure 10.5 is a list of suggested criteria for choosing products to display in a catalog.

According to Muldoon, the final selection of merchandise is best made as the cataloger creates the page-by-page layout for the catalog, a process often referred to as *pagination.*[17] Choose merchandise for the most important pages first. The front cover is the most powerful location, followed by the back cover, the inside front

[15] Tucker in Nash, 1984, p. 667.

[16] Tucker in Nash ed., The *Direct Marketing Handbook*, p. 668.

[17] Muldoon, *Catalog Marketing*, pp. 57-60.

FIGURE 10.5 ***Product Selection Checklist***

Quality:
- Suits catalog's image
- Will satisfy customers' expectations

Price:
- Correct price range
- Appropriate for target market

Availability:
- Supplier can guarantee delivery in time to meet customer fulfillment requirements
- Back-up suppliers are available

Exclusivity:
- Item not offered by other catalogs
- Can negotiate an exclusive color, style, etc.

Uniqueness:
- Item not available in retail stores

Vendor Cooperation:
- Will be able to fill orders and reorders in acceptable time
- Will assist in forecasting sales, inventory requirements, market trends, etc.
- Items have sold well in previous/other catalogs

Photographic Potential:
- Will photograph accurately

Cross-Sellability:
- Will encourage sale of other items in catalog

Merchandise Mix:
- Appropriate number and type of merchandise categories
- Appropriate number of items within each category

Profit Potential:
- Will generate a satisfactory level of sales
- Will generate a satisfactory margin

Vendor Selection Checklist

Minimum-Order Requirements:
- Small enough not to produce excess inventory

Returns and Exchanges:
- Will accept return of unsatisfactory or unsold merchandise

BackUp Inventory:
- Will keep 2 to 3 times initial order in stock for reorders

Advertising Allowances:
- Conditions for and amount of advertising allowance available

Photographic Allowances:
- Will furnish photograph or cash allowance to help defray costs of photography

Source: Adapted from Katie Muldoon, *Catalog Marketing* (New York: R. R. Bowker, 1984), pp. 46–48.

cover, the inside back cover, the center spread, and the pages around the order form.

If merchandise is to be used on the cover, it should be selected with great care to excite interest and convey the overall image. Additionally, the inside front cover—the inside of the cover and the page facing it—helps set the tone for the rest of the catalog and should display merchandise carefully chosen to be representative of merchandise categories and price points.

The back cover has special importance because it may provide the customer's first view of the catalog. The center pages may get special attention because the catalog easily falls open there. Similarly, the pages near the order form may receive closer scrutiny; these pages are an especially good location for impulse merchandise.

Pricing Decisions[18]

Pricing often represents a difficult set of decisions for the catalog marketer because these decisions not only determine the financial viability of the catalog but are an important component of the image the catalog conveys. In making pricing decisions the cataloger must consider the objectives of the catalog, select an overall pricing policy, and determine by what process actual prices will be set.

Catalog Objectives and Pricing Decisions. Pricing decisions are actually out of the hands of the catalog manager for two types of catalogs. Consumer catalogs whose main objective is to attract customers to retail stores will ordinarily use the prices set by the store, and add shipping and handling charges for merchandise purchased through the catalog. Likewise, business product catalogs whose main purpose is to support the field sales force or the dealer network will use already-established prices.

For catalogs whose primary objective is to sell merchandise, the catalog manager will ordinarily be responsible for setting a broad approach to prices. The manager will have to consider financial objectives and/or constraints such as return-on-investment targets, profit expectations, and investment pay-back commitments. Prices must also support the overall image strategy. A catalog that has to generate substantial cash flow to meet financial objectives and that wishes to present a value orientation to a mass market should engage in *penetration pricing*. This approach to pricing involves using low prices to achieve a high volume of sales.

If there is no overwhelming pressure for immediate financial achievement and if the intent is to portray an upscale image for the non-price-sensitive customer, the catalog may practice *price skimming*. In this case, the catalog will set relatively high prices, relying on substantial gross margins rather than sales volume for its profitability.

[18] This discussion is based on Berman and Evans, *Retail Management*, pp. 438-451.

Broad Price Policies. After the catalog marketer has established a basic approach to the pricing issue—relatively low or relatively high prices—the next step is to establish the framework within which actual prices will be set. This framework will provide a more specific statement of the role price is to play in the overall marketing strategy. The manager will arrive at this statement after considering prices in relation to:

- The target market
- The chosen image
- The merchandise mix

L. L. Bean provides casual clothing that is equally at home in the city and the country to a relatively upscale target market. Bean's standards of quality in both its merchandise and its service have always been uncompromising. None of these elements of strategy suggests extremely low prices. Yet Bean's strong commitment to giving the customer value for dollars spent has kept the company from pursuing a skimming strategy. Although Bean's excellence in both merchandise and customer service may not remind most of us of mass marketing, with a customer file in excess of 2 million, the company has been remarkably successful in penetrating a sizable portion of its potential market.

Pricing Strategies. Once the broad framework has been established, there are several ways in which the catalog manager can approach the actual setting of prices. While one orientation may take precedence, demand, costs, and competition must all be considered.

In a *demand-oriented pricing* strategy prices are based on the quantity demanded at a specific price, almost irrespective of costs. Products may be given relatively high prices to appeal to a quality-conscious or prestige-conscious customer. On the other hand, if the customer is price-sensitive, products may have to be priced at a relatively low level.

Catalog marketers are often tempted to base their pricing decisions entirely on cost. It is easy to take merchandise cost, add catalog operating expenses and a reasonable level of profit, and produce a formula for computing prices. *Cost-oriented pricing* does have the virtue of being easy to implement, but this strategy fails to take into account either customer demand or the activities of competitors. Consequently, even if it results in prices that enable the catalog to stay in business, it may not result in prices that produce an optimum level of profits. Still, it is obvious that costs provide a floor beneath which prices cannot drop over a sustained period of time if the catalog is to remain viable.

The third strategy is to use *competitive pricing*. This will require considerable comparison shopping to stay fully informed about competitors' prices for similar merchandise. Since catalog marketers cannot just walk into a rival's store and examine merchandise the way retailers do, wise catalog managers will make sure they are on the mailing list of all major competitors so they can monitor prices on a continuing basis.

By this time, you have probably recognized that each of these pricing strategies has merit, but that practicing any one to the exclusion of the other two may result in ignoring factors that are important to marketplace success. Successful pricing policies consider all three strategies—demand, competition, and costs—and make the appropriate trade-offs among them in arriving at a final price for merchandise in the catalog.

Customer Acquisition and Retention

Attracting and retaining customers are among the most important of all catalog marketing management activities. Catalog marketers may spend as much as 25 percent of net sales on customer acquisition. They obtain the names and addresses of prospective customers from many sources.

The House List. The house list is one of the chief assets of a catalog business. The catalog marketer must be concerned with three major issues in making decisions about uses of the house list.

1. *The house list should be complete and maintained with great care.* In our discussion of Bloomingdale's By Mail in Chapter 2, we noted the extensive information that can be recorded about each customer. Maintenance of the list can be done internally or by an external service firm. In either case, the catalog marketer should make sure that qualified technical personnel are responsible for the list and that there is complete backup in the event of a computer system crash or other disaster such as fire.

2. *The house list must be protected from misuse and overuse.* List rental, including ways of protecting the list from unauthorized use, is discussed in Chapter 4. Catalogers have two specific concerns with regard to renting out the house list. The first is whether to rent to direct competitors. Some catalogers do and some do not. The dangers of renting the house list to direct competitors are obvious. The second concern is how frequently to rent the list. At some point the list's productivity will begin to suffer from too-frequent mailings.

The house list is an important profit center for the successful catalog marketer. It cannot remain so, however, if short-term revenues are maximized at the expense of long-term profitability.

3. *The house list should be subjected to ongoing analysis to ensure its most profitable use.* Employing the type of analysis we discussed in Chapter 4 will enable the cataloger to mail more frequently to the most profitable customers or to mail specialty catalogs or other pieces to customers with the highest purchase probability. Lee Wards, a catalog that serves the home crafts market, provides a good example:

> Lee Wards divides its customers into approximately 2,400 individual cells based upon recency, frequency and monetary [value]. We analyze each one of these 2,400 cells to determine how many catalogs those people will or can get. The more recent they are, the more frequently customers purchase. If they are five years old and spent $10 and only bought from us once it may well be that they may only get one catalog. If they are two months old and spent $100 and bought from us six times in the last 24 weeks, they could get up to nine or 10 catalogs. They would get as many catalogs as we can print and mail.[19]

The ultimate expression of segmentation of the house list by catalogers is the establishment of a new catalog to serve a particular segment. Hanover House Industries provides an excellent example of this process.

By 1950, Hanover House had built a mail-order customer base of 500,000 through space advertising of low-priced women's apparel. Using this customer base, it introduced the Lana Lobell catalog. The success of Lana Lobell caused the company to search for other merchandise that would appeal to the same market. In 1962 it introduced the Hanover House catalog, which featured novelty and household items in the $5-and-under range. Sales were good, but profitability was unsatisfactory because of the low margins offered by products in this price range.

Hanover House was able to penetrate a more profitable segment by targeting only customers who had placed individual orders of $25 or more. The catalog designed for this market was Adam York, which contained apparel, gifts, and hard goods. The upscale customer base was further expanded with space advertising. As sales grew in each merchandise category, a new catalog was developed to serve it—catalogs such as Premiere Editions, which features only fashion apparel. At last count, Hanover House had a total of 28 catalogs.[20]

Use of Rental Lists. Most catalog marketers rely heavily on the use of rental lists to increase their customer base. Since literally thousands of lists are available, selecting the most productive ones to test is not easy. The following issues must be considered in selecting lists:[21]

- The nature and image of the catalog
- The objectives of the catalog
- The profile of the customers
- The merchandise offered
- Any limitations in terms of catalog or merchandise availability

[19] Julian L. Simon, *How To Start and Operate a Mail-Order Business*, 4th ed. (New York: McGraw-Hill, 1987), p. 332.

[20] "Market Segmentation ('Hanoverization') in Herbert Katzenstein and William S. Sachs, *Direct Marketing* (Columbus, OH: Charles E. Merrill, 1986), pp.282-284; "Hanover House Targets New Audiences," *Direct Marketing*, July 1987, p. 10.

[21] Based on Muldoon, *Catalog Marketing*, p. 150.

The better the match between the characteristics of the catalog and the rental list, the better the results are likely to be. Most catalogers constantly test new lists, but the most sophisticated list tests cannot overcome poor choice of lists to be tested.

Use of Space Advertising. An alternative method of acquiring new customers is to advertise in magazines. Actual or prospective customers acquired in this manner have already expressed their interest in the line of merchandise offered by the catalog. There are two basic approaches taken by catalogers to space advertising in magazines:

1. They use an "image" advertisement whose objective is to get the reader to request a catalog.
2. They use an advertisement whose objective is to get the reader to purchase a specific piece of merchandise.

The Lands' End advertisement shown in Figure 10.6 is an example of a space ad that does not attempt to sell a specific product, even though it explains in great detail the reasons for the quality of Lands' End shirts. This full-page ad is an exception to the rule; most advertising of this type is small in size, often only a few column inches.

The Company Store ad shown in Figure 10.7 is clearly attempting to sell two related pieces of merchandise. Therefore, the specific pieces of merchandise are fully described and all necessary information for ordering—sizes, colors, prices, and so on—must be included. Note that it is also possible to request a catalog without ordering merchandise, although that is not facilitated by the response coupon.

Not all catalogers agree how catalogs requested via space advertising should be mailed. Third-class mail is much cheaper and takes a minimum of 2 to 3 weeks. First-class mail costs more and generally arrives within 3 to 4 days. One school of thought argues that getting the catalog to the customer while his or her interest is still aroused is critical, and therefore first-class postage is worth the extra cost. It is generally agreed that near a major selling season—Christmas, for example—the cataloger should mail requested catalogs first class.

Today many catalogs are advertised in so-called catalog collections in major magazines. As you can see from Figure 10.8, a page from the March 1987 edition of *Connoisseur* magazine, there is not a great deal of space for copy in this type of advertising beyond the catalog logo and a few well-chosen words. But the cost of these insertions is relatively low, and there is an advantage in being grouped with other catalogs targeted at similar audiences. The reader returns the "bingo" card to the magazine, which in turn passes on the name and address to each of the catalogs requested.

Miscellaneous Customer-Acquisition Methods. There are a number of miscellaneous methods of customer acquisition that share the advantage of low cost. Used appropriately, they can be effective.

FIGURE 10.6 ***An Image-Oriented Space Advertisement***

If anyone offers more buttondowns, in a wider variety, better quality, or at better prices, we don't know of it.

It's possible, of course. It's a big country. But without question, Lands' End has become a major source of buttondown shirts in almost every conceivable fabric and color, for both men and women.

The real thing. $19.50.

This is the shirt that started it all. The cool, comfortable 100% cotton Oxford cloth shirt, with the neat, soft button-down collar some of you wore and remember from the Big Band days. We were among the first to bring it back, originally at $14. Even now it is still a remarkable value at just $19.50. Same generous cut, long tails, precise tailoring and all. But today, we offer it in more colors, and in both short and long sleeves. It does need ironing. But our companion shirt—a carefree cotton blend, also at $19.50—does not.

But this is only the beginning.

You should really check our Lands' End catalog for the full spell-out of our buttondown assortment. But we should mention the Hyde Park, beloved by traditionalists because it's cut from a cotton Oxford cloth as substantial as any found in the world today. So it wears longer, launders more nicely, and gives you the classic drape of an "expensive" shirt (which it isn't.)

And, for those of you who are into the thoroughly modern, we offer the Pinpoint Oxford, with a soft, silky touch that may woo you away from any other kind of dress shirt you've ever worn.

Dress-tailored sportshirts too.

Our buttondown story goes beyond Oxfords. We also offer a goodly selection of fine "dress tailored" sportshirts, the kind you can wear just as comfortably under a blazer as with your oldest, most disreputable khakis.

The buttondown sportshirts you'll find in our catalog vary, of course, with the season. In spring and summer, choose traditional favorites like Indian Madras and seersucker. And in fall and winter, glory in an assortment that includes ginghams, flannels, brushed twill Highlanders, and the undisputed king of <u>all</u> sportshirts—English Viyella.

We go far beyond shirts.

What Lands' End has goes beyond shirts, even beyond our famous soft luggage, sportswear and accessories. The Lands' End tradition affects everything we offer you.

First, *quality*. Then, *price*. And always, always *service*.

That's why we can offer a guarantee that would put lesser merchants out of business. Simply: GUARANTEED. PERIOD.

If we're new to you, we don't ask that you trust us. Simply try us. By phone, you can reach us toll-free 24 hours a day at 1-800-356-4444.

Or send in this coupon. Whether you order a shirt or not, we'll be pleased to send you a free copy of our latest Lands' End catalog.

LANDS' END®
DIRECT MERCHANTS
of fine wool and cotton sweaters, Oxford button-down shirts, traditional dress clothing, snow wear, deck wear, original Lands' End soft luggage and a multitude of other quality goods from around the world.

Please send free catalog.
Lands' End **Dept. O-01**
Dodgeville, WI 53595

Name ______
Address ______
City ______
State ______ Zip ______

Or call Toll-free:
1-800-356-4444

Source: Lands' End, Dodgeville, WI 53595

European Featherbed

Our European Featherbed is just like a giant body pillow. Place it on top of your mattress or waterbed, or on the floor and enjoy its natural warmth and body-cushioning comfort. It conforms to your body contours and cushions pressure points, such as hips, shoulders and knees. The Featherbed is filled with a blend of hand selected white goose and duck feathers. Its specially constructed feather- and down-proof shell is a soft 100% cotton fabric.

The European Featherbed provides a layer of gentle softness between you and the mattress. It's perfect for many uses. Our Featherbed Cover of 100% cotton keeps the Featherbed clean. Easily removed for machine washing.

If you're not completely satisfied with the European Featherbed, for any reason, call our toll free number and we'll send a UPS truck to your home — **at our expense** — to pick it up, and send you a refund (in full) or exchange.

TO ORDER OR TO REQUEST A FREE CATALOG CALL TOLL FREE
1-800-356-9367, Ext. X431,
or use our coupon (call 7 days a week).

FREE CATALOG
- 26 Down Comforter Styles
- Down Pillows
- Duvet Comforter Covers
- 100% Merino Wool Mattress Pads

The Company Store®

EUROPEAN FEATHERBED Style #C502
☐Twin (39" x 75") $39 ☐King (76" x 80") $69
☐Full (54" x 75") $49 ☐Calif. King (72" x 84") $79
☐Queen (60" x 80") $59 Color: White

FEATHERBED COVER Style #0603
☐Twin $19 ☐Full $29 ☐Queen $39
☐King $49 ☐Calif. King $59 Color: White

TO ORDER CALL TOLL FREE
1-800-356-9367, Ext. X431.

Use your credit card. OR ORDER BY MAIL:
☐M.C. ☐VISA ☐Am.Exp. ☐Diners Club ☐Check
Acct.#________ Exp.Dt.________
STYLE # ________
QTY. ________ x PRICE $________ =$________
STYLE # ________
QTY. ________ x PRICE $________ =$________
Delivery in MN-6% Tax, IL-5% Tax =$________
Ship., Hdlg., & Ins. Featherbed- $10 =$________
Ship., Hdlg., & Ins. Featherbed Cover-$2.50 =$________
*Federal Express Service =$________
TOTAL =$________
For delivery in WI-5% Tax =$________
Total for delivery in WI =$________

*☐We ship UPS ground service unless you request otherwise here. Federal Express Service add $8.50.

Name ________
Address ________
City,State,Zip ________

Send to: The Company Store, Dept. X431, 500 Company Store Road, La Crosse, WI 54601.

FIGURE 10.7
Advertisement Selling Specific Merchandise

Source: The Company Store, La Cross, WI 54601

FIGURE 10.8 ***A Catalog Collection Advertisment***

Source: *Connoisseur Magazine,* Hearst Magazines, a Division of the Hearst Corporation.

One method is simply to *ask current customers* for names of friends who would enjoy receiving the catalog. Sturbridge Yankee Workshop, which has a dedicated catalog following, uses this method effectively:

> About 20% of all incoming order blanks contain a friend's name. During our less busy season from January through April, we first send a postcard to the friend with a hand fill-in mentioning the original customer's name. This practically assures readership. The "one friend" may actually be a mother, or sister, or daughter, who is going to be talking or writing to the "referrer" anyway. Hand-done filled-in postcards have pulled up to 16% orders from the friends; when mechanized in any way, this pull (on comparative tests at the same season of the year) drops to about 4%.
>
> Year-round, after three mailings to the friend, the conversion of the order blank friends has been about 15%. This is the same as our conversion rate from space advertising—at half the cost.[22]

Sturbridge Yankee Workshop also uses another technique, *package inserts*:

> The package insert card is new. About one out of ten has been coming back to us. During the period from January through July, conversion of these "second friends" has been only 2-1/2%. However, based on our experience with the order card friends and with space inquiries, we expect that a Christmas catalog to them will produce another 4-1/2% minimum return, or 7% total. This works out as follows:

Return on 100 Insert Cards

Cost of cards @$10/M	=	$1.00
10% of these come back	=	.70 return postage
Cost of two catalogs in mail x 10 $.18 each	=	3.60
		$5.30 for 10 prospects
	or	$53.00 per hundred prospects

At 7% conversion (over the two mailings), the average cost of acquiring each customer is about $7.50 .[23]

Package inserts can be included in the outgoing orders of other firms for a promotional fee of $35 to $45 per thousand.[24] This is relatively inexpensive, but the timing and even the demographics of the recipients are not controllable because no selects are available. Firms with a number of catalogs often cross-sell in this way.

[22] Robert Bergman, "The Value of 'Homogeneity,' " DMA Release No. 2107, February 1978.
[23] Bergman, "The Value of 'Homogeneity.'"
[24] Muldoon, *Catalog Marketing*, p. 213

Catalog marketers frequently participate in *cooperative mailings*. Since these mailings are primarily composed of cents-off coupons, catalog offers may not receive a great deal of attention.

Billings of bank charge cards and department stores offer the opportunity to present catalog offers by using *statement stuffers*. Costs run from $25 to $50 per thousand.[25] Selects may enable the catalog marketer to reach a specified target market with statement stuffers.

Take-ones are promotional material in display racks placed in high-traffic locations such as supermarkets. The cost is $4 to $8 per month per store.[26] Good placement can result in a significant nunmber of responses.

Free-standing inserts, discussed in Chapter 12, also offer the catalog marketer access to large potential markets at minimal cost.

Home delivery, usually consisting of multiple promotions enclosed in a plastic bag, is available for prices ranging from $35 to $400 per thousand. Fees depend on weight and also on whether particular addresses are specified or complete coverage of a geographical area is requested. For a fee in the upper portion of the range, a catalog can be delivered to specific addresses.[27]

Finally, *publicity* can be a valuable source of new customers for the catalog marketer. It requires a great deal of effort, and both the timing and the actual content are outside the control of the cataloger, but publicity is received more credibly by consumers because it is editorial in nature, not paid advertising. Publicity gains in prestige when it appears in a prestigious medium.

Recent Developments in Customer-Acquisition Methods. In order to achieve favorable rates of growth, catalog marketers must continually be on the lookout for new methods of acquiring new customers. Recent innovations include:

"Ride-along" with magazines. In November 1986, *INC.* magazine was mailed in a clear plastic bag that also contained one of eight direct-mail pieces including a Saks Fifth Avenue catalog, a brochure for retirement planning seminars, and a gourmet foods catalog. The *American Bar Association Journal* had already experimented with Xerox office supply catalogs mailed to a portion of its subscribers in the same manner. Both magazines point to their ability to target desirable market segments selected from their entire subscriber list according to the cataloger's objectives.[28]

Catalog kiosks in retail stores and libraries. Described as a "catalog newsstand" by one practitioner, one version of a catalog kiosk holds 15 to 20 copies of 48 different specialty catalogs. The catalogs sell for $1 to $2, but on the cover of each are offers of $5 off on the first purchase and a free 1-year subscription to the catalog. Universal Product Codes allow the tracking of catalog movement through the

[25] Muldoon, *Catalog Marketing*, p. 214.

[26] Muldoon, *Catalog Marketing*, p. 216.

[27] Muldoon, *Catalog Marketing*, p. 216.

[28] Ronald Alsop, "For Extra Attention, Catalogs Hitch a Ride with Magazines," *The Wall Street Journal*, December 4, 1986, p. 37.

retailer's point-of-sale system. The cost for display space is roughly equivalent to prospecting postage and list rental costs.

Kiosks located in libraries feature single copies of over 1,000 catalogs bound in metal directory covers like those used in telephone booths. The catalogs are cross-referenced, allowing library patrons to use them to browse, to compare products and prices, or to order merchandise. Order cards can be mailed by the patron or left at the kiosk for collection three times a week. The firm that provides the kiosks receives a 10 percent commission on orders and, in turn, pays the library a 5 percent commission based on its receipts.

Catalog showrooms. Catalog order stores featuring the merchandise of a single cataloger have long been operated by mass merchandisers like Sears and J. C. Penney in trading areas which have insufficient market potential to support a retail store. Other firms such as Service Merchandise operate a chain of catalog showrooms. The most recent development, however, is a chain of catalog showrooms that features the catalogs of 400 large manufacturers. Orders are shipped directly from the manufacturer to the customer.[29]

The electronic catalog. Consumer access to catalogs via personal computer or cable television is still very new, although catalogs (including The Sharper Image) began to experiment with catalog presentations on cable television several years ago. At some point in the not-too-distant future electronic shopping will become a reality in many households. When it does, it will create an important new media alternative for catalog marketers.

These customer-acquisition techniques are still too new for their effectiveness to be evaluated. However, two things are certain: catalogers must continually seek new avenues of reaching qualified prospects, and they must carefully monitor the costs of the various methods of reaching prospects.

A Related Development. Paid advertising in catalogs is not a customer-acquisition technique, although some catalogers have argued that it adds interest to the catalog and thereby helps retain customers. It certainly produces revenue for the catalog.

Bloomingdale's By Mail began the trend with five pages of advertising in their 1985 catalog for products, including Calvin Klein sportswear and Lincoln-Mercury cars. By early 1987, as as many as 30 catalogs were accepting paid advertising.

According to a Bloomingdale's direct marketing executive, magazines reach populations that are demographically similar to the customer bases of catalogs. However, the catalog has several advantages over magazines as an advertising medium:

[29] "Catalogues Extending Reach Via New Distribution Outlets," *Marketing News*, February 13, 1987, p. 12.

- Media buyers can shop for a catalog whose image and product offering complements, and even enhances, the advertised product.
- Catalog readers are probably predisposed to purchase.
- The catalog marketer can offer exclusivity to advertisers for that issue of the catalog.

A limited amount of paid advertising appears to be desirable from the cataloger's standpoint. Advertisers view it as a cost-effective way of reaching target audiences that are well-defined both demographically and psychographically. While this is also a relatively new development in the catalog arena, it may have a very promising future.[30]

Tracking Customer-Acquisition Costs. Customer-acquisition costs should be evaluated separately for each medium. Both the cost of acquiring the name and the cost of converting the name to a sale should be calculated. When the effectiveness of each acquisition medium is evaluated individually, the catalog marketer can decide which media warrant the greatest expenditures.

The Sturbridge Yankee Workshop offers an important example with regard to the acquisition of new names. They have found that the faster names are followed up and the more concerned and personal the follow-up appears to be, the higher the conversion rate is likely to be.

Customer Service Policies. The competitiveness of the catalog marketplace and the high expectations of sophisticated customers have increased the importance of excellent customer service in developing and maintaining customer loyalty. Earlier in the chapter we pointed out that the fulfillment of orders and the delivery of customer service are part of the so-called back end of direct marketing (discussed in Chapter 7). The establishment of policies to guide back-end operations is an integral part of the development of marketing strategies for catalogers. Policies must be set for guarantees, order acceptance by mail and telephone, stock availability, order fulfillment, packing standards, customer returns, and customer relations. Figure 10.9 lists the specific decision areas and desirable standards. The number of issues specified in this checklist underscores the fact that excellent customer service can only be provided if catalog management pays meticulous attention to myriad details.

While the importance of customer service to the success of a catalog cannot be overstated, a mistake need not be fatal to the customer relationship if it is corrected promptly. A study of customer service in banks "found that settling a com-

[30] "Ads Where you Least Expect Them," *U.S. News & World Report*, March 9, 1987, p. 46; "Bloomingdale's Catalogues Carrying Paid Ad Inserts," *Marketing News*, February 13, 1987, p. 27.

Figure 10.9 ***Customer Service Checklist***

General Company Posture

Product Guarantees:

Do you offer product guarantees?

Are they:

unconditional?

conditional (limitations on time or reason for return)?

Performance Guarantees:

Do you provide stock availability, order turnaround time, and/or customer service problem-resolution guarantees?

Are they backed by remuneration such as discount coupons or free merchandise?

Reaffirmation of guarantees:

Do you feature your guarantees throughout the catalog, on the order form, during telephone order taking, and on shipping documents?

Do you routinely offer a true discounted price special, preferably one related to the product being ordered, during telephone order taking?

Telephone-Order Acceptance

Operator Schedules:

Are your customers able to place telephone orders at least 14 hours per day, including weekends?

Telephone Waiting Time:

Is each call answered in four rings or less?

Are customers kept on hold for more than 30 seconds?

Telephone Courtesy:

Are your operators pleasant, acting as facilitators and apologizing for errors when appropriate?

Do you measure telephone courtesy by supervisory listening-in audits and act on the findings?

Stock Availability Feedback:

Do you provide accurate stock availability and ability to ship information to customers as part of the order-taking process?

Product Information:

In response to customer questions, can your operators provide true, informed feedback on product characteristics?

Figure 10.9 (cont'd)

Stock Availability

Telephone Cancellations:

Do you measure the frequency of lost telephone orders due to poor stock availability?

Initial Fill Rate:

Do you monitor the percent of units ordered that were shipable at the time of order entry?

Back-order Activity:

Do you monitor the average number of back-order shipments as a percentage of total orders?

Cancellations:

What percent of total units ordered were ultimately cancelled because of stock unavailability?

Order Fulfillment

Throughput:

Do you measure average order throughput, receipt through shipment by week?

Shipping Modes and In-Transit Time:

Do you offer the customer options as to how the order will be shipped?

Do you audit in-transit times by mode and season and follow up on results?

Lost Shipping Orders:

Do you have controls that identify situations in which a shipping order was issued but shipment could not be confirmed within 3 days of when it should have been made?

Shipment Accuracy:

Do you routinely audit at least 2 percent of all outgoing shipments for accuracy (correct items, packing materials, and packing methods)?

Shipping Documents:

Do your shipping documents clearly state what you are shipping in this carton, what you have simultaneously shipped in other cartons on the same date, and the status of other items on the original order?

Personalization:

Do you have illustrated quality standards dealing with uniformity, positioning, materials, etc., for each product group and personalization technique?

Does an individual other than the personalizer check all personalized items for accuracy and quality?

Figure 10.9 (cont'd)

Regard for Product:

Do you use protective inner packaging such as special boxes, foam moldings, foam wrap, bubble wrap, or shrink wrap that makes it evident that packaging was used specifically for protection of this particular product?

Do you routinely test protective product packaging and correct where necessary?

Are products ever sent out dusty, dirty, wrinkled, or with product packaging bent, marked, torn, or marred?

Do you routinely sample for this as part of your outgoing shipment accuracy audit?

Do you routinely sample customers on this issue?

Shipment Packing Characteristics:

Do you use special shipping materials such as modular inner packs to control product shifting and standardization of initial product appearance upon opening or foam-in-place fill where truly appropriate for protection of highly fragile products?

Is your primary packing material messy or unattractive?

Are your shipping cartons of appropriate test strength and design to withstand transit through the parcel post and UPS shipping systems without symptoms of crushing?

Do you routinely test shipments for damage?

Customer Returns

Are return procedures and limitations clearly and concisely outlined on shipping documents?

Do you offer a UPS call tag or similar program?

Do you reimburse postage for defective returns in some manner?

Do you appropriately dispose of returns within 1 day of receipt?

Do you track rates of return by reason and consistently act on findings?

Customer Service Department

Telephone Calls:

Do you prominently feature a customer service telephone number on all shipping documents?

Do you offer a toll-free number for customer service calls?

Are customer service calls answered within 4 rings and kept on hold for no more than 30 seconds?

Are customer service personnel pleasant? Do they:

—facilitate conversations by actively listening to customers' problems?

—have a positive, non-argumentative attitude, striving to remove roadblocks while making sure the customer feels he or she is right?

Figure 10.9 (cont'd)

Do you set standards for average length of calls and monitor actual results weekly by operator?

Do you set standards for and monitor customer service call resolution—during the initial call, within the hour, same day, and longer—by operator?

Mail:

Do you respond to customer service correspondence within 2 days of receipt?

Source: Adapted from Todd H. Barr, Kurt Salmon Associates, Inc., "Customer Service: How Do You Rate?" *Catalog Age*, June/July 1986, pp. 113–115. Reprinted with permission of the author.

aint often engenders greater customer loyalty than if the problem never arose in the first place. Seventy to 80% of customers whose complaints were resolved satisfactorily were willing to buy other products, compared with only 10 to 20% of non-complainers." Even more strikingly, 30% of unsatisfied complainers were willing to buy other products. According to the president of the research organization that conducted the study, customers seemed grateful that anyone had paid attention to their complaint in the first place.[31] The success of catalogers who are renowned for their customer service suggests that the findings of this study apply to catalogs as well as banks.

Some of you may have experienced either excellent or poor service by a cataloger and be wondering whether your experience is the norm or the exception. The original version of the checklist in Figure 10.9 assigned points to each of the subcategories in each item shown here—a total of 1,000 points. Table 10.3

Table 10.3 Estimate of Customer Service Performance by Category

Customer Service Category	*Level of Service Achieved Estimated Industry Average Score*
General company posture	55%
Telephone-order acceptance	51%
Mail-order acknowledgment	18%
Stock availability	31%
Order fulfillment	45%
Product presentation	51%
Customer returns	55%
Customer service	39%
Average	44%

[31] Phillip L. Zweig, "Banks Stress Resolving Complaints to Win Small Customers' Favor," *The Wall Street Journal*, December 8, 1986, p. 29.

below shows the author's estimate of the average industry score on each major category. It suggests that the catalog industry, along with most other industries in this country, has a long way to go to in providing customer service.

Even though customer service activities generally take place in the latter stages of the transaction, the importance of serving customers well should underlie all aspects of marketing strategy and operations. According to Nash, "the place to begin good customer service is in the original advertisement or mailing piece. Don't make promises you can't keep or guarantees you can't fill."[32]

CATALOG DESIGN

Decisions about the design of the catalog should be guided by its basic concept. A catalog's overall look and the way it presents merchandise are powerful contributors to the firm's image in the eyes of the consumer. Earlier in this chapter the catalog was referred to as a "paper store." Think of catalog design as being akin to designing a retail store and arranging merchandise inside it to achieve the highest possible level of sales.

The basic design decisions are the size of the catalog, the layout format to be used, merchandise arrangement, visual presentation, and copy. In addition, an easy-to-use order form must be developed.

Size of the Catalog

There are two common catalog sizes, 8 1/2 by 11 and 5 1/2 by 8 1/2 inches. A length of 32 pages is common; printing-press requirements dictate that additions be in 8-page increments, though a plus cover will add 4 pages without violating that requirement.

The primary consideration in deciding which size to choose is the number of items and the space each will require for effective display. Housewares catalogs often are digest size (5 1/2 by 8 1/2 inches) because each item does not need a great deal of space. Fashion apparel catalogs, on the other hand, are more likely to be 8 1/2 by 11 inches to show the clothing to best advantage.

These two sizes are the most common because they can be run efficiently on modern printing presses. Other sizes are possible, but they will result in wasted paper and therefore will increase production costs. Some catalog marketers obviously feel the additional cost is worthwhile in order to be different from their competitors. For example, upscale retailers frequently make use of sizes larger than 8 1/2 by 11 inches.

[32] Edward L. Nash, *Direct Marketing: Strategy/Planning/Execution* (New York, McGraw-Hill), p. 380.

Catalog Format

When you look at a catalog, you see two facing pages—a spread. The two pages that make up each spread should be laid out as a unit rather than an individual pages. A catalog's format is made up of several basic spread designs that are used throughout. Tucker suggests that four basic spread designs are enough to establish the format for a typical catalog.[33] Once established, the format should be used consistently to provide the recognizable look that becomes an integral part of the catalog image.

There are two basic types of spread designs—grid and free-flowing. A *grid system layout* divides the pages into boxes, each of which presents one product. The grids do not all have to be equal in size (see Figure 10.10). Stone, who clearly does not like grid system designs, says that "if you opt for grid system layout, you needn't pay the price of an accomplished catalog designer; a draftsman can do a grid system well."[34] But other experts have argued that well-balanced grid spreads can be effective. A *free-flowing design,* on the other hand, allows for considerable flexibility and creativity, while still providing a design standard that gives the catalog its distinctive look (see Figure 10.11).

A special design, consistent with the overall catalog format, should be developed for the front and back covers. The cover format should be as distinctive and recognizable as creative design can make it. Within the basic cover format of prominently featuring the catalog name, colors, textures and seasonal merchandise can provide freshness and excitement.

Spread designs can be reversed for additional variety within the catalog. Space should be allowed on some spreads for the catalog logo and the toll-free telephone number.

The number of possible spread designs is immense. Common sense, especially the recognition that too many items squeezed onto a page cannot possibly be effective, will eliminate the worst ones. Beyond that, testing is necessary to determine what works best. In this case, in-mail testing may not be the most effective method. Instead, eye-movement cameras can be used to analyze the movement of customers' eyes over the page. Designs that do not allow for smooth eye movement are unlikely to be effective.

Merchandise Arrangement

The placement of merchandise within the catalog can be approached in a number of ways. One way is to arrange the merchandise by category—all shoes together, for example. This type of arrangement emphasizes the broad assortment of a product category the catalog has to offer.

[33] Jo-Von Tucker, 'Creating Catalog Continuity," *Direct Marketing*, February 1987, p. 50.

[34] Stone, *Successful Direct Marketing Methods*, 3rd ed., p. 313.

FIGURE 10-10

FIGURE 10-11

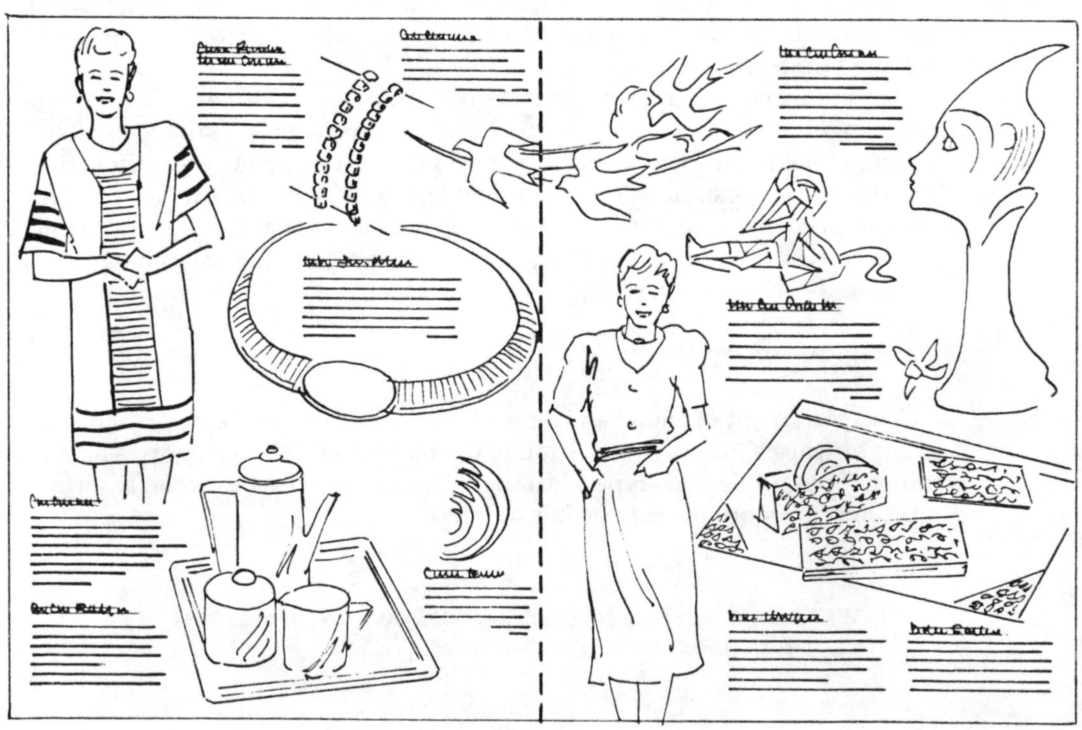

Another approach is to group items of merchandise according to typical customer use. For example, a spread might feature a man's business suit along with a matching shirt, tie, tie tack, and pair of shoes. This type of arrangement would encourage multiple-item purchases.

Another way of looking at merchandise arrangement classifies merchandise as commodity items (items regularly used and therefore repurchased on a predictable cycle), shopping items (items for which a need and an intent to buy both exist), and impulse items (items for which customers do not engage in advance planning). The developer of this classification of merchandise reminds us that retail stores place the planned purchase items (e.g., bread and milk in a supermarket) along the back or side of the store so that customers have to walk past many other items of merchandise to reach them. The same principle can be applied to merchandise arrangement in a catalog.[35]

Shopping items should be granted sufficient space for detailed graphics and persuasive copy. Since customers already have recognized a need for these products, they will be attentive to them. Consequently, the products can occupy space in some of the "lower-traffic" pages of the catalog.

Commodity products, such as business shirts for men and blouses for women, often complement a number of other products—both a suit and a pair of slacks, for example. They may be displayed several times in a single catalog, appearing each time with another item with which they are frequently used.

Impulse items should be displayed in "high-traffic" areas—the front and back covers, the inside covers, the center spread, and the pages surrounding the order form. For interest and variety, impulse and commodity items can be mixed about 50/50 on these pages.

All of these approaches to placement of merchandise emphasize the importance of understanding customer shopping and product-use behavior. They are the key determinants of merchandise arrangement within the catalog.

Visual Presentation

Most catalogs use photographs for visual presentation of their merchandise. A skilled professional photographer, preferably one experienced in catalog photography, is an absolute necessity if the cataloger wants photographs that do the best possible selling job.

Photographs can be divided into two basic categories: still-life or table-top shots and fashion shots. As the name implies, *still-life shots* show inanimate objects photographed alone or in a use setting (kitchen tools on a kitchen work space; bed linens in a bedroom setting). *Fashion shots* refer to clothing shown on a model, either in a studio setting or on location.

Good photographs have the following characteristics:

[35] Brent John Bissel, "Catalog Merchandise Floor Planning," *Direct Marketing*, March 1987, pp. 78-82.

- They show the details of the merchandise. The pose of the model, no matter how attractive, should not obscure the details of the merchandise.
- They use props to enhance the presentation and establish the size of the merchandise when necessary. Both the photograph and the copy should make it clear which items are for sale. It is very frustrating to generate many requests for, say, the necklace on page 23 when the necklace is the property of the model and therefore not for sale!
- The models are representative of the target market—or at least the way the target market would like to look. Some catalogs use their employees as models, but most use professional models.
- The backgrounds and backdrops are attractive without overwhelming the merchandise, and are appropriate to both the merchandise and the catalog image.
- The colors are right.

The last point—color—involves two issues:

1. The colors should portray the merchandise accurately. If the actual color is different from the color shown in the catalog, many items will be returned. Getting the colors right requires an understanding of color separations (described in the appendix to Chapter 9).
2. The pages should be laid out in a way that allows the printer to control the ink flow so that color from one page does not bleed onto another. This requires working closely with the printer in order to understand which pages will be next to one another on the press (a relationship quite different from the order of pages in the catalog).

Most catalogers use photographs because they show the details of the merchandise so well and seem to lend credibility to the merchandise presentation. The Banana Republic catalog, however, makes extremely effective use of illustrations to portray their merchandise (Figure 10.12). According to an executive from another catalog firm, "their merchandise frequently has subtle design features, [and] this technique is better for highlighting the feature and conveying the uniqueness."[36]

Catalog Copy

Because catalog copy must fit the space provided by the layout, it is the most disciplined form of direct-response copywriting. It must do the selling job and do it with no excess words.

Catalog copy begins with a *caption* or *headline* that focuses the reader's attention. This can be merely a description or *label*—"Power Lawn Mowers" or "Our Best Power Lawn Mowers," for example. A label headline does little to advance the sales message.

[36] William A. Dean, "Catalog Imagery," DMA Manual Release No. 1400.5, October 1986.

FIGURE 10-12 ***Using Illustrations in Catalogs***

Source: Banana Republic, Travel and Safari Clothing Co., San Francisco, CA 941045

A strong headline stresses the *benefits* to be obtained from using the product. The copywriter for the lawnmower could say, "Cut Grass-Cutting Time in Half," or even better, "New Contoured Blade Trims up to One Inch Away from Fences, Buildings." The second headline stresses a benefit and adds a reason (new contoured blade) that makes the benefit plausible. However, it may also take up more space than is available.

A *sale* headline stressing price/value is sometimes used. The headline for the lawnmower could also read "Compare at $XXX.xx." Kanter cautions, however, that sale headlines can easily be deemed misleading and are subject to strict governmental regulation.[37]

Writing catalog copy that is complete, yet concise, and that sells, but is creative, is a large order. According to Kanter, the rule is to declare the product's most

[37] Don Kanter, "Direct Response Copy-Catalogs," DMA Release No. 310.3, January 1984.

important benefit, then quickly state the secondary benefits and follow with the selling points that support the benefits. The copy must end with the necessary ordering information; sku (stock-keeping unit), size, weight, color, price, and so on.

The catalog may also include a letter, possibly on an extra sheet but more often on the inside front cover, that informs new prospects about the nature of the catalog and tells previous customers what is new and exciting in the current issue. These introductory letters can give some personal warmth to a rather impersonal medium.

The Order Form

In catalog marketing, as in all direct-response marketing, one of the cardinal rules is: *Make it easy for the customer to order*. We could well expand this to: *Make it easy for the customer to order correctly and completely*. The order blank must and easy to use and must contain all the information needed to fulfill the order quickly and accurately.

The current preference is for order forms bound into the catalog. The order panel itself is on one side; when folded, it becomes a self-mailer with the firm's address printed on the envelope portion. Many variations on this basic form are possible. Just be careful that all aspects, including folding and mailing, follow the easy-to-use rule.

The information required on an order form is rather extensive, especially if credit card orders are accepted. Both of the Suggested Additional Readings at the end of the chapter provide extensive checklists to ensure the completeness of the order form.

PRODUCING THE CATALOG

Quite a few other decisions that must be made by the catalog firm fall into the technical area of producing and mailing the catalog. These include deciding which type of printing process to use, obtaining camera-ready art, putting all material in the preferred form for the printer, and complying with postal regulations.

Other decisions are technical in nature but also affect the image of the catalog. The type of paper used and the choice of typeface fall into this category.

Many of these activities are carried out by technical experts such as printers and graphic artists, but the catalog marketer must have sufficient technical knowledge to deal with these experts in a professional manner. Entry-level catalog marketers will often find themselves working on the technical aspects of the catalog, which is excellent experience. Seminars and professional meetings, as well as careful reading of trade periodicals, can also help the direct marketer become well versed in technical processes and developments.

CATALOGS AND RETAIL STORES [38]

Throughout this chapter we have used retailing concepts to help explain the catalog marketing process. As you are no doubt aware, many retail stores also make extensive use of catalogs and many catalog firms now have an network of retail stores. The blurring of the line between catalogs and retail stores in recent years has tended to foster the mistaken impression that running a catalog business and running a retail store or chain of stores are very much alike, and therefore a firm that is successful at one should be equally successful at the other. Recent examples suggest that this is not so. Several well-known specialty firms (e.g., Esprit and Eastern Mountain Sports) have shut down their catalog operations in the last few years to concentrate on their retail stores.

Fortunately there are more instances of successful blending of these two types of retailing than there are of failures, though we should point out that many catalog firms have deliberately not developed retail outlets in order to concentrate their resources on the business they know best. The successful blendings seem to fall into two categories: retail stores using catalogs to achieve retail objectives, and firms running both catalog and retail store operations simultaneously. In this section we focus on the simultaneous operation of a full-fledged catalog and a network of retail stores.

This is not a "chicken or egg" question. It does not appear to matter which came first—the catalog or the retail stores. What is important is the realization that the two operations must be managed separately. Careful examination shows that many of the success factors for a retail store differ from those for a catalog operation. The proportion of operating expenses accounted for by various elements of cost also differs. Perhaps most important of all is the difference in the very nature of the two types of business.

Success Factors

While many of the factors that make a catalog successful are the same as those that account for the success of a retail store —the right merchandise and concerned customer service, for example—others are different:

- Since customers must come to retail stores, the location of a retail store is vitally important. Catalogs take their "paper store" to the customer.
- The catalog must accomplish all the tasks necessary to make the sale. Catalog marketers cannot offer customers fringe benefits like the sheer pleasure of shopping in an attractive retail store or the opportunity to ask for assistance while deciding whether or not to buy.

[38] This discussion is based on Robert A. Baker, A *Brief Introduction to Mail Order Advertising* (Seattle, WA: Robert A. Baker, 1983); Richard Bencin, "New Breed of Retailers Sell Customers In-Store and At-Home," *Direct Marketing*, December 1984, pp. 30-40; "MO Gains Experienced by William Sonoma and Country Curtains After They Open Stores," *DM News*, November 1, 1986, p. 36.

- A retail store is tied to one geographical trading territory. A catalog is not restricted by geography, but can target high-probability prospects anywhere in the nation.
- A retail store relies to a great extent on media advertising to attract customers. A catalog relies on mailing lists.
- Retail stores provide their customers with instant gratification because purchases are available immediately. Since catalog customers must wait for their purchases, some type of added value such as convenience or unique merchandise is required.

Cost Factors

While retail stores and catalogs have essentially the same cost elements, the importance of many of these elements is not the same for the two types of merchandisers.

The retail store will spend proportionately more on all costs associated with physical location because of the requirement for a desirable (high-traffic) location and an appropriate building with attractive interior furnishings and equipment. This means that initial capital requirements will be higher for the retail store. The nature of the retail location will also cause labor costs to be higher.

A catalog, on the other hand, will make relatively greater expenditures for customer acquisition, data processing, order fulfillment, and customer service.

Operating Philosophy

The retail store operation has traditionally been a blend of showmanship and marketing, with heavy emphasis on the showmanship. In recent years rapidly changing consumer markets and intensifying competition have changed this balance to a certain extent. However, the ability to provide a pleasant experience—even a glamorous and exciting one in up-scale retail stores—still plays a key role in the success of a retail store. This type of marketing activity is inherently unmeasurable.

Catalog merchandisers, on the other hand, are accustomed to measurability for all their marketing efforts. These efforts are based on analysis and projection, not on flair and showmanship.

This fundamental difference in approach between retail store and catalog management means that, at the operating level, it is very difficult to combine the two. Senior management must establish a coherent strategy for the dual businesses, but day-to-day operations must be managed separately.

Synergy

There are benefits to be gained from combining catalog and retail store operations under a single corporate umbrella that may indeed make the whole greater than the sum of its parts. They include heightened awareness levels created by the promotion of both catalog and store; easier retail expansion as a result of an established customer base; the ability of potential customers who are reluctant to buy by mail to visit the retail store; the opportunity to capture the names of retail store customers for the catalog mailing list; the ability of retail stores to facilitate mail-order returns and exchanges; and the ease with which a mobile customer can switch from store to catalog as location dictates.

You may be asking if retail stores do not cannibalize catalog business within their own trading territory. The answer to that is both yes and no. Two experienced firms, Williams-Sonoma (gourmet cooking equipment) and Country Curtains (curtain specialists), agree that the long-term effects are beneficial to both catalog and store. Though catalog sales may drop for a time in a geographical area where a retail store has just been established, both companies expect their business in that geographical area to increase to about seven times the level of catalog sales over the long run. Surveys by both firms suggest that retail buyers are not averse to receiving the stores' mail-order catalogs, while mail-order buyers plan to continue and even increase their mail-order purchases.

SUMMARY

The catalog segment of the direct-response industry contains some of the most rapidly growing firms in the industry. The success of the leading firms has encouraged potential competitors, many of whom have neither the financial or the marketing wherewithal to survive in today's intensely competitive catalog marketplace. Developing and marketing a catalog requires a well thought out concept, a clear definition of the target market and the desired positioning of the catalog, a sound marketing strategy, and good catalog design. This whole process depends on an in-depth understanding of the requirements for producing and mailing a quality catalog.

Discussion Questions

1. What is the nature of the appeal that catalogs have for consumers? What drawbacks do catalogs have in consumers' eyes?
2. "I think I might start a mail-order catalog. That should be a good way to keep my teenagers productively occupied." Discuss this statement made by a would-be entrepreneur.
3. Explain the steps necessary to develop and market a catalog.
4. What are the main points of similarity and difference between retailing and catalog marketing?
5. If you have not ordered something recently using a catalog's toll-free number, conduct a brief interview with someone who has. Exactly what went on during the call? Did it leave the customer with a good feeling toward the catalog company? Why or why not?

6. Bring two or three catalogs to class. If possible, select catalogs which seem to have slightly different target markets. Be prepared to discuss the image each catalog portrays to you. What are the major characteristics that convey that image?

Suggested Additional Readings

1. Lawson Traphagen Hill, *How to Build a Multi-Million Dollar Catalog Mail-Order Business by Someone Who Did* (Englewood Cliffs, NJ: Prentice Hall, 1984).
2. Katie Muldoon, *Catalog Marketing* (New York: R. R. Bowker Company, 1984).

11

Telephone Marketing

In Chapter 1 we learned that telephone is the largest of the direct marketing media, accounting for $41.2 billion in promotional expenditures in 1986. In this chapter we will discuss the multiple roles telephone marketing plays in direct-response programs. You may be surprised to discover how deeply embedded telephone marketing is in the marketing programs of many successful firms.

THE OLAN MILLS STUDIOS[1]

This family-owned firm, which has over 1,000 studios in the United States, Canada, and England, began during the Great Depression when young Olan Mills trudged the roads of rural Alabama inviting families to a portrait sitting at a local hotel. As his business grew, Mills hired door-to-door salesmen to book appointments and soon had road crews covering most of the Southeast and New England.

After World War II the firm began to experiment with telephone marketing. As a result, their operation gradually shifted from employing traveling photographers in rural areas to using permanent studios in suburban shopping centers.

Unlike most successful telephone marketers, Olan Mills does not operate a sophisticated centralized calling center. Its communicators live in the community and work out of the local studio alongside the photographer, proof consultant, and appointments secretary. This teamwork provides the highly personalized customer service the portrait business requires.

[1] The material in this section is based on Lori Kesler, "Old-Fashioned Telemarketing is Picture Perfect," *Advertising Age*, October 27, 1986, pp. S-40, S-41.

Since the 1950s, the cornerstone of the telephone marketing program has been the Olan Mills Club Plan. For $10 to $16, depending on location, a member receives three studio sittings and three free 8-by-10 portraits. After examining the six proofs made at each sitting, most customers order more than the basic package—after all, who can resist pictures of their children!

Olan Mills has experimented with direct-response space advertising in newspapers, but it has not pulled as well as the 3 percent response rate achieved by their telephone marketing program.

A DEFINITION OF TELEPHONE MARKETING

Stone and Wyman say that telephone marketing

> comprises the integrated and systematic application of telecommunications and information processing technologies with management systems to optimize the marketing communications mix used by a company to reach its customers. It retains personalized customer interaction while simultaneously attempting to better meet customer needs and improve cost effectiveness.[2]

This definition suggests several aspects of a well-planned telephone marketing program:

1. It makes use of the latest technologies, including communications hardware and software and database technology.
2. It is well planned. Telephone marketing does not consist of making a series of hit-or-miss telephone calls. Rather it is a carefully thought out and controlled marketing activity in which the persons or companies called have been identified as actual or potential members of the target market.
3. Telephone marketing is most often used as part of an integrated marketing communications program. Only rarely is it used as a stand-alone medium.
4. One of the key advantages of telephone marketing is that it allows a business to build and maintain satisfactory customer relationships. One-shot programs with only short-term objectives are not really telephone marketing.
5. Interaction with the customer or prospect is personal, even though not face-to-face. This interaction is most effective when carried out by well-trained personnel.
6. Judicious use of the telephone can often make marketing programs more effective at a lower total cost, but this is not to say it will make such programs inexpensive, as we shall see.

True telephone marketing is not a boiler-room operation in which untrained or ill-trained personnel canvass a broad population to generate an immediate

[2] Bob Stone and John Wyman, *Successful Telemarketing* (Lincolnwood, IL: NTC Business Books, 1986), p. 5.

response, with no intention of building a long-term relationship. Even get-out- the-vote operations on Election Day are more sophisticated than that today. Political operations now work from carefully honed lists of citizens who are known or likely voters for thc party or the issues.

Most of the real and perceived abuses of telephone marketing occur in consumer markets. In business markets telephone marketing is generally regarded favorably because it is a time- and cost-effective technique for both the caller and the contact.

WHAT DOES TELEPHONE MARKETING DO ESPECIALLY WELL?

Telephone marketing possesses all the special competencies of direct marketing, discussed in Chapter 1. However, as the second most intensely personal promotional medium (personal selling, of course, is the most personal), telephone marketing does some things especially well:

- It provides *immediate feedback* in two ways:
  - The two-way dialogue of telephone communications allows a rapid assessment of which aspects of the marketing program are working and which are not.
  - Sophisticated monitoring equipment gives management an up-to-the-minute accounting of the effectiveness of telephone representatives.
- It provides *flexibility.* Aspects of the program that are not working can be changed; program variations can be tested. Fixed programmatic costs are low (as distinguished from capital equipment costs, which can be substantial), so adjustments can be made immediately.
- It provides *incremental effectiveness* when used in conjunction with other media. According to Roman, telephone follow-up to a direct-mail campaign "will generate an incremental response 2-1/2 to 10 times the response achieved by mail alone. . . . The lift in response is incremental and not the result of cannibalizing responses normally achieved by mail."[3]
- It provides a method of *building and maintaining customer goodwill* between sales. This can be done by checking on customer needs and satisfaction and by notifying customers of new developments.
- It provides opportunities for greatly *increased levels of customer service.* Order verification, tracking, and complaint handling can all be done more quickly over the telephone, increasing the level of customer satisfaction.

[3] Murray Roman, *Telemarketing Campaigns that Work!* (New York: McGraw-Hill, 1983), p. xxii.

- It provides a high level of *productivity*. Depending on the market (business or consumer) and on the nature of the offer, the number of calls per hour varies from less than 3 to as many as 15.[4]
- Used correctly, it has a relatively *low cost per contact*.[5]

THE BASIC TYPES OF TELEPHONE MARKETING

There seem to be as many ways of describing basic telephone marketing approaches as there are professionals who write and talk about the subject. We will describe them as scripted, guided, and professional.

Scripted Telephone Marketing

Scripted telephone marketing is just what its name implies. The caller works from a script that is complete from "Hello, my name is . . . " to "Thank you for your time." This type of telephone marketing is much more commonly used in consumer markets than in business markets.

The major advantage of using completely scripted calls is that personnel require little training and become virtually interchangeable. Supervisory managers need not be very skilled either. However, this approach can only work for relatively inexpensive, routinely purchased products and for very simple offers. And, often it doesn't work very well even for these products.

One of our colleagues reports an experience he had with scripted telephone marketing. He had been buying *The New York Times* on his way to work every day for many years when he received a telephone call announcing that *The New York Times* was now being delivered to homes in his neighborhood and asking if he would like to subscribe. He broke into the scripted call immediately and said that he would indeed like to subscribe. The caller replied a little huffily that she had to complete the sales pitch and went right on with the script. As he tells the story, he tried to break into the script two more times, saying that he was convinced and ready to subscribe, but finally just gave up and let the caller complete the pitch before taking his order!

Actually, it is possible to do rather complex calling using a script. Computer software is now available that allows the construction of complex scripts that "branch" to different responses depending on the prospect's answer to each query. This type of sophisticated communication is also used in survey research operations.

[4] Roman, *Telemarketing Campaigns that Work!*, p. xxii.

[5] Information in this section is based on Roman, *Telemarketing Campaigns that Work!*, pp. xxi–xxii; Eugene B. Kordahl, *Telmarketing for Business*, (Englewood Cliffs, NJ: Prentice Hall, 1984), pp. ix–xi.

Guided Telephone Marketing

Guided telephone marketing programs might be compared to depth interviewing in marketing research where the questioner/ caller works from a topical guide. The guide specifies the subjects to be covered but does not provide the actual words for the caller. Guided telephone marketing has a wide range of uses: from situations appropriate for scripted approaches all the way to those that require a professional selling approach.

Professional Telephone Marketing

Professional telephone selling is essentially a personal sales call that takes place via the telephone. It requires a high level of skill and training for both telephone representatives and managers, and it is best carried out in an environment where each representative has access to the marketing database.

The professional telephone marketing approach is sometimes used in consumer markets and is fast becoming the norm in business markets. Used well, the results can be amazing. A few years ago the rule of thumb among telephone marketing managers said that supplies, reorders, and sales of products under $5,000 could effectively be handled over the telephone, but sales of higher-ticket (business) products could only be closed by a field sales representative. That rule is now being broken so frequently that it might as well be discarded. There is virtually no limit to what can be sold using a properly structured telephone marketing program.

This type of telephone selling works so well because of the increasing professionalism of telephone reps and the growing understanding by managers of the requirements for managing an inside sales force (which we will discuss in the next section). Telephone reps are being trained just as extensively and rewarded just as well as field sales reps. Some firms, in fact, are rotating personnel between the two types of selling. Others first place trainees in the telephone sales force, where they can receive more supervision and support, and later move them to the field sales force. It can work either way, if management handles it correctly. We will discuss in some detail the problems that can arise between inside and outside sales forces in Chapter 14.

DEVELOPING TELEPHONE MARKETING PROGRAMS

The basic decision variables for telephone marketing are the same as those for any other direct marketing programs: the offer, creative, timing/sequencing, customer service, and implementation. There are, however, two special considerations in this medium: preparing the script (which is essentially the copy aspect of the creative execution) and integrating the use of telephone with other media.

Preparing the Telephone Script

Despite the drawbacks of completely scripted telephone contacts, we believe it is necessary to understand script preparation for two reasons:

1. There are many situations in which good scripts delivered by callers with appropriate training are the correct approach.
2. Those who understand script development will have some insight into the professional telephone selling process.

Essentially, each call is a sales presentation and should follow the basic steps of introduction, qualification of the prospect, presentation of the sales message, meeting objectives, and closing. Bencin presents a more detailed outline for a telephone sales call[6]:

1. *Anticipate encountering a gatekeeper and be ready to get through to the decision maker.* In a business setting the gatekeeper is usually a secretary or receptionist whose job is to screen callers to prevent "nuisance" calls from going through to an executive. The caller must convince the gatekeeper that the decision maker will benefit from taking this call. Households don't usually have a gatekeeper, although more and more people are using answering machines for that purpose and the caller must be prepared to deal with that.
2. *Introduce the caller and the company.* Establish credibility at once.
3. *If the prospect has (or should have) received promotional material, or if the prospect has been referred by a third party, mention it.* This should both build credibility and jog the prospect's memory about your product.
4. *Summarize the major benefits up front.* Capture the attention and interest of the prospect.
5. *Qualify the prospect.* If the rep has not reached the right person, the time of both parties is being wasted. The dimensions on which a prospect (either business or consumer) is qualified are:

   Is the prospect's household or company a user of your product or brand?

   Are further purchases planned? Within what period of time?

   Is the person contacted the decision maker for the purchase? If not, who is?

   When and how can the decision maker be reached?

6. *Make the offer and gain the prospect's acceptance of the concept, or better, of the offer itself.* Get the prospect to commit him or herself at least to the desirability of the offer. If the prospect is prepared to accept the offer, that's great. But more often the prospect will have questions or will raise objections.
7. *Answer the questions and respond to the objections.* Both questions and objections are pretty standard across prospects. The majority of these should have been anticipated and answers/responses prepared in advance. Some of the major objections—with the proper responses—are often included in the supporting evidence

[6] Richard L. Bencin, "What's My Line?" *Direct Marketing*, June 1987, pp. 94–101.

given to provide credibility for the offer. Remember, the answers/responses should be positive, never apologetic.

8. *Repeat the order and all other relevant information such as the customer's mailing address.* Stress that this is being done to enable you to provide first-class service.
9. *For incoming calls, try to get an add-on sale.* Many firms have a daily special that all telephone reps offer to each customer. At the very least, the rep should suggest a complementary product; if the customer has ordered copier paper, for instance, the rep might ask if toner for the copier is also needed.
10. *Close on a positive note, paving the way for future calls.* Remember that one important use of the telephone is to establish and maintain customer relationships. Not all contacts will produce a sale, but all contacts are an important part of the relationship-management process.

If the call is not for the purpose of making a sale but for another objective, such as scheduling an appointment for field sales personnel or locating the decision maker in order to correctly address product information, some of these steps will not be necessary.

Figure 11.1 shows three examples of scripts. The first, the copier sales script, is designed to enable a field sales rep to schedule appointments for sales calls. With slight revision, it could be used by an inside telephone person to schedule appointments for the field salesperson. The second is a sales script for visual products. Although this script is detailed, notice that it requires considerable product knowledge on the part of the telephone rep to recommend the appropriate products to meet the customer's specific needs. Also notice that there is a free gift incentive and a 15 percent telephone discount to encourage prospects to order at the time of the call.

The third script represents a two-stage process. The first call offers an office supply catalog. The second asks for the order after the catalog has been received by the prospect. Notice that in this program monthly telephone specials give the telephone reps a good "excuse" for checking on the customer's needs each month.

You are seeing the scripts on paper, and many firms do continue to use paper scripts. However, more and more firms are using CRTs instead. The script appears on the screen, information is entered as the call progresses, and, where appropriate, the computer displays the best alternative response. This technology also facilitates checking on the inventory level of the product while the customer is on the telephone. Not only does this greatly increase customer satisfaction, but it also allows the rep to encourage choice of a substitute product if the desired item is unavailable and decreases the number of callbacks required.

These three scripts demonstrate that good scripting is not the "canned" presentations most of us find so offensive. Bencin offers a memorable quote on the subject of good vs. bad scripts: "Unfortunately, like hairpieces, we only notice the bad ones, not the good ones. When scripting is developed and presented properly, it doesn't even sound like [a script]."[7]

[7] Bencin, "What's My Line?", p. 101.

A Copier Sales Script

- Hello, Mr./Ms. ______. I'm ______ from Chicago Business Systems, Inc. I'm calling today because we have some ideas on how a ______ can increase your office productivity and reduce your operating costs.
- Mr./Ms. ______, I'd be happy to drop by and share these ideas with you at your convenience. Would a morning or afternoon be best for you?
- Fine, I'll see you (day) at (time). The spelling of my name is _____. Please call me at ______if there is a change of time, because I'm setting aside that particular time for you.
- Goodbye.

A Sales Script for Visual Products

- (Operator answers.) Hello, I'd like to speak with the person who buys your transparencies for overhead projection. Who would that person be, please? (Get spelling of name and title.)

(Note: usually purchasing, the office manager, duplicating department manager, graphic arts manager, copier key operator, or supplies manager.

- (Buyer answers.) Hello, Mr./Ms. ______, I'm ______, from Visual Products, Inc. We're the company that specializes in overhead projection supplies and equipment. Mr./Ms. ______, are you the person who determines which kind of overhead transparencies your company uses?
- (If "no" response, then determine who is responsible—also get title and department. If possible, try to get yearly volume and method of preparation.)
- (If "yes" response.) Fine. Mr./Ms. ______, our company, Visual Products, Inc., is a one-stop shopping center for overhead supplies and equipment. Many of the largest and most efficient companies in the ______ area use our products—and that's why we're the fastest growing visual products company in the U.S.!
- We offer three basic benefits to our customers: better products, faster service, and lower prices! Sound interesting? (Get prospect response.)
- (If appropriate.) Fine. My call is also very timely because we're offering not one, but two special incentives:
    - First, a special 15 percent telephone discount!

  and

    - Second, a free executive telescoping pointer or a calling card-sized calculator for first-time buyers.

FIGURE 11.1 ***Sample Telephone Scripts***

Source: From "What's My Line?" *Direct Marketing*, June 1987, p. 96, 100. © *Direct Marketing*, 224 Seventh St., Garden City, NY 11530. 800/645-6132.

FIGURE 11.1 ***Continued***

- Now, Mr./Ms. _____, if I can ask you a few questions about your current needs, I'll be able to serve you and save your company money. OK? (Get prospect acceptance.)
- Good, first:
  - How may boxes of transparencies does your company use annually?
  - How are they prepared? (Thermal, Xerox, PPC, or diazo)
  - What type do you use? (Manufacturer, number, weight, and colors)
  - Current source?
  - Current price?
  - What is the current level of satisfaction with your current supplier? (Very satisfied, slightly satisfied, slightly dissatisfied, very dissatisfied)
  - Current stock?
  - Would you be interested in more dramatic color and bold imaging in your presentations?
  - Accessories/supplies needed at this time? (Frames, markers, tape, thermal paper, other)
- We also have a special promotion on a budget-priced overhead projector. Do you need a replacement or an extra one?
- Now, let me determine the best overhead transparency/product value for you, Mr./Ms. _____. May I have a minute to figure this out for you or should I call you right back? (Get preference.)
- Mr./Ms. _____, thank you for waiting. My recommendation for your company will increase the quality of your transparencies and reduce your costs at the same time!
- I recommend:
  - Product(s)
  - Benefits (from benefit sheet)
  - Applicable free gift
  - Special telephone discount of 15 percent gives us a price of _______ for _______ boxes
- How does that sound, Mr./Ms. _____? (Get response.)
- Excellent. And we can usually provide a quick one- to two-day delivery. Also, we are always available by telephone to respond to your questions!
- So that you may receive our special telephone transparency value and free executive gift (specify), may I place your order for you?
- Fine. How do you want me to set up the account information (Bill to, ship to, etc.)?
- (Take data and reconfirm order.)

FIGURE 11.1 ***Continued***

- Thank you, Mr./Ms. ______. I know that you will be pleased with both our products and our service.
- Goodbye.

A Two-Stage Script

First pass

- Hello, Mr./Ms. ______, I'm ______ from the ABC Company.
- (If letter sent) Have you receive a letter from our president, Mr. Dee?
- (Letter sent or not) Well, as our president, Mr. Dee, has stated, ABC Company will provide to all of our *new* and *regular* customers the very best in office supply products, the lowest *overall* prices, fast delivery, and an *unconditional guarantee* of customer satisfaction.
- And, in addition to our *regular low prices*, Mr./Ms. _________, ABC Company will offer a monthly selection of office supplies at very special discounts available to our customer *only* by telephone.
- For example, this month's specials are:
- (Review *telephone* specials)
- Also, Mr./Ms. ______, as an incentive to *consolidate* your office supply purchases, we are providing free gifts for orders of _____, ______, and ______.
- (Review free gifts and order levels)
- So that we can review your current office supply needs and determine *your* free gift, may I personally send you our office supply catalog?
- Fine. I'll send one out today and give you a telephone call in a few days. Sound OK?
- Excellent. Mr./Ms. ______, have a good day. Goodbye.

Second pass

- Hello, Mr./Ms. ______, this is ______ calling back from ABC Company.
- Have you received our catalog?
- Good. As I mentioned last week, in addition to the items listed in our catalog, we're offering *special telephone discounts* on *(items)*.
- Also, remember, for *consolidated* office supply purchases of *(levels)*, we are offering free gifts. And *this month* they are *(gifts)*.
- Which items in our catalog and *telephone specials* do you think you would like to order for your company?
- (Take order, determine gift, and *review*)
- Fine, Mr./Ms. ______. We'll send this order out within _____ days. I believe you will find our merchandise excellent, our delivery service quick, and our *overall* prices to be the lowest *for the value received*.

FIGURE 11.1 ***Continued***

- And remember, if for any reason you are not 100 percent satisfied, we do provide you with an *unconditional satisfaction guarantee.*
- (Explain guarantee and provide telephone number.)
- Sound good? Fine, I thank you for your order today. I'll call you next month to advise you of the *new* telephone discounts. OK?
- Fine. Talk to you next month, goodbye.

Scripts versus Surveys. Having looked at the three scripts in Figure 11.1, you are aware that telephone scripts do not closely resemble survey research questionnaires for marketing research designed to be administered over the telephone. This subject is worth a few more words.

One of the purposes of a successful telephone contact is to obtain information that can be recorded in the firm's database. Thus asking questions and recording responses is an appropriate part of a telephone contact. *What is not appropriate is attempting to disguise the purpose of a sales call by representing it as marketing research.* The person called will not be fooled for long and the reaction to the call will immediately become negative. Firms that practice this type of deception—and it is deception—do themselves a disservice and do substantial long-term damage to both the telephone marketing and the marketing research industries.

Misrepresenting the purpose of the call is just one of the unethical practices that the Direct Marketing Association has long tried to discourage. The DMA's guidelines for acceptable telephone practices are reprinted as the Appendix to this chapter. They are worthy of careful study.

Integrating the Telephone with Other Media

You probably noticed that two of the three scripts in Figure 11.1 were part of a multimedia program, one with the field sales force and the other with a catalog. A very important aspect of telephone marketing is understanding how it can best be integrated with other media.

With Television Advertising. Some of the early direct-response television ads were hucksterism at its very worst. In fact, if you are a fan of late-night TV, you can still see some of this obnoxious advertising for products of dubious value. However, the bulk of direct-response TV advertising is now done by well-known firms marketing credible products and services.

To a certain extent, this change happened because respectable firms discovered the power of direct-response advertising. It is also important to recognize two other developments that made this change possible: 800 numbers and credit cards.

The 800 number (WATS, or Wide Area Telephone Service) has been in existence for about 15 years. It was originally viewed by businesses with a large volume of incoming (and outgoing) telephone calls as primarily a cost-saving device. The travel industry was the first to use it on a large scale as a marketing device, and many other industries soon followed. The first direct marketer to use an 800 number to facilitate ordering was JS&A in 1973. That's not very long ago when you consider how ubiquitous these numbers now are in direct-response space advertising and catalogs as well as television.[8]

Part of what makes the 800 number work so well is the ease of buying on credit cards. Over half of all U.S. households now use credit cards, and the buying power of those households is much greater than that of households that do not use credit cards (See Figure 11.2).

Put this together with the fact that calling an 800 number is free to the customer, and you have a recipe for explosive growth. We will discuss the nature and methods of direct-response TV in detail in Chapter 13.

With Space Advertising. The 800 number and the credit card have also been partially responsible for the growth of direct-response space advertising. There is another important factor at work here, however. The print media offer

While slightly more than half of all households use credit cards, only 17 percent of households with annual incomes below $10,000 do, compared to 88 percent of households with incomes of $50,000 and over. Low-income households pay for only 3 percent of their expenditures with credit cards, compared to 10 percent for high-income households.

Only 22 percent of households headed by someone without a high school diploma use credit cards, but 44 percent of households headed by high school graduates and fully 79 percent of households headed by college graduates use them. Among households using credit cards, high school dropouts charge an average of $51 a month, high school graduates charge $83 a month, and college graduates charge an average of $391 a month.

Credit card users are most likely to live in the suburbs—71 percent of suburban households use this method of payment, compared to 49 percent of urban households and 40 percent of rural households.

Households headed by those between 35 and 44 years of age are most likely to own credit cards (78 percent do), use credit cards (62 percent do), and charge the most—a monthly average of $218. The elderly are least likely to own credit cards (only 54 percent do) or use them (33 percent do). When they do use them, their average monthly charge is only $85.

Figure 11.2 ***Profile of Households That Use Credit Cards***
Source: Adapted from Martha Farnsworth Riche, "How Americans Pay," *American Demographics*, July 1986, p. 46.

[8] Allan Caplan, "Telemarketing-Inbound," in Edward L. Nash, ed., *The Direct Marketing Handbook* (New York: McGraw-Hill, 1984), p. 393.

marketers an opportunity to target selectively—newspapers by geographical area, and magazines by demographics and, even more, by lifestyles and special interests.

Space advertising offers another way besides the telephone to respond: The prospect can cut out the coupon, fill it out, find an envelope and a stamp, address the envelope, and mail it in. In this era of time pressure and immediate gratification, however, the telephone inquiry or order is increasingly popular.

With Catalogs. Telephone ordering—especially the 24-hour-a-day, 7-days-a-week variety—has also been a boon to the catalog business. According to Stone and Wyman, "catalog director after catalog director reports the average phone order to be 20% greater than the average mail order."[9] Part of that increase in average order size may well be attributable to the use of credit cards, but some of it is clearly the result of techniques, including the use of "telephone specials," that take advantage of the personal interaction between the customer and well-trained telephone personnel. Stone and Wyman cite Talbot's, an upscale apparel cataloger, as an example:

> Talbot's . . . has developed an innovative way to make all their telephone communicators familiar with the apparel they sell. They have installed a moving dress rack adjacent to their telephone center. So when a customer calls and asks a question, the telephone communicator only needs to press a button. Presto — the apparel in question is in her hands. And she can answer questions in an authoritative and meaningful way.[10]

The same authors point out the importance of presenting the 800 number properly, whether in a catalog, where the number should be repeated at intervals throughout, or in other direct-response media. See Figure 11.3 for their rules.

With Direct Mail. Telephone marketing is also a powerful force when combined with mail order. Fisher presents the results of a study that illustrates its value.[11] The objective of the program was to sell preferred credit cards. The program tested preapproved credit versus a short application (not surprisingly, preapproved credit won), first-class versus third-class mail for packages that were otherwise identical, and telephone follow-up versus no follow-up, for a total of eight test cells.

Prospects who received the first-class packages were more likely to accept the offer than those who received the third-class packages (20.6 percent versus 17.8 percent, which was significant at the .07 level in a chi-square test). Overall, telephone follow-up raised response by 35.6 percent. Even more interestingly, there was an interaction effect between telephone follow-up and first-class mail—

[9] Stone and Wyman, *Successful Telemarketing*, p. 76.

[10] Stone and Wyman, *Successful Telemarketing*, p. 76.

[11] Joseph C. Fisher, "Getting the Most Out of Telemarketing," *Direct Marketing*, June 1987, pp. 34–37.

Always show 800 as an integral part of your 800 service number. Use bold print and always include the "1" before the 800.

Be sure callers from all locations can easily identify the correct number to use.

- A single-number 800 service allows calls from inside your own state as well as from outside the state.
- If you have a separate 800 number for callers from inside your state, show it separately and specify, "In _____ State call toll free 1 800 xxx-xxxx."
- If you do not have a statewide 800 service, consider accepting collect calls (and if you do, state so clearly, giving the area code).
- You may even wish to restate your number without the area code for local callers.

State the hours when the service is available. Include the time zone if it is not a 24-hour service. If it is a 24-hour service, emphasize that.

If your 800 service is only available in certain areas, or if certain geographical areas are excluded, be sure to state so clearly. Don't forget to offer customers outside your 800 service area an alternate number.

Figure 11.3 ***Rules for Displaying 800 Numbers***
Source: Adapted from Bob Stone and John Wyman, *Successful Telemarketing* (Lincolnwood, IL: NTC Business Books, 1986), pp. 80–81.

an incremental effect of 5.1 percent over the effects of telephone alone plus first-class mail alone. This is reflected in the cost per order, which was 27 percent less than the overall average in the first-class/telephone follow-up condition.

For other types of direct mail, such as lead-generation programs, telephone marketing also increases the response rate and generally produces a higher-quality response.

Telephone marketing used in combination with other direct-response media does not cover all of the uses of the medium. Telephone is also becoming increasingly important in customer relations activities.

ESTABLISHING A TELEPHONE MARKETING PROGRAM

The first telephone marketers had little to guide them except their faith in the medium. They often had to engage in lengthy—and expensive—experimentation before their telephone programs became successful. Since much more is known today, there is no reason to reinvent the wheel when establishing a telephone marketing program, although each program will have its unique problems and successes.

In-House Agency versus Service Bureau

The first question management must settle when establishing a new program is whether to set up an in-house program or to use a service bureau. Cohen lists a number of factors that would make an outside agency the more appropriate choice for an organization:[12]

- Calling activity varies widely between high and low.
- Each contact is a single event, not part of an on-going relationship.
- It would be difficult to establish and maintain facilities, supervision, and other telemarketing center support within the organization.
- The nature of the contact requires little product knowledge or the product is not complex.
- Management requires a completed test before giving full commitment to the program.
- The telemarketing task can be performed outside the company with easy transfer of results.

Keep in mind the issue of "full commitment." We will return to the importance of management's commitment to the concept of telephone marketing later in this section.

In essence, then, the type of telephone program that is handled well by a service agency is simple, has a variable work load, and does not depend on established relationships between telephone reps and customers.

If a service bureau seems to be the correct choice, management should use the following criteria in selecting a service bureau:[13]

- *Experience.* The popularity of telephone marketing has led to a rapid increase in the number of service bureaus. Bureau management should be experienced, preferably in the type of program you are instituting.
- *Management.* Since close relationships between service bureaus and client firms are necessary to achieve the best results, be sure that you will be able to work effectively with managers and supervisors at the bureau.
- *Capabilities.* Does the bureau have the necessary equipment and personnel to handle your job during the specified time period? One useful indicator is "busy reports," which can be generated either by the bureau's own equipment or by the local telephone company. This will provide an indication of how well equipped the bureau is to handle peak periods of incoming calls.

[12] Gail Cohen, "How to Start a Telemarketing Program in Your Business," DMA Release No. 250.3, October 1986.

[13] These criteria are based on Aldyn McKean, "Selecting a T/M Outside Service," *Teleprofessional*, Summer 1986, pp. 35–43.

- *Clients.* Would any of the bureau's clients reflect badly on your own firm? Call current or past clients to find out how satisfied they were with the bureau's service.
- *Commitment.* Is telephone marketing an important part of the service bureau's business or just a sideline?
- *Controls.* Make sure that all aspects of the telephone reps' interaction with your customers and servicing of their orders will be adequately monitored. If the reps are wholly or partially compensated by commissions, be especially careful they are not permitted to engage in practices that would inflate the number of orders and result in many shipments being rejected or returned.
- *Cost.* Cost is important, but management should not choose a bureau on the basis of cost per call. That can be just as misleading as looking at only front-end costs or results for any other direct marketing medium. When a bureau will be handling inbound calls, the correct criterion is cost per order. Cost per order can be computed as:

$$\frac{\text{Cost of Advertising} + \text{Total Telephone Marketing Charges}}{\text{Total Number of Orders Generated}} = \text{Cost per Order}$$

Outbound programs should be judged on back-end results such as number of *paid* orders.

- *Telephone representatives.* Are the telephone reps (*all* of them, not just one or two stars) the type of well-trained, courteous people you want representing your company to prospects and customers?
- *Equipment.* Is the telecommunications and data-processing equipment adequate and suitable to your needs? Has it been in operation long enough to ensure its reliability?
- *Location.* It is useful if the bureau is reasonably close to your own facilities, but it is more important that it be located in an area where there is an adequate supply of qualified personnel.
- *Fulfillment capability.* Though the bureau will not ordinarily be responsible for actual order fulfillment, its responsibilities do include the correct and timely transmission of orders, leads, and so on to your firm or fulfillment house.
- *Considerations caused by the advertising medium used.* The pace and timing of inbound calling are greatly affected by the advertising medium. Responses to mail or print advertising will be received in a pattern that is fairly predictable on the basis of the mailing or publication date. Responses to television advertisements often generate high peaks of telephone activity, especially for successful commercials on prime time or weekends.

Once an outside service bureau has been selected to carry out your telephone marketing program, you must develop a plan for monitoring and exercising control over its activities. This plan will have many of the same characteristics as one for an in-house operation.

Establishing an In-House Telephone Center

Establishing an in-house telephone center is not a minor undertaking and it cannot be done overnight. It requires a great deal of advance thought and planning. Setting up a facility and managing an ongoing program involve:[14]

- Obtaining the support of top management
- Setting goals and objectives
- Integrating telephone marketing with other promotional activities, including the field sales force
- Developing scripts and guides
- Recruiting and training telephone personnel
- Supervising and motivating reps
- Planning and installing telecommunications and data-processing systems
- Designing a productive work environment
- Reporting and controlling the operation
- Testing systems and procedures

Obtaining the Support of Top Management. Whenever a new telephone marketing operation is established, there is a learning curve as personnel are trained, bugs are worked out of the equipment, lists are refined, and so forth. If top management expects a smoothly functioning operation overnight, they may lose patience and decide that telephone marketing "doesn't work." It is the responsibility of direct marketing management to help top management establish a reasonable set of expectations.

Top managers who are unfamiliar with telephone marketing may anticipate a boiler-room operation filled with fast-talking hucksters. It may therefore be necessary to convince them that telephone reps and supervisors will require training and compensation equivalent to those given field sales personnel. Top management may also view telephone marketing solely as support for the field sales force as opposed to a major element of the marketing operation with its own goals and objectives.

Unless top managers are aware of the multiplicity of roles telephone marketing can successfully play, they are likely to relegate it to second-class status. If they do this, it is unlikely that the telephone marketing program will obtain either the amount or the quality of resources necessary for success.

Setting Goals and Objectives. Each telephone marketing program will have its own specific quantitative objectives, of course, but there are usually some

[14] The activities listed are based on Cohen, "How to Start a Telemarketing Program in Your Business," and Kordahl, *Telemarketing for Business*.

strong underlying company needs that lead to the establishment of a permanent telephone center. Among the most frequently mentioned needs are:

- Decreasing sales costs
- Increasing sales revenues
- Increasing average order size
- Reducing attrition of present customers
- Obtaining new customers
- Providing information and performing other customer service activities.

The existence of a major need that is not easily satisfied in any other way is one avenue toward obtaining the support of top management and of various operating managers whose activities will be affected by the telephone marketing center. This is not to suggest that a telephone center can satisfy only one corporate need: Telephone centers often carry out multiple programs that serve multiple corporate needs. It does suggest, however, that a focused reason for the center's existence is desirable.

Integrating Telephone Marketing with Other Promotional Activities, Including the Field Sales Force. We have already discussed the synergy that comes from combining telephone marketing with other direct-response media. This cannot happen without careful coordination to ensure that appropriate levels of training and staffing will be available from the telephone center when needed.

When a firm has both inside and outside sales forces, and especially when both are compensated wholly or partially by commissions, great care must be taken to see that the two forces work together cooperatively. Since this is most often a problem for business marketers, we will discuss it at some length in Chapter 14.

Developing Scripts and Guides. This activity was discussed earlier in the chapter. The process is the same for an in-house as for an out-of-house operation.

Recruiting and Training Telephone Personnel. There are three basic personnel levels in a telephone marketing center— representatives, supervisors, and managers.

Representatives are the persons who will represent the company to its prospects and customers; they should be recruited, trained, and compensated accordingly. The most recent DMA Telephone Marketing Employment Survey[15] indicates that 95 percent of telephone reps have at least a high school diploma, 45 percent have had some college courses, and 12 percent have college degrees. The best educated, and therefore the most highly compensated, reps are engaged in

[15] "Second Annual Telephone Marketing Employment Survey," *Direct Marketing*, December 1986, pp. 54-55.

outbound calling to business customers and work for organizations that generate more than $10 million in telephone sales volume.

According to the same study, supervisors averaged just over 2 years of telephone marketing experience when they became supervisors. Again, the best educated and compensated are found in business-to-business/outbound environments in larger firms. The same is true of managers/directors, who averaged just over 3 years of experience before assuming managerial positions.

The brief experience of both the average supervisor and manager suggests just how scarce competent, experienced telephone marketing personnel are. It also indicates that both recruiting and training will have to be done with special care to ensure that these people perform up to expectations.

When recruiting telephone reps, remember that their "telephone presence" (the degree to which the person can project sincerity and knowledge) is critical. At least one interview should be by telephone to allow an evaluation of these characteristics. How important is the person's accent? If it is not so pronounced that it distracts the listener, it is probably not too important. It is said that some large telephone centers were located in the Midwest and Northwest specifically to take advantage of the flat speech patterns of these regions, which tend not to be offensive to people from any part of the country. But perhaps these companies were even more attracted to the relatively low wage rates prevailing in these areas. After all, who is offended when calling, say, Atlanta, to be answered by a person with a pleasant southern accent?

The initial training of telephone reps will vary in length and intensity according to the objectives of the program. Some of the areas covered in most training programs are:

- Orientation to the company—its history, development, and policies
- Basic selling skills
- Product knowledge
- Effective listening skills
- Telephone center procedures, including call reporting

The training program will contain a lot of role playing and/or simulations designed to let trainees practice their selling skills, reinforce their product knowledge, and become totally comfortable with the telecommunications equipment, call guides, and report formats that will be used on the job. Such a program can take from a few hours for a completely scripted calling operation to several weeks for professional selling. Whatever the length, the trainee groups should be small enough to allow for adequate individual attention and practice.

Training does not cease with the initial program. In a well-managed telephone center training is ongoing. Training programs for existing personnel can perform a number of functions, including:

- Upgrading skills and preparing employees for promotions

- Preventing formation of bad habits
- Introducing new products/programs

All good training sessions send employees back to their daily routine feeling stimulated and highly motivated to improve their performance.

Supervising and Motivating Reps. The supervisor's basic job is to maintain quality, productivity, and work force morale. Good supervisors are actively involved with reps without creating a feeling of "breathing down their necks." They both monitor calls from their station and are a visible and positive force on the floor. In addition, they must keep up with a heavy load of paperwork. According to Cohen:

> "the average supervisor also spends at least five hours a month on quality-productivity studies, performance reviews and analyses, performance improvement activities, personnel records and 32 hours on activities such as record maintenance, review of entry training, office meetings (other than the staff under them) and general administration."[16]

This paperwork load can easily detract from activities designed to motivate reps and keep morale high (and, not incidentally, to control turnover, which can become a serious problem). Books on sales force management discuss many ways to motivate sales reps, including compensation, quotas, recognition, and incentives. The principles are the same for a force of telephone reps. The differences occur because everyone is "under the same roof" and information, including productivity comparisons, is transmitted quickly.

Planning and Installing Telecommunications and Data-Processing Systems. The capital expenditures for an in-house telephone marketing center can be substantial. Currently, the cost of a telephone station is from $5,000 to $10,000, depending to a great extent on quantity (there are substantial per-unit savings for larger installations). For this reason, and also to ensure that the system is flexible enough to meet changing needs and allow for expansion, careful planning is mandatory.

New systems that do not work properly or are inadequate for the company's needs can cause snafus and out-of-service conditions that gravely damage customer relationships. There is a great deal at stake in developing the correct configurations of hardware and software that make up these systems. As call volume becomes greater, the following criteria become increasingly important:[17]

- Comfort of the telephone rep

[16] Cohen, "How to Start a Telemarketing Program in Your Business."
[17] Kordahl, *Telemarketing for Business*, p. 65.

- Ability to modify the system, during work hours if necessary, without affecting work flow
- Ease of accessing and capturing information, preferably on-line

Elements of the *telecommunications hardware system* include the telephone sets used by the reps, equipment that allows supervisors to monitor calls, and equipment for handling or distributing in-coming calls.

The greatest improvement in telephones themselves in recent years has been the development of the lightweight headset. Headsets leave the hands free and, even more importantly, reduce the fatigue and resulting stress of holding a heavy receiver over long periods of time. There are many manufacturers of this equipment and many models—under or over the head, for instance, and monoaural (one ear) or biaural models. It is often desirable to have a visual indicator, such as a light on the base of the headset, that allows other personnel to see when the rep is engaged on the telephone. But the chief criterion in choosing headsets is sound quality. Good sound quality at low sound levels causes less fatigue on the part of the reps.

Whatever their level of preparation and professionalism, telephone reps must be monitored on a continuing basis, just as a sales manager must travel with sales reps regularly. Supervisors can move around the room, plugging into a second telephone jack provided for that purpose, listening to the presentation, and critiquing or offering suggestions as soon as the call is completed. But this type of obtrusive monitoring is likely to affect the rep's presentation, and thus provide an unrealistic picture of the individual's skills.

Monitoring can also be accomplished through the telephone switching equipment. This monitoring can be done from a distance—from the supervisor's office, for example—presumably without the knowledge of the rep or the customer. Note that monitoring can be unobtrusive only if the equipment is sophisticated enough to allow the supervisor to come onto the line without an audible click or without noticeably decreasing the sound level. However you decide to monitor reps, Federal Communications Commission regulations require giving them advance warning that their calls will be monitored.

When the telephone center will be engaging primarily in outbound calling, sophisticated call-handling equipment is usually not necessary. However, for any center that handles a high volume of incoming calls, automatic call distributors (computerized, and therefore programmable, telephone switching systems) are a virtual necessity. ACDs take the incoming calls and distribute them to the reps on whatever basis meets the objectives of the center. Often this is simply first come, first served (for example, airline or hotel reservations systems), but it may be by geographical area (corresponding to field sales territories, perhaps) or by source (e.g., some reps handle calls from the 800 number used in *Business Week*, while others handle calls from the number used in *Electronics Purchasing*).

ACDs offer many features that can be of great assistance in managing a high-volume telephone center. Figure 11.4 lists some of the features that can be included

- *Uniform call distribution*—Doesn't put all the load on the first agent position. Assures even work load.
- *Queuing*—Guarantees first-come, first-served.
- *Music on delay*—Fills void of being on hold.
- *Delayed announcements*—Prepares caller for what is to follow.
- *Supervisory control with monitoring capability*—Assures quality service and aids training.
- *Detailed communicator statistics*—Important for supervision and planning.
- *Detailed trunk statistics*—Gives you control over your system's ability to produce at the proper level.
- *Night service operation*—Allows for flexible day/night operation.
- *Built-in system self-checks with fault isolation*—Saves service call time and dollars.
- *Restriction capabilities*—Isolates communicator from certain activities where needed.
- *Full outward call capability with automatic least-cost routing*—keeps toll charges at a minimum.
- *Call-waiting indication*—Advises both agents and supervision of status of incoming calls.

In addition, the system should offer the following:

- *Station activity details*—Reports hourly, daily, and by activity, what your personnel are doing.
- *Actual talk time*—Indicates success or failure of agent to meet standard time required to deliver sales message.
- *Down time and reason (equipment failure, communicator on break, etc.)*—Isolates problem to equipment or personnel.
- *Group figures of activities—trunks and stations—Quickly reports total results at any given time.*
- *Number of lost calls by disconnection or busy condition*—Alerts you to need for more telephone trunks to handle increased demand.
- *All trunks busy/peak hour reports*—Predicts scheduling needs for personnel and possible trunk expansion.
- *Number of all stations busy*—Justifies adding more communicators to your staff.
- *Department totals/reports*—Segments results by specific department, product, or service.
- *System utilization (least-cost-routing)*—Predicts need for more or less: WATS, Sprint, local lines, etc.

Figure 11.4 ***Features Available on Automatic Call Distribution Systems***

Source: Eugene B. Kordahl, *Telemarketing for Business: A Guide to Beginning Your Own Telemarketing Operation* (Englewood Cliffs, N.J.: Prentice Hall, 1984), pp. 71–72.

in an ACD system. Reports can be printed out upon request and/or on a regular basis (at the end of each shift, day, etc.). Data can also be stored on some computer medium for later retrieval and analysis.

One optional piece of equipment for telephone marketing centers that is highly controversial is computerized automatic dialing equipment. This equipment dials numbers automatically and presents a recorded message that often allows for replies from the person called. This type of calling is intrusive, annoying, and the subject of much actual and potential legislation. It is rarely used for cold calling in business markets and many direct marketing professionals believe that it should never be used for cold calling even in consumer markets because of the ire it raises.

This does not mean that there is no legitimate use for recorded messages or computerized voice-response equipment. The Campaign Communications Institute has been very successful using personal telephone contact that includes the playing of a prerecorded message (see Figure 11.5 for a sample script). And computer-generated voice response has been used in routine customer service applications such as checking on order or inventory status. Still, it is doubtful that totally nonpersonal contacts are satisfying to the customer.

COMMUNICATOR (to a person answering the phone): Hello, this is Michael Graham. I'm calling for A. B. Dick Company. May I speak to the person who buys supplies for your duplication equipment? (Notes name on record card.) That's Mrs. Smith? Thank you.

(To prospect): Hello, Mrs. Smith. I'm calling for A. B. Dick Company. Are you responsible for the purchase of supplies for your duplicating equipment?

MRS. SMITH: Yes, that's right.

COMMUNICATOR: Well, Mrs. Smith, I'm calling with our first announcement of the A. B. Dick Preferred Customer Program. Mr. Walter Whalen, our Boston branch manager, has made a special taped message describing this new service. I'd like to play that for you now—it's a little less than two minutes long—and then get your reactions after you've heard it.

MRS. SMITH: Okay.

COMMUNICATOR: Thank you very much. It'll be coming right on the line.

HELLO, THIS IS WALTER WHALEN. I'M USING THIS SPECIALLY TAPED MESSAGE APPROACH AS THE BEST POSSIBLE WAY TO SPEAK TO YOU DIRECTLY, TO TELL YOU ABOUT A NEW A. B. DICK CUSTOMER SERVICE THAT WE STARTED WITH YOU IN MIND. NOW THE REASON I FEEL IT'S IMPORTANT TO YOU IS THAT OUR NEW SERVICE WILL BE MAKING ORDERING SUPPLIES MORE SIMPLE. IT WILL ASSIST YOU IN GETTING THE BEST POSSIBLE COPIES AT THE LOWEST COST AND LET US BE OF SERVICE TO YOU IN ANY WAY WE CAN. A. B. DICK HAS ORGANIZED A PREFERRED CUSTOMER PROGRAM THAT WE FEEL IS GOING TO MAKE REORDERING AN

FIGURE 11.5 ***Personal Telephone Contact with a Prerecorded Message***
Source: Murray Roman, *Telemarketing Campaigns That Work!* (New York: McGraw-Hill Book Co, 1983), pp. 130-132.

FIGURE 11.5 ***Continued***

AWFUL LOT MORE CONVENIENT FOR YOU. UNDER THIS PLAN YOU'LL BE ABLE TO ORDER SUPPLIES BY MAIL OR PHONE. WE'LL EVEN CALL YOU PERIODICALLY AS A REMINDER AND TAKE YOUR ORDER, IF THAT'S CONVENIENT.

NOW AT THE SAME TIME, A. B. DICK WILL BE CONSTANTLY SEEKING WAYS TO PROVIDE CUSTOMERS WITH THE BEST POSSIBLE SERVICE AND SUPPLIES. FOR EXAMPLE, RECENTLY OUR CENTRAL OFFICE SOLIDIFIED ARRANGEMENTS WITH A LARGE NUMBER OF PAPER MILLS. WE'RE BREATHING A LITTLE EASIER NOW, AND WE'VE BEEN ASSURED OF A STEADY SUPPLY OF PAPER FOR OUR CUSTOMERS. IN A PERIOD OF CRITICAL SHORTAGES, WE'VE GOT PAPER SUPPLIES, AND YOU CAN HAVE THEM.

IN SHORT, WE'D LIKE TO ANTICIPATE YOUR SUPPLY NEEDS AND INVITE YOU TO RELY ON US FOR A REMINDER. STENCILS, INKS, SPIRIT MASTERS, FLUID, OFFSET MASTERS, AND, OF COURSE, PAPER. LET US WORRY ABOUT THEM FOR YOU. WHEN WE CALL, WE'D LIKE TO RUN DOWN A LIST OF YOUR SUPPLIES TO ENSURE NOTHING GETS OVERLOOKED, TELL YOU ABOUT ANY NEW PRODUCTS SO THAT YOU CAN TAKE ADVANTAGE OF THEM, JOT DOWN YOUR ORDER OVER THE PHONE, AND TAKE CARE OF EVERYTHING.

OUR CUSTOMER SERVICE REPRESENTATIVE WILL BE COMING BACK ON THE LINE NOW TO ANSWER ANY QUESTIONS THAT YOU MIGHT HAVE, AND SINCE THIS IS REALLY OUR FIRST CUSTOMER/SERVICE CALL, WE'LL TAKE AN ORDER FROM YOU IF YOU LIKE.

I KNOW THAT YOU'LL FIND OUR NEW A. B. DICK CUSTOMER SERVICE A CONVENIENCE, AND I HOPE THAT YOU'LL TAKE ADVANTAGE OF IT. THANK YOU FOR BEING AN A. B. DICK CUSTOMER.

COMMUNICATOR: Did you hear the tape all right, Mrs. Smith? Fine. Now may I just ask you a few questions to update our customer records?

MRS. SMITH: All right.

COMMUNICATOR: Do you presently have any A. B. Dick equipment?

MRS. SMITH: Yes.

COMMUNICATOR: O.K., and what kind of equipment would that be?

MRS. SMITH: The 460 Mimeograph machine.

COMMUNICATOR: And you have one of those?

MRS. SMITH: One.

COMMUNICATOR: How long have you had this machine, Mrs. Smith?

MRS. SMITH: Oh, about three years now.

COMMUNICATOR: And can you tell me, please, approximately how many copies you make per month?

MRS. SMITH: I suppose it's around 1,000 copies, or a little over that.

COMMUNICATOR: I see. Do you have any other duplicating equipment, Mrs. Smith—not necessarily A. B. Dick?

MRS. SMITH: No, we don't.

FIGURE 11.5 ***Continued***

COMMUNICATOR: All right. Now the purchase record I have before me runs through December 31. Can you tell me if you've purchased any A. B. Dick supplies or equipment since that time?

MRS. SMITH: No, I don't think so. I tried to order everything I would need at that time. But I do have another order for you when you get ready to take it.

COMMUNICATOR: O.K., fine.

MRS. SMITH: Are you ready now, or . . . ?

COMMUNICATOR: Sure.

MRS. SMITH: I need 10 reams of 8 1/2-by-14 mimeotone paper in assorted colors, 10 reams of mimeotone in 8 1/2 by 11. Let's see, I also need 2 bottles of mimeograph correction fluid 368 in blue. And 2 bottles of the mimeograph cement 268.

COMMUNICATOR: O.K., fine. Now let me check this with you: that's 2 bottles of mimeograph correction fluid 368 in blue, 2 bottles of mimeograph cement 268, 10 reams of mimeo paper 8 1/2 by 14 in assorted colors, and 10 reams of mimeotone 8 1/2 by 11—also assorted colors?

MRS. SMITH: As a matter of fact, if you could make those two of each color, that would help.

COMMUNICATOR: O.K. Let me check your address and make sure we don't have any problems with shipment. (Checks address.) O.K., fine, Mrs. Smith, thank you very much. Now since this is your first introduction to our new telephone service, we're anxious to make it work best for you. And our plan is to call you about once a month to give you information about special products and to see how we may best serve you. Generally, what's the best day and time to call?

MRS. SMITH: Ordinarily either Mondays or Thursdays are good.

COMMUNICATOR: Mondays or Thursdays.

MRS. SMITH: I'm only here in the morning.

COMMUNICATOR: Morning. O.K. In the meantime, Mrs. Smith, if you should have any needs or questions I'd like to suggest that you call our branch in Waltham. Do you have the number there?

MRS. SMITH: Yes, I do.

COMMUNICATOR: O.K., good. And ask for Mr. John Hutchinson; he'll be happy to serve you.

MRS. SMITH: O.K., thank you.

COMMUNICATOR: Thank you, Mrs. Smith.

Theoretically at least, there are three basic data-processing systems management can choose from to support the activities of a telephone marketing center:

1. A simple paper-and-pencil system—perhaps index cards with customer information on them, order forms that are physically transferred to the warehouse, and so on.

2. A batch-processing system in which all information is collected at the end of each shift and transported to a data-processing center on- or off-site, where data analysis, report preparation, and so forth are done. Printed reports, work orders, and the like are then produced and physically transmitted to the telephone center, warehouse, and field sales force.
3. An integrated management information system (MIS) in which all telephone reps and managers have on-line access to a centralized database that allows for immediate retrieval of information about customers, inventories, and so on. With an MIS database administrators are responsible for ensuring data integrity, and management can produce needed reports on demand.

Except perhaps for very small or temporary operations, the choice is only theoretical. Without downplaying the difficulties of establishing and maintaining a centralized MIS/marketing database—and the difficulties can be very great indeed—there is simply no other acceptable choice for a firm that wants the most efficient operation and the highest levels of customer service. This is true whether the firm serves a business, a consumer, or a non-profit market.

At present, numerous *software packages* are available to support telephone centers, and more are being introduced all the time. There are so many packages available that whatever the need, it is likely there is a package that will meet it. It is also possible to develop proprietary software, but this is not recommended unless a substantial block of programming time can be dedicated to this activity.

The criteria for choosing software for a telephone marketing center are no different from those for choosing software for any other application. You need to know:

- The functions the system will be expected to perform
- The number of users and the frequency and complexity of their uses
- The experience of other users with the software package
- The reputation of the software developer for installation and service
- The likelihood that the software developer will still be in existence when you need service or upgrades

Because there are so many options, and because the systems themselves are so complicated, management needs to allow sufficient time for determining the best systems configuration.

Designing a Productive Work Environment. One does not just hand a rep a telephone with a nice headset and say, "Here, go to it!" The individual telephone station itself and the overall work environment are very important to successful telephone marketing.

Reps can become stressed and fatigued rather easily because of the constant nature of telephone contact. The result can be rapid turnover. This may be acceptable in a project-oriented consumer marketing setting, but it spells disaster for a business-to-business center engaging in true professional selling. One way to decrease turnover is to provide a suitable work environment.

Designing an ergonomically correct work environment—essentially, creating an interface between workers and their equipment and surroundings that makes them more productive at the same time it protects them from harm—requires careful consideration of a number of important factors.

The design of the telephone center will have to accommodate certain necessary facilities besides the reps themselves. There must be adequate space for telephone and data-processing equipment and perhaps for fulfillment operations. Offices for managers and supervisors will also be required. The supervisor's office should be visible to as much of the floor as possible. A lounge is a virtual necessity. Reps need a comfortable, accessible place to take a break when things get too intense. A conference room for meetings and training sessions is important.

Each rep should have a designated work area—an office or at least a cubicle. Privacy is desirable, but not isolation. There should be adequate desk and storage space and a comfortable adjustable chair. Lighting and ventilation should be optimal, not merely "adequate." If a CRT is used, special attention should be paid to its height and placement.

Quietness is essential; sound must not carry from one rep's area to another. This requires partitions made of sound-absorbing material, carpeted floors, and sound-absorbing materials on walls and ceilings.

A telephone marketing center requires a substantial amount of space and a sizable investment in equipment. Careful design and choice of equipment will result in a productive work environment that returns the investment many times over.

Reporting and Controlling the Operation. We consider the telephone a direct marketing medium because it lends itself to customer contact that is measurable. However, this does not happen automatically. Good reporting procedures are critical to measurability.

The basic reporting form is the customer call report that is filled out for each customer contact. There are literally hundreds of other reports including: summary call activity reports by rep, by shift, by location; account activity reports; and profitability analyses by product, by account, by call duration (see Chapter 14 for examples). To avoid a paperwork glut and time demands on supervisors and managers that detract from their other duties, automatic paperwork should be avoided. Instead, necessary reports should be generated as required by management from the computer system that controls the telephone network.

Testing Systems and Procedures. Because a telephone marketing center is a complex operation, assume that Murphy's Law applies. Things will go wrong; there will be bugs in systems; procedures, from scripts and guides to reporting formats, will not produce the desired results on the first try. Plan for intensive testing, and allow sufficient time for tests to be completed and revisions made (and retested) before attempting a full-scale operation.

The structure of a test and the time it will take depend on what is being tested. A completely scripted program in an established telephone center can be thoroughly tested in a few hours to a few days. Often one or more lead telephone reps will test the new program and work with supervisors and managers on needed revisions.

When new programs (especially those that involve professional selling) or new equipment or systems are being tested, much more time is required. One expert[18] recommends three to six months for a test of this magnitude. Supervisors and managers should take an active role in the testing of new operations, sometimes to the extent of actually performing the initial tests themselves.

One more word of warning: If multiple operations are planned—for example, incoming calls in response to media advertising as well as for customer service, plus outgoing calls for account servicing and prospecting—test each application separately. If you are testing multiple operations, allow from 12 to 15 months for the tests to be completed.

TELEPHONE MARKETING COSTS

Part of the testing process will be to establish productivity benchmarks in areas such as number of completed calls, call duration, and account profitability. Exact standards will depend on many factors, but it is useful to have a reasonable set of expectations before embarking on a program.

Do not be misled by averages; the range in terms of cost per call is fairly wide, and costs of handling inbound calls tend to be lower than costs of making outbound calls (see Figure 11.6). Inbound callers have initiated the call with a purpose in mind. Outbound calling involves determining correct numbers, reaching the decision maker, and presenting a persuasive message—all of which add up to higher costs. Calls to or from business customers tend to be more costly than calls to or from consumers.

Likewise, the application (objective) of the call affects its cost, primarily because the application determines the complexity of the call and therefore personnel requirements and call duration. Stone and Wyman suggest that, whether in- or outbound, calls for order processing, customer service, and sales promotional pur-

Inbound	**Range of Cost**
Business	$2.50 to $5.00
Consumer	$1.50 to $3.00
Outbound	**Range of Cost**
Business	$6.00 to $10.00
Consumer	$2.50 to $ 4.00

FIGURE 11.6

Costs of Inbound and Outbound Calls

[18] Vernon D. Clifton, Sr., "Should I or Shouldn't I?" *Teleprofessional*, Summer 1986, pp. 11–12, 32.

poses tend to fall in the lower ranges shown in Figure 11.6, while calls for sales support and account management tend to fall in the higher ranges.[19]

Roman estimates that one telephone rep can complete contacts with 8 to 15 consumer decision makers or 3.5 to 7 business decision makers per hour.[20] He also notes that the range for contacts with business decision makers varies by type, with that for physicians and top managers being 2.5 to 3.5 completed contacts per hour and that for small retail store managers being 5 to 7 per hour.

The average value of a telephone sale has increased dramatically in recent years. According to Kordahl, the average value of a consumer sale was $19.95 in 1980. By 1985, it had increased to $53, and the estimate for 1990 is $124. The increase in the value of business-to-business sales is even more striking: In 1980 it was $250, in 1985 it was $1,000, and by 1990 it is expected to be $1,650.[21]

In analyzing the productivity of telephone marketing operations, it is important to look at incremental sales in any situation where telephone sales may be cannibalizing sales formerly closed in some other way—by field salespeople, for instance. This is primarily a concern in business-to-business markets, and its implications will be discussed in some detail in Chapter 14.

Again, the important point is that management must test, establish benchmarks, and control its own operations. Profitability analysis for the individual operation is the critical activity, as discussed in detail in Chapter 15.

INTERNATIONAL TELEPHONE MARKETING

Perhaps the most exciting recent development in telephone marketing is the advent of international programs, both inbound (terminating in the United States) and outbound (terminating in a foreign country). Financial service companies, firms in the travel industry, and manufacturers that engage in importing and exporting were the first to establish major international telephone marketing programs. Although there are no statistics available, growth appears to be rapid. These firms are engaging in the full range of applications that would be available to them in domestic telephone marketing programs.

Harrods, the upscale London department store, recognized that American tourist traffic would be down significantly in 1986 because of the fear of terrorism and the decreasing value of the American dollar relative to the British pound. They responded by establishing an international 800 number to allow Americans to place free calls to their store's telephone service bureau. The first program began with a space ad for cashmere sweaters (a very popular item with American tourists in Britain) in *The New York Times*. The response was about 50 percent higher than expected. The program generated over $300,000 in sales and was apparently quite profitable. Even better, it opened up a whole new market; over 40 percent of the sweater buyers had never visited Harrods. The store has since promoted other

[19] Bob Stone and John Wyman, "The Mathematics of Telemarketing," *Direct Marketing*, December 1986, p. 46.

[20] Roman, *Telemarketing Campaigns that Work*, p. xxii.

[21] Eugene B. Kordahl, "How Far Is Up?" *Teleprofessional*, Summer 1986, p. 19.

products in the same manner and has experimented with direct mail. Harrods expects to establish similar programs to reach customers in Europe and the Far East.[22]

Long & Foster, a real estate firm in Fairfax, Virginia, has targeted both military and civilian personnel relocating from Western Europe to the Baltimore/Washington, D.C. area. To develop first-hand knowledge of the market, they began by offering real estate and financial seminars on military bases and in American embassies in Europe. They introduced 800 numbers, initially in Germany and England but with more planned, so prospects could begin the process of looking for a house before leaving Europe. Brokers needed no additional training to handle these calls, which are answered in person during regular East Coast business hours. At other times, callers receive a recorded message that asks questions soliciting the basic information a broker needs to know to begin working with a customer.

Wilson Tool International, based in Minnesota, manufactures tool and die equipment for customers engaged in metal fabricating. The company has been engaged in telephone marketing to customers in the United States and Canada for several years. In 1986 Wilson added the United Kingdom, West Germany, the Netherlands, and Switzerland. Company sales representatives call on prospective customers, who then call the toll-free number to place their orders. Orders are shipped Air Express and delivered within 3 days. According to one European businessperson, "Customers have quickly learned that they can get their tools quicker from Wilson than from a company 50 miles away."

Because of time differences, the line from Switzerland, the Netherlands, and West Germany is available from 1 A.M. to 9 A.M., and the line from the U.K. from 1 A.M. to 5 P.M. Central Time. The line from Switzerland, the Netherlands, and West Germany is handled by a trained representative who speaks the languages of those countries. Wilson estimates that they would lose 85 percent of their potential market if they did not use a person fluent in these languages.

DenMat is an 11-year-old manufacturer of dental materials and supplies located in Santa Maria, California. Its target market consists of 130,000 dentists in the United States, 10,000 to 12,000 in Canada, and 4,500 in Australia. DenMat's distributor network in Australia was weak and could not maintain market share, so the company consolidated inventories in a single warehouse in Sydney and moved completely to telephone marketing. Orders are faxed to Sydney within 24 hours and shipped in 24 to 48 hours. Delivery time has been improved and operational costs have decreased. According to Chris Clarke, DenMat's director of international marketing, "The direct approach is the best. DenMat's technical specialists understand the product 95 percent, while their distributors only could convey 40 percent of the knowledge." Using outbound calling, reps contact the entire customer base every 4 to 6 weeks, checking on shipments and identifying future needs. Telephone contact is followed up by mailing information about products.

[22] Nitin Sanghavi, "Harrods Reaches Out with Its Plush Touch," *Direct Marketing*, April 1987, pp. 43–50.

Telephone marketing to the Canadian market has also been successful, with telephone reps selling more in that market in a single month than distributors sold in an entire year.[23]

While the principles of telephone marketing are exactly the same in international and domestic markets, there are a number of things besides languages and time zones that must be understood by those selling to an international market. It is imperative to be aware of cultural differences—reactions to various types of sales tactics may differ from those in the United States, for example—as well as of differences in regulation or legal requirements. Basically, a firm needs to understand marketing in the particular foreign country before it attempts to do telephone marketing to that country.

The potential benefits of international telephone marketing are tremendous, however. It is possible to better serve existing customers or to open up new markets without incurring the large costs associated with establishing foreign offices or frequent travel or both.

SUMMARY

The telephone is a valuable tool for the direct marketer and its use is growing rapidly in both consumer and business markets. The telephone, however, is so much a part of our everyday life that marketers have a tendency to understate the amount of training and experience necessary to develop a good telephone rep. Likewise, establishing a telephone marketing center is not a simple undertaking. It represents a substantial investment and requires thoughtful advance planning and skillful management of its operations.

DISCUSSION QUESTIONS

1. In your own words define telephone marketing. What is it able to do especially well?
2. What are the basic types of interaction that are possible between a telephone representative and a prospective customer? In what situations is the use of each type appropriate?
3. The telephone is rarely used as a stand-alone medium in direct marketing programs. Why do you think this is true?
4. What circumstances suggest the use of a telephone service bureau?
5. What are the decisions that management must make when establishing an in-house telephone center?
6. Have you used a toll-free telephone number recently or been solicited as part of an outbound calling program? Be prepared to discuss your experiences in class.

[23] Elaine Santoro, "Telemarketing Globalized," *Direct Marketing*, June 1987, pp. 102–110.

SUGGESTED ADDITIONAL READING

1. Richard L. Bencin, "Telefocus Marketing," *Direct Marketing*, December 1987, pp. 32–40.
2. Rudy Oetting, "Telephone Marketing: Where We've Been and Where We Should Be Going," *Direct Marketing*, February 1987, pp. 86–100.
3. Murray Roman, *Telephone Marketing: How to Build Your Business by Telephone* (New York: McGraw-Hill, 1976).
4. Bob Stone and John Wyman, *Successful Telemarketing* (Lincolnwood, IL: NTC Business Books, 1986).

APPENDIX: DMA SELF-REGULATORY GUIDELINES FOR TELEPHONE MARKETING

Article 1: Prompt Disclosure

All telephone marketing contacts should promptly disclose the name of the sponsor and the primary purpose(s) of the contact. No one should make offers or solicitations in the guise of research or a survey when the real intent is to sell products or services or to raise funds.

Article 2: Honesty

All offers should be clear, honest, and complete so that the recipient of the call will know the exact nature of what is being offered and the commitment involved in the placing of an order. Before making an offer, direct marketers should be prepared to substantiate any claims or offers made. Advertisements or specific claims which are untrue, misleading, deceptive, fraudulent, or unjustly disparaging of competitors should not be used. All documents confirming the transactions should contain the means for the consumer to contact the telephone marketer.

Article 3: Terms

Prior to commitments by customers, all telephone marketers should disclose the cost of the merchandise or service, all terms, conditions, payment plans, and the amount or existence of any extra charges such as shipping and handling.

Article 4: Reasonable Hours

Telephone marketers should avoid making contacts during hours which are unreasonable to the recipients of the calls.

Article 5: Use of Automatic Equipment

No telephone marketer should solicit sales using automatic dialing equipment unless the telephone immediately releases the line when the called party disconnects.

Telephone marketers should avoid using such devices as automatic dialers and pre-recorded messages when in violation of tariffs, state or local laws, or these Guidelines.

Article 6: Taping of Conversations

Taping of telephone conversations should be conducted only with all-party consent or the use of a beeping device.

Article 7: Name Removal

Telephone marketers should remove the name of any contact from their telephone lists when requested to do so.

When possible, telephone marketers should offer to remove consumers' names from lists that are offered to other telephone marketers.

Article 8: Minors

Because minors are generally less experienced in their rights as consumers, telephone marketers should be especially sensitive to the obligations and responsibilities involved when dealing with them.

Article 9: Prompt Delivery

Telephone marketers should abide by the FTC's Mail Order Merchandise (30 Day) Rule when shipping prepaid merchandise.

As a normal business procedure, telephone marketers are urged to ship all orders as soon as practical.

Article 10: Cooling-Off Period

Telephone marketers should honor cancellation requests which originate within three days of sales agreements.

Article 11: Restricted Contacts

Telephone marketers should avoid calling telephone subscribers who have unlisted or unpublished numbers unless a prior relationship exists.

Article 12: Laws, Codes, and Regulations

Telephone marketers should operate in accordance with the laws and regulations of the United States Postal Service, the Federal Communications Commission, the Federal Trade Commission, the Federal Reserve Board, and other applicable Federal, state, and local laws governing advertising, marketing practices, and the transaction of business by mail, telephone, and the print and broadcast media.

Source: Direct Marketing Association.

12

Direct Response in Print Media

Print direct marketing may not be the most glamorous side of the industry, but it is the lifeblood of many smaller firms and an important part of the media strategy of mid-sized and giant companies.

Consider the case of Joseph Sugarman of JS&A Associates.[1] Although his initial success came from selling one of the first hand-held calculators by mail, he soon switched to space advertising in magazines like *Scientific American* and major newspapers such as *The Wall Street Journal*. Since the early 1970s Sugarman's strategy has remained constant: locate innovative products in the general category that might be called "high-tech gadgetry," advertise them in upscale magazines and through brochures mailed primarily to his own customer base, and fulfill through the mail. This method of operation has built a business that has annual sales in the neighborhood of $50 million.

The JS&A ad shown in Figure 12.1 in some ways resembles other successful direct-response space advertising. It is straightforward in both copy and layout, focusing on the product itself. Unlike most other consumer direct-response space ads, however, it occupies a full page. This is because of the lengthy copy Sugarman uses to fully explain both the distinctive features and the benefits of the product. Also, the ad does not use a response coupon, merely a copy block with instructions for ordering by telephone and the address for those who wish to order by mail.

[1] This material on JS&A Associates is from Julian L. Simon, *How To Start And Operate A Mail-Order Business* (New York: McGraw-Hill, 1987) pp. 55–56; William A. Cohen, *Building A Mail Order Business* (New York: John Wiley & Sons, 1985), p. 23.

Vision Break-through

When I put on the pair of glasses what I saw I could not believe. Nor will you.

They look like sunglasses.

By Joseph Sugarman

I am about to tell you a true story. If you believe me, you will be well rewarded. If you don't believe me, I will make it worth your while to change your mind. Let me explain.

Len is a friend of mine who has an eye for good products. One day he called excited about a pair of sunglasses he owned. "It's so incredible," he said, "when you first look through a pair, you won't believe it."

"What will I see?" I asked. "What could be so incredible?"

Len continued, "When you put on these glasses, your vision improves. Objects appear sharper, more defined. Everything takes on an enhanced 3-D effect. And it's not my imagination. I just want you to see for yourself."

COULDN'T BELIEVE EYES

When I received the sunglasses and put them on I couldn't believe my eyes. I kept taking them off and putting them on to see if indeed what I was seeing was indeed actually sharper or if my imagination was playing tricks on me. But my vision improved. It was obvious. I kept putting on my cherished $100 pair of sunglasses and comparing them. They didn't compare. I was very impressed. Everything appeared sharper, more defined and indeed had a greater three dimensional look to it. But what did this product do that made my vision so much better? I found out.

The sunglasses (called BluBlockers) filter out the ultraviolet and blue spectrum light waves from the sun. You've often heard the color blue used for expressions of bad moods such as "blue Monday" or "I have the blues." Apparently, the color blue, for centuries, has been considered a rather depressing color.

For eyesight, blue is not a good color too. There are several reasons. First, the blue rays have one of the shortest wavelengths in the visible spectrum (red is the longest). As a result, the color blue will focus slightly in front of the retina which is the "focusing screen" in your eye. By blocking the blue from the sunlight through a special filtration process, and only letting those rays through that indeed focus clearly on the retina, objects appear to be sharper and clearer.

The second reason is even more impressive. It is harmful to have ultra-violet rays fall on our eyes. Recognized as bad for skin, UV light is worse for eyes and is believed to play a role in many of today's eye diseases. In addition, people with contact lenses are at greater risk because contacts tend to magnify the light thus increasing the sun's harmful effects.

SUNGLASS DANGER

Finally, by eliminating the blue and UV light during the day, your night vision improves. The purple pigment in your eye, called Rhodopsin, is affected by blue and ultraviolet light and the eyes can take hours to recover from the damage.

But what really surprised me was the danger in conventional sunglasses. Our pupils close in bright light to limit the light entering the eye and open wider at night like the lens of an automatic camera. So when we put on sunglasses, although we reduce the amount of light that enters our eyes, our pupils open wider and we allow more of the harmful blue and ultraviolet light into our eyes.

DON'T BE CONFUSED

I'm often asked by people who read this, "Do those Blu-Blockers really work?" They really do and please give me the opportunity to prove it. I guarantee each pair of BluBlockers to perform exactly as I described.

BluBlocker sunglasses use ophthalmic-quality CR-39 lenses with a hard anti-scratch coating. Over 85 percent of all doctors' prescriptions are now filled with CR-39. I have taken no shortcuts.

The black, light-weight anodized aluminum frame is one of the most comfortable I have ever worn and compares with many of the $200 pairs you can buy from France or Italy.

The weakest link in any pair of glasses is the hinge. So I have designed a screwless precision two-way tension hinge that not only bends when you close the pair, but is spring-loaded to bend outward too. You get a completely flexible frame that will comfortably contour to your face.

I also have two other exciting models. One is a clip-on pair that weighs less than one ounce and fits over prescription lenses and the second is a precision-molded plastic frame that looks identical to the aluminum model but without the tension hinge. All models include a padded carrying case and my personal one-year no nonsense limited warranty.

I urge you to order a pair and experience your improved vision. Then take your old sunglasses and compare them to the BluBlocker sunglasses. See how much clearer and sharper objects appear with the BluBlocker pair. And see if your night vision doesn't improve as a direct result. If you don't see a dramatic difference in your vision—one so noticeable that you can tell immediately, then send them back anytime within 30 days and I will send you a prompt and courteous refund.

DRAMATIC DIFFERENCE

But from what I've personally witnessed, once you wear a pair, there will be no way you'll want to return it.

Pilots, golfers, hunters, athletes and anyone who spends a great deal of time in the sun, who drives a car or who just wants to protect their vision—all will find BluBlocker sunglasses indispensable.

Our eyes are very important to us. Protect them and at the same time improve your vision with the most incredible breakthrough in sunglasses since they were first introduced. Order a pair or two at no obligation, today.

Credit card holders call toll free and order by product number below or send a check plus $3 for postage and handling.

Aluminum Deluxe (0029KE) **$69.95**
Clip-On Model (0028KE) **29.95**
Precision Plastic (0031KE) **39.95**

One JS&A Plaza, Northbrook, IL 60062

CALL TOLL FREE 800 228-5000

IL residents add 7% sales tax. ©JS&A Group, Inc.,1987

FIGURE 12.1 ***JS & A Space Advertisement***

Sugarman's advertising approach is distinctive and recognizable.This, coupled with his ability to locate unique merchandise that appeals to an upscale, innovation/gadget-oriented, and primarily male target market, has made him quite successful.

The Sugarman story suggests that creative use of space advertising may be one of the few remaining options for the entrepreneur who yearns to begin a mail-order business on a shoestring.

MAGAZINES AS A DIRECT-RESPONSE MEDIUM

Magazines are an advertising medium used by both general advertisers and direct marketers. In deciding to use the medium and then which magazines to advertise in, the direct marketer confronts many of the same issues general advertisers have to deal with, plus a few unique to direct marketing.

We will consider four major issues as they confront the direct marketer:

1. Determining whether magazines are an appropriate medium
2. Deciding which magazines to test
3. Specifying additional requirements such as regional editions and split runs
4. Designing and executing the advertisement

The Changing Magazine Environment

When deciding whether to use magazines as a promotional vehicle, the direct marketer must grasp the nature of the medium. Magazines have in recent years become very much a specialty medium. There are few mass-circulation magazines left—*TV Guide* and *Reader's Digest* are the two primary ones. Other staples of the 1940s and 1950s, such as *Look* and *Saturday Evening Post*, have disappeared, unable to compete with television for mass-media advertising. This type of publication also suffered from steep increases in fourth-class postal rates and intense competition among general-interest magazines in the late 1960s. Some magazines have been able to survive by changing their strategies.

After a hiatus of almost 6 years, *Life* was reintroduced as a monthly in 1978. It began publication with a circulation base of 700,000 as opposed to the 8,500,000 it had enjoyed at the height of its popularity. At a per-issue price of $1.50 ($18 for a 1-year subscription), the "new *Life*" was targeted to a more affluent population that was willing to pay top price for a magazine that was more feature-oriented (as opposed to news-oriented) and even more pictorial than the original. Nine years after its reintroduction, *Life* sold for $2.50 per copy and had a guaranteed rate base of 1.5 million and an actual circulation of over 1.7 million.[2] Other magazine survivors of the TV era include *McCall's* and *Ladies' Home Journal*, womens' magazines that refocused their editorial material to place greater emphasis on working women.

[2] "'Life Is Healthier 2nd Time Around", *Advertising Age*, September 25, 1978, pp. 1, 164; "Avoiding Mistakes Secret of Long Life," *Advertising Age*, March 9, 1987, p. s–8.

The large-circulation magazines now face intense competition from a host of specialty magazines that appeal to well-defined target markets from apartment dwellers to organic gardeners. Competition continues to intensify, with 362 new titles being introduced in 1986 alone.[3]

Other changes have occurred in magazine publishing in recent years. The physical appearance of many magazines has been greatly enhanced with modern typefaces, more sophisticated photography, streamlined graphics, and more use of color—all on heavier paper that provides a better look and more impressive feel.

Editorial policy has changed too. Recognizing that time pressure makes lengthy articles unappealing to many people, many magazines have been featuring shorter articles. Others, such as *The New Yorker*, have made small alterations in layout or type without changing their primary focus on the written word. Still others feature an occasional lengthy, in-depth article interspersed among many shorter ones. Special-feature issues, such as *Sports Illustrated*'s annual swimsuit issue are also used by many magazines. All these changes have been accompanied by increasingly aggressive marketing of both subscriptions and single copies.

Magazines as a Mail-Order and Lead-Generation Medium

Magazines allow the direct marketer to reach relatively large audiences at a *cost per contact* (but perhaps not a *cost per order* or *per lead*) that is generally lower than direct mail. Like direct mail, they allow for detailed presentation of sales appeals and high-quality color photographs and artwork. Magazines are presumed to require considerable attention from the reader, which may lead to more careful consideration of the advertising in them.

Nash suggests that there are several considerations when determining whether magazines are an appropriate medium for a particular offer:[4]

- *Economics*. If the margin is very low, or if it is a two-step offer whose objective is to get information to many prospects, magazines may be appropriate because of their low cost per contact.
- *Credibility*. If the firm and / or product are unknown, the offer may need the "halo effect" of the magazine's own credibility in order to appear credible to prospects. Magazines that are known to be selective in accepting advertising and to stand behind the claims of their advertisers have high credibility with readers. Those that lack credibility (for example, the sensationalist weeklies sold at supermarket checkout counters) are poor vehicles for mail order advertising of reputable products.
- *Lack of Satisfactory Lists*. If there are no good lists for a particular type of offer, it will be necessary to build lists by initial promotion in media that reach large

[3] Belinda Hulin-Salkin, "Style, Looks Enthrall Publishers," *Advertising Age*, September 14, 1987, p. S–1.

[4] Edward L. Nash, *Direct Marketing: Strategy, Planning, Execution* (New York: McGraw-Hill, 1982) pp. 114–116.

audiences. This may be true for a genuinely innovative product. It is frequently true for business products that may be purchased by many different people within the same organization. Direct-mail marketers and catalog marketers frequently add magazines to their media mix when they see their ability to rent high-performance lists declining. It is also possible that space advertising will attract customers who do not tend to respond to direct-mail offers.

WHICH MAGAZINE(S)?

Like the general marketer, the direct marketer looks at three basic criteria when deciding in which magazine to place advertisements: circulation, special services, and editorial policy. The direct marketer then adds a fourth criterion: *receptivity to direct-response offers*.

Circulation

Magazine circulation has three components:

1. Subscriptions
2. Single copy sales
3. Pass-along readership

Some magazines (for example, *Smithsonian*) are sold primarily by subscription, while others are sold primarily as single copies (for example, *Woman's Day*) at newsstands, store checkout counters, and other places. Some magazines have high pass-along readership (have you been in a doctor's office lately that didn't have *People* magazine in the waiting room?), while others do not. Magazine subscriptions can be either paid or unpaid; the latter—called *controlled circulation*—is primarily an issue in business markets.

There is no single answer to which type of magazine is best for a particular application. It depends on the product itself and the objectives and/or requirements of the specific direct marketing program.

The offer that needs the credibility conferred by the magazine itself will benefit from a magazine with a loyal subscriber base. The offer that has as one objective building a new mailing list or adding genuinely new respondents to an existing list will benefit from a magazine with either high single-copy sales or pass-along readership or both. Lead-generation programs, consumer or business, will also benefit from the wider exposure provided by single-copy sales and pass-along readership.

The size and composition of the magazine's circulation are also important. The most comprehensive sources of detailed data on magazine circulation are the consumer and agri-media and the business publications of Standard Rate and Data Service (SRDS). Magazines are listed according to category (general editorial, women's, men's, and so forth). Besides circulation information, each listing contains detailed information on advertising rates, sales office locations, and special services offered by the magazine. Figure 12.2 shows an example of an SRDS listing.

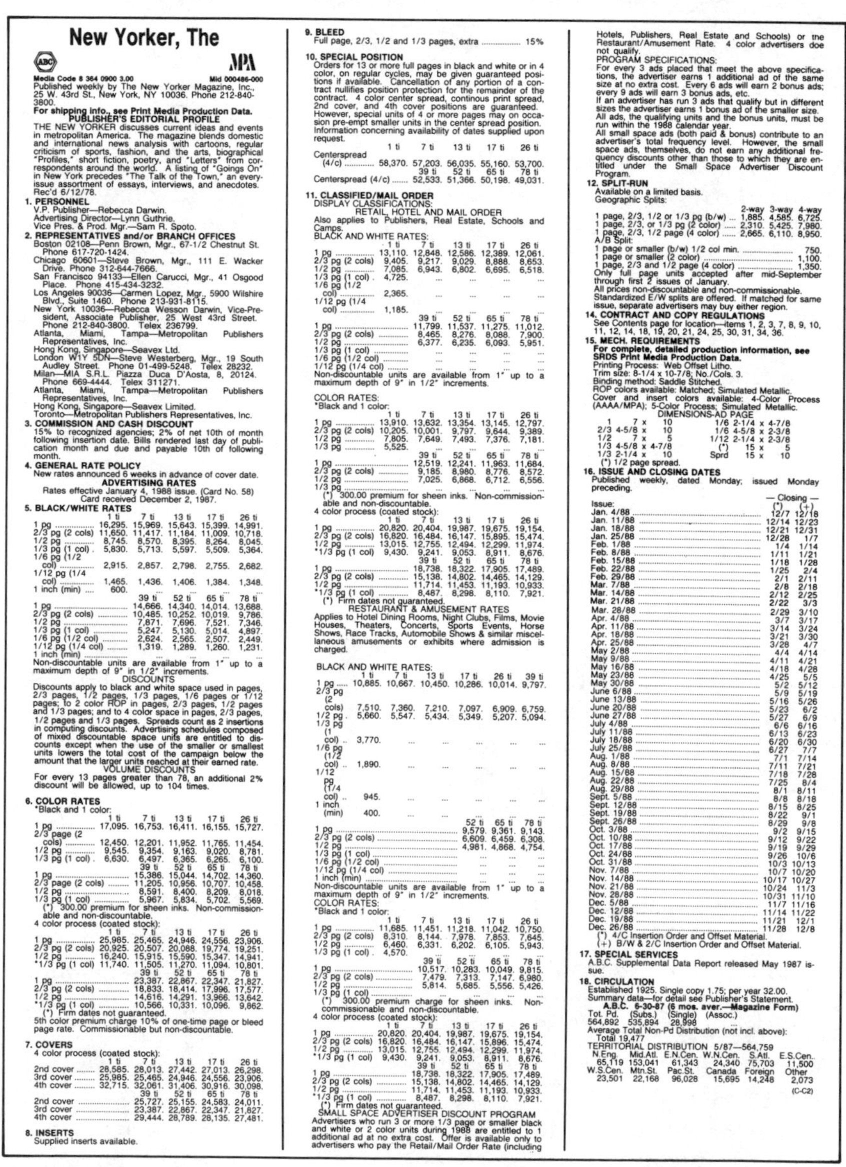

New Yorker, The

ABC — MPA

Media Code 8 364 0900 3.00 — **Mid 000486-000**

Published weekly by The New Yorker Magazine, Inc., 25 W. 43rd St., New York, NY 10036. Phone 212-840-3800.

For shipping info., see Print Media Production Data.

PUBLISHER'S EDITORIAL PROFILE

THE NEW YORKER discusses current ideas and events in metropolitan America. The magazine blends domestic and international news analysis with cartoons, regular criticism of sports, fashion, and the arts, biographical "Profiles," short fiction, poetry, and "Letters" from correspondents around the world. A listing of "Goings On" in New York precedes "The Talk of the Town," an every-issue assortment of essays, interviews, and anecdotes. Rec'd 6/12/78.

1. PERSONNEL

V.P. Publisher—Rebecca Darwin.
Advertising Director—Lynn Guthrie.
Vice Pres. & Prod. Mgr.—Sam R. Spoto.

2. REPRESENTATIVES and/or BRANCH OFFICES

Boston 02108—Penn Brown, Mgr., 67-1/2 Chestnut St. Phone 617-720-1424.
Chicago 60601—Steve Brown, Mgr., 111 E. Wacker Drive. Phone 312-644-7666.
San Francisco 94133—Ellen Carucci, Mgr., 41 Osgood Place. Phone 415-434-3232.
Los Angeles 90036—Carmen Lopez, Mgr., 5900 Wilshire Blvd., Suite 1460. Phone 213-931-8115.
New York 10036—Rebecca Wesson Darwin, Vice-President, Associate Publisher, 25 West 43rd Street. Phone 212-840-3800. Telex 236799.
Atlanta, Miami, Tampa—Metropolitan Publishers Representatives, Inc.
Hong Kong, Singapore—Seavex Ltd.
London W1Y 5DN—Steve Westerberg, Mgr., 19 South Audley Street. Phone 01-499-5248. Telex 28232.
Milan—MIA S.R.L. Piazza Duca D'Aosta, 8, 20124. Phone 669-4444. Telex 311271.
Atlanta, Miami, Tampa—Metropolitan Publishers Representatives, Inc.
Hong Kong, Singapore—Seavex Limited.
Toronto—Metropolitan Publishers Representatives, Inc.

3. COMMISSION AND CASH DISCOUNT

15% to recognized agencies; 2% of net 10th of month following insertion date. Bills rendered last day of publication month and due and payable 10th of following month.

4. GENERAL RATE POLICY

New rates announced 6 weeks in advance of cover date.

ADVERTISING RATES

Rates effective January 4, 1988 issue. (Card No. 58)
Card received December 2, 1987.

5. BLACK/WHITE RATES

	1 ti	7 ti	13 ti	17 ti	26 ti
1 pg	16,295.	15,969.	15,643.	15,399.	14,991.
2/3 pg (2 cols)	11,650.	11,417.	11,184.	11,009.	10,718.
1/2 pg	8,745.	8,570.	8,395.	8,264.	8,045.
1/3 pg (1 col)	5,830.	5,713.	5,597.	5,509.	5,364.
1/6 pg (1/2 col)	2,915.	2,857.	2,798.	2,755.	2,682.
1/12 pg (1/4 col)	1,465.	1,436.	1,406.	1,384.	1,348.
1 inch (min)	600.	...	...	...	...

	39 ti	52 ti	65 ti	78 ti
1 pg	14,666.	14,340.	14,014.	13,688.
2/3 pg (2 cols)	10,485.	10,252.	10,019.	9,786.
1/2 pg	7,871.	7,696.	7,521.	7,346.
1/3 pg (1 col)	5,247.	5,130.	5,014.	4,897.
1/6 pg (1/2 col)	2,624.	2,565.	2,507.	2,449.
1/12 pg (1/4 col)	1,319.	1,289.	1,260.	1,231.
1 inch (min)	...	...	...	...

Non-discountable units are available from 1" up to a maximum depth of 9" in 1/2" increments.

DISCOUNTS

Discounts apply to black and white space used in pages, 2/3 pages, 1/2 pages, 1/3 pages, 1/6 pages or 1/12 pages; to 2 color ROP in pages, 2/3 pages, 1/2 pages and 1/3 pages; and to 4 color space in pages, 2/3 pages, 1/2 pages and 1/3 pages. Spreads count as 2 insertions in computing discounts. Advertising schedules composed of mixed discountable space units are entitled to discounts except when the use of the smaller or smallest units lowers the total cost of the campaign below the amount that the larger units reached at their earned rate.

VOLUME DISCOUNTS

For every 13 pages greater than 78, an additional 2% discount will be allowed, up to 104 times.

6. COLOR RATES

*Black and 1 color:

	1 ti	7 ti	13 ti	17 ti	26 ti
1 pg	17,095.	16,753.	16,411.	16,155.	15,727.
2/3 page (2 cols)	12,450.	12,201.	11,952.	11,765.	11,454.
1/2 pg	9,545.	9,354.	9,163.	9,020.	8,781.
1/3 pg (1 col)	6,630.	6,497.	6,365.	6,265.	6,100.

	39 ti	52 ti	65 ti	78 ti
1 pg	15,386.	15,044.	14,702.	14,360.
2/3 page (2 cols)	11,205.	10,956.	10,707.	10,458.
1/2 pg	8,591.	8,400.	8,209.	8,018.
1/3 pg (1 col)	5,967.	5,834.	5,702.	5,569.

(*) 300.00 premium for sheen inks. Non-commissionable and non-discountable.

4 color process (coated stock):

	1 ti	7 ti	13 ti	17 ti	26 ti
1 pg	25,985.	25,465.	24,946.	24,556.	23,906.
2/3 pg (2 cols)	20,925.	20,507.	20,088.	19,774.	19,251.
1/2 pg	16,240.	15,915.	15,590.	15,347.	14,941.
*1/3 pg (1 col)	11,740.	11,505.	11,270.	11,094.	10,801.

	39 ti	52 ti	65 ti	78 ti
1 pg	23,387.	22,867.	22,347.	21,827.
2/3 pg (2 cols)	18,833.	18,414.	17,996.	17,577.
1/2 pg	14,616.	14,291.	13,966.	13,642.
*1/3 pg (1 col)	10,566.	10,331.	10,096.	9,862.

(*) Firm dates not guaranteed.

5th color premium charge 10% of one-time page or bleed page rate. Commissionable but non-discountable.

7. COVERS

4 color process (coated stock):

	1 ti	7 ti	13 ti	17 ti	26 ti
2nd cover	28,585.	28,013.	27,442.	27,013.	26,298.
3rd cover	25,985.	25,465.	24,946.	24,556.	23,906.
4th cover	32,715.	32,061.	31,406.	30,916.	30,098.

	39 ti	52 ti	65 ti	78 ti
2nd cover	25,727.	25,155.	24,583.	24,011.
3rd cover	23,387.	22,867.	22,347.	21,827.
4th cover	29,444.	28,789.	28,135.	27,481.

8. INSERTS

Supplied inserts available.

9. BLEED

Full page, 2/3, 1/2 and 1/3 pages, extra 15%

10. SPECIAL POSITION

Orders for 13 or more full pages in black and white or in 4 color, on regular cycles, may be given guaranteed positions if available. Cancellation of any portion of a contract nullifies position protection for the remainder of the contract. 4 color center spread, continous print spread, 2nd cover, and 4th cover positions are guaranteed. However, special units of 4 or more pages may on occasion pre-empt smaller units in the center spread position. Information concerning availability of dates supplied upon request.

	1 ti	7 ti	13 ti	17 ti	26 ti
Centerspread (4/c)	58,370.	57,203.	56,035.	55,160.	53,700.

	39 ti	52 ti	65 ti	78 ti
Centerspread (4/c)	52,533.	51,366.	50,198.	49,031.

11. CLASSIFIED/MAIL ORDER

DISPLAY CLASSIFICATIONS:

RETAIL, HOTEL AND MAIL ORDER

Also applies to Publishers, Real Estate, Schools and Camps.

BLACK AND WHITE RATES:

	1 ti	7 ti	13 ti	17 ti	26 ti
1 pg	13,110.	12,848.	12,586.	12,389.	12,061.
2/3 pg (2 cols)	9,405.	9,217.	9,029.	8,888.	8,653.
1/2 pg	7,085.	6,943.	6,802.	6,695.	6,518.
1/3 pg (1 col)	4,725.	...	...	...	...
1/6 pg (1/2 col)	2,365.	...	...	...	...
1/12 pg (1/4 col)	1,185.	...	...	...	...

	39 ti	52 ti	65 ti	78 ti
1 pg	11,799.	11,537.	11,275.	11,012.
2/3 pg (2 cols)	8,465.	8,276.	8,088.	7,900.
1/2 pg	6,377.	6,235.	6,093.	5,951.
1/3 pg (1 col)	...	...	...	...
1/6 pg (1/2 col)	...	...	...	...
1/12 pg (1/4 col)	...	...	...	...

Non-discountable units are available from 1" up to a maximum depth of 9" in 1/2" increments.

COLOR RATES:

*Black and 1 color:

	1 ti	7 ti	13 ti	17 ti	26 ti
1 pg	13,910.	13,632.	13,354.	13,145.	12,797.
2/3 pg (2 cols)	10,205.	10,001.	9,797.	9,644.	9,389.
1/2 pg	7,805.	7,649.	7,493.	7,376.	7,181.
1/3 pg	5,525.	...	...	...	...

	39 ti	52 ti	65 ti	78 ti
1 pg	12,519.	12,241.	11,963.	11,684.
2/3 pg (2 cols)	9,185.	8,980.	8,776.	8,572.
1/2 pg	7,025.	6,868.	6,712.	6,556.
1/3 pg	...	...	...	...

(*) 300.00 premium for sheen inks. Non-commissionable and non-discountable.

4 color process (coated stock):

	1 ti	7 ti	13 ti	17 ti	26 ti
1 pg	20,820.	20,404.	19,987.	19,675.	19,154.
2/3 pg (2 cols)	16,820.	16,484.	16,147.	15,895.	15,474.
1/2 pg	13,015.	12,755.	12,494.	12,299.	11,974.
*1/3 pg (1 col)	9,430.	9,241.	9,053.	8,911.	8,676.

	39 ti	52 ti	65 ti	78 ti
1 pg	18,738.	18,322.	17,905.	17,489.
2/3 pg (2 cols)	15,138.	14,802.	14,465.	14,129.
1/2 pg	11,714.	11,453.	11,193.	10,933.
*1/3 pg (1 col)	8,487.	8,298.	8,110.	7,921.

(*) Firm dates not guaranteed.

RESTAURANT & AMUSEMENT RATES

Applies to Hotel Dining Rooms, Night Clubs, Films, Movie Houses, Theaters, Concerts, Sports Events, Horse Shows, Race Tracks, Automobile Shows & similar miscellaneous amusements or exhibits where admission is charged.

BLACK AND WHITE RATES:

	1 ti	7 ti	13 ti	17 ti	26 ti	39 ti
1 pg	10,885.	10,667.	10,450.	10,286.	10,014.	9,797.
2/3 pg (2 cols)	7,510.	7,360.	7,210.	7,097.	6,909.	6,759.
1/2 pg	5,660.	5,547.	5,434.	5,349.	5,207.	5,094.
1/3 pg (1 col)	3,770.	...	...	...	...	...
1/6 pg (1/2 col)	1,890.	...	...	...	...	...
1/12 pg (1/4 col)	945.	...	...	...	...	...
1 inch (min)	400.	...	...	...	...	...

	52 ti	65 ti	78 ti
1 pg	9,579.	9,361.	9,143.
2/3 pg (2 cols)	6,609.	6,459.	6,308.
1/2 pg	4,981.	4,868.	4,754.
1/3 pg (1 col)	...	...	...
1/6 pg (1/2 col)	...	...	...
1/12 pg (1/4 col)	...	...	...
1 inch (min)	...	...	...

Non-discountable units are available from 1" up to a maximum depth of 9" in 1/2" increments.

COLOR RATES:

*Black and 1 color:

	1 ti	7 ti	13 ti	17 ti	26 ti
1 pg	11,685.	11,451.	11,218.	11,042.	10,750.
2/3 pg (2 cols)	8,310.	8,144.	7,978.	7,853.	7,645.
1/2 pg	6,460.	6,331.	6,202.	6,105.	5,943.
1/3 pg (1 col)	4,570.	...	...	...	...

	39 ti	52 ti	65 ti	78 ti
1 pg	10,517.	10,283.	10,049.	9,815.
2/3 pg (2 cols)	7,479.	7,313.	7,147.	6,980.
1/2 pg	5,814.	5,685.	5,556.	5,426.
1/3 pg (1 col)	...	...	...	...

(*) 300.00 premium charge for sheen inks. Non-commissionable and non-discountable.

4 color process (coated stock):

	1 ti	7 ti	13 ti	17 ti	26 ti
1 pg	20,820.	20,404.	19,987.	19,675.	19,154.
2/3 pg (2 cols)	16,820.	16,484.	16,147.	15,896.	15,474.
1/2 pg	13,015.	12,755.	12,494.	12,299.	11,974.
*1/3 pg (1 col)	9,430.	9,241.	9,053.	8,911.	8,676.

	39 ti	52 ti	65 ti	78 ti
1 pg	18,738.	18,322.	17,905.	17,489.
2/3 pg (2 cols)	15,138.	14,802.	14,465.	14,129.
1/2 pg	11,714.	11,453.	11,193.	10,933.
*1/3 pg (1 col)	8,487.	8,298.	8,110.	7,921.

(*) Firm dates not guaranteed.

SMALL SPACE ADVERTISER DISCOUNT PROGRAM

Advertisers who run 3 or more 1/3 page or smaller black and white or 2 color units during 1988 are entitled to 1 additional ad at no extra cost. Offer is available only to advertisers who pay the Retail/Mail Order Rate (including Hotels, Publishers, Real Estate and Schools) or the Restaurant/Amusement Rate. 4 color advertisers doe not qualify.

PROGRAM SPECIFICATIONS:

For every 3 ads placed that meet the above specifications, the advertiser earns 1 additional ad of the same size at no extra cost. Every 6 ads will earn 2 bonus ads; every 9 ads will earn 3 bonus ads, etc.

If an advertiser has run 3 ads that qualify but in different sizes the advertiser earns 1 bonus ad of the smaller size.

All ads, the qualifying units and the bonus units, must be run within the 1988 calendar year.

All small space ads (both paid & bonus) contribute to an advertiser's total frequency level. However, the small space ads, themselves, do not earn any additional frequency discounts other than those to which they are entitled under the Small Space Advertiser Discount Program.

12. SPLIT-RUN

Available on a limited basis.

Geographic Splits:

	2-way	3-way	4-way
1 page, 2/3, 1/2 or 1/3 pg (b/w)	1,885.	4,585.	6,725.
1 page, 2/3, or 1/3 pg (2 color)	2,310.	5,425.	7,980.
1 page, 2/3, 1/2 page (4 color)	2,665.	6,110.	8,950.

A/B Split:

1 page or smaller (b/w) 1/2 col min.	750.
1 page or smaller (2 color)	1,100.
1 page, 2/3 and 1/2 page (4 color)	1,350.

Only full page units accepted after mid-September through first 2 issues of January.

All prices non-discountable and non-commissionable.

Standardized E/W splits are offered. If matched for same issue, separate advertisers may buy either region.

14. CONTRACT AND COPY REGULATIONS

See Contents page for location—items 1, 2, 3, 7, 8, 9, 10, 11, 12, 14, 18, 19, 20, 21, 24, 25, 30, 31, 34, 36.

15. MECH. REQUIREMENTS

For complete, detailed production information, see SRDS Print Media Production Data.

Printing Process: Web Offset Litho.
Trim size: 8-1/4 x 10-7/8; No./Cols. 3.
Binding method: Saddle Stitched.
ROP colors available: Matched; Simulated Metallic.
Cover and insert colors available: 4-Color Process (AAAA/MPA); 5-Color Process; Simulated Metallic.

DIMENSIONS-AD PAGE

1	7 x 10	1/6	2-1/4 x 4-7/8
2/3	4-5/8 x 10	1/6	4-5/8 x 2-3/8
1/2	7 x 5	1/12	2-1/4 x 2-3/8
1/3	4-5/8 x 4-7/8	(*)	15 x 5
1/3	2-1/4 x 10	Sprd	15 x 10

(*) 1/2 page spread.

16. ISSUE AND CLOSING DATES

Published weekly, dated Monday; issued Monday preceding.

Issue:	Closing (*)	Closing (+)
Jan. 4/88	12/7	12/18
Jan. 11/88	12/14	12/23
Jan. 18/88	12/21	12/31
Jan. 25/88	12/28	1/7
Feb. 1/88	1/4	1/14
Feb. 8/88	1/11	1/21
Feb. 15/88	1/18	1/28
Feb. 22/88	1/25	2/4
Feb. 29/88	2/1	2/11
Mar. 7/88	2/8	2/18
Mar. 14/88	2/12	2/25
Mar. 21/88	2/22	3/3
Mar. 28/88	2/29	3/10
Apr. 4/88	3/7	3/17
Apr. 11/88	3/14	3/24
Apr. 18/88	3/21	3/30
Apr. 25/88	3/28	4/7
May 2/88	4/4	4/14
May 9/88	4/11	4/21
May 16/88	4/18	4/28
May 23/88	4/25	5/5
May 30/88	5/2	5/12
June 6/88	5/9	5/19
June 13/88	5/16	5/26
June 20/88	5/23	6/2
June 27/88	5/27	6/9
July 4/88	6/6	6/16
July 11/88	6/13	6/23
July 18/88	6/20	6/30
July 25/88	6/27	7/7
Aug. 1/88	7/1	7/14
Aug. 8/88	7/11	7/21
Aug. 15/88	7/18	7/28
Aug. 22/88	7/25	8/4
Aug. 29/88	8/1	8/11
Sept. 5/88	8/8	8/18
Sept. 12/88	8/15	8/25
Sept. 19/88	8/22	9/1
Sept. 26/88	8/29	9/8
Oct. 3/88	9/2	9/15
Oct. 10/88	9/12	9/22
Oct. 17/88	9/19	9/29
Oct. 24/88	9/26	10/6
Oct. 31/88	10/3	10/13
Nov. 7/88	10/7	10/20
Nov. 14/88	10/17	10/27
Nov. 21/88	10/24	11/3
Nov. 28/88	10/31	11/10
Dec. 5/88	11/7	11/16
Dec. 12/88	11/14	11/22
Dec. 19/88	11/21	12/1
Dec. 26/88	11/28	12/8

(*) 4/C Insertion Order and Offset Material.
(+) B/W & 2/C Insertion Order and Offset Material.

17. SPECIAL SERVICES

A.B.C. Supplemental Data Report released May 1987 issue.

18. CIRCULATION

Established 1925. Single copy 1.75; per year 32.00.
Summary data—for detail see Publisher's Statement.

A.B.C. 6-30-87 (6 mos. aver.—Magazine Form)

Tot. Pd.	(Subs.)	(Single)	(Assoc.)
564,892	535,894	28,998	...

Average Total Non-Pd Distribution (not incl. above):
Total 19,477

TERRITORIAL DISTRIBUTION 5/87—564,759

N.Eng.	Mid.Atl.	E.N.Cen.	W.N.Cen.	S.Atl.	E.S.Cen.
65,119	153,041	61,343	24,340	75,703	11,500
W.S.Cen.	Mtn.St.	Pac.St.	Canada	Foreign	Other
23,501	22,168	96,028	15,695	14,248	2,073

(C-C2)

FIGURE 12.2 ***Consumer Magazine Data from SRDS***

Special Services

Magazines offer many special services, most of which involve additional charges, that may be important to the direct marketer.

Position. Basic rates for magazine space are for ROP (run-of-press) advertising in which the publication controls the placement of the ad. Advertisers can negotiate some aspects of placement; for example, placement on right-hand pages only (left-hand pages have been found much less desirable for direct-response advertising).

For the most desirable pages in the magazine, there will be an additional charge, if those positions are even available. They are highly prized and are usually offered first to repeat advertisers. McKenzie notes that magazines may argue that their studies show readership to be relatively even throughout the publication, and that therefore position is an unimportant issue.[5] Position may or may not be important as far as readership is concerned, but direct marketers feel it is extremely important in terms of response. Table 12.1 presents a list of the most important positions in a magazine and an evaluation of their relative worth.

If a response coupon is used, it should be on the right-hand side (of a right-hand page) so it will be highly visible and easy to remove, not lost in the "gutter" at the center of the magazine. Likewise, if the ad is less than a full page, negotiate placement on the outside of the page rather than on the inside.

Many magazines have shopping pages near the end of the publication. These are similar to the classified pages in a newspaper, and offer exposure to readers who are particularly interested in mail-order shopping opportunities. The ads are

TABLE 12.1 Position Preference Sequence

Position Preference Sequence	*Position*	*Index*
1	First right-hand page and back cover	100 Approximate Response Reduction from First Choices Above, %
2	Second right-hand page	— 5
3	Third right-hand page and inside third cover	—10
4	Fourth right-hand page and page opposite third cover	—15
5	Midbook (preceding editorial matter)	—30
6	Back of book (following main editorial section)	—50

[5] Walter S. McKenzie, "Magazine Advertising," in Edward L. Nash, ed., *The Direct Marketing Handbook* (New York: McGraw-Hill, 1984,) p. 312.

usually rather small, making them feasible for the very small or beginning mail-order marketer.

Split Runs. Split runs allow the advertiser to insert different versions of the ad in the same issue of the magazine. The ads are actually inserted in every other issue of the magazine as it comes off the press, so the advertiser receives a random sample of the magazine's audience.

The ability to test in the same issue of a magazine decreases both the cost and the time necessary to evaluate a new product, offer, or creative execution. When engaging in split-run testing, keep two things in mind. First, vary only one element—the offer, the manner in which the product is positioned, price, whatever. Second, responses to the different versions of the ad must be carefully tracked. A code number printed on the response device and/or different toll-free telephone numbers are two common ways of tracking. Helpful hints for developing code numbers, commonly referred to as keys, are shown in Figure 12.3. The number of splits that can be tested in a single edition of a magazine is primarily a function of the circulation and, consequently, the sample size available for each version.

Inserts. Inserts provide high visibility for direct-response offers by "breaking" the magazine, that is, by causing the magazine to fall open at the insert. Inserts can be done in many ways. Some popular formats are postcards or business reply envelopes that are either bound in or blown in, full-page inserts with detachable response coupons, and multipage inserts which are either the same size as the publication or smaller. Remember, though, an insert adds to both the cost of the ad and its lead time. Therefore the economics of inserts must be considered carefully.

The mail-order advertising for Gevalia coffee is a good example of the creative and effective use of various magazine advertising formats, with and without bind-in inserts. Gevalia is a premium coffee produced in Sweden. When the owner of Gevalia, General Foods, decided to introduce it into the U.S. market, it was obvious that this expensive premium product could not be sold through the mass-distribution channels used for GF's extensive product lines ranging from Maxwell House coffee to Kool-Aid to Good Seasons salad dressings. Targeted marketing to an upscale audience would be required. In addition, the gross margin of the product did not favor direct mail and required a continuity offer rather than one-shot sales.

General Foods, with the aid of their agency, Wunderman, Ricotta and Klein, turned to space advertising in magazines. Tests of small space ads in upscale magazines proved successful. As a general advertiser, GF was responsive to the idea of larger "image" ads with the type of response device to be determined by the profitability of each magazine. The agency began to develop ways of using a variety of formats in different magazines—from the best to marginal publications—cost effectively.

A special envelope insert was designed by the agency art director whose background in print production proved particularly useful in this project. The en-

The functions the key in an ad must perform are:

Provide unique identification of the ad to which the individual is responding. It is helpful to know the publication that generated the response. It is preferable to know the exact issue.

Be easy to locate and identify by the fulfillment staff or the telephone respondent.

Be easy for the publication to advance with each issue. When an ad is run consistently day after day or month after month, new copy is not submitted for each insertion. The responsibility of changing the key for each insertion will be the publication's.

Make it easy to tabulate returns. This necessitates either a numerical or an alphabetical code in each key.

The key may include any or all of the following information:

- The number of the post office box.
- A code that identifies the publication. A large number of magazines suggests something like "M14"—the fourteenth magazine in the "M's" in list of magazines. Use the SRDS index or develop your own list. There are fewer newspaper possibilities: a simpler code like "WSJE" (*The Wall Street Journal* eastern edition) will usually suffice.
- A number for the specific issue of the publication. "M145" would identify the fifth insertion in the fourteenth magazine in the "M" list. Again, this can be more straightforward for newspapers: "110587"—simply month, day, year.
- A code that identifies the product. This is especially helpful when the number of ads is very great and/or there are multiple ad insertions in a single issue of a publication.

Two other keying issues are:

- Different telephone numbers may be used for different publications.
- The key in direct-mail pieces identifies the list from which the name was taken. It may also be helpful to include other information such as the date of the mailing in the key. The key is printed on the response envelope or card.

FIGURE 12.3 ***How to Key Advertisements***

Source: Adapted from Julian L. Simon, *How to Start and Operate a Mail-Order Business* (New York: McGraw-Hill, 1987), pp. 147–150.

velope, christened a "Janevelope" (can you guess the first name of the art director?), has two unique aspects. It is the smallest envelope acceptable to the USPS, and therefore covers the smallest possible portion of the ad copy. And it has a great deal of copy with an execution that mirrors that of the ad itself. Because the copy on the "Janevelope" contains the offer itself, the basic advertising copy can remain unchanged while the offer is varied for split-run tests within a magazine. This happy solution was achieved because the art director knew that inserts must be printed separately (off-line from the printing of the magazine itself) and therefore can be varied more easily than the ad itself.

Some of the variations of the basic Gevalia ad are shown in Figure 12.4: a full-page spread with the insert, and a full-page ad with a response coupon. It has also run as a two-page spread with and without the insert and as a partial-page ad with response coupon. The decision on which version of the ad to use is based on the effectiveness of the particular magazine as an advertising vehicle, the ability to purchase an insert in a particular edition (magazines limit the number of inserts they will accept for any one edition), and available positions in that edition.

Position is just as important for inserts as it is for other direct-response ads. The closer to the front of the magazine they are placed, the better. The one exception is just inside the back cover, which has been found to be equal in pulling power to the third insert placement. The Gevalia ads are often run without an insert if the first insert position is not available.

Several years of successful experience in marketing Gevalia through space advertising has allowed GF to build a database containing customer information. This database has made it easier to rent lists, refine the lists through the use of geodemographic overlays (as discussed in Chapter 4), and institute a direct-mail program. The direct mail package has the same creative execution as the space advertising, which reinforces the brand image and message, and contains the same basic continuity offer. This illustrates the strategy suggested earlier in the chapter, in which an innovative product builds its list through space advertising and then is able to use precisely targeted direct mail in a cost-effective manner.

Regional and Demographic Editions. Most major magazines offer several regional editions. Using regional editions results in a higher cost per contact but a lower total cost, which may be especially important to the small direct marketer. It allows the larger firm to gather information about the responsiveness of particular geographical markets and provides a cost-effective media buy for products with known regional appeal. Advertising in regional editions may also be used to support a television campaign or mail-order drop within that particular area. In addition, splits are often available within regional editions, allowing for testing of new products, copy, or whatever, within a geographic region. The drawback to using regional editions is that the position options within the magazine are usually limited, so the advertisement often ends up in a less favorable position.

Demographic editions offer the opportunity to reach only subscribers who possess a particular demographic characteristic —say, households with an income over $100,000 or working women. Figure 12.5 shows the various demographic edi-

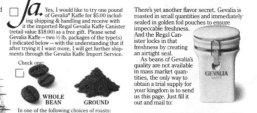

FIGURE 12.4 *Two Variations of the Gevalia Ad*

TIME Demographic Editions

TIME BUSINESS
Offers the largest all-business circulation of any magazine in the United States. All TIME Business subscriber households are qualified by industry and job title through completed questionnaires verified by the ABC. Provides in-depth reach to top, middle and technical management and professional readers in all 50 states.

Rate Base: 1,635,000
Rates based on subscription circulation only.
Space available every other week starting with the January 11, 1988 issue. (See page 6, Cycle D.) *Five week closing date* for B&W and B&1C, *seven week closing date* for 4C. (See page 4.)

	Black & White	Black & 1-Color	4-Color
Page	$44,135	$55,170	$68,860
2 Columns	33,100	41,380	55,085
1/2 page horizontal spread*	61,785	77,240	96,400
1 Column	17,655	22,070	30,990
1/2 Column	11,035	13,795	NA

*Limited availability.
See page 22 for Discount schedules.
See page 24 for new TIME Business Bonus Plan Discount.

TIME TOP MANAGEMENT
Circulates exclusively to owners, partners, directors, board chairmen, company presidents, other titled officers and department heads. Subscriber households are 100 percent qualified through completed questionnaires verified by the ABC. Provides highly refined reach targeted to top management nationwide.

Rate Base: 600,000
Rates based on subscription circulation only.
Space available every other week starting with the January 11, 1988 issue. (See page 6, Cycle D.) *Five week closing date* for B&W and B&1C, *seven week closing date* for 4C. (See page 4.)

	Black & White	Black & 1-Color	4-Color
Page	$23,185	$28,975	$36,160
2 Columns	17,390	21,730	28,925
1 Column	9,275	11,590	16,270
1/2 Column	5,795	7,245	NA

See page 22 for Discount schedules.

TIME WORLD FINANCE
A special advertising edition designed to provide unique penetration of the world's most active investment centers; to sell products and services to a significant investment community; to build corporate image in the world's most dynamic money markets. This special advertising edition circulates in the strategic triad of world finance: the investment capitals of Europe and Asia along with the New York Metropolitan area.

Rate Base: 488,000
Rates based on subscription circulation only.
Circulation area: **Asia:** 126,000 includes Japan, Malaysia, Singapore, Hong Kong. **Europe:** 267,000 includes British Isles, France, Germany, Italy, Switzerland. **New York:** 95,000 includes only top management portion of TIME New York Spot Market. Available in 1988 issues dated January 11, February 8, March 7, April 4, May 2, June 13, July 11, August 8, September 5, October 3, November 14, December 12. (See page 6.) *Five week closing date* for B&W, *seven week closing date* for 4C, full pages only. (See page 4.)

	Black & White	Black & 1-Color	4-Color
Page	$31,550	NA	$49,700

Five free copy splits available. Contact your TIME Sales Representative for complete details.

TIME TOP ZIPs
Provides national circulation exclusively to the highest-income postal ZIP Codes as ranked by estimated 1987 average household income.

Rate Base: 1,300,000
Rates based on subscription circulation only.
Available in 1988 issues dated January 18, February 1, 29, March 14, 28, April 11, 25, May 9, 23, June 6, 20, July 18, August 15, September 12, October 10, 24, November 7, 21, December 5, 19. (See page 6.) *Seven week closing date* for all colorations, full pages only. (See page 4.)

	Black & White	Black & 1-Color	4-Color
Page	$39,060	$48,830	$60,930

See page 22 for Discount schedules.

TIME CAMPUS
Circulates to America's future thought leaders and educators. Offers coast-to-coast coverage of the college market ($2 billion discretionary income) with the magazine most read by students. Contact your TIME Sales Representative for details and rates. See page 6 for availabilities.

TIME INQUIRY PROGRAM TiP
Advertisers in TIME National/4.6 or TIME Business may participate in the TIME Inquiry Program at no additional charge. TIP is a direct response service that helps generate top-quality sales leads from TIME's highly selective audience.
Available in 1988 issues dated March 21, May 16, September 19, October 17. (See page 6.)
TIP Kit and other information available on request.

FIGURE 12.5 ***Rate Card for* Time Magazine *Demographic Editions***

tions offered by *Time* magazine. Although the cost of advertising in these editions is considerably higher, remember that it is the cost per order or per lead that is the appropriate measure.

Discounts The direct marketer should also be aware that magazines offer several types of discounts.[6] If any of these apply to a particular media buy, they should certainly be used:

[6] David Kubes, "Print Ad Lead Generation and Conversion," DMA Release No. 230.3, January 1986.

- Special mail-order rates
- Dollar-volume discount
- Frequency discount
- Discount based on the total number of pages purchased
- Discount based on purchase of space in several magazines owned by the same publishing house
- Remnant space (space unsold just prior to the magazine's closing date)
- Per-inquiry rates

Editorial Policy

Editorial policy refers to the general tone of the feature articles in the magazine as well as to the actual editorials. When you pick up a copy of *The New Yorker*, you expect detailed articles on social affairs, politics, and the arts written for a well-educated and socially aware audience. When you pick up a copy of *Home Mechanix* (which has absorbed *Mechanix Illustrated*), you know you will find articles on home repairs and maintenance, automobile maintenance and safety, and do-it-yourself projects.

Both of these magazines are popular with direct-response marketers. *The New Yorker* contains numerous direct-response ads for upscale clothing and home furnishings, travel and entertainment, and gourmet foods and gifts. *Home Mechanix* ads feature tools and equipment for the house and auto and money-saving and money-making project instructions. Clearly, both are effective for direct-response advertisers who need to reach quite different target audiences.

The overall viewpoint of a magazine may be politically liberal or conservative or somewhere in between, but remember that the advertiser's concern with editorial policy does not necessarily refer directly to political ideology.

Receptivity to Direct-Response Offers

For the direct marketer the single most important criterion in choosing a magazine for promotional purposes is the receptivity of the publication's readership to direct-response offers. Stone points out that the "best" magazines, in this sense, have changed considerably over the years.[7] In the 1950s *Living for Young Homemakers*, *Harper's/Atlantic*, *Saturday Review*, and *Saturday Evening Post* produced good results. In the 1960's publications including *McCall's*, *Ladies' Home Journal*, *House & Garden*, *House Beautiful*, and *National Observer* were leaders in mail order advertising. A decade later, it was *The New Yorker*, *Country Living*, *Family Circle*, and *Smithsonian*.

[7] Bob Stone, *Successful Direct Marketing Methods*, 3rd ed. (Chicago: Crain Books 1984), pp. 131–132.

Changing demographics (primarily working women) and changing lifestyles certainly account for some of these shifts. The increasing willingness of a large segment of the population to purchase by mail the more expensive items appropriate for inclusion in upscale magazines is also a factor. The important question is not: What magazines are good for mail-order and lead-generation advertising? Rather, it is: What magazines are good for mail-order and/or lead-generation advertising *for my product category*? Some magazines may work well for certain product categories but poorly for others.

Yankee magazine has long been regarded as one of the most effective vehicles for mail-order advertising. It has a relatively upscale and devoted readership that stretches throughout the United States. Mail-order ads for foods, household items, clothing, crafts, and other products with a decidedly New England ambiance generate high response rates. However, the value of the average order generated by advertising in *Yankee* is considerably lower than that obtained through advertising in *The New Yorker*. Products that can succeed in Yankee's digest-sized format, with its black and white full-page rate of approximately $10,000, might not succeed in *The New Yorker*, with a black and white full-page rate of approximately $15,000. The reverse isn't necessarily true, though. Although most products that are at home in the sophisticated environment of *The New Yorker* would be seriously out of place in the more informal setting of *Yankee*, a few appear to do equally well in both—L. L. Bean and The Company Store (down products), for instance, are regular advertisers in both publications.

The direct marketer, then, must look not only for magazines that contain substantial amounts of direct-response advertising, but also for those that continually feature direct-response advertising for similar products. One way to ascertain this is to buy a lot of magazines and track their advertising over several months. Certainly the direct marketer should make a practice of studying the advertising of competitors and leaders in the field, but a quicker and more efficient way of finding out which magazines carry ads for products similar to your own is to consult the magazine advertising schedules which the Publishers' Information Bureau complies for virtually all advertisers who use the medium.

Which Magazine(s) . . . One More Time. So, after taking into consideration all these factors, which magazines (and a direct marketer of any size will use several), should you chose? The rule is the same as it is for any other direct marketing situation: Make the most informed choice possible and test your choices. Once you learn which type of magazine tends to work best for your product, it will become easier to select other magazines that are similar on the key characteristics. Just avoid making any long-term advertising commitments until you are sure that a particular magazine will generate a profitable level of sales or the quality and/or quantity of sales leads you desire.

DESIGNING AND EXECUTING DIRECT-RESPONSE SPACE ADS IN MAGAZINES

There are many similarities between developing copy and artwork for direct-mail pieces and for space advertisements in magazines. The ad must attract attention, arouse interest, stimulate desire, and inspire action. At the same time, an ad does not operate in the one-to-one environment of direct mail, so it cannot have the exact characteristics of a direct-mail piece.

The Elements of a Direct-Response Space Ad

A direct-response space ad has four basic elements: the headline, the copy, the graphics, and the coupon. Blattstein makes strong recommendations about each of these four elements as well as other aspects of designing and executing print ads.[8]

The Headline. In general, short headlines of 9 words or less work better. However, length is not the most important issue. Rather it is how well the headline motivates the reader by promising a desired benefit. A motivating headline leads to careful reading of the copy and then to taking the desired action.

The Copy. Again, the issue is not length; it is content. "If the body copy is well written and carries the reader along, it can't be too long. If it's clumsy and boring, it can't be too short! " If the copy is lengthy, however, consider using boldface captions at intervals throughout or breaking the copy up into separate blocks. And don't forget to make crystal clear what action you wish the reader to take and to make it easy to take that action!

The Graphics. Print is a more visual medium than direct mail, so the graphics are important. Blattstein distinguishes between "classy" and "klutzy" graphics. This isn't a matter of high- versus low-quality graphics; it is a question of the target market to which you wish to appeal.

According to Blattstein, "classy" advertising has a clean, perhaps even sophisticated, layout. The typeface used and the photographs or artwork contribute to the image of high quality and prestige.

"Klutzy" ads, on the other hand, feature "an informal layout, heavy use of spot illustration, aggressive use of headlines and captions, and a lavish sprinkling

[8] The ideas and quotations in this section on elements are from Joel J. Blatstein, "Creating Successful Direct Response Print Ads," DMA Release No. 310.4, January 1984.

of exclamation points and arrows [to] convey to the prospect the sense that he's looking at a real bargain opportunity."

The Coupon. Here the principle is the same as for an order form in a catalog or a direct-mail piece: Make it easy to fill out and return. Leave plenty of room for the name and address. Four lines are preferable; how many times have you tried to squeeze your city, state, and zip code all onto one short line? Saying "please print" is not superfluous: many orders or requests for information go unfilled because the name and address are illegible. Include the mailing address on the coupon because the reader may tear it out and separate it from the ad. The placement and emphasis given to the toll-free telephone number, if one is used, can affect the number of readers who respond by telephone as opposed to by mail.

We have already mentioned the importance of having the ad on the right page and the coupon on the right-hand side. If the magazine will not promise right-page placement, you can either prepare a second version of the ad with the coupon on the left side or move the coupon to the bottom center of the page. The coupon should not be at the top of the page. It should be a simple rectangle; would you go to the trouble of cutting out a coupon shaped like a Christmas tree and figuring out how to mail it? Finally, the coupon should have a white background so it can be written upon easily.

If you are using a bind-in card instead of a coupon, all of these design rules still hold true. In addition, the card size and height-to-width ratio must conform to postal regulations and the card stock must be heavy enough to qualify for mailing. The rule here is the same as for direct mail: When in doubt, consult your local postmaster.

The design of the card should complement the ad itself. Prepaid postage will increase the response rate. Whether it increases it enough to justify the cost is a good variable to test.

Size and Color

The general principle concerning size is: Use the amount of space necessary to present your offer effectively and profitably. While the cost of space varies greatly from one publication to another, you should neither take larger ads than are necessary in the less expensive publications nor compress an ad into too small a space to be effective in the more expensive publications.

An interesting rule of thumb is attributed to Robert Baker, "If the item is of genuine interest to 25 percent or more of a particular medium's readership, you can effectively use as much as a full page. But if your item is of limited interest, probably you should confine yourself to small units."[9] For example, stamp and coin collectors ferret out very small space ads that contain an appealing offer. Test extensively to find out which sizes work best for your offer.

[9] Quoted in Julian L. Simon, *How To Start and Operate a Mail-Order Business*, 4th ed. (New York: McGraw-Hill), p. 217.

Just as space costs money, so does color. It increases the expense of inserting each ad, as well as the original cost of producing the ad. There are some products that virtually require color—fashion items and foods, for example. Others, such as staple household items or office supplies, may be presented effectively in black and white. All other things being equal, the use of four-color will increase the response rate. But will the greater response be sufficient to recover the added expense? Only testing will tell you for sure.

Timing and Frequency

In general, the timing choices for direct-response space advertising can be described as follows:

- *Best Months:* January, February, March
- *Next Best:* September, October, November
- *Worst:* June, July, August, December
- *The "Maybes":* April, May

The same warning that applies to direct mail applies here: These are useful generalizations, but the seasonal characteristics of your products may cause a dramatically different response pattern. Test!

Stone presents some guidelines for gauging the appropriate frequency of ad insertions:[10]

- Run the first insertion in the best month for your product. If you don't know which month that is, run it in January or February.
- If the response is equal to your expectations or up to 20 percent better, run the ad again 6 months later.
- If the first insertion pulls more than 20 percent in excess of expectations, run it again in 3 or 4 months.
- If the results of the first ad are marginal, wait a year to rerun it.

Stone's rather conservative approach assumes that the readership of a magazine is finite and can quickly become saturated by a particular mail-order offer. However, if your objective is to generate leads or to build a mailing list, you will probably run the ad more frequently.

Response Patterns

Stone also points out that the pattern of responses to your magazine ad will vary according to whether the publication's sales are primarily by subscription

[10] Stone, *Successful Direct Marketing Methods*, p. 147.

(faster response) or by single copy sales throughout the week or month (slower response).[11] Responses to a weekly magazine will come in quickly—about 50 percent of the total within the first 2 weeks. Likewise, mass-circulation magazines like *TV Guide* produce a pattern that quickly peaks and then quickly drops off. A magazine that is kept longer and read at leisure will produce responses over a much longer period of time.

For a monthly magazine, a typical response pattern will look something like this:

After the 1st week	3–7%
After the 2nd week	20–25%
After the 3rd week	40–45%
After 1 month	50–55%
After 2 months	75–80%
After 3 months	85–92%
After 4 months	92–95%

Until you are able to establish a response pattern for your particular offer, this will provide a useful estimate to help you determine the ad's effectiveness before you decide whether or not to make a second insertion.

Shopping and Classified Pages

Hundreds of magazines offer either shopping pages that take ads as small as one column inch or classified pages or both. The classifieds have the same format as newspaper classifieds. With a very few exceptions, such as *The Wall Street Journal*, mail order advertising is rarely successful in the classified sections of newspapers. Ads in shopping pages and magazine classifieds, on the other hand, can be very successful, especially for the entrepreneur. Figure 12. 6 shows a shopping page from Country Living magazine (these pages are called "Country Store"). The general principles for developing ads for shopping and for classified pages are the same, although the larger ads in the shopping pages usually have illustrations, while the classifieds do not.

Cohen summarizes the advantages of classified advertising (most of which apply as well to shopping pages) as follows:[12]

- *Low cost.* As low as a few dollars per word.
- *High profit potential.* According to one source, these ads generate "dollar for dollar more inquiries or sales than any other method."[13]
- *Excellent for new businesses.* The low cost means less risk.

[11] Stone, *Successful Direct Marketing Methods*, pp. 145–146.

[12] Cohen, *Building A Mail Order Business*, pp. 161–165.

[13] Cohen, *Building A Mail Order Business*, p. 162.

FIGURE 12.6

A NEW TRADITION

...your Woodhouse custom post and beam home. Beauty and livability for today, tomorrow... and beyond.

To receive our portfolio send $10 to Woodhouse Post and Beam, Inc. P.O. Box 64, Dept. X, Mansfield, PA 16933 717-549-6232

OUTSIDE PA CALL TOLL FREE 1-800-227-4311

Woodhouse
POST & BEAM HOMES
A Division of Solar Northern Inc

"Wind Direction At A Glance"

WEATHER VANES add finishing touch to your home, garage, farm or ranch! Ornamental as well as useful. Wind direction at a glance. Balanced arrow on friction free bearing responds to slightest breeze! Made of rust-free aluminum with baked vinyl coating. Mounting hardware included. Arrow 23" long. Support 27" high. Great gifts!

SALE!

No. WVR-27 Crowing Rooster or No. WVH-25 Galloping Horse

Reg. $19.95 — NOW for limited time, ONLY $16.95 + $3 shpg

Send check, MO, MC, Visa—20 day money back guarantee

FREE 32 pg. Color **CATALOG** regular mail (No Charge or post.) Rush **FREE** 32 pg. Color **CATALOG** first class mail. Enclosed is $1 for post. & spec. hdlg., refundable with first order

HOLST, Inc. Dept. CLV-787, 1118 W. Lake, P.O. Box 370 Tawas City, Mich. 48764

Salt-Glaze Tradition

1½-gallon Watercooler $135 ppd. 16 oz. Coffee Mug $14 ppd.

Handmade and hand decorated stoneware, safe for all beverages.

Call toll free **1-800-356-5510** (WI 1-608-764-5435-Collect)

Send $2 for color catalog featuring 74 handmade items.

Allow 4-6 weeks for delivery.

ROWE POTTERY WORKS
404 England St., Dept. 564 Cambridge, WI 53523

LIGHTING Savings to 60%

Most National Brands; Stiffel, Quoizel, Murray Feiss, Westwood, Georgian, Norwell, Illuminating, Troy, Juno Trac, NuTone, Tiffanys, Crystal, and more.

Call **TOLL-FREE** with manufacturers name and style number

800-241-6111
in PA (215) 395-0596

Allied Lighting Drawer E Trexlertown, PA 18087

bent willow...

Dealer Inquiries Welcome.

it's a natural.

COUNTRY STORE

Country Curtains Dust Ruffle. Cotton and polyester ruffle attached to a sheet. Split corners to accommodate bed posts. Choose Natural or White perma press. Twin size, 15" drop length, $34.50 each; Double, 15", $38.50; Double, 20", $42.50; Queen, 15", $44; King, 15", $51. Made in U.S.A. Other sizes available. Matching bedspread. $4 p/h per order. Free 56 page color catalog. Country Curtains, Dept. 3057, Stockbridge, MA 01262

Antique Quilts from Quilts Unlimited. From their shops at Colonial Williamsburg, The Homestead Resort and Lewisburg WV (near the Greenbrier) comes this month's color photos and catalog of over 100 antique quilts. Also, beautiful selection of new crib and wall hanging quilts. Send $5 to Quilts Unlimited, P.O. Box 1210, Lewisburg, WV 24901. (304) 647-4208.

Our versatile solid pine drop leaf end table will add that special touch to any room. Constructed with wood screws and pegs-not nails-it is stained a medium walnut and handrubbed with a protective oil finish. 23"Lx24"Hx13"W (27" extended) fully assembled, $55.95 plus $11 s/h. Matching coffee table, 36"Lx18"Hx13"W (25" extended), $59.95 plus $12 s/h. Color Catalog, $2. Dealers welcome. Send CK, MC, Visa, or MO. Crossroads Country Store, Rt., 1, Box 201-B, Dept. A707, Edgemoor, SC 29712. (803) 328-8076.

Great gift idea! We have rescued and refurbished original turn-of-the-century cast iron barn pulleys from an old foundry and designed a most unique planter that will enhance your country home or patio. Ideal for live or dried arrangements. Includes: pulley, chain, ceiling hook, and two 6" antique finish buckets. (plants not included) $21.95 plus $3 s/h. CK/MO/MC VISA. Nightwatch, P.O. Box 427, Dept. CL7, Claverack, NY 12513.

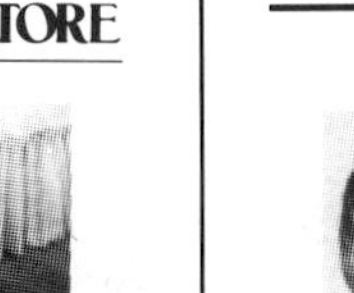

Create Braids Easily! Many styles for long and medium length hair and any texture. Step-by-step illustrated instructions in this 64-page book including basic English, French and Dutch braids to exotic styles plus Corn-rows. $5.95 plus 95¢ postage. Norton Products, Dept. CL787, Box 2012, New Rochelle, NY 10802.

Catalogue shows over 500 items. These fine quality drawer pulls, knobs, hinges, finials, and other hardware items are a must for the furniture craftsman working on a new project, or the refinisher who needs replacement hardware. $2. Horton Brasses, Nooks Hill Road, P.O. Box 120CL, Cromwell, CT 06416.

Charming Insulog™ Home. Interior has a cathedral ceiling and an open loft with its own outdoor balcony. Kits like this are available in Cedar or Pine. New full color Brochure/Plan Book, $6. Wilderness Log Homes, Route 2, Dept. GE77, Plymouth, WI 53073. 1-(800) BEST LOG; In WI: 1-(800) 852-LOGS.

Hooked on Rugs? If you want your floors to sing with interest and shimmer with color, send for Yankee Pride's catalog. Selection includes over 100 room-size rugs with the design quality and handloomed look of the custom-made. Wool hooked rugs, braids, berbers, dhurries, cotton rag rugs are realistically priced. Stair treads, chair pads, half rugs, runners, rounds, place mats, quilts, too. Full color catalog, $3. Yankee Pride, 29 Parkside Circle, Dept. LE77, Braintree, MA 02184.

FACTORY DIRECT TABLE PADS
GUARD YOUR TABLE AND SAVE!

Order with confidence from America's oldest and largest custom table pad manufacturer. No advance deposit or messy C.O.D. You pay nothing until you receive your table pads and are completely satisfied. 15 year guarantee.

Phone 1-800/328-7237 — Ext. 230
108 Briarcliff, Thomasville, North Carolina, 27360
612/646-6778 — Ext. 230

Sentry TABLE PAD CO.

Luxurious Island Hammock, made of the highest grade soft handwoven cotton rope and finest oak spreader bars. This 14½ foot hammock provides unparalleled comfort for two or more loungers. Same size and quality sold elsewhere for $100. A superb value at **$59.95** (plus $8.50 shipping). Bed size 60"w x 84"l. Includes hardware. 35" x 17" pillow $12.00. MC/Visa orders CALL TOLL FREE **800-845-1119** ext. **150**. In NY 914-895-2549.

MONEY BACK GUARANTEE.

UniqueSimplicities Inc. **P.O. Box 1185 (V), New Paltz, NY 12561**

COLONIAL MAID CURTAINS

Victorian bow tieback curtains, 190" wide, are most luxurious as well as lovely. Curtains that bring the warmth and hospitality of the Victorian period into your home.

Soft, fluffy 8" ruffles with 2-1 fullness. Highest quality no-iron poly/cotton muslin. Natural or White. 63" long, $67 pr; 84" long, $69 pr. Postage $3.50. N.Y. residents add sales tax. Send check or MC, Visa, Amex. Satisfaction guaranteed.

COLONIAL MAID CURTAINS Since 1947

Send for free color catalog.

Name ______
Address ______
City ______ State ______ Zip ______
Card # ______ Exp. date ______

COLONIAL MAID CURTAINS Dept. FAS-BG, Depot Plaza, Mamaroneck NY 10543

- *No need for layout or artwork for a classified ad.* Simply type the ad exactly as you wish it to read and submit it. Ads in shopping pages usually incorporate illustrations and are laid out like display ads.
- *Good place to test.* If successful, roll out to other magazines or progress to display advertising.
- *Builds mailing list.* Because readers of classifieds are often looking for that specific type of product or service, the quality of the responses is surprisingly high.
- *Useful supplement to display advertising.* If the response rate from the publication will not support an ROP display ad, it may well support a classified or shopping page ad. Some regular users of display ads choose to place their ads in shopping pages when available, apparently because of the quality of attention they receive from readers of those pages.
- *Lower dropoff.* The decline in response rate that ordinarily occurs with repeated use of a magazine is slower. This seems to be because not all the readers of the magazine examine these pages in every issue.

This type of advertising has disadvantages also:

- *Limited applicability.* High-cost products or others that require extensive information cannot be sold in this manner. However, even very small ads may be sufficient to generate a request for more information.
- *Limited possibilities for growth.* There are not likely to be many magazines that will be successful for any one product or service.

Cohen also points out that the classified ad must contain sufficient information and a request for action. His suggestion is to write out the ad as if you were writing copy for a display ad and then cut out every word that is not absolutely necessary.

Simon has made two useful suggestions for choosing magazines in which to test classifieds: first, the magazines should have at least three pages of classifieds; second, pick the magazines with the highest cost per word.[14] Both criteria suggest magazines that are successful for other advertisers. This would seem to be good advice in choosing shopping pages also.

Whatever the type of advertising the direct marketer chooses to place, magazines offer a variety of ways in which to reach audiences that range from large and heterogeneous to small and highly targeted. Consequently, they are part of the media plan of most direct marketers and the chief medium of many.

Let us now turn to the other major print medium, newspapers. They share with magazines the potential for reaching large audiences, but differ on many other characteristics.

[14] Simon, *How to Start and Operate a Mail-Order Business.*

DIRECT RESPONSE IN NEWSPAPERS

Newspapers, too, are an important medium for many direct marketers. Once the dominant mass medium, newspapers have found competition, especially from television, to be intense in recent years. Yet, according to *Advertising Age*, "two-thirds of all American adults still read a newspaper every weekday; 86% read a paper at least once a week; [and] newspapers are purchased regularly in 74% of all U. S. households."[15]

Numerous factors have contributed to the decline of newspapers as the primary medium for conveying both national and local news. Network and, more recently, cable television have assumed first place as providers of news for a majority of consumers. Radio is able to respond more quickly to fast-moving events. Magazines, increasing in number and ever more targeted in editorial matter, also provide competition.

The combination of rising paper and energy costs in the mid-1970s caused a steep rise in the price of newspapers and a decline in sales from which newspapers have never fully recovered. Changing lifestyles, especially time pressure and the increase in single-person households (which are less likely to subscribe to a newspaper), have also contributed to static circulation figures. Finally, the advent of *USA Today* as the first "national newspaper," with its short articles and colorful graphics, has challenged many basic tenets of the newspaper industry.

In order to meet these multiple challenges, newspapers have had to seriously reconsider the services they provide to advertisers. As a result, they now offer direct marketers a variety of ways in which to successfully reach their customers.

There are four basic types of placement within the newspaper: run of paper (ROP) advertising, freestanding inserts (FSIs), Sunday supplements, and classified advertising. Each has its own particular strengths and each tends to appeal to a different type of direct marketer. We will consider each in detail. First, however, let's look at the general characteristics of the newspaper medium.

NEWSPAPERS AS A DIRECT-RESPONSE MEDIUM

Newspapers offer a number of special advantages to any advertiser, including the direct marketer:

- *Frequency.* Most newspapers, with the exception of small suburban and rural papers, publish six or seven times per week, and some large urban papers offer both morning and evening editions.
- *Immediacy.* For black-and-white advertising, the close (the time by which the ad must be submitted for inclusion in a particular edition) is often only 48 hours prior to publication for camera-ready copy.

[15] Belinda Hulin-Salkin, "Stretching to Deliver Readers' Needs," *Advertising Age*, July 20, 1987, p. S–1.

- *Reach.* Newspapers offer high penetration of households in their primary geographical area. A 50 percent penetration of households in the locality is not uncommon, and some newspapers have a penetration of 70 percent or more.
- *Local shopping reference.* No other medium has been able to supplant the newspaper as the primary reference to local shopping opportunities. Readers expect to learn of merchandise availability, sales, and special events in the pages of their newspapers. Special sections, like the midweek food sections, provide a focused environment for the advertiser of related product categories.
- *Fast response.* Since most newspapers are a daily medium, the direct marketer knows quickly whether a particular offer is producing a satisfactory response.

At the same time, newspapers have their drawbacks. The primary one is the poor color reproduction available in the main portion of the paper. Newspapers also fail to reach some particular subgroups effectively—non–English-speaking people and single-person households are two good examples. The cost of newspaper advertising has risen sharply in recent years. Add to that their length and their high level of penetration and newspaper advertising can easily become too expensive for advertisers who need to reach a specialized market. Because newspapers are essentially a local medium, the type of advertising that does well in them is more limited than in some other media. Finally, newspapers have a life span of only about 24 hours; they are not kept around the house to give people multiple opportunities to see an offer and respond to it. Many of the services added by newspapers in recent years have been aimed at dealing with some of these disadvantages.

ROP ADVERTISING IN NEWSPAPERS

Because newspapers reach a large, heterogeneous market, they do not provide the precise targeting that most direct marketers require. Still, they are a useful medium for some types of direct-response offers.

Direct marketers who serve national or regional markets use ROP advertising in newspapers for two primary purposes: offers that are of interest to or are related to a local market and tie-ins with local retailers. Direct-response offers in newspapers are frequently for services that are being offered in a local area—for example, a seminar on buying real estate with little or no down payment or a stop-smoking clinic. Direct-response display (as opposed to classified) advertising is also being used with increasing frequency by local retailers. This advertising often has dual objectives: to generate sales and, often more importantly, to build traffic in the local retail establishment.

FREESTANDING INSERTS

Freestanding inserts, also called preprints and freefalls, have been in widespread use since the mid-1960s, and local retailers had been using them for many years prior to that time. These ads are prepared and printed in a central location and shipped to the newspapers for insertion, primarily in Sunday issues.

The volume of preprints has been growing rapidly during the last decade, reaching a volume of over $6 billion in 1986.[16] At the same time, the nature of firms using them has changed significantly. Large retailers like Sears and J. C. Penney and mail-order firms with extensive product lines like Columbia Record Club and Time-Life Books were among the first to make consistent use of inserts. Inserts in envelope form also achieved early popularity with photo-finishing chains.

Large national retailers are still massive users of FSIs. In 1984 Sears produced 54 separate inserts and distributed 50 million copies of each. K mart produces 120 million FSIs per week, covering half the population of the country.[17] Retailers like FSIs because costs are lower as a result of the centralized production. Centralized production also allows better control over the creative design and execution of the ads.

Advantages of FSIs

According to *The New York Times*, the advantages of FSIs to the advertiser are:

- Because they are distributed in the Sunday paper, readers have time to consider their propositions at leisure.
- FSIs offer a great deal of flexibility. Virtually any kind of print promotional format (reply cards or envelopes, single sheets, tabloids, catalogs, brochures, etc.) can be adapted to the FSI. Geographic and demographic options also offer flexibility in the size and type of market reached.
- FSIs reach the loyal readership of a particular newspaper and confer the credibility of that publication on the advertisement.
- Large and sophisticated advertisers, including retailers, travel and financial services firms, nonprofit organizations, and manufacturers of consumer packaged goods have consistently used FSIs successfully.

FSIs are popular with consumers according to a study by the *Courier Journal* and *Louisville Times* reported in *Editor & Publisher*.[18] This study found that newspaper inserts were better read than preprinted direct mail (that is, the same

[16] "What's Free, Full of Ads, and Read All Over?" *Business Week*, November 2, 1987, p. 122.

[17] Anna Sobczynski, "Retailers' Preprints Saturating the Land," *Advertising Age*, June 14, 1984, p. 34.

[18] "The Power of Newspaper Inserts," *Editor & Publisher*, May 4, 1985, p. 64.

type of format delivered by mail instead of in the newspaper) in all demographic categories included in the study except for women homemakers, who did read direct mail more frequently. A majority of respondents found newspaper inserts more complete, interesting, and valuable in planning their shopping. Newspaper-delivered preprints were also considered more credible than mailed preprints.

Recent Developments in the Use of FSIs

Current growth in the volume of FSIs is coming primarily from national manufacturers, who are using the medium to distribute coupons. In 1986, in what some have described as a "coupon blizzard," over 2,220 coupons per family were distributed in the United States.[19] That year FSIs distributed between 68 and 80 percent of all coupons circulated in the United States, up from 53–60 percent just one year before.[20]

For national advertisers to supply FSIs to hundreds of Sunday newspapers each week in order to distribute coupons for just a few products would hardly be cost-effective. Not surprisingly, companies have grown up to meet the coupon-distribution needs of the national manufacturer. They offer a lower CPM (cost per thousand) than advertisers could achieve on their own because of their volume and their specialization.

The three major firms that provide this service all operate similarly, although each presents a slightly different array of products and services. They solicit ads, offering geographic options; combine them into a "loose booklet" type of format; print them in a central location; and distribute them to the newspapers. On any given Sunday a newspaper may contain two, or even all three, of these inserts. Any one of them may be 30 to 40 pages long.

As this type of FSI has grown, it has broadened its scope beyond just coupon distribution. You will find mail-in refund offers, sweepstakes, and perhaps even product samples. Often you will also find a number of direct-response offers. Usually these direct marketers have purchased "remnant" space in the FSI; a considerable number of them have found this to be an effective advertising medium.

A Word About Shared Mail

A section on coupon distribution via FSIs would be incomplete without a mention of the intense competition between FSIs and shared-mail programs.

Programs generically termed *shared mail* are periodic mailings to households of a selection of coupons, direct-response offers, product samples, and perhaps other promotional vehicles. The fixed costs of distributing these promotions are shared among a number of advertisers. These programs achieve substantial

[19] Report by J. Walter Thompson based on a study by A. C. Nielsen, quoted in Jerrold Ballinger, "Direct Mail Coupon Delivery Not Keeping Up with Industry Growth," *DM News*, October 1, 1987, p. 14.

[20] Laurie Freeman, "FSI's Favored by Marketers as Product Coupons Multiply," *Advertising Age*, March 9, 1987, p. 83.

economies of scale through the large volume created by their ability to reach virtually all households in the United States.

Since the freestanding insert and shared-mail programs are after the same promotional dollars, the competition between them is fierce. This leads to many conflicting claims about the cost versus the efficiency and effectiveness of the two media. Also, as you will soon see, newspapers themselves have entered the fray, creating the possibility of three-way competition. The competitive situation differs from market to market, and it will be interesting to see how it evolves.

NEWSPAPER SUPPLEMENTS

Newspaper supplements are virtually brief magazines that, like FSIs, are produced at a central facility and distributed to local newspapers for insertion in Sunday editions. They combine the frequency, reach, and rapid response of newspapers with the high-quality graphics reproduction of magazines. Since their content is feature articles as opposed to news, they are retained longer than newspapers, giving more opportunity for exposure to the advertisements they contain. However, they lack the immediacy of the newspaper itself, since closing dates can be as much as 90 days prior to publication. There are now four major Sunday supplements, and they have little circulation overlap.

The largest is *Parade* magazine with a circulation of over 30 million each week as of late 1986.[21] It contains articles on subjects of national interest, regular features and columns, and theme sections on subjects such as food and health. Its editorial content is not localized, but it offers regional and demographic buys (the minimum circulation buy is 100,000) and split runs with buys of 2 million or more. *Parade* offers other services of interest to direct marketers, including a reader service card. A majority of the magazine's circulation is in suburbs of large cities and smaller cities.

The next largest newspaper supplement is the *Sunday Magazine* Network, with a circulation of almost 21 million. In late 1986 it was distributed in 45 newspapers in larger metropolitan areas. Its editorial content is local and its advertising is a combination of local and national ads sold through the network.

The newest of the supplements is *USA Weekend*, which is published by *USA Today* and distributed by other newspapers throughout the United States (the newspaper *USA Today* has no Sunday edition). In 1986 its circulation was over 14 million. It features articles on topics of general interest, including money management, sports, lifestyles, and celebrity interviews. There are regular columns and sections on health, automobiles, literature and travel. *USA Weekend* offers regional buys.

[21] The circulation data in this section were taken from *SRDS Newspaper Rates And Data*, October 12, 1986, pp. 748–750

Family Weekly is the smallest of the four Sunday supplements. Its circulation of about 13 million (as of 1985) is achieved through 361 newspapers serving smaller towns and rural America.

Remnant space—space unsold as the closing date nears—is available in some of these supplements. It is offered at a considerable discount, but the direct marketer may have to wait several weeks for it to become available, especially if a selective buy is desired. If there is no urgency, however, the economics of remnant space are very attractive, especially for an untried product.

Sunday supplements work very well for a wide variety of direct marketers both in testing situations and for promoting products with mass appeal over a long period of time. This means, however, that new advertisers may have difficulty obtaining the placement or even the particular edition desired. Because of the differences in reader demographics of the circulations of the four major supplements, they will probably not all work equally well for all product categories and should be tested just as carefully as any other media vehicle.

TOTAL MARKET COVERAGE

Traditional newspaper advertising, whether ROP or in some type of insert, does not completely satisfy the needs of local retailers and national manufacturers for two reasons:

1. No newspaper reaches all the households in any given geographical area; 30 to 40 percent are not likely to be reached by a specific newspaper. In markets where there is more than one daily newspaper, of course, the marketer can advertise in more than one newspaper, but this is likely to be duplicative and prohibitively expensive.
2. For retailers who only serve part of the newspaper's geographical area or for manufacturers who market to specific market segments, newspapers represent a great deal of waste circulation. For example, a seasonal promotion for snow blowers should be received by suburbanites, not urban dwellers with no driveway and very little sidewalk.

The "classic" approach to solving the problem of total coverage is to publish a weekly edition that is carrier-delivered to the entire market or mailed to all nonsubscribers. There are many variations on this basic theme. These special editions can be targeted selectively. They can be used as delivery vehicles for other types of advertising such as samples, catalogs, or coupon packs. This type of service to advertisers has been growing rapidly in recent years, with 90 percent or more of daily newspapers offering some variant.[22]

[22] Mary McCabe English, "Newspapers, Shared Mail Digging In," *Advertising Age*, June 14, 1984, pp. 17–20.

The program of the *Los Angeles Times,* which the paper calls Selective Market Coverage, or SMC, provides a comprehensive approach to reaching the desired segment of the total market in its geographical area. According to the paper's promotional material:

> Selective Market Coverage combines preprinted inserts or run of paper (R.O.P.) advertisements in *The Times* with mailing to non-subscribing households. Advertisers in the program are guaranteed from 75% to 98% market coverage in Los Angeles, Orange and Ventura counties and portions of Riverside and San Bernardino counties. The geographic area included in the program has been divided into grids which can be purchased separately or in groups. Split grids (subdivisions within grids) are also available in many areas, enabling an advertiser to zero in on specific geodemographic areas.[23]

Figure 12.7 shows a map of the area covered by Selective Market Coverage and the 130 grids that form the basis of the program. To assist advertisers in choosing which grids offer the best potential for their products and services, the *Los Angeles Times* has rank-ordered the 130 grids from highest to lowest on each of the following demographic characteristics:

- Median Household Income
- Percent of households with household incomes of $75,000 and over
- Percent of households with household incomes of $50,000 and over
- Percent of households with household incomes of $35,000 and over
- Percent of households with household incomes of $25,000 and over
- Percent of the Population Age 16 and Over Employed in a Professional/Executive Position
- Percent of the Population Age 25 and Over with 4 or More Years of College Education
- Percent of Occupied Dwelling Units Which Are Owned by the Tenant
- Median Home Value
- Percent of Households With Children Under 18
- Percent of the Population That Is Asian
- Percent of the Population That Is Black
- Percent of the Population That Is Hispanic

Other types or combinations of demographic rankings are available on request. For a particular product, the newspaper can rank-order the grids in terms of their desirability as a target market (see Figure 12.8).

For advertisers who wish to better understand the market potential for their particular product in this geographical area, the *Los Angeles Times* offers PRIZM analysis. As we described in Chapter 4, the PRIZM system groups zip codes into

[23] Los Angeles Times Marketing Research Department.

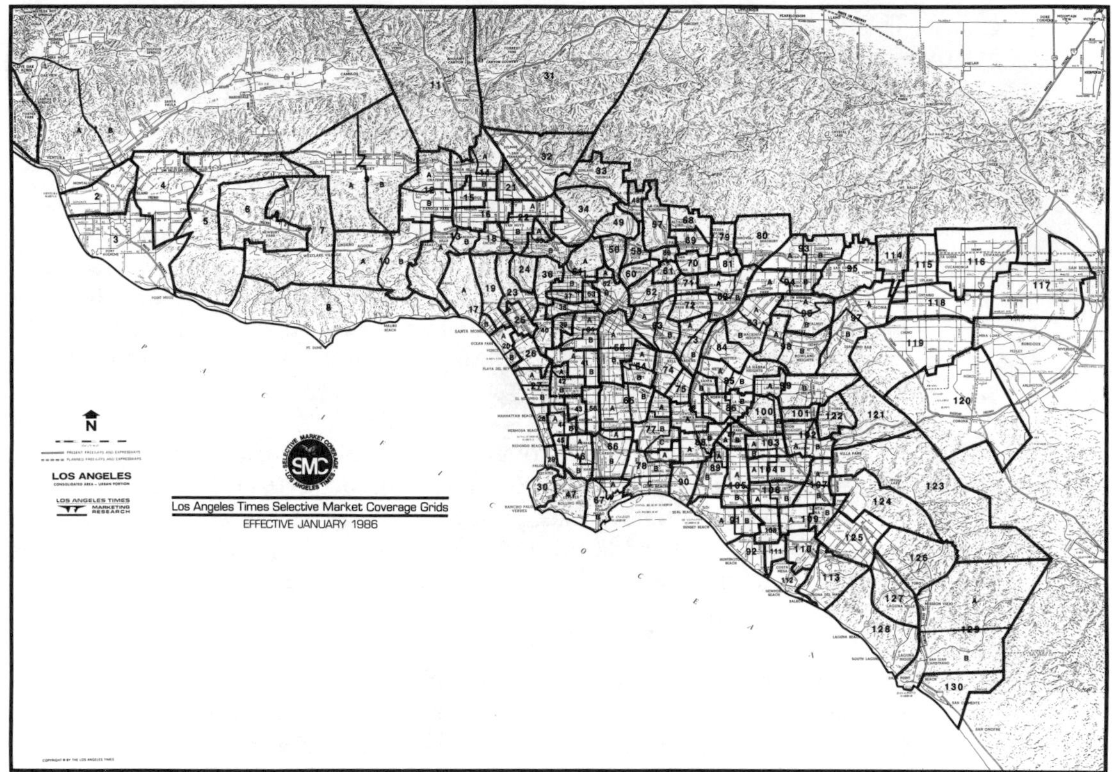

FIGURE 12.7 ***Map of Area Covered by Selective Market Coverage***

neighborhoods that can be ranked on the basis of purchase likelihood for a specific product category. Individual zip codes can then be categorized in terms of desirability. Figure 12.9 shows the results of an analysis of the market potential for European luxury cars in the Los Angeles area. Each of the over 300 zip codes has been categorized from 1—primary target market down to 4—least desirable target market. Simple demographic analysis allows the advertiser to choose the most desirable of the 130 grids. PRIZM analysis carries the process one step further by allowing the advertiser to eliminate undesirable zip codes within otherwise desirable grids, thus making the targeting more effective. Note that it would not be correct to say that PRIZM allows the ranking from 1 to 300 of all the zip codes; it merely allows them to be categorized.

The SMC program of the *Los Angeles Times* is an excellent example of several things: a newspaper providing a service to its advertisers that allows them to use advertising dollars more effectively; the selective use of direct-response techniques by a "traditional" firm (which, in this case, happens to be a direct response medium!); and a strategic response to a competitive situation.

Grids Sequenced on Median Household Income (high to low)

grid	*Median Households Income*	*Total Household (Subscribers & Mail)*	*Cumulative Total Households*
24	54,062	6,704	6,704
30	43,693	14,044	20,748
8	35,791	7,821	28,569
121	33,994	11,465	40,034
124	33,328	13,480	53,514
47	32,977	16,415	69,929
10	32,275	20,697	90,626
113	32,042	20,381	111,007
14	31,070	31,036	142,043
7	30,847	20,219	162,262
18	30,713	13,985	176,247
123	30,526	10,299	186,546
122	29,864	17,582	204,128
126	28,270	13,193	217,321
111	28,087	10,970	228,291
129	27,948	25,456	253,747
125	27,942	22,802	276,549
108	27,936	15,492	292,041
70	27,735	10,953	302,994
11	27,310	15,862	318,856
•			
•			
•			
62	13,620	26,566	2,629,567
65	13,528	47,685	2,677,252
39	13,259	17,749	2,695,001
63	13,115	51,935	2,746,936
78	12,698	64,563	2,811,499
51	12,108	51,926	2,863,425
53	11,700	21,701	2,885,126
52	11,677	54,070	2,939,196
54	11,596	56,116	2,995,312
55	10,015	57,444	3,052,756

FIGURE 12.8 ***SMC Grid Demographic Report***
Projected Weekday Distribution as of January 1986
Source: U.S. Census, 1980. Targeted Coverage Inc., estimates based on a leading mailing information supplier and the Los Angeles Times Circulation Department, as of January 1986.

FIGURE 12.9

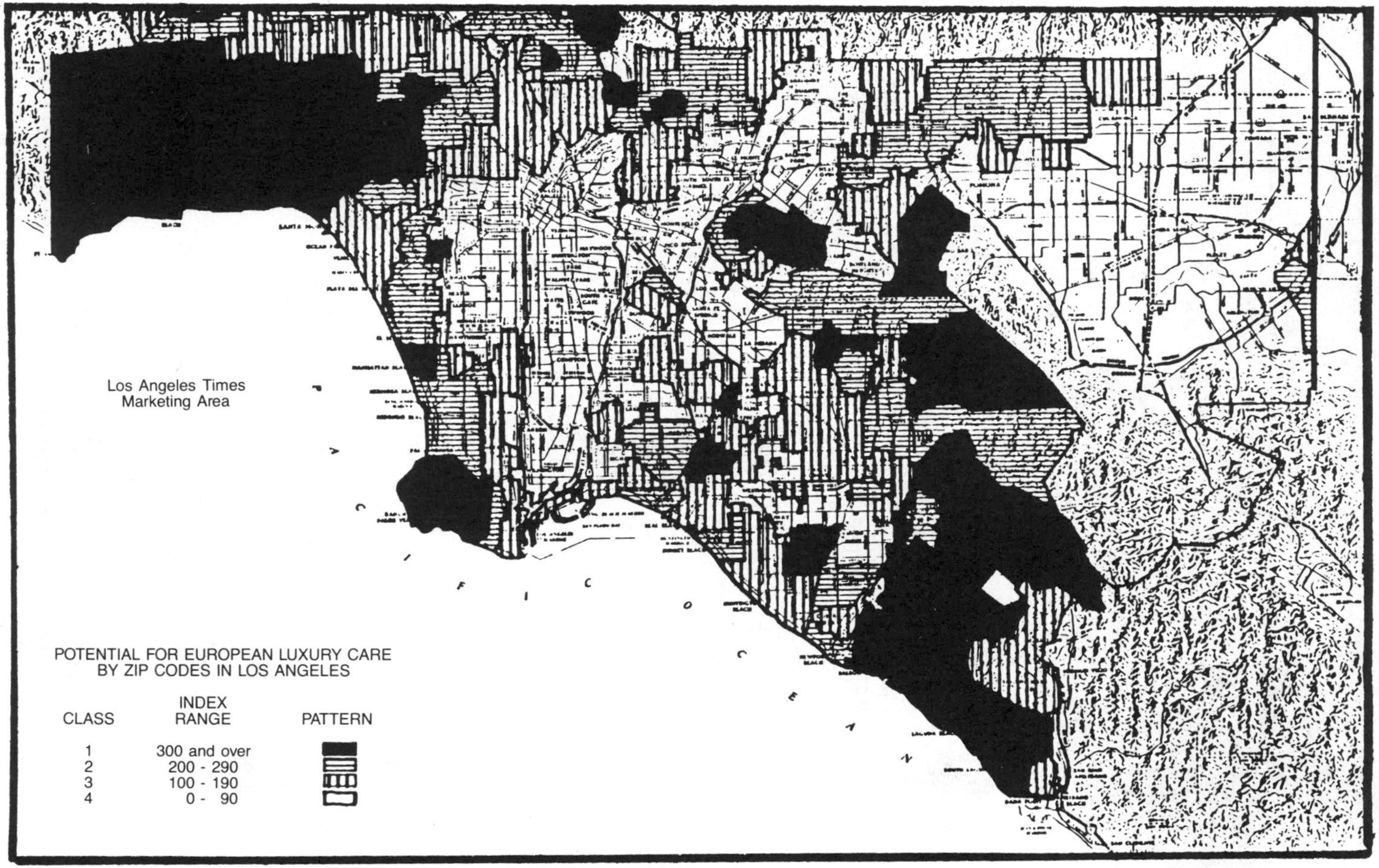

Los Angeles Times
Marketing Area

P A C I F I C O C E A N

POTENTIAL FOR EUROPEAN LUXURY CARE
BY ZIP CODES IN LOS ANGELES

CLASS	INDEX RANGE	PATTERN
1	300 and over	
2	200 - 290	
3	100 - 190	
4	0 - 90	

SUMMARY

Magazines and newspapers are important direct-response media. Both industries have undergone considerable turbulence in the past few years, and change is still occurring. Each offers specific advantages and disadvantages to the direct marketer and consequently are likely to be most effective as part of a balanced and integrated program of marketing communications. These media also offer special opportunities for the small direct marketer and the innovative or untried product. Their services for direct marketers are likely to continue to expand, further increasing their value in many direct-response programs.

DISCUSSION QUESTIONS

1. What are the major characteristics of magazines as a direct-response medium? Of newspapers?
2. What criteria should a direct marketer use in selecting magazines to test?
3. Why are the readers of some magazines more receptive than those of other publications to direct-response offers?
4. Explain the different ways in which direct marketers can advertise in newspapers.
5. Bring some direct-response ads from magazines and newspapers to class and be prepared to discuss their content and execution.

SUGGESTED ADDITIONAL READING

1. Leon Henry, Jr., "Co-ops and Inserts"; Jean Cohen, "Newspaper Advertising"; Joel Feldman, "Newspaper Preprints"; Walter S. McKenzie, "Magazine Advertising", in Edward L. Nash, ed., *The Direct Marketing Handbook* (New York: McGraw-Hill, 1984), pp. 271–316.

13

Direct Response in Broadcast Media

The hour is late. The umpteenth rerun of a once-popular movie drones on. Suddenly, the soporific monotone is broken by a loud, disgustingly awake, cheerful announcer.

With skill worthy of a master chef, he demonstrates a knife. It will cut almost anything. It is made of the finest materials, never needs to be sharpened, and comes with a lifetime guarantee. You would expect to pay much more than $19.98 for it in the stores, even if you could buy it there, which you can't. For special tasks, you also need (demonstrated in quick succession) a boning knife, a bread knife, and a frozen food knife. Each one alone is worth much more than $19.98, but you can receive them all for that one low price in this special television offer.

And to encourage you to act now, he will also include a set of lifetime-guaranteed steak knives. All you have to do is call the toll-free number. Supplies are limited, so act now!

You've seen this ad—or its first cousin—haven't you? It is, in fact, a takeoff on a famous direct-response ad that has run on late-night television off and on for many years so that it has become a stereotype. But is it representative of direct-response broadcast today? The simple answer is that this stereotype actually represents only a small portion of all direct-response broadcast advertising. It is so deeply ingrained in people's minds, however, that the simple answer does not suffice. An understanding of how direct-response advertising developed in both television and radio may help put it into perspective. First we will look at television.

There are two distinct uses of television in direct marketing—direct response and support. Like any other direct-response medium, television can be used for sales or lead generation. It also has a special capability to increase the sales or number of leads generated by advertising in other media such as direct mail or magazines. This is the support function, which will be discussed in a later section of this chapter.

THE DEVELOPMENT OF DIRECT-RESPONSE TELEVISION[1]

The tone of many early direct-response television ads can be attributed to Daniel Rubin, who sold Florida Fashions via television beginning in 1946. Rubin imitated the style of the pitchmen who worked the boardwalk in Atlantic City. He taped their sales pitches and brought some to New York to use in filming simple direct response spots. Why did these crude commercials with their rapid-fire narration, minimal sets, harsh lighting, and simple camera angles set the standards for early direct-response television? The reason is simple—they were successful. Their success attracted many imitators, but it also quickly attracted reputable advertising specialists, some of whom are still working in the field today.

Record companies were the first major direct-response television advertisers, developing the classic 120-second commercial. During the 1950s and 1960s, they were joined by companies selling products for the home—kitchen gadgets and equipment, books, tools, and inexpensive home decorating items. Another development during this period was the appearance of celebrities as spokespersons, some of whom worked for modest fees plus a percentage of sales.

In the early years of television, the supply of advertising time was considerably greater than demand. Combine crude production techniques and cheap airtime, and you have a very inexpensive advertising medium. A commercial could be produced and aired on one or two test stations for as little as $2,000. Results were available quickly—orders began to arrive in the mail about 48 hours after the commercial was aired.

Another factor that stimulated the early growth of direct- response television was per-inquiry (PI) advertising. As the term implies, the PI advertiser's payment to the station is based on a negotiated fixed payment per response. Since stations typically use PI ads to fill unsold airtime, advertisers have no control over the date and time at which they are run. This makes planning for order fulfillment difficult. In addition, responses must be carefully "sourced" by station for payment purposes. While PI deals provided inexpensive advertising opportunities during the 1950s and 1960s, they are less common today because television advertising time is in greater demand. The exception is cable networks that initially had difficulty attracting major national advertisers and used PI as an important source of advertising revenue. As cable television reaches more households and gains credibility as a medium, that situation is changing.

[1] The material in this section is based on John Witek, *Response Television: Combat Advertising of the 1980s* (Chicago: Crain Books, 1981), pp. 1-18; Sandy Davis, "Television Direct Response," in Edward L. Nash, ed., *The Direct Marketing Handbook* (New York: McGraw-Hill, 1984), pp. 317-322; Jerrold Ballinger, "The Changing Role of DR Broadcast," *DM News*, July 1, 1986, pp. 36-39.

Perhaps the greatest growth stimulant of all in recent years has been the advent of national 800-number service. While there is no question that response is greater with the use of a toll-free number, some advertisers have learned to their sorrow that impulse buying can result in high return rates, especially if order fulfillment is slow.

Support advertising was first used during the mid-1970s. Publishers like Reader's Digest and Doubleday found that the pulling power of space advertising or direct mail could be greatly increased by brief TV spots that encouraged viewers to watch for forthcoming advertising.

Once the power of direct-response television was recognized by major corporations, this kind of advertising became commonplace during prime time. Major advertisers brought a quality orientation that was almost totally lacking in early direct-response TV. Prime-time airing demanded very different products, marketing approaches, and production values. The increasing quality and credibility of direct-response TV commercials for consumers made business-to-business advertisers realize the value of prime time and weekend television for lead-generation spots.

At the same time that major national advertisers were doing their part to upgrade the quality of direct-response TV, the Federal Communications Commission and the Federal Trade Commission were engaging in regulatory and consumer protection activities that lessened many of the abuses of earlier days, and this, too, has added to the credibility of the medium. While there are still some products of questionable value and advertisers of questionable repute featured in this medium, both the broadcast and the direct marketing industries have made substantial efforts to prevent genuine abuses. The consumer's image of direct-response TV has improved in recent years, but suspicion still exists. As is true for other direct marketing media, only when this suspicion is eliminated will direct-response TV be able to achieve its full potential.

WHEN TO USE DIRECT-RESPONSE TELEVISION

Planning and executing direct-response and support TV commercials require all the detailed knowledge of the medium needed by a general advertiser plus a thorough understanding of the special requirements of direct response or support. This is a tall order, and to provide an in-depth review of the complexities of television advertising would take more space than we can devote to it. Textbooks on advertising and marketing communications cover this subject in detail. Remember as you read the remainder of this section that it covers only those aspects of planning and executing television commercials that are *essential to direct marketing applications*.

The single most important aspect of television as an advertising medium is that it reaches a mass audience; over 98 percent of all U.S. households have television sets. Astute media buying can help an advertiser reach a defined target audience, but the selectivity that can be achieved with other media is not possible with television. Also, television is an expensive medium; both production of commercials and purchase of airtime can require substantial expenditures.

As a result, products and offers must be carefully chosen if they are to be profitable. According to Nash, direct-response TV "requires products or services that either appeal to very general audiences or to audiences segmentable by program adjacencies. A kitchen knife or a set of pots may work because everyone who cooks is a prospect for it. A set of books on World War II may work best when it is adjacent to a war movie, a violent sports program, or another form of violence."[2] This does not mean that only inexpensive products can be sold via direct-response TV. Lewis points out that such products as a $500 weight-loss program, a $400 real estate home-study course, and precious gems costing $200 or more have been successfully sold through the medium.[3]

Offers must be carefully structured in order to work on TV. Those that require a great deal of explanation (e.g., a complex electronic product), lengthy legal disclosures (e.g., many financial services offers), many choices (e.g., book or record club offers), or the return of a signed contract or application (e.g., offers that require evidence of creditworthiness) are not appropriate unless they can be restructured. That is often possible, however. The complex or service product or the offer that requires a signed form may use a two-step (lead-generation) approach in which the television commercial is the first step and mail fulfillment provides the lengthy information or necessary forms. The book or record club may use a popular product as a trial offer at an attractive price. Be careful when using trial offers and incentives, however. Because television reaches a broad audience, bad credit losses and failure to complete a continuity program are likely to be higher in this medium than in any other.[4]

THE BASIC FORMATS OF DIRECT-RESPONSE TELEVISION ADVERTISING

Just as not all products or offers are appropriate for television, so, too, the general advertising approach to TV commercials will not work for direct response. Successful direct-response commercials must convey particular types of information, and experience has shown that this requires certain minimum amounts of time. The result is a formularized approach to the direct-response commercial.

You will remember that after cautioning that there is really no such thing as a "standard mail package," we then went on to use that idea as a basis for our discussion for convenience' sake. We will do the same thing here, that is, we will discuss the "classic 120-second continuity commercial," the "classic 60-second one-shot commercial," and the "classic 30-second lead generation commercial,"

[2] Edward L. Nash, *Direct Marketing: Strategy/Planning/Execution* (New York: McGraw-Hill, 1982), pp. 148-149.

[3] Donald D. Lewis, "Seven Myths That Keep You Off TV," *Direct Marketing*, January 1987, p. 58.

[4] Nash, *Direct Marketing*, pp. 149-150.

even though these formats can be, and often are, varied. However, they do provide the general structure for virtually all direct-response TV commercials. Figure 13.1 shows the three basic formats.

120–Second Continuity Commercial

A	B	C	D	E	F
5–10	15	40	20	10	20

(number of seconds)

A. Opening and basic premise of the ad
B. Introduction of series
C. Dramatization of product
D. First-installment display
E. Premiums, if any (position variable)
F. Terms of offer, ordering instructions, telephone number

60–Second One–Shot Commercial

A	B	C	D
5	10–15	30	15

(number of seconds)

A. Opening (attract attention)
B. Premise and/or mention of premium
C. Product display, possibly with premium
D. Ordering information and telephone number

30–Second Lead–Generation Commercial

A	B	C
5–10	10–20	10–15

(number of seconds)

A. Statement of problem or benefit
B. Dramatization
C. Telephone and/or address

FIGURE 13.1 ***Basic Formulas for Direct–Response Commercials***

Source: Adapted from John Witek, *Response Television: Combat Advertising of the 1980's* (Chicago: Crain Books, 1981), pp. 24–32.

The 120-second commercial is standard for continuity offers because there is so much to communicate that 2 minutes of time is usually needed. A 60-second continuity spot is rarely successful. In the same way, a minimum of 60 seconds is generally required to communicate thc information for a one-shot offer. For complex one-shot offers, 120 seconds may be required. Since a lead-generation commercial does not have to present a complete offer, just sufficient information to entice the viewer to request more, it can usually be confined to 30 seconds. Although these are generalizations rather than absolute rules, it would be a false economy to squeeze a direct-response spot into a shorter time in order to save money and end up with a commercial that does not pull. Remember, it is also necessary to allow a substantial block of time to show the toll-free number and mailing address on the screen, although the audio repetition of this information can be shorter.

The formats in Figure 13.1 have withstood the test of time and to ignore them could be dangerous. That is not to say that a knowledgeable direct marketer with a creative idea cannot structure a direct-response spot differently—so long as it is done on the basis of creativity, not ignorance!

MEDIA PLANNING FOR DIRECT RESPONSE TV

The three key media planning concepts for direct-response TV are gross rating points (GRPs), dayparts, and availability. Let's look at each in turn.

GRPs are the basic measure of television efficiency—the cumulative number of households receiving the ad during a given period of time. This measure is computed by a simple formula:

Reach (the percentage of households tuned in) x Frequency (the number of times the ad is aired) = Gross Rating Points

The objective of the direct-response media buy is to obtain as many GRPs in the most desirable dayparts as possible for the amount of money budgeted.

Broadcasters have divided the day into sections that are relatively homogeneous in terms of the type of programming offered. Finer divisions are possible, but the basic *dayparts* are morning, day, prime, and night. The significance of dayparts is that both the size and the composition of the viewing audience differ by daypart and, consequently, so do the rates charged for time in each.

Availability of time is a major concern to the direct-response TV advertiser because there are relatively few 120-second segments available, especially on network affiliates. Independent stations have more long segments to offer. Buying specific time slots is the most expensive way to purchase. Less expensive alternatives are preemptibles (the advertiser chooses a specific time but the station can replace it with a full-rate advertisement if one becomes available) and run-of-station or ROS ads (the station itself chooses the time). Per-inquiry deals, if available, lessen the risk that exists even when airtime is purchased at very favorable rates.

You may have recognized that this list of key media planning concepts omits one considered very important by the general advertiser—program ratings. While general advertisers are eager to place their commercials on highly rated programs, direct marketers generally avoid them because they are not usually good vehicles for direct response advertisements. Viewers of such programs are often too absorbed in the entertainment to pay much attention to the commercials; viewers also tend to resent the intrusion of a commercial more when they are watching a program they like; they also don't like to chance missing any of the program while placing an order. The same reasoning in reverse explains why independent stations have been such successful vehicles for direct-response ads: it's not much of a sacrifice to miss part of a rerun to place an order for an attractive product.

You have probably also realized that while the concepts of GRPs, dayparts, and availability are important to the direct-response TV advertiser, the most important concept of all is profitability, which is usually measured in terms of cost per order.

Because profitability can be measured on a station-by-station basis, direct-response television time is always purchased with a clause allowing for cancellation at any time with 48 to 72 hours notice. Direct marketers must not hesitate to cancel unprofitable advertising, but they should give the ad a chance to perform. Nash points out that response builds over time with a television campaign, but because it builds erratically, it is difficult to forecast results. A successful campaign will reach a peak after 2 to 3 weeks, plateau for several weeks, and then start to decay. The direct marketer must show some patience in the beginning, but track results carefully so the ad can be removed once results decline below the minimum acceptable profitability level.[5]

CREATING DIRECT-RESPONSE TV COMMERCIALS [6]

The aim of direct-response television creativity is to take advantage of the visual imagery unique to TV while conveying a hard-hitting sales message. The imagery and the emotion it evokes must not overwhelm the sales message; rather, the imagery should be integrated so that it becomes an essential part of the sales appeal. Direct-response TV's focus on sales (or lead generation) means that many of the

[5] Nash, *Direct Marketing*, p. 153.

[6] This discussion is based on Shan Ellentuck and James R. Springer, "Creating Successful Direct Response Broadcast Commercials," DMA Release No. 310.5, January 1984; Channing M. Hadlock, "Direct Response Television Commercial Production," DMA Release No. 440.1, January 1984; Joseph McGlone, "Broadcast Creative," in Edward L. Nash, ed., *The Direct Marketing Handbook* (New York: McGraw-Hill, 1984), pp. 517-536; Sheldon Hechtman, "How to Produce a DR Commercial," *DM News*, September 15, 1987, p. 62. .

elaborate production elements common to general television advertising will not be appropriate.

The offer is central to the creation of a successful direct-response TV commercial. All the relevant elements of the offer (as discussed in Chapter 3) must be described in sufficient detail to be clearly understood by the viewer. This description will require a substantial portion of the allotted time. As with all other direct-response media, if customers misunderstand any of the terms of the offer, back-end results will likely be disappointing.

The offer is the key to the success of the commercial in another way. Variations in the offer such as changes in price or incentive can have a substantial effect on the pulling power of the ad.

While a sound offer is essential, a number of other aspects of the commercial will have a major impact on its success:

- All copy must be clear, straightforward, and compelling. The viewer should recognize the purpose of the ad from the very beginning. Benefits of the product should be emphasized. The viewer must receive all the information necessary to make a decision and take the desired action.
- Products and incentives should be demonstrated whenever possible. Make full use of the visual aspects of the medium.
- Show the toll-free telephone number for an extended period of time. It should appear much earlier than the complete ordering information which is shown in the end tag of the commercial. Often the number is superimposed on part of the commercial itself as well as being prominently displayed on the end tag.
- If music is used, it should contribute to the mood and image, not intrude.

Direct-response TV advertisers share many creative issues with general advertisers. Should the ad be shot in a studio or on location? Should it use a celebrity spokesperson? Who will handle the actual production? The answers to these and other questions will depend on advertising objectives, budget, and the expertise of the advertiser.

TESTING DIRECT-RESPONSE TV ADs

Testing direct-response TV ads bears many similarities to test-marketing a product. Choosing representative markets and determining the length of the test must be done correctly if test results are to be valid.

Davis makes a number of recommendations on how to conduct tests of direct-response TV commercials:[7]

[7] Davis, "Television Direct Response," in Nash, *Direct Marketing Handbook*, pp. 329-330.

- Be sure objectives (to test against a control, to develop a second successful ad that can be rotated with the existing one, to develop a new creative approach) are clear.
- Use at least ten stations with a mix of network affiliates and independents. If possible, use stations on which your offer has performed well so that the station itself does not become a major variable.
- Run the test for 2 to 4 weeks.
- Run the control ad in half the stations and the test ad in the others for the first half of the test. Then switch the ads for the second half of the test. This lessens the impact of the stations chosen on the test results.
- Allow sufficient time before the start of the campaign for testing and evaluating results.

AN EXAMPLE OF DIRECT-RESPONSE TV ADVERTISING

Foster Parents Plan, a nonprofit organization that promotes sponsorship of poor children in developing countries, has been a successful user of lead-generation ads for many years. The ad shown in Figure 13.2, featuring Olympic athlete Dorothy Hamill as spokesperson, was selected for use after extensive development and testing.

FPP uses celebrity spokespersons for a number of reasons. Celebrities help to catch the attention of television viewers and motivate them to attend to the commercial instead of leaving the room or changing channels. The celebrities used must have a public image that will enhance the organization's credibility.

FPP has several categories of celebrities that have been successful in past advertisements. Dorothy Hamill was chosen as a successful young professional. Two other ads were produced using the same copy and visuals. The first featured movie and television star Shirley Jones and her husband, Hollywood agent Marty Ingels. They represented an older, established couple. The second used as spokesperson Cynthia Sykes, star of a prime-time tv medical show. The three new spots were tested against a control, the current ad featuring television personalities Steve Allen and Jayne Meadows. All these celebrities are Foster Parents. This is both a legal requirement and essential to the organization's credibility.

Foster Parents Plan has a roster of television advertising markets that have performed well in the past. Markets for a test are chosen from this roster to represent small, medium, and large tv markets. The test was run for approximately four weeks. In each set of markets a test ad and the control ad each ran for two weeks. Success was judged on the basis of cost per lead for all markets in which the ad aired. Cost per sponsor is also tracked, but FPP cannot wait 6 to 8 weeks for final conversion figures to make decisions about advertising effectiveness.

The Dorothy Hamill ad was the winner in this test but not by a large margin. A small difference in effectiveness can be viewed as a plus for the advertiser. It permits the rotation of two ads to avoid advertising "wearout." Also, it is possible that one ad pulls better in some markets while the second is better in others. Only

Figure 13.2 *Dorothy Hamill :120 Spot for Foster Parents Plan*

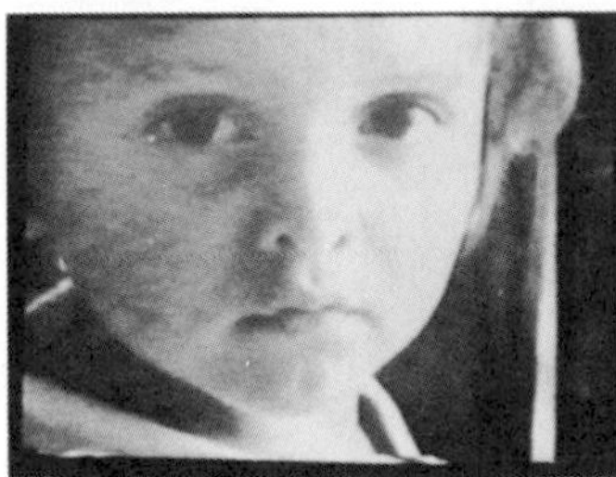

1. You know, children can really touch your heart sometimes ...

2. But the children you've been looking at are desperately poor ...

3. Hello, I'm Dorothy Hamill ... I sponsor a child in a developing country thru Foster Parents Plan ...

4. Right now one very special child is waiting for you. Please call 1- 800-621-5839 now.

5. You can choose (sex, age, country) ... You'll receive a photograph and case history and later letters ...

6. Imagine! For just 72 cents a day ... You can make it possible for a child to have ... hope.

7. It doesn't stop there ...

8. By combining your funds with those of other foster parents whole communities can change ...

9. It all starts with sponsoring just one desperately poor child overseas ...

10. Please don't wait ...

11. A desperately poor child is waiting for you ...

12. Because your love does make the difference. Call today!

direct-response television provides the market-by-market measurability that allows an advertiser to fine tune a campaign this way.

SUPPORT ADVERTISING

In addition to closing sales and generating leads, television can perform a support function in a direct-response campaign. The primary medium, the one being supported, is usually newspaper inserts, magazine ads, or direct mail. Theoretically, any medium can support any other medium, but television is most often used as the secondary, or support, medium. The purpose of using a support medium is to increase the pulling power of the primary medium by creating awareness of and excitement about the forthcoming ad.

When to Use Television Support

The direct marketer must recognize that television support cannot make an unsuccessful program successful. It can however, increase the pulling power of a marginal or successful program by 10 to 50 percent or even more.

Experts agree that there are two key requirements for television support to be successful:

1. The product or service being offered for sale must appeal to a mass audience.
2. The primary medium must reach at least 25 percent of the television market. If it does not, the expense of television cannot be justified.

Assuming these two conditions, the direct marketer must also consider several other factors:

The cost of the primary medium
The predictability of delivery of the primary medium
The distribution coverage of the primary medium
The cost of the support medium
The expected lift in the response rate[8]

Before we discuss the role these factors play, let's look at the nature of support ads.

[8] Thomas Knowlton, "Selecting the Media Mix," DMA Release No. 140.1, January 1984.

Types of Television Support Ads

Support ads are either 30 or 60 seconds long. Because their primary function is to create awareness, shorter commercials are sufficient. Support ads are also simpler in format than direct-response ads. The typical format for a 60-second spot is:[9]

A	B
10-30	30-50

A. Dramatization of the offer

B. Facts about the advertisement in the primary medium

The basic message of the support ad is: Watch for my ad in your newspaper/magazine/mailbox. If the commercial is in support of a direct mail piece, it may urge viewers to watch for an envelope with a particular message ("You may have already won thousands of dollars in our sweepstakes") or some other identifying characteristic ("Watch your mail for the purple envelope"). If you are going to use some identifying characteristic, be sure that it is distinctive enough to stand out in the mailbox clutter that is prevalent today!

To further increase excitement, and to aid in tracking the effectiveness of the support, direct marketers sometimes use a transfer device. That is, the ad may tell the viewer to mark a particular spot on the ad, to scratch an area to reveal information, to move a token from one place to another, or the like. Completing the action properly will win a prize. This additional incentive should increase the response rate.

How Much to Spend for Support Advertising

Since support advertising is not directly responsible for closing sales, the decision on how much to spend is less straightforward than for other direct-response media. There are two ways to make this decision: as a percentage of the expenditure in the primary medium and on the basis of gross rating points.

A direct marketer can decide to spend a given percentage—say, 50 percent—of the cost of the primary medium on support. While this approach has the virtue of simplicity, it has little else to recommend it. The efficiency of the television buy may differ a great deal from one market to another. That is, a given amount of money may purchase more effective reach in one market than it would in another. Since GRPs are a measure of effectiveness, they provide a better basis for expenditure decisions.

[9] Adapted from Witek, *Response Television: Combat Advertising of the 1980s*, p. 37.

One GRP equals 1 percent of the households that are watching TV at a given time. Therefore, if the direct marketer wishes to potentially reach every household in the market one time, the correct buy is 100 GRPs. The ad will be aired a sufficient number of times (frequency) so that the reach (the number of households viewing) times the frequency will equal 100. That is a commonly used support level, although the buy sometimes goes as high as 200 or even 400 GRPs.

Timing of the Ads

Timing of the support advertising is critical. If the ad is run too early or too late, it will lose much of its effectiveness. Direct marketers want their prospective customers to be looking for the ad when they read a magazine or newspaper; they cannot expect people to search through their magazine racks or coffee tables to find it.

Freestanding inserts in newspapers are the most predictable in terms of arrival and useful life, so they are the easiest in terms of establishing proper timing. As we discussed in Chapter 12, the majority of inserts appear in Sunday papers. Support advertising for these inserts should start on Friday evening and run through Sunday afternoon.

The timing of the delivery of direct mail is always difficult to predict, but the direct marketer must plan the support schedule around the expected delivery date, not the drop date. If a mailing is expected to arrive on Monday, a reasonable schedule is to begin on the preceding Friday and run through Thursday of the delivery week.

The timing of commercials supporting magazine advertising will depend on the length of time households normally retain the magazine. For a weekly magazine such as *TV Guide*, the commercials will run for less than a week. If the date of issue is Sunday, the ads may begin on Thursday and run through Monday. For a monthly magazine that is likely to be kept for a considerable period of time, the support schedule may run over several weeks. Regardless of which magazine the direct marketer uses, a small advertisement is not worth supporting.

Testing Support Advertising

Support advertising should be tested by pairing similar markets, with only one market in each pair receiving support. The markets should be matched as carefully as possible, but no pair will be exactly alike and there will be variables in the test that can neither be controlled nor precisely measured. Consequently, it is not wise to skimp on the number of markets included in the test. Eight to ten pairs will be needed in order to read the results with confidence.

Careful testing and refinements based on the results of the tests are as essential to successful use of the television medium as they are to success in any of the other direct marketing media. If the direct marketer recognizes the unique advantages of television as well as its inherent limitations, television advertising can function by itself or as a useful part of a multimedia campaign.

An Example of TV Support Advertising

The television storyboard (Figure 13.3A) and the insert shown in Figure 13.3B is an example of such a multimedia program for a chain of home-decorating stores located in the Southeast and Midwest.

Wallpapers to Go had successfully used support television prior to this particular campaign. Earlier television support ads were simple shots of rooms with changing wallpaper, fabrics, and decor. Their satisfactory experiences with support advertising prompted the firm and its agency, Grey Direct, to use a more ambitious concept that included a live model and location shots.

The version of the ad shown in Figure 13.3A was used in the markets in which all inserts were mailed as part of a shared mailing with other advertisers. This was the "Watch your mail" version. A slightly different ending that said, "Look in your newspaper, too," was used in markets where the insert was handled under a local newspaper's total market coverage (see Chapter 12 for a discussion of TMC) program, which meant that some households received it as a newspaper insert and others through the mail.

The television ad was run for 7 days in all markets to support a 3-day sale (Tuesday through Thursday). In the TMC markets, it began on Wednesday of the week prior to the appearance of the insert in the Sunday paper. In the shared-mail markets, it began on the Friday before the week of the sale.

Notice that the ad shows the insert three times—at the beginning and twice near the end. One shot of the insert near the end emphasizes the use of the coupon. What you cannot see as easily is that the 30-second informational core of the ad could be used alone—without the direct-response elements and without the promotion of the sale—as an awareness ad. So this ad could do double duty as direct-response and general advertising!

Television's versatility and power have made it a glamour medium almost since its beginning. However, it has an older cousin—radio—that can be a useful part of the direct-response media mix.

DIRECT-RESPONSE RADIO

The use of radio as a direct response or support medium bears many similarities to the use of television. Radio's special ability to reach people as they pursue many aspects of their daily lives has made it a useful direct-response medium from its inception.

Early Direct-Response Radio

One author describes an early direct-response radio operation as follows:

> Back in the wonder years of radio, in the late 1930s, the 1940s, and early 1950s, one of the most popular direct-response ads running over WCKY in Cincinnati

FIGURE 13.3A *Wallpapers to Go Storyboard*

1. Woman with flyer

2. Woman, living room background, "She did it with style" superimposed.

3. Shot of den with "She did it on a budget" superimposed.

4. Woman's head, "She did it herself" superimposed.

5. Shot of flyer.

6. Shot of wallpaper with "50% on in-stock" superimposed.

7. Scissors cutting coupon.

8. Wallpapering kit with "Free...an $8 value" superimposed.

9. End tag with Wallpapers to Go Where Beautiful Rooms Begin.

Source: Wallpapers to Go

FIGURE 13.3B *Four Page Newspaper Insert*

Source: Wallpapers to Go

peddled a lamp shade impregnated with insecticide. When the lamp was turned on, the announcer promised, the heat would activate the insecticide and kill all the bugs in the room....

WCKY was one of several 50,000 kilowatt, clear-channel stations which, since many stations were required to go off the air at sundown, were able to "skyway" their signals at night over as many as 30 states. L. B. Wilson of WCKY was one of the most colorful station managers. At one time, he was said to have 15 to 18 people in the mailroom just filling orders for products that included baby chicks and a very popular plastic statue of Jesus. Stories of closets full of "crystal-like" table cigarette lighters or leftover "collapsible" hula hoops were common station gossip through the years.[10]

Radio has changed a great deal since those early days. One difference is that stations no longer perform the fulfillment function. Marketers who do not have fulfillment capabilities hire independent fulfillment specialists to handle responses from their radio advertisements. An even more important change is that radio has lost its status as the only mass medium capable of attracting a large national audience with broad-appeal programming. The days of the *Jack Benny Show, Fibber McGee and Molly, The Green Hornet*, and *Captain Preston of the Yukon* are gone forever. With the widespread adoption of television in the 1950s, radio evolved into a low-reach–high-frequency medium that offers its own unique advantages to the direct marketer.

Radio Today

At present there are more than 8,500 radio stations selling commercial airtime in the United States.[11] Because of its size and geographical distribution, radio offers a number of advantages to all advertisers, including direct marketers.[12]

1. It is ubiquitous. Radio is available to most people at any place at any time.
2. It is selective. The limited geographical reach of most stations and their specialized programming formats attract audiences that tend to be quite homogeneous in terms of demographics and lifestyles.
3. It is economical. Radio's CPM (cost per thousand audience members) is relatively low and has increased more slowly than that of other advertising media for the last decade.[13] Despite a noticeable increase in the demand for radio advertising time in recent years, that trend is expected to continue through 1989.[14] Also,

[10] Terry Considine Williams, "Will Direct Response Radio Return to the Golden Ad Days?" *Direct Marketing*, October 1986, pp. 50, 52.

[11] Herbert Zeltner, "Interesting Times, Yes; Predictable, No," *Advertising Age*, November 30, 1987, p. S-2.

[12] Albert C. Book and Norman D. Cary, *The Radio And Television Commercial* (Chicago: Crain Books, 1978), p. 11.

[13] "Direct Response in Electronic Media," *Direct Marketing*, June 1986, p. 37.

[14] Robert J. Coen, "TV Forms Hot: Print, Outdoor Waver," *Advertising Age*, November 30, 1987, p. S-4.

production costs for radio commercials tend to be low compared to those for other media.

4. It offers rapid access. An advertiser who has an urgent need to communicate information can get a live radio commercial on the air within a few hours. Recorded commercials can be completed within a few days. Contrast this to the weeks, or even months, required for production and publication in some other media.
5. It is involving. Radio is a personal medium and listeners develop strong loyalties to specific stations. They may engage in participatory behavior such as calling the station to express their opinions or to request musical selections. Radio tends to involve listeners by encouraging them to use their imaginations to supplement the communication being received through the auditory sense.
6. It is flexible. When the situation demands it, a new radio commercial can be written and aired live within a few hours. Existing commercials can be revised quickly without incurring substantial cost. The relatively low cost and flexibility of radio make it a useful test medium for offers that may eventually be run in any medium. Commercials can be developed and refined easily and the results are available almost immediately. Experience indicates that 90 percent of the responses will be received within 5 minutes of the airing of the commercial.[15]

WHEN TO USE DIRECT-RESPONSE RADIO

Unlike with television, the successful use of radio does not require a product with broad mass appeal. Products that serve niche markets can be ideal candidates if they meet two criteria:[16]

1. The product's user profile can be matched to the audience characteristics of one or more radio stations.
2. The offer can be explained in a brief period of time. If everything else appears favorable but the offer is complex, two-step programs can be used on radio just as on television.

Media Planning for Direct Response Radio

Though there are a tremendous number of formats (i.e., type of programming offered) for radio stations, we can offer a few useful generalizations about types of stations that do and do not work. Stations that specialize in "background music" do not tend to be successful, probably because their listeners keep the volume low and don't pay close attention to what they hear. Stations that appeal primarily to teenagers are unlikely to be successful either since young people are

[15] Shan Ellentuck and James R. Springer, "Radio Advertising: What Radio Offers to Direct Marketers," in Nash, *The Direct Marketing Handbook*, p. 353.

[16] Ellentuck and Spring, "Radio Advertising," p. 349.

not generally a responsive audience. The direct marketer should look for stations that involve the audience, but not so much that people will not leave the program to respond.

As with television, radio airtime can be purchased in a number of ways. If the direct marketer is willing to pay top rates, specific time slots can be bought. Otherwise, time can be obtained at lower ROS (run of station) rates. PI time is available on many stations. Other possible arrangements are response guarantees, in which the marketer pays regular rates but unsuccessful commercials are rerun at no cost until a specified response is achieved, and barter, in which goods or services are exchanged for airtime.

Choosing the correct daypart for the media buy is important if the direct marketer is purchasing specific times. Ratings are available for radio just as they are for television, and they are equally unimportant to the direct marketer. The issue is a responsive audience, not high ratings. For example, listenership is often quite high during "drive time," but the inability of motorists to respond at the time of the commercial may produce a disappointing response rate.

Radio time can be purchased on either a network or a spot basis. Media buyers can arrange "packages" of spot purchases to meet the product's specific needs, thus avoiding a laborious and expensive station-by-station purchase. Additionally, there are so-called unwired networks. These may be oriented to a particular event—broadcast of a major sporting event, for example—or long-term media representation arrangements by a group of stations.

The cardinal rule of direct marketing—Test!—holds true for all aspects of the direct response radio program.

Radio as a Support Medium

The general principles are much the same for using support programs in print media, radio, or television. There should be a good match between the coverage of the primary medium and the secondary medium. Timing of radio support will follow the same pattern for each of the primary media that we described in the section on support television.

Creating a Direct Response Radio Commercial

Direct-response radio commercials are usually 60 seconds long. That translates into about 200 words of copy, about half of which are likely to be required to detail the terms of the offer. Only 100 words, then, are left to promote the benefits of the product in a way that moves the listener to take immediate action. The ad must attract attention with a riveting "headline" and move the listener on through the succeeding stages of interest, desire, and action. Figure 13.4 presents a sample radio script with a step-by-step analysis of its structure. The script is straightforward, informative, and contains a strong call to action.

Can you recognize your body's danger signals? Which of those aches, pains, or changes in your body should your doctor know about at once? With Better Homes and Gardens' FAMILY MEDICAL GUIDE in your home, you'll always have practical, easy-to-understand health and first-aid information on hand—when you need it. When you're confused ... when you're frightened ... when there's a medical emergency. Written by 29 of America's most prominent physicians, the FAMILY MEDICAL GUIDE gives you frank advice on hundreds of health problems—on female disorders, irregular heartbeat, loss of vigor, arthritis, strokes, cancer, allergies, and much, much more. It's profusely illustrated and contains more than 2,000 clear, simple explanations of often-confusing medical terms. Yes, you owe it to yourself and your family to examine Better Homes and Gardens' FAMILY MEDICAL GUIDE and right now you can do just that—absolutely free.

In fact, to encourage you to take advantage of this no-obligation opportunity you'll receive from Better Homes and Gardens not one but two FREE gifts ... an amazing see-through Atlas of the Human Body and Better Homes and Gardens' EAT AND STAY SLIM cookbook.

All you need do is call toll-free, 800-228-2200 and ask to have a copy of the FAMILY MEDICAL GUIDE sent to you. Then, if you agree the FAMILY MEDICAL GUIDE is a book that will prove its great value in your home time and time again, you may pay the full and complete price of $16.95 plus $1.45 postage and handling in four easy monthly payments. Four easy payments of only $4.60 each—which covers all costs. Or return it within 14 days and not owe a single penny. But no matter what you decide, the two gifts from Better Homes and Gardens are yours—free ... just for examining the MEDICAL GUIDE! So act now. Operators are standing by! Call 800-228-2200, today. Better Homes and Gardens pays for the call. 800-228-2200 ... call today!

The opening attracts attention and excites interest in the minds of the target market.

An important benefit is promised early in the script.

The participation of experts adds credibility.

Considerable detail is given about the attributes and benefits of the product.

A free trial is offered as one way to reduce perceived risk.

Two free gifts are offered as incentives.

The toll-free number is mentioned well before the end of the script to alert listeners to the fact that this is a direct-response ad.

Since the objective of this ad is to close a sale, the terms of the offer must be completely spelled out.

The call to action gives specific instructions on how to take action. The toll-free number is repeated two more times.

The ending is another call to action.

FIGURE 13.4 ***Analysis of a Direct-Response Radio Script***

SUMMARY

Television and radio are not new media to the direct-response marketer, but both have gained considerably in use and credibility in recent years. Both continue to be successful in selling a wide variety of products, but their greatest growth has apparently come as support for other direct marketing media. The direct marketer's approach to using broadcast media is more structured than that of the general marketer. The direct marketer finds the same opportunity to test, refine, and measure the effectiveness of broadcast commercials that exists in the other direct marketing media.

DISCUSSION QUESTIONS

1. What are the similarities and differences between general and direct-response advertising on television? On radio?
2. What are the major considerations when buying direct-response television time? Direct-response radio time?
3. The formularized approach described in this chapter unnecessarily hinders creativity in developing direct-response TV ads. Comment.
4. Discuss the concept of support advertising. Have you seen examples in which media combinations other than the ones described in this chapter are used as primary and support media?
5. Be prepared to discuss in class examples of direct-response television and radio ads to which you have recently been exposed.

SUGGESTED ADDITIONAL READINGS

1. Tony Everett, "TV and Direct Response: Don't Dilute the Discipline" *Direct Marketing*, June 1986, pp. 36-39.
2. Raymond Roel, "Financial Services Down Under," *Direct Marketing*, June 1988, pp. 36-40, 107.
3. John Witek, *Response Television: Combat Advertising of the 1980s*. Chicago: Crain, 1981.

14

Business-to-Business Direct Marketing

The UPS truck came to a halt, double-parking on the busy city street. The driver reached for a large light-weight box. After locating the name of a well-known public relations firm on the building directory, he took the elevator to the third floor and entered the reception area. With a puzzled frown, the receptionist verified the correctness of the address and signed for the unexpected delivery.

Several other members of the firm had seen the box arrive and curiosity drew them to the desk, where the receptionist still regarded the unidentified box with a questioning look. Scissors were found, the box was opened, and a bright maroon Mylar balloon floated gracefully into the air above the box. "Design Solutions," it said. A hanging tag on the bottom of the balloon encouraged the recipient to call for more information about a new piece of graphics-design software for personal computers.

This promotion demonstrates a number of aspects of business-to-business direct marketing:

- Its objective was to generate sales leads by getting businesspeople to call or write for additional information.
- It was planned and executed to attract attention, thereby reducing the power of the gatekeeping function in recipient firms.
- On a cost-per-contact basis, it was quite expensive.
- It showed that business promotions can be interesting and unusual; they don't have to be dull and boring.

This anecdote also suggests that a precisely targeted list enables business marketers to develop and implement high-impact promotions with a reasonable degree of assurance that they will reach a decision-maker.

The ability of well-conceived and executed business-to-business promotions to achieve important communications and sales objectives is a prime reason for the explosive growth of business-to-business direct marketing in recent years.

THE NATURE AND SCOPE OF BUSINESS-TO-BUSINESS DIRECT MARKETING

The first thing that must be understood about business-to- business direct marketing is that it is much more extensive than the relatively few suppliers of goods and services who rely solely on direct-response marketing. Fishman estimates that in 1986, 1,130 business and industrial suppliers (whom we will describe generically as "business marketers") relied primarily on mail order, generating almost $11.3 billion in sales, or 30 percent of the $37.6 billion total business-to-business mail-order sales.[1] Another 4 million businesses use direct response as a portion of their total marketing effort, and account for the remaining 70 percent. Put another way, over half of all business marketers in the United States, and an increasing number throughout the world, include direct response in their marketing activities.

Why has direct response become so important in business markets? Certainly one reason is the high and steadily increasing cost of field selling (Figure 14.1). The average cost of one sales call was almost $230 in 1985; consider that it may take several calls to close even a moderately complex sale! With expenses of that magnitude, any approach that helps reduce costs is welcome. Direct-response methods do that in two basic ways. First, they can provide qualified leads, virtually eliminating the need for unproductive cold calls. Second, they can actually sell supplies and other low-margin items which do not warrant the expense of a personal sales call.

Another reason for the growth in direct-response business-to-business marketing is more subtle—the need of large business marketers to deal with a multitude of (relatively) small customers. This is best illustrated by the micro-computer industry. There was a time when mainframe computers were sold to large firms and, within those firms, to one or a very few centralized data-processing operations. Customers were few and easily identifiable, and each controlled a huge purchasing budget. Today micro-computers are ubiquitous. They are found in firms from the very largest to the very smallest and, in most firms, in multiple organizational units and physical locations. This kind of diffused market exists in many other industries such as telecommunications, parcel delivery services, and office supplies. It creates an ideal climate for direct-response marketing because

[1] Arnold Fishman, "Business and Industrial Mail Order Trends," *Direct Marketing*, September 1987, pp. 88-94.

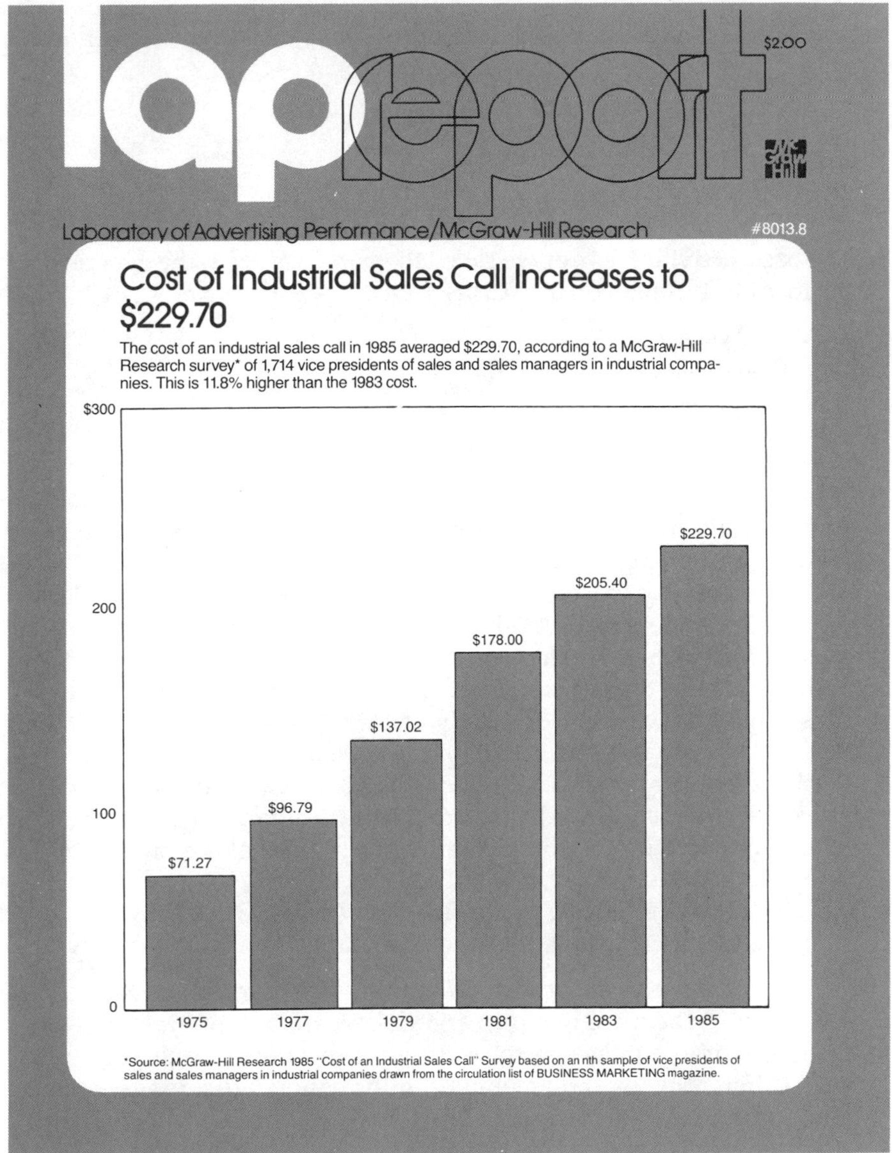

FIGURE 14.1
Source: McGraw-Hill Research/Laboratory of Advertising Performance Report.

customers and prospects are identifiable and in most instances are buying stock (as opposed to customized) items.

Whether the firm using direct-response techniques is large or small, the same basic principles apply. First we will look at the ways in which business marketers can achieve generic objectives by using direct marketing methods, and then we will briefly look at each of the major media as they are used in business-to-business settings.

ACTIVITIES OF BUSINESS-TO-BUSINESS DIRECT MARKETERS

The basic activities—or, as we called them in Chapter 1, the generic objectives—of business-to-business direct marketers are:

Lead generation
Lead qualification
Making the sale
Maintaining customer relationships

These generic objectives are precisely the same as those for direct marketing of consumer goods and services. However, the manner of implementation in business markets is often different.

The primary reason for the difference is the nature of the decision-making process in business markets. In all decisions except for the very small or the completely routine, more than one person is involved in the process. People may act in many roles in the decision process—as initiators, influencers, gatekeepers (persons who exert control, especially of information), users, or ultimate decision makers. This makes the marketing task more complex. At the same time, all businesspeople are human beings with individual outlooks and emotional reactions. The most successful direct marketing programs often operate at both levels, taking into account the complex group decision-making process and the equally complex individual objectives and reactions.

This causes business-to-business direct-response activities to differ from similar efforts in consumer markets in a number of important ways:

A single direct-response activity may require targeting several different people in the firm. There are two primary reasons for this multiple targeting. The first is the multiple purchasing roles already mentioned. Each purchasing role may need different types and amounts of information. The design engineer wants to know, in considerable technical detail, how the product will make a particular job easier or more effective. The manager of manufacturing operations may be especially concerned about integrating innovations into operations without disrupting work flows; here again, much technical information will be required. The executive who will make the final decision to purchase or not may be more concerned about costs and about the impact of new technology or products on the organization as a whole. This executive may or may not have a technical background.

In some circumstances the direct marketer might be able to combine all this information into a single mailing, although a single message would probably be less effective than multiple, precisely targeted ones. A single message is impossible, however, when various participants have different backgrounds and training (engineering versus business management, for example); are differentially acquainted with precise technical terminology; and have preferences for lengthy, detailed information versus more concisely presented information that portrays "the big picture" a decision-maker must take into account. The presence of some or all of these three conditions creates a need for multiple versions of a program to target various participants in the decision-making process.

Obtaining complete and up-to-date lists is often a problem. There are in excess of 10,000 rental lists available to business marketers. However, in large firms personnel change their titles and/or physical locations so frequently that even the best-maintained lists have a high proportion of incorrect addresses (although some misaddressed pieces will eventually be delivered). Small firms come and go so quickly that they may not even engage in the kind of activities (such as undergoing credit checks) that would make them known to some of the large business list sources like Dun and Bradstreet.

Moreover, merge/purge is less effective for business lists than for consumer lists. Business lists contain four-line addresses—name and title, corporate name, corporate address, city/ state/ zip code is a common format. However, there are many variations of this format as well as spelling or abbreviating organizational titles and corporate names. Increasingly sophisticated computer software designed to deal with business addresses can catch some of the discrepancies—V-P and Vice President will be recognized as representing the same title, for example. Still, business address merge/purge is far from error-free.

Lists are often small—perhaps only a few thousand names in very specialized industries or occupations. In one sense, this is no problem if the direct marketer wants to reach the entire universe of interest. It may even make it possible to use more expensive promotions with greater impact.

The small size of the total population presents one severe disadvantage to the direct marketer, however: the type of systematic testing and roll-out which is standard in consumer markets is often impossible. This is why many business-to-business direct-response promotions go untested. It is also why more and more business marketers are turning to marketing research, especially to focus groups, even though their drawbacks are well known. Since they cannot test the programs with any degree of statistical rigor, they feel they must better inform the planning and development stages of their programs.

We must be careful not to exaggerate these differences between business and consumer markets, however. The differences are mainly in degree, not kind. The wise marketer remembers that people do not cease being people the moment they enter their store, office, or plant in the morning. In fact, direct marketers of products that are not genuinely differentiated (such as office supplies) or of products in highly competitive markets (such as computer software) are increasingly turning to consumer marketing techniques, including colorful mailing packages and catalogs and price incentives of various types.

One of the differences of degree between business and consumer markets is the much greater use of two-step or lead-generation programs in business markets. Even though their frequency of use is considerably greater in business markets, remember that the same approaches are often used in consumer markets for expensive and/ or infrequently purchased goods and services.

LEAD GENERATION AND MANAGEMENT PROGRAMS

While no statistics are available, it is commonly believed that lead generation is the single largest direct-response activity of business marketers. To be effective, these programs must be carefully planned and monitored to include lead generation, lead qualification, and lead tracking. Depending on the program, fulfillment (for example, sending an information packet either before or after qualification) may be required. We will discuss each of these activities in detail. As we do, keep in mind the primary purpose of a lead-generation program—to generate the highest volume of sales in the most cost-effective manner by focusing expensive field sales activity on the most qualified prospects. Figure 14. 2 presents a graphic portrayal of this objective.

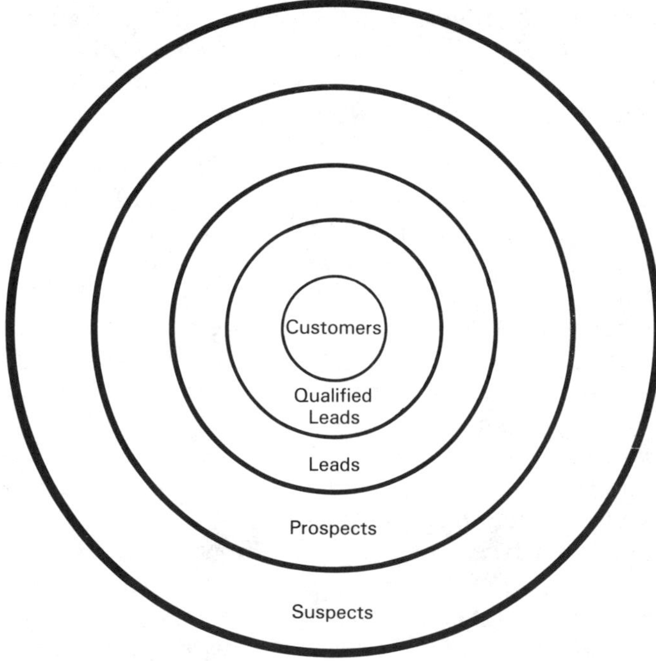

FIGURE 14.2

Suspects are merely business names, often from a compiled list. Their number may be legion; there are an estimated 8 million businesses in the United States alone. Nothing is known about the purchasing interest or likelihood of suspects.

Prospects meet predetermined qualification criteria. They may have been selected from a list by, for example, SIC (Standard Industrial Classification) code, which identifies them as a member of the industry group that is an appropriate target for the business's product or service. Many specialized prospect lists are available from list brokers; for example,lists of physicians (by medical specialty), real estate brokers (by residential or commercial), owners of business aircraft (by type and size). The majority of these are compiled lists, although some response lists are available. The number of selects varies widely.

Leads are prospects who have indicated a minimum level of interest by some type of response, usually sending or calling for additional information. *Qualified leads* represent the next stage—leads that have been contacted and meet pre-determined standards of relevancy and immediacy.

Goldburg and Emerick[2] identify the main lead qualification issues as:

Desire
Need
Authority
Money

This DNAM model is similar to the AIDA model discussed in Chapter 9, but it emphasizes the importance of decision-making authority and ability to commit funds in the purchase decision process in business markets. Contact with the lead—either by telephone or in person—is the best way to obtain qualifying information.

Some business marketers call these qualified leads referrals because they should immediately be referred to a person who can proceed to close the sale. Because this term generates confusion by suggesting third-party referrals, we prefer to use 'qualified lead,' though the importance of immediate action should not be forgotten.

The center of the bull's-eye is, of course, the customer. Creating a customer is not the end of a process, however; it is really only the beginning. Later in this chapter we will return to the importance of viewing the customer as a prospect for additional sales.

The need for an inquiry-management system that screens and verifies the quality of leads is emphasized by Posner and Walcek.[3] Their summary data show that for every 100 raw inquiries:

- 3 will purchase the advertised product within 3 months.
- 20 have a legitimate need, authority, and intention to buy within 12 months.

[2] Bernie Goldburg and Tracy Emerick, *Business to Business Direct Marketing* (Hampton, NH: Direct Marketing Publishers, 1987), p. 100.

[3] Gerald Posner and Emil J. Walcek, "Implement Lead Follow-up System for More Business-Marketing Sales," *Marketing News*, October 25, 1985, p. 22.

- 37 are gathering information to support a future purchase decision.
- 40 are collecting information or are simply curious.

An effective system quickly identifies the 23 most likely leads and refers them for personal contact. It maintains contact with the 37 longer-term prospects, but expends little or no effort on the 40 information seekers.

Lead Generation

There are many ways to generate leads—direct mail, telephone prospecting, print, broadcast, and trade shows as well as letters, specialty mailing pieces, ads, bingo cards, request forms, even fish bowls into which people drop their business cards! The medium used and the offer extended will determine both the quantity and quality of leads generated.

A recent study of lead-generation practices[4] indicated that direct mail is the most frequently used medium in all the product categories studied except for industrial services, which uses chiefly the telephone. The study also found that most firms with active lead-generation programs employ a variety of media.

When the intent is to generate a large volume of leads, trade shows and bingo cards are usually quite effective. However, many of the leads they generate turn out to be of poor quality because little effort is required of the respondent. Other media can be used in ways that generate greater or lesser numbers of leads.

It is easy to assume that the more leads you generate, the better off you are. Not so! Too many leads can be just as bad as too few, for when the volume is too great, the leads cannot be followed up effectively and you are simply wasting money.

Beyond choosing media effectively, there are a number of things a marketer can do to affect the quantity of leads. These actions were discussed in Chapter 3 as offer hardeners and softeners. Making it harder to reply—by not enclosing an envelope, not using prepaid postage on the enclosed envelope, not including a response device, using a non–toll-free number, mentioning the price, making it clear that a salesperson will call—will cut down the quantity of leads. Presumably the leads which are obtained when lead hardeners are used are of higher quality because respondents have been required to exert more effort.

How many leads should a program produce? Obviously, there's no one correct answer to that question. Management must consider the issue in planning the program and establish both quantity and quality objectives. The trade-off between the two is well stated by a representative of a large business services company:

> We see a dilemma. We want to improve both the quality and quantity of leads. To improve quality, we use targeted mailing lists or appeal more pointedly to the

[4] Jill Okun, "Lead Generation Media Usage in Business-to-Business," *Direct Marketing*, October 1987, p. 142-211.

decision-maker. To improve quantity, we use more aggressive programs. But that's the Catch 22. A major effort to improve quantity reduces quality, and most efforts to improve quality sharply reduce quantity.[5]

Lead Qualification

Whether your program is designed to produce high quantity or high quality, leads will still need to be qualified. There are a number of ways to qualify respondents, but telephone contact is by far the most common. It takes two forms: outbound calling in response to inquiries received by mail and questioning of callers who are requesting information.

The questioning need not be lengthy or complex. It should be a reasonably straightforward attempt to obtain the DNAM information described earlier in this chapter. A machine tool manufacturer used the following questions to qualify inquiries concerning one of its product lines:[6]

1. Does your firm do some type of surface grinding?
2. Do you intend to purchase some type of surface grinding equipment?
3. When do you expect to buy this equipment?
4. Are you a decision-maker in this selection purchase? If not, who is?
5. Has a budget been appropriated for this purchase?

Based on answers to these questions, the company used a simple quantitative scoring system to group the inquiries into five categories:

A—decision maker; intends to purchase within the next 9 months
B—decision maker; intends to purchase within the next 9 to 18 months
C—either not decision maker or unsure of purchase intent or purchase timing
D—not a prospect for this type of equipment
E—has already purchased

Categories A and B were immediately referred to field sales reps, all of whom had received thorough briefings on the new sales lead program, complete with specially designed promotional material. Lead categories A, B, and C were all sent packets of literature and entered into the firm's database.

Notice that the "hottest" category includes all decision makers who expect to purchase within the next 9 months, implying a fairly long purchase cycle. The specific time criterion will differ according to the nature of the product, but the concept remains the same. Leads that need immediate attention from the field sales force are usually referred by means of a prospect or sales lead card (see Figure 14.3).

[5] Quoted in Al Paul Lefton, Jr., "The Lucky Seven: How to Roll Leads into Sales," *Business Marketing*, August 1987, p. 88.

[6] Richard Manville, "Qualification Is the Key Step," *Business Marketing*, February 1987, pp. 77-92. Reprinted with permission from *Business Marketing*, February 1987. © 1987 Crain Communications, Inc.

HOT LEAD

FOLLOW-UP IMMEDIATELY!

Shown below is a **HOT SALES LEAD** produced from our advertising and publicity efforts. Product information has been sent to the prospective customer who has responded with the card shown below.

Please follow up this sales lead immediately. Complete bottom of form and return to the above address.

RETURN COMPLETED FORM TO:

SALES REPRESENTATIVE: ____________

DATE PROCESSED: ____________

We recently sent you information...

A few weeks ago, we sent you information about our Validator Coordinate Measuring Systems. To help us continue to provide the best possible service, would you please take a moment to answer the following questions:

1. **Did you receive our Validator literature?** ☒ Yes ☐ No
2. **Is the label below correct?** If not, please enter correct information here:
3. **Would you like a no-obligation demonstration of a Validator Coordinate Measuring Machine in your area?** ☒ Yes ☐ No

003-101242-102687-0075-000412
0050-0075

John Sample
Vice President Sales
ABC Computer Corp.
PO Box 123
Anywhere, USA 00000

4. **Would you like one of our representatives to contact you?** ☒ Yes ☐ No
5. **Is there any additional Validator information you would like to receive?** Prices
6. **Should we send copies of our Validator Systems literature to someone else in your plant?**
   Name ____________ Title ____________
   Name ____________ Title ____________
7. **What is your application?** Multiple - will discuss
8. **Is your Coordinate Measuring Machine requirement:**
   ☐ Immediate ☒ 1-3 months ☐ 3-6 months ☐ 6-12 months ☐ longer
9. **Approximate number of employees in your plant:**
   ☐ 1-19 ☐ 20-49 ☐ 50-99 ☒ 100-249 ☐ 250-499 ☐ 500-999 ☐ over 1000

Thank You.

Coordinate Measuring Systems, Precision Park, North Kingstown, RI 02852, Phone 401-886-2000, Telex 92-7771

DATE CONTACTED: ____________ ☐ IN PERSON ☐ BY PHONE

LEAD QUALITY: ☐ EXCELLENT ☐ GOOD ☐ FAIR ☐ POOR

PURCHASE POSSIBILITY: ☐ IMMEDIATE ☐ 3 MONTHS ☐ 6 MONTHS ☐ LONGER ☐ SOLD ☐ NONE

KEEP ON MAIL LIST: ☐ YES ☐ NO

END PRODUCT OR APPLICATION: ____________

OTHER INTERESTS: ____________

FOLLOW UP DATE: ____________

COMMENTS: ____________

Salesperson: ____________

Date: ____________

PROSPECT PRODUCTION

Identification of Qualified Sales Prospects

FIGURE 14.3 ***Sales Lead Referral Card***

Source: © 1987 Inquiry Management Institute

The machine tool manufacturer's program paid off. Because the company made sure its sales reps were committed, the lead follow-up rate went from 18 to 78 percent—a 433 percent increase! It costs this firm between $400 and $500 per field sales call, even if that call only qualifies a prospect. In contrast, the outside telephone service the company employed can qualify a lead for $9 to $12—a savings of around 4,000 percent!

There were two more measurable benefits from this program. First, the firm is saving from $4 to $6 on each category D and E inquirer to whom it does not mail a fulfillment package. Second, by analyzing the origin of its qualified leads, the firm is able to make the most effective allocation of its advertising dollars. In fact, this firm no longer uses cost per lead:

$$\frac{\text{Number of leads obtained}}{\text{Cost of promotional activity}}$$

to measure the effectiveness of its lead-generation activities. Instead it uses *cost per qualified lead*—a much more meaningful measure.

The Fulfillment Package[7]

Whether used before or after qualification by personal contact, the fulfillment package plays a key role in the process of direct marketing by fulfilling the responder's request for information. There are several things to keep in mind when developing the package.

First and foremost, it must be sent and received in a timely fashion, before the requester loses interest. Both the lead-processing system and the postage will affect the timeliness. The lead must be handled quickly, whether qualification is done before or after the package is sent, and transmitted to the fulfillment operation. Manual systems can accomplish this, but automated systems are becoming quite common. The objective should be to mail the fulfillment package no later than 48 hours after receipt of the request for information. First-class postage will speed delivery, but it is obviously expensive. The weight of the package, the value of the product being promoted, and the perceived quality of the lead are all factors to be taken into account when deciding between first- and third-class postage.

Second, the package should have an outer envelope that clearly identifies it as information that has been requested. This is essential to separate the fulfillment package from all the unsolicited mailings that cross the businessperson's desk each day. Beyond that, there is no need for elaborate graphics—a simple business envelope will suffice.

Third, the package should contain a qualification ("bounce-back") card. The card should ask whether the information is sufficient and often contains a toll-free customer service number. If the card is being used for even initial qualification purposes, the NDAM data described in the section on lead qualification should also be obtained.

[7] The material in this section is based on Gerald Posner, "Inquiry Handling—An Effective Systems Application," DMA Release 570.1, January 1984.

Lead Tracking and Follow-Up

It sounds very simple—mail a fulfillment package and then refer the leads to sales or dealer reps and they will follow through. After all, the reps' objective is to make as many sales as possible!

Unfortunately, tracking and follow-up are more complicated than that. One reason has already been mentioned—there are so many leads that it is impossible to contact them all. Another reason is that many sales reps have been burned by referrals of unqualified leads in the past and now perceive all leads to be of poor quality. Still other reps may consider the program an intrusion into the management of their sales territory. Others perceive it as a subtle form of managerial control to be resisted. And finally, sales reps despise the paperwork that lead tracking usually requires and will go to almost any length to avoid it.

How should the direct marketer approach this resistance? It isn't easy, because the sales reps are not under the direct marketer's control. The direct marketer must work through sales management and can only motivate, not issue directives.

Still, a number of things can be done to obtain the cooperation of the field sales force. First, allow them genuine input into the design of the program; then keep them informed of its progress. Nothing is more damaging to the program than for customers and prospects to be aware of it when the sales reps are not. Win the trust of the reps by demonstrating that the program will help them do their job better. Don't let it be perceived as interference or a threat to their management of their territory—or, even worse, to their commissions. In the process, be sure that the direct marketing department is seen as the resource for genuinely qualified sales leads. Finally, see that the salesperson receives full recognition for having made the sale. The cooperation of the sales force in following up on leads is essential; without that cooperation the best-designed lead-generation program will be a failure in the end. The direct marketer should not rely on sales force cooperation alone, however. The leads should be carefully tracked to ensure that they are being followed.

Overall, an effective lead-tracking or inquiry-management system must do the following:[8]

- Respond quickly and completely to an inquirer's request.
- Qualify hot prospects for immediate transmittal to the field sales force.
- Reduce selling costs by focusing sales efforts on the most promising prospects.
- Report on and contribute to ad effectiveness.
- Monitor the progress of the sales effort.
- Relate the sale to the initial inquiry.
- Serve as a marketing, research and planning tool by providing information on prospects, products, applications, and new-product ideas.

[8] Posner and Walcek, "Inquiry Handling," p. 22.

The information produced by a lead-tracking system can be aggregated in many ways to provide useful management summary reports. These reports can be developed by prospect, product, sales rep, sales territory, source of lead, and many other categories. Figure 14.4 shows three examples of the many reports that can be produced directly from the information provided by this type of marketing program.

Lead-Generation Programs for Dealer Networks

The problems of motivation and control are magnified when the leads are produced for and referred to a dealer network instead of the firm's own field sales force. The dealers, as independent businesspeople, must be handled with special care.

A carrot-and-stick approach usually works best. The carrot is genuinely qualified, fresh leads. The stick is some type of requirement of dealers that will give them a stake in the success of the program. This assumes that most lead-generation programs are initiated by the manufacturer; programs initiated and carried out by dealers themselves are comparatively rare.

There are a number of issues that must be resolved about the manner in which the program will be implemented.[9]

Who plans and coordinates the program?

Generally, programs are more effective if controlled by the manufacturer. According to the dealer development manager of Fawn Vendors, Inc., a Des Moines, Iowa, vending machine company, "If you let the dealer organization do it themselves, they don't get it done." Fawn found that dealers were not mailing out the lead generation packages which they supplied. When they switched to a centralized program, they also developed segmented mailings—an industrial segment, an office segment, and a so-called "street" segment which includes small businesses such as gas stations. Dealers can specify segments and geographical areas. They pay the total cost of each mailing and must participate in each of the three annual mailings. The firm, with the help of its direct response agency, controls the program and analyzes the results.

Decentralized programs can work, however. The Office Systems Division of 3M develops mailings from the sales support literature used by its field sales force. It supplies these mailing pieces, costing anywhere from $.75 to $4, to its dealers and they do the rest. 3M charges the dealers for the mailing pieces, so they have a strong incentive to use them. 3M also provides telephone marketing training for dealers' support personnel. Dealers seem to like the program, but results are hard to measure because much of the activity is carried out by individual dealer reps.

[9] Diane Lynne Kastiel, "Make Your Dealer a Direct Marketing Co-Star, *Business Marketing*, August 1986, pp. 60-63.

NAME OF REPORT: QUALIFICATION ANALYSIS (Q1)
FOR PERIOD: 01/01/87 THRU 03/31/87
DESCRIPTION: BY SALESPERSON

	FOR PERIOD SHOWN ABOVE											LAST 12 MONTHS					
			INQUIRIES RATED AS					RATINGS BASED ON						RATINGS BASED ON			
	TOTAL INQ	TOTAL RATED	SOLD	HOT	QUAL	FAIR	OTHER	INIT QUAL	REP QUAL	BBC QUAL	REP &BBC	TOTAL INQ	TOTAL RATED	INIT QUAL	REP QUAL	BBC QUAL	REP &BBC
JOHN SAMPLE	21	18	0	7	4	0	7	0	12	6	0	86	67	8	20	32	7
SALESMAN	10%	86%	0%	39%	22%	0%	39%	0%	67%	33%	0%	7%	78%	12%	30%	48%	10%
ELLEN WEST	26	21	2	5	8	5	1	5	7	4	5	127	91	16	41	24	10
SALESMAN	12%	81%	9%	24%	38%	24%	5%	24%	33%	19%	24%	11%	72%	18%	45%	26%	11%
ROBERT SMITH	28	22	0	8	8	4	2	2	8	8	4	130	99	6	45	32	16
SALESMAN	13%	79%	0%	36%	36%	18%	10%	9%	36%	36%	18%	11%	76%	6%	45%	32%	16%

NAME OF REPORT: UPDATED STATUS LISTING
FOR PERIOD: OCT. 1, 1986 - DEC. 31, 1987
DESCRIPTION: H,Q,F,S, FOR ALL SALES REPS

JOHN SAMPLE
ABC CORPORATION
MAPLE AVENUE
ANYWHERE, USA 00000
ID# 12345 TEL:

**CURRENT STATUS: BY SALESREP/HOT /871208
INITIAL STATUS: NEW INQUIRY - HOT
RESPONSE TYPE: WHITE MAIL
DATE PROCESSED: JUL 02 87
S.I.C.:
MARKET: COMMERCIAL
SALESREP: 10
SPECIAL INFO: # OF EMPLOYEES: 85

BY PROSPECT/QUALIFIED /871101
PRODUCT: MADISON
PACKAGE: MADISON
MEDIA: DIRECT MAIL
SOURCE OF LEAD: DESIGN NEWS
ISSUE DATE: FEB 02 87
OF LABS: 3

ELLEN WEST
DEF CORPORATION
MAIN ST.
ANYWHERE, USA 00000
ID# 67891 TEL:

**CURRENT STATUS: BY SALESREP/SOLD /870125
INITIAL STATUS: NEW INQUIRY
RESPONSE TYPE: BOUND IN POSTCARD
DATE PROCESSED: NOV 10 86
S.I.C.:
MARKET: BEVERAGE
SALESREP: 20
SPECIAL INFO: # OF EMPLOYEES: 900

BY PROSPECT/NO RESPONSE
PRODUCT: DIFFERENT
PACKAGE: DIFFERENT
MEDIA: SPACE ADVERTISING
SOURCE OF LEAD: SALES & MARKETING MGMT
ISSUE DATE: SEPT. 86
OF LABS: 6

ROBERT SMITH
GHI CORPORATION
ROUTE 1A
ANYWHERE, USA 00000
ID# 98765 TEL:

**CURRENT STATUS: BY SALESREP/NO RESPONSE
INITIAL STATUS: NEW INQUIRY
RESPONSE TYPE: READER SERVICE
DATE PROCESSED: JAN 02 87
S.I.C.:
MARKET: BEVERAGE

BY PROSPECT/QUALIFIED /870115
PRODUCT: HANNAH DESK
PACKAGE: HANNAH DESK
MEDIA: SPACE ADVERTISING
SOURCE OF LEAD: BUSINESS MARKETING
ISSUE DATE: DEC 86

NAME OF REPORT: COST PER QUALIFIED INQUIRY SUMMARY
FOR PERIOD: THRU 10/01/87
DESCRIPTION: BY MEDIA TYPE

MEDIA	COST	TOTAL $ INQ	COST PER INQ	$ QUAL INQ	COST QUAL INQ	HOT	QUAL	FAIR	SALE
						*** LEVEL OF QUALIFICATION ***			
SPACE ADVERTISING	42,000	1,909	22.00	343	122.44	89	112	91	51
DIRECT MAIL	55,000	1,280	42.96	458	120.08	44	198	168	48
EDITORIAL	5,000	243	20.57	81	61.72	18	34	20	9
PUBLICITY	5,000	107	46.27	44	113.63	11	19	7	7
TRADE SHOW	46,000	578	79.58	127	362.20	21	50	14	42

FIGURE 14.4 ***Lead Tracking Results***

Source: Epsilon Data Management, Inc., Burlington, MA 01803

Who bears the cost of the program?

If dealers bear at least some of the cost of the program, they are more likely to take an active role in it.

Gelco is a national leasing firm with local dealerships throughout the country. Gelco's direct response agency in Minneapolis develops the mailing packages. Dealers place their own names on the packages and choose the target areas for the mailings. They also pay 100% of the cost of the mailings, which typically run about $.43 apiece.

The dealers' names on the mailings give them a "local" feel, important in a service enterprise. At the same time, the content of the mailing makes it clear that a large national service network exists. Having invested in the program, dealers have a serious stake in making it work.

Who processes and tracks the leads?

While most dealers would like to see leads come directly to them, manufacturers who have tried both agree that centralized control is more effective. Just as is true with a field sales force, if leads are not tracked, they may not be followed up in a timely fashion or may not be followed up at all. Gelco, the leasing firm, has inquiries go back to its agency. The agency sends the fulfillment package within 36 hours and sends a lead report to the dealer. Regular status reports, indicating whether the prospect was contacted and whether a sale is pending or has been made, should be required of dealers.

Even if dealers pay the total cost of the mailings, dealer- directed lead-generation programs are not free of cost to the manufacturer. Basic costs of program planning and administration will be incurred. In addition, sell packages—direct-mail packages sent to dealers generally costing between $2,000 and $10,000—are extremely important in obtaining dealer cooperation. ComputerLand, the largest computer retailer in the United States, was able to obtain the participation of 200 of its 600 dealers in 1985, the first year of its lead-generation program for dealers. They paid less attention to selling dealers on the program in its second year and saw participation drop to 115 dealers. For the second year, ComputerLand omitted a training videotape and did not announce the program at its annual dealer conference. According to ComputerLand's direct marketing manager, "The difference was a decline in the company's 'merchandising efforts' to its dealers. . .Next year, we'll be putting more effort into merchandising, like we did last year."[10]

Despite the cost and effort of these lead-generation programs for dealer networks, manufacturers who have used them consider them an important aspect of their marketing/dealer relations programs. Yet, according to one direct-response agency executive, "less than 50 percent [of companies that could benefit from such

[10]Kastiel, p. 63.

programs] do it."[11] You can expect to see more lead- generation programs for dealer networks as word of their effectiveness spreads.

Shared lead-generation programs between manufacturers and dealer networks have many similarities to vertical cooperative advertising campaigns. In co-op advertising there is potential for joint benefits to be realized that exceed the total of benefits accruing to the manufacturer and the dealer network acting separately and independently.[12] There have been no quantitative analyses of the specific optimal parameters of shared lead-generation programs, but the direct marketer should be aware of the synergy possible as a result of these programs.

The Business-to-Business Marketing Database

As you read the section on lead generation and tracking programs, you may have realized what a rich source of information they provide for the direct marketer's database. Because lead generation represents a major effort in terms of customer acquisition, it may seem that it is also a logical starting point for database development for a firm that does not currently have one. Logical as that may seem, there are good reasons for the business marketer to take another approach to database development, and that is to incorporate the results of lead generation and other direct marketing programs into the base of existing customers.

Marketers who carefully analyze their sales patterns on an account-by-account basis are well aware of the 80/20 rule which states that 20 percent of customers generate 80 percent of sales. These percentages, of course, are not absolute; a firm may be startled to find that fifteen percent of its customers generate ninety-five percent of its business. However, the basic principle—that a small percentage of customers account for a large percentage of business—holds true across firms and industries, in consumer markets as well as in business markets. Thus the business marketer should carefully analyze its customer base, discover who its best customers are, and design programs based on this knowledge. Figure 14.5 contains information obtained from the analysis of a file containing 66,000 customers who generated $2 million in revenues. Only 3 percent (1,768) of the customers produce 20 percent of the revenues of this business. While the average revenue per customer is just over $30.30 (2,000,000 / 66,000), the average revenue per customer for the top 3 percent is $226.24 (2,000,000 x .2 = 400,000 / 1,768).

Two marketing approaches are suggested by this simple analysis. One is that the firm can clearly afford to expend more marketing effort on high-quality customers than on marginal ones. This type of analysis has led many firms to develop a telephone marketing program for marginal customers to keep sales costs down, while having the field sales force call on the more productive customers.

[11] Kastiel, p. 63.

[12] Paul D. Berger, "Vertical Cooperative Advertising Ventures, *Journal of Marketing Research*, August 1972, pp. 309-312.

FIGURE 14-5 ***Revenue from Customer Base by Percentile***

Number of Customers	*Cumulative Number of Customers*	*Percent of Revenue %*	*Average Revenue Per Customer $*
650.00	650.00	10.00	307.69
1118.00	1768.00	20.00	178.89
1196.00	2964.00	30.00	167.22
1996.00	4960.00	40.00	100.00
3206.00	8166.00	50.00	62.38
3799.00	11965.00	60.00	52.65
9713.00	21678.00	70.00	20.59
11268.00	32946.00	80.00	17.75
15519.00	48465.00	90.00	12.89
17535.00	66000.00	100.00	11.41

Source: Epsilon Data Management, Inc., Burlington, MA 01803.

Second, this analysis should cause marketing managers to ask which customers could be upgraded into high-performing ones. Upgrading can be done either by selling the customers a greater volume of the products they are currently buying or by cross-selling, that is, selling them other products from the existing line that they are not now buying. Targeting customers for this type of effort will take additional analysis: ascertaining the key characteristics of high-performing customers (in the way we discussed in Chapter 4) and then identifying other customers in lower-performing categories who possess the same characteristics.

When presented with this line of reasoning, business marketers (and some consumer marketers who deal directly with their customers) recognize that they have a wealth of information within their own firm that can make their marketing efforts more effective and efficient. Computerizing the information that currently exists in, for example, order files is often a monumental task, so many marketers are tempted to avoid it. But the value to be obtained from this information is very great, particularly since a company's current customers are almost invariably its best prospects.

There is a word of warning to be sounded even here, however. (These strategic insights were provided by Daniel D. Sherr of Claritas, Inc.) The contents of the database, well used, can determine the strategic marketing direction of the firm. Consequently, there is a danger in the approach just recommended, and that is that the marketing manager may prospect only for customers who have the same profile as current top-performing customers and fail to look for opportunities not represented in the current customer base. Strategic thinking, not blind following of past practices, is required. This reasoning should not be construed as a suggestion that the manager ignore the task of obtaining the greatest possible volume of sales from current customers; That is not only crucial, it is also the easier task. The more difficult task is to think strategically about the direction in which the business should be moving and then steer it in that direction.

Figure 14.6 is a graphic portrayal of sources of information for the business-to-business database and of various types of marketing programs that can be devised as a result of analysis of its information. A firm may be unable to utilize all these data sources or to implement all the types of programs. But the figure brings out a basic point: Each and every contact with a customer or a prospect provides valuable information for the database. The wise marketing manager studies the firm's marketing programs with the objective of capturing all available information. The manager then carefully analyzes the tactical and strategic needs of the firm and puts in place analyses that will guide the design and implementation of required marketing programs.

THE MEDIA OF BUSINESS-TO-BUSINESS DIRECT MARKETING

The media available to business marketers are exactly the same types of media available to marketers of consumer goods and services. However, the media weights (the amount of usage of each medium) may differ somewhat; for example, television is less likely to represent a major promotional expenditure for business marketers. Even more importantly, the way in which media are used may differ substantially.

Telephone

Telephone is the largest single business marketing medium, accounting for expenditures of $27,750,000,000 in 1984 according to *Business Marketing* magazine.[13] According to its study:

> Business-to-business sales today account for about 80 percent of all telemarketing revenues.... Much of that selling is performed by the more than 80,000 companies that have in-house telemarketing operations.
>
> A survey of telemarketing service bureaus, however, found that even their lines are tied up with business calls. Fifty six percent of the time, they are dialing for a business-to-business client.
>
> The rise of business-to-business telemarketing has been meteoric, to put it mildly. Expenditures have soared 144% in the last two years alone.
>
> But selling is only one of the many uses marketers have found for the telephone.

[13]"Here Is What Business-to-Business Marketers Spend Their Money on We Think, monograph, p. 6 *Business Marketing*, undated.

FIGURE 14.6 ***Sources and Uses of Database Information***

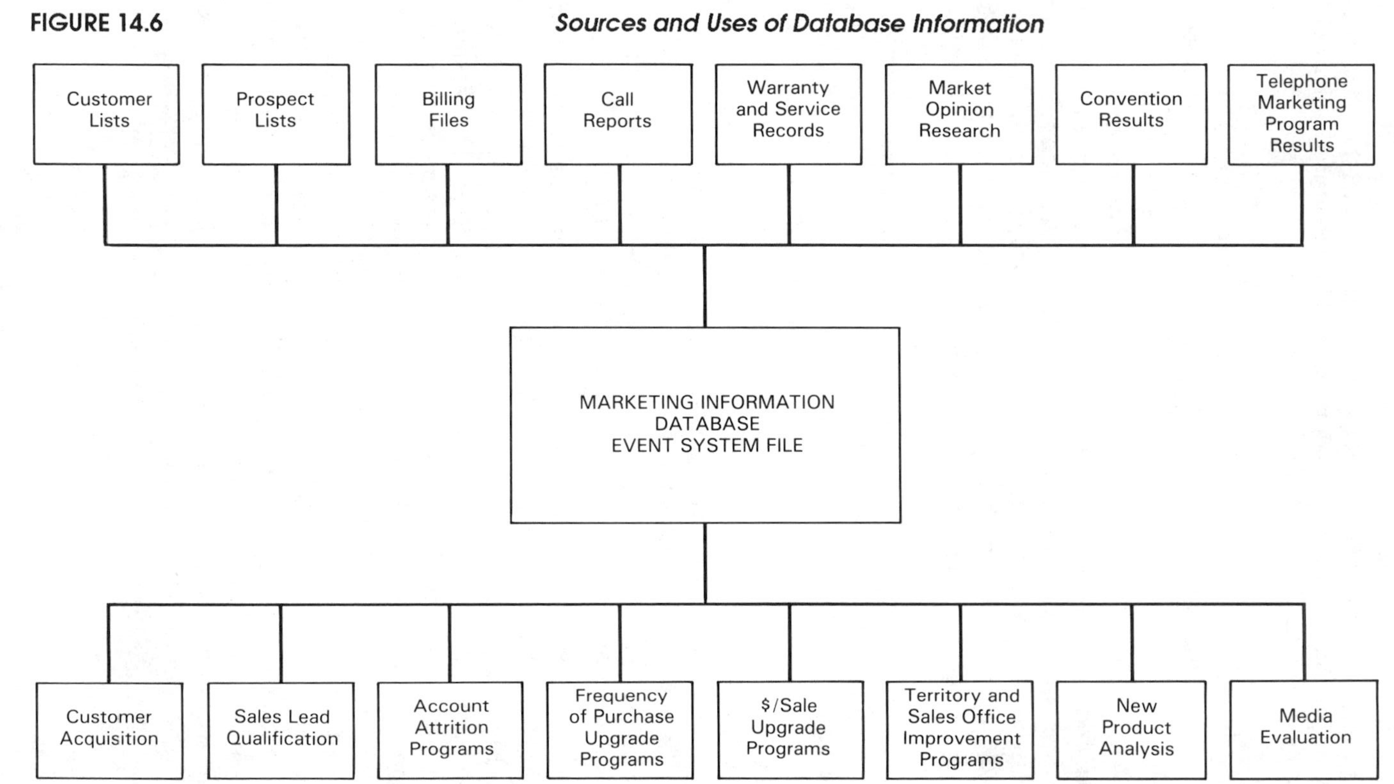

Source: Adapted from promotional material of Epsilon, Inc.

> A three-year-old study found that 63% have instituted lead- handling systems that depend on telephone prequalification. And 54 percent use the phone to conduct market research.[14]

Why is telephone marketing, both inbound and outbound, enjoying such explosive growth in business markets? The following reasons seem to be the most important.

Telemarketing allows personal contact with customers and prospects with optimum frequency at an affordable cost. Personal contact with customers and qualified prospects is desirable, often necessary, to close the sale for a business product or service. We have already mentioned that an average field sales call cost about $230 in 1985 and that multiple calls are often necessary to close a sale. A field salesperson ordinarily averages 3 or 4 calls per day; that's 600 to 800 sales calls per year.

In contrast, a telephone sales rep in a business-to-business setting can be expected to complete 35 to 45 calls per day (by "completed calls" we mean a call in which a decision maker was reached). The average telephone rep will close 2.5 sales per day at a cost per sale much lower than that of a single sales call.[15]

The relative economy of telephone selling allows customers to be contacted more frequently than would ordinarily be possible using field salespeople. If customer product usage is relatively predictable—as it is with many types of office supplies, for example—calls can be timed to coincide with reorder points. When usage is not so predictable, firms may offer a promotion of some type—a "monthly special," for example—to provide a reason for the call.

A wide variety of goods and services, covering a wide range of price points, can be sold over the telephone. In the early days of telephone marketing (maybe 10 years ago!), it was commonly assumed that only routine reorders or low-unit-value sales could be closed over the telephone. That assumption has been completely disproved over the past few years, as is suggested by the increasing value of the average telephone sale (see Figure 14.7). Two trends seem to be reflected in these figures. One is that an increasing number of items are ordered during a single telephone sales call, driving up the total value of the order. These multiple orders have been made possible by sophisticated databases that give telephone sales reps detailed information about customers'purchasing habits that can be used to upgrade the average order size.

The second trend reflected in these figures is the increasing rate of success in selling higher-priced items over the telephone. Telephone marketing is no longer limited to products priced at a few hundred dollars or less. Today, items costing

[14]Here Is What Business-to-Business Marketers Spend Their Money On, p. 7.

[15]Keith A. Stoeger, "Three, Two, One, Contact!", Direct Marketing, June 1987, pp. 114-115; "Business-to-Business Telephone Sales Should Hit $97 Billion this Year: Study," *DM News*, June 1, 1986, p. 4.

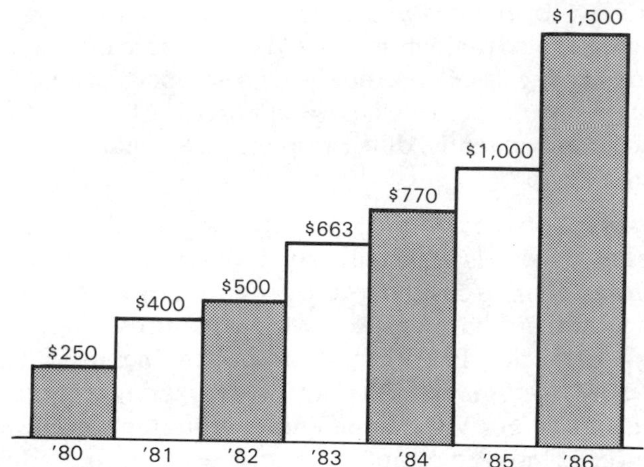

FIGURE 14.7 ***Value of the Average Telephone Sale***
Source: Business Marketing (Chicago, IL 60611).

several thousand dollars are routinely sold over the telephone, with no face-to-face contact between customer and sales rep.[16]

Telemarketing can, and usually should be, used in conjunction with other promotional media. Goldburg and Emerick have tested a variety of telephone/ direct-mail programs:

> We have tested the use of mail and phone separately and then tested mail followed by phone and the results were very different. The mail produced at 2% and the phone produced at 7.5%. You would therefore expect the combined results to be about 9.5%. The actual result of the combination of the two was almost 13%.
>
> We also tested to determine the best time to follow the mail with telemarketing. We began telemarketing about five days prior to the mail. The first scripted question asked was, "Do you recall seeing the information we sent you?" Even before the mail was dropped, about 30% of those asked indicated that they could recall receiving the mail. This may sound amusing, but some people will respond positively so as not to appear ignorant. After the mail was dropped, we continued to track the answer to this question. The favorable response peaked at almost 70% from day 11 after the mail was dropped and remained there through day 17. The response rate then began to drop. Within 30 days after the mail drop, the favorable response rate dropped to 40% and stayed there for the next 15 days. It ultimately went back to the 30% range.[17]

[16] See Stoeger, "Three, Two, One, Contact!", p. 114.
[17] Goldburg and Emerick, *Business to Business Direct Marketing,* p. 114.

Direct mail seems well suited to use in combination with aggressive outbound calling, although it is also frequently utilized to generate inbound calls. In addition, telephone marketing is often employed to support print advertising (here the calling is usually inbound) as well as to support direct-response radio for business products and, less frequently, direct-response television (again, most of the calling is inbound).

Telephone marketing can provide a cost-effective alternative to a field sales force for small businesses. This is especially true if the unit values of the small firm's products are low and/or its customers are geographically scattered.

Visualon, Inc., a Cleveland-based marketer of visual presentation products such as overhead transparencies, faced a not-unusual problem—its two major competitors, Xerox and 3M, were giants with immense marketing resources at their command. To compete effectively, Visualon offered discounted prices and a high level of customer service, including a complete line of presentation products, next-day delivery, and knowledgeable customer service reps handling incoming telephone calls. Still, the firm's small field salesforce could not produce a satisfactory volume of new business at an affordable cost, so the firm turned to outbound telephone marketing.

The outbound program tested by Visualon included a careful analysis of results by market segment. Schools, hospitals, and manufacturing firms with over 500 employees were found to be the best new business prospects. The analysis permitted the firm to specify which lists would be most useful in its business development effort.

Visualon's program also included revision of direct-mail efforts and more careful training of telephone representatives.[18]

Telemarketing is completely measurable. In Chapter 11 we discussed supervision of telephone marketing operations and examined typical reports that can be produced on demand or at standard times such as the end of each shift. This ability to monitor programs as closely as necessary provides much greater control and allows for the kind of useful testing described by Goldburg and Emerick.

One potential problem in using telephone marketing in conjunction with a field sales force is that the field salespeople see the telephone marketing operation as a serious threat, especially if they derive a large part of their compensation from commissions. Even though the telephone marketing operation may be concentrating on routine reorders and sales of lower-valued items, each telephone sale represents a potential commission lost to a field sales rep. While it is true that the telephone operation frees the field sales force to concentrate on the higher-valued, and therefore higher-commission, products, the sales reps may not accept this argument with much grace. They may argue that the program is making the easier sales and leaving them responsible for the more difficult ones.

[18]Richard L. Bencin, "Aggressive Telemarketing-Answer to Corporate Growth," *Direct Marketing*, September 1986, pp. 32-37.

There are several ways to handle this problem, all of which boil down to trying to prevent the field sales and telephone reps from competing with each other. Working out an effective approach will require the cooperation of sales management and direct marketing management to achieve mutual objectives.

The telephone reps can certainly be put on salary rather than on commission, but this won't go far to counter the field reps' objections. Some firms have found a territory bonus plan that includes both field and telephone reps to be a workable solution. If the territory sales quota is achieved, the entire group receives bonuses. If it is not, no one receives a bonus. This approach has the benefit of promoting teamwork rather than competition, but it is unappealing to some top-performing sales reps who prefer straight commission.

Although the problems associated with telephone marketing are significant, they are far outweighed by the benefits. Still, business-to-business telephone marketing has not achieved its full potential in at least two ways. First, there are many firms that could benefit from a telephone marketing program that do not yet have one. Second, there are many firms whose efforts, especially their initial ones, do not represent a competently organized, staffed, and supervised operation based on the principles we described in Chapter 11. This problem is especially acute for the business marketer who believes that a telephone service bureau cannot handle the detailed technical questions expected from customers and prospects and so begins an in-house operation with little or no experience. In this situation the astute business marketer will do everything possible to ensure that the telephone marketing operation reflects favorably on the firm and its products.

Direct Mail

According to the *Business Marketing* study cited earlier,[19] direct mail ranks second in expenditures by business marketers—$3.1 billion, or an average of 7.5 percent of company marketing budgets, in 1984. That represents sales of $31.62 billion, an increase of 11 percent over 1983. This sales figure appears to include direct-mail pieces and catalogs as well as other types of mailings.

Direct-Mail Packages. The standard direct-mail package described in Chapter 9 is also widely used in business-to-business direct mail. But extremely elaborate packages are used when the target audience and the product or service being promoted warrant it.

A good example is the package for Chase Manhattan Bank, N.A. of Europe, that is shown in Figure 14.8. Although Chase had successfully used direct mail in its retail operations for many years, this was a first for its wholesale side. It was aimed at potential customers for the bank's currency exchange services. Developed in France, the package was found to be so appealing that it was used

[19]"Here Is What Business-to-Business Marketers Spend Their Money on," p 6.

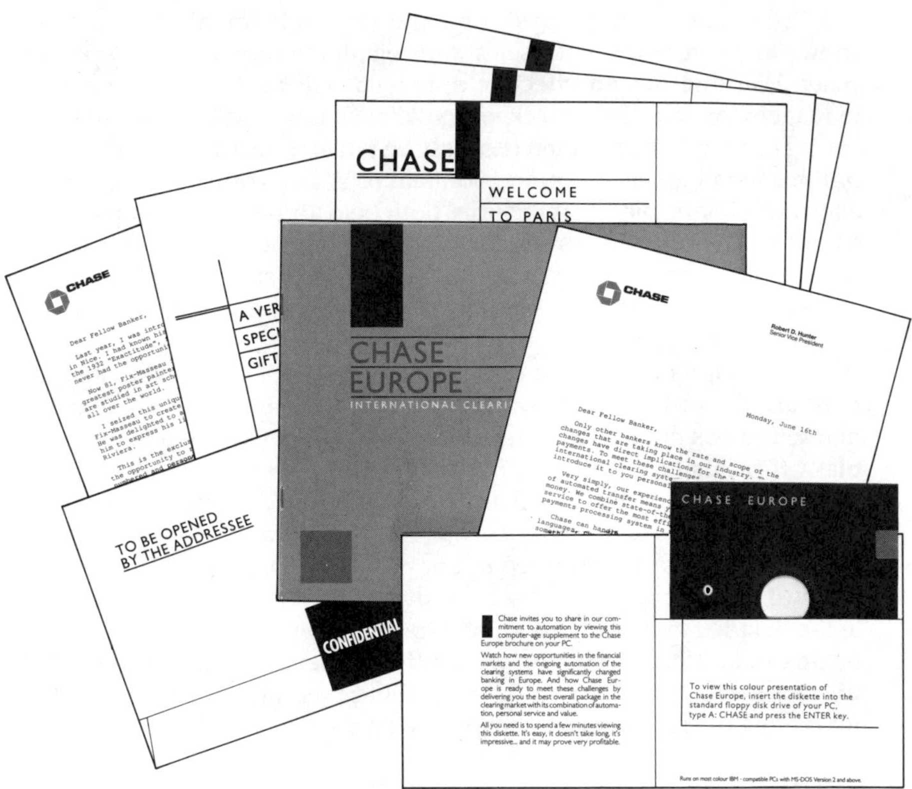

FIGURE 14.8 ***Multinational Lead Generation Package***

around the world, except in Africa and South America, where clearing services perform this specialized service.

A list of 3,500 bank presidents was developed for the program. Early in the week of the mail drop each president received a telex announcing that a special package would soon be delivered. The packages were timed to arrive at the end of that week.

The package contained a letter from a manager within the recipient's geographical area. An elaborate benefits-oriented brochure featured expressionistic artwork suggestive of Chase's corporate art collection and was designed to allow inserts inside the back cover describing services specific to that country. The enclosed floppy disk illustrated Chase's services. Finally, a hand-addressed sealed envelope marked "Confidential" contained an offer for a free limited edition lithograph by a noted French artist. When a lithograph was requested, it was personally delivered by a Chase representative, who used the opportunity to explain the bank's services in more detail.

At $50 each, the packages were expensive. However, bank management felt the expense was well justified by the 14 percent response rate.[20] Simple mailings may work well also, and at a much lower cost.

This example supports a widely held belief about business-to- business direct marketing: personalization is essential for getting communications by the gatekeeper to the ultimate decision maker. A recent study by Hennessey[21] looked at the issue differently. Instead of personalization versus no personalization, he tested two versions of personalization—name versus title only.

In a mailing to a rental list promoting a sales management newsletter, Hennessey found both a higher response rate and a higher average order size for the title-only mailings than for the ones using the recipient's name. He suggests that the high turn-over in management positions and the incompleteness of many business lists alluded to earlier in the chapter might be at least partially responsible for these unexpected results. This study certainly reinforces the importance of testing the tenets of direct marketing whenever possible.

Catalogs. It is not clear what portion of the $3.1 billion total business direct-mail expenditure is composed of catalogs, but they appear to make up an increasingly important component of business-to-business direct mail.

Business catalogs have been in existence for many years, of course. The older generation of catalogs tended to be merely listings for reference and ordering purposes. Even today, for commodity products like chemical reagents commonly used in laboratories, a simple listing with necessary technical information, such as the purity of the compound, and ordering information, such as quantity and price, is all you will usually find. Since these products cannot be differentiated in terms of physical product characteristics from one manufacturer to another, this type of marketing approach is deemed sufficient.

Specialty products, no matter what their price, are more likely to be promoted via a consumerlike catalog. These catalogs have high-quality glossy paper and make extensive use of color. Observation suggests that the trend is clearly toward more visually appealing catalogs in product categories from high tech all the way down to office supplies.

Inmac sells products ranging from diskettes to data- communications devices to the computer aftermarket by means of its catalog. The catalog is produced in French, German, and Swedish as well as in English and reaches more than half a million customers. According to one of the founders of Inmac, these are the four cornerstones of catalog success:

1. *Valid positioning.* The catalog must have a clearly defined mission that will produce a set of recognizable benefits to the businessperson. Inmac's business

[20]Claire Wilson, "Chase Mailer Chases New Business Accounts," *Advertising Age*, January 17, 1987, pp. S-4, S-5.

[21]Hubert D. Hennessey, "Comparing Personalized Name to Title-Only Labels in a Business Mailing," *Journal of Direct Marketing Research*, Spring-Fall 1987, pp. 99-102.

was founded on the realization that no one wants to take substantial time away from other activities to manage computer supplies.

2. *Targeted audience.* The catalog needs to provide a unique offer to a specific target market. Inmac started out to serve the needs of users of Digital Equipment, Data General, and Hewlett-Packard equipment.
3. *Disciplined product line.* Each item in the catalog must be submitted to profitability analysis and eliminated if its performance is unacceptable. Inmac has also observed that broadening the product offering too far—for example, including computer peripherals with computer supplies—does not work.
4. *Solid creative.* Presentation that both differentiates the product offering from that of competitors and makes the catalog clear and comprehensible is essential for a successful catalog. Achieving savings at the expense of effective presentation will be counterproductive.

These four cornerstones are just as appropriate for consumer catalogs as for business catalogs. As a matter of fact, the founders of Inmac patterned their first catalogs after the successful consumer catalog produced by Norm Thompson.[22]

Other Types of Mailing Pieces. Business marketers often use something less than a complete package, especially when the nature of the product does not warrant it or when they are exploring new markets or segments. Self-mailers are frequently employed by both manufacturers and distributors. They are particularly useful for updates of one kind or another—announcements of promotional activities or new product introductions, for example.

Card decks "are popular with neither marketers nor advertising agencies," according to an article by an agency executive[23] because they offer little opportunity for corporate or product positioning or creative execution. They do, however, pull large numbers of inquiries at a low cost. Careful tracking of responses can provide useful information for product positioning and media planning.

Newsletters. Newsletters are one good way of maintaining relationships with customers and prospects. They are relatively inexpensive and their soft-sell approach may make them especially well received.

The newsletter published by the industrial division of the Polaroid Corporation shown in Chapter 1 is a good example. In addition to articles about products and their applications, features on individual employees or customers can add human interest to the newsletter. This type of publication can portray the firm as an industry leader to its customers and/or its dealer network. If desired, a business reply card can be incorporated to allow readers to request additional information about the products and applications featured.

[22]Kenneth A. Eldred, "Three Not-So-Obvious Mistakes You Must Work Hard to Avoid," *Direct Marketing*, February 1986, pp. 70-72.

[23]Jim Morris, "Low-Cost Direct Mail Provides Ticket to High-Tech Sales," *Direct Marketing*, September 1986, p. 48-50.

Business and Trade Magazines

Not all of the money spent on advertising in business publications is direct response, although if you look in many business magazines you may get the impression that it is. There is a tremendous amount of business-to-business direct-response advertising. The majority of it is for sales lead generation. The advertising appears in both the general business press and many specialized trade publications that reach audiences that are sometimes quite small but extremely targeted. The ability of this type of magazine to reach a very selective audience can make the advertising very cost effective. Unfortunately, much space advertising in business publications suffers from a dismal sameness that is the despair of creative critics.

SUMMARY

Business-to-business direct-response promotions are growing at a rapid rate in all available media. Spurred by the high cost of field sales calls and the fragmentation of many markets, business marketers are incorporating direct marketing into their marketing programs at a rapid rate. Business-to-business direct marketing should continue to be a major growth industry for the foreseeable future.

DISCUSSION QUESTIONS

1. Why is business-to-business direct marketing growing so rapidly?
2. What are the major differences between consumer and business-to-business direct marketing? Similarities?
3. Why is a good lead generation and tracking system important to business marketers?
4. Explain the meaning and importance of qualifying a customer.
5. What is the 80/20 rule? How can it be useful to marketers?
6. Why should business marketers worry about lead-generation programs for their dealers?

SUGGESTED ADDITIONAL READINGS

1. Bernie Goldburg and Tracy Emerick, *Business-to-Business Direct Marketing* (Hampton, NH: Direct Marketing Publishers, 1987).
2. "Business-to-Business Advertising," *Advertising Age Special Report*, June 20, 1988, pp. S-1, S-26.

15

The Bottom Line of Direct Marketing—Profitability

INTRODUCTION

In any business the bottom line objective is *profit*. This is a word, however, that can have many different meanings and time horizons over which it is measured. Also, it is often a quantity which results from the optimization of other, intermediate criteria, these being quite different in various different activities. An example from general marketing is choosing advertising media to maximize *awareness*, then *recall*, and then the real bottom line: *response* (purchase), or *dollar profit from the purchase.*

Each area of direct marketing, from decisions to rent a list, mail offerings, qualify leads, etc., can be evaluated as if it is an auxiliary business of its own. An equivalent of a profit/loss statement can be generated to determine either whether to expand or reduce an activity, or more generally, what the optimal (profit maximizing) choice of level or decision should be.

Many of the specific decision-making frameworks for profit maximization have been discussed in the respective chapter on that subject (e.g., the decision making process with respect to mailing vs. not mailing a group of names, and how deep into a segmented list to mail, were addressed in Chapter 4). In this chapter we will consider some basic issues in general profitability analysis. First we talk about the revenue/contribution/profit side; then we address cost issues; finally, we discuss putting the two considerations together.

PROFIT AND CONTRIBUTION

Robert Kestnbaum lists four basic growth strategies to generate higher revenue/profits in the long run:[1]

1. Invest in new customer acquisition
2. Invest in new media for presenting offers
3. Add products or services to your line
4. Expand the number of times customers and prospects are contacted

Each of these strategies can be utilized to achieve specific financial goals:

1. Maximize sales
2. Maximize profit
3. Maximize profit as a percent of sales
4. Maximize return on investment (ROI)

Kestnbaum goes on to say that the latter goal is the most meaningful in the long run. One key to achieving this goal is to make certain that no components of revenue, contribution, or profit are overlooked in the process of evaluating this return.

Lifetime Value

A core element in determining contribution and profit is to assess the *lifetime value* of a customer. *Lifetime value* (let's say for a new customer) is defined as the net present value of all future contributions to overhead and profit. It depends on a variety of considerations. Richard Courtheoux[2] lists the following four factors as contributors to a customer's lifetime value:

1. Future forecasted revenues
2. Margin
3. Fulfillment cost expectations
4. Cost of capital

The most important use of this calculation of lifetime value is for decision making in the areas of customer reactivation and customer acquisition. Julian Simon[3] indicates how important this calculation is: "How much is it worth to you to get an additional customer? The calculation of the answer to this question is the most im-

[1]Robert Kestnbaum, "Growth Strategies for Direct Marketers," *Direct Marketing Association*, Release 110.2, January 1984.

[2]Richard Courtheoux, "The Practical Side of Database Theory: Everyday Applications," *Direct Marketing* (August-September, 1984).

[3]Julian Simon, *How to Start a Mail-Order Business*, 4th Ed. (New York: McGraw-Hill, 1987), p. 121.

portant calculation a mail-order merchant makes." Courtheoux proposes a conservative rule of thumb that one should invest no more than 40 percent of lifetime value in customer acquisition.

In the past, direct marketers would mistakenly consider only the initial profits from the current offering to represent the (potential) value of a customer. According to marketing theory, there are cases in which repeat business is not worth worrying about, and the current sale is the only real consideration. The usual example given is sales of encyclopedias. However, in direct marketing, repeat business is usually one, if not the, major consideration. Most magazine publishers would never attempt to acquire any customers if they didn't include repeat business in their calculations of customer (lifetime) value.

Looking at only the first sale is analogous to using "payback period" as the criterion for investment decision making; it is a conservative criterion, one with which the risk is minimal but for which the opportunity loss is potentially very high. After all, if one decides to incur an acquisition cost only when it is less than the expected profit on *the first sale,* one will virtually never lose money in the acquisition process. Yet, quite often the decision is made not to attempt to acquire a customer when the latter's expected profit greatly exceeds the acquisition cost.

Note that we continue to talk about *expected* or average value of a customer. This is because usually we cannot be sure of the degree to which a new customer will be profitable (or whether he or she *will* be profitable). Statistical analysis can address the issue of predicting "profitability," but it still will be a case of averaging, since two customers with exactly the same "profile" will not exhibit precisely the same purchase behavior.

Because of the need to go through an averaging process with respect to many of the parameters making up lifetime value, an amount of historical data is required. Diane Kastiel[4] notes that some formulas for lifetime value require at least two-and-a-half years of data on customers and promotions.

Just how does one figure out the (expected) lifetime value of a new customer? Suppose that we assume that the margin is the same for all products we offer. This allows us to focus on total dollar sales, multiplying by a constant to determine contribution/profit. (Actually, we can arrive at the same point by taking a weighted average of the margins of the various products we offer, where the weights are sales dollars for each different margin. Let us ignore the difficulty of projecting margins into the future). Still, how do we figure out the (lifetime) total dollars of a customer? Actually, we figure out an expected value of this quantity. We do this by using the average amount of total dollars per customer for each sale, multiplied by the number of repeats. We use our historical data base to estimate the repeat rate. For example, in the case of a magazine subscription, we can simply assume that a constant percent of customers drop out each year and/or mailing. In a more general direct marketing situation, we may take a random sample of 200 customers and compute the average repeats per customer:

[4]Diane Kastiel, "Customers' 'lifetime value' Helps Steer Direct Marketing," *Business Marketing* (February 1987), p. 34.

Number of Repeats	*Number of Customers*	*Repeats × Customers*
0	115	0
1	45	45
2	21	42
3	9	27
4	7	28
5	3	15
>5	0	0
	Total: 200	157

The average number of purchases per customer then equals:

$$n = (200 + 157)/200 = 357/200 = 1.785.$$

If it is possible that some of these customers will at some future time make another purchase, then the above value could be a slight underestimate. By the way, Simon reminds us that we should take into consideration, and view as equivalent to repeats, any purchases which come from names of friends that are provided by the customer.

To find the lifetime value of a customer one must project into the future. Courtheoux, in a release of the Direct Marketing Association, provides a methodology for projecting future customer performance.[5] It involves seven steps:

1. Segment customers into a manageable, but distinguishable number of cells, based on recency, frequency, or monetary considerations. Typically, there should be from 25 to 100 cells.
2. Choose a time period for tracking results. Six months is typical.
3. Estimate the contribution to overhead and profit by tracking all revenues and costs associated with all customers.
4. Describe movement of customers across cells.
5. Project the movement of 1000 new customers over a number of periods into the future. Proceed enough into the future so that only a small amount of contribution is potentially remaining.
6. Use the number of customers projected for each cell (from step 5) and the financial performances for each cell (from step 3) to calculate contribution for each period.
7. Apply the cost of capital to and find the net present value of the contribution stream.

Courtheoux's paper gives some examples of using this procedure, and then goes on to incorporate the results into a variety of different decision making situations.

[5]Richard Courtheoux, "Estimating and Applying Customer Name Values," *Direct Marketing Association*, Release 620.4 (January 1986).

Performance Measures for Profit and Contribution

In addition to the concept of lifetime value, there are many traditional ratios and other performance measures used to evaluate a direct marketing campaign. Here are some of the more common performance measures:

$$\%R = \text{Percent Response} = \text{Numbers of Orders/Total Quantity Mailed}$$

$$OPM = \text{Orders per Thousand} = \%R \times 10$$

$$CPM = \text{Cost per Thousand} = \text{Total Cost/(Quantity mailed/1000)}$$

$$CPO = \text{Cost per Order} = CPM/OPM$$

$$ROP(\%) = \text{Return on Promotion} = [(\text{Contribution} - CPO)/CPO] \times 100$$

$$C\$R = \text{Cost per Dollar Raised (in a fund raising campaign)}$$

$$DAP = \text{Total Dollar Amount Purchased}$$

Before leaving this section, it must be said that some contributions are qualitative (not able to be quantified). This appears to be especially true in the telemarketing arena. An example of this is reported by Stone and Wyman[6] in which an evaluation is being made of the economics of a GE Answer Center, a free telephone service provided by General Electric that allows customers to call with questions or comments about products, either before or after a purchase is made. When Powell Taylor, manager of the Center, was asked, "How do you know that the millions of dollars spent in building and maintaining the Center have been worth it?" he answered, "Surveys have shown that 95% of surveyed dealers regard the GE Center to be a 'super idea.' " Obviously, there is no simple way either to quantify the value of the Center nor to have done a quantitative analysis prior to its being built. An a priori questionnaire about the Center's impact on purchase behavior would have been speculative; likewise, an after the fact questionnaire to evaluate the incremental effect of having the Center would also be of dubious value.

COSTS

In the most general sense, contribution and profit are both defined as the difference between revenue and cost. Yet, the terms are not interchangeable; though each is not defined consistently between one discipline and another, nor often within the same discipline, the best and simplest working definition for us to use in the direct marketing environment is that *contribution is revenue less variable costs,* while *profit is contribution less fixed costs.* (*Fixed costs* are those costs not affected by the amount of revenue

[6]Bob Stone and John Wyman, "The Mathematics of Telemarketing," *Direct Marketing* (December 1986), pp. 46–52.

[or, number of orders or number of items]; typical examples are rent and management salaries. Variable costs are costs directly associated with items sold and are usually per order [e.g., paperwork], per item [e.g., wholesale cost of the item, postage], per dollar of sale [e.g., taxes]). Some fixed costs are called *overhead.*

One subtlety that needs mentioning is that some variable costs must be expressed as an expectation. For example, costs for bad debts (nonpayment) are incurred for some orders but not others. Yet, it is clear that if you had, for example, twenty weeks in which the number of orders were 200 per week, and another twenty weeks in which the number of orders were 400 per week, the average number of bad debts per week for the latter twenty would likely be about twice the average for the former twenty. In other words, we cannot predict the cost for bad debt for a given order, but the total dollar cost surely varies, *on average,* with the number of orders. Bad debt cost, expressed as an expectation per order, is thus a variable cost. Costs for lost shipments, damaged items, and returned items are other variable costs that are expressed as an expectation.

There are two key issues involved in correctly using costs in various decision-making situations. One is to make sure that all relevant costs of servicing the customer are included. The other is to include or exclude the fixed costs as relevant costs, as appropriate.

The list of all relevant costs for a direct marketing activity depends on the particular activity. In fact, there are different levels or hierarchies of costs. Consider, for example, a catalog operation. Higher level of costs might be the traditional costs including the cost of the products sold, cost of shipping and handling, cost of bad debts, costs associated with returns, and so forth. One of the costs could be "cost of producing the catalog." At a level deeper in the hierarchy, we could list the detailed costs of producing the catalog: paper, printing, envelope, photography, consultants to produce copy, and others. At yet a deeper level in the hierarchy, we could detail the costs of the photography (say, into a time component, a black-and-white versus color component, etc.) for purposes of making specific decisions about the catalog.

The most frequent error made in terms of wrong use of costs involves including the fixed cost in a decision situation in which it is unwarranted. (The converse-not including the fixed cost in a situation in which it is appropriate to include it-does not often occur). This is a problem that pervades not only direct marketing decision making, but one that affects many areas of decision making. The entire notion of a "sunk cost" needs understanding. Once a (nonrefundable) cost is incurred, it is no longer a consideration in deciding upon strategies for the future. Simon[7] says this well by noting the adage, "Sunk costs are sunk."

A typical example in which an inferior decision may be reached by misuse of the role of fixed costs is the decision how deep into a segmented list to mail. Consider the following greatly simplified description of the parameters involved. Suppose we have rented a list to which we apply our proprietary segmentation al-

[7]Julian Simon, *How to Start and Operate a Mail-Order Business,* 4th ed. (New York: McGraw-Hill, 1987), p. 136.

gorithm. Anticipated response rates for the segmented list, ranked ordered by decile, are as follows:

Decile	*Response Rate*	*Decile*	*Response Rate*
0–10	.050	40–50	.027
10–20	.042	50–60	.024
20–30	.036	60–70	.021
30–40	.031	70+	.019

There is only one product offered for $50 per unit, there are no multiple orders, and no consideration of repeat business is relevant. The product cost is $22 per unit, and all other variable costs (front end and back end, including those which are expectations) total $10 per order. Thus, contribution to overhead is $18 per order. Finally, suppose that the in-the-mail cost per thousand pieces mailed is $400.

The correct analysis of how deep into this list to mail is reasonably straightforward, given this simplified problem. In essence, we should mail any decile (we assume there is no way to segment more finely than by decile) for which the response rate, *P*, satisfies

$$18 \times (1000 \times P) > 400$$

$$\text{or} \qquad P > .022.$$

This result corresponds to mailing the top 60 percent of the rank-ordered list; the 50–60 decile response rate is .024 (higher than .022), while the 60–70 decile response rate is .021 (lower than .022).

Now suppose that the decision as to how deeply into the list to mail is made by somebody who mistakenly includes some fixed (sunk) costs in the calculation. More specifically, suppose that the list rental cost is included, $63 per thousand with some selects. After all, one might reason, this is a cost that is associated directly to a name and is thus a variable cost. Of course, this reasoning stops short of realizing that the cost is a sunk cost and does not vary with the number of names we choose to mail from the list. Suppose further that an additional $36 per thousand is allocated to the cost to cover such traditional fixed costs as rent, management salaries, copy design expenses, etc. The cost figure that would now mistakenly replace the $400 value of the earlier analysis is

$$\$400 + \$63 + \$36 = \$499.$$

With this value as input, we should mail any decile for which the response rate, *P*, satisfies

$$18 \times (1000 \times P) > 499$$

$$\text{or} \qquad P > .028.$$

This result corresponds to mailing (only) the top 40 percent of the rank-ordered list. The 30–40 decile response rate is .031 (higher than .028), while the 40–50 decile response rate is .027 (lower than .028).

Note that the mistaken use of the fixed costs has resulted in mailing the top 40 percent of the rank-ordered list rather than the top 60 percent. Consider the amount of dollar contribution lost, assuming the rented list consists of one million names. By not mailing the 40–50 decile, with response rate .027, and by not mailing the 50–60 decile with response rate .024, the number of orders foregone

$$\begin{aligned} &= (100{,}000 \times .027) + (100{,}000 \times .024) \\ &= 2700 + 2400 \\ &= 5100. \end{aligned}$$

This represents a lost contribution (excluding the in-the-mail cost)

$$\begin{aligned} &= \$18 \times 5100 \\ &= \$91{,}800, \end{aligned}$$

with an in-the-mail cost

$$\begin{aligned} &= 200{,}000 \times (\$400/1000) \\ &= \$80{,}000, \end{aligned}$$

resulting in a lost net contribution

$$\begin{aligned} &= \$91{,}800 - \$80{,}000 \\ &= \$11{,}800. \end{aligned}$$

In percentage terms, this $11,800 represents a decrease in net contribution of 8.6 percent, from $138,000 (if the top 60 percent of the rank-ordered list is mailed) down to $126,200 (mailing only the top 40 percent). In terms of the number of orders, the decrease is far more dramatic-28.3 percent, from 21,000 orders (if the top 60 percent of the rank-ordered list is mailed) down to 15,900 orders (mailing only the top 40 percent).

This example can be extended to illustrate the use of the list rental cost and the use of the other fixed costs (e.g., management salaries) in making a strategic decision. This is somewhat hypothetical, but suppose that you were allowed to segment the above list and note your segmentation results, before having to commit yourself to renting the (entire) list. The decision whether to rent the list would use the above optimal net contribution (excluding the rental cost) of $138,000 (by mailing the top 60 percent of the rank-ordered list), and subtract from it the total rental cost of $63,000 (a million names at $63 per thousand), giving a value of $75,000. Since *this amount* (not the $138,000) is greater than zero, the correct decision is to rent the list. Now suppose (very hypothetically) that the entire business of this firm consists of ten lists, each identical to the one being discussed. At $75,000 contribution per list, this results in a total contribution of $750,000. The decision whether this company should (let's say continue) in business would be decided by taking the $750,000 and subtracting from it the total of all fixed costs such as management salaries, utility bills, etc.; only continue in business if this difference (not the $750,000) is greater than zero.

If all relevant costs are included in a cost calculation and fixed costs are not included when inappropriate, the analysis has an excellent chance of leading to the truly best decision. However, the actual implementation of decision analysis still requires adapting to the particulars of the decision situation. Decisions about how deeply into a list to mail involve very different costs and benefits than decisions as to the amount of products to include in a catalog or decisions having to do with other areas of direct marketing. In telemarketing a big area of decision making is that of lead qualification, where cost per lead can be interpreted only with a number of accompanying parameters. As stated by Peg Kuman when addressing the decision of examining alternatives for lead qualification, "The Cost Per Lead (CPL) is not an absolute....the marketer is not necessarily justified in selecting the cheaper methodology. The analysis must also include the ratio of leads qualified to the original universe; the ratio of projected sales to qualified leads; and the average value of a new customer (what is popularly referred to as Average Order Size [AOS])[8]

PROFIT AND LOSS STATEMENTS

The most useful way to represent the results of many direct-marketing activities is through a profit and loss statement. This is a detailed table of sales/revenue and costs. It can also be used as the springboard for a spreadsheet analysis when different sets of assumptions are to be tested or explored. To construct a profit and loss statement one must be able to identify all relevent revenue sources and cost sources. The statement is really just an organized format for assessing the prospects and/or results of an operation (promotion, decision whether to rent a list, change of design for a warehouse, etc.). Indeed, producing a profit and loss statement is a general business tool which greatly transcends the field of direct marketing.

There is no one design for a profit and loss statement. It depends on the operation being detailed. In fact, for the same operation two different people working independently would not arrive at the same exact design. Table 15.1 lists the categories of units/dollars of a detailed profit and loss statement worksheet for a direct mail offer of one item used by Passavant in a Direct Mail Marketing Association release:[9]

[8]Peg Kuman, "The Profitability of Lead Qualification in Telemarketing," *Direct Marketing* (August 1986), p. 110.

[9]Pierre A. Passavant, "Direct Marketing Economics and Budgeting," *Direct Mail Marketing Association Manual Release 600.1* (October 1979), p. 1.

Table 15.1 Detailed Profit and Loss Statement

1. Cash selling price
2. Deferred payment price
3. + Shipping/handling

4. Avge gross order value
5. – Returns (10%)

6. Avg. net sale
7. Cost of goods per sale
8. per unrefurbished return
9. Order receipt & processing
10. Business reply postage
11. Order process & customer set up
12. Credit card fee—3.5%
13. Credit check
14. Installment billing
15. Customer service
16. Shipping & handling
17. Returns postage
18. Returns handling

18A. Returns refurbishing

19. Bad debt (3%)
20. Collection effort
21. Premium
22. Promotion (CPO)
23. Overhead

24. Total expense
25. Profit before taxes
26. Profit % to net sales

Passavant goes on to say that this table is very detailed and cumbersome if the objective is a quick review, and proposes the categories of Table 15.2 as a summarization:

Table 15.2 Summary Profit and Loss Statement

1. Selling price
2. + Shipping/handling
3. Gross order value
4. – Returns (10%)
5. Net sales

6. Cost of goods
7. Order process, shipping, return costs, customer service, credit fee
8. Bad debt (3%)
9. Premium
10. Promotion (CPO)
11. Overhead

12. Total expenses

13. Profit
14. Profit % to net sales

Table 15.3 presents the categories of a profit and loss statement put forth by David Shepard for a similar operation:

Table 15.3 Profit and Loss Statement for a Single-Shot Promotion*

1. Gross sales
2. Shipping and handling
3. Total revenue
4. Returns

5. Net sales

6. Cost of sales
7. Product
8. Net shipments
9. Nonreusable units
10. Order processing
11. Reply postage
12. Setup costs
13. Credit card costs
14. Bad check expense
15. Shipping and handling
16. Return processing
17. Postage
18. Handling
19. Refurbishing

*David Shepard, "Economics of Direct Marketing," in *The Direct Marketing Handbook*, ed. Edward Nash (New York: McGraw-Hill, 1984), p. 67.

20. Premium

21. Total cost of sales

22. Operating gross margin
23. Promotion expense

24. Contribution to overhead and profit
25. Overhead allocation

26. Profit

The two detailed profit and loss statements (Tables 15.1 and 15.3) are quite similar, but far from identical. It is natural that they are very much alike, for, after all, they are both modeling the same operation. However, the fact that both statements include the same number of entries (twenty-six) is more a coincidence than something to be clearly anticipated; in fact, Table 15.1 really has twenty-seven entries, one being 18A. The two statements differ in a variety of ways. The precise names of the categories are not the same; for example, "Gross sales" on one statement has "Avge gross order value" as its counterpart on the other statement. The order of the entries differ; "Gross sales" is the first entry on one statement, while its "Avge gross order value" counterpart is the fourth entry on the other statement. The hierarchy of the categories is not identical on the two statements. On one statement all costs (product costs, order processing costs, etc.) are listed as a subset of "Cost of sales," while on the other statement each major cost category is in equal status to sales, with subset costs within each category on a lower level. Finally, each statement covers categories that the other does not; in Table 15.3 there is no listing of profit as a percent of sales, category 26 in Table 15.1; on the two statements the position of overhead differs, so that in Table 15.1 the first profit/contribution measure (entry 25) has overhead already subtracted out, while in Table 15.3 contribution (i.e., before overhead is subtracted out) is separately listed in entry 24, as well as profit being listed in entry 26.

The key point is that the profit and loss statement is for the user's benefit and should be designed to include not only all relevant revenues and costs but also any other costs or combination of entries (e.g., "Profit % to net sales" in Table 15.1, which is just the ratio of entry 25 to entry 6) that the user believes would be enlightening.

As a final point, the reader should be reminded that the profit and loss statements presented were for situations in which no long term profit considerations were present. For decision making in situations in which customers have lasting value (e.g., if you are examining the profitability of a particular rented list, and you get to enter on your house list all names who respond), the lifetime value of a customer, and not the net contribution or profit from sales on just this one promotion, could be the relevant consideration for the optimal decision to be reached.

SUMMARY

Profitability analysis is a matter of considering the appropriate revenues and costs and determining the resulting contribution or profit. This analysis can be performed on a promotion-by-promotion (list by list, item by item, etc.) basis or by grouping elements together. For example, we might evaluate three rented lists as a tandem. For catalogs, it is often considered more strategically useful to group items by merchandise category, and construct an aggregated profit & loss statement. Also, it may be beneficial in general to aggregate profit and loss statements by profit/cost center.

Profitability analysis potentially is both prospective and retrospective. As noted by John Groman,[10] combined with the modern computer, profitability analysis can enable you to make outdated the famous quote attributed to Lord Leverhume, "I know I'm totally wasting half of my advertising expenditure but no one can tell me which half."

The role of costs in changing direct-marketing decision making is well illustrated by one of the latest innovations in the field of direct marketing—faxing direct "mail" ads through fax (facsimile) machines. As reported in Newsweek,[11] response rates from sending ads through the fax machine has reached as high as 6.75 percent. A Ft. Lauderdale restauranteur faxed his menu to offices in the area; a Texas florist plans to fax ads to various corporations. The key to this entrepreneurship is cost. First of all, the cost of the machines is dropping dramatically, and in 1988 it is projected that about 800,000 fax machines will be installed. Second, the *customer pays a significant portion of the transmission cost;* the sender pays any expenses associated with the telephone call, but the receiver (customer) pays for the thermal-coated paper. Compiled lists for fax machines are busily being prepared for rental. Marcus Smith, editor of *Postal World,* suggests that soon there will be unlisted fax numbers!

DISCUSSION QUESTIONS

1. Give three examples in which it would be clearly incorrect to include fixed costs in a decision analysis. Give three in which it would clearly be correct to do so.
2. Explain the role of cost of capital in determining the lifetime value of a customer. If the cost of capital were larger, would the lifetime value of a customer rise or fall?
3. Give three examples in which the contribution of a direct marketing activity is qualitative.

[10]John E. Groman, "Database Driven Marketing," *MDM Review,* 1 (April 1986), p. 2.

[11]Andrew Murr and John Schwartz, "A Mounting Pile of 'Junk' Fax," *Newsweek,* July 25, 1988, p. 54.

4. For the numerical example discussed in the Cost section of the chapter, why is it that mailing 33 percent fewer names than was optimal resulted not in a 33 percent drop in contribution but in only an 8.6 percent drop?
5. Discuss the similarities and differences between a profit and loss statement and the traditional "income statement."

SUGGESTED ADDITIONAL READING

1. Dick Berry, "The Art of Forecasting Direct Mail Response Rates," *Direct Marketing* (April 1986), pp. 42–57.
2. John F. Tighe, "Getting to the Silent Majority," *Advertising Age* (June 30, 1986), p. 36.
3. James S. Gould, "Pencils in Packages: How Good Are They?" *Direct Marketing* (October 1986), pp. 72–78.
4. Herbert Katzenstein and William Sachs, *Direct Marketing* (Columbus, Ohio: Merrill Publishing Co., 1986), pp. 155–176.

16

A Look Ahead

At the Massachusetts Institute of Technology is an institute called the Media Lab that is dedicated to the continuing development of electronic communications technologies. The vision of the future that pervades the work of the Media Lab is one of man-machine interaction that extends the capabilities of both to an extent that would be impossible for either alone. Among other outcomes, this would lead to totally personalized communications utilizing electronic communication technology. According to Media Lab director Nicholas Negroponte, "Monologues will become conversations; the impersonal will become personal; the traditional 'mass media' will essentially disappear."[1]

Among the specific technologies being investigated at the lab are:

- A personalized newspaper that selects items of interest to the particular individual from on-line databases and holds them for retrieval on a touch-sensitive screen at the individual's discretion.
- Interactive television that allows the viewer to select what programming will be viewed during which time period regardless of when it has been broadcast.
- Speech recognition capability for personal computers that permits not only conversation between the computer and the user but also recognition by the computer of numerous other individuals who regularly interact with the user.
- Feature-length movies on compact discs that permit the audience to interact with the show.

[1]Stewart Brand, *The Media Lab: Inventing the Future at MIT*, (New York: Viking Penguin, 1987), p. 5.

- Computed holograms that allow the projection of three dimensional images in space so that they can be examined from all angles.
- Simulated environments that capture all the sensory elements of the actual environment.

To the extent that some or all of these technologies are applied over the next few decades, they will revolutionize human communications and will have a tremendous impact on all types of advertising. This kind of futuristic technology opens many exciting vistas. However, before we become too excited about future prospects, two words of warning are in order.

First, the speed at which any technology will evolve is unpredictable. We have seen a tremendous acceleration in the rate of technological development in recent years, but some major breakthroughs still must occur before some of the technologies listed can become commercial realities.

Second, some technologies are available for many years before they achieve widespread adoption among the consuming public. There are a variety of reasons for this slow diffusion of technology. Later in the chapter we will examine videotex, which exemplifies the long lag between technological availability and widespread adoption.

Even though widespread adoption of the electronic technologies being explored at Media Lab may not be just around the corner, they are intriguing possibilities for future innovation in direct marketing.

THE ELECTRONIC TECHNOLOGIES

A number of electronic communications technologies are currently available to the direct marketer. These vary greatly in their current penetration of the market and in the accuracy with which their future impact can be estimated.

Cable Television

Cable television is so widely available that it hardly seems to qualify as a new technology. It has been estimated that 70 percent of all U.S. households had access to cable by the end of 1987.[2] However, in areas with access, not all households subscribe to cable TV. A penetration rate of 35 to 50 percent is not uncommon, so that approximately 48 percent of all U.S. households were receiving cable in 1987.[3] Since well over 90 percent of all U.S. households have one or more television sets, there is a clear opportunity for cable to increase its penetration.

[2]Wayne Walley, "Industry Pushing Its New Image to the Public," *Advertising Age*, March 30, 1987, p. S-1.

[3]Walley, "Industry Pushing Its New Image," p. S-1.

Cable television offers a number of important opportunities to direct marketers. One has already been mentioned—the availability of per-inquiry advertising, especially on newer networks that have not yet obtained a strong advertiser base.

A broader issue, however, is the increasingly specialized target markets reached by cable. CNN (news), ESPN (sports), HBO and Showtime (feature-length movies), MTV (music videos), and the Disney Channel (family entertainment) are just a few of the services available. Each appeals to an identifiable consumer group of interest to both direct and general marketers.

For example, Lands' End, whose catalog includes classic active-wear designs, first experimented with TV advertising in the summer of 1987 with a spot on a rugby game telecast on ESPN. This was a natural because Lands' End designed and made the rugby shirt for one of the teams competing in the game. The ads produced both sales and catalog requests. Without divulging specific numbers, a company spokesman indicated that the experiment was successful enough that Lands' End would be receptive to similar opportunities.[4]

Cable television, of course, delivers the home shopping programs that have aroused so much interest in consumers, marketers, and the financial community during the past few years.

Televised Shopping Programs

By 1988, an estimated 56 million households were being reached by home shopping programs, up from only 3 million in 1985 when Home Shopping Network was introduced. Anticipated sales in 1988 were $2.55 billion, a 45 percent increase over 1987.[5]

Although initially a vehicle for the sale of merchandise of uncertain quality at discount prices, the home shopping channels have broadened their merchandise offerings and provided entertainment-oriented programming environments in order to increase audience involvement and interaction. Game-show formats and celebrity presenters are used on some channels. Promotional techniques that have been successful include prizes and special offers, contests, and discount coupons.

A study by Jones Intercable in California quoted in *Marketing News* found that 6 percent of cable TV shoppers purchase from the home shopping services. Of those purchasers, 64 percent purchase once a month or more, 66 percent watch more than one hour per week and 71 percent make purchases of $20 or more.[6] Another survey of the home shopping market found that almost 73 percent of the purchasers were women, 53 percent of whom were between the ages of 25 and 44

[4]Dan Abramson and Linda Lynton, "Fear of Shopping," *DM News/Catalog Business*, October 1, 1987, p. 29.

[5]Joanne Cleaver, "Consumers at Home with Shopping," *Advertising Age*, January 18, 1988, p. S-16.

[6]Joe Agnew, "Home Shopping: TV's Hit of the Season," *Marketing News*, March 13, 1987, pp. 1, 20.

and 60 percent of whom had at least some college education. Their annual household income averaged $40,500; they made six purchases per year and spent $179. It was found that 52 percent watched the shows in the hope of finding bargains, but almost 24 percent watched for the entertainment value.[7]

This is no arena for the proverbial kitchen-table start-up direct marketing business. One executive indicates that a 24-hour home shopping service needs to reach between 2 and 3 million homes in order to have a market of sufficient size. Production costs run at least 15 percent of gross sales. Merchandise return rates average between 7 and 8 percent, and when puffery is used to sell products, can go up to 40 to 45 percent. Operating and telephone costs amount to an additional 10 to 15 percent of sales.[8]

The demographics of the home television shopper are so similar to those of catalog customers that a blurring between the two types of businesses is inevitable. As of late 1987, all three of the largest home shopping networks were using either catalogs or direct mail as another way to reach their customer base. And more catalog firms are beginning to experiment with television as a shopping medium.

The J. C. Penney Company's Teleaction service may be an indicator of things to come. Customers will receive this service over cable TV and will be able to flip from one item of merchandise to another using a touch-tone telephone. Unlike other television shopping services, the viewer will be able to control the type and sequence of items presented. Note, however, that this type of system—generically referred to as *teletex*—is not interactive; communication is one-way only. This service will feature the products of a large number of retailers, and viewers will be able to place their orders by pressing other telephone buttons.

The exact shape this industry will take is uncertain. However, its success to date certainly suggests that there is a potential for electronic shopping. In the words of one industry observer:

> We're in the middle of a major shift in consumer habits, but a few things seem clear. One is that consumers are accepting it as a credible way of retailing....They are making inroads into traditional retailing....because [they are] treating people well.[9]

Videocassette and Videodisc

As videocassette recorders have become commonplace in the U.S. household, marketers have begun to experiment with videocassettes as a sales tool. Royal Silk was one of the first major catalogers to develop a videocassette. Promoted in its first catalog of 1987, the video sold for $5.95. It ran 35 minutes and had three sections, beginning with a fast-paced fashion display, moving on to a section describ-

[7]Sydney P. Freedberg, "Home-Shopping Shakeout Forces Survivors to Find Fresh Approach," *The Wall Street Journal*, November 4, 1987, p. 39.

[8]"Catalogers: Look Out for the Plight of the 90's," *Direct Marketing*, July 1987, pp. 120, 127.

[9]Agnew, "Home Shopping," p. 20.

ing the care of silk garments, and concluding with a sales presentation. The video was shot on location in Hawaii and cost between $40,000 and $50,000—less than the average 60-second television commercial. By late in the year it had sold about 4,500 copies and was generating average orders somewhat higher than the norm for the paper catalog.[10]

Fashions, which look better in motion and which can be presented in glamorous settings, seem a natural for videos. Videos also appeal to other marketers of upscale consumer goods. Both Commodore Business Machines and Apple Computer have tried them for their personal computers. Apple's tape is a soft-sell educational approach aimed at the first-time computer buyer, advertised in magazines for $3.95. Commodore's tape, which is more sales oriented, features the visual display capabilities of its Amiga 500 computer. It is so effective in putting the computer through its paces that Commodore expects it to be an important sales aid for its retail distributors.[11]

Other business marketers are beginning to view videos as a useful component of their marketing program. Complex products such as insurance or computers are prime candidates for videos because of the medium's ability to use visuals to demonstrate or convey a complex message. Business-to-business videos are shorter than consumer videos (5 to 10 minutes) and are most likely to be effective if used as one aspect of a marketing program. The usual sequence is to mail the videos to a prospect who has already been qualified and then follow-up either through a field salesperson or a telephone rep.[12]

Even when they do not make an explicit sales presentation, videos may play a useful role. A manufacturer of industrial ladders developed an 18-minute video dealing with safety on the production floor. It was offered by both direct mail and print, and persons who responded were qualified by telephone. Qualified prospects received the video to use at corporate safety meetings. Follow-up included both direct mail and telephone. This multi-media program was successful in opening numerous new accounts with major companies.[13]

Videodisc technology has caught on much more slowly with the general public, although it has been used for several years by retailers with extensive product lines. Sears, for example, has experimented with the videodisc because it has random access capability—that is, it allows viewers to go directly to the portion of the presentation that interests them. Though this is a very attractive attribute, the fact that few laser disc players are available has been a serious drawback. Now that compact disc with video (CDV) is on the horizon, this type of technology may find useful applications. It could then join the videocassette, according to an executive of Royal Silk, as "a new medium where [direct

[10]Jon Boorstein, "Talking Catalogs," *DM News/Catalog Business*, October 1, 1987, p. 32.

[11]Cleveland Horton, "Commodore, Apple Offer Video Promos," *Advertising Age*, November 23, 1987, p. 54.

[12]Judith Graham, "Selling Through Video Wins Proponents," *Advertising Age*, January 18, 1988, pp. S-2, S-6.

[13]Richard L. Bencin, "Telefocus Marketing," *Direct Marketing*, December 1987, p. 35.

marketers] can generate new names, generate new markets and....stand out among other competitors."[14]

Facsimile Transmission

Facsimile equipment (or *fax* as it is better known) transmits written and graphic communications between two fax machines over telephone lines. This equipment became commonplace in business a few years ago, but was rarely seen as a potential direct-response medium before a recent campaign by AT&T on behalf of the fax equipment it markets and the international fax service it provides.

Direct-mail pieces urged business executives to respond by fax if they wished further information about AT&T's equipment or services. Executives who responded received promotional material that same day, also via fax. The campaign was supported by print and television advertising and by special promotional material prepared for the AT&T sales force.[15]

While fax technology itself may not be appropriate for many direct-response programs, this example does suggest the creative possibilities inherent in the new technologies.

Electronic Data Transmission and Retrieval

Computer hackers have been fans of electronic bulletin boards ever since the first modem was invented. In their early years electronic bulletin boards primarily carried communications between computer users. As such, they quickly became a useful medium for individuals to sell or trade computer-related items. Only in recent years have they come to be regarded as a direct marketing medium with commercial potential.

Advertising Age estimates that there were over 2,000 computer bulletin board systems (known to aficionados as *BSSes*) in the United States in 1987. Typically, they offer a menu of services, including electronic mail/mailboxes, local news and event listings, and several categories of retail advertising such as automobile, employment, and restaurant sections. Users—who are predominantly male, young, and upscale—seem quite willing to purchase from these advertisers.[16]

Since increasing amounts of data are being transmitted directly from one business to another electronically, this technology is also likely to provide interesting promotional opportunities for business marketers. The Sheraton Corporation has taken advantage of this potential with a sweepstakes promotion aimed at travel agents in the United States and countries throughout Western Europe.

[14]Janice Steinberg, "Retailers Page Through Videolog Possibilities," *Advertising Age*, January 18, 1988.

[15]Alison Fahey, "AT&T Campaign Offers the Facts of Fax," *Advertising Age*, March 14, 1988, p. 46.

[16]Len Strazewski, "Computer Bulletin: More Consumer Advertisers on Home Networking Systems," *Advertising Age*, December 14, 1987, p. 82; R.C. Morse, "Videotex Systems for Lead Generation and Direct Sales," DMA Release 1500.3, July 1985.

Computerized reservation services were one of the first large-scale applications of electronic data transmission systems, so travel agents have long been accustomed to them as part of their daily work lives. Sheraton and its agency, HBM/Creamer Direct, decided to take advantage of this mode of communication in a campaign to increase the number of bookings made by travel agents at Sheraton properties worldwide.

The sweepstakes format was chosen because travel agents already receive steep discounts and/or free airline travel and lodging as employment benefits. What they need most in order to take advantage of the travel opportunities is cash—hence the sweepstakes with cash prizes.

The program was first implemented in the United States and its success there led to its subsequent roll-out in a number of Western European countries. The program was announced to travel agents by a direct-mail piece (see Figure 16.1) that contained an explanatory letter, a brochure with contest details, a starter entry card that required no reservation, and materials for other agents in the office. The program was supported by print ads in trade publications (Figure 16.2) and an 800 number through which agents could request additional information.

Details of the program were varied slightly from country to country to conform to local laws, an extremely important consideration in any sweepstakes promotion. Basically, though, each time the agent booked a reservation at a Sheraton Hotel via the computerized reservation system, he or she could request a form (actually, a postage-paid return postcard) on which to record the reservation information. The return cards were handled by fulfillment houses that generated the entries for the sweepstakes drawings, fulfilled inquiries about the program, and assisted in tracking and compiling management reports.

Prizes were $50,000 first prize and five $1,000 second prizes for a 13-week contest in the United States. In Europe a $1,000 weekly prize was awarded in each country, with a $5,000 prize in each country at the conclusion of the program. These were significant enough prizes to generate enthusiasm about the program. In both Europe and the United States the names of weekly contest winners were posted on the electronic mail facility of the computerized reservation system to keep the level of interest and enthusiasm high throughout the campaign.

As more and more people and companies encounter electronic data transmission in their regular daily activities, direct marketers will discover how to make both the home and office CRT another important medium of promotion.

Videotex

Videotex is the electronic communication technology that has most excited the direct marketing community for the past few years. It offers great potential but, in the United States at least, that potential is far from realization.

Videotex has been described as

> an interactive medium that can deliver text and other visual information directly to consumers.... The user interacts with the system via a handheld keypad,

FIGURE 16.1 *The Sheraton Travel Agency Sweepstakes Mail Package*

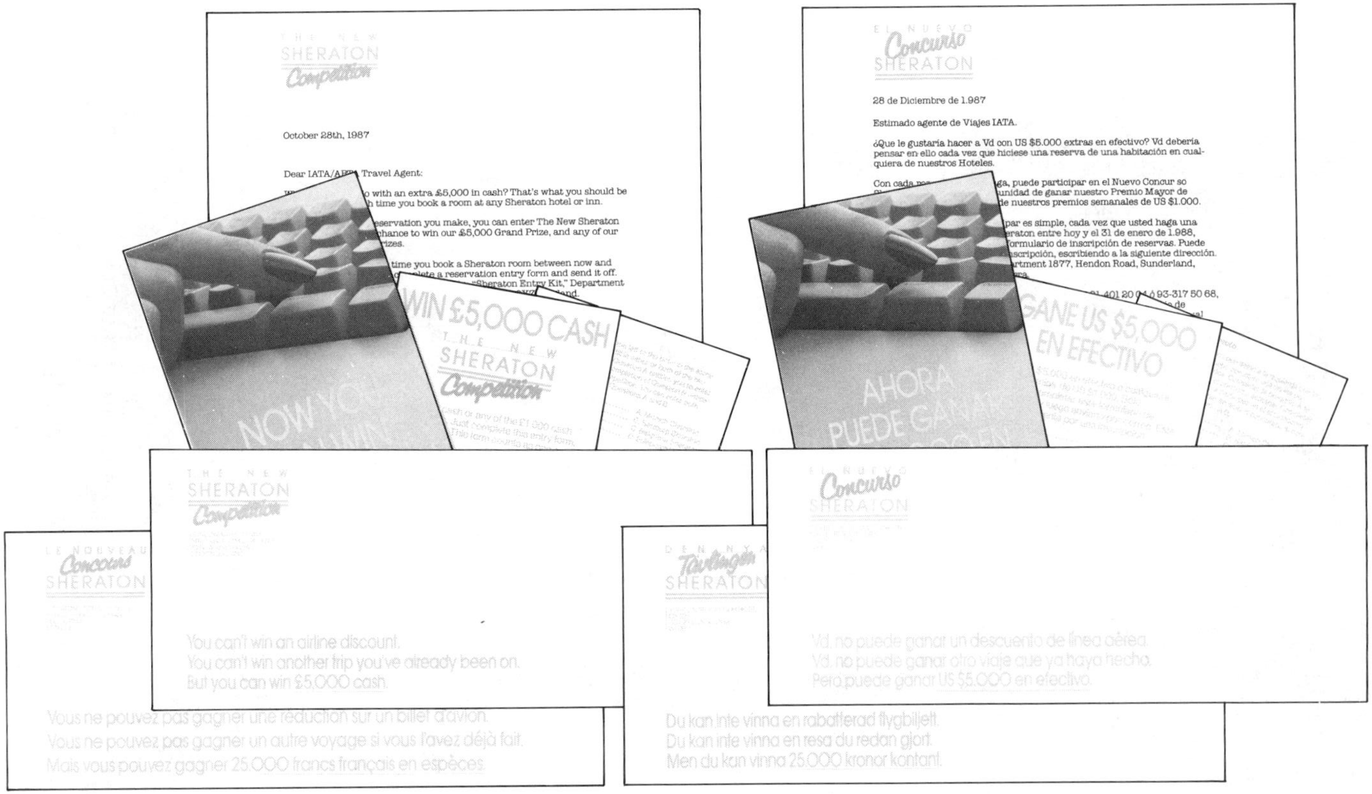

THE NEW SHERATON Competition
October 28th, 1987
Dear IATA/ABTA Travel Agent:
WIN £5,000 CASH
NOW YOU
EL NUEVO Concurso SHERATON
28 de Diciembre de 1.987
Estimado agente de Viajes IATA.
¿Que le gustaría hacer a Vd con US $5.000 extras en efectivo? Vd debería pensar en ello cada vez que hiciese una reserva de una habitación en cualquiera de nuestros Hoteles.
GANE US $5.000 EN EFECTIVO
AHORA PUEDE GANAR
You can't win an airline discount.
You can't win another trip you've already been on.
But you can win £5,000 cash.
LE NOUVEAU Concours SHERATON
Vous ne pouvez pas gagner une réduction sur un billet d'avion.
Vous ne pouvez pas gagner un autre voyage si vous l'avez déjà fait.
Mais vous pouvez gagner 25.000 francs français en espèces.
DEN NYA Tävlingen SHERATON
Du kan inte vinna en rabatterad flygbiljett.
Du kan inte vinna en resa du redan gjort.
Men du kan vinna 25.000 kronor kontant.
Vd. no puede ganar un descuento de línea aérea.
Vd. no puede ganar otro viaje que ya haya hecho.
Pero puede ganar US $5.000 en efectivo.

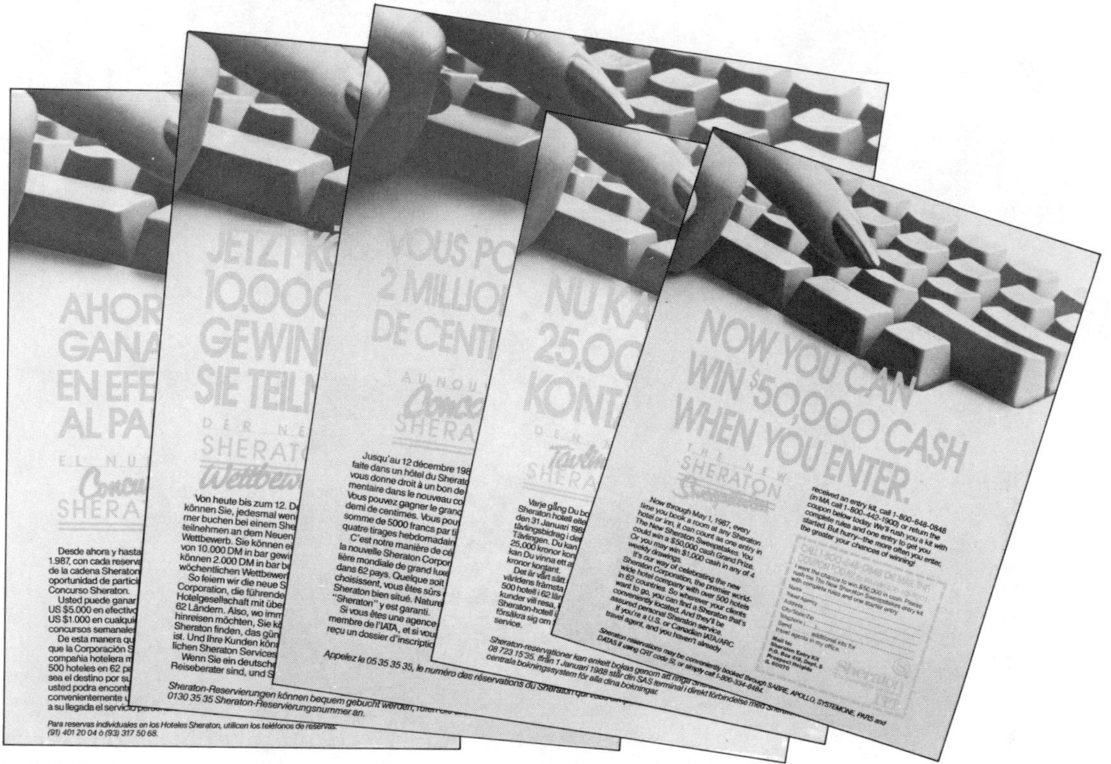

FIGURE 16.2 ***The Sheraton Travel Agent Sweepstakes Print Ads***

> push button console or full alpha-numeric keyboard. Desired information is retrieved interactively from the videotex center directly or through gateways to other information sources. Requested information is displayed on a television screen, computer terminal or other video device.[17]

While there are successful videotex suppliers in the United States, development has been more rapid and penetration more extensive in Europe, especially in France.

The basis of the French system has been the elimination of the paper telephone book and the provision—by French Telco, the state-owned and -operated telephone system—of Minitel terminals to access the electronic telephone book. Not having to print and distribute telephone books and provide associated directory assistance services saves French Telco a substantial amount of money. The consumer has immediate access to completely up-to-date telephone listings. Even more important, however, the consumer now has a computer terminal with communications capability.

As of June 1986, over 1.8 million Minitel terminals were in use and more than 3 million hours had been spent by users on the 3,000+ services available on the sys-

[17]W. Wayne Talarzyk and Robert E. Widing II, "Videotex: Are We Having Fun Yet?" Working Paper No. 87-72, College of Business, The Ohio State University, June 1987, p. 2.

tem.[18] Some of the services are provided by major French businesses, including banks, newspapers, and retailers. Airline, hotel, and restaurant reservations can be made on the system; you can even use it to call a cab. Many businesses have been established just to serve the Minitel marketplace, including electronic catalogs. The system also makes available electronic communications services such as electronic mail, bulletin boards, games, and, of course, the electronic equivalent of dating services.

A large number of services are also available to the French business community, which is a major user of Minitel. Small businesses were the first to take advantage of services such as consumer credit checks, check verification, and electronic ordering from suppliers. Penetration is rapidly increasing in larger businesses, partly because of an aggressive marketing program by the telephone company.[19]

Several videotex services exist in the United States, the three largest being CompuServe, The Source, and Dow Jones News/Retrieval. All the services together are estimated to have about one million subscribers.[20] Generally, these videotex services tend to offer news, data bases, financial information and services, travel services, electronic shopping, and the like over telephone lines to personal computers that have modems attached.

Interesting and useful though these services may be, do many people really require them? More importantly, do they need them enough to buy a personal computer if they do not already own one? Or even a modem? For most people the answer is no. Videotex provides little, if anything, that cannot be obtained in other ways,—albeit more slowly and less conveniently.

That may be the key reason for the success of the French system as opposed to the lackluster performance of videotex in the United States. The electronic telephone book provides a basic necessity via videotex, giving consumers a reason to adopt it, to familiarize themselves with it, and, in time, to access other services as well—best of all, with little or no investment on their part. So far, no equally compelling reason to be has been provided for widespread consumer adoption of videotex in the United States, nor has a single unifying force like the French telephone company emerged to provide such a reason.

Videotex services can be used in environments other than the home, however, to deliver a wide variety of promotional messages. Most of the original video kiosks were used simply to deliver product or directory information in high-traffic areas such as airports and shopping malls. Transactional capabilities were soon added, so that customers could make purchases via the kiosk and have the merchandise delivered to their homes.

[18]George Nahon and Edith Pointeau, "Minitel Videotex in France: What We Have Learned," *Direct Marketing*, January 1987, p. 64.

[19]Nahon and Pointeau, "Minitel Videotex in France," pp. 64-71. 125.

[20]Bill Saporito, "Are IBM and Sears Crazy? Or Canny?" *Fortune*, September 28, 1987, p. 75.

The most recent development in public-access video is personalized interactive video (PIV). PIV is a combination of videotex and the massive data-storage and random-access capabilities of laser disc technology. The ability to store large amounts of data and access it rapidly allows a PIV system to deliver customized messages at or near the point of purchase, where they are most likely to be acted upon by customers. A number of systems were in test or small-scale use in mid-1988. Photo center kiosks, located in mass merchandise outlets and supermarkets, can receive film for processing, sell additional film and other photographic supplies, cross-sell related products, and collect consumer data. In supermarkets a system being tested by a large food products manufacturer can plan menus based on criteria supplied by the customer, provide recipes and cooking instructions for a specified number of diners, and dispense coupons for the products specified in the recipes—a service truly custom-tailored to the needs of the individual customer.[21]

There is certainly some type of future for videotex in the United States, both in the home and in public places. Which systems will take priority and how rapidly they will develop is still open to question, however.

The Telaction home shopping service discussed earlier is a new entrant into the home videotex field. So, too, is a joint venture between IBM and Sears called Prodigy that began tests in early 1988. Videotex is an exciting new communications medium for the direct marketer, one that warrants observation and experimentation, but not yet complete commitment.

The electronic communications technologies constitute the most glamorous trend that will affect the future of direct marketing. However, there are two other areas that should also be examined—the increasing quantitative sophistication of direct marketing and major legal and regulatory issues that are expected to persist into the early 1990s. First we will look at two major areas in which advanced quantitative methods, in combination with computer technology, will affect direct marketing—decision support systems and artificial intelligence.

QUANTITATIVE ADVANCES IN DIRECT MARKETING

Direct marketing, as we have stressed throughout this book, is an information-intensive activity. One of the direct marketer's chief aims must be to use that information effectively. Since the volume of information has become so great and the decisions to be made on the basis of that information so complex, there is a need for decision aids that can handle large quantities of data. Decision support systems represent one useful approach.

[21]John L. Stanton and Richard J. George, "Personalized Interactive Video: The Next Frontier in Direct Marketing," *Proceedings of the Direct Marketing Symposium*. Cincinnati, OH: April 27-29, 1988.

Decision Support Systems

According to Little, a marketing decision support system (MDSS) is "problem-solving technology...that consists of people, knowledge, software, and hardware successfully wired into the management process."[22] He goes on to state that an MDSS is made up of a database, models that specify relationships between certain data elements, and optimization (for example, linear programming) routines that supply a "best" solution to a specified problem.[23] Sophisticated decision support systems allow managers to ask "what if" questions (for example: What if I increased the advertising budget by $x? and What if I tested X names from Y lists, with each list having a certain set of characteristics?) and receive answers quickly and in an easily interpretable form. A good MDSS allows a manager who is not a computer expert to manipulate the system without extensive training and without intervention by a programmer.

A customized MDSS, complete with extensive industry-specific and product-specific models, is obviously an expensive undertaking. However, before you assume that an MDSS is possible only in large organizations that are well-equipped with both cash and technical expertise, consider the possibilities available with a personal computer and off-the-shelf software.

A hypothetical but realistic example shows the type of analysis that can be performed using a popular spreadsheet program.[24] The necessary facts about the fictional business are presented in Figure 16.3. Using these data, a model of the firm was constructed. Specifically, the analyst utilized the capacity of the spreadsheet software to describe relationships between data items by means of simple algebraic formulae. After constructing the model and inputting the data represented by the information in Figure 16.3, the analyst could examine different courses of action the business might follow.

Three alternative scenarios were proposed and analyzed:

1. *No-Change Scenario.* Continue 6 mailings per year at level necessary to maintain 6 percent growth rate.
2. *Growth Scenario I.* Mail 6 times per year to sufficient names to achieve a 20 percent growth in sales.
3. *Growth Scenario II.* Mail 10 times per year to buyers' list, and 6 times per year to in-house prospects and rental lists, with an objective of 21 percent overall growth.

The income statements, balance sheets, and selected financial ratios resulting from each scenario are shown in Figure 16.4.

[22]John D. C. Little, "Decision Support Systems for Marketing Managers," *Journal of Marketing*, Summer 1979, p. 9.

[23]Little, "Decision Support Systems," pp. 9-11.

[24]Opportunities Unlimited," *Direct Marketing*, February 1988, pp. 82-87.

FIGURE 16.3 ***Operating and Financial Characteristics of Hypothetical Business Marketer***

The Business

Founded	1967
Sales for most recent fical year	$8 million
Pretax profits	4–5% of sales
Long-term debt	$1 million
Projected growth rate	6% per year
Product line	5,000 stock-keeping units

Customer and Prospect Base

In-house prospect list	100,000
Buyers list	
Last 24-month purchasers	72,000
Last 3-month purchasers	21,600
Total prospect universe	2,500,000
Universe of prime prospects	1,000,000

Current Promotional Strategy

96-page catalog 6 times per year to buyers list, in-house prospect list and 125,000 rental names

Historical Response Rates

Buyers list	8.5%
In-house prospect list	2.0%
Rental lists	0.8%

Average Order Size

Buyers list	$150.
In-house prospects	$130.
Rental lists	$120.

Promotional Costs

Buyers and in-house prospects	$.42 per issue
Rental names	$.50 per issue (includes cost of list rental @$80/m)

Annual Customer Attrition Rate	
	18%
Order Processing Cost	
	$13 (includes no allocation of overhead)
Returns and Allowances	
	7% of sales
Ratio of Inquiries to New Accounts	
	40%

Under the No-Change Scenario, the firm's profits, in both absolute and percentage terms, decline steadily over the 6-year projection. Worse still, both the current ratio (current assets to current liabilities) and the acid-test ratio (cash and receivables to current liabilities) increase sharply, although the debt to equity ratio declines. Decreasing profits and the worsening of two important ratios measuring liquidity suggest the eventual failure of the firm.

The projected results of Growth Scenario I are even worse. Profits become negative in the third year, and the loss increases for each of the remaining 3 years. The high cost of bringing in new customers, coupled with the rise in fixed costs necessary to service the increased business activity, makes the firm unprofitable with no apparent likelihood of a turn-around.

The third scenario represents an attempt to balance growth and profitability objectives. Growth Scenario II attempts to obtain more business from existing customers, and therefore to avoid excessive customer acquisition costs. The result is increased profitability for the first 5 years with a decline in the sixth. Financial ratios remain acceptable. Although this is a much better outcome than the preceding two scenarios, longer-term results will not be satisfactory unless some changes are made in strategy.

At this point the spreadsheet analysis can mimic a formal MDSS if the analyst asks the right what-if (sensitivity) questions. What if I am able to lower customer acquisition costs by 1.5 percent per year? 1 percent? 2 percent? What if I can reduce the customer attrition rate from the current 18 percent to 15 percent? What if I can increase the ratio of inquiries to new accounts from 40 to 45 percent? What if I can decrease the order-processing cost from $13 to $12?

This type of analysis will give the direct marketer much useful guidance. It is unlikely to give a "best" (optimal) result; that would happen only by accident. The number of reasonable individual changes (that is, it may be reasonable to decrease the order processing cost to $12, but it probably is not reasonable to

FIGURE 16-4A

Results of No-Change Scenario Projection Model at 6x Mailing, 6% Growth

	1987	1988	1989	1990	1991	1992
Income Statement						
Sales	7,788	8,295	8,827	9,385	9,969	10,579
Cost of Sales %	60.0%	60.5%	61.0%	61.5%	62.0%	62.5%
Cost of Sales $	4,673	5,018	5,384	5,772	6,181	6,612
Gross Profit	3,115	3,276	3,442	3,613	3,788	3,967
Variable Expenses $	1,257	1,338	1,424	1,514	1,608	1,706
Gross Margin	1,859	1,938	2,018	2,099	2,180	2,261
Advertising	983	1,037	1,091	1,148	1,206	1,265
Fixed Overhead	500	533	567	603	640	679
Income Before Tax	375	369	361	349	335	317
	4.8%	4.4%	4.1%	3.7%	3.4%	3.0%
Income Tax (36%)	135	133	130	126	120	114
Net Income	240	236	231	223	214	203
	3.1%	2.8%	2.6%	2.4%	2.1%	1.9%

Balance Sheet	1987	1988	1989	1990	1991	1992
Assets						
Cash	200	213	227	241	256	272
Acounts Receivable	863	919	978	1,040	1,105	1,172
Inventory	779	836	897	962	1,030	1,102
Prepaid Advertising	164	173	182	191	201	211
Total Current Assets	2,006	2,141	2,284	2,434	2,592	2,757
Fixed Assets - Net	500	530	562	596	631	667
Total Assets	2,506	2,672	2,847	3,030	3,223	3,424
Liabilities						
Notes Payable - Bank	1,000	778	564	369	195	47
Accnts Payable & Accrual	379	397	426	455	487	520
Total Current Liabilities	1,379	1,176	990	824	682	567
Shareholders' Equity	1,127	1,496	1,857	2,206	2,541	2,857
Total Liabilities & Equity	2,506	2,672	2,847	3,030	3,223	3,424

Key Ratios	1987	1988	1989	1990	1991	1992
Current Ratio	1.45	1.82	2.31	2.95	3.80	4.86
Acid Test Ratio	0.77	0.96	1.22	1.55	1.99	2.55
Debt to Equity Ratio	1.22	0.79	0.53	0.37	0.27	0.20
Customers	72,000	76,762	81,782	87,060	92,595	98,387
House Acquisition Cost	$10.93	$11.12	$11.32	$11.56	$11.83	$12.12
Rented Acquisition Cost	$37.01	$37.63	$38.25	$38.87	$39.48	$40.10
Current Value (000)	4,252	4,383	4,509	4,628	4,737	4,837
Employees	46	49	52	55	59	62
Square Footage	31,152	33,178	35,307	37,539	39,874	42,315

FIGURE 16-4B

Results of Growth Scenario I
Projection Model at 6x Mailing, 20% Growth

	1987	1988	1989	1990	1991	1992
Income Statement						
Sales	7,788	9,108	10,998	13,399	16,262	19,549
Cost of Sales %	60.0%	60.5%	61.0%	61.5%	62.0%	62.5%
Cost of Sales $	4,673	5,510	6,709	8,240	10,082	12,218
Gross Profit	3,115	3,598	4,289	5,159	6,180	7,331
Variable Expenses $	1,257	1,483	1,800	2,197	2,668	3,205
Gross Margin	1,859	2,114	2,489	2,961	3,512	4,126
Advertising	983	1,460	1,962	2,487	3,033	3,601
Fixed Overhead	500	585	706	860	1,044	1,255
Income Before Tax	375	69	(179)	(386)	(566)	(730)
	4.8%	0.8%	-1.6%	-2.9%	-3.5%	-3.7%
Income Tax (36%)	135	25	(64)	(139)	(204)	(263)
Net Income	240	44	(114)	(247)	(362)	(467)
	3.1%	0.5%	-1.0%	-1.8%	-2.2%	-2.4%

Balance Sheet	1987	1988	1989	1990	1991	1992
Assets						
Cash	200	234	282	344	418	502
Accounts Receivable	863	1,009	1,219	1,485	1,802	2,167
Inventory	779	918	1,118	1,373	1,680	2,036
Prepaid Advertising	164	243	327	414	506	600
Total Current Assets	2,006	2,405	2,947	3,617	4,406	5,305
Fixed Assets - Net	500	579	693	837	1,008	1,206
Total Assets	2,506	2,984	3,639	4,454	5,414	6,511
Liabilities						
Notes Payable - Bank	1,000	1,351	2,090	3,169	4,551	6,211
Accnts Payable & Accrual	379	437	532	652	797	964
Total Current Liabilities	1,379	1,788	2,621	3,822	5,348	7,175
Shareholders' Equity	1,127	1,196	1,018	632	67	(664)
Total Liabilities & Equity	2,506	2,984	3,639	4,454	5,414	6,511

	1987	1988	1989	1990	1991	1992
Key Ratios						
Current Ratio	1.45	1.35	1.12	0.95	0.82	0.74
Acid Test Ratio	0.77	0.70	0.57	0.48	0.42	0.37
Debt to Equity Ratio	1.22	1.49	2.58	6.05	80.40	-10.81
Customers	72,000	76,762	88,359	105,991	129,003	156,863
House Acquisition Cost	$10.93	$12.23	$12.87	$13.04	$12.98	$12.87
Rented Acquisition Cost	$37.01	$37.63	$38.25	$38.87	$39.48	$40.10
Current Value (000)	4,252	4,147	4,426	5,000	5,799	6,763
Employees	46	54	65	79	96	115
Square Footage	31,152	36,433	43,992	53,595	65,048	78,198

FIGURE 16-4C

Results of Growth Scenario II
Projection Model at 10x Mailing, 21% Growth

Income Statement	1987	1988	1989	1990	1991	1992
Sales	7,788	10,972	12,626	14,704	17,169	19,992
Cost of Sales %	60.0%	60.5%	61.0%	61.5%	62.0%	62.5%
Cost of Sales $	4,673	6,638	7,702	9,043	10,645	12,495
Gross Profit	3,115	4,334	4,924	5,661	6,524	7,497
Variable Expenses $	1,257	1,768	2,041	2,380	2,781	3,238
Gross Margin	1,859	2,566	2,883	3,281	3,744	4,259
Advertising	983	1,292	1,617	1,957	2,310	2,678
Fixed Overhead	500	704	811	944	1,102	1,284
Income Before Tax	375	570	456	380	331	298
	4.8%	5.2%	3.6%	2.6%	1.9%	1.5%
Income Tax (36%)	135	205	164	137	119	107
Net Income	240	365	292	243	212	191
	3.1%	3.3%	2.3%	1.7%	1.2%	1.0%

Balance Sheet Assets	1987	1988	1989	1990	1991	1992
Cash	200	282	324	378	441	513
Accounts Receivable	863	1,216	1,399	1,630	1,903	2,216
Inventory	779	1,106	1,284	1,507	1,774	2,082
Prepaid Advertising	164	215	269	326	385	446
Total Current Assets	2,006	2,819	3,277	3,841	4,503	5,258
Fixed Assets - Net	500	691	790	915	1,063	1,232
Liabilities						
Notes Payable - Bank	1,000	1,288	1,305	1,509	1,863	2,344
Accnts Payable & Accrual	379	525	609	714	839	983
Total Current Liabilities	1,379	1,814	1,914	2,222	2,702	3,328
Shareholders' Equity	1,127	1,697	2,153	2,533	2,864	3,162
Total Liabilities & Equity	2,506	3,510	4,067	4,755	5,566	6,490

Key Ratios	1987	1988	1989	1990	1991	1992
Current Ratio	1.45	1.55	1.71	1.73	1.67	1.58
Acid Test Ratio	0.77	0.83	0.90	0.90	0.87	0.82
Debt to Equity Ratio	1.22	1.07	0.89	0.88	0.94	1.05
Customers	72,000	76,762	86,177	99,328	115,843	135,422
House Acquisition Cost	$10.93	$9.54	$10.02	$10.30	$10.49	$10.66
Rented Acquisition Cost	$37.01	$37.63	$38.25	$38.87	$39.48	$40.10
Current Value (000)	4,252	6,372	6,814	7,521	8,428	9,484
Employees	46	65	74	86	101	118
Square Footage	31,152	43,887	50,503	58,816	68,678	79,968

decrease it to $2) that could be effected are likely to number in the hundreds. Each of those individual changes could be combined with another individual change (a two-way combination of changes), which would increase the number of potential adjustments in strategy to several thousand. And that figure doesn't even consider three-way and greater combinations! It takes the optimization routine of a true MDSS to deal with this kind of complexity.

Yet the advantages that can be derived from the type of analysis just illustrated should not be understated. It shows that our hypothetical business marketer is courting disaster if the current 6 percent growth rate objective is followed blindly—and that is valuable information to gain from a relatively simple, low-cost analysis.

This approach assumes that all the relevant relationships in a particular situation can be quantified and, as a result, precise mathematical solutions can be obtained. Frequently, however, that is not the case. It was the desire to try to replicate the human reasoning process as it muddles through to a solution to an imprecisely specified problem that stimulated the quest for artificial intelligence.

Artificial Intelligence and Expert Systems

While there is no universally accepted definition of artificial intelligence (AI), it is commonly understood to mean computer systems that can emulate the reasoning, and even the learning, power of the human brain. While there was considerable progress in the field of artificial intelligence in the 1980s, the learning, reasoning machine is still far from a reality.

Progress has come primarily in the sub-field of AI known as *expert systems*. According to one expert:

> Expert systems are interactive computer programs that apply a variety of knowledge elements, such as facts, rules, and models, in a manner that supports and enhances problem-solving in specific domains. The term "expert" is intended to imply both narrow specialization and a high level of competence. Expert systems are often referred to as "knowledge-based systems" because their performance critically depends on their ability to represent and manipulate knowledge.[25]

In other words, expert systems mimic the decision-making activities of experts in particular specialized fields of knowledge. This is by no means a simple accomplishment, but it is considerably less complex than mimicking reasoning and learning.

[25]Mark Stefik, et.al., "Basic Concepts for Building Expert Systems," in Frederick Hayes-Roth et.al., eds. *Building Expert Systems*, Reading, MA: Addison, Wesley, 1983, quoted in Arvind Rangaswamy, Raymond R. Burke, Jerry Wind, and Jehoshua Eliashberg, *Expert Systems for Marketing*, Cambridge, MA: Marketing Science Institute Report No. 87-107, 1987, p. 2.

Expert systems are just beginning to penetrate the field of marketing. A system called PROMOTER[26] provides a means of evaluating the effect on sales of manufacturers' trade promotions either alone or in combination with consumer promotions. ADCAD is a system for selecting advertising copy strategies and communication approaches.[27]

The MORE/2 system, which is described in the list segmentation section of Chapter 4, is an expert system for direct marketing applications that is well known to the authors. Some portions of this system involve mathematically precise calculations; some require making judgments with incomplete information about a complex set of alternatives. The latter endeavor requires a set of decision rules that incorporate the kinds of knowledge and skills possessed by an expert direct marketer.

Many other problems of direct marketing besides list segmentation are appropriate candidates for the application of expert systems. According to one group of experts,[28] the types of problems that are suitable for expert systems methodology are:

- *Those characterized by logical rather than arithmetical relationships.* Logical relations can be simply characterized as those in which IF one condition exists, THEN a particular action should be taken.
- *Semi-structured rather than structured or completely unstructured problems.* Semi-structured environments offer the opportunity for successful application of knowledge-based decision rules.
- *Problems characterized by incomplete knowledge.* When knowledge is incomplete, it is difficult to identify all the important variables and/or to specify all the important relationships among them.
- *Situations in which management wishes hands-on access to the MDSS.* These include both time-sensitive and complex decision-making situations.

A number of key direct marketing decisions fit these criteria rather well. Choosing between alternative offers or creative executions and developing positioning and promotional strategies are just a few of the reasonable applications.

The environment in which direct marketing managers must analyze data and make decisions is complex and constantly changing. In earlier chapters we dealt with some aspects of change: evolving consumer lifestyles and purchasing patterns, developments in production and information technology, fragmented markets, and increasing costs of servicing customers, to name just a few. In the final section of this chapter we will look briefly at another major aspect of change—legal and regulatory issues affecting direct marketing that are expected to persist into the next decade.

[26]Magid M. Abraham and Leonard M. Lodish, "PROMOTER: An Automated Promotion Evaluation System," *Marketing Science*, Spring 1987, pp. 101-122.

[27]Rangaswamy et al., *Expert Systems for Marketing*, pp. 1-50.

[28]Rangaswamy et al., *Expert Systems for Marketing*, pp. 13-14.

MAJOR LEGAL AND REGULATORY ISSUES FACING DIRECT MARKETING

Direct marketing firms must contend with legal and regulatory issues that are either common to all businesses or are specific to a product line or an industry. As direct marketers, they must also deal with issues that are of general concern to the direct marketing industry. At least two such issues have concerned the industry for a number of years and it seems certain they will continue to do so. These are privacy and the state collection of sales or use taxes from direct marketers operating outside their borders.

The Issue of Privacy

Whether the United States Constitution provides an implicit guarantee of a right of privacy is a complex legal question. In any case, privacy is a pressing concern of many people and organizations, and the Direct Marketing Association has taken a strong stand on the need for the industry to protect the privacy of the individual:

> The Direct Marketing Association recognizes the need for businesses to protect the personal privacy of individuals and their need to provide safeguards for the proper handling of personal data contained in data files. DMA strongly believes that good business practices require respect for such expectations of the individual.[29]

Two general privacy issues summarize the major concerns of individuals and legislators: first, list rental and databased marketing practices, and second, media intrusiveness.

While objections to the basic idea of list rental are voiced rather frequently, list rental is generally believed to be valid and to warrant protection as a kind of "commercial free speech." At the same time, no list owner is required to rent a list, and potentially useful lists of governmental entities are sometimes unavailable because of public pressure. The DMA's Mail Preference Service, described in Chapter 9, is one important response by the industry to the concerns of people who do not wish to receive unsolicited mailings.

When the issue is broadened to encompass the entire activity of databased marketing, it becomes more volatile because of the extent of the information contained in many databases. After examining a number of court cases, Posch concludes that "'Privacy' is not and should not be of major concern to database marketers who subscribe to sound professional ethics."[30] The position of the DMA is that these sound ethics include collecting only needed data by fair and legal

[29]Direct Marketing Association "Guidelines for Personal Information Protection, DMA," p. 1.

[30]Robert Posch, "Nuisance/Privacy Infractions—Part Two," *Direct Marketing*, Janary 1988, p. 103.

methods; ensuring the completeness and accuracy of data; allowing individuals to challenge the accuracy of data and to correct inaccurate data; transferring data between direct marketers only for direct marketing purposes; recognizing especially sensitive types of data; and protecting data from unauthorized use while in storage or transit.[31]

The second privacy issue that is of special concern to direct marketing is the perception that telephone is an especially intrusive medium that should be regulated. While the "commercial free speech" argument appears to apply to valid telephone sales contacts, this has not lessened the annoyance of many consumers or the desire of many state legislatures to regulate telephone marketing practices.

Most annoying of all to many consumers is computerized equipment that dials the call and presents a pre-recorded message. Some direct marketers feel that the indiscriminate use of computerized telephone calling systems is threatening, not just the use of this equipment itself, but the entire telephone marketing industry. Some states, including Florida and Massachusetts, already have laws regulating one or more forms of telephone marketing, and all the others have one or more bills on this issue pending in their state legislatures.

Continuing advances in information and telecommunications technology suggest that these privacy-related issues will not soon disappear. For example, the use of bar codes on almost all consumer goods will increasingly present both direct and traditional marketers with opportunities to develop databases of unrivaled size and specificity. Their potential advantages in developing more precisely targeted marketing programs are immense, but so is their potential for generating increased pressure for regulation.

The Use Tax Issue

The crux of this issue is whether direct marketers must collect sales taxes (in this context they are referred to as *use taxes* for arcane legal reasons) on goods and services sold in states other than the one(s) in which the direct marketer has some type of business location.

States have long tried to capture these taxes, but in 1967 the U.S. Supreme Court held that a firm that has no presence in or connection with a state does not have to collect that state's sales tax. However, Congress could pass legislation permitting states to require the collection of the taxes.

This type of legislation is supported, not surprisingly, by many state governors who believe that they are losing substantial tax revenues as a result of not being able to tax mail-order sales. It is also supported by major retailers, some of whom are also in the mail-order business, because they believe that direct marketers have an unfair price advantage in that their out-of-state customers do not have to pay sales tax.

[31] "Guidelines for Personal Information Protection," pp. 2-4.

Also not surprisingly, direct marketers oppose this legislation. They argue that collecting these taxes—more than 4,000 individual taxes, according to one industry source[32]—would be an administrative nightmare. The number of tax rates is much larger than the number of states because both sales tax rates and the types of products that are taxable vary from state to state. Direct marketers also argue that the states might realize little net revenue because the cost of collecting the taxes will be so high. It is not possible to estimate how much passage of such a bill would harm the direct marketing industry in terms of higher costs and/or lost sales, but both Williams-Sonoma and The Talbots have conducted tests that showed a sales decline of 15 percent or more when customers were asked to compute the amount of tax due. Sales fell less when the tax was simply added to the purchase price.

Whatever the precise figures, the effect on the industry is unlikely to be positive, especially in the short run. However, government's search for new sources of tax revenue is probably override industry concerns in the near future.[33]

SUMMARY

Direct-response marketing is changing the face of marketing as it has traditionally been practiced. The gradual inclusion of elements of direct response into traditional marketing programs is blurring the sharp dividing line between the two. Rapid technological advances, including the widespread adoption of new communications technologies, will hasten the recognition of the importance of two-way interactive communications between marketers and individual customers and further increase the value of measurable, controllable marketing programs to consumer and business marketers alike.

DISCUSSION QUESTIONS

1. Which electronic communications technologies are direct marketers using? Can you think of applications in addition to the ones described?
2. What do you think the future of videotex will be in the United States?
3. What is a management decision support system? How can an MDSS be used by a direct marketer?
4. How would you describe the concerns of the American public about direct marketing and invasion of privacy?

[32] "New Software Package is Designed to Help DM'ers Deal with Use Tax," *DM News*, December 1, 1987, p. 18.

[33] Jim Emerson, "Taxation and Legislative Worries Continue to Haunt Direct Marketers," *DM News*, April 1, 1988, p. 14; Steven W. Colford, "Taxing Mail-Order," *Advertising Age*, September 14, 1987, p. 37; Emanuel Soshensky, "Sales Tax Showdown," *DM News/Catalog Business*, December 1, 1987, pp. 44, 52-53.

SUGGESTED ADDITIONAL READINGS

1. Stewart Brand, *The Media Lab: Inventing The Future At MIT* (New York: Viking Penguin, 1987).
2. Richard J. George, "An International Perspective of In-Home Electronic Shopping," in Kenneth D. Bahn, *Developments in Marketing Science*, Vol. III (Montreal: Academy of Marketing Science), pp. 56-60.
3. Arvind Rangaswamy, Raymond R. Burke, Jerry Wind, and Jehoshua Eliashberg, *Expert Systems for Marketing* (Cambridge, MA.: Marketing Science Institute Report No. 87-107, 1987).

Case 1

JESSICA'S COTTAGE
Maintaining the Momentum of a New Catalog

Lynn Woufe, President of WarmWear, Inc., was deep in thought as she drove the winding mountain road on a spring evening in 1982. She was pleased with the success of the company's new mail-order catalog, Jessica's Cottage. Launching a specialty catalog featuring flannel sheets had been viewed as a risk by the company's directors, but sales for its first year would exceed the forecasted $1 million. Ms. Woufe realized that her task now was to build on the catalog's initial success so it could make an important contribution to WarmWear's overall growth and profitability. With a long weekend ahead, she had borrowed a friend's mountain cabin so she could have three quiet days to develop a marketing plan for the catalog's second year of operations.

COMPANY BACKGROUND

WarmWear, Inc. markets thermal underwear, outdoor clothing, and work clothing through a mail-order catalog. Located in Tacoma, Washington, it does business throughout the United States and Canada, although sales are concentrated in colder regions. It is vertically integrated with a manufacturing plant for thermal underwear in Richland, Washington and another for outerwear in Bend, Oregon. The company is privately held so exact sales figures are not divulged, but the trade press estimated that its 1980 sales were approximately $25 million.

Ms. Woufe had joined WarmWear soon after it was founded in 1966. Prior to that she had been a management trainee at a large Seattle department store and a circulation assistant for a company which published a number of trade journals. Ms. Woufe enjoyed the entrepreneurial environment of the small mail-order firm and her creativity and hard work played an important role in WarmWear's early growth. She liked to describe herself as an "intuitive marketer" who relied on instict and experience instead of as an "analytical marketer" who relied on research and numbers. Her promotion to president of the company came in 1976 when its founder retired. Ms. Woufe felt that her challenge was to accelerate WarmWear's growth rate by expanding the current business and by adding new catalogs when attractive opportunities arose.

This case was prepared by Associate Professor Mary Lou Roberts as a basis for class discussion rather than to illustrate effective or ineffective handling of an administrative situation.

THE CATALOG CONCEPT

The idea for Jessica's Cottage came into being while Ms. Woufe was visiting her mother's distant cousin in England early in 1980. After a long day of travel she had arrived at Cousin Jessica's country home late on a rainy English night, cold and tired. The elderly woman quickly took Ms. Woufe to her room and urged her to get a good night's sleep. Although the room was cold by American standards, she slipped between flannel sheets and found them warm and soothing.

Her reaction to the experience was so strong that she became intrigued with the idea of a catalog featuring all-cotton flannel sheets. When she returned to Tacoma, she developed the concept fully and presented it to the WarmWear board of directors.

Ms. Woufe's presentation emphasized two aspects of the current environment that seemed to support her concept—the increasingly strong preference of upscale consumers for natural fibers instead of synthetic ones and household energy conservation resulting from the energy crisis of the mid-1970's. She also pointed out that the new catalog could utilize the talents of existing WarmWear managers. Only one new manager would be needed to head product development and procurement. After considerable discussion of the concept and the first-year marketing plan, Ms. Woufe's proposal was approved by the board.

The overall concept was well expressed in the catalog's first print advertisement. The ad was written as a letter from "Jessica" herself and featured a silhouetted picture of a charming English stone house. The copy read:

Dear Friend:

I'll never forget the night I came to the moors in Yorkshire. I had planned and saved for years for my trip to England. Then, out of the blue, I got a chance to spend a few days in an honest-to-goodness 13th century cottage in Yorkshire's wild north country. I just knew it could be the thrill of a lifetime!

The trouble started after I left London. Suddenly the weather turned shivering cold and wet. Thick damp mists swirled down the hills and covered the lonely road winding through the moors. I lost my way twice.

As a result, it was almost midnight when I finally saw the cottage. By then I was too tired and miserable to care about picturesque charm and history. I knew how the English are about central heating. All I could think of was how uncomfortable I was going to be in a drafty stone cottage.

Sure enough, when I got to my room it was freezing. A wonderful old-fashioned housekeeper said, "Don't you worry, mum. You'll be snug and warm as toast in this bed."

And you know, she was absolutely right. That bed was heavenly! When I crawled in I was dumbfounded to discover how marvelously cozy it was even with so little heat.

There was a big, puffy down comforter on top. Underneath, the sheets and even the pillowcases were flannel. And not that flimsy, pilled kind we used to have at summer camp. These were luxuriously soft, rich real English cotton flannel.

I felt utterly pampered in plush comfort. And I never slept better in my life because I wasn't buried under layers of heavy bedclothes.

Then and there I decided that I was going to have sheets like that on my bed at home. What a great way to save on heating costs at night and still feel rich and special.

When I got home I soon learned that was easier said than done. The flannel sheets in stores had polyester in them. They didn't feel or look the same at all.

Finally, I got so frustrated I went to WarmWear, a company here in my home town manufacturing the world's warmest underwear, and suggested they sell real English flannel sheets and matching pillowcases. They loved the idea. You can imagine how surprised I was when they asked if I would like the job. They said they were sure they'd never find anyone more enthusiastic than I was!

That's how Jessica's Cottage was born. We talked it over and added some other things to go with the sheets. I'm a great believer in quality and sensible prices so I was very picky about my choices. I am pleased and proud of our selections. I hope you will be too.

THE MARKETING PLAN

In addition to creative promotional strategy the marketing plan was designed to emphasize both the quality and value of the product offering.

Product Line

The Jessica's Cottage product line emphasized flannel sheets, but it also contained percale sheets, down comforters, blankets, and a few decorative items for the bedroom. All items were unique and the highest possible quality for that price point. Each item was tested in WarmWear's quality-control laboratory before being added to the product line.

All of the sheets were manufactured in England to WarmWear's specifications. This meant that sheets had to be ordered well in advance of the major selling season and inventoried. Reorders took at least six weeks to arrive from England. The sheets were stocked in twin, full, queen, and king sizes in white, yellow, bone, blue, and rose. A tattersall print was also available.

Marketplace

It was extremely difficult to forecast demand for the initial year. The market for all-cotton flannel sheets was virtually nonexistent in 1980. One trade source estimated it to be about $500,000.

Flannel sheets were available in the United States both in retail stores and through mail-order catalogs. The sheets that were sold in retail outlets were made of blended fabrics, not 100 percent cotton. They were given little merchandising or promotional support. There were perhaps 12 to 14 major catalog marketers including L. L. Bean and Lands' End. There were two other specialty catalogs that featured flannel sheets: Lucy Stewart and Garnett Hill. None of them had patterned flannel sheets.

The market for bedding is both a comfort-oriented and a fashion-oriented one. Ms. Woufe felt that the entry of Jessica's Cottage into this market would continue the movement toward the fashion end of the spectrum.

Price

Prices for the flannel sheets ranged from $22.00 and $24.00 for twin flat and fitted, respectively, to $30.95 and $32.95 for king flat and fitted. Percale sheets ranged from $9.99 for solid-color twin sheets to $23.50 for king-sized prints. Sheet casings in percale were priced at $38.95 for twin up to $60.95 for king. Flannel sheet casings ranged from $62.95 for twin size to $80.95 for king. Down comforters began at $95.00 for a 50 percent down/50 percent goose feather twin and went up to $295.00 for a 100 percent down king-sized comforter. Blankets ranged from $30.00 for a twin-sized cotton thermal blanket to $130.00 for a king-sized merino wool blanket.

Ms. Woufe did not want Jessica's Cottage to become enmeshed in the price competitiveness typical of the bedding industry. She counted on its unique merchandising approach and strong overall marketing strategy to avoid having to cut prices and thus margins.

Promotion

Space advertising was used in magazines such as *Woman's Day* and *House and Garden* as well as in *The Wall Street Journal*. The advertising was initially budgeted at $45,000, but strong initial sales caused the budget to be increased; $200,000 was actually spent in the first year.

Space advertising was used instead of list mailings for two reasons. WarmWear had built its business on space advertising. The company had not used rental lists until it had been in business for 5 years. One of Thermoware's special strengths was therefore its effective use of space advertising. the second reason for using space advertising was concern that the best lists were being overused so that good mail-order customers were receiving too many catalogs from too many different companies. The company knew that the traditional industry return on mailing lists is 2 percent while the return on inquiries from space advertising ranges from 4 percent to 20 percent, depending on the product and the offer.

The magazines Jessica's Cottage advertised in were those that had a high volume of sales at newsstands. A magazine whose sales come primarily from subscriptions is read by the same people each month. A magazine with circulation based to a large extent on newsstand sales is read by different people each month, providing a fresh audience for advertisements.

The advertisement itself was considered unique and extremely appealing. "Jessica's story" made it fun to read. Management felt strongly that it was preferable to a more traditional product-oriented space advertisement. The uniqueness and high attention-attracting value was considered important for a relatively expensive, infrequently purchased product.

The original budget projected a space advertising cost of $2 for each inquiry. So successful was the campaign that the actual cost was 70 cents per inquiry.

The Catalog Itself

The first catalog was issued in September 1981. The letter from "Jessica" appeared on the inside front cover. To maintain the warm, personal, informal style, a story was created for each product. The stories not only described the products, they also explained their uses and benefits.

The products were all shown in use in room settings rather than as a pile of different-colored sheets as was done in competitive catalogs. The digest-sized catalog was printed on very heavy, high-quality, glossy paper stock. This not only gave the best possible color reproduction but also conveyed a high-quality image. The cost to produce each catalog was 14 cents.

FIRST-YEAR RESULTS

First-year results were very impressive. Sales increased constantly through the winter months, and then decreased as the season ended. The breakdown of demand for products was 80 percent flannel sheets, 10 percent comforters, and 10 percent specialty items. By late October, Jessica's Cottage had depleted its inventory of popular items and had to scramble to obtain additional merchandise.

Response to the storytelling space advertisement was exceptionally favorable. The conversion rate of inquiries to orders averaged about 5 percent. All catalogs were mailed first class. Ms. Woufe believed that the added postage costs were a necessary element of her marketing strategy. "A person who orders a catalog and then receives it 6 weeks later probably won't even remember requesting it or would have lost interest because of seasonality of the product."

The average order was $100, nearly double WarmWear's average order. Thirty-five percent of customers used a toll-free number to place their orders; the remaining customers used the mail. In spite of the unconditional satisfaction-or-money-back guarantee, the refund rate was only 2.5 percent of sales.

Because flannel sheets are expensive, Ms. Woufe expected the typical customer to be a woman between the ages of 45 and 50, in a middle- to upper-income bracket, living in the northern United States. Actual first-year sales results revealed the following:

Age	*% of Sales*
30-35	35
36-54	30
55-65	35
Sex	
Women	95

Sales were not concentrated in any particular geographical region. Customer income was not known.

The only major failure during the first year was the mailing to 400,000 names on the WarmWear house list. WarmWear's customers tend to be relatively young, active people who spend a lot of time outdoors. They are in the middle- to upper-income ranges, are predominantly male, and are concentrated in geographical regions with colder climates. For reasons Ms. Woufe described as "different economic bases," the conversion rate was only .5 percent. As a result, Jessica's Cottage lost money on the mailing to the WarmWear list.

THE PROBLEM

As the first year was drawing to a close Ms. Woufe felt extremely satisfied with results so far. Now the problem was, "How do we keep it up?"

Case 2

GEMINI ENTERPRISES (A) Testing and Evaluating Results from a Mail-Order Campaign

Gemini Enterprises is a 10-year-old midwestern electronics firm with 1984 sales of about $40 million. The industrial division manufactures a wide variety of electronic products ranging from simple flow meters through complicated electronic devices used for testing and quality control of other electronic products such as microcomputers. These products are sold to scientific laboratories and manufacturing installations throughout the United States.

Gemini's 4-year-old Consumer Products Division has a limited line of products marketed primarily to the upscale "electronic household." These include cardiac and blood pressure monitoring devices, home security systems, and a variety of remote control and/or programmable devices for everything from garage door openers to coffeepots.

Gemini has a substantial research and development division that is charged with the improvement of existing products and the development of new ones. Recently, the R&D division had produced a product prototype that, for the first time, appeared to hold substantial promise in both the industrial and the consumer markets.

THE ETB

While working on improved methods for the control and sequencing of CAM (computer-aided manufacturing) devices, R&D had developed a product they called an electronic telephone book (ETB).

The ETB could store up to 250 names, addresses, and 10-digit telephone numbers with special purpose storage for access numbers such as those used by Sprint and MCI. It could access numbers by name, by area code alone, or by telephone number with or without area code. Once the number was located, a function key allowed the device to automatically dial the number from any Touch-tone

This case was prepared by Paul D. Berger, Professor of Quantitative Methods, and Mary Lou Roberts, Associate Professor of Marketing, as a basis for class discussion rather than to illustrate either effective or ineffective handling of an administrative situation.

The authors wish to thank Persoft, Inc., of Woburn, Massachusetts, a company at the forefront of the development of multivariate statistical analysis applied to list segmentation and other direct marketing activities. Certain aspects of this case are based on Persoft's promotional materials.

telephone in the United States. Another function key activated the user's access code, so that with the use of two-function keys in sequence, the user could automatically dial the complex access code plus the 10-digit telephone number.

In addition, a simple conversion device allowed the electronic telephone book to be connected to an IBM PC or an Apple IIe or Macintosh. The user could then obtain a hard-copy printout of any or all the names and numbers stored on the system.

The marketing department at Gemini was intrigued by the possibilities of this new product. Investigation of the marketplace quickly determined that there were similar products but that none of them had a storage capacity of more than 100 names and numbers. Even more important, none of them had the capability of producing hard copies of the stored information.

After discussions with both the research and development engineers and the operations manager for the Electronic Controls Division, two more things became clear. First, the division had the ability and the production capacity to manufacture both the electronic telephone book and the computer interface device in reasonable quantities. Second, the advanced design of the ETB would allow it to be sold profitably at a price substantially below that of existing products. Consequently, top management felt that every business telephone and one or more users in every household with an income of $25,000 or more was a potential customer for this product. They were eager to penetrate this large potential market quickly before their competition developed a similar product.

MARKETING AT GEMINI

Because of the complexity of most of its industrial products and their applications, Gemini sold primarily through its own force of 60 sales reps. In 1982 the company had begun to work with the new Corporate Direct Marketing Department to support the field sales activities. The direct marketing group had several specific responsibilities relative to the industrial product line:

1. To maintain Gemini's database of approximately 35,000 current customers.
2. To generate sales leads for new Gemini products from the existing customer base.
3. To generate sales leads for potential new customers of both new and existing products.
4. To develop sales support material for the field sales reps.

Most of the lead generation had been accomplished through mailings. The group had experimented briefly with telemarketing for sales lead generation but had not been satisfied with the results. They had also tested a catalog featuring their less complex, lower-priced products with little success. Consequently, they had decided to stick with lead-generation campaigns for specific products, usually new products or improved models of existing products. They mailed to a combination of their house list, Dun and Bradstreet lists selected by SIC code, and subscription lists from various technical trade journals.

Gemini's consumer products had been sold by direct mail from the beginning. The majority of sales were achieved as a result of the company's own solo mailing. These were usually high-quality 8 1/2-by-11-inch packages with cover letter, four-color product brochure, response card, and often a lift device of some kind. Gemini used a variety of rental lists for these mailings, including catalog lists, major credit cards, and upscale magazine subscribers, plus its own house list. Over time the house list had grown to approximately 100,000 names.

On several occasions Gemini had been able to include its products as bill stuffers in department store and credit card billings. Since Gemini handled fulfillment for these orders, the company was able to capture those names and addresses for its house list.

Since all consumer products were marketed directly, the Consumer Products Division was also a major user of the services of the Corporate Direct Marketing Department. The department supported the consumer products marketing by:

1. Maintaining their database and the associated mailing list.
2. Assisting in the creative design and handling production of the direct-mail packages.
3. Recommending rental lists for mailings.
4. Performing analyses of information in the database upon request.
5. Recommending ways in which the database could be used to increase the effectiveness of consumer-products marketing efforts.

TARGETING THE ETB MARKETING EFFORT

After considerable discussion about the broad and diverse market for the ETB, Gemini top management decided to test the system in the consumer marketplace. Faced with this task, the Consumer Products Division's first step was to ask the direct marketing operations people to look over the database and to identify those characteristics that they believed would enable targeting of the users and households that had the greatest potential for being purchasers of the ETB. Ted Smith, a senior analyst in the Corporate Direct Marketing Department, was put in charge of the analysis.

The results of Smith's initial effort identified the following characteristics (in order in which they appeared on the database):

Characteristic

1. Consecutive nonresponse to previous Gemini mailings
2. Proportion of mailings in which there were purchases
3. Consecutive responses
4. Gemini credit card holder'? (yes/no)
5. Time since first Gemini purchase
6. Time since most recent Gemini purchase
7. Total dollars of all (mail) purchases
8. Dollars of most recent Gemini purchase
9. Age
10. State of residence

These 10 characteristics are labeled "major characteristics" by Gemini. There are 11 other characteristics based on census block group data (discussed below). These are labeled characteristics 11 through 21.

Census block group data are data that characterize "districts" or (broadly speaking) "neighborhoods," and give a finer breakdown than zip codes. For each "block group" 180 different variables were determined, and these variable values were associated with each name, depending on the block group in which that person resided. These 180 variables were of three types:

1. *Residence measures.* Variables relating to types of residences, age of physical structures, etc. Specific examples of variables are "% occupied by a renter with rent greater than $400," and "% of people in condominiums built before 1975."
2. *People measures.* Variables relating to the people in the block group. Specific examples of variables are "% males," "% Irish," and "% persons under 21, male, divorced."
3. *Socio-economic measures.* Variables relating to education, job status, and income. Specific variables are "% adults in retail trade," "% adults in military," and "mean family income."

A factor analysis was performed to identify systematic relationships among the variables. A separate factor analysis was performed for each of the three types of variables. The number of variables of each type and the number of factors resulting were:

Type	*No. of Variables*	*No. of Factors*
1. Residence	81	4
2. People	49	3
3. Socio-economic	50	4
	180	11

These 11 factors became characteristics 11–21 for the ETB analysis.

Questions

1. Which of the above characteristics do you think are the most important ones for predicting who will purchase the ETB and who will not?
2. Which of these characteristics do you believe are the three most important ones?
3. If you were Ted Smith and were responsible for answering questions 1 and 2, how would you go about doing so?

GEMINI ENTERPRISES (B)

Suppose that the Gemini analyst, Ted Smith, addressed questions 1 and 2 by examining the data in the company's house list and considering the relationship of the 21 characteristics developed in Section A to purchase of similarly priced upscale electronics products. Of course, as the results of mailings of ETB literature are received, the relationships of the 21 characteristics to purchase of the ETB *specifically* could be explored and utilized for future in-house list mailings and decisions about which lists to rent.

Mr. Smith's first task was to carefully choose from Gemini's product portfolio a product line he felt was most similar to ETB in terms of function, cost, and importance. This turned out to be a combination phone answering machine/kitchen appliance operator. Smith believed that whatever relationships existed between the 21 characteristics listed in Section A and the propensity to purchase this product would to the largest degree available be relevant for the ETB.

Every fifth name was selected out of a recent mailing of 50,000 names promoting the phone machine/appliance operator. Each name was in the database, and data on all major characteristics were available, along with the record of whether a purchase had been made.[1] The 10,000 names were culled from the master file and isolated in a separate file. Smith was now ready to analyze the data.

Questions

4. What factors should be considered in finding a "similar product"?
5. How concerned should Smith be about the recency of the mailing he is analyzing?
6. Is a sample size of 10,000 adequate? Or unnecessarily large?
7. The sample of 10,000 is not a "random" sample in the strict definition of the term. What biases might appear in any analysis of these data? Can you suggest a preferable method for selecting the sample of 10,000?

GEMINI ENTERPRISES (C)

Mr. Smith's first step in the analysis was to generate a frequency distribution of each major characteristic. The Gemini data were routinely coded as output into a fixed set of categories for each characteristic. For example, characteristic 7, total dollars of all (Gemini) mail purchases, is represented by the categories (with the corresponding percents for the 10,000 names):

Categories of Total Dollars (rounded to the nearest $)	*Percent*
$0	42.3
1–49	2.4
50–99	5.1
100–149	6.6
150–249	8.3
250–499	12.8
500–999	12.2
1000+	10.3
	100.0

[1] Actually, when a multiple purchase was made, it was duly recorded as such; however, only one such event occurred for the 10,000 names.

What was of more interest to Smith was the percent of each category that made the purchase. This is noted in the following table:

Total Dollars	*Purchase Percent ("response rate")*
$0	2.2
1–49	3.1
50–99	3.2
100–149	3.6
150–249	3.4
250–499	4.1
500–999	4.8
1000+	3.9

Questions

8. On the basis of these two tables, what was the overall "response rate" (percent who purchased) among the 10,000 names?

9. In the last table in Section C it can be seen that generally a higher value for total dollars is associated with a higher purchase likelihood. However, the $1000+ category appears to belie this generalization. Is the difference of 0.9 percent between the 500–999 category and the 1000+ category "significant?" Or is the difference small enough so that it could easily be the result of "statistical error?"

GEMINI ENTERPRISES (D)

Mr. Smith examined the table of response rates for each of the major characteristics and chose to retain all of them in his subsequent analysis. He decided on a multiple regression approach. Each of the first 10 major characteristics was represented by a set of categorical (dummy) variables. For example, "total dollars" for its eight categories had variables V7a, V7b, . . . ,V7g, where

V7a = 1, if person's "total dollars" is from $1 to 49; 0, otherwise
V7b = 1, if person's "total dollars" is from $50 to 99; 0, otherwise

.

.

.

V7g = 1, if person's "total dollars" is $1000+; 0, otherwise

Major characteristic 1, consecutive nonresponse, had 8 categories: 0,1,2,3,4,5,6,7+, and variables V1a, . . . ,V1g.

Major characteristic 2, proportion of mailings with a purchase, had 5 categories: 0, .01–.20, .21–.40, .41–.60, .61+, and variables V2a, . . . ,V2d.

Major characteristic 3, consecutive responses, had 3 categories: 0,1,2+ and variables V3a, V3b.

Major characteristic 4, Gemini credit card holder, had two categories: yes and no, and one variable, V4.

Major characteristic 5, time since first Gemini purchase, had 8 categories: 0, 1–2 months, 3–4, 5–6, 7–12, 13–24, 25–36, 37+, and variables V5a, . . . V5g.

Major characteristic 6, time since most recent Gemini purchase, had 8 categories: same as for characteristic 5, and variables V6a, . . . ,V6g.

Major characteristic 7, total dollars, had the 8 categories noted earlier, with variables V7a, . . . ,V7g.

Major characteristic 8, dollars of most recent purchase, had 8 categories: 0, 1–14, 15–49, 50–99, 100–149, 150–249, 250–499, 500+, and variables V8a, . . . ,V8g. ("0" was for no purchase at all.)

Major characteristic 9, age, had 13 categories: 1–18 years, 19–22, 23–26, 27–30, 31–35, 36–40, 41–45, 46–50, 51–55, 56–60, 61–65, 66–70, 71+, with variables V9a, . . . ,V9(el).

Major characteristic 10, state, had 32 categories, some consisting of one state, some of two, three, or four states, with variables V10a, . . . ,V10z, V10aa, . . . ,V10ee.

The 11 census block group characteristics (characteristics 11 through 21) were continuous variables, V11–V21, each ranging from -10 to +10. There were then 96 actual independent variables in total. The dependent variable was a "1" if the person mailed indeed made a purchase (within 4 months), "0" otherwise.

Questions

10. For each major characteristic the number of categorical variables is one fewer than the actual number of categories (the first category always being "the dummy"). Why is this necessary?
11. A rule of thumb in performing regression analyses is to have a minimum sample size at least 10 times the number of independent variables, with some authors suggesting 25 times as many. Is Smith all right with regard to sample size?
12. Should Mr. Smith use "standard" multiple regression (i.e., all 96 variables used in the regression equation) or a form of stepwise regression? Discuss the relative merits of each choice.
13. Of the 10 major characteristics, numbers 4 (credit card status) and 10 (state of residence) are qualitative (non-numerical) in nature and must be represented by categorical (dummy) variables. However, the other 8 major characteristics are quantitative (numerical) in nature, and thus can routinely be represented by continuous variables. Why, then, did Mr. Smith

choose to represent these 8 characteristics by categorical variables? Discuss the advantages and disadvantages of this choice.

GEMINI ENTERPRISES (E)

Mr. Smith decided to perform a stepwise regression analysis, and with a "Pin" of.05 (i.e., bringing a variable into the regression equation only if it would enter with a significance of less than .05), the following variables entered the regression equation:

V2a,	V2b,	V2c,	V2d			
V3a,	V3b					
V4						
V7a,	V7b,	V7c,	V7d,	V7e,	V7f,	V7g
V8a,	V8c,	V8e,	V8f,	V8g		
V9h,	V9i,	V9j,	V9k			
V10c,	V10m,	V10t				
V13						
V16						
V17						

Question

14. What is the interpretation of V8a, V8c, V8e, V8f, V8g, being significant, but V8b and V8d *not* being significant and not entering the equation?

GEMINI ENTERPRISES (F)

Mr. Smith used the regression equation to get a "predicted purchasability index" for each of the 10,000 names in the sample, and was about to compare the predictions with the actual result of who purchased and who did not when he recalled having read that he should not use the same names to test out a prediction equation that were used to generate the equation. Therefore, he took the *other* 40,000 names (from the original list of 50,000 names) and compared for each of *them* the predicted purchase index and the actual purchase/no purchase result.

Questions

15. Why do you think the literature Smith had read suggested using different names to evaluate a prediction equation than those used to generate the equation?

16. Once Smith has the prediction for each name, and the corresponding actual result for each name, how should he proceed to evaluate the equation?

GEMINI ENTERPRISES (G)

Mr. Smith had the 40,000 names arranged in descending order of predicted purchase index. He then drew up a table showing what proportion of total sales (from all 40,000 names) would have been captured versus mailing to a given proportion of names from *the rank-ordered list*:

Top % of List Mailed	*% of Total Sales*
5	11.2
10	22.1
15	32.7
20	42.2
25	51.0
30	59.1
35	65.8
40	71.1
45	76.2
50	81.0
55	85.0
60	87.3
65	89.2
70	91.1
75	92.7
80	94.2
85	95.7
90	97.2
95	98.6
100	100.0

Questions

17. Graph the curve from the above table of data. Let "% of Total Sales" be the vertical axis. What would the graph look like had the prediction equation had no value at all? What would the graph look like had the prediction equation been (theoretically) ideal?

18. If we had a new (or the same) list of names that was expected to have the same properties and interrelationships to purchase likelihood of the ETB that the above list has to the combination phone answerer/appliance operator, how deep into the list (i.e., what portion of the list), after it is rank-ordered by the above prediction equation, should Smith mail if postage plus brochure costs $2 per name and contribution per ETB is $23 (not counting the postage plus brochure cost)?

Case 3

HARBOR SWEETS, INC.
Sales Growth and Expense Control in a Mail-Order Firm

Eighty of the one hundred and fifty employees of Harbor Sweets gathered on the production floor for a nonmandatory general meeting. As he entered the room, Ben Strohecker, founder of Harbor Sweets, exchanged warm greetings with his employees. On the front wall hung a flip chart showing Harbor Sweets' operating results for the month of February 1984. Ben began the meeting by pointing to the financial statement and simply asking, "What can we do about earnings?" This year earnings were only 3.8 percent of net sales ($77,000) instead of the projected 6.2 percent ($157,000). There were a few moments of silence as Ben waited for a reply from his employees. Finally, a voice from the back corner suggested, "Maybe we should be more careful with the WATS line." Another person added, "Freezing wages might help." Ben walked over to a blank flip chart and with a colored marker boldly wrote down the two suggestions. More hands went up; a lot of people were anxious to voice their expense control strategies. One by one each proposal was jotted down for everyone to see. (See Figure C3-1 for all suggestions given that evening.) Now it was up to Ben to decide which, if any, of the suggestions should be implemented to help control expenses and bring net profit back into line (Figure C3-2).

COMPANY HISTORY

Ben Strohecker, who had been marketing director for Schrafft's Candy Company, enjoyed making his own candy as a hobby. He experimented in his kitchen on evenings and weekends, trying to make the "best candy in the world." To help him in this pursuit he asked friends and acquaintances, "If you could eat only one more piece of candy in your life, what would it be?" On the basis of their replies, Ben decided to produce three types of candy made of only the purest-quality ingredients: pecan halfs in caramel covered with dark chocolate; a bittersweet dark chocolate flavored with peppermint starlights or orange crunch; and a triangular-shaped "sweet sloop"—Harbor Sweets' almond butter crunch dipped in white chocolate

This case was prepared by Jill Barlow, Brian Duftler, and Sharon Silver under the direction of Associate Professor Mary Lou Roberts as a basis for class discussion rather than to illustrate either effective or ineffective handling of an administrative situation. All figures are used with the permission of Harbor Sweets, Inc.

with a splash of dark chocolate and chopped nuts on the bottom. Ben believes that people can detect even small differences in quality, although they may not be able to say exactly what they are. "We will buy anything that will improve the quality of our product, regardless of the cost," he says.

Ben's first box of candy was "test marketed" at a local church fair. He was astounded when this 10-ounce box of chocolate sold for a very high price. In addition, friends and neighbors who had received the chocolates as a personal gift from Ben just couldn't get enough. "People kept asking for another box," he stated.

When he was completely satisfied with the feedback, Ben was able to realize his lifelong dream: starting his own business. He left Schrafft's and established his operation in an old warehouse in Salem, Massachusetts. His motto was: "Volume will follow excellence."

The Harbor Sweets establishment has been described by one visitor as "a cross between Willy Wonka's chocolate factory and Santa's workshop." Bright, smiling workers in white caps and red aprons bustle about. With its immaculate white walls and tabletops, accented by brightly colored red chairs and red-and-white-striped curtains, the Harbor Sweets retail shop is the essence of a candyland setting.

Every bit of this unusual operation is a reflection of Ben Strohecker's personalty. Wearing duck shoes, wide-whale cords, and a multicolored plaid shirt, he oversees this cheery workshop in the most informal way. Based solely on trust, the company runs without any sign of time clocks. Workers come in, take breaks, eat lunch, and, in general, schedule their own time. "Whatever you put on your time card, you get paid for," says Ben.

Automation and machinery are minimal. Some of the machinery is modern, some antique. Ben Strohecker feels that machinery often restricts the way candy is made. For example, his foiling machine was not able to wrap the triangular-shaped sweet sloop. Rather than change the shape of the chocolate, he decided to have every sloop hand wrapped. He refuses to sacrifice quality to automation.

The most impressive aspect of Harbor Sweets is the spirit and cooperation evident among employees. Side by side work a member of the exclusive Eastern Yacht Club and a recent immigrant from the Dominican Republic, a handicapped person and the wife of the mayor of Salem. Most employees work part-time on flexible schedules. For example, Sis and Sue share the job of production manager. Sis works Mondays, Tuesdays, and Wednesday afternoons, while Sue works Wednesday mornings, Thursdays, and Fridays.

Before coming to Harbor Sweets none of the 150 employees on the payroll had ever made a piece of candy. Today, from production line worker to top management, all are energetic and enthusiastic. As someone once said, "The workers seem to take as much pleasure in the company's triumphs as does the owner himself." Perhaps this is the outcome of Ben Strohecker's firm rule that "If working at Harbor Sweets is no longer fun, then you're fired!"

CHANNELS OF DISTRIBUTION

Catalog

The Harbor Sweets catalog is consistent with the overall corporate image. Its handwritten copy and charming gift items are in keeping with the Harbor Sweeets homey, "handmade" atmosphere. (See Figure C3-3.)

In fiscal 1983–1984 mail-order sales were 33 percent of total sales. Three regular issues of the catalog are printed each year—Fall (Christmas), Valentine's Day, and Spring (Easter, Mother's Day, and Father's Day). In addition, Harbor Sweets typically issues a few special catalogs each year. For fiscal 1983–1984 one special issue was an America's Cup catalog featuring nautical chocolates, a tie-in with the prestigious yacht race held every 4 years in nearby Newport Beach, Rhode Island.

Also new in 1983–1984 was Harbor Sweet's custom catalog (see Figure C3-4). This features chocolates custom-designed for nonprofit institutions around the country (see below, under "Custom Distribution," for further details). To encourage participation in the catalog and to help the institutions recover their mold costs, Ben donates 5 percent of gross sales to the participating institution, based on individual items sold. If this catalog is successful, it will become a regular part of Harbor Sweets' offering and will help to even out the seasonality of the mail-order business. Ben originally intended to mail the catalog to only a portion of his previous buyers, and therefore budgeted it at $10,000. He decided instead to mail to all 22,000 previous buyers at a cost of $26,000 for production and mailing.

The catalog business generates a large percentage of sales for Harbor Sweets. The total mailing consists of 75,000 names, 22,000 of which are previous buyers. Ben prefers to do all catalog design and list management internally. He started his mailing list with the 75 names and addresses on his Christmas card list. As the popularity of his chocolates grew, so did his list. He tried renting lists, but this proved unsuccessful, so he decided that in the future he would only invest in "sure things" to increase sales. He has also sold his chocolates by featuring them in other firms' catalogs. However, he is phasing out this channel of distribution.

Harbor Sweets' own mail-order business continues to grow. Many additions to the mailing list come from people returning the response cards included in each box of chocolates (see Figure C3-5). Harbor Sweets are shipped all over the world, but the list is heaviest in the Northeast. The catalog image clearly caters to New England tastes.

Fairs

Ben Strohecker sold his first chocolates at a church fair. The fairs in which Harbor Sweets are now involved are mostly social fund-raisers for charitable organizations such as the Junior League, Planned Parenthood, and private schools or institutions such as symphony orchestras. In 1983–1984, this channel of distribution ranked third in size, generating 13.5 percent of the total sales.

Retail Operations

Just inside the Harbor Sweets entry is a small reception area. This is the Harbor Sweets retail store. During the Christmas season hordes of people wait patiently in long lines outside the factory door. Visitors to Salem love to visit Harbor Sweets, and everyone is welcomed graciously. About 4.5 percent of the candy is sold in this difficult-to-locate waterfront setting.

Wholesale

About 33 percent of Harbor Sweets' sales come from the wholesale business. Ben Strohecker is extremely selective about which stores will carry his chocolates.

"We turn down about ten outlets for each one who wants to buy," he says. Most of the shops that feature Harbor Sweets are high-quality gift shops. Ben explains his strategy: "We prefer high-priced specialty stores since we want to be a low-priced gift in a high-priced shop." He has been approached by some major department stores, but except for a custom piece for Saks, he does not do business with them. Ben knows from his experience at Schrafft's that department stores often do not pay their bills promptly and that department store people are no fun to do business with. "We don't sell to anyone, anytime, if we don't think it will be an enjoyable experience. I'm too old for that." He does not want the wholesale business to exceed 40 percent of the total.

Custom Distribution

The Museum of Fine Arts in Boston, the Metropolitan Opera in New York, the Pittsburgh Symphony, the Field Museum in Chicago, Colonial Williamsburg, and the Smithsonian Institution are a few of Harbor Sweets' customers. Harbor Sweets has created highly detailed souvenir chocolate pieces for each of these institutions. The institution pays all the development costs (mold costs) in addition to paying for the actual finished chocolates. The chocolates are then sold by the organization as a fund-raising device. One of the most popular chocolates was featured by the Museum of Fine Arts in Boston. The Egyptian shawabti statue of a servant was buried along with the dead man in order to do his bidding in the underworld and to drive off demons. The chocolate reproduction of a gold shawabti was made from an exact reproduction in bronze. The plastic molds were made from a brass casting that the artist copied from a Xerox of the original statue. Included in every box was a description and explanation of the ancient relic, which made eating a yummy mummy an educational experience.

Ben is currently developing about 20 other accounts, although he doesn't allow this channel of distribution to exceed 12 percent of sales. This business helps even out the seasonality of the mail-order business. Harbor Sweets of Marblehead is clearly identified as the maker of each box of custom candy.

Miscellaneous Sales

Employees are entitled to purchase chocolate at 20 percent over cost. Total employee sales, sampling, and product replacement costs contributed $41,000, or 3.3 percent, to total sales in 1983–1984.

THE DECISION

Ben Strohecker is faced now with an important management decision. Although the employees clearly feel that internal cost control will solve the problem, he wonders whether he has been concentrating his efforts on the most profitable channels of distribution.

FIGURE C3-1 ***Complete Contents of Flip Chart***

- Communicate HS location
- Fair returns—mints in cold storage need refreezing
- Broken mug returns
- Keep things neat
- Too many people vs. work space:
  reduce size of mfg. operation and open second operation in another location—simulate competition between two
- Reduce employee candy sampling
- Time clock
- Closer supervision in production—mini supervisor at each table
- Make standards clearer in the fall
- Ben: more visible on the floor
- Less chatting
- Be stricter and meaner! Crack down on lazies!
- Train 5 new people a week—not all new employees at once
- Overemploying
- Mail list duplication
- Cash register
- Freeze wages
- Raise employee prices

FIGURE C3-2

Harbor Sweets Comparative Income Statement

	1980 $	1982 $	1983 $
Sales			
Mail Order	119,515	282,800	403,609
Fairs	68,636	158,100	163,994
Retail Shop	6,328	32,300	55,152
Wholesale	156,184	351,100	398,071
Custom		103,600	141,004
Catalog	11,306	14,100	15,860
All other	14,421	31,800	41,351
TOTAL SALES	401,490	973,900	1,219,041
Cost of Sales			
Ingredients	67,035	140,337	142,976
Cash Discounts		(1,946)	(2,416)
Packaging	41,606	112,513	145,194
UPS		30,236	35,892
Labor—Direct	63,297	167,536	211,908
Labor—Shipping	22,318	17,531	18,014
Payroll and Tax		37,630	40,723
Depreciation		5,083	
Replication and Returns			9,268
All Other (including repairs)	6,453	667	568
Inventory Change	(11,310)	(23,912)	(20,773)
TOTAL COST OF SALES	189,566	491,790	581,353
Marketing			
Mail Order	58,588	78,797	121,122
Fairs		66,355	71,708
Retail Shop		2,089	6,938
Wholesale and Cat.	8,006	24,109	42,854
Custom		55,571	14,834
All Other	3,814	22,618	21,730
TOTAL MARKETING	70,408	203,339	279,186

Figure C3-2 continued

	1980 $	*1982* $	*1983* $
Administrative			
Salaries—Administration/Office	52,406	100,732	146,654
Computer Payroll		1,430	1,698
Carpentry and Supplies		14,430	13,122
Rent, Secretary, Stenographer	3,312	12,566	14,066
Maintenance	2,407	8,904	11,671
Insurance and Employee Benefits	6,906	10,887	14,254
Professional Fees	7,099	7,629	10,191
Utilities	1,032	7,937	8,577
Office Supplies	2,242	3,898	3,754
Payroll Taxes	12,146	11,899	16,811
Manufacturing and Office Equipment	5,499	4,538	3,643
Communication Services		1,234	2,192
Meetings, T&E		4,012	5,100
Dues, Fees		1,829	1,485
Bonuses	5,158	9,235	20,045
IRA, Amortization, MC	2,990	6,281	7,774
Interest	2,832		
TOTAL ADMINISTRATIVE COSTS	103,979	205,564	277,037
TOTAL OPERATING EXPENSES (Marketing and Administration)	174,387	408,903	556,223
TOTAL EXPENSES	363,953	900,693	1,137,576
Net Income Before Taxes	37,537	73,207	81,465

Figure C3-2 continued

BALANCE SHEET
June 30, 1983

ASSETS

Current Assets:				
Cash on hand			1,099	
Cash—Savings			58,511	
Accounts Receivable	57,592			
	2,863		54,729	
Merchandise and Supplies Inventory—Note 1			76,697	
Prepaid Expenses			5,267	
Total Current Assets				196,904
Fixed Assets—Note 1	*Cost*	*Accumulated Depreciation*		*Net Book Value*
Machinery and Equipment	41,901	15,204		26,697
Molds and Dies	6,622	3,657		2,965
Leasehold Improvements	16,374	11,350		5,024
Production Fixtures	7,295	2,459		4,836
Office Furniture and Equipment	12,317	1,671		10,646
Automobile and Boat	13,743	7,286		6,457
TOTAL FIXED ASSETS	98,252	41,627		56,625
Other Assets:				
Deposits			150	
Intangibles—Net—Note 1			215	
TOTAL OTHER ASSETS				365
TOTAL ASSETS				253,894

Figure C3-2 continued

LIABILITIES AND STOCKHOLDERS' EQUITY				
Current Liabilities				
Notes Payable—due within 1 year—Note 2			5,416	
Accounts Payable			32,825	
Customers' Deposits			1,035	
Withheld and Accrued Payroll Taxes			10,553	
Accrued Salaries and Expenses			15,796	
Accrued Massachusetts Corporation Excise Tax			10	
				65,635
Long-Term Liabilities				
Notes payable—due after 1 year—notes				9,699
Stockholders' Equity				
Capital Stock—Common—No Par Value				
Authorized	12,500 shares			
Issued and Outstanding	1,978 shares	48,752		
Retained Earnings (Deficit)		129,808		
TOTAL STOCKHOLDERS' EQUITY				178,560
TOTAL LIABILITIES				253,894

FIGURE C3-3 ***Cover and Selected Pages from Christmas Catalog.***

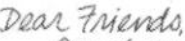

Dear Friends,

One of our neighbors popped in the other day and, looking over our shoulder, announced, "You have never had a more exciting catalogue!"

Now you know we devote our main attention to our original hobby of making the best piece of candy in the world... regardless of cost... and if you've visited us you've seen all the fresh butter and cream going into those shiny copper pots... but it sure is fun working with local craftsmen developing new gifts and containers to go with these Harbor Sweets.

Many of our fellow "Cottage Industry" folks are nationally famous - like Chris Gurshin and his Country Primitive Art (pages 8+9) Joyce Howell and her designs (page 12) and Sandy Boynton - World Famous Author and Artist... wait til you see what she's done - just for us! (page 7).

Have a wonderful Holiday,
Ben Strohecker

P.S. So many items are "limited editions". Please order soon.

Sweet Sloops Set Sail

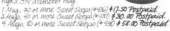

Back to Basics... we've offered other designs, but this is still the most popular. The Waechtersbachs prove their ceramic craftsmanship in this 3¾" high x 3¼" diameter mug.

1 Mug, 20 or more Sweet Sloops (#436) **$17.50 Postpaid.**
2 Mugs, 40 or more Sweet Sloops (#437) **$30.00 Postpaid.**
4 Mugs, 80 or more Sweet Sloops (#438) **$58.00 Postpaid.**

"For me who hides Sweet Sloops under my pillow and dust ruffle, the thought of merely sharing the gems is intolerable."

Kathy Hunt
Troy, Michigan

A Sweet Carafe

This shiny copper carafe holder looked nautical enough to catch our eye (everything nautical catches our eye). Filled bottom to top with Sweet Sloops or after they are gone, there's room for a ½ litre of wine (a bit over a pint). Includes brass plate. Handsome! 30 or more Sweet Sloops in ½ litre carafe (#413) **$29.50 Postpaid.** 60 or more Sweet Sloops in 1 litre carafe (#414) **$39.50 Postpaid.**

Sweet Treats

Great for Stocking Stuffers

An assortment of Sweet Sloops, Sand Dollars, Mini Barque Sarah and Marblehead Mints, all in bright taster boxes. A great way to keep everybody happy with their own Harbor Sweet. Nautically packaged in white fishnet, pulled into a bag with Red Satin Ribbon. 12 boxes (3 each of 4) 18 pieces. (#484) **$16.00 Postpaid.** 24 boxes (6 each of 4) 36 pieces (#486) **$29.00 Postpaid.**

A Reindeer Basket

An Assortment of Taster Boxes

A Guaranteed Conversation Stopper!! Designed to hold Christmas mail, provide a festive touch to a plant, or of course, to be a home to your Harbor Sweets. Hand sewn from quilted cotton. Contains 5 each of 4 taster Boxes - Sweet Sloops, Sand Dollars, Mini Barque Sarah and Marblehead Mints. 20 boxes, 30 pieces. (#483) **$41.50 Postpaid.**

Marblehead Nostalgia

Our talented friend, Joe Gallen captured this scene looking across our Harbor from "The Neck." The timing of the sun, barely under a cloud, casting a wake through the peaceful evening waters is unlike anything we've ever seen. We were delighted he allowed us to offer it. 11" x 14" mounted flat in a beveled mat, ready for framing, with a gift box of 16 or more Sweet Sloops. (#420) **$27.50 Postpaid.**

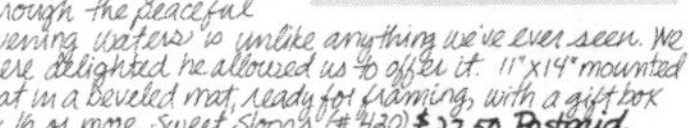

Gift Notes and Sweet Sloops

Our famous friend, Anne Bell Robb captured the magic of Marblehead Harbor in the same soft "Primitive" style which characterizes her paintings of Williamsburg and Charleston. The sailboat is our "Sweet Sloop," a classic Herreshoff 12½ built in 1942. 5 note/envelope set and gift box of 16 or more Sweet Sloops (#424) **$15.00 Postpaid.**

FIGURE C3-4 ***Cover and Selected Pages from Custom Catalog.***

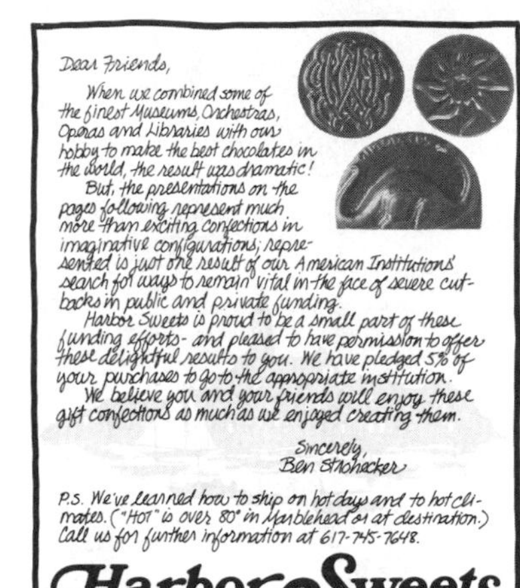

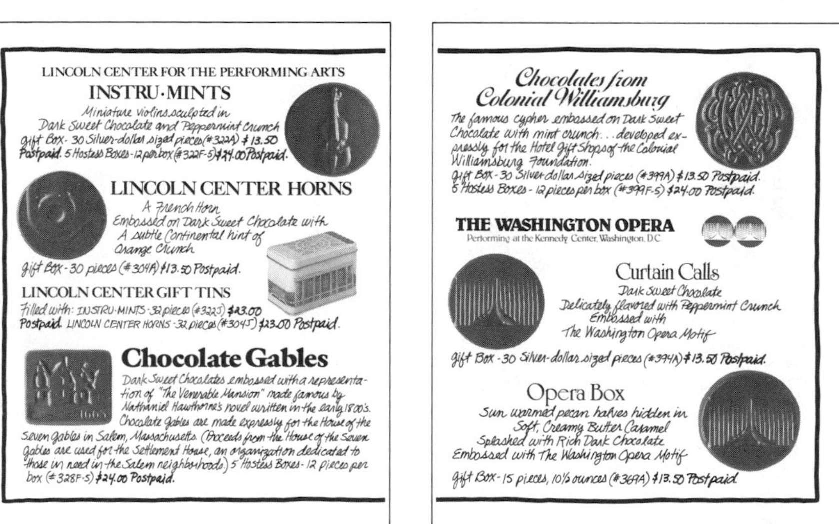

FIGURE C3-5 ***Response card.***

From____________________

____

____

NO POSTAGE NECESSARY IF MAILED IN THE UNITED STATES

BUSINESS REPLY CARD
FIRST CLASS PERMIT #224 MARBLEHEAD, MA

Postage will be paid by:

HARBOR SWEETS®
BOX 150
Marblehead, Massachusetts
01945

Please let us know if your Harbor Sweets package was not received in satisfactory condition.

____

____

____

Please send me ☐ Information on Harbor Sweets Gift Packages
☐ Name of nearest shop selling Harbor Sweets

My address______________________________

____

____

Harbor Sweets®

Harbor Sweets Inc., P.O. Box 150, Marblehead, MA 01945. 617-745-7648.

Case 4

JORDAN MARSH
Use of Direct Marketing Techniques by a Department Store

The Lucite plaque on the desk says "No Surprises." This statement is a reflection of the management philosophy of Don O'Brien, director of marketing of Jordan Marsh, New England's dominant retailer. He believes in well-thought-out strategy, careful planning, and meticulous execution—hence "No Surprises."

It is March 1982 and Don O'Brien and his staff have reviewed all the image-building campaigns run by Jordan Marsh since 1980 with special emphasis on the most recent, "Jack and Jill II." Each campaign has contributed in its own way to the upgrading of Jordan Marsh's image. Proposals for the fall 1982 campaign are on his desk. Now he must decide which campaign proposal to implement.

COMPANY BACKGROUND

In 1851 Eben Dyer Joran and Benjamin L. Marsh established the Jordan Marsh Company. Today Jordan Marsh is the area's largest full-line department store. It has 17 stores that occupy almost 4 million square feet and employ over 10,000 people. Stores are located in 5 states, with the flagship store in Boston's Downtown Crossing. Its parent company is Allied Stores Corporation, which operates 23 department store divisions and whose total sales for fiscal 1982 were $3.2 billion. Joran Marsh New England is the corporation's largest single division.

Directly across the street from JM's Boston store is one of its oldest competitors, Filene's, which was established in 1849. Because of their closeness to one another and their long history of success in serving the greater Boston market, most people think that Filene's is JM's chief competitor. Elliot Stone, president of Jordan Marsh, disagrees, saying, "They just happen to have more stores in the same malls we do than any other retailer."

With the construction of Boston's Prudential Center came two new retail competitors to the Boston area: Lord and Taylor in 1968 and Saks Fifth Avenue in 1971. JM differed from all three major retail competitors in that it was more concerned with functional than with fashion items. Mr. Stone recalls:

This case describes Jordan Marsh's strategy as of early 1982. Their strategy continues to evolve as the market place continues to change.

This case was prepared by Anne Heneberry, Christiana Maharas, and Laura Preskin under the supervision of Associate Professor Mary Lou Roberts, as a basis for class discussion rather than to illustrate either effective or ineffective handling of an administrative situation. All figures are used with the permission of Jordan Marsh.

> We were primarily noted for a strong home furnishings business, moderately priced stuff for the middle-of-the-road customer. We had more mundane pots and pans than anybody...In our apparel area we did a large volume, but the business was strictly with people who had a moderate degree of fashion awareness—not particularly attuned to the trendy things.

In 1973 something happened that made all Boston-area retailers sit up and take notice. In Chestnut Hill, a nearby suburb of Boston, a store that was bound to change the way Boston shopped opened its doors. This was the renowned Bloomingdale's. There is a certain mystique about Bloomingdale's; it is not so much trendy as trend-setting. It has been described as being "by far the nation's most talked about retailer" and "like no other store in the world." The imminent arrival of "Bloomies" caused concern among many Boston-area retailers.

The 1970s also brought increasing competition from two new sources. Specialty stores, such as The Crate and Barrell, Ann Taylor, The Gap and The Limited, were springing up all over the area. Off-price stores were also becoming commonplace. Major off-price retailers included Anne & Hope, Marshall's, and Loehman's. These competitors, plus a changing marketplace, raised doubts about whether JM could retain its market share.

THE CHANGING MARKETPLACE

Population changes in Boston reflected demographic changes that had occurred throughout the United States in the late 1970s and early 1980s. The population of JM's trading territory had grown in size and changed in composition. The city had undergone extensive urban renewal, and its high-technology and service industries had created many new jobs. The people drawn to this environment were younger, more affluent, and more cosmopolitan than the "typical Bostonian" of earlier years.

Boston had long had a traditional, conservative fashion image, but this change in demographics created a more fashion-conscious population. The new atmosphere was a signal to retailers to modify their marketing and merchandising strategies.

As President Stone explained the change, "Sixty percent of the disposable income for general merchandise is in the hands of the customer who ranges in age from 25 years to 45 years." Another significant segment is the 55- to 65-year-olds, empty-nesters who have reached their peak in earnings. This segment, Stone reasoned, contains many better-merchandise customers. Stone also felt that the lower-income population is no longer as likely to shop the upstairs floors of the conventional department stores. Two-income families, on the other hand, are willing to buy what they want when they want it. Stone reasoned that JM must capture a large share of these affluent segments if it was to prosper in the 1980s.

UPGRADING THE IMAGE—MERCHANDISE AND FACILITIES CHANGE

The parent corporation, Allied Stores, was aware of JM's stagnant image and the changing Boston marketplace. JM's merchandise mix emphasized items that appealed to budget-conscious customers who were low in fashion awareness. The downtown store was large—1.7 million square feet—but poorly organized and merchandised. The customer entering the store was confronted by rack after rack, table after table, of merchandise. The visual merchandising lacked the kind of impact that would draw a customer into a department and make him or her want to buy. The store itself was poorly organized, forcing customers to walk back and forth between the main store and an annex to find the items desired. In this era the JM shopping experience was not an exhilarating, or often even a successful, one; it was an exercise in frustration.

Allied Stores recognized the need for an experienced retailing executive who could bring a strategic marketing perspective to JM. Don O'Brien had come to retailing with a background in newspapers and retail advertising. He had served as advertising manager, sales promotion manager, and general merchandise manager at various Allied stores. Just prior to coming to JM he had worked at Hecht's in Washington, D.C., and Gimbels, New York.

Don O'Brien knew that the first priority was to bring in merchandise that would appeal to the affluent segments that were JM's new target. Only after a sizable proportion of this merchandise was in place could the message about "the new JM" be communicated to these targets. JM was able to trade up about 20 percent of its merchandise in the first year. At the same time JM was increasing the efficiency of its sales promotions and establishing long-term goals aimed at attracting these new customers.

Looking back at that hectic first year, Don O'Brien points out one critical element of the strategy that he and Elliot Stone implemented. While JM had targeted new segments, the store did not alienate its existing base of customers who had been loyal JM shoppers for many years. By gradually revising the merchandise mix, JM was able to retain its big customer base while simultaneously attracting new customers. Don O'Brien says that

> Success in this business is more than a fresh merchandising strategy. There has to be the proper customer base first and foremost. Then there are several disciplines involved and they all have to mesh together.
>
> Presentation and display, advertising, housekeeping, motivating sales personnel, resource structure, customer service, vendor relations, are among the disciplines necessary to bring it all together for retailers, above and beyond a strong merchandising plan and the management to carry out that plan.

At the end of his first year these disciplines were in place.

Enter Elliot Stone, a man regarded as a wunderkind of retailing, who was to coordinate the efforts that would successfully transform JM into an updated, upscale store.

Elliot Stone began his retailing career as an executive trainee and later boys' wear buyer at R. H. White of Boston. He also served in various merchandising and store management positions at Gimbel's of Pittsburgh, Maas Brothers, and JM, New England. From 1975 to 1979 he was president of Gimbel Brothers Inc., in New York City. In 1979 he returned to JM as president and chief executive officer. In 1982 he was elected vice president of Allied Stores Corporation.

Stone felt that JM had to "make important statements in merchandise to show we back up what we believe." With designer names such as Norma Kamali, Gucci, Burberry of London, Liz Claiborne, and Baccarat, the consumers were sure to get the message.

Unfortunately, not everyone was happy with the prospect of trading up. Buyers were forced into a difficult position: They had to create relationships with new vendors while simultaneously conducting business with lower-prestige vendors. The latter had been selling large quantities to JM, and now were finding themselves being phased out. Buyers were also upset because they were being forced to sell brand-new lines with which they had little or no experience. These problems were eased by broadening communications throughout the store to ensure that everyone understood the new strategies.

Housing the new merchandise was another problem. The year 1976 marked the reconstruction of the flagship store. The building was reduced from 1.7million square feet to 850,000 square feet. As a result, as new lines were introduced, some old lines had to be discontinued. The emphasis of the reconstruction was on merchandise presentation. This renovation turned the cluttered, voluminous JM of the past into the eye-pleasing and exciting department store of today. Branch stores were also renovated to convey this same comfortable, tasteful, updated image.

THE DIRECT MARKETING CAMPAIGNS

One element of JM's strategy was to decrease reliance on newspaper advertising. JM, like most other major retailers, devoted a large portion of its advertising budget to newspaper ads that promoted specific items to a broad market. These ads reached many people who were not potential customers for that particular item. Consequently, JM reallocated approximately 40 percent of its total advertising budget to direct-mail campaigns.

Stone and O'Brien were aware that most retailers concentrated on "item promotions," newspaper advertisements that featured specific merchandise currently available for sale. In the past JM had carried this one step further by featuring mostly sale or promotional items, thereby strengthening its appeal to the price-conscious customer.

The store's new strategy was completely different from this traditional retailing approach. Its aim was to develop a total customer perception of JM based on five specific image dimensions:

- Forward fashion
- In-store excitement
- Unique merchandise
- Customer service
- Value for dollars spent

Management viewed this image as an umbrella (see Figure C4)—a favorable overall perception of JM that would allow them to attract prime segments immediately and to target other key segments for future growth. One of these prime segments made up the bulk of JM's existing customer base—the budget-conscious shoppers. The new prime segment was the "luxury empty nesters." Other segments, such as large and small sizes, would be developed as specialty businesses.

Direct marketing techniques were vital to this strategy. However, Don O'Brien points out that JM's objective in using direct marketing techniques differed from that of the typical direct marketer. "Our primary objective is to traffic the stores rather than to sell specific products," he said.

Orient Expressed

In September 1980 JM created an aura of in-store excitement by sponsoring a two-week extravaganza entitled "The Orient Expressed." Don O'Brien refers to this as "the two-by-four we used to get the elephant's attention,"—the elephant, of

FIGURE C4–1 Jordan Marsh's Marketing Strategy

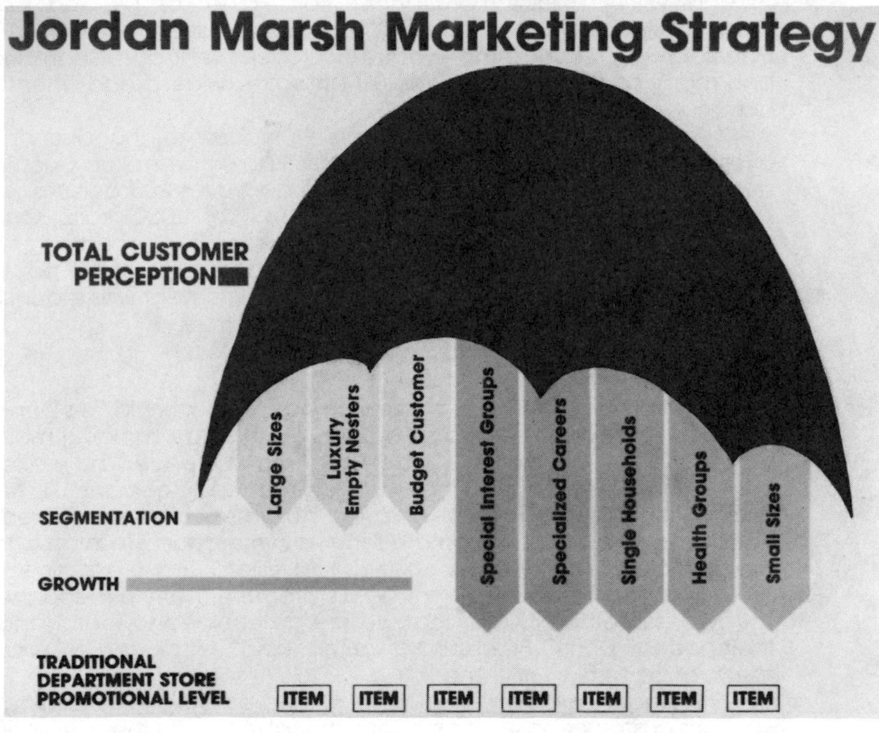

course, being the upscale market that JM was trying to attract. This promotion brought with it unique merchandise from Hong Kong, China, and Kyoto, Japan (Boston's sister city). The campaign required the assistance of the Hong Kong Trade Development Council, the Kyoto City Government and Chamber of Commerce, and many of JM's own resources. It attracted widespread attention in the Boston community.

A direct-mail promotion featured unique merchandise and many special events both inside and outside the store. Over one million people came into the store to witness the spectacular show biz of over 200 artisans, entertainers, and demonstrators from Japan and China and over 1,000 props. Outside the store a sports day was conducted along Boston's waterfront consisting of traditional Oriental games. In addition to all this, JM took advantage of the popularity of Shogun by sponsoring this television miniseries. The excitement was mounting.

"Jack and Jill I and II"

JM's first overall image campaign was "Jack and Jill." As Don O'Brien explains, "Jack and Jill were created as an approach to a changing market, to the baby boom of the 1950s, to the 24- to 39-year-old audience who make up over 50 percent of the whole market." The catalog featured Jack and Jill, representatives of an emerging lifestyle. They were young, attractive, career- oriented, and somewhat hedonistic. The catalog promoted the new merchandise in an attempt to change the upscale customer's perception of JM. Elliot J. Stone explained that "'Jack and Jill' was an extreme way of making a statement that we recognized the lifestyle of the two-career family and that we are determined to merchandise our stores to their needs." Don O'Brien sums it up this way: " 'Jack and Jill' was a lifestyle statement, not a fashion statement."

Ordinarily, a department store mails a catalog to its existing customers only. But JM's customer base was inadequate for reaching the newly targeted segment; there were not enough "Jacks and Jills" among existing customers. So lists were purchased from the *Boston Phoenix* (a lifestyle oriented newspaper), *Harpers Bazaar*, and *Metropolitan Living*. The catalog was also inserted in the New England edition of *the New York Times*. "Jack and Jill" was designed to attract the new customer and to pave the way for the upcoming markets, namely the "young professional" and the two-income family.

From the very beginning the new couple in town received a lot of attention from both the press and the public. "Jack and Jill" were described in a March 1981 edition of the *Boston Globe*, as follows:

> The new couple in town is Jack and Jill. They have fun. They live in a \$199,500 condominium. They do not wear wedding rings. They interact. They do not have furniture. They buy modular groups from a large midtown department store. Their four-piece modular group costs \$1,699.95. They buy and buy and buy. The spaghetti on their plate is the product of \$297 worth of equipment and accessories. They have a dog named Freckles. He is never in the way . . .

The consumer reaction was both positive and negative. Some Jordan Marsh customers praised the catalog, while others sent their charge cards back snipped in half. A small group of customers actually picketed in front of JM's downtown store. Some protested on the grounds that Jack and Jill were not wearing wedding rings. Others felt that the entire campaign was sexist.

In terms of professional recognition, "Meet Jack and Jill," the first catalog, won a national DESI award for graphic design and second prize in a national competition for best home furnishings catalog. "Even though they recognized this was not a home furnishings book," Don O'Brien explains, "they thought it was so innovative that they gave us second prize anyway."

Despite the negative feedback received from "Meet Jack and Jill," the Jack and Jill team turned out a second catalog in the late spring of 1982 entitled "Going in Style." In this catalog Jack and Jill have sold their Beacon Street condominium and have moved into the Charlestown Navy Yard apartments, a renovated historical area. Their dog Freckles has come along, and he is no longer a pup. Moving into a new apartment resulted in purchasing new modular units, accessories, and appliances (including a computer in the kitchen). In this edition we also have the opportunity to meet Jack and Jill's black neighbors. Richie and Delores not only share Jack and Jill's upscale lifestyle, but are even more affluent. The champagne glasses used at their "Hasta la Vista" party cost $33 each, while the wine glasses on Jack and Jill's dining room table cost only $17.50.

After settling into their new apartment, Jack and Jill needed a vacation. They embarked on a trip to Peru. The shooting of all the ads was done in Peru. Each location corresponded to a different page in the catalog. Even with careful planning, the jungle provided many surprises. They included 1 1/2-inch-long deadly ants crawling on the trees where the models posed and carnivorous piranha fish that filled the waters of the Amazon beneath a small boat on which the models had to stand.

Jack and Jill became celebrities as more people became interested and involved with their life. Postcards reading, "Have a wonderful time. Wish you were here. Love, Jack and Jill" were sent to the homes of media representatives. The couple became soap opera figures as people wondered what would happen to them next. Would there be wedding bells for Jack and Jill next year? Would they become parents the following year?

Puttin' on the Ritz

In the fall of 1981 JM made its first high-fashion statement with its "Puttin' on the Ritz" catalog. For the first time JM used television advertising to support a direct-mail campaign. This campaign made the store the label ("This is the Place") instead of using designer names. This campaign led JM into a traditional Christmas season.

All Systems Go

In the spring of 1982 JM produced another campaign entitled "All Systems Go." This campaign featured high technology and made a high-fashion statement. The "Jack and Jill" models appeared in the catalog as well as in spot commercials on television, which supplemented and supported the campaign. The catalog and television commercials featured an assortment of electronic and computer equipment. The merchandise was displayed in a setting alive with contemporary graphics. Success of "All Systems Go" was evidenced by the fact that JM sold out of personal computers for two consecutive Christmases.

THE CURRENT SITUATION

Looking back over the past 2 years, Don O'Brien recognized that JM had made considerable progress toward its overall image objective. This was reflected in double-digit sales growth, as well as in the volume of traffic in the stores, which increased noticeably after each direct marketing campaign. He also recognized, however, that each campaign could only address two, or at most three, of JM's image dimensions. As a result, some of those dimensions had been emphasized repeatedly while others needed to be prominently featured in upcoming campaigns.

There was considerable sentiment among the marketing staff in favor of a "Jack and Jill III." The proposed campaign would find Jack and Jill pursuing their careers and, of course, "dressing for success." In their off-hours they would continue to enjoy their fun-loving lifestyle.

Since the new campaign would be carried out in the fall, there was also support for a campaign with a New England motif, full of historical sites and preparations for a traditional Thanksgiving and Christmas. Tentatively entitled "New England Celebrates," it would reinforce JM's image as a proponent of time-honored New England values of quality and service.

Don O'Brien wondered whether he should approve one of these proposals or look for a totally new approach to the continuation of JM's image-building strategy.

Case 5

SHAKER WORKSHOPS, INC. Potential Acquisition of a Mail-Order Firm

THE CONCEPT

The concept was simple: create a synergy by merging the talents of three men. The implementation was more complicated.

In 1970 a real estate agent (Mr. R), a museum curator (Mr. M), and an accountant (Mr. A) formed Shaker Workshops, Inc. This company was designed to market Shaker-style furniture. The idea was that Mr. R would sell old houses and convince the residents to purchase Shaker furniture. Mr. M would determine what kind of furniture to market, and serve as a full-time authority on Shaker style. Mr. A, a Harvard Business School graduate, would keep track of the books and arrange the financing.

SHAKER HISTORY

In 1774 Ann Lee, who later came to be known as Mother Ann Lee, founded the faith that was dubbed Shakerism. The Shakers landed in New York from England and spread their religious faith north and south, traveling as far west as Ohio. In their search for God the Shakers believed in leading a simple life free of pride, greed, and sex, which they saw as the cause of man's misery on earth. Inspired by these convictions, the Shakers upheld four fundamental principles: confession of sins, community of goods, celibacy, and withdrawal from the sinful world. These beliefs affected every aspect of their lives, even the furniture they built. A succession of wars and numerous economic and social changes finally led to Shakerism dying out around the turn of this century. Only two small villages remained in 1970.

MANUFACTURING AND RETAIL OPERATIONS

In 1970 Shaker Workshops, Inc., was strictly a middleman. The company did not manufacture furniture, it marketed it. Inventory was obtained through subcontractors. Subcontracting had many advantages and disadvantages. Production of fur-

This case was prepared by Brad Pogachefsky and Nikki Sossin under the supervision of Associate Professor Mary Lou Roberts as a basis for class discussion rather than to illustrate either effective or ineffective handling of an administrative situation.

niture in general, and curved Shaker furniture in particular, requires special equipment and tools, as well as skilled labor. By using subcontractors, the company did not have to pay or train skilled laborers, nor did it have to store raw materials and purchase equipment. When the company needed certain components of furniture, all it had to do was order them. This convenience had its price. Shaker Workshops was forced to pay a premium for the furniture. The company was also unable to realize any economies of scale. In an industry with average net earnings before taxes of 10 percent, economies of scale and cost efficiencies are critical to profitability.

Once the individual components of the furniture were received by Shaker Workshops from the subcontractors, the furniture was assembled at the company's factory/warehouse in West Concord. The assembled furniture was then shipped to the company's retail storefront in fashionable downtown Concord, a wealthy suburb of Boston. Only a few pieces of each type of furniture were stocked at the retail storefront. Therefore stockouts were frequent, forcing the company to continually run a truck to and from the factory/warehouse in West Concord. The average cost of transportation and packaging, as a percentage cost of goods sold, is 7 to 10 percent. Since Shaker Workshops was forced to pay for transportation and packaging twice,— once from the subcontractors to the West Concord factory, and once from the factory to the downtown Concord retail storefront,— the average cost of transportation and packaging for the first 5 years of business was over 11 percent. Again, in an industry with an average net earnings before taxes of 10 percent, economizing on transportation and packaging expenses is critical to profitability.

In 1974 the company established a West Coast subsidiary, another retail store outside San Francisco. The partners decided to open this outlet because 20 percent of their mail-order business came from the California area. However, this was not enough business to justify opening a store in California. No Shakers had ever lived on the West Coast; very few West Coast residents even knew what Shaker-style furniture was! Since this store was located so far from the factory, transportation costs were grossly increased. Also increased were the company's phone bill and traveling and administrative expenses. The California subsidiary was closed in the spring of 1975.

THE CATALOG

Mr. A knew that direct-mail advertising is especially effective when applied to products and services whose markets are highly segmented. Direct mailings enable a marketer to reach only those consumers he knows are interested in his product. The mailings, if properly targeted, are very exact. For example, if one has a product that is used to restore the teakwood on Rolls-Royce automobiles, it would be wasteful to advertise this product on television. Most viewers do not own Rolls-Royces. Assuming one could obtain a list of all Rolls-Royce owners, it would be much more efficient to reach these consumers via the mail.

Shaker furniture represents a very small segment of the entire furniture market. The furniture is used most often in traditional-style homes, and the market is not concentrated in one regional area. Therefore Mr. A's decision to use direct marketing techniques was more logical than Mr. R's idea of selling the furniture to new homeowners. However, when the direct mailing piece is the only selling tool, it must present the product effectively and make it easy for the customer to buy it. Shaker Workshops' catalogs did not accomplish this.

The company's first catalog was more like a museum history book than a sales catalog. Of its 27 pages, 20 were devoted to script about the history of the Shakers and their furniture. There was no order form or self-addressed, stamped envelope attached to the catalog. The ordering process required two pages of instruction (not an effective use of space). This was not an easy catalog to order from (800 numbers were not widely used at the time). The second year's catalog still did not have an order form attached, nor a self-addressed, stamped envelope. It did display more of the furniture that was for sale than the first year's catalog. However, the photos were poorly laid out. It was often hard to see what was actually for sale. Procedural mistakes persisted throughout the succeeding catalogs.

The implementation of Shaker Workshops' direct marketing effort was not handled well either. To generate inquiries for its catalog the company advertised in both *Yankee* and *Early American Life* magazines. It also obtained a mailing list from Hancock Shaker Village, a Massachusetts museum. In its first year it mailed around 10,000 catalogs from the office by hand, causing a long delay between inquiry and receipt of the catalog.

THE DEGENERATING SITUATION

In 1972 Shaker Workshops showed a small operating profit (Figure C5-1). Pleased with their success, Mr. M spent a year developing a line of scented herbs to add to the catalog. When his partners did not share his enthusiasm, Mr. M left the firm.

At this point in the company's development the remaining partners recognized two distinct problems in their operation. First was the need for a marketing expert. Second, they felt that to increase quality and decrease costs, they should manufacture the furniture themselves.

They solved their first problem by persuading a college classmate of Mr. A's to join them. Mr. C (the classmate) had been working for a local advertising agency that specialized in industrial print advertising and the development of sales support material. He had little retail or mail-order catalog experience. He worked with Shaker part-time in 1973, full-time in 1974, and part-time thereafter.

In order to begin manufacturing furniture themselves, in 1974 and 1975 the partners purchased tools and production machinery. Mr. C loaned Shaker $25,000 to finance these acquisitions.

After Shaker showed a large operating loss in 1974, Mr. A and Mr. R had an argument. What caused the final split in late 1974 or early 1975 is unclear, but the outcome was resolved by a flip of a coin. Mr. R won the toss and he bought Mr. A's share of the business.

A PROSPECTIVE PURCHASER

Dick Dabrowski first heard about Shaker Workshops, Inc., through the industrial grapevine in December 1979. Mr. Dabrowski, who had never taken a business course in his 4 years as a political science major at the University of North Carolina, began his career as an assistant buyer in Jordan Marsh's record department.

He left there after 2 years and began working at Woodcraft Supply Corporation, the largest supplier of specialty woodworking hand tools in the United States. Sales were conducted both through a mail-order catalog and retail stores. In 1979, just before Mr. Dabrowski left, Woodcraft was doing an annual business of over $5 million.

Mr. Dabrowski studied the reproduction kit furniture industry and saw that three or four firms had the entire market to themselves. That's when the idea of purchasing Shaker Workshops, Inc., occurred to him. Mr. Dabrowski met with Mr. R early in 1980 to discuss Mr. R's proposal that Mr. Dabrowski should buy 60 percent of the company's business for a "bargain price" of $50,000.

After reviewing the company's December 31, 1978, balance sheet, Mr. Dabrowski felt unsure about this offer. He knew that in October 1979, because no federal taxes had been paid for several years, the IRS had impounded all cash funds. He and his lawyer went to the tax revenue office at the Massachusetts state capitol to see what, if any, state taxes were due. They discovered that Shaker Workshops had substantial accrued liabilities for unemployment compensation, state withholding taxes, and state sales taxes. These liabilities appeared on the 1978 balance sheet, but substantial penalties associated with them were not shown.

After his visit to the state capitol, Mr.Dabrowski returned home to sort out his thoughts. He sat down and listed, in order of importance, what he saw as the positive and negative aspects of the failing business.

Positive

1. Shaker Workshops was an established business. The groundwork had been done. He didn't have to start from scratch.
2. Since blueprints for the furniture already existed, he would be saved the expense of hiring a draftsman.
3. The company name capitalized on the positive association potential customers might have with the Shaker Church and community. People would be more inclined to purchase Shaker furniture from Shaker Workshops than from "Josephine's Furniture Shop."
4. There was a mailing list of approximately 35,000 names on file. The only problem was that the file consisted of small pieces of paper stuffed in paper bags.
5. There was tooling worth approximately $10,000 left from the factory. The balance sheet showed this tooling and shop machinery as assets, though Mr. Dabrowski discovered that most of it was the property of Shaker's production manager. He had loaned Shaker $10,000 with the shop machinery as collateral. When the loan was not repaid a year later, he assumed ownership of the machinery.

Negative

1. There was no "salable" furniture in inventory, which consisted of mixed sets of right arms and left legs and other such combinations. There was also no main inventory sheet. Mr. Dabrowski had no way of knowing exactly what was there without going through it piece by piece himself.
2. No kits were left in inventory, although kits were the essence of the business.
3. The company had virtually no machinery (the production manager owned it).
4. Some customers were still waiting for refunds on furniture they had returned to the company.
5. There were unpaid taxes.

6. Because of slow order fulfillment and unpaid refunds, the company had, over 10 years, developed a bad reputation.

All in all, it appeared that Shaker Workshops had total assets worth $15,000 in 1978. Since $8,000 of this consisted of personal loan notes made to the officers/owners of the company, assets were, realistically, around $7,000.

Liabilities, on the other hand, totaled close to $89,000. The balance sheets did not accurately portray what had happened year to year. Shaker Workshops' books were done on a calendar year basis instead of on an August 1 through July 31 fiscal-year basis, which would reflect mail-order sales more accurately.

Following the advice of his lawyer, Mr. Dabrowski hired a business consultant to "work out the numbers," that is, to see if the company could be a profitable acquisition. He needed the consultant for an objective analysis of this crazy situation. Mr. Dabrowski was very enthusiastic about the idea, but the consultant's advice would keep him in check. While waiting to hear from the consultant, Mr. Dabrowski sat back and did a little thinking on his own. He was at a crossroad. Should he walk away from the whole situation, wiping his hands clean of Shaker Workshops and forgetting about the designs, lists, and other assets of the business? Or should he buy the 60 percent of the business Mr. R was offering him for $50,000? Or should he start a completely new Shaker furniture business? He just didn't know.

FIGURE C5–1

SHAKER WORKSHOPS, INC.

Balance Sheet
December 31, 1978

Exhibit A
Page 1 of 2
Unaudited

ASSETS

Current Assets:			
Petty Cash		$ 110.00	
Advances to Officers		8,239.44	
Unexpired Insurance		1,398.00	
Merchandise Inventory		19,324.53	
Savings Account		125.08	
Total Current Assets			$ 29,197.05
Property and Equipment:			
Machinery and Equipment	$ 21,679.25		
Less Allowance for Depreciation	10,522.33	$ 11,156.92	
Office Equipment	$ 2,325.63		
Less Allowance for Depreciation	1,694.73	630.90	
Leasehold Improvements	$ 8,231.00		
Less Allowance for Depreciation	6,720.50	1,510.50	
Total Property and Equipment			13,298.32
Other Assets:			
Lease and Utility Deposits			515.00
Total Assets			$ 43,010.37

Exhibit A
Page 2 of 2
Unaudited

LIABILITIES AND STOCKHOLDERS' EQUITY

Liabilities:			
Current Liabilities:			
Bank Overdrafts		$ 1,645.16	
Accounts Payable		20,801.33	
Customers' Deposits		10,129.54	
Accrued Interest Payable (Notes 2 & 3)		5,505.50	
Withholding Taxes Payable		7,348.54	
Accrued Payroll Taxes		4,720.03	
Accrued Taxes Payable		263.00	
Sales Taxes Payable		7,824.24	
Other Accrued Expenses		18,299.18	
Total Current Liabilities			$ 76,536.52
Other Liabilities:			
Note Payable - Other (Note 3)		$ 10,000.00	
Note Payable - Stockholder (Note 2)		20,000.00	
Total Other Liabilities			30,000.00
Total Liabilities			$ 106,536.52
Stockholders' Equity:			
Capital Stock: Common, No Par Value			
Authorized: 7500 Shares			
Issued and Outstanding: 262 Shares		$ 57,818.68	
Retained Earnings:			
Balance, December 31, 1977-Deficit	$(121,819.59)		
Net Profit for the Year	474.76		
Balance, December 31, 1978-Deficit		(121,344.83)	
Total Stockholders' Equity			(63,526.15)
Total Liabilities and Stockholders' Equity			$ 43,010.37

FIGURE C5–1 continued

Year End Balance Sheets
Month Ending 12/31

	1971	1972	1973	1974	1975	1976	1977
Cash	$ 5,024.56	$ 3,664.87	$ 5,078.76	($ 563.33)	$ 5,970.79	($ 2,724.92)	($ 8,355.88)
Accounts Rec.		(100.00)	405.73		1,779.6t	3,353.60	300.97
Inventory	24,109.24	26,547.20	59,548.56	75,811.49	32,479.88	41,125.56	29,187.16
Advances	236.21	91.34	234.85	1,503.56	2,446.83	7,627.94	6,836.20
Other	42.60		2,564.71				
Total	$29,412.61	$30,203.41	$67,832.61	$76,751.72	$42,677.15	$49,382.18	$27,968.45
Office Equip.	$ 632.01	$ 2,764.31	$ 2,205.25	$ 2,575.63	$ 2,775.61	$ 2,325.63	$ 2,325.63
Tools	1,239.17	1,522.91	2,217.38	3,272.23	4,044.49	4,583.21	4,561.81
Shop Machinery				2,924.28	3,139.28	17,096.04	17,255.70
Leasehold Imp.			1,668.54	4,886.02	7,075.27	9,899.01	10,278.12
Truck			5,092.00	5,092.00	5,092.00	5,092.00	5,092.00
Product Develop.				1,083.95	1,283.95	1,322.27	1,322.27
Reserve for Dep.	(857.01)	(1,942.37)	(3,288.30)	(6,725.43)	10,514.82)	(11,102.49)	(13,911.83)
Reserve for Amor						(4,557.90)	(6,615.54)
Total	$ 1,014.17	$ 2,344.85	$ 7,894.87	$13,108.68	$12,895.78	$24,657.77	$20,308.16
Deposits	$ 284.00	$ 284.00	$ 370.00	$ 1,750.00	$ 715.00	$ 515.00	$ 515.00
Prepaid Int.			526.91	346.26	165.61	348.14	102.39
Org. Exp.	519.98	401.91	283.11	164.31	45.51		
Total	$ 803.98	$ 685.91	$ 1,180.02	$ 2,260.57	$ 926.12	$ 863.14	$ 617.39
Catalogs on Hand				$ 3,001.78	$ 342.91	$ 964.69	$ 113.27
Prepaid Adv.							
Ins. Unexpired				1,367.53	1,553.25	1,015.58	1,281.16
Prepaid Exp.				49.35	49.35	184.79	184.79
Claim for Tax Refund				2,146.43			
Total				$ 6,565.09	$ 1,945.51	$ 2,165.06	$ 1,579.22
Grand Total	$31,230.76	$33,234.17	$76,907.50	$98,686.06	$58,444.56	$77,068.15	$50,473.22
Acc'ts Payable	$ 3,024.54	$ 8,253.03	$43,657.30	$59,587.93	$35,068.13	$53,369.65	$37,884.93
Sales Tax Pay.	423.36	603.10	1,079.44	695.03	2,505.59	5,121.09	6,786.94
Payroll Tax W/H	523.30	559.98	1,285.21	2,002.08	5,037.01	6,048.11	6,588.17
Accrued Exp.	399.98	1,548.66	1,961.50	15,883.61	20,924.72	30,103.50	27,671.17
Pro. St & Fed Tax			495.49	394.50	270.31	498.31	498.31
Customer Deposits	773.53	870.57	7,182.22	5,132.79	1,198.57	5,948.81	4,036.86
Gift Certificates			157.00				
Total	$ 5,144.71	$11,835.34	$55,818.16	$83,695.94	$65,004.33	$101,089.47	$83,466.38
Notes Payable	$	$	$ 4,221.35	$37,774.03	$11,326.71	$ 7,268.64	$ 3,576.73
JFC	9,547.02	3,529.12					
RSB	10,242.32	5,354.69	4,080.83				
Dodd	3,300.00	3,120.00			15,000.00	15,000.00	15,000.00
Total	$23,089.34	$12,003.81	$ 8,302.18	$37,774.03	$26,326.71	$22,268.64	$18,576.73
Capital Stock	$20,618.68	$20,618.68	$20,618.68	$51,818.68	$57,818.68	$57,818.68	$57,818.68
Surplus (Deficit)	(17,621.97)	(11,223.66)	(7,831.52)	(74,602.59)	90,705.16)	(104,108.64)	(109,388.57)
Total	$ 2,996.71	$ 9,395.02	$12,787.16	($22,783.91)	$32,886.48)	($ 46,289.96)	($ 51,569.89)
Grand Total	$31,230.76	$33,234.17	$76,907.50	$98,686.06	$58,444.56	$77,068.15	$50,473.22

Year End Income Statements
Cumulative 12 Months Ending 12/31

	1971	1972	1973	1974	1975	1976	1977
Sales	$34,690.76	$142,203.08	$225,617.69	$256,885.79	$192,523.79	$196,523.00	$144,640.48
Cost of Sales	(23,089.72)	(79,018.43)	(107,300.33)	(136,011.90)	(87,483.38)	(143,289.00)	(105,529.69)
Gross Total	$11,601.04	$ 63,184.65	$118,317.36	$120,873.89	$105,040.41	$ 53,234.00	$ 39,110.79
Rent	$ 3,541.56	$ 5,782.29	$ 6,698.30	$ 12,350.00	$ 8,131.20	753.00	$ 574.56
Interest	300.00	287.71	738.25	3,702.95	3,917.03	2,769.00	3,501.86
Office Supplies	1,647.74	1,885.71	3,997.48	3,426.39	4,167.94	3,293.00	1,596.75
Depreciation	925.59	1,203.43	1,464.73	3,555.93	3,908.19	148.00	147.84
Insurance	160.16	1,270.03	1,209.84	1,824.65	1,540.00	509.00	440.88
Taxes	261.00	(29.34)	911.15	751.69	294.16	35.00	228.00
Electricity				1,328.55	970.46	181.00	231.75
Telephone	} 811.29	} 1,970.38	} 2,887.34	4,624.56	2,742.16	3,273.00	3,535.02
Heat				490.62	828.28	83.00	111.60
Catalog Print.	6,725.55	8,065.87	11,350.53	11,027.11	4,475.87	6,620.00	1,852.95
Total	$14,372.89	$ 20,436.08	$ 29,257.62	$ 43,082.45	$ 30,975.29	$ 17,664.00	$ 12,221.21
Freight Out	} $ 690.96	} $ 3,172.73	} $ 5,408.13	$ 11,851.82	$ 6,430.27	$ 4,109.00	$
Freight In				1,280.92	326.77		
Packaging	1,123.37	317.12	4,158.49	5,813.20			
Postage	880.69	2,607.34	3,929.73	3,607.85	1,647.92	4,657.00	1,198.23
Total	$ 2,695.02	$ 6,097.19	$ 13,496.35	$ 22,553.79	$ 8,404.96	$ 8,766.00	$ 1,198.23
Payroll	$ 8,422.30	$ 17,109.43	$ 38,485.93	$ 68,024.29	$ 43,151.08	$ 33,848.00	$ 22,950.96
Payroll Tax	686.86	1,415.41	3,713.58	5,416.28	3,536.40	3,044.00	586.46
Advertising	2,496.15	5,628.08	13,258.29	31,086.01	8,265.23	10,358.00	2,352.09
Prototypes	448.75	907.39	1,310.90	----			
Dues & Sub.	69.00	36.00	110.92	303.58			45.50
Commissions		76.25	445.24	1,380.45	950.93	495.00	919.75
Travel		735.49	4,177.39	6,209.27	1,218.34	1,190.00	1,083.40
Legal & Acc't			4,806.35	4,501.72	2,422.80	1,355.00	1,656.62
Consult/Draft.	232.02	524.07	4,704.34	2,120.44	120.00	919.00	110.00
Total	$12,355.08	$ 26,432.12	$ 71,022.94	$119,042.04	$ 59,664.78	$ 51,199.00	$ 29,704.78
Penalties	$	$	$	$ 63.76	$ 404.45	$ 1,481.00	$ 1,131.76
Truck Expense			79.18	2,217.08	4,108.27		
Contributions			25.00	60.00			
Equip. Rental				621.40			
Misc.				339.99	67.79	2,009.00 *	134.74
Total			$ 104.18	$ 3,302.23	$ 4,580.51	$ 3,490.00	$ 1,266.50
Total Expenses	$29,422.99	$ 52,965.39	$113,881.09	$187,980.51	$103,625.54	$ 81,119.00	$ 44,390.72
Income (Loss)	($17,821.95)	$ 10,219.26	$ 4,436.27	($ 67,106.67)	$ 1,414.87	($ 27,885.00)	($ 5,279.93)

* inc. amort. of $1,992.00

Case 6

SIMPLEX TIME RECORDER CO. Growth of the Telemarketing Support Group

DEFINITION OF THE PROBLEM

In February 1984 Michael Rague, supervisor of special projects at Simplex Time Recorder Co., was reviewing the first year of operations at the company's new telemarketing division in Acton, Massachusetts. There was no question that the new sales approach by telephone had been a huge success in the area of time clocks. The company was selling more clocks than ever before. By generating leads, the system was also helping to cut down on the amount of cold calling done by the field sales representatives. In addition to substantially reducing the cost per sales call, the system was helping the company to better forecast demand. Still, Mike was concerned about one aspect of the system that wasn't performing up to expectations: the telemarketing of service contracts.

The first year's efforts to sell service contracts over the phone had been largely unsuccessful. Mike attributed this to the fact that there was no set price for the service contracts as there was for the time clocks. Many factors had to be taken into consideration before a price could be set for full-service contracts, and the telemarketing system had not been able to handle the pricing problem effectively. Later on in the month Mike was going to have to make a recommendation to the retail sales manager, Mike Gallant. Was it possible to handle the many variables involved in selling the service contracts over the phone, or were these better left to the field sales representatives?

COMPANY HISTORY

In 1888 Edward G. Watkins invented the first modern time clock and shortly thereafter founded the Simplex Time Recorder Co. In the early years of the company's history Watkins worked on building a reputation for quality and dependable service that has remained intact to the present. In order to maintain this reputation, growth at the company came slowly as a result of internal growth and the careful acquisition of time clock companies.

Since this case was written, Simplex has drastically reduced its telemarketing group and moved out of the Acton facility. A small telemarketing group engaged exclusively in the sale of time cards is now in operation at its Gardner, Massachusetts headquarters.

This case was prepared by Jon Hughes and Simon Zafet under the supervision of Associate Professor Mary Lou Roberts as a basis for class discussion rather than to illustrate either effective or ineffective handling of an administrative situation.

In 1942 Edward Watkins died and passed control of the company on to his son, Curtis G. Watkins. Following in his father's footsteps, Curtis Watkins continued a policy of gradual and carefully planned growth, always paying close attention to quality and service. In 1958 the company acquired IBM's Time Equipment Division, making Simplex the dominant firm in the time recorder industry, a position the company maintains to this day. Further growth in the time clock market led Simplex into the international market with subsidiaries in Western Europe, Canada, and Australia. At the time of his death in 1967, Curtis Watkins had diversified the company into the master clock, fire alarm, and security systems markets, in each of which the company soon achieved a market leader position.

Once again the company was passed from generation to generation as Watkins's son, Edward G. Watkins, became chairman in 1967. Edward Watkins continued the tradition of growth and quality by integrating technological developments into Simplex products. This resulted in the new line of electronic time recorders that Simplex now offers.

SIMPLEX PRODUCT LINE

Simplex markets an array of time clocks designed to fit every need. The basic line starts with the JCP Cordless model, which is a portable time clock designed for rugged use in places where electricity is difficult to get. Model HA2GD is designed for controlling documents and correspondence by clearly printing the exact time and date. Another time clock, Model HA11, is used to record only the date of the transaction (for example, as a date validator in a check-clearing system). The product line also includes Model HA17, a numbering time stamp that can be used, for example, to number and date purchase orders. Model HA32G is an automatic time/date and numbering stamp. These models are for use in smaller businesses where the number of employees is not over 20 and the volume of work is not excessive (see Figure C6-1).

For more complex applications, Simplex offers Model Series 5000/6000 and Models ETC and TMT 7100. Models 5000/6000 are designed for documenting employee attendance; they provide indisputably accurate records enabling a company to more effectively control labor costs. The series includes Model 5000, an automatic attendance recorder, and Model 6000, an automatic attendance recorder with "up the card" time registration (allowing a single vertical daily schedule to be programmed).

Models ETC and TMT 7100 are Simplex's answer to the minicomputer age. Both models are programmable, calculating actual elapsed time worked by employees while differentiating between regular hours, overtime hours, and special overtime hours. These models can be connected with the main computer system, allowing direct calculation of payroll costs. In addition, Model TMT 7100 provides information for a variety of management reports (such as total overtime hours or detailed/cumulative payroll information) regarding a specific employee (see Figure C6-2).

FIELD SALES FORCE

The need to create a more efficient way to support the growth of the sales force became evident at the beginning of 1978. The company sales force had grown with the business recovery that had taken place in the late 1970s, and the company

FIGURE C6–1 ***Part of the Simplex Product Line***
Source: Simplex Promotional Materials

Time and Date Stamp

The Simplex Time and Date Stamp is the ideal product for controlling documents and correspondence. It clearly prints the exact time and the date that correspondence is received or sent, when transactions take place, or the start and stop time of any activity.

This stamp is available with or without a clock dial, with either regular time or military time (0-23 hours) and with custom inscription dies.

Facsimile Print
Actual size
Model HA2G D.

FEB 9 3 14 PM '84

Custom inscriptions engraved to your requirements can be added above and/or below print line.

Date Stamp

The Simplex Date Stamp is used when it is necessary to capture only the date of the transaction. Often used as a bank validator with optional removable inscription keys.

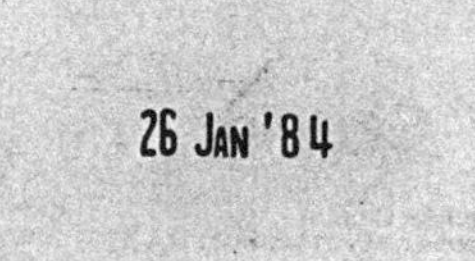

Facsimile Print
Actual size
Model HA11

Optional custom inscriptions available.

Numbering Stamp

The Simplex Numbering Stamp imprints a six digit number which automatically advances with each registration. Provides a convenient and secure method of document number control. Ideal for purchase order numbers, invoice numbers, deed numbering and many other control applications. Optional key switch restricts use to only authorized keyholders. Optional custom inscriptions are available for use above and below the number.

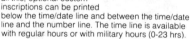

475362

Facsimile Print
Actual size
Model HA17

Automatic Time/Date and Numbering Stamp

The ultimate - Simplex' automatic Time/Date/Numbering Stamp does it all. Controls transactions and documents with a consecutive number, the date and the exact hour and minute. In addition to all this, optional custom inscriptions can be printed below the time/date line and between the time/date line and the number line. The time line is available with regular hours or with military hours (0-23 hrs).

000044

FEB 9 7 01 AM '84

Facsimile Print
Actual size
(Regular hours - Model HA32G)
(0-23 hours - Model HA38G)

FIGURE C6–2A ***Computerized Models***
Source: Simplex Promotional Materials

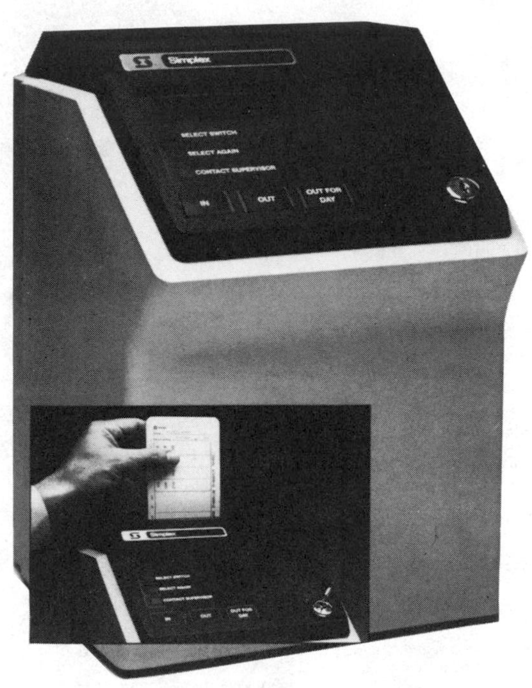

7 features of The New Simplex TMT 7100

1 **Time Totalization**
- Eliminates hand totaling
- Insures accuracy
- Controls overtime
- Saves management time

2 **Management Reports**
- Added labor cost control
- Obtain group totals by departments
- Enables more efficient man-power allocation

3 **Holiday Scheduling**
- Schedules up to 16 holidays
- Automatically totals in holidays
- Eliminates past hassles

4 **No Overpunch**
- Card-reader ends errors
- Eliminates hassles over checks

5 **Employee Lock Out**
- No use of clock after hours
- Better management control

6 **Battery Backup**
- Keeps time during power failures
- Continues operating
- No extra cost

7 **Magnetic Striped Card**
- Card remembers totals
- Card remembers schedules

FIGURE C6–2B

Electronic Time Calculator

Finally---Fast efficient and economical collection and calculation of attendance data.

Improved Time Card Document

- Easy to read format with daily totals.
- Machine memory of last print placement assures no over-print.
- Abnormal registrations printed in red (late arrivals, early de-partures, etc.)

Accurate Calculations

- Error prone manual elapsed time calculations eliminated by microprocessor computations.
- Disputes with employees reduced by clear illustration of daily totals.

Conforms to Your Work Schedules

- Up to 12 fixed work schedules handled simultaneously.
- Flexible and irregular schedules unlimited with Simplex' time grid.
- 24 hour shifts and rotation of shifts handled automatically.

Conforms to Your Payroll Policies and Practices

- Rounding of arrivals and de-partures.
- Authorized and unauthorized overtime periods.
- Authorized arrival-departure periods.

Easy To Implement

- Employees adapt easily to familiar IN-OUT registration procedures.
- Installs quickly; requires no connection to other equip-ment.
- Master clock and/or computer interfacing is easily accomplished.

Supervisory Tools

- Time Card format with totals precalculated, aids super-visors in controlling labor distribution, overtime and attendance abuse.
- Management reports can be generated upon demand by authorized managers for all users.
- Reports provide listings of employees individual total time as well as listing of employees present or absent by department or by individuals.
- ETC can be efficiently inter-faced with most computing systems through an RS-232C interface.

was concerned that it was losing touch with the marketplace. Furthermore, Simplex management had become increasingly aware that the costs associated with the field sales force were getting out of hand and becoming a deterrent to the overall growth of the company.

The salesmen themselves often complained of having to handle large numbers of small customers while being under constant pressure to make frequent calls on their best customers. The rural salesmen pointed out that it often took them 2 hours to travel from one customer to another, which significantly reduced the number of customers they could contact in a given day. A more efficient system was needed to help all salesman determine how frequently to call on each individual account. In addition, if salespeople knew specific customer needs in advance of the sales call, they could feature the appropriate model in their sales presentations. This would increase their overall sales productivity by cutting down on unnecessary sales calls and by making sales presentations more effective. It often happened that more than one salesman would approach the same prospect, sometimes with the same sales presentation. This was not only ineffective for Simplex, it was confusing and annoying to customers.

Besides servicing existing accounts, salespeople were also responsible for generating new accounts. Simplex salespeople, unlike many other field sales forces, were eager to develop new accounts. They knew that the expected replacement cycle for time clocks was 8 years. This severely limited the amount of repeat business a salesperson could expect from existing accounts. However, salespeople experienced problems in prospecting for new accounts similar to those they had in handling existing accounts—inadequate knowledge about which firms represented the best targets and what their specific needs were.

Finally, salespeople were eager to concentrate on the electronic time clocks. They spent a great deal of time determining which existing accounts were the best candidates for the higher-priced models. They also preferred to prospect for new accounts that seemed likely to purchase the higher-end models.

By 1980 management was seriously concerned about the set of problems caused by increased sales force size and an expanding product line. Cost per sales call was continuing to increase. The costs of servicing small-ticket items, such as the basic time clocks and supplies for them, was becoming prohibitively expensive.

Another problem was the time that elapsed between placement of the order and customer receipt of the merchandise. During the 1970s this time had increased from an average of 2 weeks to over 3 weeks. This was resulting in considerable customer dissatisfaction. During the same period Simplex saw its inventory level increase substantially.

Management also knew there was a problem in managing Simplex's geographic sales regions. There were 12 sales regions and 140 sales representatives covering the entire United States. Occasionally, sales representatives found themselves calling on the same accounts. Management knew this problem would worsen as growth continued.

Sales growth was also causing pressure for increased decentralization of inventories to provide faster customer service. If management chose to maintain inventory at more locations, costs would increase and control would become much more difficult.

DEVELOPMENT OF TELEMARKETING SYSTEM

The early stages of the telemarketing operation took place at company headquarters in Gardner, Massachusetts, early in 1982. The feasibility of the idea was tested by providing a single 800 number and using it in an advertisement for Simpex's basic models in *The Wall Street Journal*. The response was so great that by May six full-time telemarketing representatives were handling the inquiries from that single number. By October Mike Rague and Mike Gallant were in the process of choosing a telephone system to be used at the new telemarketing division in Acton, Massachusetts.

By January 1983 the system had been chosen and operations begun. The system being used was an ACD (automatic call distribution). It consisted of a computer that accepted all calls coming in on the 800 numbers. Using the area code of the incoming call as a basis, the computer directed it to the telemarketing representative responsible for that territory.

Simplex divided the United States up into 12 regions, and broke each one of these up into different territories. Each region is assigned field sales representatives according to its size. The telemarketing sales representatives are similarly allocated, with some regions having more representatives than others. Each rep works hours corresponding to the business day in his region. For example, the reps for the West Coast come into work at noon and leave a 8 P.M., whereas the reps for the East Coast work 9:00 A.M. to 5:00 P.M.

The system also handles other functions vital to the sales effort. Records of the number of calls coming in and going out, the amount of time spent on each call, and actual sales figures are made available to management on a daily basis. This information is then be used to evaluate sales performance, to estimate inventory requirements, and to update customer files.

FACILITIES

The actual facilities at division headquarters in Acton are specifically designed for a telemarketing operation. The office area is open and spacious, with sales reps separated by special sound-absorbing partitions. Office furniture and headsets are designed with comfort and mobility in mind. This is very important for good performance since the sales reps are sitting down for 7 hours a day. The open atmosphere is also important to smooth operations. It fosters camaraderie among the sales reps and also works as a motivational device for management. With quotas and performance levels posted openly, a desire to perform well is instilled in each sales rep.

PERSONNEL

Currently there are 36 telemarketing sales reps working at the Acton division; 22 of whom are full-time reps and 14 of whom work part-time as lead qualifiers for the electronic models.

The job of a telemarketing sales rep at Simplex is supportive in nature. Commissions are based on how well the field sales force in that person's territory does for the year, not on how many time clocks the person sells over the phone. As a result, the two sales forces, telemarketing and field, are not in direct competition with each other.

The objectives for the telemarketing sales reps are to sell as many of the basic low-sales-effort models as possible, and to get qualifying information on the electronic models to the field sales force. This way the field sales force will not be waiting their $200 sales call on customers who could have been serviced over the phone.

Each telemarketing sales rep is responsible for a territory that is based on area codes. In turn, each territory is broken up according to the type of order than the customer wishes to place. The result is that for each territory there will be at least two sales reps: one who handles the 800 number for time cards, and another who handles the 800 number for all time clocks. Depending on the size of the region, there may be other reps to handle any overflow.

When a call is transferred to the appropriate sales rep by the computer, the sales rep follows a specific routine. First a number of qualifying questions pertaining to the higher-end models such as the TMT 7100 are covered by the sales rep. If the customer qualifies for one of these, then the information is recorded. (see Figure C6-3), the customer is told that he can expect to hear from a field sales rep, and the information is passed on to one of the two on-line operators. If the customer does not qualify for the high-end models, then the rep will try to sell one of the low-end models directly over the phone. If the customer feels that he has enough information, the case will be handled in the same manner as the electronic models. Otherwise a lead slip is filled out.

Sales reps handle up to 75 calls per day and therefore have little time to run forms to the order-entry personnel. Instead, runners periodically pick up the forms from the sales reps and deliver them to the order-entry personnel. The information is keyed into the on-line order-fulfillment and inventory-control system. All leads are sent to the appropriate sales offices. Orders are forwarded to the appropriate warehouse.

The sales rep position at Simplex is highly regarded and applicants undergo extensive interviewing and training before they are hired. It is a high-pressure position, and this is reflected in the starting salaries, which average $18,000. As is true of the industry as a whole, about 75 percent of the sales reps at Simplex's telemarketing division are women.

THE INITIAL ATTEMPT TO TELEMARKET SERVICE CONTRACTS

Full-service contracts are an important source of revenue for Simplex. With the life of a clock being 8 years on average, it is essential for Simplex to supply any service needed on the clock during that period. Unfortunately, Simplex did not have as dominant a position in this area as it did in time clocks themselves.

Many small operators were competing with Simplex in the service area. Several of these were former Simplex service reps who had branched off on their own. While these small operators were less dependable than Simplex, they could offer a lower price because they didn't have the support costs Simplex had. Simplex had an extensive training program, supplied its service reps with cars, and had a full inventory of replacement parts.

To combat these higher costs, Simplex decided to try to sell its full-service contracts through the telemarketing system. In this way the company wouldn't need to waste service reps' time selling the contract but could have them perform the actual service full-time. This system also cut down on the amount of traveling the service reps would need to do. Instead of having the rep travel to the site, diagnose the problem, travel back to pick up the necessary parts, and then return to make the repairs, the customer could call the 800 number for service and give a description of the problem to the sales rep, who would then send the information to the appropriate service rep. The service rep could then make a well-prepared service call and make the repair on the first trip out. If the problem needed immediate at-

FIGURE C6–3 ***Telemarketing Contact Report Form***
Source: Simplex Promotional Materials

322476

Simplex SALES/SERVICE ACTION NOTICE REGION ____ BR# ____

IMMEDIATE ☐ POTENTIAL ☐

HQ TELEMARKETING# 1-800-343-6186

DATE OF SVC. CALL __/__/__

COMPLETED BY T.R. NAME ____ EMP. NO. ____

CUSTOMER # ____ CUSTOMER # ____

SHIP TO - CUSTOMER NAME ____ BILL TO-SAME AS SHIP TO UNLESS SHOWN ____

STREET ____ STREET ____

CITY ____ CITY ____

STATE ____ ZIP ____ STATE ____ ZIP ____

CUST. CONTACT AND LOCATION ____

TEL. NO. ( ) ____

EQUIP. RECORD

MODEL NO. ____ SERIAL NO. ____ AGE (YRS.) ____

☐ DAY ☐ DATE ☐ MONTH ☐ YEAR

HOURS: ☐ 1-12 ☐ 0-23 MIN: ☐ 0-59 ☐ .1 ☐ .01

☐ SYMBOL ☐ 2 COLORS ☐ BELLRINGER ☐ TAM

MOTOR: ☐ IMPULSE VOLTS ____ ☐ SYNC.

TRIGGER: ☐ AUTO ☐ MANUAL

MY INSPECTION REVEALED: ☐ EXCESSIVE WEAR ☐ EXTERNAL ABUSE ☐ UNIT IN SHOP ☐ OTHER (EXPLAIN BELOW)

RECOMMENDATION: ☐ QUOTED PRICE $ ____ ☐ SHOP WORK ☐ NEW EQUIP. ☐ SYSTEM UPDATE

INSCRIPTION PLATE: ☐ UPPER ☐ LOWER ☐ IMPRESSION ATTACHED

TIME CARD # ____

☐ STD. ☐ SPEC. ☐ COPY ATTACHED

LOANER PROVIDED ☐ YES ☐ NO

TYPE ____ SERIAL # ____

CONDITION, RECOMMENDATIONS, SPECS. AND COMMENTS ____ SA # ____

TYPE OF BUSINESS ____ NO. OF EMPLOYEES ____

TO BE COMPLETED BY HQ TELEMARKETING

EQUIP. ORDER NO. ____ **P.O. NO.** ____ **TELEMARKETING REP.** ____

INITIAL CALL DATE __/__/__ **FOLLOW-UP DATE** __/__/__ **FIELD REP.** ____ # ____

EQUIPMENT & MODEL NUMBER QUOTED

	DEL. IN BRANCH	NO. OF UNITS	LIST PRICE	SELLING PRICE
CLOCK				
CLOCK				
CARDS				
RACK				
TCP				
MISC.				
TRADE IN				

EXTENDED WARRANTY ☐ **SERVICE AGREEMENT** ☐ **$**

INSTALLATION YES ☐ **NO** ☐ **TAM $**

TOTAL DISCOUNT $ ____
BOTTOM LINE $ ____
TOTAL REVENUE $ ____

OV-0012 R1

TELEMARKETING ☐ **BRANCH SALES** ☐

tention, the sales rep could give the information to the service rep within an hour of the call.

Unfortunately, the first year of operations with the sale of service contracts did not work as well as expected. Unlike sales of time clocks, the full-service agreements did not have a set price attached to them. A number of variables had to be ccn-sidered in order to come up with a price for the service contracts. These included the type of clock being services, the number of clocks the customer was using, the distance that the area sales rep had to travel to reach the customer, and the amount of competition in the area. Without the available information on these variables, the sales reps were finding it almost impossible to come up with an acceptable price. Somehow they needed to develop an average price per service call or to customize their service pricing strategy. Mike Rague knew that unless some of this information could be collected and made readily accessible to the reps, the telemarketing of service contracts would have to be dropped.

Index